COMMEMORATIVE ESSAYS

COMMEMORATIVE ESSAYS

PRESENTED TO

SIR RAMKRISHNA GOPAL BHANDARKA

BY

RAMKRISHNA GOPAL BHANDARKAR

GYAN

Published by

Gyan Publishing House
5, Ansari Road
Daryaganj, New Delhi-110002
Phone: 011-47034999, 9811692060
E-mail: books@gyanbooks.com

Distribution Network
gyanbooks.com
India, USA, Canada, UK, Australia

ISBN: 978-93-6280-654-3 (HB)
First Published, 1917

2nd Impression 2024

Printed at: Gyan Press, Delhi.

COMMEMORATIVE ESSAYS
Author: RAMKRISHNA GOPAL BHANDARKAR

COMMEMORATIVE ESSAYS

PRESENTED TO

SIR RAMKRISHNA GOPAL BHANDARKAR

K. C. I. E., M. A. (Bom.), Ph. D. (Gottin. & Cal.), LL. D. (Bom. & Edin.),
Honorary Member of the Royal Asiatic Society of Great Britain
and Ireland, of the German Oriental Society, of the American
Oriental Society, and of the Italian Asiatic Society; Corresponding Member of the French Institute and of the
Imperial Academy of Sciences, St. Petersburg;
Foreign Member of the Royal Bohemian Society
of Sciences; Sometime Vice-Chancellor of
the University of Bombay; and late
Professor of Oriental Languages
Deccan College,
Poona.

तेजस्वि नावधीतमस्तु

Bhandarkar Oriental Research Institute, Poona

1917

BORN
8th OF JULY 1837

This Volume

of Essays written by

his Friends, Pupils, and Admirers

from Different Lands

IS DEDICATED

as a Mark of Respect and Affection

TO

SIR RAMKRISHNA GOPAL BHANDARKAR

upon the Completion of his 80th Year

on Friday the 6th of July

1917

ILLUSTRATIONS

CONTENTS

Veda and Antiquity

THE PRINCIPLES TO BE FOLLOWED IN TRANSLATING THE ṚGVEDA

BY A. A. MACDONELL

IT is now one hundred and twelve years since the first authentic information about the *Ṛgveda* reached European scholars through Colebrooke's essay on the Vedas in *Asiatick Researches.* Not, however, till the middle of the nineteenth century did a portion of the text of the *Ṛgveda* supplemented by Sāyaṇa's commentary become accessible by the publication, in 1849, of the first volume of Max Müller's edition. In the following year was begun Wilson's translation which was based on Sāyaṇa's interpretation. No other method was at that time possible because only a fraction of the text was known and no other aids, such as treatises on Vedic grammar, as yet existed. Wilson's version was carried on by him, and after his death by others according to the same plan, till it was completed by the appearance of the sixth and last volume in 1888. All the Vedic literature known to Sāyaṇa had by the end of the nineteenth century been published and at the present time lies open to the use of Sanskrit scholars. Two questions now arise. Can the traditional method of translation, which was a necessity in 1850, be considered at all adequate to-day? And if it is not adequate, what method should be substituted for it in producing a new version? Before supplying definite answers we must examine in its chronological order the traditional material available for exegesis, and test its value by examples as far as the space at our disposal will allow.

The investigation of the Brāhmaṇas has shown that, being mainly concerned with speculation on the nature of sacrifice, they were already far removed from the spirit of the composers of the Vedic hymns, and contain very little capable of throwing light on the original sense of those hymns. They only give occasional explanations of the sense of the Mantras and these explanations are often very fanciful. How completely they can misunderstand the meaning intended by the seers appears sufficiently from the following two examples. The *Śatapatha Brāhmaṇa* (vii. 4, 1, 9) in referring to the refrain of Ṛv. x. 121, *kásmai devā́ya havíṣā vidhema* 'to what god should we offer worship with oblation', says 'Ka is Prajāpati: to him let us offer oblation.'[1] Another Brāhmaṇa passage, in explaining the epithet 'golden-handed' (*híraṇya-pāṇi*) as applied to the sun, remarks that the sun had lost his hand and had got instead one of gold.[2] Quite apart from the linguistic evidence,[3] such interpretations show that there was already a considerable gap between the period of the Brāhmaṇas and that of the Mantras.

We next come to the *Nighaṇṭus* which constitute, as far as they go, the oldest Vedic lexicographical material extant. They are, however, so limited in scope as to be of very little use in the interpretation of Vedic words. Of their five sections the first three contain sixty-nine lists of the synonyms of certain well-known nouns and verbs. Thus the list beginning with *rebháḥ* ends with the explanation *iti trayodaśa stotṛnāmāni ;* and that commencing with *cikyat* ends *ity aṣṭau paśyatikarmāṇaḥ.* The meanings they thus assign are often so vague and general as to leave the specific sense of the terms enumerated quite uncertain. Thus among the synonyms of *vā́c* 'speech' appear such words as *ślóka, nivíd, ṛ́c, gā́thā, anuṣṭúbh,* which denote different kinds of verses or compositions and can never have been employed to express the simple meaning of 'speech.' As there is a wide gap between the Mantras and these lists, even the general meanings may sometimes be wrong. The remaining two sections of the *Nighaṇṭus* consist of nine mere lists of words of different senses which

1 This led later to the employment of Ka not only as an epithet of Prajāpati (AB. iii. 22, 7), but as a name, used by itself, of the supreme god (MS. iii. 12, 5). See Macdonell, *Vedic Mythology*, p. 119. Cp. ŚB. ii. 5, 2, 13.

2 See Max Müller, *History of Ancient Sanskrit Literature*, p. 433, note.

3 See Macdonell, *Vedic Grammar for Students*, p. 1.

are not explained in any way. As even the first three sections are far from containing all the difficult words in the Veda, it is obvious that the help afforded by this vocabulary to the interpreter of the *Ṛgveda* is of a very limited and meagre kind.

This vocabulary brings us to Yāska, the oldest surviving representative of the commentators; for it was he who explained the *Nighaṇṭus* by adducing in illustration a large number of verses, chiefly from the *Ṛgveda*, which he interprets. In this sense his *Nirukta* is the earliest continuous Vedic commentary; but the total number of the Mantras explained by him constitutes only a very small portion of the *Ṛgveda*. He is a learned interpreter working with the materials which scholarship had accumulated before his age. He also enjoys a great advantage in point of time compared with the later compilers of detailed and continuous commentaries, belonging as he did to quite a different period, in which Sanskrit was still in process of natural development. In all cases of difficulty his method of interpretation is based on etymology. When, however, he positively states that a word which does not occur in later Sanskrit has a particular sense that suits the passage, we may often assume that such a statement is based on traditional authority even though he may support the meaning he assigns by an etymology. Thus when he asserts that *śvaghnín* means a 'gambler' (v. 22) there seems no ground for doubting the assertion. But when the sense appears to rest solely on etymology and does not suit the passage, it is doubtful whether he has any such authority behind him. And when, as is often the case, he offers two or more explanations derived from mere etymology, we must suppose him to be purely conjectural. Thus the doubtfulness of much of his explanation shows that he was not the depository of any certain interpretation of the hymns handed down by tradition from the period when they were intelligible to every one who recited them.

This conclusion is corroborated by the fact that the seventeen predecessors whom Yāska mentions often give conflicting explanations of the same Vedic term. Thus

Aurṇavābha, he tells us (Nir. vi. 13), interprets *nā́satyau*, an epithet of the Aśvins, as 'true, not false' (*satyau, na asatyau*), Āgrāyaṇa as 'leaders of truth' (*satyasya praṇetārau*), while Yāska himself thinks it may mean 'nose-born' (*nāsikā-prabhavau*). Again, Krauṣṭuki took *draviṇodā́s* to be a name of Indra, but Śākapūṇi regarded it as a name of Agni.[1] Another, Kautsa, actually asserted that the science of Vedic exposition was useless, because the Vedic hymns and formulæ were obscure, unmeaning and mutually contradictory. Yāska moreover mentions several different schools of interpretation, the Nairuktas or etymologists, the Aitihāsikas or legendary writers, the Yājñikas or ritualists, the Parivrājakas or ascetic mendicants. Each of these explained difficulties according to its respective bias. Thus he tells us (Nir. xii. 1) the various views as to who the Aśvins were: "'Heaven and Earth' say some; 'Day and Night' say others; 'Sun and Moon' say others; 'two kings, performers of holy acts' say the Aitihāsikas."[2] From this it is clear that in and before Yāska's time there existed no uniform tradition of interpretation from the period when the hymns of the Ṛv. were still understood, but that on the contrary there then prevailed wide-spread divergences in the explanation of the obscurities of those hymns.

We now come to Sāyaṇa, the author of the great commentary on the *Ṛgveda*. This work differs from the *Nirukta* in being continuous, inasmuch as it explains every *ṛc* of the Ṛv., while the former comments on only about 600 isolated stanzas out of a total of about 10,500 in the *Ṛgveda*. It is also more detailed inasmuch as it comments on practically every word of the text, which is not the case in the *Nirukta*. Sāyaṇa labours under the disadvantage of having lived nearly 2000 years later than Yāska and having had much less ancient exegetical material avail-

1 An examination of all the passages of the Ṛv. in which this term occurs decisively proves that it is an epithet of Agni.

2 Several other examples of such divergent interpretations will be found in Muir's article, *On the Interpretation of the Veda*, J. R. A. S. 1866, p. 18ff.

able for his explanations than Yāska must have had. There is no reason to suppose that he had at his disposal any other authorities than those whom he quotes; on the contrary, it is highly probable that, as he seems in all important cases to adduce older texts in support of his views if he can, he had no such evidence when he adduces none. Thus he quotes Yāska in passages explained by that commentator; for example, on Ṛv. i. 44, 1 Yāska's five etymological explanations of Agni's epithet *jātávedas*.[1]

Sāyaṇa commonly follows Yāska, but in several cases he disagrees with him. Thus on Ṛv. i. 174, 2 he explains the word *dā́naḥ* as a verb in the 2. sing. impf. meaning either 'thou didst subdue' or 'thou didst cause to cry,' while Yāska explains it as an adjective meaning 'liberal-minded' (*dāna-manaḥ*). *Dasrā́*, a frequent dual epithet of the Aśvins, is explained by Yāska (vi. 26) as *darśanīyau*[2] 'to be seen, sightly'; but by Sāyaṇa sometimes in the same sense, in other passages as 'destroyers of enemies', or 'destroyers of diseases', or as 'gods having the name of Dasrā.' *Dívişṭi* means, according to Yāska, in the plural 'longings after the sky,' but according to Sāyaṇa on the same passage (viii. 4, 19) 'sacrificial rites which are the causes of obtaining heaven,' and elsewhere as 'sacrificial days' or 'people who desire heaven, priests.' *Aminá* is explained by Yāska (vi. 16) as either 'of unlimited measure or quantity' or 'uninjured,' and by Sāyaṇa on the same passage as 'uninjurable,' but in another passage where it is applied in the same way, as an epithet of Indra in two new alternative meanings (unknown to Yāska), 'going everywhere' or 'beloved by all.'[3]

Sāyaṇa further explains many words differently in different passages, though according to the context the meaning must be the same. Thus *ásura* is most variously

1 Here he picks out only one of these explanations, analysing the compound as a Tatpuruṣa, *jātānāṁ veditā*, though strictly speaking it is a Bahuvrīhi as the accent shows, 'he who has knowledge of created things.'

2 Of course an impossible etymology.

3 A good example of how conjectural Sāyaṇa often is.

rendered as 'expeller of foes,' 'giver of strength,' 'giver of life,' 'hurler away of what is undesired,' 'giver of breath or water,' 'thrower of oblations, priest,' 'taker away of breath,' 'expeller of water, Parjanya,' 'impeller,' 'strong,' 'wise' and 'rain water' or 'a water-discharging cloud.'[1]

Thus it is clear that when Yāska gives two or more alternative explanations of a word in the same passage he can be following no certain tradition and all but one sense must necessarily be wrong, and even that one may possibly be so. A similar remark applies to Sāyaṇa. Again, in the many cases in which Sāyaṇa contradicts Yāska, he is not following the tradition, or if he is right the tradition is wrong. Moreover, when Sāyaṇa gives divergent interpretations of the same word in parallel passages, one or other of such interpretations must be wrong. It is thus evident that of about a large number of the most difficult words neither Yāska nor Sāyaṇa possessed any certain knowledge either from tradition or etymology. Many of their etymological explanations are, moreover, obviously not only grotesque but impossible, as will be shown below. Thus a translation of the Ṛv. based solely on the interpretation of the Vedic commentators cannot possibly be satisfactory. The guidance of these writers is indeed invaluable in the interpretation of the Brāhmaṇas and Sūtras, because they lived in the atmosphere of the ceremonial represented by that class of literature. But they are removed both in language and thought from the atmosphere prevailing in the hymns of the *Ṛgveda*. How otherwise could it have been asserted even before the time of Yāska that the Vedic hymns were unmeaning? In fact the very excellence of these writers as expositors of the ritual literature was actually a drawback when they interpreted the older literature of the Mantras. Their familiarity with classical Sanskrit led them to see its ordinary idiom in the Vedic hymns also. Thus Sāyaṇa constantly explains Vedic forms as irregularities from the point of view of Sanskrit, when they are perfectly regular ancient forms. For instance, in

1 Cp. Muir, *op. cit.* p. 74 f.

his comments on Ṛv. viii. 45, 17, he explains *kṛṇávate*, the normal 3. sing. Ātm. pres. subjunctive of *kṛ* 'to do', as the dat. sing. pres. part. for *kṛṇvaté* and goes on to say that this dat. stands for the inst. and then for the locative! Again, since these commentators regarded the forms of sacrifice known to them as having existed from the beginning of the world, they naturally took for granted that the ancient seers of the Ṛv. sacrificed in the same way as they themselves did. As their own mythology and cosmology (though in reality differing largely in many respects from those of the Ṛv.) seemed to them to be revealed truth, they naturally saw them in the old hymns also. Thus Sāyaṇa considers the dwarf incarnation of Viṣṇu to be referred to in Ṛv. i. 22, 16ff.; yet Yāska (xii. 19) seems to know nothing of that incarnation, which in any case can be shown to have been a gradual mythological development of the post-Ṛgvedic period.[1] Sāyaṇa also (on Ṛv. i. 114, 6) identifies the Rudra of the hymns with the husband of Pārvatī, who is unknown to the Ṛv.[2] And just as he was blinded by the theology of the Brāhmaṇas, he was misled by the etymological fictions of the *Nirukta*.

The traditional method of interpreting the Ṛv. that prevails in India by no means presents a unique state of things. The sacred books of other ancient nations have been as a rule explained in the same way by later generations according to the system of theology and the level of scholarship prevailing at the time. In every case such interpretation has been given out as a tradition, or in other words has claimed for itself an antiquity and a value which have often fallen greatly short of the truth. The interpretation of the Hebrew Books of the Old Testament according to the Talmud and the Rabbis affords quite a parallel case. But have we any reason to expect that any other method can yield more certain results? The method of natural science which has led to such an astounding advancement of knowledge, for instance in the sphere of

1 See Macdonell, *Mythological Studies in the Ṛgveda*, J. R. A. S. 27, 168 ff.; *Vedic Mythology*, p. 41.

2 Cp. Muir, *Sanskrit Texts*, iv, 57 and 257.

physics, chemistry, and medicine, during the preceding and the present century, is fundamentally the same as that which has been applied in modern European scholarship. To this have been due such marvellous achievements as the decipherment of the cuneiform writings of Persia and of the rock inscriptions of India, and the discovery of the languages concealed under those characters which had for many centuries been absolutely unintelligible to the natives of those countries. The application of this method has also resulted in extraordinary progress being made in the study of the literature of other ancient civilizations, such as that of the Babylonians, Egyptians, Hebrews, and Homeric Greeks. Considering that the aids accessible to the Vedic researcher are more abundant than in the aforesaid cases, there is good ground for supposing that the ultimate achievements will be correspondingly greater. The essential nature of the critical method is the patient and exhaustive collection, co-ordination, sifting and evaluation of the facts bearing on the subject of investigation. The sole aim here being the attainment of truth, it is a positive advantage that the translators of ancient sacred books should be outsiders rather than the native custodians of such writings. The latter could not escape from religious bias; an orthodox Brahman could not possibly do so.

The modern critical Vedic scholar has at his disposal for the purposes of interpretation practically all the traditional material accessible to Sāyaṇa in the 14th century. But over and above this common material the scientific scholar possesses a number of valuable resources which were unknown to the commentators. These are the evidence of the *Avesta*, of Comparative Philology, of Comparative Mythology, of the anthropology of ancient peoples, besides the application of the historical method to traditional evidence as well as to classical Sanskrit as throwing light on the Veda. Let us examine the value of each of these resources in succession.

The *Avesta* is capable of elucidating questions of language, metre, mythology and 'cult' in the Ṛv. Thus it shows, for example, that the Vedic imperative form *e-dhi* is based on *az-dhi* (Av. *zdi*), and that *sed*, the weak form of the perfect of *sad*, stands for *sazd* (Av. *hazd*).[1] Again, the parallel metre of the *Avesta* shows that the cæsura in the Triṣṭubh Pāda must originally have come after the fourth syllable only, and never after the fifth.[2] The evidence of the Avestic Mithra proves that Mitra was a sun-god, a fact which is not clear from the Ṛv. itself.[3] The parallelism of the Avestic Ahura indicates that the term Asura originally applied to the highest gods and only later came to mean demon. It incidentally disproves the etymology of Yāska who says (Nir. iii. 8): "it is well known that he (the Creator) formed the *Suras* (gods) from *su* 'good,' in which their essence consists, and that he formed the *Asuras* from *asu* (*a+su*, 'not good'), and that in this consists their essence." The statements of the *Avesta* about *haoma* show that the preparation and cult of Soma were pre-Indian.

Comparative Philology not only throws direct light on the origin and meaning of many Vedic words, but negatively supplies a check on wild and impossible etymologies. Thus the word *sarvátāti* (in the loc. sing.) is explained etymologically by Yāska (xi. 24 on Ṛv. i. 95, 15) by *sarvāsu karmatatiṣu* 'in all extensions (=performances) of works' (*tati* being here intended as a noun from *tan* 'to stretch'); Sāyaṇa follows his explanation, but adds 'or at all sacrifices.' But we know from the cognate languages that this word (with its doublet *sarvá-tāt*) is a derivative, not a compound, of *sárva* 'whole' (Lat. *salvo-*) with the suffix *-tāti* (or *-tāt*) which appears in Vedic, Avestic, Greek, and Latin: Av. *haurva-tāt*, Gk. ὁλό-τητ- (cp. Lat. *juven-tāti* 'youth'), meaning 'wholeness', 'complete welfare'. This meaning is shown, by a comparison of all the passages in which the word occurs, to be applicable practically everywhere: Sāyaṇa himself cannot help once (on Ṛv. iii. 54, 11) giving it the similar meaning of 'every desired good', though he elsewhere renders it by 'sacrifice', or 'every worshipper'

1 Cp. Macdonell, *A Vedic Grammar for students*, p. 19.

2 *Op. cit.*, p. 440, foot-note 3.

3 Cp. *Vedic Mythology*, p. 30.

(*sarvaḥ stotā*), 'battle', or 'extension of all enjoyments'.

The verb *spaś* 'to see', of which several forms occur in the Ṛv.,[1] Sāyaṇa regularly explains as meaning either 'to touch' (*spṛś*) or 'to injure' (*bādh*): *ánu-spaṣṭa*, which he renders by *dṛṣṭi-gocara*, is the only form in which he assigns its real meaning to this verb, doubtless because the only form surviving in classical Sanskrit is the participle *spaṣṭa* 'clear'. But the sense 'to see' suits perfectly in all passages of the Ṛv., and Comparative Philology shows that this root is an Indo-European root meaning 'to see', as is proved by the Av. *spas*, Lat. *spec-io*, Old German *speh-on*, Eng. *spy*. The noun *spáś* 'spy' Sāyaṇa continues to explain by *spṛś* or *bādh*, while he gives it the various senses of 'ray', 'ray or spy', 'form' (*rūpam*) 'injurious follower'; and the nom. *spáṭ* he renders in one passage (v. 59, 1) by *spraṣṭā hotā* 'the priest who touches', but in another (viii. 50, 15) by *sarvasya jñātā*, 'the knower of everything'. Here again the meaning 'spy' suits the context everywhere, and the evidence of cognate languages corroborates this sense: Av. *spas*, Eng. *spy*, Lat. *au-spec-* 'augur' (that is, 'inspector of birds').

The plural form *ūtáyaḥ* Sāyaṇa generally (and correctly) renders by 'aids', but once (on Ṛv. i. 84, 20) as *gantāraḥ* 'goers' or *dhūtayaḥ* 'shakers' (meaning the Maruts). The latter etymology, which implies the dropping of a single initial consonant, can be shown by the laws of Vedic phonology to be impossible.[2]

Comparative Mythology proves that the nature of various deities cannot be fully understood from Vedic evidence alone because they are derived from earlier periods. Thus the original character of Yama can only be ascertained by taking the conception of the Avestic Yima into consideration. Again the trait of paternity in the Dyaus of the Ṛv.[3] is shown by the Greek ζεῦ πάτερ and the Lat. *Juppiter*, as parallels of *dyàuṣ pitar*, to be not purely Vedic, but inherited from the remote Indo-European period.

1 See *Vedic Grammar for Students*, p. 431.

2 Cp. *Vedic Grammar for Students*, 15 k.

3 Cp. *Vedic Mythology*, § 11.

The evidence of ethnology indicates that the notion of Heaven and Earth being universal parents is a very primitive one, and must have been inherited by the Ṛv. from a very early age.[1] It further enables us to understand the meaning of various phenomena of the funeral ceremony, such as the wife's lying down on the pyre beside her dead husband, or the taking of the bow from his hand,[2] and explains the history of widow-burning in Vedic India.[3]

The value of the historical method in utilizing classical Sanskrit as an aid in the interpretation of the Ṛv. is perhaps best brought out by showing the lack of it in Sāyaṇa's explanations. This weakness is apparent in the first place on the linguistic side. Taking his stand on the later language he constantly treats the older normal Vedic forms as irregularities. Thus *vīrayā́*, the instrumental case used adverbially, of the denominative fem. *vīrayā́* (formed from *vīrá*[4]) is explained (iii. 90, 1) as the dat. masc. *vīrā́ya* (from *vīrá*), 'to the hero' (Vāyu). The subjunctive form *áyaḥ*[5] Ṛv. (viii. 2, 40) is rendered by *agamayaḥ*, and thus taken not only to be an ind. impf., but also to have a causative sense. On the other hand, past augmented forms are often explained as imperatives, as *ákṣan* 'they have eaten' (Ṛv. x. 15, 12), aor. of *ghas*,[6] by *adantu* 'let them eat.' Sāyaṇa does not recognise the root *vakṣ* 'to grow' (the Indo-European evidence of which, though it is extinct in classical Sanskrit, is proved even by the English *wax* 'to increase'), from which several forms occur in the Ṛv.[7] These are all explained by him as formed from *vah* to 'carry' (once from *vac* 'to speak'). The 3. pl. perf. *vavakṣúḥ* he renders as a pres. desiderative, 'they wish to bring'[8]; and the 2. sing. perf. *vavákṣitha* as 'thou wishest to carry', once even as a 2. sing. imperative, 'do thou desire to carry'.

Sāyaṇa, moreover, often imports later ideas into the Ṛgveda. Thus (on i. 114, 6) he accounts for Rudra's be-

1 *Loc. cit.*
2 *Op. cit.*, §71.
3 Cp. *History of Sanskrit Literature*, p. 126.
4 See *Vedic Grammar for Students*, p. 77.
5 *Op. cit.*, p. 130.
6 *Op. cit.*, p. 381.
7 *Op. cit.*, p. 415.
8 The desiderative could only be *vivakṣanti*.

ing called the father of the Maruts[1] by a fantastic later story telling how Indra divided the fœtus of Diti into forty-nine parts, all of which were by Parameśvara (Rudra), at the request of Pārvatī, turned into sons (the Maruts). Of all this the Ṛv. knows absolutely nothing; besides there the number of the Maruts is thrice seven or thrice sixty, but never forty-nine.[2] Mātariśvan, who in the Ṛv. is a producer of fire, sometimes identified with Agni, but in the later Saṁhitās and the Brāhmaṇas becomes a name of wind, and is also so regarded by Yāska, is by Sāyaṇa (on i. 71, 4) said to mean the principal vital air divided into the five airs. In commenting on vii. 59, 12 he explains *tryàmbaka* as 'the father of the three gods Brahmā, Viṣṇu and Rudra.' This triad, however, does not exist in the Ṛv., the only one there being Sun, Wind and Fire.[3]

The question now arises, what are the principles to be followed, in translating the Ṛv. anew, by the scientifically trained Vedic scholar who possesses the advantages above described over the traditional commentator, and who, moreover, has at his command the results of special and detailed researches, covering the whole field of Vedic study, accumulated during the last forty years.

The greater part of the hymns of the Ṛv., being simple and straightforward, a new scientific translation will here be in agreement with the traditional interpretation. But owing to the isolation of the Ṛv., as by far the oldest product of Indian literature, it contains a large amount of material which, as we have seen, the commentators did not understand. The interpretation of this material must be based on an exhaustive examination of the Ṛv. itself by a complete collection and comparison of the facts it contains, mainly in the spheres of grammar (including syntax), vocabulary, accent, and metre.

The very foundation of a scientific translation must be a strict adherence to the rules of Vedic grammar. The commentators had no such work for the Veda as was available for classical Sanskrit in Pāṇini's great treatise. In

1 Cp. *Vedic Mythology*, pp. 74 and 78. 2 *Op. cit.*, p. 78.
3 *Op. cit.*, p. 93 (bottom).

the course of the last sixty years every single form occurring in the Ṛv. has been registered, and those which are irregular or obscure have been discussed in many articles and monographs. All this material has been gathered together and arranged by myself in my *Vedic Grammar* (1910). Vedic syntax has been thoroughly investigated by Professor Delbrück as a whole, and in detail by others: the results of these researches have been embodied in a chapter of my *Vedic Grammar for Students* (1916). It will no longer be possible to render forms like *vavákṣitha* and *vavakṣúḥ* as desideratives, nor the subjunctive *áyas* as an imperfect indicative, nor the injunctive *dhīmahi* as an indicative present, nor the instr. fem. *vīrayā́* as a dat. masc., nor the aorist subj. *rāsate* by the ind. pres. (*dadāti*), as Sāyaṇa does. I remember a good example of the pitfalls into which a translator who has not a thorough knowledge of Vedic grammar may stumble. A pupil of mine, who was a very good Sanskrit scholar, once spoke with much contempt of previous translators of Ṛv. x. 129, and volunteered a rendering of his own. This contained two serious grammatical errors: he took (against the Padapāṭha) a fairly well known verbal form for a particle (against sandhi and accent), and mistranslated another verbal form, because he was unacquainted with the use of separable prepositions. It sometimes, however, happens that though every grammatical form in a sentence is perfectly certain, the sentence, as a whole and taken by itself, is susceptible of two or three interpretations: a comparison of parallel passages and of the context can then alone decide.

The vocabulary of the Ṛv. presents peculiar difficulties to the translator, because the meaning of many words can only be ascertained by an exhaustive examination of all the passages in which they occur, and even then doubt may sometimes remain. A very valuable foundation was here laid by Professor Roth, who followed this comparative method, in the large St. Petersburg Dictionary. It is of course impossible that a single scholar, investigating the whole vocabulary of the Ṛv. in this way, should have arrived at certainty in all cases. A number of minute researches as to the exact sense of individual words have therefore since been undertaken by various scholars. But a great deal still remains to be done in the critical re-examination of results already arrived at. Let us take the word *jātávedas* as an example of the comparative method. A scrutiny of all the very numerous passages in which it occurs shows that it is an exclusive epithet of Agni. We also find that in one passage (vi. 15, 13) its sense is explained in the Ṛv. itself: *sá rā́jā víśvā veda jánimā jātávedāḥ* 'that king Jātavedas knows all created beings,' this meaning being further corroborated by the Tatpuruṣa compound *jāta-vidyā́* 'knowledge of created beings.' The accent shows us that the word is a Bahuvrīhi; and an examination of the use of Vedic compounds proves that it is a Tatpuruṣa Bahuvrīhi, 'possessing a knowledge of created beings,' and cannot be a Karmadhāraya Bahuvrīhi (like the classical Sanskrit *jāta-rūpa* 'possessing innate beauty'), because the latter type has not yet come into use in the Ṛv. Yāska, being unacquainted with the comparative method, is uncertain about the exact meaning, and gives as many as five interpretations: *jātāni veda, jātāni vā enaṁ vidur, jāte jāte vidyata iti vā, jātavitto vā jātadhano, jātavidyo vā jāta-prajñānaḥ.* Again a comparison of the passages in which the word *uru-gāyá* appears indicates that it is predominantly an epithet of Viṣṇu connected with his taking (*vi-kram*) his three strides, and means 'wide-going.' In reviewing parallel passages, the careful examination of the context in the same hymn is a valuable expedient: thus the variation of this epithet in the Viṣṇu hymn i. 154 by *uru-kramá* 'wide-striding' confirms the sense of 'wide-going.' Yāska (ii. 7) correctly renders the word by *mahāgati* 'having a large gait.' Sāyaṇa, however, explains it variously, in three stanzas of the same hymn (i. 154), with the renderings—*1. urubhir, mahadbhir, gīyamānaḥ, atiprabhūtaṁ gīyamano vā ; 2. bahubhir gīyamānaḥ ; 3. bahubhir, mahātmabhir, gātavyaḥ, stutyaḥ*—here at least always as if the word were derived from *gā* 'to sing'; but elsewhere he fluctuates more: 'wide-going or much praised' (iii. 6, 4), 'of great renown' (iv. 3, 7), 'great goer'

(iv. 14, 1) 'moving in many places or of great renown or one who by his powers makes all his enemies howl' (viii. 29, 7). This is typical of his way of explaining the individual passage before him without reference to others that are parallel. Occasionally, however, he adduces one other passage in support of his interpretation; thus (on i. 60, 1) he explains *rāti* as 'friend,' and then adds, "some say it means 'son'," quoting in proof of this view Ṛv. iii. 2, 4; but on looking up that verse we find to our surprise that his rendering there is 'giver of desired objects.' This example illustrates well how far removed Sāyaṇa's manner of interpretation is from the comparative and critical method. The evidence showing that *urugāyá* means 'wide-going' is confirmed by its use as a neuter substantive both in the Ṛv. and later in the sense of 'wide space for movement,' 'free movement.'

Many words occur only once in the Ṛv. and are unknown in the later language. In these cases our only aids are etymology and context, but several examples could be quoted where these are sufficient, though the sense of many must necessarily remain obscure. The meaning is here sometimes ascertainable, because the component parts of the word are clear, as for instance when they are a preposition and a verbal root, inflected forms of which are found elsewhere in the Ṛv. Thus *ni-varta*, taken with the context (in x. 19, 6) evidently means 'one who causes to return.' Etymology is of course valuable in many other cases when applied according to scientific principles, but is hazardous and often leads to absurdities when used by those who are ignorant of such principles. Thus Sāyaṇa's derivation of *nápāt* (on viii. 17, 13) as 'one who causes not to fall' (*na pātayitā*), that is, 'one who establishes' (*avasthāpayitā*), highly improbable in itself as a Sanskrit etymology, is impossible, because *nápāt* = Lat. *nepōt*, as an Indo-European word, could not be thus derived.

Again, stringent observance of the laws of the Vedic accent, which have been fully ascertained by the labours of various scholars and are summed up in my two Vedic grammars, must be observed in translating the Ṛv. I have met with many mistakes caused by the neglect or ignorance of these rules. One of the most frequent of these is due to overlooking the accent of the vocative case; thus Griffith (x. 15, 14) renders the nom. *sva-rā́ṭ* as if it were the voc. *svá-rāṭ*. Other errors result from the confusion of such forms as *mā́* 'not' and *mā* 'me', *té* 'those' and *te* 'of or to thee', *yuvábhyām* 'for you two' and *yúvabhyām* 'for the two youths'. Another example is Wilson's 'rendering of the words *prathamajā́ bráhmaṇaḥ* by 'the first-born of Brahmā' in accordance with Sāyaṇa's explanation: *brahmaṇaḥ, sarvasya jagataḥ sraṣṭuḥ, prathamajaḥ, prathamam utpannāḥ*. Here quite apart from the importation of the later idea of the personal creator Brahmā as a masculine, who is never mentioned in the Ṛv., the accent of *bráhmaṇaḥ* shows that the word is a neuter and not a masc. (*brahmáṇaḥ*).[1]

Even the evidence of Vedic metre, the laws of which have been fully established by the researches of several scholars, must be taken into consideration by the translator, because the separation of internal Pādas and the position of the cæsura may often help in deciding the syntax and the resultant meaning of sentences. To show how this criterion may apply would, however, require a more elaborate proof than can here be presented.

The question still remains to be answered, what should be the attitude of the translator of the Ṛv. towards emendations of the text? Now it has been proved that the Saṁhitā text was constituted with such extraordinary care[2] that even slight irregularities and inaccuracies, going back to the original authors, which might easily have been removed by the redactors, were left unaltered by them; and that primarily by the aid of the Pada text, it has been preserved since then with scrupulous care. The Saṁhitā text therefore possesses an extraordinary degree of authenticity. Advancing study has proved many emendations, made by earlier scholars owing to imperfect knowledge, to be unnecessary. Conjectural corrections of the text

1 See *Vedic Grammar for Students*, p. 259.

2 Cp. *History of Sanskrit Literature*, p. 48.

should, therefore, be resorted to only in extreme cases. No other product of ancient literature has ever been handed down without mistakes, and it cannot be supposed that the text even of the Ṛv. should have remained entirely free from any corruption.

Thus in some cases emendation is required by grammatical considerations, in order to produce any sense at all. Again, the Pada text, though it contains some undoubted misinterpretations and misunderstandings, is the earliest attempt at exegetical explanation, going back almost to the time when the Saṁhitā text was constituted; its phonetic analyses should, therefore, not be rejected except after very careful scrutiny.

Such are, in the opinion of the present writer, the principles to be followed at the present day by a translator of the Ṛv. while utilising the aid to be derived from every possible source. A new translation can of course not be final, but will only represent a summary of all the exegetical material now available. Much investigation still remains to be done. Complete success, especially in a field in which the workers are so few, can only be attained by the efforts of several generations of scholars. The Psalms and Prophetic Books of the Old Testament have absorbed the energies of Hebrew scholars for centuries, and yet the sense of many passages remains obscure. Greek scholars have for centuries worked at the lexicographical interpretation of Homer, and yet his vocabulary is not entirely explained, though his language presents incomparably fewer difficulties than the hymns of the *Ṛgveda*. Even if a final translation of the latter should ever be made, it will necessarily contain an irreducible minimum of passages that can never be understood, simply because the circumstances to which they allude will for ever remain unknown.

ON SOME RIVER-NAMES IN THE ṚGVEDA

BY M. AUREL STEIN

THE historical interest presented by Hymn x. 75 of the Ṛgveda, the famous *Nadī-stuti* or 'Song of the Rivers', has been recognized ever since the critical study of Vedic literature began. The numerous ancient river-names of North-Western India therein mentioned furnish an indication, more definite than can be found elsewhere, of the area once occupied by, or familiar to, the Indo-Aryan people to whom we owe the oldest literary remains of India as contained in the Vedic Saṁhitās. In the present note, which regard for manifold urgent tasks resulting from my third journey of exploration in Central Asia obliges me to keep short, I do not intend to discuss the entire list of those river names nor its quasi-historical import, but merely to put on record a few observations which occurred to me long ago while my work still lay in the Panjāb. They concern the river-names recorded in a verse of the hymn which reads thus—

इमं मे गङ्गे यमुने सरस्वति शुतुद्रि स्तोमं सचता परुष्ण्या ।
असिक्न्या मरुद्वृधे वितस्तयार्जीकीये शृणुह्या सुषोमया ॥

No question of text or interpretation affects the general meaning of the verse, which may be rendered as follows—

> "Attend to this my song of praise, O Gaṅgā, Yamunā, Sarasvatī, Śutudrī, Paruṣṇī; together with Asiknī, O Marudvṛdhā, and with Vitastā, O Ārjīkīyā, listen with Suṣomā."

The identity of the first four rivers here enumerated and also of the Vitastā is subject to no doubt. They correspond to the present Ganges, Jumna, Sarsūti, Sutlej, and Jehlam (the ancient Hydaspes, still called Vyath in Kāśmīrī). The order in which the first four are mentioned exactly agrees with their geographical sequence from east to west. Hence Professor Roth, who was the first to discuss the passage critically in his epoch-making treatise *Zur Geschichte und Literatur des Weda* (1846) pp. 136 sqq., was justified in looking for the three rivers *Paruṣṇī*, *Marud-*

vṛdhū and *Asiknī*, which figure in the list between them and the Vitastā, among those of the 'Five Rivers' of the Panjāb that intervene between the Śutudrī : Sutlej in the east and the Vitastā : Jehlam in the west. Guided by this sure indication he succeeded in correctly identifying the *Asiknī* with the Chenāb or Candrabhāga, whose classical name *Akesines* is undoubtedly derived from the Vedic by a kind of 'popular etymology' attested in a gloss of Hesychios (ii. p. 1150, ed. Alberti Σανδαρόφαγος [the exact Greek rendering of Candrabhāga] ὑπὸ 'Αλεξάνδρου πόταμος μετωνομάσθη καὶ ἐκλήθη 'Ακεσίνης).

No such definite evidence is available regarding the *Paruṣṇī*, in which Roth, following Yāska's Nirukta, ix. 26, was prepared to recognize the Irāvatī, the present Rāwī; but until a survival of the name *Paruṣṇī* can be traced in some way this identification, though probable, cannot be considered as certain. The main argument in its favour is that the Beas, the only other Panjāb river of any importance between the Sutlej and the Chenāb, is repeatedly mentioned in other hymns of the Ṛgveda under its proper ancient designation of *Vipāś*.

As regards the *Marudvṛdhā*, which figures in the list between the Asiknī: Akesines and the Vitastā: Hydaspes, and is nowhere else mentioned in Vedic literature, Roth had to content himself with the conjectural suggestion that by it may be meant the united course of the Akesines and the Hydaspes. For a record of other conjectures equally unsupported by philological or geographical evidence, Zimmer, *Altindisches Leben*, p. 12, and Macdonell-Keith, *Vedic Index*, ii p. 135, may be consulted. It is unnecessary to discuss them in detail; for, a reference to the map will show us a solution which seems to impose itself both by regard for geographical position and by the obvious explanation it furnishes for a local name surviving to the present day.

If we pay attention to the position occupied by the name *Marudvṛdhā* in the list, and bear in mind the fact that the narrow Doāb between the Chenāb and the Jehlam leaves no room for any stream to descend independently to the Indus, it is obvious that we have to look for the Marudvṛdhā either among the western main tributaries of the Chenāb or else among those which join the Jehlam from the east. Now, among all the affluents in question there is none comparable in importance and volume to the glacier-fed river which joins the right bank of the Chenāb or Candrabhāga, as it is still known in the mountains, in the alpine territory of Kishtwār, and which in the Survey of India maps is shown as the 'Maroowardwan River'. In its course of about one hundred miles it gathers, as can clearly be seen in sheets 28, 45, 46 of the 'Atlas of India' the greatest part of the drainage from the almost continuous chain of glacier-girt peaks which stretches from the big snowy massif of Amarnāth (17,900 ft. above the sea) in the extreme north-east of Kashmīr proper, to the head-waters of the Bhutñā River, culminating in the ice-clad Nun-kun Peaks, well over 25,000 feet high. Narrow and deep-cut in its lowest portion, the valley of *Maruwārdwan* opens out above the point (about 75°46′ long. 33°40′ lat.) where its two main branches meet, and throughout a total length of about forty miles affords ample space for cultivation at an elevation of between 6,000 and 9,000 ft. On the west this portion of the valley immediately adjoins the watershed towards the eastern part of the great Kashmīr valley watered by the Jehlam or Vyath (Vitastā).

It does not require elaborate philological argument to prove that in the name *Maruwārdwan*, which according to the information received by me in Kashmīr is borne by both the valley and its river, we have the direct phonetic derivative of a form closely linked with the Vedic *Marudvṛdhā*. Among all my Kashmīr tours I never managed to visit the valley in person,—a fact which the absence of any reference to it in Kalhaṇa's *Rājataraṅgiṇī* may help to excuse. But I have reason to believe that the form of the name recorded by the Survey of India during its Kashmīr operations in the late fifties of the last century is a substantially correct rendering of the name as used by the neighbouring hill population. Leaving aside the ending

-wan to be accounted for presently as a determinant derived from Skr. *vana* 'forest', we clearly have the correct phonetic derivative of *Marud,* the first part of the compound, in *maru-*. In *-wārd* it is equally easy to recognize the derivative of a Vṛddhi form **vārdha,* in which *dh* has become dis-aspirated in agreement with a phonetic rule of Kāśmīrī (comp. Sir George Grierson's *Phonology of the Modern Indo-Aryan Vernaculars, Z. D. M. G.*, l. p. 9).

The use of this Vṛddhi form may possibly be connected with the fact that the second half of the compound, in the form *Wārdwan,* is applied independently to the chief group of hamlets in the western or main branch of the Maru-wārdvan valley, while *Maru,* the first half, is used in a corresponding fashion for the inhabited lower portion of the eastern branch of the valley drained by the Fariābādī tributary. I owe the confirmation of the record presented by the 'Atlas of India' to the kindness of that veteran geographer and scientist, Colonel H. H. Godwin-Austen, F. R. S., who conducted the survey operations in these mountain regions more than half a century ago, and who still remembers accurately all the essential features of their topography.

To this splitting-up of the local name *Maru-wārdvan* we have an exact parallel in the use of the names *Candra* and *Bhāga* for the two main branches of the Candrabhāga at its head-waters, as attested by the Survey of India maps. In the same way, far away in the south, the two main feeders of the Tuṅgabhadrā River each bear one half of the name, being known respectively as the Tunga and the Bhadrā. I cannot spare time to trace further this curious bifurcation of river-names, prompted by a kind of 'popular etymology'. But I have little doubt that it is widely spread and could be illustrated outside India.

It is equally easy to account for the addition of the determinant *-wan,* Skr. *vana,* at the end of the compound. The name *Maru-wārdwan* applies primarily to the valley, and it seems quite appropriate that the latter should be designated as the 'forest of the Marudvṛdhā', seeing that its lower and middle portions have their sides clothed with dense forests of deodars and firs duly marked in the Survey map. Skr. *vana* always takes in Kāśmīrī the form *wan* (see Grierson, *Phonology*, etc. *Z. D. M. G.*, l. p. 12; also my notes on modern Kāśmīrī forms of local names containing Skr. *vana*, *vanikā*, in *Rājat.* viii. 1438, 1875-77), and this we find duly in *Maḍ'wāḍwan*, the Kāśmīrī form of the name *Maruwārdwan* as heard by me in Kashmīr and probably used by the Kāśmīrī-speaking population of the valley. Kś. *Maḍ'wād-* represents the correct phonetic derivative from a Skr. **Marudvārdha*, through intermediary forms **Marduwārdha* > **Maḍḍuwāḍḍha*, since Skr. *rd* > Prk. *ḍḍ* becomes *ḍ* in Kś., and Skr. *rdh* > Prk. *ḍḍh* similarly results in Kś. *ḍ* (comp. Grierson, *Phonology*, l. c., §§ 53, 86, 87). Attention must also be paid, as Sir George Grierson points out to me, to the undoubted fact that there is continual interchange between dentals and cerebrals in Kāśmīrī.

Before leaving the riverine system of the Chenāb I may here conveniently call attention to another tributary the name of which, perhaps, also claims an ancient ancestry. I mean the *Ans* River, which receives the southern drainage of the Pīr Pantsāl range between the Rūprī and Gulābgarh passes, and joins the Chenāb above Riassi just where it makes its final southward bend to reach the Panjāb plain. The mere fact that the bed of the Ans River forms a straight continuation northward of the line followed by the Chenāb after the bend just mentioned suffices to attest the relative importances of this tributary. Is it possible that we have in its name a lingering trace of the ancient designation *Asiknī* once applied to the whole river where it emerges from the mountains?

Phonetically the suggested derivation would present no difficulty. Under the influence of the stress accent thrown on the first syllable (see Grierson, *Phonology*, *Z. D. M. G.*, xlix. pp. 395 sq.) *A'siknī* would be liable to assume the Apabhraṁśa form **A'snī*. This, again, through phonetic changes well attested in the development of modern Indo-Aryan vernaculars, might become **A'ssī*, and finally, with the nasalized long vowel often resulting from the simplification of a double consonant, take the form *Ā̃s*, which I assume to be the true pronunciation of the name recorded as *Ans* in the Survey maps (comp. Grierson, *Z. D. M. G.*, l, p. 22; thus, *e. g.*, Skr. *nidrā* > Prk. *niddā* becomes *nī̃d* in Hindī).

Of the river-names mentioned in our verse there still remain two for discussion. The last of them is *Suṣomā* found likewise in a few other Ṛgveda passages, and for this Vivien de Saint-Martin long ago indicated what appears to me the correct identification. He took it to be the present *Sohān* River (also spelt *Suwan*), which flows from the outer Hazāra hills through the Rawalpindi District and reaches the Indus north of the Salt Range (comp. V. de Saint-Martin, *E'tude sur la géographie, etc., du nord-ouest de l'Inde*, 1860, p. 35). The Greek form of the name, Σόανο or Σόαμος, as recorded by Megasthenes (see Arrian, *Indika*, iv. 12; Schwanbeck, *Megasthenes* 31), proves the antiquity of the change of medial Skr. *ṣ* into *h*, so common in the vernaculars of the north-west of India. For the reduction of the *ō* into *ā* in the second syllable of the name, Grierson, *Phonology*, *Z. D. M. G.*, xlix. p. 409 may be compared. Possibly the correct pronunciation of the name is *Sohā̊n* which would represent a closer approximation to the original.

With the Suṣomā : Sohān we have reached the extreme west of the Pañcanada or Panjāb proper. If we are right in assuming for the remaining *Ārjīkīyā* the same exact geographical sequence from east to west observed in the preceding river-names we must clearly look for it between the Vitastā in the east and the Suṣomā in the west.

There is no river of any importance crossing the much-broken plateaus and low hill chains of the Salt Range which fill the area between those two rivers. Hence we are led to look for the *Ārjīkīyā* among the chief tributaries which the Vitastā receives on its right bank before it emerges from the mountains above the town of Jehlam. Of these there are two of considerable size. One is the Kishangangā, the *Kṛṣṇā* of the *Rājataraṅgiṇī*, which drains the high snowy ranges north of Kashmīr and at the confluence, near Muẓaffarābād, rivals the Vitastā in volume. The other is the Kunhār River, Albērūnī's *Kuśnārī*, which gathers the mountain streams of the big Kāghān Valley in the north and joins the Vitastā some five miles below Muẓaffarābād. Both Kishangangā and Kunhār would be important enough to figure in our Vedic 'Catalogue of Rivers'; but I am quite unable to trace in the case of either, any designation ancient or modern that might be connected with the name *Ārjīkīyā*.

None of the Ṛgveda passages which mention the Ārjīkīyā again, or give the obviously related ethnic designation of Ārjīkas and Ārjīkīyas (comp. Macdonell-Keith, *Vedic Index*, i. pp. 62 sqq.), helps us to a definite location. Professor Hillebrandt, when discussing these names in his *Vedische Mythologie*, i. pp. 126 sqq., thought that he could locate them near Kashmīr, owing to the connection he assumed between Ārjīka and the chief Ἀρσάκης, whom Arrian mentions as the brother of Ἀβισάρης chief of the Abhisāras, i. e. the tribes occupying the outer hills south of Kashmīr between the Chenāb and the Jehlam. But this supposed connection fails us, since I have shown elsewhere that by Ἀρσάκης is meant the chief of Uraśā or Hazāra, the name of whose territory figures as Ἄρσα or Οὐάρσα in Ptolemy's Geography (comp. my note on *Rājat.* v. 217).

I may conclude this note with a brief general observation. The analysis of the river-names given in our Ṛgveda verse has proved that, leaving aside the still uncertain Ārjīkīyā, they follow each other in strict order from east to west. The exact geographical knowledge thus indicated, ranging over a great extent of country, might at first sight cause surprise, since it seems impossible to suppose that the composer of the *Nadī-stuti* could have had before him topographical record in the shape of either text or map. Yet the difficulty is easily removed in the light of actual travel experience. During my Central-Asian explorations I have again and again come into contact with men, whether Turkīs of the Tārīm Basin engaged in long journeys as traders and caravan-men, or nomadic Mongols, who, wholly illiterate and unable to keep any but mental records, could yet without any apparent effort give a brief but accurate account of the successive stages, with passes, streams, and other natural features, which they had passed on journeys extending over far more than a thousand miles. It is probable that in India also, in spite of all modern changes, similar geographical knowledge of a wholly empiric kind might still be gathered from pilgrims, traders, and others accustomed to distant peregrinations. It is safe to assume the same facility of obtaining exact information in ancient times, so that the only difficulty which the composer of the Hymn is likely to have experienced when recording the river-names, was how to fit their sequence with his metre.[1]

1 This paper was written in the autumn of 1916 as a special contribution to this volume, but unfortunately and through reasons for which the present difficulties of communication are mainly responsible, its publication occurred in another place sooner than was intended. A. S.

CHALDEAN AND INDIAN VEDAS

BY BAL GANGADHAR TILAK

ONE of the most important events of the latter half of the nineteenth century is the discovery of the Chaldean literature as embodied in the cuneiform inscriptions excavated in Mesopotamia and deciphered with great skill, ingenuity, and perseverance by European scholars. These ancient records conclusively show that the country at the mouth of the Euphrates was, so far back as 5000 B.C., colonised by a people of the Turanian race who went there by sea from some distant province, presumably situated in Northern Asia. These people not only developed a civilization of their own in Mesopotamia, but what is to the point, have left there a record of their religious beliefs and culture in the form of brick-inscriptions, which M. Lenormant has aptly described as the Chaldean Veda.

This ancient civilization at the mouth of the Tigris and Euphrates gradually spread northwards and was the parent of the Assyrian civilization which flourished about 2000 years before Christ. It is believed that the Hindus came in contact with Assyrians after this date, and as a natural result of this intercourse Hindu culture was largely influenced by the Assyrian. Thus Rudolph von Ihering, starting with the theory that the original Aryan home was in an uncultivated mountain district in Central Asia, has, in his work on the *Evolution of the Aryans* (Eng. trans. by Drucker, 1897, pp. 11, 223–4), come to the conclusion that the Aryans were originally a nomadic race unacquainted with agriculture, canals, navigation, stone-houses, working in metals, money transactions, alphabet and such other elements of higher civilization, all of which they subsequently borrowed from the Babylonians. But this conclusion is not accepted by other scholars, who think that von Ihering has gone too far in the matter. It is, however, still believed that in the matter of magical charms and formulæ, cosmography, cosmogony, astronomy and chronology the Hindus were more or less indebted to the Babylonians, and that this borrowing was the result of an intercourse between the two races at a date later than 2000 before Christ.[1] When it was therefore pointed out that the word *manā* in the phrase *sácā manā́ hiraṇyáyā* (Ṛv. VIII. 78. 2) corresponded with Latin *mina*, the Greek μνᾶ and the Phœnician *manah*, and it must therefore have been borrowed by the Indians from the Babylonians, and that, if so, a later date must be assigned to the Ṛgveda, Professor Max Müller declined[2] to accept the inference and contended that the word might be of Aryan origin and that it might, as interpreted by Sāyaṇa, mean 'ornaments' or 'beautiful appendices'. For Professor Max Müller believed, and rightly, that the Ṛgveda, the oldest of the Vedas, cannot be assigned to a date later than 2000 years before Christ. The learned Orientalist was aware that the word *manā* was to be found not only in the Babylonean but also in the Accadian tongue. But he seemed not to have realised the importance of this fact; for in that case, the Accadian being a still older language, it was not necessary to assign a later date to the Ṛgveda even if the word *manā* (cf. Kanarese and Marāṭhī *maṇa*, English corruption 'maund') was found to be of foreign origin.

In my *Orion or the Antiquity of the Vedas*, I have shown that Vedic culture or civilization can be carried back as far as, if not further than, 4500 B. C., when the Vernal equinox was in Orion. This makes the Vedic and the Chaldean civilizations almost contemporaneous, and it is not unnatural to expect some intercourse either by land or by sea between the Chaldean and the Vedic races even in those ancient times. No evidence has, however, yet been adduced to prove the existence of an intercourse between these two races in the fourth or fifth millennium before Christ by tracing Vedic words or ideas in the Chaldean tongue, or vice versa. If this evidence is discovered the existing theories about the inter-relation

1 For a summary see the article on *Hinduism* in Hastings' Encyclopædia of Religion and Ethics, Vol. VI. p. 688f.

2 *India : What can it teach us ?* Edition 1883, pp. 125-26.

between these two oldest civilizations will have to be greatly modified or revised. But without going so far into the subject I wish in this essay to confine myself to the words and ideas which I have found common to the Chaldean and the Indian Vedas, stating at the same time what little has been done by the previous scholars in this direction.

Professor A. H. Sayce, in his *Hibbert Lectures*, 1887, pages 137-138, observes that in an ancient list of Babylonian clothing *sindhu* is mentioned as a name for muslin or woven cloth, and that it corresponds to the *śadīn* of the Old Testament and the *σινδών* of the Greeks. The learned Professor has further stated that this 'muslin' or woven cloth must have been called *sindhu* by the Accadians (Chaldeans), because it was exported from the banks of the Indus (*Sindhu*) to Chaldea in those days (cf. the word *calico* from *Calicut*). He has further noted that this intercourse between the two countries must have been by sea, for had the word passed by land, i. e. through Persia, the initial *s* of the word would have become *h* in Persian mouths.

Here then we have two words: *manā* borrowed by the Vedic people from the Chaldeans, and *sindhu* borrowed by the Accadians or Chaldeans from the Indians, proving either that these races were neighbours to each other even in Vedic times or that the Chaldean traders had made their way to the mouth of the Indus or to the Western coast of India, each people borrowing from the other according to necessity.

More recently, the excavations made in Asia Minor during the summer of 1907 have brought to light documents which contain the terms of a treaty between the king of Hittites and the king of Mitani (Northern Mesopotamia), of the time of *circa* 1400 before Christ. In these treaties the deities of both these nations are invoked; and among the Mitani gods Hugo Winkler has found the names of Mitra, Varuṇa, Indra and Nāsatyas or Aśvins, one and all of which are Vedic deities. It is, therefore, quite clear that in the fourteenth century B. C. and earlier the rulers of Northern Mesopotamia worshipped Vedic gods. The names of these rulers, it is true, appear to be Persian and not Vedic. But it does not affect the conclusion that Vedic culture and worship were known to and had influenced the Mesopotamian rulers in the fourteenth century before Christ.[1]

This takes us back to B. C. 1400 or 1500. But we can go still further back and show, that the intercourse between Chaldea and India existed from a time far anterior to the reign of the Mitanic kings. M. Lenormant has justly observed that while the Aryans worshipped the good and beneficient deities in nature, the Mongolians (to which race the Chaldeans belonged) always tried to propitiate the malevolent spirits; and hence while *sacrifice* formed the main feature of the Vedic religion, *magic and sorcery* was the main characteristic of the religion of the ancient Chaldeans. Not that there were no Chaldean hymns to the sun-god, but even these were used for magic purposes.[2]

This shrewd generalisation of the French savant at once enables us to lay our hand upon the Atharva Veda, if we wish to find any parallels to the Chaldean magic formulæ in the Vedic literature. The Vedic religion is very often called the *trayī-dharma* or the religion based only on the three ancient and older Vedas. The Atharva Veda finds no place amongst these three, and there is an old tradition that in point of importance and authority the Atharva does not stand on a par with the Ṛg, the Yajus and the Sāman. Historically speaking it is now further ascertained that the Atharva Veda is much more recent than the three other Vedas. But though comparatively younger, we must at the same time remember that even this recent Veda must be placed at least some twenty-five centuries before Christ in as much as it is

1 H. Jacobi's paper in the *Journal of the Royal Asiatic Society* for July 1909, pp. 721-726.

2 Lenormant's *Chaldean Magic*, Engl. Trans., pp. 145f, 179 and 319.

mentioned by name and cited in the Brāhmaṇas and the Upaniṣads.[1]

If we therefore discover any names of Chaldean spirits or demons in the Atharva, it could only mean that the magic of the Chaldeans was borrowed, partially at least, by the Vedic people prior to the second millennium before Christ, and that this could not have been done unless the Chaldean people were either the neighbours of Vedic tribes or traded with them even in those ancient days.

Now let us take for comparison Atharva Veda v. 13. It is a hymn against snake poison; and verses 6,7,8 and 10 therein (omitting the accents) run as follows—

असितस्य **तैमातस्य** बभ्रोरपोदकस्य च ।
सात्रासाहस्याहं मन्योरव ज्यामिव धन्वनो वि मुञ्चामि रथाँ इव ॥ ६ ॥
आलिगी च **विलिगी** च पिता च माता च ।
विद्म वः सर्वतो बन्ध्वरसाः किं करिष्यथ ॥ ७ ॥
उरुगूलाया दुहिता जाता दास्यसिक्न्या(*v. l.* क्न्याः) ।
प्रतङ्कं दद्रुषीणां सर्वासामरसं विषम् ॥ ८ ॥

....

ताबुवं न **ताबुवं** न घेत्त्वमसि **ताबुवम्** ।
ताबुवेनारसं विषम् ॥ १० ॥

The verses have been translated into English by Bloomfield,[2] Whitney, Griffith and other scholars; but none of them has attempted to explain the derivation and meaning of the words printed in black in the original and

1 Bloomfield's Introduction to Atharva Veda in S. B. E. Vol. XLII.

2 In the S. B. E. series vol. XLII, p. 28—

I release thee from the fury of the black serpent, the *Taimāta* the brown serpent, the poison that is not fluid, the all-conquering, as the bow-string (is loosened) from the bow, as chariots (from horses). 6.

Both *Āligī* and *Viligī*, both father and mother, we know your kin everywhere. - Deprived of your strength what will ye do? 7.

The daughter of *Urugūlā*, the evil one born with the black—of all those who have run to their hiding-place, the poison is devoid of force. 8.

....

Tābuvam (or) not *Tābuvam*, thou (O serpent) art not *Tābuvam*. Through *Tābuvam* thy poison is bereft of force. 10.

italics in the translation. Their very sound betrays, to a Sanskrit reader, their foreign origin. But hitherto not only commentators but even translators have failed to explain their true import or origin. The word *Taimāta* again occurs in Atharva Veda V. 18. 4; while *Āligī*, *Viligī* and *Urugūlā* do not again occur in the Atharva Veda. According to *Kauśika Sūtras* these hymns are recited while performing certain manœuvres in the process of removing the snake poison. But the *Sūtras* do not give any information regarding the origin of the above mentioned words. Griffith says that *Taimāta* and *Apodaka* (waterless) are some unidentifiable varieties of snakes and that *Āligī*, *Viligī* and *Urugūlā* similarly indicate some other unknown species of serpents. Whitney considers *Taimāta* as a derivative from *Timāta*, while the word *Urugūlā* is translated by him as " the broad-knobbed one." *Āligī* and *Viligī* (the father and mother) he does not attempt to explain at all. The word *asiknī*, which means black, suggests that *Urugūlā* is a word borrowed from black races (cf. *asiknīḥ viśaḥ* in Ṛv. VII, 5. 3). But in the absence of any definite knowledge about the magic and sorcery of the black races, it was impossible to trace the origin of these words. The discovery of the Chaldean literature now supplies us with the means of accurately ascertaining the parentage of some of these words. For instance, the serpent *Taimāta* is, I am sure, no other than the primeval watery dragon *Tiāmat* generally represented as a female but sometimes even as a male monster snake in the Chaldean cosmogonic legends; and the word *Apodaka* in the Vedic text indicates that a land species of the same (as opposed to aquatic) is intended to be coupled with it. Tiāmat is the well-known Chaldean androgynous dragon whose fight with Marduk is the subject of some of the cuneiform tablets[1] of the creation legends. As regards *Urugūlā* the word appears as *Urugala* or *Urugula* in the Accadian language. Literally, it means " the great (*gal* = *gula*) city (*uru*)", but is generally

1 See Sayce's *Hibbert Lectures* pp. 370–384, and *Chaldea*, Story of Nations Series, Chap. VI, p. 16.

used to denote the great nether world, the abode of the dead—a place visited by Istar in her search for her lover Dumuzi or Tamuz.[1] Personified, it means the deity of the nether world, and a female snake can be fitly described as *Uru-gula's* daughter.

I have not been able to trace *Āligī* and *Viligī*, but they evidently appear to be Accadian words, for there is an Assyrian god called *Bil* and *Bil-gi*. At any rate there is no doubt that *Taimāta* and *Urugūlā* are, in spite of a little difference in spelling, the same as *Tiāmat* and *Urugal* or *Uru-gula* in the Accadian legends, and that these names must have been borrowed by the Vedic people from the Chaldeans, coming in contact with them either as their neighbours or as tradesmen in those early days. When the old religion of sacrifice was thus tampered with, and hybrid hymns incorporating foreign magical incantations and formulæ were tried to be introduced in the Vedic literature, it was natural that the Veda which contained these incantations should come to be looked upon with scant respect or even with contempt by the orthodox Vedic community, who must then have regarded the Atharva Veda as a novel departure in their religious observances. There are some other words in the Atharva Veda, especially in the poison and witchcraft hymns, which on their face appear to be foreign importations. For instance we may cite *Tābuvam*[2] in the hymn we are considering and *Kanaknakam* and *Taudi* in Av., X, 4. Again the word *Kimīdin* which occurs both in the Ṛg and the Atharva Veda, (Ṛv. VII, 104. 23 ; Av. I. 7. 1) and which indicates goblins, or evil spirits, is derived by Yāska (VI. 119) from *kim idānīm* (what now?), and

1 Jensen's *Kosmologie der Babylonier*, pp. 217-222 ; *Chaldea*, S. N. Series pp. 157, 326f, and 367f.

2 I think *Tābuvam* is derived from the Polynesian word *tabu* and means, pertaining to or resulting from *tabu*, i. e. contact with unclean, unholy, or interdicted thing, in which case the disease or evil requires to be treated with sacred incantations. The exorcist asks whether the poison is or is not of *Tābuvam* character. For the use of *tabus* in Babylonia see *Thompson's Semitic Magic*.

explained by observing that these ghosts were believed to wander about in search of "what is now happening." This derivation is obviously fanciful; and as the word has a foreign ring, I believe that it is a Chaldean word. For *Ekimmu* and *Dimme* are Accadian words for spirits and *Kimm-dimm* may well have been a word compounded from them to express ghosts of all kinds.

It may be further noted that the Kirātas, evidently some non-Aryan tribe, are mentioned as dealing in medicinal herbs in Av. x. 4. 14; and Griffith, in a note to Av. v. 13. 5, interprets *Kairāta* as a variety of snake found among the Kirātas, the barbarous tribes who inhabited woods and mountains and lived by hunting (the *Kirrhadae* of Arrian). It is therefore not to be doubted that the magic and witchcraft hymns in the Atharva Veda do contain some foreign words. But we in India have not the means to thoroughly investigate all of them. We have no library in India, much less an Assyrialogist we can refer to or consult, for obtaining the requisite information on these matters. The Mleccha-prasiddhārtha-prāmāṇyādhikaraṇa in Jaimini's sūtras (i. 3. 10) shows that even the orthodox Mīmāṅsakas would not have hesitated to recognise the foreign origin of such words if they had but been able to ascertain it definitely.

The Bible often refers to Chaldea and Babylonia. But no one ever dreamt that the account of creation and deluge in the Old Testament could have been, in the main, borrowed by the Hebrew priests from Chaldean sources. A great sensation was therefore caused in Europe when the Chaldean cuneiform tablets of the creation legend were discovered, their translation published and the Hebrew word *Têhom*, which is translated as 'deep' or 'waters' in the first verses of Genesis, Chap. I, was found to be no other than Assyrian *Tamtu* or the Chaldean *Tiūmat.* Even so late as 1902, Professor Delitzsch's lectures on *Babel and Bible* (Eng. trans. New York 1903) were received and criticised in the same spirit. But it may now be taken as established that the Biblical stories of creation and deluge together with the institution of sabbath and even the story of the fall of man by the serpent are all of Chaldean origin. It was further pointed out by Professor Delitzch, the well-known Assyriologist, that the word *Jehovah*, God's secret name revealed to Moses, was also of Chaldean origin, and that its real pronunciation was *Yahve*, and not *Jehovah*; and this derivation is now accepted even by the compilers of the present Biblical dictionaries. But the matter does not really end at this point. Jehovah is undoubtedly the same word as the Chaldean *Yahve*. But we have still to inquire whether the word can or cannot be traced further back. And here we derive great help from the Vedic literature. The word *yahu* (Zend, *yazu*), *yahva*, *yahvat* and the feminine forms *yahvī* and *yahvatī* occur several times in the Ṛgveda; and Grassmann derives them from the root *yah* = to hasten or to drive quickly. The Nighaṇṭu also tells us that the word *yaha* means water (Nig. I. 12) or strength (Nig. II. 9); while the adjective *yahva* (Nig. III. 3; Nir. VIII, 8) means 'great.' *Yahva* in this sense is applied in the Ṛgveda to Soma (Ṛv. IX. 75. 1), to Agni (Ṛv. III. 1. 12) and to Indra (Ṛv. VIII. 13. 24). It is needless to give further quotations. I may only mention that *yahva* in one instance (Ṛv. X. 110. 3) is used in the vocative case, and Agni is there addressed as "O *Yahva!* you are the sacrificer of the gods." This clearly shows that the word was not only familiar to the Vedic sages, but that it was applied by them to their gods to signify their might, power or strength; and Griffith has translated it by the English word 'Lord' in several places. Besides, in the Vedic Sanskrit we have several other words derived from the root *yah* and so cognate to *yahva*, viz. *yahu*, *yahvat*, *yahvī* and *yahvatī*. It is not, therefore, unreasonable to conclude that *yahva* was originally a Vedic word, and though Moses may have borrowed it from the Chaldeans, yet the Chaldean tongue, in which the various other cognate forms of the word are wanting, cannot claim it to be originally its own. Like the word *sindhu* the Chaldeans appear to have themselves borrowed it from the Indians in their mutual intercourse at some remote period of antiquity.

We might say the same about the Chaldean word *Apsu*, or *Abzu*. It is written as *Zu ab* and read as *Abzu*. It denotes the primeval chaos or watery abyss, and is represented as the husband of *Tiāmat*. Marduk had therefore to fight with them both to rescue the powers of light from their clutches. Dr. Jensen[1] has critically examined the various meanings of this word in the Chaldean literature. But it is unnecessary to go into these details; for the word and its denotation are well established in usage. It is the primeval abyss from which the gods of light have to be rescued by Marduk for the benefit of mankind. This conquest of Marduk over *Apsu* and *Tiāmat* is celebrated in a Chaldean Epic which is now available in translation.[2]

I have shown above that the word *Taimūta* occurs in the Atharva Veda, and that it must have been borrowed from the Chaldean. Such is not however the case with *Apsu*, the husband of *Tiāmat*. In the Ṛgveda we have not only the word *apsu* in several places but the main features of the Tiāmat-Marduk struggle are also to be found in the Vṛtra-Indra fight so fully described in the Vedas. I have shown elsewhere[3] that Indra's fight with the Vṛtra was for the release of captive waters, and that after the fight these waters, till then enveloped and hemmed in by Vṛtra, the Vedic Tiāmat, were set free, by Indra, to flow (*sartave*).[4] For this very reason Indra is described in the Ṛgveda as *Apsu-jit*.[5] It is usual to explain the compound word

1 In his *Kosmologie der Babylonier*, pp. 243–253.

2 See Sayce's *Hibbert Lectures*, pp. 379–384 ; Jensen's *Kosmologie der Babylonier*, pp. 273–288 ; also *Chaldea*, S. N. Series, Chap. VI.

3 See *Arctic Home in the Vedas*, Chap. IX, pp. 233–296.

4 Ṛgveda i. 32. 12. Curiously enough the same phrase occurs in the Chaldean Creation Tablet No. 4, line 140, where Marduk after defeating Tiāmat, is said to have ordered her (Tiāmat's) waters, which were not coming out, to come forth. The line is so rendered by Dr. Budge; but Jensen, following the Hebrew tradition, translates it to mean "ordered the waters not to come forth" (*Kosmologie der Babylonier*, p. 288). Vedic tradition and phraseology both support Dr. Budge's rendering and I prefer it to Jensen's. Prof. Sayce (*Hibbert Lectures*, 1887, p. 383) follows Dr. Budge, and Jastrow (*Babylonia and Assyria*, p. 438) follows Jenson.

5 Ṛv. VIII 13. 2; VIII. 36. 1 ; IX. 106. 3.

Apsu-jit by treating its first member as a locative of *ap*,= water and translate it as meaning "conqueror *in* waters" But it will be easily seen that in spite of the Vārtika on Pāṇini VI. 3. 18, this is rather a forced construction, and that it is better to take *Apsu* as a word by itself and translate *Apsu-jit* as "conqueror of *Apsu*." The same remark applies to the words *Apsu-ja* and *Apsu-kṣit* and the like. It may be further noted that the phrase *apsavam arṇavam*[1] also occurs in the Ṛgveda, and there, *apsavam*, which is an adjective, evidently means "of or relating to *Apsu*". Similarly the word *apsumat* is also found in the Vedic literature (Ait. Brāh. VII. 7), and it is there applied to Agni. In this word we cannot take *Apsu* as a locative of *ap*; and if we have thus a direct authority for treating *Apsu* as a separate word by itself, there is no reason why we should not take *Apsu* as a word by itself, and not as the locative of *ap*, in such words as *Apsu-jit* and *Apsu-kṣit*. *Apsu* taken as a separate word, may be derived either from *ap* = water and *su* = to beget, or from *psu*, which, according to Nig. III. 7, means shape or form. In the latter case *Apsu* would mean a shapeless or formless chaos, which is the meaning assigned to it in the Chaldean literature. Anyhow there is little doubt that *Apsu* in *Apsu-jit* is the same word as the Chaldean *Apsu* or *Abzu* which was conquered by Marduk, the Chaldean Indra. The word is evidently Vedic, but owing to the ignorance of its true significance, the Indian etymologists have treated it as the locative of *ap* in compounds like *apsu-jit*. The light thrown by the Chaldean literature on the subject enables us now to rectify the error and understand *Apsu-jit* in its proper and legitimate sense. Tiāmat was the orginal Chaldean word for the primeval abyss. But when the Vedic word *Apsu* was borrowed it became necessary to differentiate between the two, and this seems to have been done by making one the husband of the other.

Another Vedic word on which new light is thrown by the Chaldean literature is *uru*. In the Vedic literature

1 Ṛv. X. 55. 37.

the word occurs several times by itself and also in compounds like *uru-krama* (Ṛv. I. 90. 9) *uru-kṣaya* (Ṛv. X. 118. 9), *uru-gāya* (Ṛv. I. 154. 1) and several others. The word *uru* in these compounds is generally taken as an adjective meaning "wide." Thus *uru-gāya* is translated by "wide-going" and so on. But it seems to me that if we take *uru*, as in the Chaldean, to mean the nether world, the above Vedic words can be better interpreted. In the Ṛgveda *uru-gāya* is not only applied to Viṣṇu but also to Indra and Soma. Now we know from the Ṛgveda that Viṣṇu and Soma are the deities who helped Indra in the conquest of the waters of *Apsu*. All these deities can therefore be aptly described as *uru-gāya*, that is, those who traverse the nether world of waters and conquer, along with Indra, the powers of darkness therein. In other words, we can now take *uru-kṣaya* as a synonym for *apsu-kṣit* and *uru-krama* as synonymous with *apsu-sad* or *apsu-jit*. The word *uru* appears to have the same meaning in *uru-lokam* in Ṛv. X. 128. 2. But a still more important word is *Uru-aśī*, (Urvaśī), the name of a well-known nymph. Yāska[1] would have us believe that the word *uru* in *Uru-aśī* means a thigh, and there is an etymological myth which tells us that *Uru-aśī* was born from the thigh of Nārāyaṇa.[2] But all these strange derivations become unnecessary if we take *uru* in *Uru-aśī* to mean the nether world or its waters as in the Chaldean. *Uru-aśī* would then mean a watery nymph or a nymph of the nether world and can thus be properly described as *ap-saras*. There are a few other words in the Ṛgveda on which new light may be thrown by the discovery of Chaldean literature. For instance *sinīvālī*[3] looks to me like a foreign word, and *tur-pharītū* in that well-known un-

1 Nir. v. 13. 2 Cf. Kālidāsa's Vikramorvaśīya, i. 3.

3 *Sin bubbuli* in Chaldean may mean 'disappearance of the moon'; and *tur-parattu* may mean 'son of waters'. *Sindhu-mātarau*, sons of ocean, is one of the epithets of Aśvins in the Ṛgveda. The word *sina* appears in Ṛgveda ii. 30. 2 and there it is said to be brought to or presented to Vṛtra. Can *sina* here mean the moon? Owing to her waning she may be properly said to be handed over or delivered to Vṛtra, the demon of darkness.

VEDIC CONCEPTION OF THE WORLD.

(FROM THE *ARCTIC HOME IN THE VEDAS.*)

VṚTRA TRIUMPHANT.

VṚTRA SLAIN.

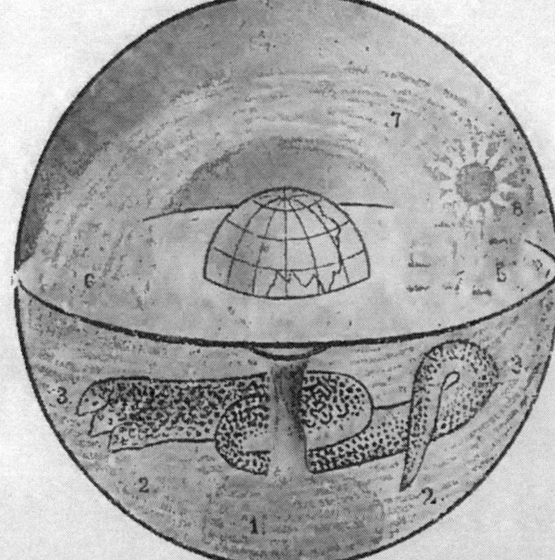

1 Varuṇa's tree in the Nether World.
2 The cosmic waters (stagnant, Chald. *Apsu*) enveloped by Vṛtra.
3 Vṛtra as Serpent (Chald. *Tiāmat*).
4 The sun in stagnant waters in the clutches of Vṛtra.
5 The sunrise mountains.
6 The sunset mountains.
7 The Cosmic waters set free to move in the Heavens.
8 The sun moving with released waters in the Heavens.

BABYLONIAN CONCEPTION OF THE WORLD.

(FROM JENSEN'S *COSMOLOGIE* DER *BABYLONIER.*)

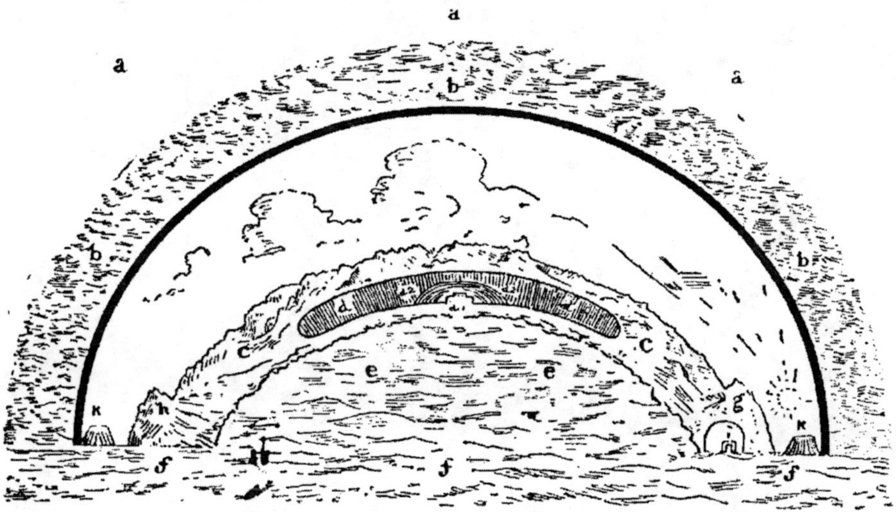

a Inside of the Heavens.
b The Heavenly Ocean.
c The Earth.
d The Kingdom of Death.
*d*1 Palace of Death.
*d*2 The seven walls of Death's Kingdom.

e The prime Hidden place.
f The Ocean (*Apsu*) round the world.
g The sunrise mountain.
h The sunset mountain.
i The meeting-place with the House of Fates.
k The damm of the Heavens.

Between pp. 40 and 41]

intelligible verse (Ṛv. X. 106. 6) also wears a suspicious look. I shall not, therefore, be surprised if that verse is found to contain some words of foreign origin. On the other hand *itu* meaning 'a month' in the Chaldean language seems to me to be the same word as the Vedic *ṛtu* meaning 'a season' or 'a month.'

Lastly I may here mention that we find a very close resemblance between the Chaldean and the Vedic legends regarding the place and movements of cosmic waters, their conquest by the powers of light, viz. by Indra or Marduk, and also between the cosmographic ideas of the two nations, that is those relating to the arrangement of the whole universe, as may be seen by a comparison of the illustrative diagram of "the world according to Babylonish ideas" given by Jensen at the end of his book, and the one given by me in my *Arctic Home in the Vedas* at the end of Chapter IX.[1] Dr. Jensen has also discussed the sevenfold division of the earth's continents by the Babylonians, and pointed out its resemblance with the Paurāṇic account of the seven continents.[2] But I think that the parallel can be carried much further; for I have shown elsewhere that this sevenfold division is to be found not only in the Purāṇas but also in the Vedas.[3] It is really interesting to note that there are not only seven Heavens and seven Hells in the Chaldean mythology, but that the serpent Tiāmat killed by Marduk is sometimes represented as having seven heads, while Indra is called *Sapta-han* or the "Killer of Seven" in the Vedas,[4] and the closed watery ocean, the doors of which Indra and Agni opened by their prowess, is described as *sapta-budhna* (seven-bottomed) in Ṛv. VIII. 40. 5. Again there are indications in the ancient Chaldean literature of a dark intercalary winter month and of the sun-hero being affected with a kind of skin

1 Compare also Maspero's *Dawn of Civilization*, Eng. translation, Vol. II, pp. 542–543.

2 *Kosmologie der Babylonier*, pp. 163–184.

3 Cf. *Arctic Home*, pp. 340f.

4 Ṛv. X. 49. 8.

disease or lost for a part of the year,[1] thus corroborating the theory of a common Arctic home for all. But the subject, howsoever interesting it may be, cannot be discussed at the end of this paper. My object was simply to draw the attention of Vedic scholars to the importance of the comparative study of Indian and Chaldean Vedas by pointing out some words which, in my opinion, are common to both, and which fairly establish the case of mutual, and not merely one-sided, indebtedness between the almost contemporaneous Aryan and Turanian people. What effect it may have on the current theories about the inter-relation between the two ancient cultures must be left for the scholars to decide. When two civilizations are contemporaneous it is natural to expect some borrowings from each other; but when both are equally old it is difficult to see why, supposing the borrowing is proved, one of them alone should be considered to have borrowed from the other and that too only in later times.

1 In Gilgames and Istar myths. In Ṛv. vii. 100. 6 Viṣṇu is said to be affected with skin disease (*śipiviṣṭa*). Compare *Arctic Home*, pp. 330-32. See also Plunket's *Ancient Calendars*, pp. 4 and 14. The intercalary or the thirteenth month was called *se-dir*, the dark month of sowing.

BRĀHMAṆA-QUOTATIONS IN NIRUKTA

BY P. D. GUNE

YĀSKA'S Nirukta is a running commentary upon the Nighaṇṭavaḥ or collections of difficult Vedic words. These latter consist of five parts or chapters, containing synonyms in the first three, difficult Vedic words in the fourth and names of deities and other words connected with them in the fifth. Yāska takes each of these words, first gives its meaning, then the derivation or derivations and lastly quotes the Vedic passage or Nigama in which it occurs. This is generally his method. In deriving he often gives divergent views, sometimes with names, e. g. *iti Audumbarāyaṇaḥ*, *iti Āgrāyaṇaḥ*, etc., but often without them. Occasionally, as in the Daivatakāṇḍa, he mentions schools[1] of interpretation such as that of the Yājñikāḥ, the Parivrājakāḥ, the Naidānāḥ, the Aitihāsikāḥ, or simply like *atha adhyātmam*, *eṣa cākhyānasamayaḥ*. Very often he quotes Brāhmaṇa passages in corroboration of, or simply as alternative to, his view. He indicates these passages in one of these ways : 1 by introducing them with the words *athāpi Brāhmaṇam bhavati* ; 2 by closing them with the words *iti ca Brāhmaṇam* ; or 3 by putting *iti vijñāyate* after them. But he is not—as no Ācārya ever was—in the habit of indicating from what particular source he was quoting. Perhaps in his days there was no necessity of doing so, for, those for whom his book was meant had, like himself, committed to memory most of the old literature; and they could easily know where the quotation was from. There are a few Pandits even to-day who could do the same.

There are about fifty passages from the Brāhmaṇas in the body of the Nirukta, indicated by one of these three ways. The second way, however, is more than twice as frequent as the last. Only a few of these passages have yet been identified—some of them by Roth in his Erleuter-

1 About these schools see Sieg, *die Sagenstoffe des Ṛgveda*, introduction.

ungen. The following is an attempt to identify as many others as possible under the present circumstances. Quotations from the Nirukta follow Roth's edition, giving chapter and section only. It would not be difficult to trace the quotations in other editions of the Nirukta, as they also mention this manner of division of the book. In quoting from the Brāhmaṇas the old natural division is resorted to, as this is bound to be given in any edition of them, be it European, or Bengali or Marathi.

1. तद्यदाभिर्वृत्रमशकद्धन्तुं तच्छक्करीणां शक्करीत्वं इति विज्ञायते (i. 8)—This passage, with slight change, is found in the Kauṣ. Br.—एताः शक्कर्यः। एताभिर्वा इन्द्रो वृत्रमशकद्धन्तुं। तद्यदाभिर्वृत्रमशकद्धन्तुं तस्माच्छक्कर्यः (xxiii. 2). The same derivation is found in the Tāṇḍ. Br. in different words—तस्मा एतच्छन्दोभ्य इन्द्रियं वीर्यं निर्माय प्रायच्छदेतेन शक्नुहीति तच्छक्करीणां शक्करीत्वम् (xiii. 10. 1). In the Aitareya the same derivation is given, but the Śakvarīs are connected with Prajāpati—यदिमांल्लोकान्प्रजापतिः सृष्ट्वेदं सर्वमशक्नोद्यदिदं किंच तच्छक्कर्योऽभवंस्तच्छक्करीणां शक्करीत्वम् (v. 7).

2. तस्मादेते व्यक्ततरे इव भवत इति ह विज्ञायते (i. 9)—Not traced.

3. ऋच्छन्तीव ख उदगन्तामिति ह विज्ञायते (i. 9)—Not traced.

4. पर्याया इव त्वदाश्विनम् (i. 9)—This is found in the Kauṣ. Br. xvii. 4.

5. उरु प्रथस्वेति प्रथयति प्रोहाणीति प्रोहति (i. 15)—Though the usual expression, indicating that this is a quotation from a Brāhmaṇa, does not occur at the end, we know the fact from the previous sentence which runs—अथापि ब्राह्मणेन रूपसंपन्ना विधीयन्ते. Roth has indentified these sentences as occurring in Vāj. Saṁ. i. 22 and ii. 15. The first part of the quotation occurs in Tait. Saṁ. i. 1. 8. 1, i. 2. 12. 2, vi. 2. 7. 3; Mait. Saṁ. i. 1. 9, i. 5. 5, etc.; Kāṭh. i. 8; Tait. Br. iii. 2. 8. 4. For the latter part Bloomfield's Concordance refers to Vāj. Saṁ. ii. 15, not quite to the point.

6. ओषधे त्रायस्वैनम् (i. 15)—This is an often recurring sentence in the various Saṁhitās of the Yajurveda. Vāj. Saṁ. v. 42. Compare Tait. Saṁ. i. 2. 1. 1, 1. 3. 5. 1, vi. 3. 3. 2, etc.; Mait. Saṁ. i. 2. 1, iii. 9. 3, etc.; Kāṭhakam ii. 1, etc. See Bloomfield's Concordance. Also Mantra Br. i. 6. 5 and 6. Śatapatha Br. iii. 1. 2. 7 has ओषधे त्रायस्व (without एनम्) and स्वधिते मैनं हिंसीः together; again at iii. 6. 4. 10 and iii. 8. 2. 12 and often.

7. स्वधिते मैनं हिंसीः (i. 15)—An often occurring formula in the Yajurveda. Vāj. Saṁ. iv. 1, v. 42, vi. 15; Tait. Saṁ. i. 2. 1. 1, 1. 3. 5. 1, vi. 3. 3. 2, etc.; Mait. Saṁ. i. 2. 1, and about a dozen times more; Kāṭhakam ii. 1, etc. It occurs in some places of the Saṁhitās together with No. 6 as one running proverb. Of the Brāhmaṇas it occurs some thrice in the Śat. Br. iii. 1. 2. 7, etc. Also Mantra. Br. i. 6. 5 and 6.

8. अग्नये समिध्यमानायानुब्रूहीति (i. 15)—Roth identifies this as from Śatapatha Br. p. 31 Weber (a very curious way of quoting!); Tait. Saṁ. vi. 3. 7. 1; Mait. Saṁ. i. 4. 11; Śat. Br. i. 3. 5. 2 and 3, ii. 5. 2. 19, etc; Tait. Br. iii. 3. 7. 1. See Bloomfield, Concordance.

9. एतद्वै यज्ञस्य समृद्धं यद्रूपसमृद्धं यत्कर्म क्रियमाणमृग्यजुर्वाभिवदतीति च ब्राह्मणम् (i. 16)—The Gopatha has this full quotation at ii. 2. 6 and ii. 4. 2. The Aitareya has it almost at half a dozen places, but without the words यजुः—यत्कर्म क्रियमाणमृगभिवदति (i. 4, i. 13, i. 16, i. 17, etc.).

10. तद्यदेनांस्तपस्यमानान्ब्रह्म स्वयम्भ्वभ्यानर्षत्त ऋषयोभवंस्तदृषीणामृषित्वमिति विज्ञायते (ii. 11)—Tait. Ār.. ii. 9 has the passage as it is in our Nirukta. Only भवन् and तत् are combined as भवन्तत्.

11. यदवृणोत्तद्वृत्रस्य वृत्रत्वमिति विज्ञायते यदवर्तत तद्वृत्रस्य वृत्रत्वमिति विज्ञायते यदवर्धत तद्वृत्रस्य वृत्रत्वमिति विज्ञायते (ii. 17)—In Tait. Saṁ. this passage occurs at ii. 4. 12. 2 as यदिमाँल्लोकानवृणोत्तद्वृत्रस्य वृत्रत्वम्.

12. तस्मात्पुमान्दायादोऽदायादा स्त्रीति विज्ञायते तस्मात्स्त्रियं जातां परास्यन्ति न पुमांसमिति च (iii. 4)—The language—विज्ञायते and इति च—shows that these are quotations from the same source, and it is a fact: यत्स्थालीं रिञ्चन्ति न दारुमयं तस्मात्पुमान्दायादः स्त्र्यदायादा यत्स्थालीं परास्यन्ति न दारुमयं तस्मात्स्त्रियं जातां परास्यन्ति न पुमांसम्—Mait. Saṁ. iv. 6. 4. The last sentence is repeated again at Mait. Saṁ. iv. 7. 9.

13. सोऽर्देवानसृजत तत्सुराणां सुरत्वमसोरसुरानसृजत तदसुराणामसुरत्वमिति विज्ञायते (iii. 8)— Tait. Br. ii. 3. 8. 2 has a similar idea—तस्यासुरेवाजीवत् तेनासुनाऽसुरानसृजत तदसुराणामसुरत्वम्.

14. विपक्वप्रज्ञ आदित्य इत्युपनिषद्वर्णो भवति (iii. 12)—Not traced.

15. नेमे देवा नेमेऽसुराः (iii. 20)— Durga says इति ब्राह्मणवाक्यमेवेदं वाजपेये मैत्रायणीयानाम्। अर्धतो देवा अर्धतोऽसुरा आसन्नित्यर्थः। In Mait. Saṁ. ii. 9 we have देवाश्च वा असुराश्चास्पर्धन्त नेमे देवा आसन्नेमेऽसुराः with an आसन् in the middle.

16. नेमानि क्षत्राणीति च ब्राह्मणम् (iii. 20, etc.)—Not traced.

17. नाभ्या सन्नद्धा गर्भा जायन्त इत्याहुः (iv. 21)—Tait. Saṁ. vi. 1. 7. 2 has a similar idea but quite different words—यदबद्धमवदध्याद्गर्भाः प्रजानां परापातुकाः स्युर्बद्धमवदधाति गर्भाणां धृत्यै.

18. पञ्चर्तवः संवत्सरस्येति च ब्राह्मणम् (हेमन्तशिशिरयोः समासेन) (iv. 27)—A passage similar in meaning is found in Ait. Br.—द्वादश मासाः पञ्चर्तवो हेमन्तशिशिरयोः समासेन तावान्संवत्सरः (i. 1), identified by Roth. पञ्चर्तवः संवत्सरस्य comes, by the bye, very often in Śatapatha Br., sometimes in an expression like—द्वादश वै मासाः संवत्सरस्य पञ्चर्तवः etc. (i. 3. 5. 11, i. 7. 2. 8, xii. 3. 2. 1, etc.).

19. षष्टिश्च ह वै त्रीणि च शतानि संवत्सरस्याहोरात्रा इति च ब्राह्मणम् [समासेन] (iv.27)—अहोरात्रा stands here collectively ; day and night are regarded as one. Three hundred and sixty of such are contained in one year. This is apparently from Goptha Br., although with insignificant changes—त्रीणि च ह वै शतानि षष्टिश्च संवत्सरस्याहोरात्राणि (i. 5.5). The change consists in the inversion of words denoting number and the form अहोरात्राणि. In the Ait. Br. we have त्रीणि च वै शतानि षष्टिश्च संवत्सरस्याहानि (ii. 17) where besides the inversion we have for अहोरात्राः अहानि. A play upon this number is repeated in Ait. Br. v. 12 in connection with the स्तोत्रिय verses. The Śat. Br. i. 3. 5. 9 has त्रीणि च वै शतानि षष्टिश्च संवत्सरस्याहानि ; xii. 3. 2. 3 has रात्रयः for अहानि.

20. सप्त च वै शतानि विंशतिश्च संवत्सरस्याहोरात्रा इति च ब्राह्मणम् [विभागेन] (iv. 27)—This is found word for word in the Ait. Br. ii. 17. In Gopatha, too, we find it in the following form—सप्त च वै शतानि विंशतिश्च संवत्सरस्याहानि च रात्रयश्च (i. 5. 5), Śat. Br. xii. 3. 2. 4, i. 5. 5. 4, Ait. Ār. iii. 2.

21. वरमाहारमाहार्षीरिति च ब्राह्मणम् (v. 4)—Not traced.

22. गायतो मुखादुदपतदिति च ब्राह्मणम् (vii. 12)—The word विपरीता that immediately precedes is, I think, to be taken with the previous sentence त्रिगमना वा विपरीता—meaning that गायत्री is to be derived from त्रि and गमन and their order reversed. Durga is silent on the point.

23.* गायत्रीमेव त्रिपदां सतीं चतुर्थेन पादेनानुष्टोभतीति च ब्राह्मणम् (vii. 12).

24.* यत्त्रिरस्तोभत्तत्त्रिष्टुभस्त्रिष्टुत्त्वमिति विज्ञायते (vii. 12).

25.* जलगल्यमानोऽसृजदिति च ब्राह्मणम् (vii. 13).

* These sentences about metres in general are found in almost the same form in the 3rd खण्ड of the दैवतब्राह्मण of the सामवेद. The questions arising out of the identity of the passages will be dealt with at the end.

26. समुद्रादूध्येषोऽद्भ्य उदेतीति च ब्राह्मणम् (vii. 17)—Kauṣ. Br. xxv. 1. समुद्रादूध्येषोऽद्भ्य उदेति is exactly quoted by Yāska.

27. अथापि ब्राह्मणं भवति अग्निः सर्वा देवता इति (vii. 17)—This is one of those almost proverbial Brāhmaṇic passages which are many times repeated in different Brāhmaṇas. It cannot therefore, with any amount of certainty, be said that it is taken from one particular Brāhmaṇa and not from another. In this respect it is like another pithy and proverbial saying यज्ञो वै विष्णुः of the Brāhmaṇas. It is found in Aitareya, Śatapatha, Tāṇḍya and other Brāhmaṇas. Roth has already referred to Ait. Br. i. 1, where this passage occurs, with a वै after अग्नि which Yāska has not got. Tāṇḍya Br. ii. 1. 12 has अग्निर्वै सर्वा देवताः like the Ait. Br. In the same way the Gopatha Br. ii. 1. 12, and the Ṣaḍviṁśa Br. iii. 7. The Śatapatha Br. i. 6. 2. 8 agrees with the other Brāhmaṇas in having वै after अग्नि. So Mait. Saṁ. i. 4. 14.

28. यत्तज्जातः पशूनविन्दतेति तज्जातवेदसो जातवेदस्त्वमिति ब्राह्मणम् (vii. 19)—Not traced.

29. अथापि ब्राह्मणं भवत्यग्निर्वा इतो वृष्टिं समीरयति धामच्छदिव खलु वै भूत्वा वर्षति मरुतः सृष्टां वृष्टिं नयन्ति यदा खलु वा असावादित्यो न्यङ्‌रश्मिभिः पर्यावर्ततेऽथ वर्षतीति (vii. 24)—In Tait. Saṁ. ii. 4. 1. 2 after saying अग्नये धामच्छदे पुरोडाशमष्टाकपालं निर्वपेत् etc. the passage reads—अग्निर्वा इतो वृष्टिमुदीरयति मरुतः सृष्टां नयन्ति यदा खलु वा असावादित्यो न्यङ्रश्मिभिः पर्यावर्ततेऽथवर्षति धामच्छदिव खलु वै भूत्वा वर्षति. The only difference is the position of धामच्छदिव etc. and the absence of the word वृष्टिं after सृष्टाम्.

30. यदस्य दिवि तृतीयं तदसावादित्य इति हि ब्राह्मणम् (vii. 28)—Not traced.

31. आप्रीभिराप्रीणातीति च ब्राह्मणम् (viii. 4)—Roth refers to Ait. Br. ii. 4 where the passage is found in exactly the form in which Yāska quotes it. It occurs besides in Kauṣ. x. 3. 2. in the same form.

32. आग्नेया वै प्रयाजा आग्नेया अनुयाजा इति च ब्राह्मणम् (viii. 22)—Not traced.

33. छन्दांसि वै प्रयाजाश्छंदांस्यनुयाजा इति च ब्राह्मणम् (viii 22)—The Śatapatha Br. i. 3. 2. 9 has only छन्दांसि ह्यनुयाजाः and that more than once.

34. ऋतवो वै प्रयाजा ऋतवोऽनुयाजा इति च ब्राह्मणम् (viii. 22)—The Bibl. Ind. edition reads पशवः before अनुयाजाः which is hardly likely according to the context. The first part ऋतवो वै प्रयाजाः is found in Kauṣ. Br. iii. 4 ; also Śat. Br. i. 3. 2. 8, where ऋतवो हि प्रयाजाः is the reading. Mait. Saṁ. 1. 4. 12 has first part only.

35. पशवो वै प्रयाजाः पशवोऽनुयाजाः इति च ब्राह्मणम् (iii. 22)—The first part only in Kauṣ. Br. iii. 4.

36. प्राणा वै प्रयाजाः प्राणा वा अनुयाजा इति च ब्राह्मणम् (viii. 22)–The Bibl. Ind. edition reads अपाना before अनुयाजाः which would be in accordance with the Kauṣ. Br. vii. 1 and x. 3. The Ait. Br. seems to combine the two expressions into the one प्राणा वै प्रयाजानुयाजाः (i. 17). At Ait. Br. i. 11 there is another similar sentence—प्राणा वै प्रयाजाः प्रजाऽनुयाजाः differing in the latter part only. The Śat. Br. has the whole passage with अपानाः for प्राणाः before अनुयाजाः (xi. 2. 7. 27).

37. आत्मा वै प्रयाजा आत्मा वा अनुयाजा इति च ब्राह्मणम् (viii. 22)—The Bibl. Ind. edition reads प्रजाः before अनुयाजाः while in the Tait. Saṁ. vi. 1. 5. 4 the passage runs thus—आत्मा वै प्रयाजाः प्रजाऽनूयाजाः which is in accordance with the Bibl. Ind. edition of the Nirukta ; only, in the latter part we have a Saṁdhi प्रजाऽनूयाजाः and a long ऊ.

38. यस्यै देवतायै हविर्गृहीतं स्यात्तां मनसा ध्यायेद्वषट्करिष्यन्निति ह विज्ञायते (viii. 22)—This is to be seen in the Gopatha Brāhmaṇa ii. 3. 4 as follows—यस्यै देवतायै हविर्गृहीतं स्यात् तां मनसा ध्यायन् वषट् कुर्यात् ; only, the verb in the Nirukta passage appears in the Brāhmaṇa as a participle and vice versa. The idea and the words are however quite the same. In the Ait. Br. iii. 8 the passage occurs in exactly the same form as in the Nirukta except the word मनसा.

39. उरु मे कुर्वित्यब्रवीत्तदुलूखलमभवत्। उरुकरं चैतदुलूखलमित्याचक्षते परोक्षेणेति च ब्राह्मणम् (ix. 20)—In Śatapatha Br. vii. 5. 1. 22 we read उरु मे करदिति तदुरुकरमुरुकरं ह वै तदुलूखलमित्याचक्षते परोक्षम् etc.

40. यदरुदत्तद्रुद्रस्य रुद्रत्वमिति काठकम् (x. 5)—Not traced.

41. यदरोदीत्तद्रुद्रस्य रुद्रत्वमिति हारिद्रवकम् (x. 5)—Identical with Tait. Saṁ. i. 5. 1. 1. हारिद्रवकम् = मैत्रायणीयानां शाखाभेदः says Durga.

These are highly suspicious passages. Because when Yāska quotes from the two Saṁhitās he always says इत्यपि निगमो भवति and does not at all give the names of them. In the case of quotations from Brāhmaṇas, he never mentions them by the Śākhā to which they belong, but simply in a general way, as said above.

42. तद्यदेनं प्राणैः समैन्धंस्तदिन्द्रस्येन्द्रत्वमिति विज्ञायते (x. 8)—Not traced.

43. आदित्यो दक्ष इत्याहुः (xi. 23)—Not traced.

44. या पूर्वा पौर्णमासी साऽनुमतिर्योत्तरा सा राकेति विज्ञायते (xi. 29)—Durga rightly says ब्राह्मणमुदाहरन्ति, thus paraphrasing इति विज्ञायते and recognising that this was another way of indicating a Brāhmaṇa quotation. Roth has identified the quotation as from the Ait. Br. vii. 11. It is found also in the Ṣaḍviṁśa Br. iv. 6. in exactly the same form ; and in the Gopatha Brāhmaṇa ii. 1. 10.

45. या पूर्वामावास्या सा सिनीवाली योत्तरा सा कुहूरिति विज्ञायते (xi. 31)—Identified by Roth, Ait. Br. vii. 11. This also occurs in exactly the same form in Ṣaḍ. Br. iv, 6 and in Gopatha Br. ii. 1. 10.

46. सविता सूर्यां प्रायच्छत्सोमाय राज्ञे प्रजापतये वा इति च ब्राह्मणम् (xii. 8)–For the fable or legend contained in this quotation Roth refers to Ait. Br. iv. 7—प्रजापतिर्वै सोमाय राज्ञे दुहितरं प्रायच्छत्सूर्यां सावित्रीं etc. But in the Kauṣ. Br. it occurs in a form which is more akin to our quotation, than the Ait. Br. अथ यत्र ह तत्सविता सूर्यां प्रायच्छत्सोमाय राज्ञे (xviii. 1).

47. अथोरामः सावित्र इति पशुसमाम्नाये विज्ञायते (xii. 13)—Roth has referred to Vāj. Saṁ. xxiv. 1 to 40 which is so to say a catalogue or collection of the names of beasts. Compare also Vāj. Saṁ. xxii. 59 ; Tait. Saṁ. v. 5. 22. 1.

48. कृकवाकुः सावित्र इति पशुसमाम्नाये विज्ञायते (xxi. 13)—Vāj. Saṁ. xxiv. 35. ; Tait. Saṁ. v. 5. 18. 1 ; Mait. Saṁ. iii. 14. 15 and 175. 9.

49. प्राशित्रमस्याक्षिणी निर्जघानेति च ब्राह्मणम् (xii. 14)—According to Roth this legend is referred to in the Śat. Br. But it is Kauṣ. Br. vi. 13 that contains this passage as in the Nirukta–only the word प्राशित्रं is not in the same sentence—and is evi-

dently the source of our quotation. The Gopatha Br. also has the legend, but not in these words—स [प्रजापतिः] यज्ञमभ्यायम्याविध्य तदाविद्धं निरकृन्तत् तत्र प्राशित्रमभवत्तदुदयकृत्तद्भगाय पर्यहरंस्तत्प्रतीक्षेत। तस्य चक्षुः परापतत्तस्मादाहुरन्धो वै भग इति (ii. 1. 2). The same legend is found in the Śatapatha thus—ते होचुर्भगायेनद्दक्षिणत आसीनाय परिहरत तद्भगः प्राशिष्यति तद्यथाहुतमेवं भविष्यति तद्भगाय दक्षिणत आसीनाय पर्याजन्हुस्तद्भगोऽवेक्षांचक्रे तस्याक्षिणी निर्ददाह। तथेतन्नूनं तदास तस्मादाहुरन्धो भग इति (i. 7. 4. 6).

50. अग्निः पशुरासीत्तमालभन्त तेनायजन्तेति च ब्राह्मणम् (xii. 41)—Identified by Roth, Ait Br. i. 16. In Tait. Saṁ. this is found as अग्निः पशुरासीत्तेनायजन्त v. 7. 26. 1, without the words तमालभन्त.

51. अथापि ब्राह्मणं भवति सा वै वाक्सृष्टा चतुर्धा व्यभवत्। एष्वेव लोकेषु त्रीणि पशुषु तुरीयम्। या पृथिव्यां साग्नौ सा रथन्तरे यान्तरिक्षे सा वायौ सा वामदेव्ये या दिवि सादित्ये सा बृहति सा स्तनयित्नावथ पशुषु ततो या वागत्यरिच्यत तां ब्राह्मणेष्वदधुस्तस्माद्ब्राह्मणा उभयीं वाचं वदन्ति या च देवानां या च मनुष्याणामिति (xiii. 9)—Mait. Saṁ 1. 11. 5 has it with insignificant verbal changes as follows:—no एव after एषु, तुरीयाणि between त्रीणि and पशुषु, वाते for वायौ, no आदित्ये after दिवि, ब्राह्मणे न्यदधुः for ब्राह्मणेषु etc., and lastly यश्च वेद यश्च न for या च देवानाम् etc. It is too much to say that this may be an inaccurate quotation; presumably it is from another recension.

52. एतद्ध वा एतदक्षरं यत्सर्वां त्रयीं विद्यां प्रतिप्रतीति च ब्राह्मणम् (xiii. 10)—This is taken from the Kauṣ. Br. vi. 12.

These quotations show us that Yāska knew most of the—one is tempted to say almost all the—Brāhmaṇas. His very words बहुभक्तिवादीनि ब्राह्मणानि भवन्ति (vii. 24) point to the same fact. More precisely, we can say that he knew the two Brāhmaṇas of the Ṛgveda, viz. the Aitareya and the Kauṣītaki (nos. 4, 46, 49, speak expressly for the latter), the Brāhmaṇas—where they exist apart from their Saṁhitās—of the Yajurveda, most probably the Pañcaviṁsa or Tāṇḍya and the Ṣaḍviṁśa Brāhmaṇa of the Sāmaveda, and the Gopatha Brāhmaṇa of the Atharvaveda. Nos. 9, 19, and 38 above specifically point to the Gopatha Brāhmaṇa as their source. See also Keith, Veda of Black Yajus School Translated, p. clxx, where he makes so much of the non-occurrence of the words *Yajur vā* in Ait. Br. i. 4, upon which Nirukta i. 16 appears to be based. The Nirukta indeed agrees with the Gopatha vii. 6 (see supra) in saying *Ṛgyajur vā abhivadati*, but all the Nirukta Mss. do not contain the words *Yajur vā*.[1] The Gopatha no doubt is a late Brāhmaṇa; its style shows it. Its first sentence ब्रह्म ह वा इदमग्र आसीत् reads like the opening of an Upaniṣad. It is, as Keith says, probably of composite redaction. But that affects neither our position nor the date of Yāska, which is as unsettled as any thing can be.

Yāska, himself a Yajurvedī, quotes from the various Saṁhitās of that Veda. He draws mostly upon Taittirīya and Maitrāyaṇī Saṁhitās, and presumably upon the Kāṭhaka Saṁhitā, which unfortunately is not yet available to scholars in its entirety for verification. It is not true to say therefore, as Keith does, that many parallels to the Taittirīya Saṁhitā look like inaccurate quotations from it. Of inaccuracy there can be no question, until we prove it by facts and figures. Presumably they are quotations from other recensions not yet wholly available to us.

Lastly we have to consider certain passages from the third Khaṇḍa of the दैवतब्राह्मण, that are identical with some passages in the seventh Adhyāya of the Nirukta. The passages in question are—1 अथातो निर्वचनम् 2 गायत्री गायतेः स्तुतिकर्मणः 3 गायतो मुखादुदपतदिति ह ब्राह्मणम् 4 उष्णिगुत्स्नानात्स्निह्यतेर्वा कान्तिकर्मणोऽपिवोष्णीषिणीवेत्यौपमिकम् 5 ककुप् ककुद्रूपिणीत्यौपमिकम् 6 ककुप् च कुब्जश्च कुजतेर्वोब्जतेर्वा 7 अनुष्टुबनुष्टोभनात् 8 अन्वस्तौदिति ह ब्राह्मणम् 9 पिपीलिका पेलतेर्गतिकर्मणः 10 पिपालिकमध्येत्यौपमिकम् 11 बृहती बृंहतेर्वृद्धिकर्मणः 12 विराड् विरमणाद्विराजनाद्वा 13 पंक्तिः पंञ्चिनी पञ्चपदा 14 त्रिष्टुप् स्तोभ इत्युत्तरपदा 15 का तु त्रिता स्यात्तीर्णतमं छन्दो भवति 16 त्रिवृद्वज्रस्तस्य स्तोभमिवेत्यौपमिकम् 17 जगती गततमं छन्दो जज्जगतिर्भवति क्षिप्रगतिर्जज्मला (?) कुर्वन्नसृजतेति ह ब्राह्मणम्.

This corresponds, with very slight verbal changes and a few omissions, to Nirukta vii. 12. The order there is गायत्री, उष्णिक्, ककुप्, अनुष्टुप्, बृहती, पंक्तिः, त्रिष्टुप्, जगती, विराट् and पिपीलिका; while the order in the above passage is गायत्री, उष्णिक्, ककुप्, अनुष्टुप्, पिपीलिका, वृहती, विराट्, पंक्तिः, त्रिष्टुप् and जगती. I shall now quote the Nirukta passage without further comments,

1 My friend Prof. Rajwade who is editing the Nirukta for the Anandashram Series tells me that one of his best Mss. omits the words *Yajur vā*.

because the similarity is too obvious to be specially pointed out—गायत्री गायतेः स्तुतिकर्मणस्त्रिगमना वा विपरीता गायतो मुखादुदपतदिति च ब्राह्मणम् । उष्णिगुत्स्नाता भवति स्निह्यतेर्वा स्यात्कान्तिकर्मण उष्णीषिणीवेत्यौपमिकमुष्णीषं स्नायतेः । ककुप् ककुभिनी भवति ककुप् च कुब्जश्च कुजतेर्वोब्जतेर्वा । अनुष्टुबनुष्टोभनाद्गायत्रीमेव त्रिपदां सतीं चतुर्थेन पादेनानुष्टोभतीति च ब्राह्मणम् । बृहती परिबर्हणात् । पंक्तिः पञ्चपदा । त्रिष्टुप् स्तोभत्युत्तरपदा । का तु त्रिता स्यात्तीर्णतमं छन्दस्त्रिवृद्वज्रस्तस्य स्तोभनीति वा । यत्त्रिरस्तोभत्तत्त्रिष्टुभस्त्रिष्टुप्त्वमिति विज्ञायते vii. 12 जगती गततमं छन्दो जलचरगतिर्वा । जल्गल्यमानोऽसृजदिति च ब्राह्मणम् । विराड् विराजनाद्वा विराधनाद्वा विप्रापणाद्वा विराजनात्संपूर्णाक्षरा विराधनादूनाक्षरा विप्रापणादधिकाक्षरा । पिपीलिकमध्येत्यौपमिकम् । पिपीलिका पेलतेर्गतिकर्मणः vii. 13.

In the Nirukta this derivation of metres belonging to different gods (आग्नेभक्तीनि etc.) is quite in place. But what is their place in the Brāhmaṇa of the Sāmaveda? As the name of the Brāhmaṇa in question shows, it has to do with deities of the various songs in that Veda. In the beginning of his commentary on that Brāhmaṇa Sāyaṇa rightly observes—तत्रादौ साम्नां निधनभेदेन देवताभिधानाय ता एवानुक्रमते. And at the end of the first sentence of the Brāhmaṇa 'अग्निरिन्द्रः प्रजापतिः सोमो वरुणस्त्वष्टाङ्गिरसः पूषा सरस्वतीन्द्राग्नी' he says 'एताः सामदेवता इति शेषः.' In the first Khaṇḍa, the deities of the songs are given; in the second Khaṇḍa after describing the 'colours' of the various metres, their deities are given. This really ought to close the Brāhmaṇa; but here follows the third Khaṇḍa, the greater part of which we have quoted above. Here, as usual, Sāyaṇa has his introductory remarks and he almost apologetically observes—अथ सामाश्रयाणां छन्दसां कथनप्रसङ्गेन तेषामेव निर्वचनं दिदर्शयिषुरादौ प्रतिजानीते—now, after having mentioned the metres upon which the songs depend he incidentally wishes to show their derivation, and begins. The word प्रसङ्गेन is important as showing how Sāyaṇa has to invent an excuse. Derivation is, indeed, not an uncommon phenomenon in the Brāhmaṇas; but it is never indulged in for its own sake. We find for instance the names of deities, or songs derived, but only as a corroboration of the function or *viniyoga* that is mentioned. And nowhere do we find a continuous string of derivations as in this Brāhmaṇa. Again a Brāhmaṇa quoting from another Brāhmaṇa for corroboration is a phenomenon that I have not found in the other extant Brāhmaṇas. Words like तस्योक्तं ब्राह्मणम् that one often meets with in the Ait. Br., for instance, mean something like तस्योक्तं रहस्यं or तस्योक्तो विनियोगः etc. They do not refer to a Brāhmaṇa in the sense of a theological work. We have therefore no hesitation in saying that the whole of the third Khaṇḍa of the Daivata Brāhmaṇa is an imitation of the Nirukta and quite out of place in the Brāhmaṇa.

Some few quotations have necessarily remained unverified, but it is hoped that, as more Saṁhitā and Brāhmaṇa texts are discovered and printed, these may also be traced.

SOME AVESTAN TRANSLATIONS

BY J. H. MOULTON

I have essayed a hard task in trying to put some typical Gāthā extracts into English verse. But I have some hope that they may become a little easier in this form. Of Professor Mills's version (in *Sacred Books of the East*) it has been too truly said that the English needs the help of the original to be intelligible. My own prose in *Hibbert Lectures* on "Early Zoroastrianism" is I hope less difficult, and it embodies Bartholomae's researches, which were not available for my predecessor. But the use of rhythm and rime, and a greater freedom in rendering, may make the impression of the Hymns a little truer.

We have to remember that Zarathushtra was not writing poetry for poetry's sake. The verse form was mainly intended as a help to memory. If therefore the English version has little claim to be poetry, the translator may fairly claim that he had no right to put into his original what was not there. Only an Edward Fitz-Gerald may do that!

The selection in the first two cases was dictated by the striking character of the contents, in which the very greatness of the Prophet's theme lifted his verse into poetry. To quote my own words (*Early Religious Poetry of Persia*, p. 84)—

> "Versified summaries of the most eloquent sermons, composed to help the faithful to retain their essence in the memory, have almost as little chance of rising into literature as the mnemonic stanzas by which at school we painfully acquired the mysteries of Latin genders. 'Almost'—for after all the Prophet was in deadly earnest, and he preached on great themes, and spiritual fervour can make literature *malgrè lui*, even under such unfavourable surroundings."

Yasna 31. 1–8

1. Mindful of a heavenly calling, we
    the words of Truth assert—
Hard the words, when Falsehood's followers
    Right's domain conspire to hurt,

Welcome words, when to the Wisest men
their willing mind convert.

2. Since, for all this truthful teaching, souls
to higher things are blind,
Come I to you, good and evil, judge
by Mazdah's will assigned,
Set to order life's renewal, that the Right
its way may find.

3. Tell us, Wisest, let us know it—be the word
from thine own tongue,
By thy Fire and by thy Spirit what thou
dealst to right and wrong,
What thy true decision tell me—to convert
mankind I long.

4. For the prayer to Right and Mazdah, and
whatever Lords there be,
Destiny and Duty invoking, Best Thought,
do thou seek for me
Heaven's All Might, for war with Falsehood,
so to win the victory.

5. Show me then, O Right, my portion, heaven-
ordained, that I may know,
Fixed my mind and wary ever, though men
grudge that it be so:
Tell what shall be, what shall not be; Wisest
Lord, thy wisdom show.

6. He that as a man of knowledge hath the skill
true words to rede,
Heir of Utmost Good, that redes me Weal
and Life Indeed,
His the Wisest Lord's Dominion, which Good
Thought for him shall speed.

7. His the primal thought, ordaining "Let the
blest worlds teem with Light."

His the craftsman hand that stablished,
Wisest Lord, the heavenly Right.
Changeless aye Thy Spirit, enriching homes
for Goodness in the height.

8. Thee as First, Thee Last—my soul's grasp
fastened on the mystery;
Father of Good Thought, Thou camest to the
seeing of mine eye;
Author sole of Right, Thou judgest deeds
of our mortality.

Yasna 44. 1–5

1. This I ask thee—tell me truly, tell me
duly, Holy Lord—
How to worship with a service worthy
thee, O King adored.
Teach me, Wise One, as the heavenly may
the earthly, as to friend
Friend may speak—so may the kindly Right
its timely succour bring,
And with heaven's Good Thought to reward
in its gracious power descend.

2. Tell me duly, tell me truly as I pray,
O Holy King:
When the Highest Life is dawning, at thy
Kingdom's opening,
Shall the dooms of heaven's tribunal give
to every man his due?
Surely he, the holy prophet, to his watchful
soul doth lay
All men's sin, yet ever friendly doth
the worlds of life renew.

3. This I ask thee—tell me truly, tell me duly
as I pray:
Who the Sire from whose begetting Right
was on Creation Day?

Who their several paths appointed where
the Sun and Stars should go?
By whose power is yon Moon waning, by that
power once more to wane?
These things, Wisest, I am yearning, these
and more beside, to know.

4. This I ask thee, Lord of Wisdom—truly
make the mystery plain:
Who this world beneath, above us, safe
from falling did sustain,
Nether Earth and vault of Heaven? Who
the Waters hath upborne,
Who the Plant-world? Who yoked swiftness
to the clouds and to the wind,
Who is he, O Wise Creator, from whose soul
Good Thought was born?

5. Tell me truly as I ask thee—Lord,
illuminate my mind:
Light and Darkness, who hath made them?
Who such wondrous skill might find?
Who the hours of sleep and waking hath
ordained with wisest skill,
Dawn of day, and noon's refreshment, and
the late approach of eve,
Set to call the man of knowledge hests of
duty to fulfil?

The next specimen, a complete hymn, is given to illustrate the humbler purpose of the Gāthās. Yasna 47, the opening hymn of the *Gāthā Spentā-mainyū*, is a very palpable verse summary. In the little book just quoted (pp. 108 f.) I have noted that the hymn is almost a neophyte's first lesson, bringing together a maximum of characteristic terms. Note how in the first stanza we have all the six leading *ahuras* (Amesha Spenta), the triad of Thought, Word and Deed, and the Holy (Kindly) Spirit. Later we have the Ox and the Fire, and the Demon world represented by Ill Thought and Falsehood (*Druj*). There is also the technical (and much disputed) word *rānōibyā*, "the two parties", followers respectively of Asha and Druj, to whom falls the *vanghāu vīdāiti*, "partition in good", i.e. of good and evil severally.

Yasna 47

1. By his kind Spirit, by Best Thought and Deed
And Word, with Right, the Wise Lord gives his meed
Through Power and Piety—Weal and Life Indeed.

2. This kindliest Spirit's Best doth one fulfil
With tongue by Goodness' words, with hand by will
Of Piety's lore :—Mazdah Right's sire is still.

3. Blest Father of the Spirit that hath made
Luck-bearing cattle, and their peaceful glade
By the kind Mother, through the Good Thought's aid.

4. From this have fallen the lovers of the Lie,
Not so the Right's men. Rich or poor, may I
To these show love, to those show enmity.

5. Thy promised Best, by this kind Spirit due
To men of Right—Lord, is't thy will a crew
Of Liars enjoy it, Ill Thought's comrades true?

6. Through this kind Spirit, Lord, and by thy Fire,
With Right and Piety, thou giv'st both their hire—
Sure *this* shall turn all that the Truth desire!

Last come the three specially sacred formulæ, of which only the third is even partially a "prayer" in the usual sense: the first two are rather creeds. I have represented the translation defended in my *Early Zoroastrianism*, pp. 160f. and 390. The third, as I read it, is a rallying-cry to the people. The *Ahuna Vairya* is a declaration that Zarathushtra is Teacher in this life, and judge in the Hereafter by Asha's appointment: he will offer to Mazdah the treasure of his faithful people's merits, which by their outweighing the counter-accumulation of Ill Thought will establish the

Kingdom, the final victory of Good over Evil. This is done by one whom Mazdah appointed (I take *dadat* as singular, not plural) to be "shepherd" of the faithful "poor." The *Ashem Vohū* is a concise play on two meanings of *aša*: he who lives in accordance with "Right" gets his "rights" in the end.

Ahuna Vairya

As here our chosen Master he,
By Right he there our Judge shall be.
Life-works that from Good Thought arise
He offers to the Only Wise,
To the great Lord his Kingdom sure
Who made him shepherd of the poor.

Ašem Vohū

Right is the highest good, and so our rights
Meet heart's desire when Right
has reached its heights.

Āairyəmā išyō

Hither come, dear Brotherhood,
Come to aid the people's good,
Zarathushtra's faithful men,
Faithful women, and again
Goodness' self. What soul doth light,
On the precious meed of Right,
(Rise, my prayer, to the Wise Lord),
Grant him thine own blest Reward.

By way of foil, I append a translation from the Later Avesta, a very much easier matter. I have translated a good many more striking passages in *Early Religious Poetry*, chap. ix. I now select the first part of the *Hom Yasht* (*Ys.* 9. 1–15), the verse of which is preserved throughout, though very haltingly in the last section, where the subject changes from Aryan folklore to Magian ritual: probably this is connected with later date, and a period when the language was archaic and the prosody largely lost. I have not attempted to mend the metre there, but in the earlier cantos I have sometimes struck out apparent glosses, so as to make the lines scan.

To Haoma (Ys. 9)

1. At the hour of due libation,
Haoma came to Zarathushtra,
Busily the fire attending,
While the holy Hymns he chanted.
Of him then asked Zarathushtra:
"Who art thou, O man? for never,
Never in the world of matter,
Or in that self-dowered existence,
Deathless, sunny, saw I fairer."

2. Then to me he made an answer,
Haoma, holy, death-averter:
"Zarathushtra, I am Haoma,
Haoma, holy, death-averter.
Call me to thee, O Spitama,
Press me, ready for the drinking;
Praise me, with what praise the Saviours
Of the coming age shall utter.*

3. Then made answer Zarathushtra: *
"What man first, O glorious Haoma,
Pressed thee for the world material?
What the boon by him achievéd?
What the guerdon that befel him?

4. Then to me he made an answer,
Haoma, holy, death-averter:
"'Twas Vivahvant, first of mortals.
This the boon by him achieved,
This the guerdon that befel him:
To him was a son begotten,
Yima of fair flocks, all-shining.
Never mortal born had glory
Like to his, whose face was sunlight.
For he made through his dominion,

Men and cattle all unfading.
Plants and waters drought-defying,
Food to eat imperishable.

5. In swift Yima's great dominion
Neither winter was nor summer,
Neither age nor death befel them,
Neither sickness (?) demon-given.
Fifteen years in age—so seemed it—
Son and father walked together.*
While he reigned, of fair flocks shepherd,
Son of Vivahvant, great Yima."

[6 and 7 = 3 and 4. Āthwya was the second.]
To him was a son begotten
Of a noble house, Thraetaona.

8. He the Serpent slew, Dahaka,
Triple-jawed and triple-headed,
Six-eyed, thousand-powered in mischief,
Falsehood-demon very mighty,
False, a pest to all creation.
Him the mightiest fiend of falsehood
Angra Mainyu's self had fashioned,
To material creation
Foe, for death of Asha's creatures.

[9 and 10=3 and 4.]
10. Thrita was the third to press me,*
Thrita, strongest of the Sāmas.
This the boon by him achieved,
This the guerdon that befel him:
To him were two sons begotten,
Urvākshaya, Keresāspa—
One a Judge, just dooms to issue,
But the other, wonder-worker,
Curly-headed, young, club-bearer,

11. He that smote the Horned Serpent,
Horse and man alike engulfing,

Belching poison, yellow-sicklied:
Flowed the yellow poison o'er him,
Fathom deep, a flood of mischief.
On his back did Keresāspa
Boil him flesh in iron caldron
At the noon-day hour of eating.
Then the ill beast, scorched and sweltering,
Shot away beneath the caldron,
Spilled away the seething water.
Headlong fled away affrighted
Manly-minded Keresāspa.

[12 and 13 = 3 and 4]

Pourushaspa fourth of mortals
Pressed me for the world material.
This the boon by him achieved,
This the guerdon that befel him,
That to him wert thou begotten,
Even thou, O Zarathushtra,
Of the house of Pourushaspa,
Foe to fiends, the Good Law's champion.

14. Famous thou in Aryan country,
First of men, O Zarathushtra,
First to chant *Ahuna Vairya* *
Four times, with the ordered pauses,
Stressed the second half in utterance.

15. All the demons, Zarathushtra,
Thou hast driven in earth to hide them:
Erstwhile bold, in guise of mortals,
Round about this earth they wandered.
Thou the strongest, thou most vigorous,
Thou the keenest, thou the swiftest,
Thou the mightiest victor ever
That the spirits Twain have fashioned.

One or two notes may be appended on the lines marked with*.

2. *Aparacit* is a gloss, due to ignorance that *Saošyantc* is a future already and does not need the adjective.

3. *Nəmō Haomāi* is *extra metrum*, if not to be simply omitted.

5. *Kaṭarascit* is a gloss, which adds nothing to the sense.

10. Since there is no reason why the formula should be always identical, we may drop *astvaiθyāi gaeθyāi* this time, and so restore the metre.

14. Since the Ahuna Vairya is essentially a declaration of spiritual allegiance to Zarathushtra as "shepherd of the poor," there is considerable *naïveté* in the great discovery here assigned him. It is perhaps contributory evidence for a thesis otherwise probable, that when the Yasht was composed the formula was already unintelligible.

HŪṆAS IN AVESTA AND PAHLAVI

BY J. J. MODI

THE writer of the article on the Huns in the Encyclopædia Brittanica[1] says that the authentic history of the Huns in Europe practically begins about the year A. D. 372, when Balamir or Balambir led a westward movement from their settlements in the steppes on the north of the Caspian sea. A side issue of this movement was the downfall of the Gupta dynasty in India, regarding which Mr. Vincent Smith[2] in his History of India says—

> The Golden age of the Guptas comprised a period of a century and a quarter (A. D. 330–455), covered by three reigns of exceptional length. The death of Kumāragupta I, which can be fixed definitely as having occurred early in 455, marks the beginning of the decline and fall of the empire...........When Skandagupta (455–480 A. D.) came to the throne, in the spring of 455, he encountered a sea of troubles. The Puṣyamitra danger had been averted, but one more formidable closely followed it—an irruption of the savage Huns, who had poured down from the steppes of Central Asia through the north-western passes, and carried devastation over the smiling plains and crowded cities of India. Skandagupta, who probably was a man of mature years and ripe experience, proved equal to the need, and inflicted upon the barbarians a defeat so decisive that India was saved for a time.

The Bhitari[3] stone pillar inscription of Skandagupta takes a note of this victory over the Huns.[4]

Then there were fresh inroads between A.D. 465 and 470. Skandagupta was succeeded on the throne by his son Puragupta (480–485), who was succeeded by his son Narsiṁhagupta Bālāditya. In or about 484, there were other stronger and further inroads of the Huns under their king Toramāna, who had established himself in Mālwā (500 to

1 Ninth Ed. Vol. XII. p. 381. 2 Third Edition (1914) pp. 308 ff.

3 A village in the Sayyidpur Tahsil of the Ghazipur district in the N. W. Provinces.

4 Corpus Inscriptionum Indicarum, Vol. III, Inscriptions of the Early Gupta kings and their successors, by John Faithful Fleet, (1888), Inscription No. 13, Plate VII, pp. 52-56.

510). This Toramāna was succeeded by Mihiragula or Mihirkula.

The above-mentioned Bālāditya was the king of Magadha at this time and Yaśodharman (Vikramāditya) was the ruler of Mālwā in Central India. Round the names of these two kings there rages a conflict of opinions among scholars, as to which of these two Rājas, defeated Mihirkula and put an end to the Hūṇa supremacy in India. Dr. Rudolf Hoernle[1] says it was Yaśodharman. He rests for his authority on epigraphical, numismatic, and literary evidence, of which the first is the most important. The inscriptions of Yaśodharman on his two *raṇa-stambhas* or "Columns of Victory in War," commemorate this victory.[2] The second column, which is much mutilated, is, as it were, a duplicate. Mr. Vincent Smith,[3] on the other hand, advocates, that it was Bālāditya who defeated the Hūṇa king. He rests for his authority on the statement of the Chinese traveller Hiuen Tsang[4] who represents Bālāditya as defeating Mihirkula.

This question has been also indirectly touched by Professor K. B. Pathak[5] and Babu Manmohan Chakravarti.[6] In the solution of this question, the Persian history of the Sassanian times has also been appealed to. I do not wish to enter into the controversy, but simply say that, on weighing the arguments on both sides, I am inclined to believe that the credit of the defeat of the Huns belongs to Yaśodharman. The authority of the Chinese traveller is second-hand and late. His statement that Mihirkula, the Hūṇa king who is the hero of this controversy, lived 'some centuries ago'[7] should make one pause before taking him

1 Journal, Royal Asiatic Society, 1909, pp. 88–144.

2 Fleet's Gupta Inscriptions, No. 33 and 34, pp. 142–50.

3 History of India, 3rd edition (1914) pp. 318-21.

4 Si-yu-ki, Buddhist Records of the Western World, by Samuel Beal Vol. I, (1884) pp. 165–71.

5 Journal, B. B. R. A. Society, Vol. XIX, pp. 35–43.

6 Journal of the Royal Asiatic Society for 1903, pp. 183–86.

7 Beal's Buddhist Records, Vol. I, p. 169.

as an authority. By that statement, he carries the date of Bālāditya also 'some centuries ago,' which is against chronological facts. Thus, the authority of a pilgrim-traveller who speaks in later times, and that on second-hand hearsay information, and whose statement on the fact of the date of a king is incorrect, must be set aside, when placed by the side of the contemporary evidence of the inscriptions of the king who claims the victory. If Yaśodharman had not been the real victor, he would not have dared to get that inscription put up. He ran the risk of being taken for a braggart or a boaster by his contemporaries,—princes and peasants alike. The court-poet, while preparing the inscription verses, may praise the king and even make a god of him if he liked, but he would not dare, and his royal patron himself would not allow him to dare, to attribute to the king, in the inscription, a feat or a deed which the king did not do. Exaggeration in praise is one thing but a false statement is another thing. The latter would lower the king in the esteem of his people who knew all the contemporary events.

The above Hun kings, Toramāna and Mihirkula, speak of themselves on their coins, as "Shāhi" kings. We learn from Firdousi, that the king of the Haetalite Huns, who helped Firuz, was spoken of as the Shāh of Haitāl.[1] He is also spoken of as the Chagāni Shāhi.[2] So, I think, the term "Shāhi," used by the Hun kings of India, refers to the title which they had assumed, and that the Huns who settled in India were of the same tribe as those who invaded Persia.

Though the above historical references and the epigraphical evidence speak of the inroads of the Huns in the 5th and 6th centuries after Christ, looking to the history of this great nation of the Huns, who had a running history of about 2000 years, it appears, that there were inroads of these people in times much anterior to these later times of the Guptas. According to M. Deguignes the his-

1 Mecan's Calcutta edition of the Shah-nameh, Vol. III, p. 1589.

2 Ibid.

tory of the Huns is the history "of a nation almost ignored which established at different times powerful monarchies in Asia, Europe and Africa. The Huns, who, later, bore the name of 'Turks', natives of a country situated in the North of China, between the rivers Irtush and Amur, made themselves, by degrees, masters of the whole of the great Tartary. Since 200 B. C. several royal families have successively reigned in their vast countries. They had empires more extensive than that of Rome, some illustrious emperors, some legislators and conquerors, who have given rise to considerable evolutions."[1] The Huns in their long history of about 2000 years, and in their distant marches of more than 2000 miles, one way or another in the East or in the West, in the North or in the South, were known under a dozen different names at different times and different places.

The history of Persia, the history which one may perhaps like to call comparatively the pre-historic history of Persia, points to the existence of the Huns centuries before Christ. The Avesta writings clearly show this. These writings show that the name of the Huns, by which these people are known, is a very old name of times long anterior to Christ; and this further confirms the views of M. Deguignes in the matter.

The Huns are spoken of in the Avesta as the *Hunus.* We find the following references to them.

I. We read thus in the Ābān Yasht—

(53) Tāṁ Yazata takhmō Tusō rathaeṣtārō barēṣaēṣu paiti aspanāṁ zāvarē jaidhyantō hitaēibyō dravatātem tanubyō pouru-spakhṣtīm tbiṣayantāṁ paiti-jaitīm duṣmainyavanāṁ hathrānivāitīm hamerethenāṁ aurvathanaṁ tbiṣyantāṁ. (54) Āat hīm jaidhyat avat āiyapteam dazdi mē vanguhi sevistē Ardvīsūra anāhitē yat bavāni aiwi-vanyāu aurva *Hunavō* vaeskaya upa dvarem

1 I give my own translation from "Histoire Générale des Huns, des Turcs, des Moguls, et des autres Tartares, occidentaux etc., avant et depuis Jesus Christ jusqu'à present," par M. Deguignes (1756), Tome I, Partie I, Préface, p. V.

khṣathrōsaokem apanōtemem kanghaya bērēzantya aṣavanaya yatha azem nijanāni Tūiryanāṁ dakhyunāṁ pancasagnāi satagnāiṣca satagnāi hazangragnāiṣca hazangragnāi baēvaregnāiṣca baēvaregnāi ahaṅkhṣtagnaiṣca. (55) Dathat ahmāi tat avat āyaptem Ardvīsūra anāhita hadha zaothrō barāi arēdrāi yazemnāi jaidhyantāi dāthriṣ āyaptem.

Translation:—(53) The brave warrior Tusa invoked her (Ardvīsūra) riding on horse-back and praying for strength to his horses, strength to [his own] body, great watchfulness over those who annoyed him, power to strike his enemies, power to run down his foes, adversaries and annoyers. (54) Then he asked of her: O good beneficient holy Ardvisura! give me this gift, that I may be the overcomer of the brave *Hunus* of Vaēśaka[1] at the gate of the lofty [fort of] Khṣathrōsaoka of the high and holy Kanga[2], [and] that I may kill the fifties and the hundreds, the hundreds and the thousands, the thousands and the ten-thousands [and] the ten-thousands and the innumerables of [the people of] the country of Turan. (55) Holy Ardvīsūra granted the desire of him who carried offerings, gave gifts, made invocations [and] sought the fulfilment of desires.

II. We further read in the Ābān Yasht :

(57) Tāṁ yazenta aurva *Hunavō* Vaēskaya upa dvarem khṣathrō-saokem apanōtemem Kanghaya berezantya aṣavanaya sateē aspanāṁ arṣnaṁ hazangrē gavaṁ baēvarē anumayanaṁ. (58) Āat hīm jaidhyen avat āyaptem dazdi nō vanguhi seviṣtē Ardvīsūra anāhitē yat bavāma aiwivanyāu takhmem Tusem rathaēṣtārem yatha vaēm nijanāma airyanāṁ dakhyunaṁ pancasagnāi satagnāiṣca satagnāi hazangragnāiṣca hazangragnāi baēvarēgnāiṣca

1 Dr. West is wrong in translating "Hunavō Vaēskaya" as the "Hunus in Vaēska" and thus taking Vaēska to be the name of a place (Legends relating to Keresasp. Pahlavi Texts, Part II, S. B. E. XVIII, p. 371, n. 4).

2 Firdousi places the fortress of Kang (Kangdez) at about a month's distance from China. Maçoudi (II, p. 131, ch. 21) also places it (Kenkeder) in China.

baēvaregnāi ahaṅkhṣtagnāiṣca. (59) Nōit aēibyaścit dathat tat avat āyaptem Ardvīsūra anāhita.

Translation:—(57) The brave *Hunus* of Vaēsaka invoked her (Ardvīsūra) at the gate of the lofty [fort of] Khṣathrōsaoka of the high and holy Kanga, with one hundred horses, one thousand oxen, [and] ten thousand lambs. (58) Then [thus invoking] they asked of her: "O good beneficient holy Ardvisura! give us this gift; that we may be the overcomers of the brave warrior Tusa [and] that we may kill the fifties and the hundreds, the hundreds and the thousands, the thousands and the ten-thousands, [and] the ten-thousands and the innumerables of [the people of] the country of Iran." (59) Holy Ardvīsūra did not grant this gift to them.

We gather the following facts from the above passages of the Ābān Yasht on the *Hunus*: (1) Vaēsaka was one of the brave leaders, or rather the family of the leaders, of the *Hunus*. This Vaēsaka of the Avesta seems to be the same as Visak of the Pahlavi Bundehesh (chap. xxxi, 16, 17),[1] one of the ancestors of the Turanians, an uncle of Afrāsiāb[2] and the father of Pirān, the Turanian Nestor. He is the Viseh of Firdousi's Shah-nameh. (2) An Iranian hero Tusa[3] was a great enemy, or rather Tusa's family and descendants were great enemies of Vaēsaka or of Vaēsaka's family and descendants. We learn from Firdousi, the special reason why these two families were so very hostile. In the war between the Iranian Naodar the father of Tusa, and the Turanian Afrāsiāb the nephew of Viseh, Bārmān,

1 Vide my Bundehesh p. 169.

2 According to M. Gabriel Bonvalot, travellers are, even now, shown at Samárkand, a place known as that of the Cemetry of Aprosiāb (Afrāsiāb). The present ruins of Samarkand include the ruins of Afrāsiāb and are known as the city of Afrāsiāb (Through the Heart of Asia by M. Gabriel Bonvalot, translated from the French by Pitman, Vol. II, pp. 7 and 31). For further particulars about him, vide my Dictionary of Avesta Proper Names, p. 130. Vide also Tārikh-i-Rashid by Elias, pp. 286–7.

3 It is this Tus that is said to have been the founder of the city of Tus, the birth-place of the great Firdousi Tousi.

a son of Viseh was killed. Naodar was killed by Afrāsiāb in revenge.[1] (3) The head-quarters of this Hun hero Vaēsaka and his tribe was, at that time, at a place called Kanga, somewhere in Central Asia. It is the Kangdez, i.e. the Fortress of Kang of the Shah-nameh. (4) The time of this war between the Iranian Tus and the Turanian Hun Vaēsaka or Visa, was long anterior to that of king Viṣtāsp, who, according to later Pahlavi writers, lived, at least, about seven centuries before Christ. Thus, we see from the Avesta, that the *Hunus* or the Huns appear first in history as fighting with the Iranians long before the 7th century before Christ.

III. The next reference to the Hūṇas in the Avesta is in the Meher Yasht (x. 113) where we read as follows—

Tat nō jamyāt avanghē Mithra Ahura berezanta yat berezem barāt aṣtra vācim aspanāṁca srifa khṣufsāṅ aṣtrāu kahyāṅ jyāu ṅivaithyāṅ tigrāunghō astayō tadha *Hunavō* gouru-zaothranāṁ jata paithyāunti frā-varesa.

Translation:—May the great Mithra and Ahura come to our help there where the weapons of war jingle (lit. raise loud noise), the hoofs of horses rattle, the daggers clink, [and] bows shoot forth sharp arrows. There [by the arrival of Mithra and Ahura for assistance] the *Hunus*, the mala-fide offerers of sacrifices, go about smitten and with dishevelled hair.

The word *Hunu* in the Avesta also means a son. It is used for bad or wicked sons. It is the Sanskrit *sūnu*, Eng. son. So, Darmesteter, Kavasji E. Kanga, Harlez, Spiegel and others take the word here as a common noun in the sense of 'sons' or 'descendants.' But, I think, there is here a clear reference to the battles with the *Hunus* or Huns.

In the present passage there is an invocation to Mithra and Ahura for help in the battle field, so that, with their help, certain persons may be smitten. These persons, all the translators take to be the descendants or sons (*hunu*) of some evil-minded persons. I would ask: Why are Mithra and

1 Le Livre des Rois, par M. Mohl, Vol. I, p. 422.

Ahura invoked for smiting the children of the evil-doers and not the evil-doers themselves? One cannot admit the justice of such an invocation. So I submit that it is clear that it is the evil-doers themselves, the *Hunus*, against whom the invocation is made. We are not in a sure and certain position to determine the time of this reference to the Huns.

IV. We read as follows in the Jamyād Yasht about a great Iranian hero Keresasp—

41. Yō janat *Hunavō* yat pathanya nava *Hunavaś*-ca Nivikahē *Hunavaś* ca Dāṣtayānoiṣ.

Translation:—Who (Karesāspa) smote the *Hunus*, the nine highway men, the *Hunus* of the Nivika, the *Hunus* of the Dāṣtaya tribe.

Other translators like Kanga, Darmesteter, Spiegel, have taken the word *Hunu*, which occurs thrice in this passage, as a common noun for 'sons or descendants.' West[1] and Harlez have taken the word in its first place, as a proper noun for the *Hunus*, and in the next two places, for common nouns. I think that it is a proper noun in all the three places and refers to a fight with the *Hunus*.

Harlez gives the following note over the word *Hunus*: "Personages légendaires inconnu. Les légendes recueillies dans les Shahnāmeh parlent aussi de brigands tués par des héros et de brigands au nombre de cinq ou sept."[2]

Harlez supposes this name to be legendary, but it seems to be a reference to the Huns. The time of this reference seems to be well-nigh the same as, or even a little anterior to, that referred to in the Ābān Yasht. The Haoma Yasht (Yaçna IX 6–13) places Keresasp's time long before Zoroaster. The Ābān Yasht (Yt. V, 37) places his time somewhat before that of Afrāsiāb, the nephew of the Vaēsaka or Visa above referred to. The Rām Yasht (Yt. XV, 27) also places him before Zoroaster.

1 Legends relating to Keresasp, Pahlavi Texts Part II, S. B. E. Vol. XVIII, p. 370.

2 Le Zend Avesta, p. 546, n. 5,

Keresasp was a great Iranian hero who is more than once referred to in the Avesta. Some of his exploits are referred to in the Zamyād Yasht. One of these exploits was, as said above, that of smiting the *Hunus*. It seems that these exploits were described at some length in the Sudgar Nask, one of the lost books out of the twenty-one books of the Avesta that are believed to have been extant at one time. Though almost all the Nasks have been lost, we know from the ninth book of the Dinkard what their contents were. Similarly, we find therein, in brief, the contents of the Sudgar Nask.[1] In the contents of the fourteenth Fargard Ad-fravakhṣyā we find the exploits of Keresasp. Therein, we find that the above-mentioned exploit with the Huns, referred to in the Zamyād Yasht, is described thus—

> "When the Veskō progeny who (were descendants) of Nīvīk [and] Dāṣtānik [were] slain by him."[2]

Here in the Pahlavi passage, we do not find the word *Hunu* repeated as in the Zamyād Yasht with the two proper names Nīvīka and Dāṣtāyana, i. e. the word for 'son,' as understood by the different translators, has not been given. Dr. West has himself added the word 'descendants' This fact seems to me to show that the word *Hunu* in the Zamyād Yasht is used as a proper noun for the *Hunus* or Huns in all the three places and not as a common noun in the sense of 'sons.'

The Pahlavi legend is also preserved in the Pahlavi Rivāyet accompanying the Dādistān-i-Dini.[3] Therein,

1 For the Pahlavi Text, vide Dinkard compiled by Mr. D. M. Madon, Vol. II, pp. 802–803 and West's Dinkard (S. B. E. XXXVII, Pahlavi Texts Pt. IV, pp. 197–99) Bk. IX, Ch. XV. Vide also West's legend relating to Keresasp in the S. B. E. Vol. XVIII (Pahlavi Texts, Pt. II, pp. 370–72). For the Persian rendering of the legend, vide the Saddar Bundehesh (Chap. XX, pp. 86–92), edited by Ervad Bomanji N. Dhabhar. For the translation of this Persian legend, vide Ervad Edalji Kersaspji Antia's Paper "The Legend of Keresasp," in the Spiegel Memorial Volume edited by me (pp. 93–98).

2 West S. B. E. XXXVII p. 198, XVIII, p. 372.

3 For the Text of this, vide "The Pahlavi Rivāyet accompanying the Dadistān-i-Dinīk," edited by Ervad Bomanji N. Dhabhar (1913) pp. 65 to 74, No. XVII.

where the particular exploit of Kerasasp in connection with the *Hunus* mentioned in the above passage of the Zamyād Yasht is referred to, we do not find the name *Hunu* but we find that the persons whom Kerpsasp smote are spoken of only as *rūçdâr*,[1] i. e. highway men, which is a Pahlavi equivalent of the Avesta 'Pathan.'

In the Persian Legend of Keresasp, which is the rendering of the above Pahlavi Revāyats, we find the word *rāh-dār* which is the same as Pahlavi *rūçdăr*.

These Pahlavi and Persian renderings of the original exploit show, that the *Hunus* or Huns, with whom Keresasp fought, were by profession, as it were, highway men. The Avesta Zamyād Yasht, gives the number of their leaders as nine (*nava*). The Pahlavi Revāyat gives no number. But the Persian Revāyat has reduced the number to seven.

Now, what was the time of this fight of the Iranians with the Huns referred to in the Zamyād Yasht? From the fact that this war or battle was led by Keresasp, we may properly conclude that it referred to times long anterior to king Viṣtāsp and Zoroaster, i. e. long anterior to at least about B. C. 700.

V. The next references to the Huns are in the Farvardin (xiii. 100) and Zamyād (xix. 86) Yashts, where we read thus about king Viṣtāsp (Guṣtāsp)—

Yō hīm stātaṁ hitaṁ haitīm uzvazat haca *Hunū-iwyō.*

Translation:—Who (King Vīṣtāsp) separated it (i. e. the Zoroastrian religion referred to in the preceding para), strong holy-existing from [the influence of] the *Hunus*.

Darmesteter, Spiegel, Harlez and Haug very properly take the word *Hunu* in this passage for a proper noun, but Kanga takes it for a common noun.

In the Farvardin and Zamyād Yashts, king Viṣtāsp or Guṣtāsp, the patron of Zoroaster and of the Zoroastrian religion, is spoken of, as said above, as separating the religion of Iran from the influence of the *Hunus*. In the Goṣ

1 Ibid p. 69, l. 7.

Yasht[1] Viṣtāsp prays for overcoming eight foreign kings or chiefs. Among them, one is Khyaona Arejatāspa, who is spoken of in the Pahlavi Aiyādgār-i-Zarirān (Memoirs of Zarir) as Arjāsp-i-Khyōnān Khudāi[2], i.e. Arjāsp the king of the Khyaonas. We find a similar prayer in the Aṣiṣvang Yasht.[3] Viṣtāsp had to fight three wars with this Turanian king Arjāsp. Firdousi refers to these at some length. The wars were due to the appearance of Zoroaster as a prophet in the court of Viṣtāsp. According to Firdousi, Zoroaster advised his royal patron to free himself from the yoke and influence of this Turanian king. So, taking the above passage of the Farvardin Yasht in connection with the passage of the Goṣ Yasht above referred to and with the Pahlavi writing of the Aiyādgār, it seems that Arjāsp the Tụranian with whom Viṣtāsp fought, and his tribesmen the Khyaonas, were all Huns.

From the passages of the Yashts, at least of the Farvardin and Zamyād Yashts, we find that the *Hunus* or Huns lived in the time of king Viṣtāsp and Zoroaster, which, if not anterior to, was at least not later than, that of the 7th century before Christ.

These *Hunus* seem to have belonged to the same group of hostile tribes to which the Varedhakas and the Khyaonas belonged. King Viṣtāsp, the patron king of Zoroaster, who is represented as opposing the *Hunus*,[4] is also represented as opposing the Varedhakas[5] and the Khyaonas.[6]

According to Darmesteter, the Varedhakas referred to in the Avesta as a hostile tribe like the *Hunus*, may be the later Vertae. Similarly the Khyaonas were the Chionitae. They lived somewhere on the western coast of the Caspian.[7]

1 Yt. IX. 31, 32.

2 Vide my "Aiyādgār-i-Zarirān, Shatrōiha-i-Airan and Afdiya va Sahigiya-i-Seistan" (1899) p. 5.

3 Yt. XVII, 49–50.

4 Farvardin Yasht 100.

5 Gosh Yasht, 31; Aṣiṣavang Yasht 51.

6 Ibid and Zamyād Yasht 87.

7 Darmesteter, S. B. E. Vol. XXIII, p. 117 n. 6, Yasht IX, 100 n. 6.

From this rather long examination of the Avesta passages we find that the *Hunus* were known in Persia as a wandering and pillaging nation or tribe before the 7th century of the Christian era.

Among the several passages of the Avesta which we have examined we find that there is some difference about the meaning of the word *Hunu* in some passages. But there are some for which there is no difference, especially the passages referred to in the Ābān Yasht and which referred to the war between the Iranians of Tusa and the *Hunus* of the Turanian Vaēsaka.

The early Huns, i. e. the Huns of the times of the Avesta, seem to have professed well-nigh the same religion as that of the early Iranians. We see this from the ceremonial form of their prayers, referred to in the Ābān Yasht (Yt. V. 53, 58). We see, from the passages of this Yasht given above, that both the Iranian Tusa and the *Hunus* of Vaēsaka invoke Ardvīsūra with the same ceremonial offering. They both offer 100 horses, 1000 oxen and 10000 lambs. Secondly, we learn from the Pahlavi Aiyādgār-i-Zarirān that Arjāsp raised a war against Viṣtāsp because the latter acknowledged the new religion of Zoroaster. Why should he have done so had they professed different religions? Though hostile and though differing in the details of their belief, they seem to have followed a common religion, a religion the main elements of which were the same. Had it not been so, there was no special reason for Arjāsp to declare war for the sake of religion. We read in the Pahlavi Aryādgār: "Arjāsp, the king of the Khyaonas, had the startling news that king Viṣtāsp had, with his sons, brothers and family, chiefs and equals, accepted from Oharmazd this holy religion of the Mazdayasnāns. Thereby he was much distressed."[1] Further on, we read the following message of Arjāsp to Viṣtāsp: "I have heard that Your Majesty has accepted from Oharmazd the pure Mazdayasnān religion. If you will not think of it, great harm and unhappiness may result to us from that (religion). But

1 Vide my Aryādgār-i-Zarirān etc. p. 3.

if it please Your Majesty, and you give up this pure religion, and be of the same religion with us, then we will pay homage to you as a king."[1] These passages show that Arjāsp resents Viṣtāsp's forsaking the common ancestral religion and adopting the new Mazdayasnān one of Zoroaster. Again, according to the Iranian tradition, recorded in the Pahlavi Bundehesh, the Iranians and the Turanians at first belonged to the same group. They had a common ancestor. This fact also shows that they had well-nigh the same religion. We find from the above passages of the Farvardin (100) and the Zamyād (86) Yashts that with the help of king Guṣtāsp, Zoroaster separated the good elements from the bad ones, and rejecting the latter purified the old religion. That was his great work of reform. Firdousi (Calcutta ed. III. p. 1548) represents even the later Huns as praying in fire-temples with *bāz* and *barsam*, the sacred requisites of Zoroastrian worship. According to Firdousi, king Behramgore sent the queen of the Khokan of the Hunnic Turks to the fire-temple of Azor Goushasp as a state prisoner to serve there.

We also learn from Indian history based on epigraphical, numismatic, and literary materials that Mihirakula was a foreign Hun king whom the Indian king Yaśodharman, or as said by Mr. Vincent Smith, both Yaśodharman and Bālāditya combined, defeated. Rājataraṅgiṇī,[2] the history of Kāśmīr by Kalhaṇa, refers to this Mihirakula at some length. We learn the following facts from this work about Mihirakula. (1) He founded the temple of Mihireśvara and the city of Mihirapura. (2) He allowed the Gandhāri Brahmans, a low race, to seize upon the endowments of the more respectable orders of the Hindu priesthood. (3) These Gandhāri Brahmans of Mihirakula had the custom of the

1 Ibid p. 5.

2 Bk. I, stanzas 306 et seq., Troyer's French Translation of 1840, Vol. I, pp. 33 et seq. Vide also Sir Aurel Stein's Text and Translation and Wilson's Essay on the Hindu History of Kāśmīr in the *Asiatick Researches*, Volume V (pp. 1-11), n. 23.

next-of-kin marriages among them.[1] (4) A number of flesh-devouring birds followed the army of this king.[2]

The very name Mihirakula is, as said by Dr. Stein, Iranian. The names of the temple and city founded by him are Iranian. The marriage custom attributed to him is the matriarchal custom alleged to be tribal with some Persian people.[3] The reference to the flesh-eating birds points to the Iranian custom of the disposal of the dead. All these facts and references point to an inference that the religion of this Hun king, Mihirakula, had many elements which were common to the religion of the early Iranians.

According to the Iranians of the Avestic[4] times, the people of the then known world were divided into five groups: (1) the Airyas, (2) the Turyas, (3) the Sarimyas or the people who dwelt in Syria, (4) the Sāini, or the Chinese and (5) the Dāhæ. Of these five stocks, the first three are traced from the three sons of king Faridun, the Thraētaona of the Avesta. These three sons were Salam, Tur and Irach. From Salam descended the stock of the Sarimyas, from Tur that of the Turanians and from Irach that of the Iranians. Viṣtāsp came from the stock of Irach and Arjāsp from that of Tur.

Vaēsaka, the typical Hūṇa or Hun, and Tusa, the typical Iranian, descended, according to the Pahlavi Bundehesh, from a common ancestor. The following geneological tree, prepared from the account of the Bundehesh, gives their descent from Gayomard, supposed to be the

1 The stanza referring to this custom is omitted in Dr. Stein's Text but is found in Troyer's Text, p. 38. Dr. Stein refers to this omission in the foot-note. As to Mihirkula, Dr. Stein also thinks that the name is Iranian.

2 Rāj., stanza i. 291.

3 For this custom see a Paper on "Royal Marriages and Matrilineal Descent" by Miss Margaret Murray (Journal of the Anthropological Institute of England, July-December 1915.)

4 Farvardin Yasht, Yt. XIII, 144.

first king of the countries, of which Airyana Vaeja or Iran formed a part.

- Gayomard
  - Masya
    - Sīyāmak
      - Fravāk
        - Hoshang
          - Yanghad
            - Vivanghāo
              - Takhmorup
              - Yima (Jamshed)
                - Vanfraghesna Āspiyān
                  - Ramaktorā Āspyān
                    - Geraftorā Āspyān
                      - Sapidtorā Āspyān
                        - Sihaktorā Āspyān
                          - Bortorā Āspyān
                            - Soktorā Āspyān
                              - Purtorā Āspyān
                                - Barmayun
                                - Katayun
                                - Faridun, descended from Purtora from a line of ancestors who lived for 1000 years
                                  - Salam
                                  - Tur, the ancestor of the Turanians
                                    - Dorosasp
                                      - Spaenasp
                                        - Turk
                                          - Zadsan or Zaesam, descended from a line of ancestors
                                  - Erach, the ancestor of the Iranians
                                    - Ganzah
                                      - Fraguzaga
                                        - Zushak
                                          - Frazusag
              - Spitur
              - Narsih
        - Taz
          - Virafsang
            - Zainigāo
              - Khrutasp (or Mardās)
                - Dahak (Zohak), the Arab of the Semetic group from Babylon

- *Zadṣan or Zeaṣam, descended from a line of ancestors*
  - Visak
  - Paṣang
    - Afrāsiāb

- *Frazuṣag*
  - Bitarg
    - Thritak
      - Buterak
        - Mamak Sozak
          - Manosh Kharnak
            - Manosh Kharnar
              - Minocher
                - Nodar
                  - Tus

THE EARLY HISTORY OF THE INDO-IRANIANS

By A. BERRIEDALE KEITH

IT is a curious characteristic of all the peoples of Indo-European speech that they should have failed in the early days of their development to fashion for themselves a script, and that they should have owed their alphabets to the invention of others. Moreover even when they came into contact with peoples who used writing, they showed a disinclination to avail themselves of the discovery: this is clear not only in Iran and India, but beyond all in Greece, where we now know there existed linear scripts not later than 1800 B. C., but of these the invading Greeks, Ionians, Achaians, and Dorians made, it would seem, no use whatever, leaving to Phoenicia the honour of bringing into use the script from which is derived the writing of Greece.[1] In close connection with this failure on the part of the Indo-Europeans stands the absence of annals of their early history, a fact which leaves us in the most tantalising darkness as to the development of the nations. The example of Egypt which, first of nations, could boast the invention of a chronology indicates how little faith can be placed in oral tradition as to historical personages. The account of the early history of Egypt given by Herodotos and Manetho proves how folk-tales of all sorts became associated with the great names of the past, and, but for the happy discovery of original monuments, our knowledge of Egyptian history would be one mass of grave error. It is not surprising therefore that the ingenuity of many generations of scholars has failed to make anything satisfactory out of the legendary history of Greece: the objections which, in point of theory, could be adduced against the possibility of attaining definite results from tradition have been enforced and made insuperable by the discovery through the excavations in Crete of a civilisation of the existence of which no hint was contained in

1 Cf. A. J. Evans, *Scripta Minoa* (1909); H. R. Hall, *Aegean Archaeology* (1915).

the tradition. In India the case is even worse than in Greece, where the epic is the oldest recorded literature: the legends, out of which scholars are now engaged in seeking to extract results which the nature of the case forbids us to attain, are recorded in works, the epics and the Purānas, of late and uncertain date. Happily these speculations are of minor importance in the case of India, as they have not affected in any degree the correct dating of the religious literature of the Vedic period. In the case of Iran, however, misplaced confidence in the Parsi tradition, which dates Zoroaster three hundred years before Alexander, has resulted in endless confusion and difficulty.[1]

The defects of tradition are in some measure made good in the case of Greece by synchronisms with Egypt and by references in Egyptian monuments, and within the last few years evidence has accumulated bearing on the early history of the Indo-Iranians. Unfortunately this evidence is in the main of a kind peculiarly difficult to estimate precisely: it consists of the occurrence of names of deities and men in the records of non-Indo-European peoples, and it is obvious at once how great a difficulty there is in determining whether in the names cited we are to see renderings of Indo-Iranian names, or names of other origin. It is indisputable that, in being reproduced in a foreign speech, names may suffer considerable change, and with some ingenuity and a free use of the constructive imagination it is not difficult for any scholar to excogitate etymologies for such words which will make them fit in with his preconceived theories of the linguistic connections of the words. No more convincing proof of this fact can be adduced than the famous controversy over the language of the Scyths of Herodotos, as evidenced by the personal names and the names of deities given by him: they have been shown conclusively in the eyes of one set of scholars to be Iranian, while another school has found

1 Cf. E. Meyer, *Zeitschrift für vergleichende Sprachforschung*, xlii. 2; J. H. Moulton, *Early Zoroastrianism*, pages 18 ff.; A. B. Keith, *Journal of the Royal Asiatic Society*, 1915, pp. 798, 799.

explanations of them all from Finno-Ugrian, while yet others fall back on the theory of a mixed race.[1] To add to the difficulty it must be remembered that the languages in which these names occur are by no means very well known: the controversy over the character of Hittite is still unsolved, and perhaps likely to remain unsolved.[2]

The oldest evidence yet adduced is that derived from the names of Kassite princes and certain words preserved in a glossary giving the Babylonian equivalents of certain Kassite words.[3] In two names of kings, Burna-buriaš and Nazi-bugaš, have been seen as elements the Iranian farna- and baga-, but clearly without any cogency. More noteworthy is Šuriaš, since it is explained as meaning the sun, and E. Meyer[4] has yielded to the temptation to accept equation with the Vedic Sūryas; but, apart from the odd fact that the termination of the nominative should be reproduced, it is clear that in the absence of any further evidence it is illegitimate to accept the proposed identification. Such confirmation would indeed be forthcoming if the views of Scheftelowitz regarding other Kassite words could be adopted, but even E. Meyer admits that this is out of the question. He, however, adduces in support of his acceptance of Aryan influence the fact that the horse appears freely in Babylonian records under the Kassite dynasty which from 1760 B. C. onwards controlled Babylon, and that its description as "the ass of the mountains" shows its origin. But this argument lacks all cogency, since it is certain that the horse was introduced into Babylon, if not under Hammurabi himself, at any rate under his son, probably not later than B. C. 2000.[5] Nor of course

1 E. H. Minns, *Scythians and Greeks*, pp. 85, 86.

2 Cf. A. H. Sayce, *Journal of the Royal Asiatic Society*, 1914, pp. 965–72; 1916, pp. 253 ff.

3 Published by F. Delitzsch, *Die Sprache der Kossaeer* (1884). See Scheftelowitz, *Zeitschrift für vergleichende Sprachforschung*, xxxviii. 270 ff., and M. Bloomfield, *American Journal of Philology*, xxv. 10 ff.

4 *Geschichte des Altertums*³, I, ii. 654.

5 A. Ungnad, *Orientalistische Literaturzeitung*, x. 367 f.

can the slightest value be placed on the view[1] that white slaves from Gutium and Subarti, who are mentioned under the reign of the last king but one of the dynasty of Hammurabi, were Aryans, or on the wild guess[2] of Brunnhofer which finds a reference in the Ṛgveda to the capture of Babylon by the first Kassite king.

Much more substantial is the evidence which is to be derived from the records of the Mitani in Northern Mesopotamia, a people whose affinity to the Hittites and perhaps to the Kassites has been affirmed with a fair amount of plausibility: at any rate they were certainly not Indo-Europeans. But in a treaty with the Hittite king Subbiluliuma, concluded some time after 1380 B. C., Mattiwaza invokes the gods Mitra, Varuṇa, Indra and the Nāsatyas by names which are very slightly different from the Vedic.[3] To this falls to be added the fact that Dušratta, the Mitani king, brother-in-law of Amenhoteb III of Egypt (c. 1414–1379 B. C.), his brother Artašumara, his father Šutarna, and his grandfather Artatāma, bear names which have an Iranian sound, and the eye of faith has even seen the Aryan type in the features of Teie, the wife of Amenhoteb III, a princess of Mitani. More important is the suggestion of Winckler,[4] that the name Harri used of the Mitani is really the Aryan name, a view which he supports by the fact that the Susan version of the inscriptions of Darius

1 J. Kennedy, *Journal of the Royal Asiatic Society*, 1909, pp. 1112, 1113.

2 H. Brunnhofer, *Iran und Turan*, p. 221.

3 H. Winckler, *Mitteilungen der Deutschen Orientgesellschaft*, No. 35; *Orientalistische Literaturzeitung*, xiii. 296 ff. A.H. Sayce (*Journal of the Royal Asiatic Society*, 1909, pp. 1106, 1107) denies the Aryan character of the Mitani royal names. Artatāma's name is often wrongly read as Artatama. Mattiwaza and Sa-uš-ša-tar are declared Aryan by Meyer, but this is not certain. W. Max Müller (*Orientalistische Literaturzeitung*, xv. 252 ff.) finds Mitra in the name Mitrašama of an Egypto-Semitic stele in Palestine.

4 Followed by Meyer, *Geschichte des Altertums*,[3] I. ii. 677. The suffix found in *Marianni* is comparable with that found in Našatiana (=Nāsatyā) in the list of gods. It may be Aryan; cf. E. Leumann, *Zur nordarischen Sprache und Literatur*, pp. 5 ff.

likewise aspirates the name of the Aryan claimed by the king: he also finds in *marianni*, a word applied to the warriors of the Mitani, the Vedic *marya* 'the manly.' It is however impossible to accept the further suggestion that the Horites of *Genesis* are to be brought into this connection, if for no other reason than that their princes bear true Semitic names. On the other hand, as we might expect, there are other traces in the Amarna correspondence, which represents the period before and after 1400 B.C., of Aryan names among the princes in Syria such as Šuwardata, Jašdata, Artamanya, Ruṣmanya, Arzawiya, Biridiya or Biridašya, Namyawaza, Teuwatti, Šubandhi and Šutarna, most if not all of which have a fairly clear Aryan appearance.[1] Definitely Iranian in type are the names of princes of Kommagene recorded for us in 854 and about 740 B.C., Kundašpi and Kuštašpi, doubtless Vindāspa and Vištāspa: from 838 B.C. onwards the Medes appear in conflict with Assyria, and as early as 745 B.C. the name Mazdaka is found, doubtless denoting a worshipper of Mazdāh, whose name in the archaic form Assara Mazāš is actually found in a record of Assurbanipal (B.C. 668-626).

What are the historical conclusions to be drawn from these facts? In the first place it is essential to note that we have no proof of the existence of any actual Aryan tribe in Northern Mesopotamia and Syria: the presence of princes of Aryan name in these petty states is not proof of migration on a great scale: we may rather think of restless adventurers and mercenaries of the type familiar in European no less than in Asiatic history. It follows, in the second place, from the sudden appearance of these names in history that we may properly assume the appearance of Aryans in these regions as a recent matter. The question, therefore, presents itself from what side the Aryans entered the country. The possibility that they came by sea may fairly be dismissed: in the reigns of Merenptah and Ramses III from 1229 B.C. onwards we have recorded raids and even settlements on the Syrian coast by foreign

1 E. Meyer, *Zeitschrift für vergleichende Sprachforschung*, xlii. 17–19.

adventurers and tribes as a result and sign of the great migration of peoples which took place in the thirteenth century, and it is possible, though not certain, that the Philistines were to some extent Aryan in blood.[1] But if this had been the case in the earlier period, we should doubtless have a record of it in the Amarna correspondence. Of the land routes, that through Asia Minor naturally suggests itself, and it might be regarded as plausible if we could accept the view of Kretschmer[2] which ascribes the second city of Troy to the Phrygians. But this view may fairly be dismissed as impossible: the history of Asia Minor is doubtless not perfectly known, but there is adequate evidence to show that the first important influx of Aryans was only caused by the migrations of peoples which produced the settlements on the coast of Syria, and that the first entrance of the Phrygians and cognate tribes into Western Asia Minor falls after B. C. 1400.[3] A third possibility is that to which Hirt[4] has lent the weight of his authority: in his opinion the original home of the Indo-European people is to be found in Europe, perhaps more specifically in northern Germany, and the Indo-Iranians entered their future homes via the Caucasus. This hypothesis is however subject to a grave objection, which Hirt has not overcome in any degree. If his view were correct, we ought to find that Armenia shows early traces of Aryan population, but this is very far from being the case. On

1 They may, of course, have been pre-Hellenic Cretans or other Islanders. Crete itself, from the earliest times known to us, had both a dolichocephalic (Mediterranean) and a brachycephalic (Armenoid, akin to the Alpine race of Europe) population. To which of these belonged the names in *ss* and *nth* (*nd*) spread over Greece, Asia Minor, and the islands is not known. Cf. R. M. Burrows, *Discoveries in Crete*, pp. 165, 166. Most authors assume the existence of one race only, but withou warrant.

2 *Einleitung in die Geschichte der griechischen Sprache*, pp. 180, 181, who relies on the untrustworthy argument of continuity of culture.

3 E. Meyer, *Geschichte des Altertums*³, I. ii. 693.

4 *Die Indo-germanen*, i. 178 ff,

the contrary Armenia seems to have been distinguished by a remarkably vigorous non-Aryan population which produced the interesting kingdom of Van to contend not unsuccessfully for a couple of centuries with Assyria; and the entry of the Indo-European Armenians, who seem to have been closely connected with the Phrygians, falls no earlier than about B. C. 700. The Ossetes who have occasionally been regarded as the remnants of the Indo-Iranians coming from the west are now doubtless correctly held to have been Alani, later Iranian invaders from the east.[1] Nor is this objection to Hirt's view to be removed by any other considerations available. Even if we could prove early Babylonian influence on India we could not be certain that this fact would establish the view that the Indo-Iranians entered their future homes by the route south of the Caspian, as it is impossible to define the distance to which Babylonian culture could be carried. But in any case the proof of such influence is wholly inadequate. The solitary *manā* of the Ṛgveda has of course repeatedly been equated with the Babylonian mina, but no explanation has been offered of the fact that, if borrowed, this valuable unit was not retained: similarly *paraśu*, axe, is compared with Sumerian *balag*, and Akkadian *pilakku*, and *loha* with the Sumerian *urudu*, copper, in both cases wholly without cogency, since in both cases, even if we accept the identification,—a course open to grave doubt,—there is not the slightest evidence to show in which language the words are primitive, and it is perfectly possible that the borrowing, if any, may be from a third source altogether.[2] More serious perhaps is the famous argument of Oldenberg[3] that the seven Ādityas are strange gods in India, pointing to a borrowing from a people which worshipped the seven planets, and gave a moral fervour to their religion otherwise lacking in Indian religion. The theory must be re-

1 E. Meyer, *Geschichte des Altertums*^{3}, I. ii. 890, 891.

2 Cf. S. Feist, *Kultur der Indo-germanen*, pp. 71ff. *loha*; is not Ṛgvedic.

3 *Die Religion des Veda*, pp. 103 ff., *Zeitschrift der Deutschen Morgenländischen Gesellschaft*, l. 43 ff.

jected, if for no other reason than that the worship of the seven planets cannot be proved early enough for Babylon to render the view even possible.[1] Nor can we accept the derivation either of Aššur from Asura[2] or of Asura from Aššur.[3] There is no identity of character in the two conceptions, and the similarity of name is far from close. The Indo-Iranian Asura has an obvious derivation from *asu*, and, while the name of Aššur is less certainly interpreted, it is important to note that its oldest form seems to have been Ašir, and in Palestine we have the place name Ašer, and among the Amorites, the sacred post, the Ašera, and the divinity which took up its abode therein.[4] Nor do we need to fly to Babylon for an explanation of the 360 day year of Vedic India, or the sacredness of the number 7.[5]

There remains therefore the obvious conclusion that the Aryans of Mitani and Syria penetrated these lands from the east, their progress being rendered possible by the confusion and disturbance caused by the Kassite overthrow of Babylonia. But, accepting this simple and satisfactory view, the question arises in what light we are to regard the gods of the king of Mitani, and the Aryan names. Are they early Indian, or early Iranian, or do they belong to the period before Indian and Iranian were differentiated? The view that the gods were Indian, brought by an East Iranian tribe, is adopted by Jacobi[6] as the only solution of the non-Iranian form of the name Našatia, coupled with the Arta- found in the names of the kings of Mitani. This view receives some support from J. Hope Moulton,[7] who thinks a retrograde movement by tribes dissatisfied with India possible, and who strengthens his opinion by

1 E. Meyer, *Geschichte des Altertums*³, I. ii. 593.

2 H. M. Chadwick in J. H. Moulton, *Early Zoroastrianism*, p. 32.

3 F. W. Thomas, *Journal of the Royal Asiatic Society*, 1916, p. 364.

4 E. Meyer, *Geschichte des Altertums*³, I. ii. 608.

5 A. B. Keith, *Journal of the Royal Asiatic Society*, 1916, p. 355.

6 *Journal of the Royal Asiatic Society*, 1909, pp. 721 ff.

7 *Early Zoroastrianism*, pp. 25 ff.

the acceptance of a suggestion that the data of the *Tištrya Yašt* are best explained on the view that the observations recorded were made in India at some time between B. C. 1800 and 900. This argument must be deemed wholly invalid, and the main suggestion must be regarded as distinctly improbable. The view of Oldenberg[1] that we have to deal with proto-Iranian deities is thus in itself the natural one, and it certainly gains plausibility from the fact that Indra and the Nāsatyas are known as demons, Indra and Nāonhaithya, in Iran, while the omission of Agni who is clearly a specifically Indian development of the worship of fire tells in the same direction.

E. Meyer[2] on the other hand lays considerable stress on the fact that the go's are Aryan, not Iranian, and he finds in them a vivid pre..ntation of the reality of the Aryan period which can be reconstructed from the agreement of Indian and Iranian, but of which the first direct proof is afforded by these names. He has been accused of inconsistency in this regard by Jacobi, and it is clear that his expressions of opinion on this topic have not been altogether happily worded. But the real meaning of his view is clear: he holds indeed that the period when the Aryans as an undivided people in the strict sense were living together in a country where Soma grew, probably Bactria and the western Hindu Kush, did not last so late as 1400 B. C., and he accepts the view that the Indians must have invaded India not later than B. C. 1500. But the spread of the people over Iran and India did not at first and in itself cause complete severance: this was a gradual development, doubtless beginning in the period of the united people and gradually increasing until in Iran the divergence was brought to its full development by Zoroaster. For the old suggestion, which saw in the division of the Aryans into Indians and Iranians the result of a

1 *Journal of the Royal Asiatic Society*, 1909, pp. 1095 ff.

2 *Sitzungsberichte der Königl. Preussischen Akademie der Wissenschaften zu Berlin*, 1908, pp. 14–18 ; *Zeitschrift für vergleichende Sprachforschung*, xlii. 24–27, *Geschichte des Altertums*,[3] I. ii. 900.

definite religious split due to the activity of Zoroaster, we must substitute the conception of a difference of religious outlook, commencing in the period of united life, and intensifying with the separation of the elements of the people in space. The gods of Mitani are therefore best described as Aryan gods, and the language as an Aryan dialect, differing as it does both from Iranian and Vedic as known to us: unlike the former it keeps *s* between vowels in Našatia, while unlike the latter it has Arta– not Ṛta–, though in this case the argument is difficult to press, for in Mitani script it was impossible to reproduce Ṛta correctly: Suwardata seems clearly equivalent to the Vedic form *suvar-datta*, though that name is not found in Vedic texts. Similarly the name Assara Mazāš, which we must assume to have been borrowed at a much earlier date than that of its appearance, can be explained easily as Aryan: it is doubtless not a very perfect phonetic representation of the original, but the *s* is retained while the *z* is clearly Aryan, the speech whence it was taken being therefore older than either Iranian or Vedic. We need not of course postulate that the precise dialect whence these names come was the parent of Iranian and Vedic: it presumably was a dialect of Western Aryan origin.

The value of this result lies in the main in the fact that it enables us to view in a new light the long continued controversy over the place of origin of the Indo-Europeans. The evidence indicates that the entry of Aryans into Iran took place from the north-east, and that it conformed therefore to the general trend of the movements of the Iranian tribes throughout history. It still remains open of course to hold that in the first place the Indo-Iranians came from Europe, and Moulton[1] has deduced from the similarities of German and Sanskrit in certain respects, such as the treatment of the aspirate mediæ, that we have to recognise first a migration from Europe of the primitive Iranian people, and then the migration at a very rapid rate of a Germanic tribe which imposed its language on

1 *Essays and Studies presented to William Ridgeway* pp. 249–260.

this population and passed on into India, leaving the Iranian population gradually to absorb those members who stayed in Iran. This argument however is untenable: all the Indo-European languages have certain special points in which they agree with one or another of the group, and to deduce racial mixture and migration from these facts is quite impossible.

Moreover the hypothesis of an Asiatic origin of the Indo-Europeans has derived a good deal of additional plausibility from the discovery of Tocharian. It is indeed necessary not to overrate the importance of this evidence as Feist[1] is inclined to do. When we remember the wanderings of the Gauls it is quite unscientific to assert that the Tocharian speech could not represent a migration from Europe into Asia. But a priori it is not so probable as the movement from east to west, and while the claim of South Russia to serve as the original Indo-European home is discounted by the fact that it is essentially a place of passage and not a permanent abode, the alternative claim of Germany must be held to be shattered by the fact that at the hands of the Germans the Indo-European speech has suffered such striking alteration in its sounds, an occurrence which is most easily explained by the hypothesis that in Germany this speech was imposed by a small minority on a pre-existing population. The fact that Tocharian in its treatment of the gutturals, and to some extent in its retention of the vowels *e* and *o* beside *a* ranks with the *centum* speeches of Europe makes it reasonable to suppose that the Indo-European home lay in the plateau of central Asia, the source of the later Mongolian invaders of the west. The Tocharian speech may represent the language of the portion of the people who remained there after the *centum* speakers, and part of the *satem* speakers, had migrated west by a route north of the Aral and the Caspian, and the Aryans had moved south-west, while their nomads, the Scoloti and other Scythian tribes wandered on the steppes through which the earlier migrants

1 *Kultur der Indogermanen*, p. 519.

had moved. This is a conjecture of E. Meyer's[1] and while neither it, nor the suggestion that the Tripolje culture of South Russia[2] marks, in the period about 2500–2000 B.C., the march of Indo-European tribes westwards, can lay claim to more than plausibility, it is one which could effectively be used to solve many problems of linguistic history. Moreover this explanation accounts well for the close similarity between the accounts of the early Indo-Europeans and especially the nomadic tribes and those of the Mongols: as regards manner of life, religion and funeral customs similarity of circumstance would produce similarity of result.[3]

It is not of course to be assumed that the Indo-Europeans entered empty lands: the strong differentiation of the Indo-European speeches, and the character of the peoples are a priori proofs to the contrary, which are strengthened by anthropological and historical evidence. It is not impossible that we find in Tocharian a relic of a speech which has been overwhelmed by Indo-European. It shows a comitative suffix *aśśäl*, which most curiously must be identified with the *aššil* added in the Mitani record to the names of Mitra and Varuṇa, no doubt to indicate them as a pair.[4] Whatever the explanation may be, it must in any event be remembered that the period of Indo-European unity need not be placed earlier than 3000 B. C. and that this is a comparatively late date in the history of man on this earth.

1 *Geschichte des Altertums*,[3] I. ii. 890 ff.

2 Described by E. W. Minns, *Scythians and Greeks*, pp. 133 ff.

3 The evidence is well given by E. W. Minns, *Scythians and Greeks* pp. 85 ff., but he, writing in the main before the Tocharian evidence was known to him, is inclined unduly to accept the parallelism as proof of Mongolian elements in the Scyths of Herodotos. This need not in itself be doubted, but the weight of the evidence is misconceived. Similarly the tracing of certain features in early Buddhism to Mongolian sources rests on a false ignoring of the fact that the culture of nomads is practically identical whatever the race.

4 The conjecture of Hall (*Journal of Hellenic Studies*, xxix. 21) that the suffix denoted the plural of each word is clearly an error.

THE LAND OF SEVEN RIVERS

BY N. G. SARDESAI

THE word *Sapta-sindhu* has been generally used in the Ṛgveda in the sense of seven rivers. Thus Ṛv. i. 32.12 extols Indra for having let the seven rivers flow (*ávāsṛjas sártave saptá síndhūn*); in i. 35. 8 the light of the sun is said to have illumined the eight quarters, the three desert regions, and the seven rivers (*aṣṭaú vyàkhyat kakúbhaḥ pṛthivyā́s trī́ dhánva yójanā saptá síndhūn*); and in i. 71. 1 all offerings are said to wait upon Agni "as the seven mighty rivers seek the ocean" (*samudráṁ ná sravátas saptá yahvī́ḥ*). It is usual to suppose that the seven rivers meant are the five rivers of the Panjab (Vitastā, Asiknī, Paruṣṇī, Vipāś and Śutudrī) together with the Indus and the Sarasvatī, the river Kubhā in some enumerations taking the place of the last-named. If it is only a question of somehow making up a given number, we shall have no reason to quarrel with either of these enumerations or even suggest a third made up of the Ganges, the Jumna and the five rivers that give the Panjab its name. But there is another passage in the Ṛgveda[1] where Sapta-sindhu is the designation of a land or country[2] watered by seven rivers. The passage (viii, 24. 27) reads thus—

य ऋक्षादंहसो मुचद्यो वार्यात् सप्तसिन्धुषु ।
वधर्दासस्य तुविनृम्ण नीनमः ॥

Translation: Who would free [us] from ruinous woe or from the Ārya [enemy] in the Seven Rivers; thou O valiant hero, bend the Dāsa's weapon [down].

Scholars have been for the most part content to regard the Panjab as the modern equivalent of the ancient Sapta-sindhu, but the difficulties in the way of this identification

1 Cp. also Atharva Veda iv. 6. 2, though the passage is not decisive.

2 In the Avesta Hapta-hindu is the regular name of a country once inhabited by the Aryans; compare Vendidad i. 19.

are quite on the surface. The Panjab[1] (*Pañc+ap*) derives its name from only five rivers and they do not all flow into the sea, as Ṛv. i. 71. 1 requires it. And to bring in distant or imaginary rivers to complete the number is a questionable process which does not explain why no trace of the ancient name of the country survives in its modern equivalent; for, established names are tough things and die very hard. To obviate this difficulty, some scholars[2] have imagined the seven rivers to be atmospheric streams; but even so it would not be unreasonable to enquire after their terrestrial analogues; for, things celestial always have their analogues on earth. Further if the Ṛgveda—though not in its present form at least in its ideas and back-ground—is to be regarded as an Indo-Germanic product, would it be right to confine all the Vedic literary and religious activity to the Panjab and the country adjoining? Would it not be nearer the mark to look up for the 'land of the seven rivers' somewhere in the central Asian plateau which, if not the cradle of the Aryan race, was at least, we might presume, a place of long sojourn in the course of the Aryan migrations from their Arctic home?

Curiously enough there is in central Asia, in Russian Turkestan, North of the Ala Tau Range, East of the Lower Illi River, and West of the Lepsa river, a country[3] which is even now called 'the land of the seven streams', this being the literal meaning of its current Russian name 'Semiretchenski-krai'. Lake Balkash forms a part of its Northern boundary and the seven rivers—Lepsa, Baskan, Aksu, Sarkau, Biyen, Kartal, and Koksu—which give the country its name do all flow into this Lake: at least for a part of the year; for when not in floods the minor rivers

1 The name is unknown to the Ṛgveda. Its earliest mention is in the Vājasaneyī Saṁhitā xxxiv. 2, where we are told—

पञ्च नद्यः सरस्वतीमपियन्ति सस्रोतसः ।
सरस्वती तु पञ्चधा सो देशेऽभवत्सरित् ॥

Compare also Atharva Veda VI. 98. 3.

2 For example, B. G. Tilak in the *Arctic Home*, p. 288ff.

3 See annexed map.

SEMIRETCHENSKI-KRAI
OR
LAND OF THE SEVEN RIVERS

To face page 94]

loose themselves in the sands. Traces of an ancient Aryan colonization of the land are still discernable there. The Aryan Tajik, the aborigines of the fertile parts of Turkestan and now known as Galchas, constitute in fact the intellectual element of the country and are the principal owners of the irrigated land. The country,[1] we must remember, is and has always been a theatre of a series of violent earthquakes, and in the course of centuries topographic changes small and great are almost inevitable. The sand storms which, as geologists tell us,[2] affected the stretch of country from Arabia to Mongolia must have produced certain other alterations in the physicial features[3] of the land; but the main feature which gave the country its name, and the name itself, have survived, and if an expedition such as that of Sir Aurel Stein is sent to explore the land much new light might be forthcoming. Above all it would be necessary to find out if the names of these seven rivers, in the native pronunciations[4] of them, afford any basis for fruitful philological deductions.

If the suggestion as to a possible location for the Land of Seven Rivers that I have thrown out is at all found worthy of a serious consideration it would follow that when, in the course of their migrations, the Aryan people came and settled in the Panjab they found the country, in its physical features and especially the river system, so much like their original Sapta-sindhu that it is likely that they might have transferred many of their original geographical names to this new land of their adoption, very much like what the English colonists did when they,

1 For fuller description see Asia, vol. I, pp. 130 ff., by A. H. Keane; Edward Stanford, London. 1916.

2 Modern Science in Modern Life, vol. i. pp. 161 ff., Greshman Publishing Co., London, 1910.

3 Cp. the 'desert regions' or 'dry promontories' mentioned above in Ṛv. i. 35. 8.

4 That foreigners absolutely maltreat the native names was never brought home to the writer of this paper so vividly as when he discovered that what is written in the maps as *Socka Boemi* and pronounced by the ordinary rules of orthography was really, in the native Javanese pronunciation, *Sukha-bhūmi.*

a couple of centuries ago, occupied and colonised America or Australia. This probably led to a gradual effacement of all the memory of their original home ; so that later Brāhmaṇic and Paurāṇic texts, and even Avestic texts for the matter of that, when they speak of the Sapta-sindhu or the Land of Seven Rivers, always mean by it India, or more correctly, the Panjab and the Gangatic Basin.

Epics and Purāṇas

TATO JAYAM UDĪRAYET

PAR M. SYLVAIN LÉVI

CHACUN des livres du Mahābhārata débute par une bénédiction liminaire uniforme :

Nārāyaṇaṁ namaskṛtya Naraṁ caiva narottamam
Devīṁ Sarasvatīṁ caiva tato jayam udīrayet.

La même formule reparaît vers la fin du dernier chant (XVIII. 232) dans une sorte d'appendice qui traîte de la récitation du Mahābhārata. Cette bénédiction d'aspect assez banal ne paraît pas avoir attiré l'attention[1]; on la lit et on la traduit sans s'y arrêter. L'interprétation communément admise a été suivie avec docilité par la traduction de P. C. Roy: *Having bowed down to Nārāyaṇa, and Nara the most exalted male being, and also to the goddess Sarasvatī, must the word* success *be uttered* (les légères variantes de style qu'on relève d'un chant à l'autre dans la traduction anglaise de cette formule n'en affectent pas le sens). Le commentateur Nīlakaṇṭha signale pourtant la possibilité d'une autre interprétation pour le dernier pāda : *tato vyāptas tayaiva Sarasvatyā parama-kāruṇikayā janabodhāyāviṣṭo jayam 'Jayo nāmetihāso'yam' iti vakṣyamāṇatvāj Jaya-saṁjñaṁ Bhāratākhyam itihāsaṁ vā*

Aṣṭādaśa purāṇāni Rāmasya caritaṁ tathā
Kārṣṇaṁ vedam pañcamaṁ ca yan Mahābhārataṁ viduḥ
Tathaiva Viṣṇudharmāś ca Śivadharmāś ca śāśvatāḥ
Jayeti nāma teṣāṁ ca pravadanti manīṣiṇaḥ

iti Bhaviṣyavacanāt purāṇādikaṁ vā

Caturṇāṁ puruṣārthānām api hetau jayo'striyām

iti kośād anyaṁ vā puruṣārtha-pratipādakaṁ granthaṁ Śārīrakasūtrabhāṣyādirūpam udīrayet uccārayet.

En commentateur honnête, Nīlakaṇṭha essaie de donner une valeur positive au mot *tataḥ*, que P. C. Roy néglige,

1 Bühler en a toutefois reconnu et signalé la valeur religieuse: It is a characteristic mark of the works of the ancient Bhāgavata sect, where it is invariably found, frequently with the variant *devīṁ Sarasvatīṁ Vyāsaṁ* instead of *caiva* (Indian Studies, no. II, p. 4, n. 2).

et qu'on rend ordinairement par "ensuite, après cela (= après ce triple namaskāra)." Il rattache par un lien immédiat cet adverb au nom de Sarasvatī qui le précède, et il explique : "sous l'influence de cette divinité qui est toute compassion." Quant au mot *jaya*, au lieu de lui attribuer ici son sens usuel de "victoire" il le considère comme une désignation du Mahābhārata lui-même, et il cite à l'appui le texte exprès du poème qui déclare par deux fois : "ce récit a nom Jaya" I. 2302, XVIII. 194 (la même désignation est appliquée à un épisode de l'épopée, le Vidulāputrānuśāsana V. 4639). Il cite l'autorité du Bhaviṣyapurāṇa qui applique le nom de Jaya non-seulement au Mahābhārata mais encore aux dix-huit Purāṇas, au Rāmāyaṇa, aux Viṣṇudharmās et aux Śivadharmās. Il va même jusqu'à proposer d'étendre cette désignation à l'œuvre philosophique de Vyāsa, le Śārīrakasūtra, et subsidiairement au commentaire (de Śaṅkara etc.) sur la foi d'un lexique qui définit ainsi le mot *jaya* : "tout ce qui cause les quatre fins humaines."

On peut taxer ici Nīlakaṇṭha d'un excès de subtilité ; on peut lui reprocher d'attribuer au mot *jaya* un sens purement scolastique, ou même imaginaire, que rien ne justifie dans l'usage réel de la littérature et de la langue. C'est pourtant par un sentiment profond des réalités de la langue qu'il a été conduit presque instinctivement à écarter le sens adopté plus tard par P. C. Roy et les Occidentaux. Je ne crois pas qu'on puisse trouver en sanscrit un exemple authentique du verbe *udīrayati* construit directement avec le mot qu'il s'agit d'exprimer. Je n'ai pas besoin de rappeler que *ud-īrayati* signifie au sens propre "produire la mise en branle, faire monter en l'air, décocher, lancer," et de là, au sens figuré, "pousser, émettre (un son)." Mais, dans ce dernier cas, le verbe est toujours suivi d'un mot qui précise l'idée de son : *na tāṁ (vācam) udīrayet*, Manu ii. 116 ; *vācam udīrayan*, Rāmāyaṇa ii. 57. 3 ; *udīrayāmāsuḥ......ālokaśabdam*, Raghu ii. 9 ; *mantram udīrayan*, Yājñavalkya i. 136. On ne dira pas plus en sanscrit *jayam udīrayet* qu'en français "pousser la victoire" pour exprimer l'idée de "pousser un cri de victoire."

Mais avant d'adopter le sens indiqué, assurément contourné, qui est proposé par Nīlakaṇṭha, il convient d'examiner si le texte ne peut pas fournir un sens plus simple et plus vraisemblable. Directement sans aucun prévention, on traduirait: "En adorant Nārāyaṇa, et Nara le meilleur des mâles, et aussi la déesse Sarasvatī, qu'on fasse de là saillir la victoire." N'oublions pas que le couple Nara-Nārāyaṇa est identique au couple Arjuna-Kṛṣṇa; l'idée est proclamée à maintes reprises dans le Mahābhārata, p. ex. I. 218, 7889; 224, 8161; 228, 8302; III. 47, 1888; V. 96, 3496; 111, 3824; VII. 11, 422; 77, 2707; etc. Cette équivalence reconnue évoque aussitôt, en parallèle avec la bénédiction liminaire, une autre formule qui traverse tout le poème, qui en exprime toute l'inspiration, et qui subsiste encore dans la conscience de l'Inde comme la leçon la plus haute du Mahābhārata : *yataḥ Kṛṣṇas tato jayaḥ*, I. 205, 7513 ; IV. 68, 2531; VI. 21, 771 ; 23, 821 ; IX. 62ψ, 3491 ; XIII. 168, 7746: "unde Kṛṣṇa, inde victoria." Dans plusieurs cas, la formule est complétée par une formule analogue, *yato dharmas tataḥ Kṛṣṇo*......VI. 23, 821 ; IX. 62ψ, 3491; les deux se combinent à leur tour en série continue, *yataḥ Kṛṣṇas tato dharmo yato dharmas tato jayaḥ* XIII. 168, 7746—"unde Kṛṣṇa, inde jus; unde jus, inde victoria;" d'où résulte enfin la formule *yato dharmas tato jayaḥ* VI. 65, 2695. Sous cette forme, la maxime semble proclamer une leçon de morale absolue: Le droit donne la victoire. Mais c'est fausser le Mahābhārata dans son principe même que de l'interpréter ainsi. Sans doute le Mahābhārata est une épopée didactique et moralisante; mais l'épopée et la morale y portent la puissante empreinte de l'organisation sociale et religieuse de l'Inde; elle est, comme toutes les créations du génie hindou, une œuvre de caste et de secte. Elle est bien le cinquième Veda, comme elle s'appelle et comme on l'appelle, parce que les quatre Vedas des brahmanes enseignent la vie sainte, ou plutôt la vie sacrée, et qu'elle enseigne avec une égale autorité la vie guerrière aux kṣatriyas. Elle est bien aussi le Kārṣṇa Veda, "le Veda de Kṛṣṇa" puisqu'elle prêche aux kṣatriyas, comme une garantie de succès et de salut, le culte de Kṛṣṇa. Le succès pour le kṣatriya, c'est la victoire, *jaya*; le salut pour le kṣatriya, c'est le dieu des kṣatriyas, Kṛṣṇa. "Où est Kṛṣṇa, là est la victoire"; car, "si on a Kṛṣṇa, on a tout"—*yataḥ Kṛṣṇas tatas sarve*; "Où est Kṛṣṇa, là est la règle (dharma)," la règle propre des kṣatriyas, celle qui leur prescrit de combattre et de vaincre ou mourir, celle qui leur assigne pour fonction de manier le bâton du commandement, *daṇḍa*, le bâton qui frappe le méchant et qui impose le respect des lois. Le Mahābhārata dans son ensemble est l'illustration et le développement de ces principes; ils convergent et s'illuminent dans la Bhagavadgītā; cet incomparable dialogue, souvent considéré comme un hors-d'œuvre sublime, est tout au contraire le cœur et le noyau de l'ouvrage. Les deux inséparables, en qui s'incarnent Nara et Nārāyaṇa, divinités tutélaires de l'œuvre, Kṛṣṇa et Arjuna, se recueillent, face à face, à l'heure des décisions suprêmes; le parfait chevalier interroge le Bienheureux, Bhagavat, maître parfait de chevalerie; il apprend à suivre sans hésitation sa loi propre dans l'ensemble de la loi universelle; il doit verser sans scrupule le sang, et de ses proches même, si le triomphe du bien l'exige. Les spéculations métaphysiques des brahmanes, conçues par répugnance à l'action, s'harmonisent pour le kṣatriya avec la nécessité d'agir. Arjuna, le parfait chevalier, est aussi le parfait dévot; libre d'opter entre l'alliance effective des divinités et la simple assistance de Kṛṣṇa comme cocher de char, il choisit Kṛṣṇa comme la promesse infaillible du succès. Les critiques de l'Occident, habitués à considérer le Mahābhārata comme un traité de morale absolue, ont été souvent choqués de certains actes commis par les Pāṇḍavas et qui s'accordent mal avec l'idéal de l'honneur chevaleresque: Yudhiṣṭhira emploie un subterfuge pour se débarrasser de Droṇa; Bhīmasena porte à Duryodhana un coup déloyal. L'auteur de l'épopée n'hésite pas à reporter sur Kṛṣṇa lui-même la responsibilité de ces actes (VII. 190, 8748; IX. 58, 3246); sa sagesse transcendante connaît et utilise les transactions nécessaires de la vie pratique. La fin justifie les moyens, quand la fin est la victoire du droit.

On n'hésitera donc pas, il me semble, à traduire ainsi

la bénédiction liminaire : "En adorant Nārāyaṇa, et Nara le meilleur des mâles, et aussi la déesse Sarasvatī, qu'on fasse venir d'eux la victoire !"

Si l'interprétation que je propose est exacte, les combinaisons laborieuses échafaudées autour du Mahābhārata tombent. On est allé jusqu'à présenter le Mahābhārata comme le retournement artificiel d'un poème antérieur qui aurait eu pour héros Duryodhana et ses frères. Il est à la fois plus simple et plus honnête de prendre le poème, tel qu'il est, pour essayer d'en concevoir la genèse. Que l'Inde ait eu des rhapsodes ou des jongleurs qui colportaient des récitations épiques, rien de surprenant ; la vie féodale devait aboutir à l'éclosion du genre sur le sol indien. Juchés dans leurs châteaux-forts, les rājas d'autrefois, comme les Rajpouts modernes, assisaient à s'en délasser entre deux expéditions au récit des exploits légendaires ; ils guettaient avec une curiosité impatiente le barde vagabond qui connaissait les preux d'autrefois. Mais l'épopée n'est pas une simple collection de chants épiques enfilés bout à bout ; c'est une composition savante organisée avec art autour d'une donnée centrale, inspirée par un sentiment dominant qui la pénètre et la traverse. Dans l'Occident, où l'unité du groupe s'affirme dans le sentiment national, c'est l'âme de la nation qui inspire le poète. L'Iliade, l'E'néide, glorifient la Grèce et Rome ; la Pucelle de Chapelain comme la Henriade de Voltaire prétendaient glorifier la France. La foi religieuse est aussi un des liens les plus forts de la collectivité ; l'épopée peut lui emprunter aussi son inspiration : la Jérusalem Délivrée, le Paradis Perdu, la Messiade sont écrites à la gloire du christianisme. L'Inde n'a jamais su dégager sa conscience nationale ; elle n'a reconnu son unité que dans son organisation sociale et dans son panthéon. Le Mahābhārata découle de cette double source : il glorifie la caste des kṣatriyas et le rôle idéal qui lui est assigné dans l'ensemble de la société hindoue ; il enseigne aussi aux kṣatriyas la gloire du dieu qui leur garantit le succès et le salut. L'adoration à Kṛṣṇa, qui a accompli tant de miracles dans la littérature de l'Inde au cours des siècles méritait de donner à la société brahmanique son épopée ; l'Inde des brahmanes y a concentré tout ce qu'elle recélait de grâce, de tendresse, de douceur, d'humanité. Le charme exquis de cette figure héroique et galante pouvait seul faire échec au Bouddha. L'un incarnait l'idéal d'une communauté mélancolique, sassée des douleurs de la vie, sans autre consolation que l'espoir du néant. L'autre devait attirer à lui les âmes éprises d'action, d'aventures, de grands coups, de fêtes galantes. Tous deux également accueillants acceptent les prosélytes de l'Inde et du dehors. Ménandre, le roi philosophe, incline au bouddhisme ; mais vers le même temps un autre Grec, Héliodore, de Taxila, ambassadeur du roi Antalcidas auprès d'un prince indien, se réclame du dieu des kṣatriyas, et dresse un pilier à Garuḍa en l'honneur de Vāsudeva, dieu des dieux. Quand les Kuṣāṇas constituent un empire scythique dans l'Hindoustan, un des successeurs de Kaniṣka s'attribue aussi le nom de Vāsudeva. Dans l'excessive pénurie des documents historiques, ces menus indices, joints aux témoignages indigènes (inscr. de Ghosundi, de Nānāghāṭ), laissent entrevoir l'active propagande des Bhāgavatas en concurrence avec les Bouddhistes.

Pour le procédé de composition aussi, l'épopée de Bhāgavata semble entrer de propos délibéré en concurrence avec le bouddhisme. Le Mahābhārata s'enorgueillit d'être une "cent-milliade" (śatasāhasrī), autrement dit, une œuvre gigantesque qui dépasse la mesure ordinaire des ouvrages humains *(iti Śrī-Mahābhārata-śatasāhasryāṁ Saṁhitāyāṁ Vaiyāsikyām......parvaṇi......adhyāyaḥ)*. La désignation était consacrée dans l'usage dès le Ve siècle ; l'inscription de Śarvanātha, trouvée à Khoh et datée de 214 (ère de Cedi ?), cite expressément le Mahābhārata comme "la collection de cent-mille" *(uktaṁ ca Mahābhārate śatasāhasryāṁ Saṁhitāyāṁ,.........)*. Mais cette désignation rappelle inévitablement ceux des ouvrages fondamentaux de la littérature bouddhique, la "cent-milliade" Śatasahasrikā, comme on l'appelle par excellence, ou pour l'énoncer par son titre complet, la Perfection de la Sapience en cent-mille [lignes], Śatasahasrikā Prajñāpāramitā. Pour passer dans l'usage courant, l'œuvre a dû subir des réductions successives, en vingt-cinq mille, en huit mille (aṣṭasahasrikā ; c'est la forme classique du traité), en sept cents, en cinq cents lignes. La Śatasahasrikā s'y prêtait d'ailleurs sans difficulté ; il suffisait d'élaguer les tautologies, les homonymes, les redondances, les répétitions qui l'enflent et la grossissent ; il est évident que l'auteur s'est proposé d'atteindre à tout prix les dimensions démesurées qu'il s'était assignées. Dans son effort continu vers le beau, l'Inde a manifestement passé par la stage intermédiaire du colossal ; avant de goûter et de réaliser la beauté dans l'équilibre harmonieux des lignes, l'esprit humain se laisse d'abord éblouir par le prestige de la masse. Dans la littérature profane, la Bṛhatkathā présentait un cas analogue ; Guṇāḍhya, le Vyāsa des contes, s'était piqué d'écrire une "Grande Histoire" ; mais son œuvre n'avait pas pour sa sauvegarde, comme la Śatasāhasrī de Vyāsa et comme la Śatasahasrikā bouddhique, le zèle pieux des copistes ; il n'a survécu que dans des adaptations réduites : Kṣemendra en a tiré un bouquet (Mañjarī) ; Budhasvāmin en a versifié l'abrégé (Ślokasaṁgraha); Somadeva se donne formellement pour un abréviateur (*saṁgrahaṁ racayāmy aham*).

Mais c'est au bouddhisme encore qu'il faut revenir pour trouver le paralléle le plus frappant du Mahābhārata. L'école des Mūla-Sarvāstivādins qui employait le sanscrit comme langue sacrée et qui se faisait gloire d'une forte culture littéraire, s'est donné un Vinaya immense, double au moins en étendue du Vinaya des Sarvāstivādins qui lui-même surpasse d'autant les Vinayas des autres écoles : Sthavira (Pāli), Dharmagupta, Mahīśāsaka, Mahāsaṁghika. Son Vinaya est plus grand que la Śatasahasrikā même ; la traduction tibétaine occupe treize volumes dans le Kanjour, tandis que la Śatasahasrikā n'en fait que douze. Autour de brèves et sèches prescriptions de la discipline monastique, le rédacteur a accumulé les récits, les contes, les jātakas, les épisodes, sans compter une véritable biographie du Bouddha, une sorte de Buddhavaṁśa, qui peut faire pendant au Harivaṁśa, complément organique du Mahābhārata. Avec toutes ses surcharges, tous ses épisodes, avec sa masse touffue et luxuriante, le Mahābhārāta porte à sa base sur un Vinaya, le code de la discipline kṣatriya à l'usage des Bhāgavatas.

ANCIENT INDIAN GENEALOGIES—ARE THEY TRUSTWORTHY?

BY F. E. PARGITER

GENEALOGIES of the royal dynasties of ancient India are to be found in the Epics and Purāṇas, and profess to give the names of the kings who reigned in various kingdoms in Northern, Eastern and Western India. They do not pretend to mention every king, but only those who left some memory behind them.

Those dynasties are assigned to two great stocks, one the Solar race that claimed descent from Manu, who was said to be son of Vivasvant (the Sun), and the other the Aila or Lunar race which claimed descent from Soma (the Moon). The Solar race held three kingdoms, those of Ayodhyā, Videha and Vaiśālī, but the line of Ayodhyā being the greatest was known specially as the Solar race. The Lunar race began with Purūravas Aila and soon branched out into the five tribes of the Pauravas, Yādavas, Ānavas, Druhyus and Turvasus. The Pauravas established themselves in all the middle region of North India, the Yādavas in Western India and the north-west portion of the Dekkhan, the Ānavas in the Panjab and in the Eastern region, and the Druhyus in the extreme North-west of India with offshoots that spread out into the countries beyond. They all belonged to the Lunar race, but this title was appropriated to the Paurava line and especially to its main branch which reigned at Hastināpura. All those dynasties go back to very early times, and are dealt with in the genealogies. The question naturally arises whether the genealogies are worthy of credence.

They are plainly open to the objection that the long lists of kings are rather shadowy, and that their earliest portions are mythical and enveloped in fable. Such of course they must be, because genuine traditions of the earliest times can hardly be anything better, since there were no means in India of making permanent records contemporaneously; and because such traditions cannot escape the natural tendency in men to make mistakes, to magnify the past and to distort ancient stories into fables. But to acknowledge these limitations is not the same thing as to declare that those traditional genealogies are unworthy of any trust whatever.

It was the vogue half a century ago to treat the earliest traditions as mere fables and explain them away by theories or presumptions. In all ages the world has had its full share of vigorous life and martial exploits; large tribal movements occurred in early times and wars of conquest, as well as peaceful periods that ministered to national welfare. Great men lived and performed great deeds in those times. There was ample material for true songs and ballads in their honour, and it was but natural that such songs should have been composed and handed down. It has now been found that the old accounts in other countries which were discredited half a century ago were based on genuine tradition, because excavations and discoveries have gone far to rehabilitate the general trustworthiness of those accounts. Men in ancient times knew the difference between truth and falsehood as well as we do, for truth was praised and falsehood condemned as far back as literature can testify. It is absurd to suppose then, that men in old times discarded the truth and carefully handed on what was spurious. In fact, the position has been reversed now, as compared with that of fifty years ago. It is no longer correct to declare that the person who seeks information from ancient tradition should first prove that it is worthy of attention, for now the duty rather lies on the person, who pronounces a tradition to be worthless, to give reasons for his assertion.

Civilization in India is very ancient and many kingdoms existed in very early times. Where kingdoms and a degree of civilization flourished, tradition could and naturally would remember the names of the kings, because a large part of knowledge in ancient times consisted of historical tradition, without the multitudinous subjects with which we are overburdened. It is not credible then that the memory of distinguished kings of earlier times should be wholly lost in their own nation, and the presumption is that ancient tradition about kings is *primâ facie* deserving of attention. Accordingly the ancient Indian genealogies are presumably genuine tradition in their main outlines, while of course judgment may be reserved on various particulars, knowing how human testimony is liable to develop mistakes in details in the course of time.

There is however a further objection whether the genealogies, supposing they were genuine, may not have been tampered with or at least corrupted so as to vitiate their value, as we have them now. Certainly spurious genealogies, both royal and private, have been fabricated in past times; but before any one would think of fabricating a false thing the real and true thing must have existed, and the real thing must have had such a value that there was a strong incentive to make and put forward a spurious thing as genuine. False genealogies presuppose and imitate genuine genealogies. It is incredible that any one would construct a false genealogy before real genealogies existed. Real genealogies must have existed from the earliest times, because, as soon as any chieftainship or kingship was established in any tribe or people, a real genealogy of the chiefs or kings who succeeded must in the nature of things have come into existence. Chieftainships began as soon as tribes developed any kind of collective existence, and as they generally tended to become hereditary, genealogies of the ruling families must have been coeval with the origin of civilization. The fact that the original founder is often wrapped in fable, such as that he was the offspring of the sun or moon or some superhuman being, does not militate against this conclusion, because such fables merely touch the origin of the family: the succession of chiefs or kings, when such rule was once established, was real, that is, there would be a real genealogy.

Real genealogies then must have existed from the earliest stage of civilization, before fictitious genealogies could have been thought of, and long before falsehood could have been attempted successfully. The occasions when spurious lineages are generally constructed are the rise of new chiefs or kings, because their families and dignity need to be enhanced by devising connexions with earlier and greater dynasties. It is the *novus homo* who requires a spurious genealogy. Instances of spurious genealogies have been detected in medieval and modern India, and false descents have been alleged in some of the smaller ancient genealogies in some of the Purāṇas; but these are clearly later productions.

Real genealogies moreover would have been carefully preserved by the kings and their priests and bards, because ancient lineage has always been a source of pride, and ancestral fame always a theme for poetic laudation. Bards and ballad-makers have always existed, who not only ministered to the pride of kings but also gratified popular interest by reciting old ballads and traditional tales; and such recitals are alluded to in Sanskrit books. In such dynasties there would have been no occasion for making false genealogies while the dynasty lasted, and little or no motive for falsification after it had passed away.

Mistakes, omissions and corruptions might and no doubt did creep into the genealogies during the lapse of time, and it may even be conceded that attempts may have been made to remove unpleasant facts from them. These may be cited as instances. The Kānyakubja dynasty which culminated in Viśvāmitra, and the Kāśī dynasty have been wrongly alleged in some of the Purāṇas to have been descended from the successors of Bharata the great and pious monarch of the Paurava race; and the genealogy of the Ayodhyā line given by the Rāmāyaṇa is incorrect both in respect of its arrangement of the kings and also by its omissions. The errors in the Rāmāyaṇa appear to have been due to the lack of the historical sense among ancient brahmans, for it is mainly brahmanical; but the wrong descent of the Kānyakubja and Kāśī lineages is hardly explicable except on the supposition that there was some tampering. Still, whatever the causes were, those errors failed to establish themselves, because the majority of the authorities have preserved different accounts which appear on examination to be more trustworthy. There appears to have been a sufficiently strong body of traditional knowledge in North India to prevent false particulars from being successfully introduced to any serious extent. There were bards, not only in the royal courts, but also elsewhere. An error might have prevailed in one place but could hardly have gained acceptance everywhere among all the bards; and the errors cited above illustrate this. The wrong derivation of the Kānyakubja dynasty from Bharata's successors had some attraction, because several brāhman families did originate from them, and Viśvāmitra's brahmanhood would have appeared less revolutionary if he also had that descent; yet the majority of the genealogists have ignored it, and even two of the books which give the wrong version give also the true version. The Rāmāyaṇa has been probably the most famous poem in India for much more than a thousand years, and its authority would (one might think) have overborne every other work; yet all the Purāṇas, even those which have erred in the Kānyakubja matter, disregard its version of the Solar dynasty and give another version, which appears to be correct, for it is corroborated by incidental references in various other books. Even the Rāmāyaṇa therefore with all its fame could not establish an incorrect genealogy.

Fictitious genealogies do occur in Sanskrit books and the difference between them and the royal genealogies is very striking. They are those which appear in connexion with Dakṣa in the accounts of creation, the genealogies of the Pitṛs, those which explain how the various kinds of fires developed, and such like. They are all brāhmanical compositions, obviously imitated from the dynastic genealogies, and bearing their spuriousness on their face. Moreover attempts to construct real genealogies out of insufficient materials are also found, such as the so-called vaṁśas of the Bhārgavas, Ātreyas, Vasiṣṭhas and other brahman families found in the Brahmāṇḍa, Vāyu, Matsya and Liṅga Purāṇas. These are not proper genealogies. They contain here and there a piece of genealogy comprising a few generations, but all the rest of the vaṁśas is merely a list of rishis and gotras compiled with no clear arrangement. The pieces of genealogy given do not appear to be original, but seem to have been constructed from information collected from various books, information that can be generally found elsewhere now. Those brahman vaṁśas were manifestly compiled in imitation of the royal genealogies at a much later date, and since there were no real brahmanical genealogies preserved by tradition, the compilers simply put together, as best they could, all the scraps of information they could find.

Such fictitious genealogies and brahmanical vaṁśas would never have been fabricated, unless real genealogies had existed before them and been famous. Manifestly there were no real and famous genealogies except those of the royal dynasties, which were all kṣatriya. Consequently these latter were the originals which the former tried to imitate. These spurious genealogies then offer strong testimony to the antiquity and genuineness of the royal genealogies; and their defects and inaccuracies, compared with the abundant, simple and generally natural details of the kṣatriya genealogies, reveal plainly what spurious work was like.

The royal genealogies were kept up and preserved, not by brahmans as brahmans, because such matters were not their province, but naturally by men connected with the courts, where the succession of kings was a subject of continuous importance and interest. Those men were royal bards, and may even have been brahmans; yet, if brahmans were the custodians of the genealogies, they did their duties not as brahmans but as court functionaries. The rishis or strict brahmans of ancient times did not busy themselves with such mundane affairs, except rarely and in special circumstances. They did not take any pains to preserve even their own vaṁśas, since no genuine brahmanical genealogies are to be found. Had such once existed, they would certainly have been preserved by the brahmans who have been the custodians of Sanskrit literature for at least two thousand years. The only real genealogies they have preserved are the kṣatriya genealogies of the ancient dynasties. Since the brahmans preserved the Vedas and other brahmanical works with verbal accuracy, there is no improbability in believing that bards and genealogists and paurāṇikas could have preserved those genealogies with substantial faithfulness. For these and other reasons also, the discussion of which would much augment this paper, there seems to me to be no reasonable doubt that the royal genealogies are really ancient and substantially worthy of acceptance. And this conclusion is corroborated by the fact that those genealogies, and they alone in Sanskrit writings, describe how what we know of the Aryan occupation of India took place, namely, by the diffusion and domination of the Aila or Lunar race over North India and the north-west of the Dekkhan. Their harmony with positive ethnological facts is unimpeachable testimony to their trustworthiness.

Pāli, Buddhism and Jainism

THE HOME OF LITERARY PĀLI

By GEORGE A. GRIERSON

SCHOLARS are not agreed as to the home of literary Pāli. The three most important theories are those of H. Oldenberg, R. Otto Franke, and E. Windisch.

According to Oldenberg,[1] 'the home of the Pāli language must be looked for more to the south than to the north of the Vindhya mountains.'

Franke,[2] after considering the dialectic peculiarities of all the available coins and inscriptions in the Pāli language, comes to the following conclusions:—(1) that the language of the inscriptions of the eastern parts of Northern India differs from Literary Pāli in such important particulars that Literary Pāli cannot have had its home there; (2) that as regards the language of the Kharoṣṭhī documents of North-Western India, there are both points of agreement with, and points of difference from, Literary Pāli. Hence, though the North-West was not the home of Pāli, the gap between the two dialects is not so great as in the East; (3) that the language of the inscriptions of the Deccan shows marked points of difference from Literary Pāli. He is thus unable to accept Oldenberg's theory; (4) that the language of the inscriptions of the Western Madhyadeśa shows most points of agreement with Literary Pāli, though there are some points of difference. Taking the inscriptions of the fourth group in detail, and comparing the language of each with Literary Pāli, he finally decides that the home of Literary Pāli was South to the South-East of the Kharōsthī country, South of Mathurā and perhaps also South of Sanchī and Bharaut, or at all events not in the immediate neighbourhood of these places, West or South-West of the Pāli of the North-East, North of Nāsik, and East of Girnār. In other words, the original

1 *Vinaya piṭaka*, p. liv.

2 *Pāli and Sanskrit*, chapter x, esp. p. 138. Franke on the whole agrees with Westergaard and E. Kuhn.

home was as nearly as possible the country between the middle and western Vindhyas. So far he considers his points as proved, and he adds the conjecture that the city of Ujjayinī probably occupies the centre of the tract.

Windisch[1] lays stress on the fact that Franke's conclusions are mainly negative. The home was not in the East, or North-West, or South, and therefore it must have been where he puts it, as this was the only remaining possible location. He then urges that Literary Pāli, as its name implies, was a literary language, and was therefore, like all literary languages, a more or less mixed form of speech. But, as this mixed language must have had for its basis some particular dialect, he contends that this was the dialect spoken by the Buddha himself,—the language of Magadha. As a literary language this was influenced by the languages spoken to its West, and especially by the other great literary language, Sanskrit. This accounts for the retention of a Sanskrit *r* instead of the Māgadhī *l*, and for the use of *o* instead of the Māgadhī *e* in the nominative singular of *a*-bases. In other respects Literary Pāli agrees very well with the peculiarities of Māgadhī Prākrit as described by the grammarians. The Buddha himself, in the course of his travels, would have picked up dialectic peculiarities of the places where he preached, and it is the Buddha's language that it was intended to preserve in Pāli.[2]

It seems to me that Windisch's explanation is the right one. It is the only formula that explains the Indian tradition, according to which Literary Pāli is described as Māgadhī. From inception to conclusion, his arguments are eminently cautious and reasonable; and, accepting the fact that Literary Pāli was a mixed form of speech having

1 *Ueber den sprachlichen Charakter des Pāli,* in *Actes du XIVe Congrès International des Orientalistes* (Algiers, 1905), part I. pp. 252ff., esp. pp. 277ff.

2 It is worth noting that, according to Mārkaṇḍeya, the peculiarities of Māgadhī Prākrit extended much further west in connexion with Paiśācī Prākrit. Thus (xx, 2, 3,) Śaurasenī Paiśācī changed *s* to *ś* and *r* to *l* and the latter change also took place in Pāñcālī Paiśācī (xx, 14).

as its basis the language of Magadha, the object of the present paper is to see if we can trace this development any further, and ascertain the locality in which it is probable that Literary Pāli received its final form.

It is generally accepted that in Aśoka's time Māgadhī, the language of his court, was employed as a κοινή, spoken and understood over the greater part of India, and certainly as far North-West as Shāhbāzgaṛhī. It had its variations, just as at the present day the modern κοινή, Hindostānī, as spoken in Delhi differs from that spoken in Eastern Bengal or in Madras. As in the case of Hindostānī, wherever it was used it imported peculiarities from the local dialect, but in the main it was the same language throughout. There is no reason for supposing that this was not the case before Aśoka's time. A κοινή does not establish itself in a moment or at the command of a king, but by gradual growth, and that being the case, we are justified in assuming that the Buddha found his native language a useful κοινή that could be employed wherever he preached.

Sten Konow, in his article on *the Home of Paiśācī*,[1] draws attention to the many points in which Pāli agrees with Paiśācī Prākrit. These are—

1 The hardening of sonant mutes.

2 The retention of intervocalic consonants.

3 The employment of *svarabhakti* in words such a *bhūriya*, *sināna*, and *kasaṭa*.

4 The change of *jñ*, *ṇy*, and *ny* to *ññ*.

5 The preservation of *y*, instead of changing it to *j*.

6 The termination *o* of the nominative singular of *a*-bases, not the Māgadhī *e*.

7 General agreement of the inflexional systems.

To these may be added—

8 In the Standard Paiśācī of Kekaya, but not in the sub-dialects of Śūrasena and Pañcāla, the retention of the Sanskrit *r*, and its non-change to the Māgadhī *l*.

1 ZDMG. lxiv (1910), p. 114 ff.

Konow places the home of Paiśācī in and about the Vindhyas and perhaps further to the South and to the East, and argues (p. 118)—in this supporting the above-mentioned theory of Franke—that it follows that Pāli is based on an Aryan dialect spoken in the same neighbourhood.

While I agree with Konow as to the close relationship between Paiśācī and Pāli, I am compelled to differ from him altogether as to the home of the latter. In a paper[1] entitled *Paiśācī, Paiśācas, and 'Modern Piśāca'*, I have discussed this question at considerable length and believe that I have proved that there was once a tribe or group of tribes in the extreme North-West of India, to which was given the name of 'Piśāca' by those who lived farther to the East; that these people spoke a language called by the Prākrit grammarians 'Paiśācī Prākrit'; and that traces of this particular Prākrit are still to be found in considerable numbers in the languages spoken on the North-Western Frontier at the present day. While I admit that it is probable that these Piśācas spread down the Indus into Rājputānā and along the Konkan coast, I maintain that the nidus in India from which they spread was the North-West, and that, though they may have carried their language with them, this North-West was its proper home.

I do not propose to repeat here the arguments used in that paper. They are there for those who wish to discuss them; but I mention one, because it involves a new piece of evidence that was not available when the paper was written.

As Konow points out (p. 100), the later Prākrit Grammarians knew numerous Paiśācī dialects.

Hemacandra knew three, but does not say where they were spoken.

Mārkaṇḍeya (17th century) mentions the following—

1 Kāñcīdeśīya
2 Pāṇḍya
3 Pāñcāla
4 Gauḍa

1 ZDMG, lxvi (1912), pp. 49 ff.

5	Māgadha	8	Śaurasena
6	Vrācaḍa	9	Kaikaya or Kaikeya
7	Dākṣiṇātya	10	Śābara
		11	Drāviḍa

Of these (sūtra 8) he says that only three were civilized (*nāgara*). The rest were local dialects of no importance. The three were Kaikeya, Śaurasena, and Pāñcāla.

Rāmatarkavāgīśa (? 17th century) knows two Paiśācikas, one Kaikeya and the other (?) Caska. He adds that if other Prākrit dialects, e. g. Māgadhī, are used incorrectly, they become *aśuddha Paiśācika.*

Lakṣmīdhara gives the following list of countries in which Paiśācī was spoken (quoted from the Mysore Edition of 1889)—

1	Pāṇḍya	6	Kuntala
2	Kekaya	7	Sudheṣṇa
3	Bāhlīka	8	Boṭa
4	Siṁha(la)	9	Gandhāra
5	Nepāla	10	Haiva
		11	Kannojana

The first thing that strikes one about these three lists is the great extent of country that they cover. If we are to accept them in their entirety, Paiśācī Prakrit was spoken over nearly the whole of India and also in Tibet. It would, in fact, be more of a κοινή than modern Hindostānī. In the second place they do not agree. There is only one name, Kekaya, common to all three, and it is the only one which, according to Mārkaṇḍēya, has a dialect of importance. This Kekaya (with which we may also count Gandhāra) lies in the extreme North-West of India, in the very locality where I, for independent reasons, have located the Piśācas. The remaining names seem to be what Rāmatarkavāgīśa calls *aśuddha Paiśācikas*, i. e. are either not Paiśācī at all but are corruptions of the local dialects, or else, what is more probable, local varieties of Pāli, the language of the, to them, heretical Buddhists. This would account for the presence in the lists of names such as Boṭa (Tibet), Pāṇḍya, or Drāviḍa, names that indicate localities in which certainly no Aryan language was the vernacular.

Mārkaṇḍeya treats this Kekaya Paiśācī as the standard. Moreover, according to him, it was in this dialect that Guṇāḍhya's *Bṛhatkathā* was composed. In the 9th sūtra of his chapter xix he says that in Kekaya Paiśācika the word *kvacit* becomes *kupaci*, and as an example he quotes "*Bṛhatkathāyām, 'kupaci pisālam'.*" Lakṣmīdhara mentions another country in the same neighbourhood, Gandhāra. It adjoined Kekaya, and the boundaries between the two fluctuated from time to time. For our present purposes, in discussing the language of Kekaya, we shall be perfectly safe in including under this name so much of Gandhāra as lay to the East of the Indus.

We have thus arrived at the following facts—

1 Literary Pāli is a mixed dialect based upon Māgadhī.

2 It is closely connected with Paiśācī Prākrit.

3 Standard Paiśācī Prākrit was spoken in, and was almost certainly the local dialect of, Kekaya and eastern Gandhāra, lying in the extreme North-West of India.

Let us now see if this leads us to any conjecture, less securely founded, but reasonable. From very ancient times the greater Kekaya, as defined above, was famous for its learning. We are told in the Chāndogya Upaniṣad (V. 11) how five theologians came to a Brahman with hard questions, which he was unable to answer for them. So he sent them to Aśvapati the king of Kekaya, who solved all their difficulties. It was at Śalātura, not far from Takṣaśilā that Pāṇini himself was born, and it is not unfair to assume that it was at the Takṣaśilā University that he was educated. This University was famed in early Buddhist times. According to the Jātakas it was the only great University in India. Numerous pupils went to it from Eastern India, from Magadha and Benares.[1] The Buddha himself, as a

1 Jātakas 61, 222, 336, 374, 487, 489, 506, 522, 536, 546.

Bodhisatta, studied there in several previous births.[1] In many cases he went there in a former birth as one of the numerous sons of Brahmadatta, king of Benares,[2] and in other births he was even a professor there.[3] In fact a perusal of the Jātakas shows that during the period in which they were composed Takṣaśilā was considered to be the only place in India where a Buddhist could get a complete education. Finally, in Jātaka 229, the Bodhisatta is represented as king of Takṣaśilā.

When we consider the undoubted fact that Paiśācī Prākrit was the vernacular language of the country round Takṣaśilā, and that it is closely connected with Pāli, we have a strong reason for concluding that Literary Pāli is the literary form of the Māgadhī language, the then κοινή of India, as it was spoken and as it was used as a medium of literary instruction in the Takṣaśilā University. It was the language of educated Buddhists and, in a polished form, would naturally be used by them for literary purposes.

The origin of modern literary Hindī presents a striking parallel to that suggested above for Pāli. The language of the country round the great university town of Benares is quite different from that of Delhi. Nervertheless Hindostani, the κοινή founded on the speech of the Delhi market, has been adopted in Benares as an important vehicle of literary expression, and, under the form of Hindī, bears all the hall-marks of the Sanskritizing influence of the University in which it has been nurtured and from which it has gained universal acceptance. Moreover, many books written by eminent Hindī writers display idioms and a vocabulary which clearly belong to the Awadhī and the Bhojpurī spoken in or not far from Benares, and which are strange to the language of the Upper Dōāb.

1 Jātakas 80, 99, 117, 130, 149, 150, 163, 165, 173, 175, 180, 185, 200, 211, 214, 251, 259, 276, 284, 313, 319, 323, 328, 337, 346, 348, 356, 376, 380, 392, 402-3, 411, 413-4, 418, 423, 431, 440, 443, 445, 447, 453, 467, 474, 478, 488, 498, 499, 524, 527-30, 537.

2 Jātakas 50, 55, 96, 101, 132, 151, 160, 181, 252, 260, 262, 269, 282, 289, 310, 349, 355, 362, 415-6, 456, 468, 525.

3 Jātakas 71, 97, 338, 353, 377.

THE CAKKAVATTI

(Dīgha, xxvi.)

BY T. W. RHYS DAVIDS

ASOKA states in his Edicts that it was the horrors of actual warfare, as brought to his notice during his conquest of Kaliṅga, that led him to the propagation, in those Edicts, of the Dhamma—the Norm—as the only true conquest. So the Buddha is represented in this Suttanta as setting out his own idea of conquest (not without ironical reference to the current idea) and then as inculcating the observance of the Dhamma—the Norm—as the most important force for the material and moral progress of mankind.

The whole is a fairy tale. The personages who play their part in it never existed. The events described in it never occurred. And more than that. A modern writer, telling a story to emphasise a moral, would always, like the creator of the immortal Dr. Teufelsdröckh, endeavour to give probability, vraisemblance, to the characters and events of his tale. Here the very opposite would seem to be the case. Recourse is had rather to the shock of improbability. This is in accord with the procedure in other cases (for instance in the story of Sharp-tooth the Priest, or in that of the Riddles of the God).[1] The point of the moral—and in this fairy tale the moral is the thing —is the Reign of Law. Never before in the history of the world had this principle been proclaimed in so thorough-going and uncompromising a way. But of course it is not set out in such arguments as we find in modern treatises on ethics or philosophy. The authors are not writing a monograph on history or ethics. They are preaching a gospel; and their method is to state their view, and leave the hearer to accept it, or not, just as he pleases.

The view was, so to speak, in the air at that time. The whole history of religion, in India as elsewhere, had been the history of a struggle between the opposing ideas,

1 Kūṭadanta and Sakka-Pañha (*Dīgha Nikāya*, v, and xxi).

or groups of ideas, that may be summed up by the words Animism and Normalism. Animism has now become a well-known term. It is based on the very ancient hypothesis of a soul—a subtle, material, homunculus or mannikin supposed to dwell in the heart of a man. This afforded what seemed a simple and self-evident 'explanation' of many mysterious things. When in his dream a man saw another, whom, when the dreamer woke, he knew to have been dead, he at once concluded, on the evidence of the dream, that the person he saw in his dream was still alive. It is true he had seen the body dead. But it was self-evident that a something he knew not what, but very like the body, was still alive. He did not reason much about it, or stay to weigh the difficulties involved. But he was much too frightened of it to forget it. Once formed, the hypothesis was widely used. When a man awoke in the morning after hunting all night in his dreams, and learnt from his companions that his body had been there all the time, it was of course his 'soul' that had been away. In a similar way death and trance and disease could be ascribed to the absence of the 'soul'. 'Souls' were believed to wander from body to body. Animals had souls, and even things, when they were uncanny, or when they seemed to have life and motion and sound. The awe-inspiring phenomena of nature were instinctively regarded as the result of spirit action: and rivers, plants and stars, the earth, the air and heaven became full of souls, of gods, each of them in fashion as a man, and with the passions of a man.

But wide-reaching as this hypothesis was, it could not cover everything. From the earliest times of which we have any record we find in India as elsewhere quite a number of religious beliefs and ceremonies which were not explained, and could not be explained, by the hypothesis of a soul. In other words they are not animistic. The first impression we get is that of the bewildering variety of such beliefs. But they can be arranged, with more or less exactitude, into over-lapping groups: and behind all the groups can be discerned a single underlying principle. That principle is the belief in a certain rule order, law. We have no word for such a belief in English and this, since the theory is as important, in the ancient Indian religions, as Animism, is a pity. I have suggested in my lectures on Comparative Religion in Manchester, to call it Normalism.[1]

Of course the men who held the beliefs, and practised the ceremonies so-named, had no clear conception of the theory of Normalism, just as they had no clear conception of the theory of Animism. But they unmistakeably held the view that things happened, effects were brought about without the agency of a soul or god, and quite as a matter of course; and they regarded that as the rule in such and such a case. Now we do not ourselves believe in the rule or in any one of the rules, thus laid down—(any more than we believe in the hypothesis of a homunculus within the heart). But the word Animism has been found most useful in clearing up our appreciation of ancient views. Its usefulness is limited, it is true. It covers rather less than half of the main beliefs recorded in the most ancient literatures of the world. The other half would be covered by the corresponding hypothesis of Normalism.

This is not the place to raise the question of the importance of Normalism in the general history of religions. Perhaps one of the reasons why, in Europe, so much more attention has been paid to Animism, may be that the general trend of belief in Europe is itself predominantly animistic. But it is at least certain that in the far East, and more especially in China and India, Normalism is the more important of the two.

In China it is the basis of the theory of the Tao (the way), which finds its earliest expression in the famous tractate of Lao Tsu, but was undoubtedly earlier than that, and is taken for granted also by Confucius. The Tao is quite Normalistic; and though much abused in later times in the official circles of Taoism, the early form

1 *Journal, Manchester Egyptian and Oriental Society*, 1914-15.

of it has never ceased to influence the various intellectual centres of Chinese belief. The theory of Yang and Yin, also so widely, indeed universally held, in China, and also going back to very early times, is equally Normalistic. No one of these three conceptions was ever personified. All three rested on the idea of law or rule independent of any soul.

In India our earliest records, the thousand and more Vedic hymns, seem at first sight to be altogether animistic. They consist almost exclusively in appeals to various gods. The European books on Indian religions are concerned, when treating of the Vedic period, with descriptions of these gods, based on the epithets applied to them, the acts attributed to them, and so on. But these poems make no pretention to being a complete statement of the beliefs of the tribes whose priests made use of the poems. Other poems, not included in our present collection, were doubtless extant in the community at the time when the collection was made. Other beliefs, not mentioned in the poems, were widely influential among the people. What we have is not complete even as a summary of the theosophy, or the ritual, or the mythology of the priests; and it refers only incidentally to other beliefs, unconnected with gods, of great importance as a factor in religion and daily life.

This conclusion might be justified as rendered necessary by a critical consideration of the simple known facts as to the composition of the anthology we call the Ṛgveda. It is confirmed by the discovery in later Vedic books, especially in the manuals of domestic rites, of customs and beliefs that must evidently go back to the Ṛgveda period, (though not referred to in that collection), and even of one or two such cases that certainly go back to an earlier period still. We have space here for only one or two sample instances, and even they can only be treated in the merest outline.

Take the case of ṛta. The meaning of the word would seem to have passed through some such evolution as 'motion, rhythmic motion, order, cosmic order, moral order, the right.' In those slowly moving ages a long period must be postulated for the growth and consolidation of such ideas. The word is found, incidentally mentioned, at the end of its career, in the Avesta and the Veda. It must have been in full use before the Persian Aryans had separated from the Indian Aryans. The idea may therefore with reasonable probability be traced back to the third millennium before Christ. The use of the word died out in India before the time of the rise of Buddhism. Of the pre-Buddhistic Upaniṣads it occurs only in one—the Taittirīya. In the peroration to that work ṛta is placed above, before the gods. The word occurs, it is true, in three or four isolated passages of post-Buddhistic works, but these are archaisms. It has not been traced in either the Buddhist or the Jaina canonical literature.

The process of the gradual decline in the use of an abstract word is precisely analogous to the process of the gradual decay and death of a god.[1] The word covers not one idea only, but a number of connotations. The implications involved in it are constantly, though imperceptibly, changing. Sooner or later one or other phase of it over-masters the others, and some new word, or words, emphasising some one or other of the various connotations of the older word, come gradually into use as more adequate or more clear. When that process is complete the older word is dead. But it lives again in the newer word or words that have taken its place, and would never have been born or thought of unless the older word had previously lived. It was so with ṛta—a broader and deeper conception than the Greek moira; and more akin to the Chinese Tao. Like these, ṛta was never personified and it lives again in the clearer and more definite (though still very imperfect) phrases of the Suttanta before us now.

The case of ṛta is by no means unique. I have elsewhere discussed at some length another case, that of *tapas* or self-mortification, austerity.[2] It was held in India from

1 See *Buddhist India*, p. 234. 2 *Dialogues of the Buddha*, i, 213 f.

Vedic times onwards that *tapas* (originally 'burning glow,' but afterwards used of fasting and other forms of self-mortification) worked out its effects by itself, without the intervention of any deity. This is only the more remarkable since it is almost certain that in India, as elsewhere, the ecstatic state of mind which rendered such austerity possible was originally often regarded as due to the inspiration of a spirit. But it is, so far as I know, never mentioned that the supernormal effects of the austerity were due to the spirit from whom the inspiration came. The effects were due to the austerity itself. Very often indeed there was no question of any deity's help in the determination to carry out the self-torture—just as in the case of the *pujārī's* at the *ghāts* in modern India.

Even the very sacrifice itself—made to gods, supposed to give sustenance and strength to gods, accompanied by hymns and invocations addressed to gods—was not entirely free from such normalistic ideas. The hymns themselves already contain phrases which suggest that their authors began to see a certain mystic power over the gods in a properly conducted sacrifice. And we know that afterwards, in the Brāhmaṇas, this conception was carried to great lengths. So also we have evidence of a mystic power, independent of the gods, in the words, the verses, that accompany the sacrifice. It is no contradiction of this that we find this mystic power itself deified and becoming, indeed, in the course of centuries of speculation, the highest of the gods. And it is significant, in this connection, that the string of Bṛhaspati's bow is precisely ṛta.

It would be tedious (and it would also, after the above instances, be, I trust, unnecessary) to quote the very numerous other instances in Vedic works of a slighter character and less importance, showing the existence of a theory of life the very opposite of Animism. They are naturally only quite incidental in the Ṛgveda itself, and occur more and more frequently in the later books, being most numerous in the Sūtra period. Many of these can be classed under one or other of the various meanings given by anthropologists to the ambiguous and confusing word 'magic'[1]—the 'magic' of names, or numbers, or propinquity, or likeness, or association, or sympathy, and so on. Many will also be found in the long list of practices from which it is said in the Sīlas (one of the very earliest of our Buddhist documents, earlier than the Piṭakas) that the Samaṇa Gotama refrains.[2]

The above suffices to show something of the position of Normalism in pre-Buddhistic India. Our present Suttanta shows the stage it had reached in the period of the early Buddhists. It is a stage of great interest—differing, as it does, from the line of development followed by Normalism in other countries.

1 For some of these divergent and contradictory meanings see *Proceedings of the Oxford Congress of Religions*, 1908.

2 *Dialogues of the Buddha*, vol. 1, pp. 16-30.

SAGE AND KING IN KOSALA-SAṀYUTTA

BY MRS. RHYS DAVIDS

THE fame of Gotama Buddha is world-wide and crescent. The religious and philosophical doctrines associated with his name were at one time paramount in India—they were Indian culture. Few will be ignorant of or dispute either of these two statements. Yet it is singular to note how slight and confined to how few are the movements on foot in our centres of learning, European and Indian, to acquire and to spread a better based and more intimate knowledge (1) of the earliest known, least apocryphal sources and methods of those doctrines, (2) of the earliest documentary evidence extant of the social and political atmosphere in which they arose. We know the methods of Sokrates, we know the very words, let alone the character of the conversations and discourses ascribed to the Christ. How much is present to our mind of how, as preserved in the larger literature of the Nikāyas, the Sakyamuni dealt with his numerous interlocutors? We know the Sokratic Athens; we can almost see the hasty Herod, the reluctant Pilate, the contending Pharisee and Sadducee. Which of us has a mental picture of those two loyal inquirers and patrons, King Pasenadi of Kosala and Sudatta, whom for his philanthropy men called Anāthapiṇḍika: 'Feeder of the forlorn'? Yet there are no other Indian laymen of so early a date, concerning whose life and character so much relatively early documentary evidence is extant. Chandragupta, compared with these, is but a name; Asoka lives chiefly in the records of his edicts. But in the Suttas of the Nikāyas, aided by the Vinaya, "the King, the Kosalan Pasenadi" walks and talks before us with all the strong and the weak points of his Kṣatriyan characteristics. And we have documentary evidence of a similar kind for the character of the commoner.

But for the piety and support of these two men, it is conceivable that the Saṅgha, in Asoka's day, might not have been in such a position as to make it expedient for that ruler to patronize and propagate it. It is to aid a little in familiarizing some readers with the Pasenadi of Pāli literature and with the methods used in his case by India's greatest teacher, that the following selection from the Kosala-Saṃyutta (ed. Feer, Pāli Text Soc.) is here offered. It will serve at least to fill out a little the brief outline of the King's career sketched in my husband's *Buddhist India*.

In these Suttas and in Buddhaghoṣa's Commentary[1] the Kosalan Pasenadi[2] stands out as a very real, if average aristocratic despot. He is shown combining, like so many of his class all the world over, a proneness to affairs of sex with the virtues and affection of a good 'family man,' indulgence at the table with an equally natural wish to keep in good physical form, a sense of honour and honesty, shown in his disgust at legal cheating, with a greed for acquiring wealth and war indemnities, and a fussiness over lost property, a magnanimity towards a conquered foe with a callousness over sacrificial slaughter and the punishment of criminals. Characteristic also is both his superstitious nervousness over the sinister significance of dreams due, in reality, to disordered appetites, and also his shrewd, politic care to be on good terms with all religious orders, whether he had testimonials to their genuineness or not.

In all these respects then the Pasenadi is a typical Kṣatriya, with the qualities and defects of his class. Indeed it would seem that he shows some complacency in ranking himself as a good type of a prosperous monarch (3, § 5), greatly busied over the pleasures and duties, the advantages and disabilities, of a ruler who, as in his case, had inherited a kingdom of expanded dimensions,[3] and had 'won security therein' (3, § 5). Nevertheless in one important respect he is revealed as superior to the average

1 *Sāratthappakāsinī*. The Pali Text Society is preparing an edition.

2 Probably an official, possibly a clan name, as we might say the Egyptian Pharaoh, or the Rumanian Hohenzollern. He is elsewhere called Agnidatta (*Divyā*: 620; *Bud*: *India*, 10).

3 Cf. *Buddhist India*, p. 25.

king, and that is in his discernment—according to his lights—of, and his inclination towards, that which was good and righteous (2, § 4), and also in his appreciation of the man who, in a transcendent degree, embodied all that was good and righteous.

These were matters, as the Sage reminded him (2, § 1), that were anything but easy for one in his position to recognize. Living amidst luxuries and distractions, flattery and lies, the Pasenadi had the strength of mind to secure time for solitary meditation (1, § 4—§ 6), and to face the bed-rock questions of life and death, good and evil. Hence his conscience was alert, and swift in response to the spur, lightly or heavily applied, of the Sage's admonition. Frequently thus admonished, he remained a loyal upāsaka of the master during practically the whole of his long public ministry. In the opening Sutta, his first meeting with the young and new teacher is given. After that the title *bho Gotama* is changed once for all to the *bhante* of the disciple. And in the eloquent valediction put in his mouth, in the Dhammacetiya-sutta of the *Majjhima*, as spoken just before he went forth to meet desertion and a lonely death, he asserts that both he and his teacher are octogenarians. Viewed as a historical fact, this friendly intercourse is thus made to cover more than forty years. Did ever monarch do himself such high credit for so long a period?

Such was the Kosalan Pasenadi, the most powerful king of his day in India, whose realms extended from the Ganges to Himalaya, and were bound west and east by (probably) the Jumna and the Gandhak.

In the counsels which he sought and found, most of the methods employed by the Sage are illustrated. In discussing those methods in his introduction to the Kassapa-Sīhanāda Sutta (*Dialogues of the Buddha*, i, 206 f.) Rhys Davids shows how, in conversing with one whose standpoint differed widely from his own, the Buddha invariably put himself as far as possible in the mental position of the questioner, accepting his starting points, attacking no cherished convictions, even adopting the very phraseology of the other, but, partly by a re-creating of the meaning of terms, partly by appeal to matters of common agreement, bringing him to a fresh and a higher conclusion. Several of the Suttas here presented exemplify these words. Both Sage and King were of the same social class and country,[1] and of the same age, yet it were hard to find two persons more sharply contrasted in opinions and outlook than these two. Note then how the sage, who, save to help and uplift his fellow-beings, had entirely done with the world, stooped at every interview to the King's outlook and stock of ideas, and grafted his admonitions on that stock and in that soil:—

His Majesty has been gluttonous. Abstemiousness is gently enjoined, not as favouring spiritual growth,[2] but because he will thus more lightly bear advancing age. How should he most wisely direct his almoners to proceed in the matter of doles etc.? Use the same tests as you do in passing young men for your army. He has decided that nothing is so precious to any man as his own soul. Then see that you hurt not the soul, so precious to him, of another man. He has been busy after the manner of kings? Well, you often receive reports from special king's messengers of an approaching crisis. *I* am such a messenger, and I tell you, you have no time to be busied over so much that kings hold important. In the face of *this* great crisis,—the brevity of this life,the approaching of death—what alone remains for you to be busied withal?

The sympathetic appeal of such advice *ad* this specific *hominem* must have been very vital and rousing. In his graver and sadder moods the king is met by the 'common sense', which opens the casement of sorrow's private cell, and lets in the bracing, if bitter wind of the 'common lot' . . . 'life is but death' . . . 'the best are not exempt.'

1 As the King reminds him (Dhammacetiya-sutta)—
Bhagavā pi khattiyo, aham pi khattiyo; Bhagavā pi Kosalako, aham pi Kosalako.

2 Cf. the rebuke to Dāsaka (XVII,) Belaṭṭhakāni (CI) in my *Pss. of the Brethren.*

But nowhere is he advised to leave the world, or be aught but diligent over his kingly duties.

Sycophancy is as wholly absent in the Sage's replies and comments on the King's acts, as is the rudeness of a Diogenes. Whether surfeited or chastened, self-complacent or vexed, the King and his actions meet with unfaltering 'sweet reasonableness,'[1] courtesy and magnanimity. Not always is the guiding hand applied heavily. There is a pretty touch of irony in speaking of the liability of wealth to be 'confiscated by kings or by thieves' to a monarch who had just absorbed a millionaire's intestate property (2, § 9). Both King and Sage indulge in covert humour when comparing the unknown character, concealed (we should say) beneath a cowl, to the disguises and transformations carried out in the career of thieves as chartered spies. And it lends no small charm as well as verisimilitude to these little Sutta-etchings, when we discern the Teacher and the King, who in comparison was but as an average nice boy, finding themselves here on common ground—that of men of experience wary of judging by appearances, and together amused at the parallel drawn by one of them.

But perhaps the most impressive feature in these brief records is the several social deals to which the Sage points the way in reply to the King, or in comment on his acts. We note him condemning the methods of military aggressiveness, upholding the dignity of woman as daugher, wife and mother, and enjoining those public works for the people's good (3, § 4) such as would come under that righteous living, which it was alone of real importance for the king, confronted by the brevity of life (3, § 5), to be occupied withal. Thus it was all very well for the king to spare the life of his conquered foe, but in confiscating his war material, and indeed in waging war, he did but sow the seeds of retaliatory violence (2, § 5). Again, that a daughter might prove a greater blessing to a king than a son, that the birth of one was anyway not to be considered a disappointment and failure in achieve-

1 Matthew Arnold's ἐπιείκεια applied to Christ.

ment—these are startling words to hear coming from that time and that country, nay, and not from ancient India only. The Buddhist Canon contributes its quota—not a great one for a compilation by male and monastic editors—of blows and kicks at woman—'*dulce monstrum.*' And it would scarcely have surprised us to come upon a Sutta stating that the birth of a daughter was due to the Karma of some shortcomings in the parents' antecedents, let alone those of the baby's former lives. But in the verse on Mallikā's infant daughter and the disappointed parents (2, § 6,) we seem to hear the real voice of a teacher who transcended the bounds of time and tradition, of one worthy to rank as guide and healer of men and women of all ages and every race.[1]

1 The selection mentioned on p. 2 above will appear in the writer's forthcoming translation of the Sagāthavagga of the Saṁyutta-Nikāya to be published by the Pāli Text Society. It could not unfortunately be included here.

जैनतत्त्वज्ञानम्

ॐ नमः परमात्मने ।

यच्चैतन्यमहोऽग्रतः प्रतिहताः सर्वेऽपि तेजस्विनो
यच्छक्तेः पुरतः समस्तभुवनस्थामाऽप्यकिञ्चित्करम् ।
विश्वैश्वर्यसुखाकरोऽपि च यदानन्दोदधौ बिन्दुवद्-
यश्चिन्तास्मृतिगोचरोऽपि नतरां प्रत्यक्षगम्यः पुनः ॥ १ ॥

तस्मै जगद्विचित्राय जगदीशाय शम्भवे ।
ब्रह्मणे परमेशाय सद्भक्त्या विदधे नमः ॥ २ ॥

अयं तावदारम्भः सङ्क्षेपेण परिदर्शयितुं जैनदर्शनतत्त्वम् । दर्शनानि च षट् । यदाहुः श्रीहरिभद्रसूरयः षड्दर्शनसमुच्चये–

बौद्धं नैयायिकं साङ्ख्यं जैनं वैशेषिकं तथा ।
जैमिनीयं च नामानि दर्शनानाममून्यहो ॥

अस्य च जैनदर्शनस्य प्रकाशयिता परमात्मा रागद्वेषाद्यान्तररिपुजेतृत्वाद-न्वर्थकजिननामधेयः । जिनोऽर्हन् स्याद्वादी तीर्थकर इति चानर्थान्तरम् । अत एव तत्प्रकाशितं दर्शनमपि जैनदर्शनमर्हत्प्रवचनं जैनशासनं स्याद्वाददृष्टि-रनेकान्तवाद इत्याद्यभिधानैर्व्यपदिश्यते ।

अत्र दर्शने नव तत्त्वानि पदार्थाः परिकीर्तिताः सन्ति । तानि चामूनि । जीवोऽजीवः पुण्यं पापमाश्रवः संवरो निर्जरा बन्धो मोक्षश्चेति । यदाह जैनागमः श्रीसूत्रकृताङ्गसूत्रम्[1]—

नत्थि जीवा अजीवा वा णेवं सन्नं निवेसए ।
अत्थि जीवा अजीवा वा एवं सन्नं निवेसए ॥ इति ॥

तत्र चेतनालक्षणो जीवः । चैतन्यं ज्ञानमुपयोग इति हि पर्यायाः । सर्वत्रापि चेतनावत एव जीवस्य भावात् । चेतनायाः जीवस्वरूपत्वाज्जड-मात्रस्य चेतनाराहित्याच्च । अनेनैव जडचेतनयोर्मुख्यत्वेन भेदसिद्धिः । ज्ञानरूपत्वेऽपि जीवस्य यन्न भवति सकलवस्तुविषयक आलोकस्तत्रेदं कारणं

१ इत्यादिगाथाकदम्बकं द्वितीयश्रुतस्कन्धे पञ्चमाध्ययने ।

वेदितव्यम् । अनादिकालविपरिवर्तमानविविधकर्मसन्ततिभिः सामस्त्येन सम्बद्ध एव जीव एताभिश्च कर्मसन्ततिभिः समाच्छादितत्वान्न शक्नोति समस्तपदार्थान् साक्षात्कर्त्तुम् । तदुक्तम्—

न सर्वमपि वेत्त्येष प्राणी कर्मावृतो यथा ।
नार्कस्याऽभ्राभिभूतस्य प्रसरन्त्यभितः प्रभाः[1] ॥ इति ॥

तथा च कर्मप्रतिबन्धराहित्य एव सति निरभ्रदिनकर इव सर्वत्र प्रकाशमयो भवितुमर्हति जीवः ।

तत्र जीवा द्विविधा मुक्ताः संसारिणश्च । मुक्ताः सकलकर्मपरिक्षयेण सिद्धनिरञ्जनपरब्रह्मस्वरूपं प्राप्ताः । संसारिणः पुनः कर्मप्रतिबद्धाः । तेऽपि द्वेधा स्थावरास्त्रसाश्च । तत्र स्थावराः पृथ्वीजलतेजोवायुवनस्पतिभेदभिन्नाः पञ्चधा । त्रसा द्वीन्द्रियत्रीन्द्रियचतुरिन्द्रियपञ्चेन्द्रियभेदैश्चतुर्धा । तत्र घर्षणच्छेदनादिभिरचैतन्यमप्राप्तानां पृथिव्यादीनां पञ्चानां त्वगिन्द्रियस्यैव सद्भावेनैकेन्द्रियत्वम् । एते चैकेन्द्रियाः प्रत्येकं द्वेधा सूक्ष्मा बादराश्च । सूक्ष्माख्यनामकर्मोदयात् सूक्ष्माः । ते च सकललोकव्यापिनः । सकललोकाकाशस्तैर्जीवैः परिपूरित आस्त इत्यर्थः । बादराख्यनामकर्मोदयाद् बादराः । ते च प्रतिनियतस्थलवर्तिनो गम्याः[2] । तत्र सूक्ष्मत्वं प्रतीतम् । बादरत्वं च स्थूलत्वम् । स्पर्शनरसनेन्द्रियाभ्यां द्वीन्द्रियाः कृमिपूतरकचन्दनकशङ्खकपर्दजलौकाप्रभृतयः । स्पर्शनरसनघ्राणैस्त्रीन्द्रिया कुंथुमत्कुणयूकामत्कोटकेन्द्रगोपकादयः । स्पर्शनरसनघ्राणनेत्रैश्चतुरिन्द्रिया भ्रमरमाक्षिकामशकवृश्चिकप्रमुखाः । स्पर्शनरसनघ्राणनेत्रश्रोत्रैः पञ्चेन्द्रियाश्चतुर्धा तिर्यञ्चो मनुष्या नारका देवाश्च । तत्राऽद्या मीनमकरगजसारसहंसादयः । मनुष्याः प्रतीताः । नारका अधोलोकवर्तिनः । देवाः प्राधान्येनोर्ध्वलोकवर्तिनः । केचिद् भुवनपत्यादयो देवा अधोलोकेऽपि । द्वीन्द्रियत्रीन्द्रियचतुरिन्द्रियाणां त्रयाणां विकलेन्द्रियसंज्ञास्ति ।

एकेन्द्रिया विकलेन्द्रियाश्च विशिष्टमनोज्ञानरहितत्वेनासंज्ञिन उच्यन्ते यस्मात् ते सम्मूर्च्छिमा गर्भजत्वाभावात् । देवा नारकाश्चोपपातजा उक्ताः । देवा हि देवशय्याभ्यन्तर उपपतन्ति । नारकाश्च वज्रकुड्यस्थवातायनसदृशनिष्कुटेषु । तिर्यक्षु च केचिद् गर्भजाः केचित् सम्मूर्च्छिमाश्च । मनु-

१ श्रीविनयविजयोपाध्यायकृतलोकप्रकाशे द्रव्यलोके द्वितीयसर्गे ७० ।

२ सूक्ष्मबादरनामधेये कर्मणी वक्ष्यमाणाष्टविधकर्मान्तर्गतनामकर्मभेदौ ।

ष्यास्तु गर्भजाः । ये तु श्लेष्मादिषु गर्भजमनुष्यसम्बन्धिषु चर्मचक्षुरदृश्या अन्तर्मुहूर्तभवस्थितिका मनुष्यजातीया उत्पद्यन्ते ते सम्मूर्च्छिमा एव। देवगतौ देवा देव्यश्च सन्ति न कश्चिन्नपुंसकः । नारकाः सम्मूर्च्छिमाश्च नपुंसका एव । सम्मूर्च्छिमव्यतिरिक्ताश्च तिर्यञ्चो मनुष्याश्च पुंस्त्रीनपुंसकाः ।

जीवानां शरीरं पञ्चधा । औदारिकं वैक्रियमाहारकं तैजसं कार्मणं च । तत्र प्रथमं मनुष्यपश्वादीनां सर्वेषां देवनारकव्यतिरिक्तानाम् । वैक्रियं च ह्रस्वदीर्घदृश्याऽदृश्यभूचरखेचरादिनानाविधरूपकरणसमर्थं भव(जन्म)स्वभावतो देवानां नारकाणां च । तथाविधशक्तिमहिम्ना मनुष्यादेरपि । आहारकं वपुश्चतुर्दशपूर्वविद्याबलेन सकलपदार्थान् समधिगच्छतां महापुरुषाणां परमर्षीणां भवति । एतेन च जीवन्मुक्तानां देहवतां सर्वज्ञपरमात्मनां पुरस्सरं प्रेषितेन सूक्ष्मार्थसन्देहापगमो भगवन्महार्द्धिदर्शनं च शक्यते कर्तुम् । तैजसकार्मणे च सर्वस्य संसारिजीवस्य भवतः । तैजसेन मुक्ताहारपरिपाकादिकार्यं भवति । कार्मणं शरीरं पुनः क्षीरनीरवद् अन्योन्यं परिश्लिष्टा जीवप्रदेशैः कर्मप्रदेशा एव । एतद्बलेन जीवस्य भवान्तरे गतिर्भवति ।

तथाविधानां पृथिव्यादीनां सचेतनत्वं दुर्गममपि युक्तिशास्त्रबलेन शक्यते प्रतिपत्तुम् । तत्र वनस्पतेस्तावत् सचेनतत्वं स्फुटत्वात् समर्थ्यते । मूले सिक्तेषु तरुषु यो रसः फलादिषु स्फुटतया परिदृश्यतेऽसौ नोच्छ्वासमन्तरेणोर्ध्वं प्रसर्पुमर्हत्यस्मदादिषूच्छ्वासे सत्येव रसप्रसर्पणोपलम्भात् । मृत्तिकादावुच्छ्वासाभावे रसप्रसर्पणाभावाच्च । तस्माद् रसप्रसर्पणेनाक्षिप्यमाण उच्छ्वासस्तरुषु निःसन्देहं सात्मकत्वं प्रसाधयति । एवं नृणामिव द्रूणामपि दोहदोत्पत्तिदर्शनात् संकोचविकासादिसंज्ञाबलाच्च वनस्पतीनां चेतनावत्त्वं सुश्रद्धानम् । पृथिव्यादीनामपि—सात्मिका पृथ्वी विद्रुमशिलादिरूपा छिन्नाया अप्यस्याः पुनस्तत्स्थान एव समानजातीयाङ्कुरोत्थानाद् अर्शोऽङ्कुरवत् । भौममम्भः सचेतनं क्षतभूसजातीयस्य स्वभावस्य सम्भवाद् दर्दुरवत् । नाभसमपि जलं सात्मकम् अभ्रादिविकारे स्वतः सम्भूय पातान्मीनादिवत् । तेजः सात्मकम् आहारोपादानात् तद्वृद्धौ विकारविशेषोपलब्धेश्च नरवत् । सचेतनो वायुरन्यप्रेरितत्वे सति तिर्यग्गतिमत्त्वाद् गोवत्—इत्यादिप्रमाणबलेनागमवचनाच्च सचेतनतां कक्षीकुर्वन्ति धीराः ।

१ दृष्टिवादो नाम शास्त्रमासीत् । तस्य चतुर्दशपूर्वात्मको विभागः ।

ये तु जीवपदार्थमेव नेच्छन्ति तेषां बन्धमोक्षादिव्यवस्थानुपपत्तिः। इष्टापत्तौ जगद्वैचित्र्यं कस्माच्छक्येतोपपादयितुम्। एको राजा एको रङ्कः कश्चिद् धनी कश्चिद् दरिद्रोऽन्यो नीरोगः परो रोगी अपरः प्रज्ञावान् इतरोऽतिस्थूलमतिरित्याद्येवमनन्तविश्ववैचित्र्यं जीवपदार्थमपलेपुषामशक्यं साधयितुम्। आत्माभिसंश्लिष्टकर्मवैचित्र्यव्यतिरेकेण तदनुपपत्तेः। यदाह प्रथमकर्मग्रन्थे प्रथमगाथावृत्तौ श्रीमान् देवेन्द्रसूरिः—

> क्ष्माभृद्रंककयोर्मनीषिजडयोः सद्रूपनीरूपयोः
> श्रीमद्दुर्गतयोर्बलाबलवतोर्नीरोगरोगार्तयोः।
> सौभाग्यासुभगत्वसङ्गमजुषोस्तुल्येऽपि नृत्वेऽन्तरं
> यत्तत्कर्मनिबन्धनं तदपि नो जीवं विना युक्तिमत्॥ १॥

ननु पृथिव्यादिभूतेभ्यो गुडपिष्टोदकादिभ्यो मदशक्तिरिव चेतना समुद्भवतीति मतं तदपि न विचारसहम्। अचेतनेभ्यो भूतेभ्यश्चेतनोत्पत्तिविरोधात्। अन्यथा घटादीनामपि सचेतनत्वप्रसक्तेः। पृथिव्यादिचतुष्टयस्य विशिष्टाभिसम्बन्धे सति चेतनाविर्भाव इति चेन्न। यो हि येषां न धर्मस्तेषां सत्यपि सम्बन्धे तद्धर्मप्रादुर्भावानुपपत्तेः। प्रत्यक्षसिद्धो ह्ययमर्थः। न हि तिलव्यतिरिक्तेभ्यः केभ्यश्चिदपि तैलप्रादुर्भावः। नास्ति च पृथिव्यादिः प्रत्येकं चेतनाधर्मवान् नातस्तत्सम्बन्धेऽपि चेतनोद्भवो युक्तिमान्। मदशक्तिदृष्टान्तोऽप्ययुक्तः। मदशक्तेरचेतनत्वेनाचेतनेभ्यः पिष्टोदकादिभ्य उत्पादस्य युक्तत्वेऽपि जडेभ्यो भूतेभ्यश्चैतन्यशक्त्युत्पादस्याऽसिद्धेः। एतेन देहात्मनोरैक्याभिमानोऽपि प्रत्युक्तः। मृतदेहे चेतनानुपलम्भात्। इन्द्रियाण्येवात्मेत्यपि न युक्तम्। चक्षुर्दृष्टस्यार्थस्य चक्षुर्व्यपगमे स्मरणानुपपत्तेः। न हि चक्षुर्दृष्टमर्थमन्यदिन्द्रियं क्षमते स्मर्तुम्। अन्यदृष्टस्यार्थस्यान्येन स्मरणायोगात्। तस्माद् इन्द्रियव्यतिरिक्तममुमेकं पदार्थमभ्युपगन्तुमर्हन्ति प्रेक्षावन्तः। यो हि ज्ञानस्वरूपो येन च प्रेरितानि करणानि स्वस्वविषयं परिच्छेत्तुं प्रभवन्ति यः पुनरेकस्येन्द्रियस्य व्यपगमेऽपि तदुपलब्धमर्थं स्मृतिविषयीकरोति स एव देहादिव्यतिरिक्तो जीवपदार्थः। उक्तं च न्यायदर्शने गौतमीये तृतीयाध्यायस्य प्रथमान्हिके प्रथमसूत्रम्—दर्शनस्पर्शनाभ्यामेकार्थग्रहणादिति।

उक्तो जीवः। अथाजीवतत्त्वव्याख्यावसरः। अजीवस्य लक्षणं चेतनात्यन्ताभावः। जडोऽचेतनोऽजीव इति चानर्थान्तरम्। स च पञ्चधा—धर्मा-

स्तिकायोऽधर्मास्तिकाय आकाशास्तिकायः पुद्गलास्तिकायः कालश्च । अत्रास्तिकायो नाम प्रदेशसमूहात्मकः । प्रदेशसमूहात्मकाः पदार्थाः पञ्चैव सन्ति जीवो धर्मोऽधर्म आकाशं पुद्गलश्च । तत्र प्रत्येकं जीवस्यासंख्येयाः प्रदेशा एतावन्तश्च धर्मस्याऽधर्मस्य च । आकाशस्याऽनन्ताः प्रदेशाः । पुद्गलस्य पुनः संख्येया असंख्येया अनन्ताश्च । कालस्तु प्रदेशरहितः । अनागतस्य कालस्याऽनुत्पन्नत्वादुत्पन्नस्य च विनष्टत्वाद्वर्तमानस्य च समयस्य प्रदेशराहित्यात् । एवं च पञ्चास्तिकाया ज्ञेयास्तदात्मकोऽयं लोकः । अत्र धर्माधर्मौ न पुण्यपापरूपौ शुभाशुभरूपौ जीवसम्बद्धाऽदृष्टरूपौ वा प्रत्येतव्यौ किन्तु लोक आकाशवद् व्यापकावेतन्नामानौ पदार्थौ जैनप्रवचने प्रज्ञप्तौ । तत्सद्भावे किं प्रमाणमिति चेदागम एव प्रमाणम् । स्वीकुर्वते हि सर्वेऽपि दार्शनिकाः स्वस्वाभिमतमागमं प्रमाणम् । न हि स्वर्गनरकाद्यतीन्द्रियपदार्थाभ्युपगम आगममन्तरेण वर्तते किञ्चिच्छरणम् । स्वर्गाद्यनुमापकान्यप्यनुमानप्रमाणानि न स्वातन्त्र्येण चित्ताश्वासहेतवः किन्त्वागमप्रमाणस्य सकाशाल्लब्धप्रसादान्येव भवन्ति । ननु जैनदर्शनादन्यत्र न क्वापि दर्शने धर्माधर्मौ पदार्थौ स्वीचक्राते ततः कथमागममात्रेण तत्राश्वाससम्भवः । युक्तिं हि काञ्चिदाचक्षीतेति चेत् तर्ह्यवधेयमिदम् । गतिलक्षणस्तावद् धर्मास्तिकायः । प्रमाणं चात्र गतिपरिणतयोर्जीवपुद्गलयोरलोके गमनविरहान्यथानुपपत्तिः । न चालोकाभिमुख्यविरहादेव तत्राऽगतिरिति वक्तव्यम् । सिद्धपरमाण्वादीनामलोकाभिमुखत्वात् । न च क्रियाविशेषे देशविशेषस्य हेतुत्वादलोकदेशस्य गत्यहेतुत्वेनैवोपपत्तौ व्यर्था धर्माधर्मपरिकल्पनेति युक्तं वक्तुम् । सहकारिण एव तत्र विशेषकत्वात् । सहकारिणमन्तरेण केवलदेशत्वरूपेण हेतुताकल्पनायां मानाभावात् । स्थितिलक्षणोऽधर्मास्तिकायः । तत्रापि स्थितिपरिणतयोर्जीवपुद्गलयोरलोके स्थितिविरहान्यथानुपपत्तिः प्रमाणम् । अयं भावः । स्वभावतः संचरतां जीवपुद्गलानां पानीयमिव मीनानां धर्मास्तिकायः साहाय्यकं करोति । अधर्मास्तिकायः पुनस्तेषामेव मीनानां स्थलवत् पान्थानां छायावद् वा स्थितौ सहायो भवति । इदं तात्पर्यम्—गतिस्थितिपरिणामे सत्येवैतौ सहायौ । अन्यथा जीवादीनां सदा गतिस्थितिप्रसङ्गात् । एतयोर्लोकव्यापिनोः सदा सत्त्वात् ।

इदं चात्र ध्येयम् । अर्हत्प्रवचने लोकोऽलोकश्चेति द्वौ प्रज्ञप्तौ । तत्र

लोकश्चतुर्दशरज्ज्वात्मको जीवाजीवैश्च संव्याप्तः । लोके पुनस्त्रयो विभागाः । ऊर्ध्वलोकोऽधोलोकस्तिर्यग्लोकश्च । ऊर्ध्वाधोलोकयोर्देवनारकनिवासः प्रागुक्त एव । तिर्यग्लोकः पुनरयं यत्राऽस्मदादयो वर्तन्ते । भारतवर्षादिक्षेत्रसमूहात्मको योजनशतसहस्रनिष्कम्भो वृत्तो यस्य नाभौ मेरुर्वर्तते । एवम्भूतश्च जम्बूद्वीपः । असौ तद्द्विगुणविष्कम्भेण लवणसमुद्रेण परिवेष्टितः । एवंरीत्याऽसंख्येया द्वीपा उत्तरोत्तरसमुद्रेण परिवेष्टिताः । त असंख्येया द्वीपसमुद्रा द्विद्विगुणविष्कम्भा वलयाकृतयो वेदितव्याः । अयं सर्वोऽपि तिर्यग्लोकः । इत्येवमुक्तो लोकः । अलोकः पुनः केवलाकाशात्मकः । अलोके हि जीवपुद्गला धर्माधर्मौ च न सन्ति किन्तु केवलमाकाशमेव । एवं च धर्माधर्मानभ्युपगमे लोकालोकव्यवस्था न स्यात् । जीवपुद्गलानां सर्वत्राऽप्यस्खलद्गत्यादिसम्भवेनालोकत्वेनाभिमतस्यापि लोकत्वप्रसंगप्राप्तेः । धर्माधर्मसद्भावे तु यत्रैव लोके तौ स्तस्तत्रैव पुद्गलानां गत्यादिसम्भवात् तदन्यत्र जीवादिगमनाभावेन केवलाकाशरूपत्वप्राप्तेः सुतरामलोकत्वसिद्धिः । अलोकश्चानन्तः । सर्वव्यापि सर्वाधारः स्वप्रतिष्ठमनन्तप्रदेशमाकाशं प्रसिद्धमेवं । दिक् तु नार्थान्तरमाकाशात् । वर्तनादिलक्षणः कालः । वर्तना च नवपुराणादिपरिणामः । तत्र चार्धतृतीयद्वीपसमुद्रान्तर्वर्ति कालद्रव्यं हेतुः ।

१ लोकस्य चतुर्दश भागाः क्रियन्ते ते प्रत्येक रज्जुनाम्नोच्यन्ते ।

२ लोकसम्बद्ध आकाशो लोकाकाशः । अलोकसम्बद्ध आकाशोऽलोकाकाशः । एवं चैकमप्याकाशं धर्मास्तिकायादिसम्बन्धसत्त्वासत्त्वाभ्यां द्वेधा विभज्यते । आकाशं ह्यवकाशदम् । अलोके पुनर्जीवपुद्गलानामभावादवकाशदायित्वगुणश्चरितार्थो न भवत्याकाशस्य । न च तद्गुणस्याऽचारितार्थ्येऽलोकाकाशस्याकाशत्वं भज्येत । अलोकाकाशो ह्यवकाशं दातुं सर्वदा स्थित एव परं तत्रावकाशग्राहक एव कश्चिन्न स्यात् तदास्य कोऽपराधः । यदि जीवादिपदार्था अलोके भविष्यन्नवश्यमसौ तेषामदास्यताऽवकाशम् । अतोऽवकाशग्राहकाभावकारणेनाचरितार्थेनाप्यवकाशदत्वगुणेनालोकाकाशस्य सुस्थमाकाशत्वम् ।

देहादिव्याप.. तद्वेष्टको लवणोदधिस्तद्वेष्टको धातकीखण्डस्तत्परिवेष्टकः कालोद-
प्रथमान्हिके प्रथ. रावर्तस्याऽर्धभागः । एवं च द्वौ समुद्रौ सार्धौ द्वौ द्वीपौ तथा चार्ध-
उक्तो जीवः । -वर्धतृतीयौ द्वीपौ तौ च समुद्रौ चार्धतृतीयद्वीपसमुद्रौ । इदमेव
त्यन्ताभावः । जडोऽचे लक्षयोजनप्रमाणम् ।

स्पर्शरसगन्धवर्णवन्तः पुद्गलाः । ते द्विधा । अणवः स्कन्धाश्च । तत्र स्कन्धात् पृथग्भूता अबद्धा अप्रदेशाः परमाणवः । द्वौ प्रदेशावारभ्य संख्येया असंख्येया यावदनन्ताश्च प्रदेशा यत्र सन्ति ते द्विप्रदेशिकाः संख्येयप्रदेशिका असंख्येयप्रदेशिका यावदनन्तप्रदेशिकाः स्कन्धा उच्यन्ते । अत्रेदं ज्ञेयम् । यो घटपटादिस्कन्धेषु सम्बन्धः परमोऽणुः स प्रदेश उच्यते । स्कन्धात् पृथग्भूतस्तु स एव परमाणुः । जीवादीनां प्रदेशास्तु जीवादिभ्योऽभिन्ना न पृथग् भवितुमर्हन्ति । यथा पृथग्भूतः केवलः परमाणुः स्वतन्त्रद्रव्यमेवाथ च स्कन्धसम्बन्धे सति प्रदेशशब्देन व्यपदिश्यते तथा जीवादिप्रदेशाः स्वतन्त्रतया द्रव्याणि न । अत एव पुद्गलप्रदेशेभ्यो जीवादिप्रदेशानां विजातीयत्वं विज्ञेयम् । अत एव च जीवादिप्रदेशाः परस्परं सम्बद्धा एकीभूता इव सर्वदाऽवतिष्ठन्ते ।

उक्तोऽजीवपदार्थः । वस्तुत एतौ द्वावेव पदार्थौ । नाभ्यामतिरिच्यते कश्चिदर्थः । ये च धर्माधर्माकाशकालपुद्गलजीवा उक्तास्तानि षड्द्रव्याण्यपि पूर्वोक्तरीत्या जीवाजीवान्तर्भूतान्येव । यान्यपि पुण्यादितत्त्वानि दर्शयिष्यन्ते तान्यपि यथासम्भवं जीवाजीवयोरन्तर्भवन्ति न पृथग्भवितुमर्हन्ति । ज्ञानादिरूपादिगुणानामुत्क्षेपणादिकर्मणां च कथञ्चिदभेदेन जीवाजीवद्रव्यान्न सर्वथा पृथग्भावः साधीयान् । सामान्यविशेषावपि वस्तुस्वरूपावेव । समवायसम्बन्धोऽपि नैयायिकवैशेषिकाभिमतो न द्रव्याद् भेदेन स्थातुमर्हति । अभावं तु भावात्मकमाचक्षत एवार्हताः । यदाहुस्तार्किकसार्वभौमाः श्रीयशोविजयगणयो न्यायालोके---एवमप्यभावस्याधिकरणात्मत्वसिद्धिः । एवं च स्थितेऽपि द्वौ पदार्थाविति सिद्धान्ते गोबलीवर्दन्यायेन विशेषप्रतिपत्त्यर्थं संसारनैर्गुण्योपदर्शनद्वारेण निःश्रेयसमार्गसम्मुखीकरणार्थं च युक्त एव पृथगुपन्यासः पुण्यादितत्त्वानाम् ।

तत्र पुण्यं स्वर्गैश्वर्यादिप्रशस्तफलसम्पादनप्रगुणाः प्रशस्ता जीवाभिसंसृष्टाः कर्मवर्गणाः । तद्विपरीतं पापम् । आश्रूयतेऽनेन कर्मलक्षणमुदकं जीवरूपतडागे इत्याश्रवः । कर्मोपादानहेतुरित्यर्थः । कर्मोपादानं च मिथ्यात्वाविरतिकषाययोगैर्भवति । तत्र मिथ्यात्वं वस्तुस्वरूपाद्विपरीतप्रतिभासः । हिंसानृतस्तेयाब्रह्मपरि-

१ आदिपदाद् धर्माधर्माकाशाः ।

२ मुद्रितपुस्तके दशमपत्रे प्रथमपृष्ठ उपान्त्यपङ्क्तौ ।

३ वर्गणः समुदायः ।

४ आगम्यत आनीयत इति यावत् ।

ग्रहेभ्यो न विरतिरविरतिः। कषायाः क्रोधमानमायालोभाः । मनोवाक्कायव्यापारा योगाः। शुभा योगाः पुण्यस्याशुभा योगाः पापस्य हेतवोऽवसेयाः। संवरः पूर्वोक्तानां मिथ्यात्वादीनां कर्मोपादानहेतूनां विरोधः । अयमर्थः । यथा सरोवरोऽप्रतिरुद्धै-र्द्वारैः प्रविष्टेन जलप्रवाहेण परिपूर्यते प्रतिरुद्धेषु तु द्वारेषु मनागपि न तत्र जलप्रवेशो यथा यानपात्रे रन्ध्रद्वारेण जलं प्रविशति कृते तु रन्ध्रपिधाने न तत्प्रवेश एवं-रीत्या आश्रवद्वारैरप्रतिरुद्धैः कर्मद्रव्यप्रवेश आत्मनि भवति सम्यग्दर्शनविरति-क्षमादिगुप्तिभिश्च क्रमेण पूर्वोक्तानां मिथ्यात्वादीनामाश्रवद्वाराणां प्रतिरोधे कृते न मनागप्यात्मनि कर्मद्रव्यं प्रविशति । तथा हि । सम्यग्दर्शनेन पूर्वोक्तल-क्षणमिथ्यात्वाद्विपरीतलक्षणेन मिथ्यात्वं निगृह्यते । हिंसादिविरत्या च तद-विरतिः प्रतिरुध्यते । क्षमया क्रोधो मृदुत्वेन मान आर्जवभावेन माया संतोषेण च लोभः पराभूयते । मनोगुप्त्या मनोयोगनिग्रहः । वाग्गुप्त्या वाग्यो-गनिरोधः । कायगुप्त्या च काययोगप्रतिरोधः ।

उक्तावाश्रवसंवरौ । निर्जरा तपसा कर्मनिर्जरणम् । देशतः कर्मोपक्षयः। अथ बन्धतत्त्वम् । अञ्जनचूर्णपूर्णसमुद्गकवन्निरन्तरं पुद्गलनिचिते लोके कर्मयो-ग्यपुद्गलैरात्मनः क्षीरनीरवद् वन्ह्ययः पिण्डवद् वान्योन्याभिसंश्लेषात्मकः सम्बन्धो बन्धः। स चतुर्धा–प्रकृतिः स्थितिरनुभागः प्रदेशश्च । तत्र प्रकृतिरष्टधा। ज्ञानावरणं दर्शनावरणं वेदनीयं मोहनीयमायुष्कं नाम गोत्रमन्तरायं च । तत्र चक्षु-रावारकपटादिवद् ज्ञानावारकं कर्म ज्ञानावरणम्। एतस्यैव कर्मणो महिम्ना विदु-षोऽपि कदाचित् स्मृतिभ्रंशादयो जायन्ते । यथा यथा परिपुष्टं भवत्येतत्कर्म तथा तथा ज्ञानमात्रा ह्रासमापद्यते । यथा यथा चेदं कर्म शिथिलीभवति तथा तथा ज्ञानप्रकाशो विशेषतः प्रसरति । सामस्त्येन चास्य कर्मणः परिक्षये सकलप-दार्थप्रकाशः प्रादुर्भवति। दर्शनावारकं कर्म दर्शनावरणम् । एतत्कर्मबलेन निद्रादयो भवन्ति । अन्धत्वबधिरत्वादिकमप्येतन्निबन्धनम् । सुखासुखजन-नस्वभावं कर्म वेदनीयम्। अत एव तत् सातवेदनीयमसातवेदनीयमिति द्वेधा। मदिरावन्मोहयमानं कर्म मोहनीयम् । यथा मदिरापानाद् विमूढीभूतः पुमां-स्तत्त्वविवेकविकलो भवति तथा मोहनीयकर्मणापि प्राणी सदसत्स्वरूपपरिज्ञा-नशून्यो भवति । एतद् द्विधा दर्शनमोहनीयं चारित्रमोहनीयं च । प्रथमं त्रेधा मिथ्यात्वं सम्यक्त्वं मिश्रं च। तत्र प्रथमे द्वे प्रागुक्ते । मिश्रं पुनर्गुणस्थानक्रमारोहे श्रीरत्नशेखरसूरिराह–

जात्यन्तरसमुद्भूतिर्वडवाखरयोर्यथा ।
गुडदध्नोः समायोगे रसभेदान्तरं यथा ॥
तथा धर्मद्वये[1]श्रद्धा जायते समबुद्धितः ।
मिश्रोऽसौ भण्यते तस्माद्भावो जात्यन्तरात्मकः ॥

अथवा नालिकेरद्वीपवासिनो मोदकादाविव सत्यमार्गे न रागो न च द्वेष इत्येवम्भूतो योऽध्यवसायस्तन्मिश्रमोहनीयमित्यप्याहुः । अयमत्र भावार्थः— मिथ्यात्वपुद्गलकदम्बकं मदनकोद्रवन्यायेन परिशोधितं सद् विकाराजनकत्वेनाशुद्धं सम्यक्त्वमुच्यते । तदेव मिथ्यात्वपुद्गलकदम्बकं किञ्चिद्विकारजनकत्वेनार्धविशुद्धं सन्मिश्रमुच्यते । यदा तु सर्वथाऽप्यशुद्धं तत् तदा मिथ्यात्वमिति । चारित्रमोहनीयं पुनः क्रोधादिकषायहास्यादिनोकषायरूपम् । तत्र क्रोधादिकषायाश्चत्वारः प्रागुक्ताः । हास्यादयस्तु नव—हास्यं रतिररतिर्भयं शोको जुगुप्सा पुरुषवेदः स्त्रीवेदो नपुंसकवेदश्च । एते कषायसहचारित्वान्नोकषाया उच्यन्ते नोशब्दस्य साहचर्यवचनत्वात् । कषायोद्दीपनाद्वा नोकषायाः । आयुष्कर्म सुरनरतिर्यङ्नरकायुर्भेदाच्चतुर्विधम् । नामकर्म समासतो द्विधा शुभमशुभं च व्यासतस्तु नानाविधम् । यथा चित्रकृद्विविधं चित्रं निर्माति तथा नामकर्माप्ययं मनुष्योऽयं बलवानयं पशुरसौ निर्बलः स रूपवानेष कुरूपोऽसौ सुस्वरः स दुःस्वर इत्याद्यनेकप्रकारं विपरिणामं जीवेषूपजनयति । गोत्रं कर्म द्वेधा । उच्चगोत्रं नीचगोत्रं च । उच्चनीचगोत्रव्यवहारः सर्वत्र प्रकारान्तरेण सम्भवति । अन्तरायं कर्म पञ्चधा । तत्र सत्यपि देये वस्तुन्यागते च गुणवति पात्रे जानन्नपि दानफलं यदुदयान्नोत्सहते दातुं तद्दानान्तरायम् । तथा विशिष्टेऽपि दातरि विद्यमानेऽपि च देये वस्तुनि याञ्चाकुशलोऽपि याचको न लभते यदुदयात्तल्लाभान्तरायम् । यस्योदयात्सत्यपि विभवादौ सम्पद्यमानेऽपि चाहारमाल्यादौ विरतिहीनोऽपि न भुङ्क्ते तद् भोगान्तरायम् । सदपि वस्त्राभरणादि नालमुपभोक्तुं यस्योदयात्तदुपभोगान्तरायम् । यदुदयाच्च बलवान्नीरोगोऽपि तृणकुब्जीकरणेऽप्यशक्तः स्यात्तद्वीर्यान्तरायम् ।

१ धर्मद्वय इति सत्यतत्त्वेऽसत्यतत्त्वे च ।

अथ केन प्रकारेण पूर्वोक्तं कर्माष्टकं बध्यते तदुपदर्श्यते। ज्ञानस्य ज्ञानवतां ज्ञानसाधनानां च दर्शनस्य दर्शनवतां दर्शनसाधनानां च मात्सर्याऽन्तरायोपघातादिकरणेन ज्ञानावरणदर्शनावरणयोर्बन्धः । दुःखशोकतापाक्रन्दनवधपरिदेवनान्यात्मपरोभयस्थान्यसातवेदनीयस्य कर्मणो बन्धहेतवः । भूतानुकम्पादानक्षान्त्यादयः सातवेदनीयस्य । परमर्षीणां धर्मशास्त्रस्य देवतादीनां चावर्णवादो दर्शनमोहनीयस्य। कषायोदयात् तीव्रसंक्लिष्टपरिणामश्चारित्रमोहनीयस्य। बह्वारम्भपरिग्रहत्वं नारकस्यायुषः । माया तैर्यग्योनस्य । अल्पारम्भपरिग्रहत्वं स्वभावमार्दवार्जवं च मानुषायुषः । सरागसंयमदेशसंयमबालतपआदयो देवायुषः । मनोवाक्काययोगवक्रत्वपरप्रतारणाद्योऽशुभस्य नाम्नः । विपरीतं शुभनाम्नः । परनिन्दात्मश्लाघा सदसद्गुणाच्छादनोद्भावने च नीचगोत्रस्य । विपरीताश्चोच्चगोत्रस्य । विघ्नकरणमन्तरायस्य ।

उक्तः प्रकृतिबन्धः। स्थितिबन्धस्तु आत्मगृहीतानां कर्मपुद्गलानां स्थितिकालनियमनम्। आद्यानां तिसृणां कर्मप्रकृतीनामन्तरायस्य चोत्कृष्टा स्थितिस्त्रिंशत्सागरोपमकोटीकोट्यः । सप्ततिसागरोपमकोटीकोट्यो मोहनीयस्य। नामगोत्रयोर्विंशतिः सागरोपमकोटीकोट्यः। आयुष्कस्य त्रयस्त्रिंशत्सागरोपमाणि। जघन्या स्थितिः पुनर्वेदनीयस्य द्वादशमुहूर्ताः । नामगोत्रयोरष्टौ। शेषाणामन्तर्मुहूर्तम् । कर्मपुद्गलानामेव शुभोऽशुभो वा घात्यघाती वा यो रसः स एवानुभागबन्धो वा रसबन्धो वा। कर्मपुद्गलानामेव स्थितिरसनिरपेक्षं दलिकसंख्याप्राधान्येनैव यद् ग्रहणमसौ प्रदेशबन्धः । प्रकृतिस्थितिरसप्रदेशाश्च

१ क्रियते कषायादिदोषैः कर्मद्रव्यमात्मना बध्यते इति कर्म । तच्च पुद्गलरूपम्। अत एव निगडादिनेव कर्मणा बध्यते जीवः। नैयायिकास्तु जीवस्य गुणः कर्म सौगताः वासनास्वरूपं कर्म कापिलाः पुनः प्रकृतिविकारः कर्म ब्रह्मवादिनश्चाविद्यास्वभावं कर्मेति परिभाषन्ते । परन्तु पूर्वोक्ताऽनुभवेन पौद्गलिकरूपमेव कर्मेति सिद्धान्त आर्हतानाम् ।

२ सागरोपमोऽतिदीर्घतमः कालविशेषः । अस्य स्वरूपं पञ्चमकर्मग्रन्थे देवेन्द्रसूरिनिर्मिते द्रष्टव्यम् ।

३ कोट्या गुणिता कोटी कोटीकोटी ।

४ अतिसूक्ष्मतमः कालः समयशब्देनोच्यते यस्मात् सूक्ष्मसमयो नास्ति । नवभ्य एकसमयोनमुहूर्तान्तं यावदन्तमुहूर्तं भवति ।

मोदकदृष्टान्तेन भाव्याः । तद्यथा । मोदको वातपित्तकफान्यतमविनाशिद्रव्योत्पन्नस्तदन्यतमं यथोपशमयत्येवं ज्ञानावरणादिकर्मणोऽपि ज्ञानाच्छादनस्वभावा प्रकृतिः । एवं शेषमप्यूह्यम् । स एव मोदको यथा मासं पक्षमेकदिनमपि वा तिष्ठति तथैव कर्मणोऽपि ज्ञानावरणादेस्त्रिंशत्सागरोपमकोटीकोट्यादिः स्थितिः । रसः पुनर्मोदके स्निग्धमधुरादिरूप एकगुणो द्विगुणस्त्रिगुणोऽपि वा भवति तथैव कर्मणोऽप्येकस्थानिकद्विस्थानिकत्रिस्थानिकादिरूपः । प्रदेशा यथा मोदका एकप्रसृतिप्रमाणाः प्रसृतिद्वयत्रयसेतिकादिप्रमाणा वा भवन्ति तथा कर्मण्यप्यल्पबहुबहुतमादिरूपा वेदितव्याः ।

नवमं तत्त्वं मोक्षः । सकलकर्मक्षयो मोक्षः । स च केवलज्ञाने सत्येव । केवलज्ञानं च ज्ञानावरणदर्शनावरणान्तरायाणां मोहनीयकर्मप्रक्षयादनु प्रक्षये जाते प्रादुर्भवति । एतत्कर्मचतुष्काच्छेषं कर्मचतुष्कमघातिशब्देनोच्यते । अघातिकर्माणि भवाधारत्वाद्भवोपग्राहिशब्देन व्यपदिष्टानि । सत्स्वेतेषु हि भवरूपः प्रासादोऽवतिष्ठते । एषां च प्रक्षये स प्रासादस्तत्क्षणमेव भज्यते ।

केवलज्ञानिनो द्वेधा तीर्थङ्कराः सामान्यकेवलिनश्च । येषां तीर्थङ्करनामकर्मोदयो नास्ति ते केवलिनः सामान्यकेवलिन उच्यन्ते । ये तु तीर्थङ्करनामकर्मोदययुक्तास्ते तीर्थङ्करा ईश्वराः परमेश्वराः । तीर्थं प्रवचनं तत्प्रकाशकत्वात् तीर्थङ्करत्वम् । तीर्थं साधुसाध्वीश्रावकश्राविकालक्षणश्चतुर्विधः सङ्घस्तत्स्थापकत्वाद्वा तीर्थङ्करत्वम् । तीर्थङ्कराश्च तीर्थङ्करनामकर्मोदयमहिम्ना परमातिशयसाम्राज्यचमत्कृतसकलसुरासुरनरेन्द्रयोगीन्द्राः देवेन्द्रैरहमहमिकया परिषेव्यमाणा धर्मदेशनाद्वारेण जगज्जनाननुगृह्णन्ति । एतेषां परमात्मनां शिष्यीभूयैतेषामुपदेशमवलम्ब्य ये महाप्राज्ञा विशिष्टशक्तिसम्पन्नाः परमपुण्यभाजो द्वादशाङ्गीं ग्रथ्नन्ति ते गणधरा उच्यन्ते । अङ्गानि चामूनि । आचाराङ्गं सूत्रकृताङ्गं स्थानाङ्गं समवायाङ्गं भगवती ज्ञानधर्मकथोपासकदशाऽन्तकृद्दशाऽनुत्तरोपपातिकदशा प्रश्नव्याकरणं विपाको दृष्टिवादश्चेति । तत्र दृष्टिवादो व्यवच्छिन्नः । शेषाणि चाङ्गानि तत्कालापेक्षया सङ्क्षिप्तानि वर्तन्ते सम्प्रति । अन्यान्यप्युपाङ्गादीनि बहून्यागमशास्त्राणि गणधरशिष्यप्रशिष्यगुंफितानि सन्ति वर्तमाने ।

स च केवली भगवानायुःपरिसमाप्तौ सत्यामघातिकर्मप्रक्षय एव देहपञ्जरान्निर्गत्य समश्रेण्योर्ध्वं याति यावल्लोकान्तमेकसमयेन तथा स्वाभाव्यात् ।

लोकान्तात् परतो धर्मास्तिकायाभावान्न गमनसम्भवः । लोकान्तादधःपातोऽपि गुरुत्वाभावादसम्भवः । प्रेरकाभावाच्च तिर्यग्गतिरप्यसम्भविनी । ऊर्ध्वमधस्तिर्यग्गमनं हि जीवानां कर्मजन्यम् । क्षीणसकलकर्मणां पूर्णब्रह्मणां सिद्धानां तु स्वभावत एवोर्ध्वगतिः । ते सिद्धाः कुत्र समवस्थिता इत्यत्राह भगवानुमास्वातिस्तत्त्वार्थसूत्रपर्यंते—

मनोज्ञा सुरभिस्तन्वी पुण्या परमभासुरा ।
प्राग्भारा नाम वसुधा लोकमूर्ध्नि व्यवस्थिता ॥
नृक्षेत्रतुल्यविष्कम्भा सितच्छत्रनिभा शुभा ।
ऊर्ध्वं तस्याः क्षितेः सिद्धा लोकान्ते समवस्थिताः ॥

घातिकर्मचतुष्कप्रक्षये क्रमतश्चत्वारोऽक्षय्याः सदावस्थायिनो गुणाः सम्पद्यन्ते । तथा हि । ज्ञानावरणविध्वंसे केवलज्ञानं दर्शनावरणविनाशे केवलदर्शनं मोहनीयनिर्घाते परमोज्ज्वलं चारित्रम् । एते गुणास्तु जीवन्मुक्तानां देहवतां प्रत्यक्षीकारनिर्देश्यानां परमात्मनां घातिकर्मप्रक्षयसमुत्थाः सम्भवन्त्येव । आयुःपरिसमाप्तौ चाघातिकर्मप्रक्षयजन्या अन्ये पुनरनन्तसुखादिगुणा अमीषां प्रादुर्भवन्ति । मुक्तीभूतानां भगवतां परब्रह्मणां देहेन्द्रियाद्यभावादैन्द्रियकसुखासम्भवेऽप्यात्मस्वभावं सुखमाविर्भवति । तस्यानन्तभागेऽपि सकलभुवनेन्द्राणामैश्वर्यसुखमहाकरो नोपपद्यते । अकर्मकीभूतः परमात्मा न पुनः कर्मवानर्हति भवितुम् । न हि क्षीरात् समुद्धृतमाज्यं पुनः क्षीरतां व्रजति । यथा च रसेन्द्रेण नीताः शातकुम्भतां धातवो न पुनरावृत्तये भवन्त्येवमकर्मकीभूतो निरञ्जनः सिद्धो न भवेत् पुनः कथमपि कर्मवान् । एतेनेदमपि प्रज्ञप्तं भवति । मुक्तिं प्राप्य न पुनरधोऽवतारः सम्भवति । आह च महर्षिरुमास्वातिर्वाचकमुख्यस्तत्त्वार्थसूत्रपर्यन्ते—

दग्धे बीजे यथाऽत्यन्तं प्रादुर्भवति नाङ्कुरः ।
कर्मबीजे तथा दग्धे न रोहति भवाङ्कुरः ॥

परमात्मानो हि परमवीतरागाः । न तस्मादेषां संसारेण किमपि प्रयोजनं येन पुनः संसारमाविशेयुरिति जैनसिद्धान्तः । इदमपि जैनसिद्धान्ताभिमतम् । कर्मक्षयस्य करणेन भवतीश्वरो न पुनर्नित्यमुक्तः कश्चिदेकः सनातन ईश्वरः । उक्तं हि सम्मतिप्रकरणवृत्तौ[1] न्यायचक्रवर्तिना श्रीमदभय-

[1] मुद्रितपुस्तक १२१ पृष्ठे ।

देवसूरिणा—तन्न रागादिक्लेशविगमः स्वभावत एवेश्वरस्येति युक्तमिति । उपायबलेन ह्युपेयसिद्धिरुपायव्यतिरेकेणोपेयसिद्धेरसम्भवात्। तथाचेश्वरत्वमपि यदि नोपायसिद्धं तर्हि सर्वेषामपि तत्सम्भवः स्यान्न वा कस्यापि । उक्तं हि सौगतेन धर्मकीर्तिनाऽपि—

नित्यं सत्त्वमसत्त्वं वाऽहेतोरन्यानपेक्षणात् ।
अपेक्षातो हि भावानां कादाचित्कत्वसम्भवः ॥

अत एव जैना ईश्वरं प्रतिपद्यमानाः सेवमाना उपासीना ध्यानगोचरीकुर्वाणा अपि नाचक्षते जगत्कर्तारम् । तेषां ह्ययमेवाऽभिप्रायः । परमवीतरागस्येश्वरस्य न किञ्चिज्जगत्सृष्टौ प्रयोजनं सम्भवति । परमकृतार्थत्वात्। न च निष्प्रयोजनस्य जगत्सृष्टिचेष्टोपपत्तिमती । ईश्वरस्यानादितया स्वीकर्तॄणां जगतोऽप्यनादित्वेन स्वीकारे न किञ्चिद् दूषणापातः । प्रतिक्षणं विपरिणममानमपि जगद् द्रव्यशक्तितः सनातनमेव । समूलनाशायोगात् । मुक्तेरनादित्वेन मुक्तिस्थानामप्यनादित्वात् सुतरामीश्वरस्याऽनादित्वसिद्धिर्जैनप्रवचनेऽपि । मुक्तेरनादित्वादेव च संसारस्याऽप्यनादित्वं सुतरां सिध्यति।

ईश्वरस्य वीतरागत्वेन निग्रहानुग्रहकारित्वाभावेऽपि तदुपासना परमावश्यकी । शुद्धालम्बनेन मनसः शुद्धिभावेन सर्वार्थसिद्धेः । यादृशं ह्यालम्बनं तथारूप उपरागो मनस्युपजायते । यथा चाग्निं सेवमानस्य शीतार्तिरुपशाम्यति तद्वद्वीतरागं परमेश्वरमुपासीनस्य रागार्तिरुपशाम्याति ।

अन्यच्च। आर्हतानामयं मूलमन्त्रः—सर्वे खलु भावाः स्याद्वादमुद्राङ्किताः । स्याद्वादमन्तरेण वस्तुस्वरूपानुपपत्तेः । स्याद्वादो हि सापेक्षतयैकस्मिन् धर्मिणि सदसत्त्वनित्यानित्यत्वाद्यनेकधर्माभ्युपगमः । सर्वं हि वस्तु स्वरूपेण सत् पररूपेण चासत् कटककुण्डलादिपर्यायेण चानित्यं स्वर्णमृत्तिकादिमूलद्रव्येण च नित्यं सर्वेषां प्रतीतिपथमारोहति । इदं च तत्त्वं श्रीहरिभद्रसूरिपादैरनेकान्तजयपताकायां बहु विवेचितमस्तीति तद्विषयिणी जिज्ञासा तत एव सम्यगुपशाम्यति । अधिकजिज्ञासुमहाशयैः कर्मग्रन्थतत्त्वार्थसूत्रलोकप्रकाशविशेषावश्यकादयो ग्रन्था अवलोकनीयाः । इह त्वेतावदेव वक्तुमुचितं मत्वा विरमति—

विजयधर्मसूरिः ।

Philosophy

ANCIENT INDIAN LOGIC: AN OUTLINE

BY SATIS CHANDRA VIDYABHUSHAN

THE system of Philosophy called Nyāya[1] in India approaches the science known as Logic in Europe. This system was founded by a sage named Akṣapāda of the clan of Gautama who is traditionally known to have resided in Mithilā (modern Darbhanga in North Behar) probably until his retirement into Prabhāsa,[2] the well-known sacred place of pilgrimage in Kathiawar on the sea-coast. This Akṣapāda, better known as Gautama, is supposed to have lived about 550 B. C., as Jātukarṇya, his contemporary, was a pupil of Āsurāyaṇa and Yāska,[3] whose date is generally fixed as the middle of the 6th century before Christ.

The Pāli canonical scriptures such as the Brahmajāla-sutta, Udāna[4] etc. composed about 500 B. C. mention a class of Samaṇas and Brāhmaṇas who were *takki* or *takkika* (logicians or rather sophists) and *vimaṁsi* (casuists) and indulged in *takka* (logic or sophism) and *vimaṁsā* (casuistry), alluding perhaps to the followers of Akṣapāda-Gautama. 'Anumāna-sutta' is the title of a chapter of the Majjhima Nikāya, while the word 'vāda' in the sense of discussion, occurs in another chapter of the same Nikāya.[5] The Kathāvatthuppakaraṇa,[6] another Pāli work which was composed in the reign of Aśoka about 255 B. C.,

1 Logic is designated in Sanskrit not only by the word 'Nyāya' but also by various other words which indicate diverse aspects of the science. For instance it is called 'Hetuvidyā' or 'Hetu-śāstra' the science of causes, 'Ānvīkṣikī' the science of inquiry or inference, 'Pramāṇa-śāstra,' the science of evidences or proofs, 'Tattva-śāstra,' the science of categories, 'Tarka-vidyā,' the science of reasoning, 'Vādārtha,' the science of discussion, and 'Phakkikā-śāstra,' the science of sophism.

2 Vide Rāmāyaṇa, ādikāṇḍa, sarga 48, verses 11-15; and Brahmāṇḍa Purāṇa, adhyāya 23, verses 201-203.

3 Vide Satapatha Brāhmaṇa, Yājñavalkya kāṇḍa.

4 Brahmajāla-sutta 1-32; Udāna vi. 10.

5 Majjhima Nikāya, Vol. I, 15th sutta, and Vol. II, 6th sutta.

6 Kathāvatthuppakaraṇa, chapter I.

mentions *paṭiññā* (a proposition), *upanaya* (an application of reason) and *niggaha* (occasion for rebuke) etc., which are technical terms of the Nyāya philosophy of Akṣapāda-Gautama. In the Pāli Dhammasaṅgaṇī[1] composed about 450 B. C. there is a division of knowledge (viññāna) into six kinds, viz. visual (cakkhu) auditory (sota), olfactory (ghāṇa), gustatory (jivhā), tactual (kāya) and mental (mano). The Pāli Milinda Pañha,[2] composed about 100 A. D., mentions Logic under the name of 'Nīti' while the Buddhist Sanskrit work, Lalitavistāra, which was translated into Chinese *circa* 221–263 A. D., designates it as 'Hetuvidyā.'[3] In the Mādhyamika Kārikā[4] of Nāgārjuna, dated about 300 A. D., we come across some technical terms of Logic such as *punarukta* (repetition) in chap. ii., *siddhasādhana* (proving the proved) in chap. iii., and *sādhya-sama* (petitio principii) in chap. iv.; but an explicit reference to 'Nyāya' (Logic) is to be found in another Buddhist Sanskrit work called Laṅkāvatāra Sūtra (composed about 300 A. D.) where teachers of Logic are mentioned by the name of *naiyāyika* (logicians).[5] About 400 A. D. began a period when a large number of Buddhist writers gave their undivided attention to the study of Nyāya and laid the foundation of the Mediæval School of Indian Logic.

Although the Jainas claim that in the 12th *aṅga* (book) of their scripture called Dṛṣṭivāda, there was embodied a treatise on Logic, yet as that aṅga disappeared, according to their tradition, by 474 A. D., we cannot say anything about the treatise. In the Jaina Prākrit scriptures such as Nandī Sūtra, Sthānāṅga Sūtra, Bhagavatī Sūtra etc., compiled by Indrabhūti Gautama about 500 B. C., there is a

1 Vide Dhammasaṅgaṇī as well as Aṅguttara Nikāya, III., 618.

2 Vide Rhys Davids' Introduction to Questions of King Milinda in the S. B. E. series.

3 Lalitavistāra, chap. XII., p. 179, Rajendralal Mitra's edition.

4 Vide Satis Chandra Vidyabhusana's *Indian Logic: Mediæval School*, p. 68.

5 Laṅkāvatāra Sūtra, chap. II. As to the date of this work, vide my article in J. A. S. B. Vol. I. No. 6, 1905; and also my article in J. R. A. S. for October 1905.

division[1] of *hetu* or the means of knowledge into preception (pratyakṣa), inference (anumānā), comparison (upamāna) and verbal testimony (āgama), which indicates that this doctrine was either borrowed by Indrabhūti from Akṣapāda-Gautama or was the common property of both. Hetu used in the sense of inference (anumāna) is classified, in the Sthānāṅga Sūtra already referred to, according to the following types—1 This *is*, because that *is*: There is a fire, because there is smoke. 2 This *is not*, because that *is*: It is not cold, because there is a fire. 3 This *is*, because that *is not*: It is cold here, because there is no fire. 4 This *is not*, because that *is not*: There is no śiṁśapā tree here, because there are no trees at all.

Umāsvāti, who flourished in Pāṭaliputra and attained nirvāṇa in 85 A. D., was the famous author of the Tattvārthādhigama Sūtra which follows the Anuyogadvāra Sūtra, Sthānāṅga Sūtra, Nandī Sūtra etc., in its treatment of the doctrines of *jñāna* (knowledge) and *nyāya* (the method of comprehending things from particular stand-points). *Jñāna* is divided into *pratyakṣa* (direct knowledge) and *parokṣa* (indirect knowledge). Direct knowledge, which is acquired by the soul without the intervention of external agencies, is of three kinds, viz. *avadhi* (the knowledge of things beyond the range of our perception), *manaḥparyāya* (the knowledge derived from reading the thoughts of others) and *kevala* (the unobstructed, unconditional and absolute knowledge). Indirect knowledge, which is acquired by the soul through the medium of the senses and the mind, includes *mati* (knowledge of existing things acquired through the senses) and *śruta* (knowledge of things—past, present and future—acquired through reasoning and study). In the Anuyogadvāra Sūtra as well as in the Tattvārthādhigama Sūtra, *naya* is divided into seven kinds as follows—1 *Naigama*, the non-distinguished (a method by which an object is regarded as possessing both general and specific properties, no distinction being made

1 Vide Sthānāṅga Sūtra, p. 309-310, published by Dhanapat Sing, Calcutta.

between them, e. g. when we use the word 'bamboo' we indicate a number of properties some of which are peculiar to the bamboo while others are possessed by it in common with other trees). 2 *Saṁgraha*, the collective (a method which takes into consideration generic properties only, ignoring particular properties). 3 *Vyavahāra*, the practical (a method which takes into consideration the particular only, e. g. in being asked to bring a plant one can bring only a particular plant but cannot bring plant in general). 4 *Ṛjusūtra*, the straight expression (a method which considers a thing as it exists at the moment without any reference to its past or its future: it recognises only the entity (bhāva), and not its name (nāma), image (sthāpanā) or the causes which constituted it (dravya), e. g. the fact that a cowherd is named Indra does not make him Lord of the heavens, or the image of a cowherd cannot perform the functions of a cowherd, etc.). 5 *Sāmprata* (a method which consists in using a word in its conventional sense, even if that sense is not justified by its derivation, e. g. the word *śatru*, according to its derivation signifies a 'destroyer' but its conventional meaning is an 'enemy'). 6 *Samabhirūḍha* (a method which consists in making nice distinctions between synonyms, selecting in each case the word which on etymological grounds is the most appropriate). 7 *Evambhūta* (a method which consists in applying to things such names only as their actual condition justifies, e. g. a man should not be called *Śakra*, strong, unless he actually possesses the *śakti*, strength, which the name implies).

Bhadrabāhu, who is said by some authorities to have lived during 433-357 B. C. but who according to others lived in the 6th century A. D., gives in his Daśavaikālika Niryukti an example of a syllogism consisting of 10 parts. About the 5th century A. D. some of the Jaina philosophers devoted themselves to the cultivation of Nyāya and cooperated with the Buddhists in founding the Mediæval School of Indian Logic.

The Nyāya Philosophy or Logic, encouraging as it did independent discussion, could not at its early stage acquire great popularity in a country where the authority of the Vedas was accepted as final. The sage Jaimini[1] in his Mīmāṅsā Sūtra distinctly says that as the Veda has for its sole purpose the prescription of actions, those parts of it which do not serve that purpose are useless. We are therefore not surprised to find Manu[2] enjoining excommunications upon those members of the twice-born caste who disregarded the Vedas and Dharma-sūtras relying upon the support of Hetuśāstra or Logic. Similarly Vālmīki[3] in his Rāmāyaṇa discredits those persons of perverse intellect who indulge in the frivolities of Ānvīkṣikī, the science of Logic, regardless of the works of sacred Law (Dharma-śāstra) which they should follow as their guide. Vyāsa[4] in the Mahābhārata relates the doleful story of a repentant Brahman who, addicted to Tarka-vidyā (Logic) carried on debates, divorced from all faith in the Vedas and was, on that account, turned into a jackal in his next birth as a penalty. In another passage of the Śāntiparva[5] Vyāsa warns the followers of the Vedānta philosophy against communicating their doctrines to a Naiyāyika or Logician. Vyāsa does not care even to review the Nyāya system in the Brahma-sūtra (ii. 2.17), seeing that it has not been recognised by any worthy sage. Stories of infliction of penalties on those given to the study of Nyāya are related in the Skanda Purāṇa[6] and other works; and in the Naiṣadha-carita, we find Kali satirizing the founder of Nyāya philosophy as 'Gotama' the 'most bovine' among sages.

There were nevertheless persons who welcomed the science of Logic, and applied its principles to systematize other branches of learning, and when Logic, instead of relying entirely upon reasoning, came to attach due weight

1 Mīmāṅsā-sūtra i. 2. 1.

2 Manu-saṁhitā ii. 11.

3 Rāmāyaṇa, Ayodhyā Kāṇḍa, sarga 100, verse 36.

4 Mahābhārata, Śāntiparva, adhyāya 180, verses 47-49.

5 Adhyāya 246, verse 18.

6 Kālikā Khaṇḍa, chap. 17.

to the authority of the Vedas, it came to be regarded as an approved branch of learning. Thus the Gautama Dharma-sūtra[1] prescribes a course of training in Logic (Nyāya) for the king, and acknowledges the utility of that science (Tarka) in the administration of justice, though in the case of conclusions proving incompatible, ultimate decision is directed to be made by reference to persons versed in the Vedas. Manu[2] says that dharma or duty is to be ascertained by logical reasoning not opposed to the injunctions of the Vedas. He recommends Logic (Nyāya)[3] as a necessary study for a king, and a logician to be an indispensable member of a legal assembly. Yājñavalkya[4] counts Nyāya or Logic among the fourteen principal sciences, while Vyāsa[5] admits that he was able to arrange and classify Upaniṣads with the help of Ānvīkṣikī or Logic. In the Padma Purāṇa[6] Logic is included among the fourteen principal branches of learning promulgated by God Viṣṇu, while in the Matsya Purāṇa[7] Nyāya-vidyā together with the Vedas is said to have emanated from the mouth of Brahma himself. In fact so wide-spread was the study of Nyāya that the Mahābhārata is full of references to that science.

In the Ādiparva[8] of the Mahābhārata Nyāya or Logic is mentioned along with the Veda and Cikitsā (the science of medicine), and the hermitage of Kāśyapa is described as being filled with sages who were versed in the logical truths (nyāya-tattva), and knew the true meaning of a proposition (sthāpanā) objection (ākṣepa) and conclu-

1 Gautama-Dharma-sūtra, chap. XI.

2 Manu-saṁhitā, Book XII, verse 106.

3 Manu-saṁhitā, Book VII, verse 43, and Book XII, verse 111.

4 Yājñavalkya-saṁhitā, chap. I, verse 3.

5 Mahābhārata quoted by Viśvanātha in his Vṛtti on the Nyāya-sūtra i. 1. 1.

6 Padma Purāṇa, vide Muir's Sanskrit Texts, Vol. III, p. 27.

7 Matsya Purāṇa, iii. 2.

8 Mahābhārata, Ādiparva, adhyāya 1, verse 57; and adhyāya 70, verses 42–45.

sion (siddhānta). The Śantiparva[1] refers to numerous tenets of Nyāya supported by reason (hetu) and scripture (āgama), while the Aśvamedhaparva[2] describes the sacrificial ground as resounding with arguments and counter-arguments employed by logicians (hetuvādin) to vanquish one another. In the Sabhāparva[3] the sage Nārada is described as being versed in Logic (nyāyavid) and skilful in distinguishing unity and plurality (aikya, and nānātva), conjunction and co-existence (saṁyoga and samavāya), genus and species (parāpara) etc., capable of deciding questions by evidences (pramāṇa) and ascertaining the validity and invalidity of a five-membered syllogism (pañcāvayava-vākya). In fact the Nyāya (Logic) was in course of time deservedly held in very high esteem.

The work in which Akṣapāda or Gautama embodied his teachings on Logic is called the Nyāya-sūtra. It is divided into five books, each containing two chapters called *āhnikas* or diurnal portions. It is believed that Akṣapāda finished his work on Nyāya-sutra in ten lectures corresponding to the āhnikas referred to above. We do not know whether the whole of the Nyāya-sūtra, as it exists at present, was the work of Akṣapāda, nor do we know for certain whether his teachings were committed to writing by himself, or transmitted by oral tradition only. It seems to me that it is only the first book of the Nyāya-sūtra containing a brief explanation of the sixteen categories that we are justified in ascribing to Akṣapāda, while the second, third and fourth books which discuss particular doctrines of the Vaiśeṣika, Yoga, Mīmāṅsā, Vedānta and Buddhist Philosophy bear marks of different hands and ages. In these books there are passages quoted almost verbatim from the Laṅkāvatāra Sūtra,[4] a Sans-

1 Mahābhārata, Śāntiparva, adhyāya 210, verse 22.

2 Mahābhārata, Aśvamedhaparva, adhyāya 85, verse 27.

3 Mahābhārata, Sabhāparva, adhyāya 5, verses 3–5.

4 Nyāya-sūtra iv. 2. 26 which quotes the Laṅkāvatāra Sūtra (dated about 300 A. D.).

krit work of the Yogācāra Buddhist Philosophy, from the Mādhyamika Sūtra[1] of Nāgārjuna and from the Śataka[2] of Āryadeva—works which were composed in the early centuries of the Christian era. The fifth book, treating of the varieties of futile rejoinders and occasions for rebuke, was evidently not the production of Akṣapāda who dismissed these topics in the first book without entering into their details. The last and the most considerable additions were made by Vātsyāyana otherwise known as Pakṣila Svāmin who, about 400 A. D., wrote the first regular commentary, 'Bhāṣya,' on the Nyāya-sūtra, and harmonished the different, and at times conflicting, additions and interpolations by the ingenious introduction of Sūtras of his own making which he fathered upon Akṣapāda.

Vātsyāyana, otherwise known as Pakṣila Svāmin, must have flourished before Diṅnāga,[3] as the latter criticises him in connection with the explanation of the Nyāya-sūtra i. 1. 4, and possibly also before Vasubandhu[4] whose theory of syllogism, so antagonistic to that of Akṣapāda, has not been controverted, nay even referred to, by Vātsyāyana in his commentary on Nyāya-sūtra i. 1. 37. The Nyāya-sūtra, as has been already observed, contains certain aphorisms which refer to the doctrines expounded in such well-known Buddhist works as the Mādhyamika-sūtra,[5] the Laṅkāvatāra-sūtra[6] etc. These aphorisms do not constitute an essential part of the Nyāya-sūtra and were evidently interpolated into it before or during the time of Vātsyāyana who wrote a commentary on it. Vātsyāyana must therefore have flourished after the composition of the

1 Nyāya-sūtra ii. 1. 39 and iv. 1. 68 which criticise the Mādhyamika Sūtra.

2 Nyāya-sūtra iv. 1. 48 which criticises the Śataka of Āryadeva.

3 Compare Pramāṇa-samuccaya, chap. 1—

न सुखादि प्रमेयं वा मनो वास्तीन्द्रियान्तरम् ।
अनिषेधादुपात्तं चेदन्येन्द्रियरुतं वृथा ॥

4 Vide Nyāyāvatāra, verse 20.

5 Nyāya-sūtra iv. 1. 39, iv. 1. 48, ii. 1. 19, iv. 2. 32, ii. 1. 37, and Mādhyamika-sūtra, chaps. 1, 7, and 2.

6 Nyāya-sūtra iv. 2. 26, iii. 2. 11; and Laṅkāvatāra, chaps. 2 and 6.

Buddhist works, the doctrines of which are referred to and criticised in the Nyāya-sūtra. Hence the earliest limit of his age is A. D. 300, when the Mādhyamika Sūtra and the Laṅkāvatāra are supposed to have been composed.[1] As Diṅnāga[2] lived about 500 A. D. and Vasubandhu[3] about 480 A. D., Vātsyāyana who preceded them could not have lived after the latter date. Taking the mean between the earliest and the latest dates of his age, we may approximately place Vātsyāyāna at about 400 after Christ.

Vātsyāyana, also designated as Drāmila (same as Drāviḍa), was in all probability a native of Drāviḍa (the Deccan) of which the capital was Kāñcīpura, modern Conjeeveram. The title Svāmin appended to Pakṣila in the name 'Pakṣila Svāmin' also points to the same country as his birth-place. We may add that Kāñcī was a centre not only of Brahmanic learning, but also of Buddhistic culture, and it was here that Diṅnāga (500 A. D.) and Dharmapāla (600 A. D.) and other Buddhist logicians lived the flourished. It may be of some interest to note that Vātsyāyana makes a reference to the boiling of rice[4] which is a staple food of the people of Drāviḍa at about 400 A. D., when Candragupta II, called Vikramāditya, was king of Magadha. This Vātsyāyana should not be confounded with the sage or sages of that name who compiled the Artha-śāstra and the Kāma-sūtra.[5]

Diṅnāga, a famous Buddhist logician, having criticised the Nyāya-sūtra as explained by Vātsyāyana, Uddyotakara, a Brahman logician, wrote a sub-commentary on it called the Nyāya-vārtika. In it he mentions a Buddhist treatise on Logic called the Vāda-vidhi[6] which is only another name for the Vāda-nyāya by Dharmakīrti.

1 Vide my *Indian Logic*: *Mediæval School*, pp. 68-72.

2 Loc. cit. pp. 80-81

3 Loc. cit, pp. 75-76.

4 Nyāya-bhāṣya, ii. 1, 40.

5 Vide my paper *Vātsyāyana, author of the Nyāya-bhāṣya* in the Indian Antiquary for April 1915.

6 Nyāya-vārtika 1. 33, pp. 121 (Bib. Ind. ed.)

On the other hand Dharmakīrti in his Nyāya-bindu mentions a Śāstra which evidently refers to the Nyāya-vārtika, and to Śāstrakāra who seems to be the same as Uddyotakara.[1] Hence we conclude that Dharmakīrti and Uddyotakara were contemporaries who flourished about A. D. 633.[2] Among the important men who lived in the same age, we may mention Subandhu the author of Vāsavadattā, Bāṇa the author of Harṣa-carita, and king Śrī Harṣa of Thāneśvar during whose reign (629-644 A. D.) the Chinese pilgrim Yuan Chwang travelled through India.

The name Bhāradvāja as applied to Uddyotakara is derived from the family to which he belonged, while he is called Pāśupatācārya on account of his having been a preceptor of the Pāśupata Śaiva sect.[3] Nothing is definitely known as to the place where Uddyotakara was born. The only place mentioned by him is Śrughna which is situated on the Western Jumna Canal, 40 miles north of Thāneśvar. It seems to me that Uddyotakara, while writing the Nyāya-vārtika, resided at Thāneśvar which was connected with Śrughna by a high road. It is not unlikely that Uddyotakara received sometime in his career patronage at the court of Thāneśvar.[4]

Dharmakīrti and other Buddhist logicians having compiled treatises subversive of the interpretation of Uddyotakara and Vātsyāyana, a Brahman philosopher of great erudition named Vācaspati Miśra wrote, in support of the Brahman commentators, an elaborate gloss on the Nyāya-vārtika called the Nyāya-vārtika-tātparya-ṭīkā. Vācaspati, who is reputed to be a native of Mithilā (modern district of Darbhanga in North Behar), must have flourished in the 10th century A. D., as he compiled his Nyāya-sūci-nibandha in the year 898 which, if referred to

1 Nyāyabindu, chap. iii., pp. 110-11 (Bibl. Ind.)

2 See my *Indian Logic: Mediæval School*, p. 105.

3 Vide Nyāya-vārtika, colophon.

4 Vide my article *Uddyotakara, a contemporary of Dharmakīrti* in J. R. A. S. for July, 1914; and Nyāya-vārtika 1. 33.

Śaka era, corresponds to A. D. 976.[1]

Vācaspati in his turn was criticised by a host of Buddhist logicians, and it was to vindicate him against their attacks that Udayanācārya, a Brahman logician of Mithilā and the well-known author of Kusumāñjali and Ātmatattva-viveka, wrote a sub-gloss on Vācaspati's work, called the Nyāya-vārtika-tātparya-ṭikā-pariśuddhi. This Udayana was the author of another work called Lakṣaṇāvali, in the introduction to which he says that he composed the book in the Śaka year 906, corresponding to A. D. 984.[2]

Another Brahman logician who fought hard against the Buddhists was Jayanta, author of Nyāya-mañjarī, who seems to have been a native of Kāśmīr and to have flourished in the 11th century. He quotes Vācaspati Miśra[3], and is himself quoted in the Ratnāvatārikā[4] by the Jaina philosopher Ratnaprabha (1181 A. D.) and in the Syādvādaratnākara, chap. II.[5] by Deva Sūri (1086-1169 A. D.). The Nyāya-mañjarī is an independent commentary on the Nyāya-sūtra, in which Jayanta reviews the interpretations and criticisms of all his predecessors.

These are the principal Brahman commentators on the Nyāya-sūtra. Subsequently there arose a host of commentators whose names are not mentioned here as they belong to the modern school of Nyāya in respect of their style and method of interpretation. The name of Bhāsarvajña, author of Nyāya-sāra is not mentioned here as he really belongs to the Mediæval School.

From the short account given above it is evident that there is only one original treatise on Logic called the Nyāya-sūtra which presents the ancient school. The works of Vātsyāyana and his followers, though very comprehensive and ingenious, are mere commentaries.

1 न्यायसूचीनिबन्धोऽसावकारि सुधियां मुदे । श्रीवाचस्पतिमिश्रेण वस्वङ्कवसुवत्सरे ॥

2 तर्काम्बराङ्कप्रमितेष्वतीतेषु शकान्ततः । वर्षेषूदयनश्चक्रे सुबोधां लक्षणावलीम् ॥

3 Nyāya-mañjarī, p. 312 (Bib. Ind. ed.).

4 (Ratnāvatārikā, chap. IV) तथा च जयन्तः—
स्वरूपाद्भवत् कार्यं सहकार्य्युपबृंहितात् । न हि कल्पयितुं शक्तं शक्तिं etc.

5 यदत्र शक्तिसंसिद्धौ मज्जत्युदयनाद्रिपः । जयन्त हन्त का तत्र गणना त्वयि कीटके ॥

PRABHĀKARA'S THEORY OF ERROR

BY GANGANATHA JHA

PRABHĀKARA, like others, has divided cognitions into the two broad classes of 'valid' and 'invalid' cognitions; but his explanation of 'valid' and 'invalid' is entirely different from that provided by any other philosopher. That cognition he regards as 'valid' which bears directly upon its object, while 'invalid' cognition is that which does not so bear upon its object. In short, he would regard all *anubhūti*, 'apprehension,' as 'valid' and all 'remembrance' as 'invalid.' In accordance with this view Prabhākara defines 'Pramāṇa' as *anubhūti;* i. e. 'valid cognition' is apprehension, as distinguished from remembrance, which is not valid, since it stands in need of a previous apprehension and is brought about only by impressions left on the mind by that apprehension.

The question now arises—If 'apprehension' and 'valid cognition' are convertible terms, how should we account for the wrong or erroneous apprehensions that we have in our ordinary experience? For example we sometimes *apprehend* (a) a piece of shell as silver; (b) we perceive the conch as yellow, when our eye is affected with bile; (c) some derangement in vision makes us see two moons; and (d) in dreams we have the cognition of things not existent at the time. Are all these *apprehensions* valid?

Prabhākara's answer to this question is that these conceptions are not right or valid; they are erroneous; but they are erroneous, not because there is anything inherently invalid in them; but because they involve more factors than mere apprehension. The judgment 'this is silver' involves (1) the notion of 'this,' which is direct apprehension, and (2) the notion of 'silver,' which, in the absence of actual silver, can be only due to the remembrance of silver seen elsewhere,—this remembrance having been brought about by the perception of the quality of bright whiteness which is common to the thing before the eyes and the silver previously seen. Now so far as the notion of 'this' is concerned—and it is only this notion that is *apprehension*—it is quite valid; there is nothing erroneous in it; the error comes in only in the notion of 'silver,' which is of the nature of remembrance, and as such by its very nature invalid. Thus we find that, in the case cited, what is wrong and invalid is not the apprehension, but the remembrance and the mixing up of the two in the form 'this is silver.'

This explanation cannot dispose of case (b), viz. the erroneous cognition of the *white* conch as *yellow*, as there is no element of remembrance involved in it. Prabhākara's explanation of this erroneous cognition is still bolder. The notion is not erroneous, he says. We *perceive* the conch—there is nothing wrong in this; and we *perceive* the yellowness: Is this wrong? No, says Prabhākara. In any case how do we know that a certain cognition of ours is wrong? Only by finding out later, on a closer examination of the thing, that it is not as we perceived it. Now in the case of the yellow conch, the man perceives the conch as yellow,—and when he picks up the conch and looks at it closely, he still finds it to be yellow; and in as much as in actual experience his judgment, 'this conch is yellow,' is found to be in agreement with the nature of the thing as *he* perceives it, the cognition must be valid, at least so far as the man is concerned. This cognition has been likened by Prabhākara to the cognition of water as 'hot'; as a matter of fact water is not hot, it is cold, and yet it is felt as hot by reason of the heat of fire-particles hanging in it; in the same manner the conch is not yellow, it is white; and yet it is seen as yellow by reason of the yellow colour subsisting in the bile in the perceiver's eye. This cognition is further analysed: what happens is that the man perceives the conch, but fails to perceive the quality of whiteness; similarly he perceives the yellowness of the bile in his eye, but fails to perceive the substance to which that yellowness belongs. As no substance can be without qualities and no quality can subsist without a substance, the two perceptions coalesce and give rise to the notion of the yellowness as belonging to the conch.

In the next case (c) of a person seeing two moons, what happens is as follows:—Rays of light emanate from the two eyes; and by reason of some derangement in the adjustment of the action of the two eyes, the two sets of rays fall upon the moon, not simultaneously as generally happens, but at different times; so that there is no chance of the two images of the moon on the two retinas coalescing and providing the vision of a single moon; hence it is only natural that the nerves leading up from the two retinas to the brain being active at different points of time, the perception produced is that of two moons. In this case therefore there are two distinct perceptions, and both of them are right.

In dreams, case (d), the things perceived are generally real things that we have seen before, and which are remembered during sleep. So that the whole being only remembrance, it is only natural that it should be invalid. There is no direct apprehension in dreams; hence there is no valid element in them.

Thus it is found that whenever we have actual apprehension there is nothing wrong in it; error comes in only when some element of remembrance creeps into it. All cognitions *per se* are valid; and it is a misnomer to use the expression 'wrong cognition.'

[*Sources of information*—(1) *Bṛhatī*—Prabhākara's commentary on Śābara-Bhāṣya, Ms. pp. 3-7; (2) *Ṛjuvimalā*—commentary on the above, Ms. pp. 54–61; and (3) *Prakaraṇapañcikā*, Chaukhambha Sanskrit Series, pp. 32 and 63].

MĀṬHARAVṚTTI AND THE DATE OF ĪŚVARAKṚṢṆA

BY S. K. BELVALKAR

THE object of this paper is to announce the discovery of a very rare and ancient work on the Sāṅkhya philosophy and, in the light of the data furnished by it, to examine the date of Īśvarakṛṣṇa and other problems connected with the development of the Early Sāṅkhya.

In the catalogue of Sanskrit manuscripts from Gujarat, Cutch, Sindh and Khandesh compiled under the superintendence of Dr. G. Bühler, fasc. iv, Bombay (1873), on page 8 we find the entry of a Sāṅkhya work called Vyāsaprabhākara by Vyāsa. The Ms. (with another copy (2) of the same work) belonged to one Gopal Bhaṭṭa of Surat and is dated Saṁvat 1457. This Ms. was later acquired by Dr. Bühler for the Government of Bombay and it now figures as No. 107 of the Deccan College Collection of 1871-72, where however the query which followed the name of the work as given in the earlier list is omitted while Kapila instead of Vyāsa is given as the author of the work in question. So ancient a Ms. of a Sāṅkhya work ascribed to Vyāsa or to Kapila himself naturally evoked curiosity.[1] On examination however it was discovered that the work contained in the Ms. was no other than the Māṭharavṛtti of Māṭharācārya.[2]

Manuscripts of the Māṭharavṛtti are extremely rare. There is one (3) mentioned in Dr. P. Peterson's Second Report, List p. 21, and now forming No. 119 of A 1883-84, and there is another (4) with two more copies (5-6) given

1 My attention was first drawn to it by my friend Mr. R. D. Ranade M. A. now Professor of Philosophy at the Fergusson College, Poona.

2 The colophon reads—इत्याचार्येश्वरकृष्णप्रोक्तायाः सांख्यसप्तत्याः वृत्तिराचार्यमाठरकृतिः समाप्ता । स्वस्ति श्रीमनणहिलपुरे.........illegible.........श्रीकपिलमुनिना व्याहृतं सांख्यशास्त्रं वर्षलोकाधिपमुनि(*v.l.* पृथ्वीधरशर)मितेऽब्देऽखयत्कार्त्तिकादौ संवत् १४५७ वर्षे लिखितमिदम्॥ Vyāsaprabhākara seems to have been once the owner of the Ms., as his name appears on fol. 1*a*, which Dr. Bühler's Pandit seems to have mistaken for the name of the work itself.

in Bühler's Gujarat Catalogue above cited, fasc. iv, p. 10. This last belonged to one Balkrishna Joshi of Ahmedabad. No other Mss. of the work are anywhere known to exist.

Of the six Mss. of the Māṭharavṛtti above recorded, two, as just stated, are available at the Deccan College Mss. Library. The remaining four could no longer be traced. I caused careful inquiries to be made at Surat (for the second copy of 'Vyāsaprabhākara') and at Ahmedabad (for Balkrishna Joshi's three copies of the Māṭharavṛtti) but to no purpose.[1] All the more thankful must we therefore be to the accident which has made the Deccan College Library the envied possessor of the only two Mss. of this work now extant, seeing that the Māṭharavṛtti is no other than the lost original of the Sāṅkhya-kārikā-vṛtti translated into the Chinese by Paramārtha between A. D. 557 and 569.

Paramārtha[2] was a Brahman of Ujjain born in A. D. 499 who, upon the invitation of the emperor Wu-ti of the Liang dynasty, went over to China in A. D. 546 and devoted the rest of his life to the translation into Chinese of such Sanskrit works as he had brought with him from India.[3] Paramārtha died at Canton in the year 569, aged 71; and as he might be presumed to have brought with him to China only such Sanskrit works as had already an established reputation in India, we may roughly regard 500 A. D. as the *terminus ad quem* for the vṛtti which he translated into Chinese.

That this vṛtti translated into Chinese was identical with—or at any rate exhibited many points of contact

1 Professor A. B. Dhruva for instance writes from Ahmedabad to say that Balkrishna Joshi, 'through his friend or relative Uttararam Joshi, delivered many of his Mss. to Dr. Bühler; and the remnant—probably trash—was divided by his widowed niece-in-law (Balkrishna Joshi's last heiress) amongst a few Brahmans as a pious gift supported by the attractive accompaniment of a pice each!' A few months ago, at Barodā, I was shown the first few pages of a Sāṅkhya Ms. which on examination proved to be a fragment of Māṭharavṛtti. This may have been one of these pious gifts.

2 J. R. A. S., 1905, pp. 33ff.

3 In all he translated 505 different works.

with—the Bhāṣya of Gauḍapāda edited by H. H. Wilson, Oxford (1837), was suspected by Beal, Kasawara, and others long ago,[1] and is placed beyond doubt by Dr. Takakusu, who, after a searching comparison of the Bhāṣya of Gauḍapāda with the vṛtti translated into Chinese, arrives at the conclusion[2] that in citations, illustrations, and even entire passages, the coincidences between the two commentaries are so numerous and far-reaching as to preclude the possibility of their being explained away as merely accidental. This raises a chronological problem ; for, as Gauḍapāda the teacher's teacher of Śaṅkarācārya cannot be placed as early as cir. 500 A. D., and as it would be impossible to suppose that an author like Gauḍapāda could merely plagiarize, it is necessary to believe that by the time of Gauḍapāda (cir. 700 A. D.) the original vṛtti had become to such an extent defective and corrupt that Gauḍapāda could safely complete and rearrange it and give it out in an improved form as his own work. The Chinese translation does not give the name of the author of the original vṛtti ; and as this writer, whatever his name, must have lived between 546 A. D. (the date of Paramārtha's reaching China) and 450 (Dr. Takakusu's date[3] for Īśvarakṛṣṇa the author of the Kārikās), the learned doctor, rather than postulating, in the brief space of less than a hundred years (450-546), two different and important Sāṅkhya writers, simply identified[4] the author of the Kārikās with the author of the vṛtti, believing that by thus making Īśvarakṛṣṇa himself the author of both the Kārikās as well as their vṛtti he could partly take the edge off Gauḍapādācārya's subsequent appropriation of another's work as his own.

1 Max Müller : Six Systems of Indian Philosophy, p. 292.

2 Bulletin de l'E'cole Française d'Extrême-Orient, t. iv (1904), p. 24.

3 Dr. Takakusu's latest pronouncement on the subject in the J. R. A. S. for 1914, pp. 1013 ff., does not materially affect this conclusion, which however has latterly been called into question. See below p. 176.

4 Op. cit. p. 58, 60.

The present discovery of the lost original of the Chinese translation and its identification with the Māṭharavṛtti of Māṭharācārya[1] compels us to modify this conclusion in many important particulars. To begin with, we must now be prepared to admit the existence of two Gauḍapādas, one the celebrated teacher's teacher of Śaṅkarācārya and the other a namesake of his and the author of the so-called Gauḍapādabhāṣya and perhaps also of the commentary on the Uttara-gītā. It is too much to expect that the great Gauḍapāda would lend his name to a work like the Bhāṣya of Wilson's edition, which is merely a paltry abstract of the Māṭharavṛtti with an occasional addition here and there.[2] That the author of this abstract was *a* Gauḍapāda who, albeit later than the famous Gauḍapāda, must nevertheless have lived before the 11th century follows from Alberuni's reference[3] to a philosophical work composed by 'Gauḍa the anchorite' and from Maladhāri-Rājaśekhara Sūri's mention,[4] in his Ṣaḍdarśana-samuc-

1 That the Māṭharavṛtti *is* the original of the Chinese follows from the close verbal correspondence that runs through them page after page, such occasional variation as is to be found in the Sanskrit original and the French translation of the Chinese translation of the same in the Bulletin for 1904, pp. 978-1064, being no more than what could be explained away as the result of such genuine differences in reading as exist even in the Corean and Japanese recensions of the Chinese text itself. The point will be fully dealt with in my forthcoming edition of the work; an instance or two must therefore here suffice. The introduction to Kārikā 1 in the Gauḍapādabhāṣya does not contain the dramatic dialogue between Kapila and Āsuri; but the French on p. 979 of the Bulletin—"O Āsuri, tu t'amuses à mener la vie d'un maître de maison!" etc.—is a word-for-word translation of the original—भो भो आसुरे । रमसे गृहस्थधर्मेण । etc. Similarly, the Māṭharavṛtti (see below, p. 176, note 2) gives, like the Chinese text, a gloss on the last three Kārikās, which is absent in Gauḍapāda.

2 Dates make it impossible that the Māṭharavṛtti (ante 500 A. D.) be an enlargement of the Gauḍapādabhāṣya (post 700 A. D.), and the close correspondence of the two precludes the possibility of their being independent works.

3 *India*, Vol. 1. p. 132 (Trübner Series).

4 तर्कग्रन्था एतदीया माठरस्तत्त्वकौमुदी । गौडपादात्रेयतन्त्रे सांख्यसप्ततिसूत्रयुक् ॥ Maladhāri-Rājaśekhara Sūri lived about A. D. 1350.

caya, of a Sāṅkhya writer Gauḍapāda as distinct from Māṭhara. As often happens in such cases, the so-called Gauḍapādabhāṣya, the abridgment of the Māṭharavṛtti, effectively supplanted the older work.[1]

More important than this is the light which the Māṭharavṛtti throws upon the vexed question of the date of Īśvarakṛṣṇa. Dr. Takakusu assigns him to cir. 450 A. D., and the main points in his argument[2] may be thus summarised: (1) Between 546 and 569 A. D. Paramārtha, the Chinese translator, wrote a life of the celebrated Buddhist philosopher Vasubandhu, and he is thus our earliest authority for Vasubandhu. Paramārtha mentions Vasubandhu's death at the age of 80, which must have taken place before Paramārtha left for China. This gives cir. 420-450 for Vasubandhu. (2) Vasubandhu's teacher Buddhamitra, Paramārtha tells us, was defeated by the Sāṅkhya philosopher Vindhyavāsa, who however died before Vasubandhu could make amends for his teacher's discomfiture. Vindhyavāsa was thus an older contemporary of Vasubandhu and is known to have composed a work on Sāṅkhya. Elsewhere Vindhyavāsa is described as a contemporary of the Gupta king (Bālāditya) and is spoken of as a pupil of Vṛṣagaṇa or Vārṣagaṇya, while another (less reliable) account of a hundred and fifty years later makes a pupil of Vārṣagaṇya the author of a work called *Hiraṇya-saptati*. Putting all these accounts together we get Vindhyavāsa an older contemporary of Vasubandhu and the pupil of Vṛṣa or Vārṣagaṇya as the author of a Sāṅkhya work called Hiraṇya-saptati. (3) Now the commentary translated into Chinese, while explaining the phrase शिष्यपरम्परयागतम् in the last but one Kārikā, makes Īśvarakṛṣṇa, the author of the *Sāṅkhya-saptati*,

1 Mss. of Gauḍāpada's Bhāṣya are also scarce, though the work has been published four or five times: Wilson (1837), Tookaram Tatya's Reprint (1887), Jibanand (date ?), and Ben. Sk. Series (1906²). I have also to report a Bengali translation of the same. Of Mss. I have so far secured and collated only four.

2 J. R. A. S., 1905, pp. 33 ff.

the pupil of Po-p'o-li; and if we were once to make the supposition that Hiraṇya-saptati is a byname for Sāṅkhya-saptati and that the Chinese word Po-p'o-li can somehow stand for Varṣa,[1] there then remains nothing in the way of the eventual identification of Vindhyavāsa with Īśvarakṛṣṇa, which gives for the latter the date assigned by Takakusu.

Īśvarakṛṣṇa's date thus depends upon that of Vasubandhu and upon the identity between Īśvarakṛṣṇa and Vindhyavāsa the rival of Vasubandhu. Now the date of Vasubandhu has been recently made the subject of much discussion, a convenient summary of which is given in Vincent Smith's Early History, 3rd ed. (1914), pp. 328-34. And although, in the very nature of things, it is vain to expect that any one theory could satisfactorily explain all the names and allusions occurring in the Chinese reports of Paramārtha, of Hiuen Tsang and his pupil Kuei-chi, and of Itsing and others, it is clear that the general trend of the evidence is for assigning Vasubandhu somewhere between A. D. 280 and 360; and Vindhyavāsa by all accounts was Vasubandhu's older contemporary.

But it seems to me that Vindhyavāsa cannot be identified with Īśvarakṛṣṇa. As we learn from Māṭhara, the Sanskrit original of Po-p'o-li, the teacher of Īśvarakṛṣṇa, is Devala[2], and not Vṛsa or Vṛṣagaṇa, and this disturbs one factor of the identity. Next as to the Hiraṇya-saptati being a byname for Sāṅkhya-saptati there is no positive proof for it except that in the interest of our identity we would rather wish that it were so. This is arguing in a circle. We have reasons to suppose that the accounts of the Chinese pilgrims

1 Takakusu's procedure here (Bulletin, 1904, p. 30) is a mere *tour de force*. He equates Po-p'o-li, on the ground of a presumed scribal error, with Po-so-li and then, by another error of the scribe, with Po-li-so, Va-li-so, Varṣa.

2 The vṛtti on शिष्यपरम्परयागतम् etc. in the Sanskrit original runs thus—कपिलादासुरिणाप्राप्तमिदं ज्ञानमतः पञ्चशिखेन तस्माद्भार्गवोलूकवाल्मीकिहारीतदेवलप्रभृतीनागतम्। ततस्तेभ्य ईश्वरकृष्णेन प्राप्तम्। तदेव षष्टितन्त्रमार्याभिः संक्षिप्तम्। Compare Bulletin (1904), p. 1059-60, for the French translation of the Chinese, which is rather defective.

are not always strictly accurate, and Kuei-chi (to judge from the French translation of his statements on the question given by Dr. Takakusu in the Bulletin for 1904 pp. 38-39) does not profess to be narrating sober truth unmixed by legendary elements. It is permissible therefore to suppose that the Hiraṇya-saptati was a distinct work, so named either because (as Kuei-chi himself affirms) the work brought to its author a reward of three lacs of gold, or possibly because the work had something to do with *Hiraṇya* or *Hiraṇya-garbha* (one of the cardinal principles of the Sāṅkhya) just as Vasubandhu's rival work, Paramārtha-saptati, had something to do with the *parama-artha* or supreme reality, whatever that might mean for the Buddhist. It seems to me more probable however to regard the Hiraṇya-saptati of Vindhyavāsa[1] as some kind of a commentary on Īśvarakṛṣṇa's Sāṅkhya-saptati; and this will afford the most natural explanation of the confusion which some compilers of catalogues[2] and other writers[3] make between the author of the Kārikās and of the commentary on them. It must also be borne in mind that the name Vṛṣa, Vṛṣagaṇa, or Vārṣagaṇya does not occur in the *guru-paramparā* from Kapila to Īśvarakṛṣṇa as preserved in the Māṭharavṛtti.[4] Clearly therefore Vindhyavāsa and his teacher Vṛṣa or Vārṣagaṇya have to be ranked amongst the successors of Īśvarakṛṣṇa;[5] and as Vindhya-

1 It is worth noting that Bhoja's Rājamārtaṇḍa has preserved two quotations from Vindhyavāsin *apud* Yogasūtra iv. 22—सत्त्वतप्यत्वमेवपुरुषतप्यत्वम् and बिम्बे प्रतिबिम्बमानच्छाया सदृशच्छायान्तरोद्भवः प्रतिबिम्बशब्देनोच्यते. This is clearly the language of a commentator.

2 J. R. A. S., 1905, p. 47, note 3.

3 Loc. cit. pp. 162, 355, 356.

4 See note 2 on p. 176 above. Some of these names are also mentioned in the Ṣaḍdarśana-samuccaya—सांख्यानां मतवक्तारः कपिलासुरिभार्गवाः । उलूकः पञ्चशिखश्चेश्वरकृष्णस्तु शास्त्रकृत् ॥

5 This is not essential for the argument. That a commentary should be written on the Kārikās and the same translated into Chinese as early as cir. 560 carries the date of Īśvarakṛṣṇa more than a couple of centuries earlier, especially if it is remebered that the Māṭharavṛtti is confused and often misunderstands the Kārikās. Compare below, p.181, n. 2.

vāsa was an older contemporary of Vasubandhu, and as Vasubandhu is more probably to be placed cir. 300 A. D., this might give for Īśvarakṛṣṇa a date as early as the first or the first half of the second century of the Christian era.

Īśvarakṛṣṇa's Kārikās is the earliest work on the Sāṅkhya philosophy that has been preserved to us; but the Sāṇkhya as a philosophy is presupposed by Buddhism[1] and in the Mahābhārata, Sāṅkhya is *par excellence* the philosophy of the Epic,[2] occupying therein the same position of pre-eminence that Vedānta did in later times. Sāṅkhya in fact claims a pedigree still higher, seeing that the latest phase of Upaniṣad thought is co-eval with the beginnings of Sāṅkhya speculation, and even exhibits doctrines and terminology that later became exclusively characteristic of the Sāṅkhya.[3] Kapila is a name hallowed by

1 Buddhistic books acknowledge Kapila as a teacher of remote antiquity and the 4th of the 62 current heresies mentioned in the first Suttanta of the *Dīgha Nikāya* Garbe (Sāṃkhya Philosophie, p. 5, n. 1) identifies with the Sāṅkhya. It is sometimes objected to this (e. g. Rhys Davids: American Lectures on Buddhism, pp. 25ff.) that the heresy in question regards the soul and the *world* as both eternal, and not the soul and the *Prakṛti*; but that is due to the *schema* under which the 62 heresies are grouped by the Buddha. Max Müller (Six Systems, p. 314, Chips, i. 226, and elsewhere) and Oldenberg (Buddha, Eng. Trans. p. 92, note) fail to see any real correspondence between Buddhism and the Sāṅkhya, while Jacobi in his paper on the "Ursprung des Buddhismus aus dem Sāṃkhya-Yoga" has tried to prove that in its psychological technicalities at any rate Sāṅkhya must have preceded Buddhism. If we bear in mind that the original Sāṅkhya need not necessarily have been the Sāṅkhya of the Kārikās any more than Upaniṣadic Vedānta the Vedānta of Śaṅkarācārya or the original Buddhistic *nirvāṇa* the nihilistic *nirvāṇa* of Nāgārjuna, there need not be felt any more hesitation in admitting the priority of Sāṅkhya over Buddhism. Compare Dahlmann, *Nirvāṇa*, pp. 128 ff.

2 Compare ये चाप्यन्ये मोक्षकामा मनुष्यास्तेषामेतद्दर्शनं ज्ञानदृष्टम् (ii. 323. 86), and xii. 307 towards the end. The Sāṅkhyas are often described in the epic as मार्गज्ञाः, कुशलाः, महाप्राज्ञाः, etc. and the epic cosmology is pervaded through and through with Sāṅkhya technicalities.

3 Compare Garbe: *Die Sāṃkhya Philosophie*, pp. 18–21. *Maitrī*, *Śvetāśvatara*, and *Praśna* are the main Upaniṣads to be considered in this connection.

hoary tradition and his system of philosophy, before it assumed its stereotyped form in the Kārikās of Īśvarakṛṣṇa, must have undergone, in the course of centuries of its historical existence, several processes of reduction, modification or amplification for which no definite documentary evidence is forth-coming. There are a few vague and scattered hints, and in what remains of this paper an attempt will be made, on the basis of such hints, to determine the chief land-marks in this progressive philosophical evolution.

The Kārikās of Īśvarakṛṣṇa profess to give in essence the same doctrine as that contained in the Ṣaṣṭitantra[1] save its illustrative anecdotes and its argumentative portions. As to the exact nature and authorship of this Ṣaṣṭitantra there is still a good deal of confusion. Three quotations[2] from the work at the most are preserved in later commentaries, and from them it cannot be decided whether the work was in prose or verse; and as to its authorship, while from the Bhāmatī one might be led to ascribe it to Vārṣagaṇya, the Chinese tradition as quoted by Takakusu (Bulletin, 1904, p. 59) expressly credits Pañcaśikha with that honour. As usual in such cases Dr. Schrader[3] has sought to explain away the contradictions by taking refuge in the supposition of two different Ṣaṣṭitantras, one in prose and belonging to Vārṣagaṇya[4] and the other in verse of undermentioned authorship, but presumably older.

1 Compare Kārika 72 (73)—

सप्तत्यां किल येऽर्थास्तेऽर्थाः कृत्स्नस्य षष्टितन्त्रस्य ।
आख्यायिकाविरहिताः परवादविवर्जिताश्चापि ॥

2 The first is the stanza गुणानां परमं रूपं etc. cited in Vyāsa's Bhāṣya on Yoga-sūtra iv. 13 as expressly coming from the Ṣaṣṭitantra; the same stanza is quoted in the Bhāmatī to Brahma-sūtra ii. 1. 3 as belonging to वार्षगण्य, the योगशास्त्रं व्युत्पादयिता. The second occurs in Gauḍapāda's and Māṭhara's com. to Kārikā 17—तथा चोक्तं षष्टितन्त्रे पुरुषाधिष्ठितं प्रधानं प्रवर्तते । The last, not quite so explicit, occurs *apud* Kārikā 50 in Gauḍapāda (शास्त्रान्तरे) and in Māṭhara (ग्रन्थान्तरे).

3 Z. D. M. G. for 1914, vol. 68, 1, p. 110.

4 Besides the stanza गुणानां परमं रूपं two other quotations from Vārṣagaṇya, both in prose, have been hitherto traced, one in the Vyāsa-bhāṣya to Yoga-sūtra iii. 53 (मूर्तिव्यवधिजातिभेदाभावान्नास्ति मूलपृथक्त्वम्) and another in Vācaspati's com. to Kārikā 47 (पञ्चपर्वाऽविद्या).

When we have no definite information regarding one Ṣaṣṭitantra it is too much to ask us to believe in the existence of two works bearing identical names. If, following the Chinese accounts, Vārṣagaṇya is to be regarded as the teacher of Vindhyavāsa, the older contemporary of Vasubandhu, it is then not likely that the work of so late a writer as Vārṣagaṇya should have served as the basis for Īśvarakṛṣṇa's Kārikās; and in that case Vācaspati's assigning the stanza गुणानां परमं रूपं to Vārṣagaṇya—a stanza mentioned in the Vyāsabhāṣya as coming from the Ṣaṣṭitantra—must be put down as an evident oversight. The question of the authorship of the Ṣaṣṭitantra must therefore, for the present, remain undecided.

Fortunately for us the *Ahirbudhnya-Saṁhitā* recently published by the Adyar Library gives us, in chapter xii, stanzas 18–30, a rather detailed notice of the contents of the Ṣaṣṭitantra. It ascribes the work to the 'great and omniscient sage' and explains that the Ṣaṣṭitantra was so called because it had sixty topics or sections: thirty-two devoted to what we might term metaphysics (*Prākṛtam maṇḍalam*) and twenty-eight to Yoga and ethics (*Vaikṛtam maṇḍalam*). The notice is interesting[1] because it presents to us a phase in the development of the Sāṅkhya philosophy when Sāṅkhya and Yoga were not absolutely separated from each other[2] and when the system contained, along with its positive contribution to philosophy, a detailed examination with a view to refutation (the *paravāda* of Īśvarakṛṣṇa's last Kārikā[3]) of the various 'first

1 For a critical study of the question see Dr. Schrader's article, 'Das Ṣaṣṭitantra' in Z. D. M. G. for 1914, vol. 68, 1, pp. 100–110; and the same writer's Introduction to the Ahirbudhnya-Saṁhita, p. 110 ff.

2 It was probably the Yoga-sūtras of Patañjali (cir. 150 B. C.) that raised the Yoga to the dignity of an independent Darśana; and if so, the Ṣaṣṭitantra must be placed prior to B. C. 150. Many passages from the Sāntiparvan of the Mahābhārata suggest the contents of the Ṣaṣṭitantra.

3 What the *ākhyāyikās* alluded to in the Kārikā can be one can very well imagine from the Mahābhārata xii. 307. The whole adhyāya purports to be *Sāṅkhya-nirūpaṇa* and affords room for many an illustrative anecdote here and there.

principles' adduced by the earlier darśana-kāras,[1] such as, Brahma, Puruṣa, Śakti, Niyati, Kāla, Akṣara, Prāṇa, Sāmi or Svāmin, Bhūtas, etc. As Īśvarakṛṣṇa expressly tells us that he had retained the doctrinal part of the Ṣaṣṭitantra entirely unchanged, and as Īśvarakṛṣṇa's Kārikās are avowedly atheistic,[2] we must imagine that, after a critical review of the different first principles, the Ṣaṣṭitantra, in supramundane matters like the existence of God etc., came to a purely negative conclusion.

The Mahābhārata[3] presents to us the same intimate relation between Sāṅkhya and Yoga as the Ṣaṣṭitantra ;[4] but we can hardly say that the Sāṅkhya of the Mahābhārata is atheistic. The difference between the traditional Sāṅkhya of the Kārikās and the Mahābhārata Sāṅkhya can well be seen from the Bhagavadgītā where, in addition to the doctrine of the three guṇas (chapters xiv and xvii in particular), of causation through *pariṇāma* (xiii. 19–20, xviii. 14, and elsewhere), of the *akartṛtva* of the Puruṣa (iii. 27 f., xiv. 19, etc.), and of the cosmic evolution through Ahaṅkāra, Buddhi, and the five Bhūtas[4] (vii. 4), we find,

1 That there were regular darśanas with Kāla, Svabhāva, Niyati, etc. (cp. Śvetāśvatara i. 2) as first principles is well brought out in Dr. Otto Schrader's Inaugural dissertation, "Ueber den Stand der Ind. Philosophie zur Zeit Mahāvīras und Buddhas."

2 For the brilliant recovery from Gauḍapāda-bhāṣya and Māṭharavṛtti of the missing Sāṅkhya Kārikā 62 (कारणमीश्वरमेके पुरुषं कालं परे स्वभावं वा । प्रजाः कथं निर्गुणतः व्यक्तः कालः स्वभावश्च ॥) dealing with the subject, see 'Sanskrit Research,' vol. i, no. 2, pp. 107—117. One notices from this how very confused and disarranged the Māṭharavṛtti had been by A. D. 500.

3 My references throughout are to the Kumbhakonam edition based on South Indian texts and printed at the Nirnaya Sagar, Bombay.

4 नास्ति सांख्यसमं ज्ञानं नास्ति योगसमं बलम् ।
तावुभावेकचर्यौ तावुभावनिधनौ स्मृतौ ॥
पृथक् पृथक् प्रपश्यन्ति येऽप्यबुद्धिरता नराः ।
वयं तु राजन् पश्याम एकमेव तु निश्चयात् ॥ शान्तिपर्व ३२१ । २–३

5 Some minor difference in the enumeration of the eight-fold Prakṛti, which the commentators try to gloss over, serves only to strengthen the view of the primitive nature of this Sāṅkhya system.

so to say, a sort of a theistic apex to the system in Śrīkṛṣṇa or Parameśvara,[1] from whom the beginningless Puruṣa and Prakṛti are said to proceed as parallel 'modes' or manifestations (vii. 5f, xiii. 19, etc.). Other accounts from the Mahābhārata somewhat vary in detail. In fact the Epic itself admits[2] the existence of minor differences in the Sāṅkhya school; but the main conclusion as to the theistic nature of the Epic Sāṅkhya stands unshaken.

In his successive studies on the subject[3] Dahlmann has urged many a cogent reason to prove that the Sāṅkhya of the Mahābhārata—*ānvīkṣikī brahma-vidyā*, to give it its other significant title—was the parent of three parallel systems: 1 the classical Vedānta with the Māyā doctrine, 2 the classical Sāṅkhya of the Kārikās, and 3 the primitive form of Buddhism; and it is difficult to resist the temptation to accept this conclusion in the main. Accordingly it would seem that the theistic nature of the Epic Sāṅkhya was later (e. g. in the Ṣaṣṭitantra) deliberately dropped and the system reduced, by stern logic,[4] to its bare negative character. Later still, the intimate combination of the Sāṅkhya with the Yoga was dissolved, the two figuring thereafter as independent systems, the Yoga accepting the theism renounced by the Sāṅkhya.

Dahlmann stops with the Epic Sāṅkhya; but it itself is undoubtedly a composite product, as is plain even from its composite name in the Epic: *ānvīkṣikī brahma-vidyā*. It is *ānvīkṣikī* or based on reason in preference to revelation; and it treats of *Brahma* or the highest spiritual prin-

1 Compare—पञ्चविंशतिमो विष्णुः (xii. 308–38) and again—

पञ्चविंशतिमस्तात.....................।
अनादिनिधनोनन्तः सर्वदर्शी निरामयः ॥ शान्ति० ३१० । ३९

2 Compare (xii. 323. 58 ff.)—

पञ्चविंशं यदेतच्चे प्रोक्तं ब्राह्मणसत्तम ।
तदहं न तथा वेद्मि तद्भवान्वक्तुमर्हति ॥ etc.

3 Das Mahābhārata (1895), Nirvāṇa (1896), Genesis des Mahābhārata (1899), and Sāṁkhya Philosophie (1902).

4 Logic, or an explanation of supra-mundane things on the basis of reason also, was an early and well-known characteristic of the Sāṅkhya. Cp. the Vedānta-sūtra description of the Sāṅkhya Pradhāna as *aśabda* I. i. 5, and *ānumānika* I. iii. 3.

ciple very much after the fashion of the Upaniṣads. We might imagine that the cosmological problem with which philosophy began in India was worked out in some of the primitive Upaniṣads from within outwards,[1] while it was the reverse process from *mṛdādi-vikāras* back to the underlying noumena that was pursued by those other Upaniṣads where it is usual to see the beginnings of Sāṅkhya philosophy. Schrader in his book cited above at p. 181, note 1, argues for the thesis that it was the first adhyāya of the Śvetāśvatara, and especially the passage भोक्ता भोग्यं प्रेरितारं च मत्वा सर्वं प्रोक्तं त्रिविधं ब्रह्ममेतत् which formed the nucleus of all later Sāṅkhya speculation. Others choose other passages. Be that as it may, it should be quite evident that this primitive Sāṅkhya did not yet possess pronounced opinions even on such vital question as the unity or plurality of souls or of the absolute unrelatedness of the soul with the matter or Prakṛti. And hence resulted the blending together of the primitive Vedānta and the primitive Sāṅkhya of the Upaniṣads into the full-fledged system of the Mahābhārata with its added theistic apex.

We have accordingly reasons to assume the following broad stages in the development of the Sāṅkhya philosophy: 1 the primitive and undefined Sāṅkhya of the Upaniṣads; 2 its alliance with the equally primitive Vedānta of the Upaniṣads resulting in the Sāṅkhya-Yoga or the *Ānvīkṣikī brahma-vidyā* of the Mahābhārata; 3 the carrying out to their logical conclusions the basic principles of the Sāṅkhya, viz. a material first principle and the doctrine of evolution,[2] leading to a denial of theism; 4. the bifurca-

1 Introspection and observation of the psychic states of dream, sleep, trance, etc. supplied the material of this philosophy.

2 The South Indian recension of the Mahābhārata has preserved (xii. 326-28) a badly mutilated prose dialogue between Kapila and Āsuri, his first pupil, where we find the following significant description of the process whereby the Non-manifest becomes the Manifest: अव्यक्तं व्यक्तमुपलक्ष्यते यथर्तवोऽमूर्तयस्तेषु पुष्पफलैर्व्यक्तिरुपलक्ष्यते तद्वद्व्यक्तगुणैरुपलक्ष्यते—"As the seasons, themselves non-manifest, make their presence manifest in and through the flowers and the fruits, even so does the Non-manifest through the qualities of the Manifest."

tion of the system on this ground into *nirīśvara* and *seśvara* or Sāṅkhya and Yoga; and 5 its assuming a stereotyped form in the Kārikās of Īśvarakṛṣṇa. Then followed a long period of lull broken in by an occasional digest or a commentary until we come to Vijñānabhikṣu who, strangely enough, tried to retrace the steps and turn the system into the *ānvīkṣikī brahma-vidyā* of the Mahābhārata, which in fact was its earliest systematic starting-point.

Space forbids any very detailed treatment of these stages by citing illustrative texts bearing upon each: nor is that here necessary. It is enough to know that, through all these twenty-five and more centuries of the historical existence of the Sāṅkhya, the system was not stagnant, but that there were some inner changes and development going on. And the same should be true in the case of every philosophical system with a history. Indian commentators as a rule lack this historical perspective. As truth is—or ought to be—one, and as great Sages, through their instinctive vision, cannot but have perceived that one truth, all texts early and late must, in the opinion of these commentators, mean the same thing. Hence their frantic attempts at a *samanvaya* or securing harmony in the texts. But this method, perfectly intelligible as it is to the eye of faith, must give way before the light of reason. We must in other words learn to study our philosophy historically; and it may be that, after this alliance with reason, faith could be based on foundations all the more deep and durable.

History and Archæolgy

VIKRAMA ERA

By D. R. BHANDARKAR

IT is not the object of this article to discuss all the questions connected with this era. I intend here touching upon the theory that has recently been propounded regarding its origin and giving the latest information available from epigraphic sources.

According to tradition Vikrama Saṁvat was founded by a king called Vikramāditya who is presumed to have flourished cir. 57 before Christ. This tradition was, no doubt, accepted by many scholars and antiquarians when Indian epigraphy was in its infancy. But with the find of many inscriptions it had to be rejected. An attempt, however, is recently being made to revive this theory and proof is being adduced to show that there was a king of the name of Vikramāditya in the first century before Christ. It was first broached by Rao Bahadur C. V. Vaidya in an article published in the *Indian Review*, December 1909. The same view has been put forth by Mahāmahopādhyāya Haraprasad Shastri in his paper on the Mandasor inscription of Naravarman.[1] It has, therefore, become necessary to reconsider this question and find out how far their evidence is trustworthy. They both rely on a verse from Hāla's *Gāthā-saptaśatī* (v. 64) which runs thus—

Saṁvāhaṇa-suha-rasa-tosieṇa denteṇa tuha kare lakkham ।
Calaṇeṇa Vikkamāitta-cariam aṇusikkhiaṁ tissā ॥

Evidently this verse makes mention of Vikramāditya and refers to his munificent nature. And as Hāla, the author of the *Gāthā-saptaśatī*, is ordinarily spoken of as a Śātavāhana, and as this name occurs in the dynastic list of the Āndhrabhṛtyas given in the Purāṇas, and is placed there before that of Gautamīputra Śātakarṇi who, we know, lived about 125 A. D., it is argued that the work was composed about the beginning of the first century after Christ. And when such a work alludes to Vikramāditya,

1 *Ep. Ind.* Vol XII . p. 320.

it is concluded that there was really a king of this name living in the first century B. C., as reported by the tradition. Hence both Mr. Vaidya and M. M. Haraprasad Shastri hold that the tradition gives a correct account of the origin of the Vikrama era and that it was, therefore, initiated by a king called Vikramāditya.

Now even supposing for the moment that there was such a king as Vikramāditya living circa 57 B. C., it does not necessarily follow that the era was founded by him. It is true that even in inscriptions the era is associated with the name of Vikramāditya. But these are records of a late period, and, in fact, it is in Amitagati's *Subhāṣita-ratna-sandoha*[1] composed in Vikrama Saṁ. 1050 that we hear for the first time of a prince Vikrama in connection with it; and from the actual wording of the date by this Jaina author it seems that the era was believed in his time not to have been founded by Vikramāditya but rather started to commemorate his death. All the earlier inscriptions going back to the 5th century A. D. give an entirely different name for the era. What that name is will be stated further on, but it is sufficient here to say that they give not even the least inkling of its being associated with Vikramāditya. If this is what epigraphy tells us, it is rash to assume that the era was known to be connected with this king even long prior to Vikrama Saṁ. 1050. And if, as we know from epigraphy, this era had an altogether different name and had absolutely no connection with Vikramāditya, it is not reasonable at all to infer that it was established by him.

But is it a fact that the *Gāthā-saptaśatī* was such an early work as has been assumed? In the first place, that its author, Hāla, was a Śātavāhana is a mere tradition and must be set aside like all other traditions about the ancient literates of India. Introductory verse 13 of Bāṇa's *Harṣa-carita*, no doubt, speaks of a Śātavāhana having composed a *Kośa* of songs, but there are no grounds to

1 R. G. Bhandarkar's *Second Report* (1882-83), p. 228.

suppose that this *Kośa* is Hāla's *Sapta-śatī*, as has been well pointed out by Prof. Weber.[1] The internal evidence afforded by the work points, on the other hand, to a much later date for its composition. Only two points may be here noticed. The first is the reference to Kṛṣṇa and Rādhikā contained in verse I. 89, and the second to a week-day, Tuesday, in III. 61. The earliest mention of Rādhikā that I have been able to trace is in the *Pañcatantra*[2] which was compiled in the 5th century after Christ. Similarly the practice of citing the week-day in dates or for other general purposes came into vogue in the 9th century, though the earliest instance of its use is found in the Eraṇ inscription of Budhagupta dated A. D. 484.[3] And we shall not be far wrong if we assign Hāla of the *Gāthā-saptaśatī* to the commencement of the 6th century. If we take this to be his period, there is nothing strange in our finding a verse, in his anthology, descriptive of the liberality of Vikramāditya. Because whether we take this Vikramāditya to be Candragupta II of the Gupta dynasty with Sir Ramkrishna Bhandarkar[4] or with his grandson Skandagupta with Prof. K. B. Pathak,[5] he cannot be pushed later than A. D. 475. And it is quite possible that after the death of this Vikramāditya his generosity stuck to the memory of the people and became the subject of encomium with subsequent poets. Thus we find a reference to Vikramāditya's liberality not only in the work of Hāla but also in one of the introductory verses (v. 10) of the *Vāsavadattā* by Subandhu, who has to be placed about the close of the 6th century A. D. at the latest.

The theory that Vikramāditya was the originator of the Vikrama Saṁvat must, therefore, be given up, and the sooner we consign it to the region of oblivion, the better. Let us now see what the inscriptions have to say regarding

1 *Ueber das Saptaçatakam des Hāla*, pp. 2-4.
2 *Pañcatantra I* (Bom. Sk. Series No. IV), p. 38.
3 *Jour. R. A. S.*, 1912, pp. 1044-5.
4 *Jour.* B. B. R. A. S., Vol. XX. p. 398.
5 *Meghadūta* (Second Edition), Intro. p. xi.

the origin of this era. In 1885 an inscription was discovered by Dr. J. F. Fleet at Mandasor, the principal town of the district of the same name of Scindia's Dominions in the Western Malwa Division of Central India. It contains two dates, the first of which is expressed in the words—

> *Malavānāṁ gaṇa-sthityā yāte śata-catuṣṭaye* ।
> *tri-navaty-adhike'bdānāṁ*—

Though the credit of finding the inscription certainly belongs to Dr. Fleet, Dr. P. Peterson was the first to publish this date and demonstrate that it was a year of the Vikrama era. The latter translated it by—"when four hundred and ninety-three years from the establishment [in the country ?] of the tribes of Mālavas had passed away."[1] Dr. Fleet's rendering of the verse is—"when, by (*the reckoning from*) the tribal constitution of the Mālavas, four centuries of years, increased by ninety-three, had elapsed."[2]

Soon thereafter, another inscription from Mandasor was published by Dr. Fleet, giving the date in the words—

> *Pañcasu śateṣu śaradāṁ yāteṣvekānna-navatisahiteṣu* ।
> *Mālava-gaṇa-sthiti-vaśāt*—

The last phrase Fleet translated by 'from (the establishment of) the supremacy of the tribal constitution of the Mālavas,'[3] adding in a note that 'it is very difficult to find a really satisfactory meaning' for the word *vaśāt* in the passage.

Now, in the first place, it is not permissible to take *sthiti* in the sense of *sthāpanā* (=constitution) as both Drs. Peterson and Fleet have done. Secondly, even if we take the word in that sense, it does not suit the expression *Mālava-gaṇa-sthiti-vaśāt* of the second Mandasor inscription. For what is meant by saying that five hundred and eighty-nine years had elapsed in consequence of (*vaśāt*) the

1 *Jour. B. B. R. A. S.*, Vol. XVI. p. 381.

2 *Ind. Ant.*, Vol. XV. p. 201; *Gupta Inscrs.*, p. 87.

3 *Gupta Inscrs.*, p. 158.

tribal constitution of the Mālavas? Prof. Kielhorn obviates this difficulty by taking the phrase to mean "by, or according to, the reckoning of the Mālavas." He thus makes *gaṇa* equivalent to *gaṇanā*, which is objectionable. For, the word *gaṇa* has never the sense of *gaṇanā*, and when placed in juxtaposition with *Mālava*, must signify 'a tribe' and 'a tribe' only.

In 1913 a third inscription was found at Mandasor. It was discovered by me during my touring season 1912–13. The date of this record is set forth in the verse—

Śrī(r)-Mālava-gaṇ-āmnāte praśaste Kṛta-saṁjñite [।]
Eka-ṣaṣṭhy-adhike prāpte samā-śata-catuṣṭaye [॥]

In this verse there are two expressions which are worthy of consideration. The first is *Mālava-gaṇ-āmnāte*, which doubtless corresponds to *Mālavānaṁ gaṇa-sthityā* and *Mālava-gaṇa-sthiti-vaśāt* of the first two Mandasor inscriptions. Now, what does *Mālava-gaṇ-āmnāta* signify? The natural sense of *āmnāya*, as specified e. g. in the *Amarakośa*, is *saṁpradāya* (=traditional usage). The phrase must therefore mean "traditionally handed down by the Mālava tribe." This, I think, is clear and indisputable, and the other two similar phrases must be so interpreted as to correspond to this. The word *gaṇa* must, therefore, be taken to signify 'a tribe' in all the three expressions, and *sthiti* of one inscription to be equivalent to *āmnāya* of the other two. The word *sthiti* must thus mean some such thing as 'a settled rule or usage', which, doubtless, is one of its senses given by the St. Petersburg dictionary. This lexicon even quotes Sanskrit texts in support of this meaning, but does not at all give the word the sense of *sthāpanā* (=constitution, establishment), which is noteworthy.

The second expression in the verse cited above is *Kṛta-saṁjñite*, which qualifies the phrase expressing the date. As the word *saṁjñita* shows, the year 461, which is the date, is itself intended to be called Kṛta. But, as indicated by *Śrī-Mālava-gaṇ-āmnāta*, the date is clearly a year of the Vikrama era. Obviously, therefore, Kṛta appears to be the name of the years of this era. There were at least two instances of the occurrence of the term Kṛta in this sense in inscriptions before the discovery of the new Mandasor epigraph, but its real significance was not apprehended. They are the Bījaygaḍh stone pillar inscription of Viṣṇuvardhana, and the Gaṅgdhār stone inscription of Viśvavarman. In the first the date is specified in the words *Kṛteṣu caturṣu varṣa-śateṣvaṣṭā-viṅ(ṁ)śeṣu 400 20 8, etc.*[1] The second sets forth the date in the verse: *Yāteṣu catuḥ(r)ṣu Kri(Kṛ)teṣu śateṣu sau*[*m*]*-yeṣvāśīta-sottara-padeṣviha vatsa*[*reṣu*].[2] Dr. Fleet, who has edited both of these records, translates the word *Kṛteṣu* by "fully complete," but admits that it involves a straining. Besides, with this meaning the word is made redundant by *yāteṣu*, which is used along with it in the second inscription. But now that we know that Kṛta was the name of Vikrama Saṁvat, the occurrence of the term in the Bijaygaḍh and Gaṅgdhār records becomes perfectly clear and intelligible.

In connection with this discussion it is necessary to take into consideration a fourth inscription, which I discovered in December 1915 at Nagarī, seven miles north of Chitorgaṛh in the Udaipur State, Rājputānā. The most important part of it consists in the specification of the date, which has been expressed in the following words:

Kṛteṣu caturṣu varṣa-śateṣu ekāśīty-uttareṣvasyāṁ Mālava-pūrvvāyāṁ 400 80 1 Kārttika-śukla-pañcamyām.

The first portion of the date speaks of four hundred and eighty-one Kṛta years as having elapsed at the time of the gift recorded in the inscription. There can be no doubt that the term Kṛta of the Nagarī epigraph also has to be taken in the sense of Vikrama Saṁvat and that consequently the year 481 is of the Vikrama era. The second portion of the date makes mention of the lunar day in the words: 481 *Kārttika-śukla-pañcamyāṁ*, i. e. on the 5th day of the bright half of Kārttika of the year 481. The most

1 *Gupta Inscrs.*, p. 253. 2 *Ibid.*, p. 75, ll. 19-20.

interesting expression is that which qualifies *pañcamyāṁ*, viz. *Mālava-pūrvvāyāṁ*. What is the meaning of the word *pūrva* in this expression? At first sight it seems tempting to take it in the sense in which the word has been used in the phrase *etasyāṁ pūrvāyāṁ*, which we meet with in Kuṣāna and Gupta inscriptions. But a little reflection will convince anybody that it cannot suit here, because this phrase always follows the specification of the date and not precedes it as in the present record. It is worthy of note that Apte's dictionary gives 'established, customary, of long standing' as one of the significations of *pūrva*. Unfortunately, no reference has been cited in support of it. But the sense suits here most excellently, and, what is more, the phrase *Mālava-pūrvvāyāṁ* of our record is thereby brought into consonace with the expressions *Mālavānāṁ gaṇa-sthityā*, *Mālava-gaṇa-sthiti-vaśāt* or *Mālava-gaṇāmnāte* of other inscriptions. *Mālava-pūrva* thus means "established or customary among the Mālavas." Now it deserves to be noticed that the expression *Mālava-pūrvvāyāṁ* qualifies *pañcamyāṁ (tithau)*. This, therefore, clearly shows that the Mālavas had their own peculiar system of reckoning the *tithi* of the Kṛta (i. e. Saṁvat) year. We know that the years of the Vikrama era found in the old inscriptions present different methods of computation. Thus while some are according to the Kārttikādi, others are according to the Caitrādi, system. Some *tithis* again conform to the Pūrṇimānta and some to the Amānta arrangement of the lunar months. The Mālava system may have represented one of these two pecularities or perhaps even a combination of both. Whatever the method of their computation was, this much is certain that not only the *tithis* but even the years were affected thereby. And this is the reason why we find the phrases *Mālava-gaṇa-sthiti* and *Mālava-gaṇāmnāta* used in connection with the (Vikrama) years as distinguished from the *tithis*. In the Nagarī epigraph too, the year 481 has for the same reason been expressly included in the specification of the *tithi*. As just stated, the Malavas had nothing to do with the foundation of the Vikrama era. The old name of the Vikrama eras was Kṛta, whatever that name may mean. The connection of the Mālavas with this era was only in regard to the system of reckoning the *tithis* and thereby the years also. In my paper on the Mandasor inscription of Naravarman I had suspected this, but this is now unmistakably demonstrated by the expression *Mālava-pūrvvāyāṁ* of the Nagarī record used as an adjective of *pañcamyāṁ (tithau).*

NEW LIGHT ON GUPTA ERA AND MIHIRAKULA

BY K. B. PATHAK

I propose in this paper to determine the starting point of the Gupta era with the help of Jaina authors who preceded Albērūnī, without relying in any way on the conflicting statements made by that celebrated Mahomedan writer, both as regards the origin and the epoch of the era so well known to the students of Indian epigraphy. I hope to be able to elucidate the problem, which has given rise to so much controversy, with greater precision and accuracy than have attended the efforts of those scholars who have already discussed this interesting chronological question. There are four important passages in Jaina literature. Of their value as contributions to the study of Indian history it is impossible to speak too highly. The first passage[1] is the one in which Jinasena says that he wrote in Śaka 705. This has elicited an interesting discussion and taxed to the utmost the ingenuity and learning of scholars in their attempts to identify the contemporary reigning sovereigns mentioned therein. The second, third and fourth passages are prophetic, in which future events are announced. Some of these events are historical, though they are mixed up with many legendary details. In the second passage[2] we are told by Jinasena that the Guptas reigned 231 years and were succeeded by Kalkirāja, who reigned 42 years and that his successor was Ajitañjaya. The third passage[3] is the one in which Jinasena's pupil Guṇabhadra says that Kalkirāja was the father and predecessor of Ajitañjaya, that he was a great tyrant who oppressed the world and persecuted the Jaina community of Nirgranthas, and that he reigned 40 years and died at the age of 70. As regards the date of Kalkirāja we learn from Guṇabhadra that the tyrant was born when one thousand years of the *Duḥśama kāla*, commencing from the Nirvāṇa of Mahāvīra,

1 Ind. Ant. vol. xv p. 143.

2 Ibid.

3 Given at the end of this paper.

had elapsed and when there occurred the union of a saṁvatsara with Maghā-nakṣatra, that is to say, when there occurred a Māgha-saṁvatsara. The fourth[1] passage, which is an illuminating commentary on the second and third passages is found in the *Trilokasāra*, in which Nemicandra reproduces some of these details of the story of Kalkirāja and adds that the Śaka king was born when six hundred and five years and five months had passed by from the Nirvāṇa of Mahāvīra, and that king Kalkirāja was born when three hundred and ninty four years and seven months had gone by from the rise of the Śaka king, that is, when three hundred and ninty four Śaka years and seven months had elapsed. If we add 605 years and 5 months to 394 years and 7 months—

years	months
605	5
394	7
1000 years	

we get 1000 years, the interval of time, according to Guṇabhadra and Nemicandra between the Nirvāṇa of Mahāvīra and the birth of Kalkirāja. The most interesting and important point which is worth noticing here is the fact that the date of Kalkirāja, who immediately succeeded the Guptas, is given in terms of the Śaka era; he was born when 394 Śaka years and 7 months had gone by and when, according to Guṇabhadra, there occurred a Māgha-saṁvatsara.

Before discussing the historical inferences which these facts suggest we should know the dates of the three Jaina authors on whose statements we place our reliance. Jinasena wrote in Śaka 705. He must have died about Śaka 760, the latest date which can be assigned to his unfinished work, the Ādipurāṇa; and his pupil Guṇabhadra must have completed his Uttarapurāṇa only a few years later.[2] He was far advanced in years, when after finishing the re-

1 Also given at the end of this paper.

2 See my paper entitled 'Bhartṛihari and Kumārila' Journal B. B. R. A. S., vol. XVIII p. 213.

maining chapters of the Ādipurāṇa, he undertook to write his own portion of the Mahāpurāṇa.[1] And the use of the past tense आसीत् with reference to Guṇabhadra in the concluding praśasti[2] written in the time of his pupil Lokasena clearly indicates that the former had long been gathered to his fathers by Śaka 820 (A. D. 898). It is obvious, therefore, that he wrote shortly after Śaka 760, in the latter half of the ninth century.

As regards the date of the Trilokasāra, we know that its author Nemicandra enjoyed the patronage of Cāmuṇḍarāja (A. D. 778).[3] This statement is confirmed by Nemicandra himself who, in the concluding praśasti of his Gomaṭasāra, Karmakāṇḍa, ninth chapter, thus praises Cāmuṇḍarāja—

जम्हि गुणा विस्संभा गणहरदेवादि इड्ढिपत्ताणं ।
सो अजियसेणणाहो जस्स गुरू जयउ सो राऊ ॥

[वृत्तिः] गणधरदेवादीनां ऋद्धिप्राप्तानां गुणा यस्मिन्विश्रांताः सोऽजितसेननाथो यस्य व्रतगुरुः स राजा सर्वोत्कर्षेण वर्तताम् ।

सिद्धंतुदयतडुग्गयणिम्मलवरणेमिचंदकरकलिया ।
गुणरयणभूषणंबुहि मइवेला भरउ भुवनयलं ॥

[वृत्तिः] सिद्धांतोदयाचले उदितनिर्मलवरनेमिचंद्रकिरणैर्वर्धिता गुणरत्नभूषणांबुधेश्चामुंडरायसमुद्रस्य मतिवेला भुवनतलं पूरयतु अथवा भुवने अतिशयेन प्रसरतु ।

In his Purāṇa completed in Śaka 700 Cāmuṇḍarāja tells us that he was the disciple of Ajitasena and had the title of Guṇaratnabhūṣaṇa. From Śrāvaṇa Beḷgola inscrip-

1 Compare, Uttarapurāṇa, chapter 57—

जिनसेनानुगायास्मै पुराणकवये नमः ।
गुणभद्रभदन्ताय लोकसेनार्चितांघ्रये ॥

2. Compare—

प्रत्यक्षीकृतलक्ष्यलक्षणविधिर्विश्वोपविद्यान्तरात्
सिद्धांताब्ध्यवसानयानजनितप्रागल्भ्यवृद्धेद्धधीः ।
नानानूननयप्रमाणनिपुणोगण्यैर्गुणैर्भूषितः
शिष्यः श्रीगुणभद्रसूरिरनयोरासीज्जगद्विश्रुतः ॥

3 Nagar Inscrip. 46, Epi. Car. Vol. VIII—

त्रिलोकसारप्रमुख [प्रबन्धान्]
[विरच्य सर्वान्] भुवि नेमिचन्द्रः ।
विभाति सैद्धान्तिकसार्वभौम-
श्चामुण्डरायार्चितपादपद्मः ॥

tions, we learn[1] that Cāmuṇḍarāja was the minister of king Rācamalladeva, an ornament of the Gaṅga dynasty, which was uplifted by the sage Siṁhanandin. This was the Gaṅga king Rācamalla IV who was reigning in A. D. 977.[2] These facts are also alluded to in the Sanskrit commentary on the Gomaṭasāra, which opens thus—

श्रीमदप्रतिहतप्रभावस्याद्वादशासनगुहाभ्यंतरनिवासिसिंहायमानासिंहनंदिनंदितगंगवंश-ललामराजसर्वज्ञाद्यनेकगुणनामधेयभागधेयश्रीमद्राज(च)मल्लदेवमहीवल्लभमहामात्यपदविराज-मानरणरंगमल्लासहायपराक्रमगुणरत्नभूषणसम्यक्त्वरत्ननिलयादिविविधगुणनामसमासादितकी-र्तिकांतश्रीमच्चामुंडरायप्रश्नावतीर्णैकचत्वारिंशत्पदनामसत्वप्ररूपणद्वारेणाशेषविनेयजननिकुरंब-संबोधनार्थं श्रीमन्नेमिचंद्रसैद्धांतचक्रवर्ती ....इष्टविशिष्टदेवताविशेषं नमस्करोति ।

The Kannaḍa poet Ranna, who adorned the court of the Cālukya king Tailapa II, who was born in A. D. 949 and who wrote his Gadāyuddha in A. D. 982, had Ajitasena for his teacher and Cāmuṇḍarāja for his patron.[3] These facts lead to the conclusion that Nemicandra lived in the latter half of the tenth century. It is thus clear that Jinasena, Guṇabhadra and Nemicandra preceded Albērūnī who wrote in the first half of the eleventh century.

In order to enable Sanskrit scholars to realise the importance of the facts which Jaina literature holds in store for them, I must repeat here the exact words of Jinasena (Harivaṁśa, chapter 60)—

गुप्तानां च शतद्वयम् ।
एकत्रिंशच्च वर्षाणि कालविद्भिरुदाहृतम् ॥ 487 ॥
द्विचत्वारिंशदेवातः कल्किराजस्य राजता ।
ततोऽजितंजयो राजा स्यादिन्द्रपुरसंस्थितः ॥ 488 ॥
वर्षाणां षट्शतीं त्यक्त्वा पंचाग्रां मासपंचकम् ।
मुक्तिं गते महावीरे शकराजस्ततोऽभवत् ॥ 552 ॥

Guṇabhadra says that when one thousand years of the *Duḥśama kūla*, commencing from the Nirvāṇa of Mahāvīra, had elapsed Kalkirāja was born. Jinasena says that the Śakarāja was born when 605 years and 5 months had passed by from the Nirvāṇa of Mahāvīra. If we subtract

1 Mr. Rice's Śrāvaṇa Beḷgola Inscriptions, Introd. p. 34.

2 From Mr. Rice's Mysore and Coorg inscriptions.

3 Karṇāṭaka-kavi-carita, p. 54.

605 years and 5 months from one thousand years, the re-

years	months
1000	0
605	5
394	7

mainder is 394 years and 7 months. It is thus clear that, according to Jinasena and Guṇabhadra, Kalkirāja was born when 394 years and 7 months had passed by from the birth of the Śaka king. Nemicandra says exactly the same thing when he tells us that, after the lapse of 605 years and 5 months from the Nirvāṇa of Mahāvīra, the Śaka king was born, and that, after the lapse of 394 years and 7 months from the birth of the Śaka king, Kalkirāja was born. Guṇabhadra adds that when 394 years of Śaka era and 7 months more had passed by, there occurred a Māgha saṁvatsara—

चतुर्मुखाव्हयः कल्कीराजोद्वेजितभूतलः ।
उत्पत्स्यते मघासंवत्सरयोगसमागमे ॥

This is a prophecy put into the mouth of Gautama-Gaṇadhara who says—

"There shall be born the king Kalkin, named Caturmukha, the oppressor of the world, on the occurrence of the union of a saṁvatsara with the Maghā-nakṣatra." When a saṁvatsara becomes मघानक्षत्रयुक्त, it is named माघसंवत्सर. After the nakṣatra the word मघा takes the termination अण् according to the sūtra of this Jainendra Vyākaraṇa—

गुरूदयात् भाद् युक्तोद्बः (iii. 2. 5.)

गुरुर्बृहस्पतिः तस्योदयो यास्मिन् नक्षत्रे तद्वाचिनो मृदः भासमर्थाद् युक्त इत्येतस्मिन्नर्थे यथाविहितं त्यो भवति यो युक्तोर्थः स चेदब्दः स्यात् । गुरूदयेन पुष्येण युक्तोब्दः पौषः संवत्सरः । फाल्गुनं वर्षम् । शव्दार्णवचंद्रिका, Benares ed p. 86.

Guṇanandin thus explains the Jainendra sūtra—

गुरुर्बृहस्पतिस्तदेति यस्मिन् नक्षत्रे तद्वाचिनो भासमर्थात् युक्त इत्येतास्मिन्नर्थे यथाविहितं त्यो भवति योऽसौ युक्तः स चेदब्दः संवत्सरः स्यात् । इत्यण् । एरित्यखम (iv. 4. 150) तैष पौषं भे (iv. 4. 157) इति यखम् । पौषः संवत्सरः पौषं वर्षम् । एवं-फाल्गुनः संवत्सरः फाल्गुनं वर्षम् । Jainendraprakriyā, part ii. p. 162, Benares ed.

Hemacandra, who owes his explanation to Śākaṭāyana, says—

उदितगुरोर्भाद्युक्तेऽब्दे (vi. 2. 5.)

उदितो गुरुर्बृहस्पतिर्यस्मिन् भे नक्षत्रे तद्वाचिनस्तृतीयान्ताद् युक्तेऽर्थे यथाविहितं प्रत्ययो भवति सचेद्युक्तोऽर्थोऽब्दः संवत्सरः स्यात्। पुष्येणोदितगुरुणा युक्तं वर्षं पौषं वर्षम्। फल्गुनीभिरुदितगुरुभिर्युक्तः फाल्गुनः संवत्सरः। उदितगुरोरिति किम्। उदितशनैश्चरेण पुष्येण युक्तं वर्षमित्यत्र न भवति। भादिति किम्। उदितगुरुणा पूर्वरात्रेण युक्तं वर्षम्। अब्द इति किम्। मासे दिवसे वा न भवति। Bṛhadvṛtti vi. 2. 5.

From the Jaina grammatical sūtras[1] and commentaries cited above it is obvious that Guṇabhadra's expression मघासंवत्सरयोगसमागमे means "on the occurrence (समागमे) of the union (योग) of मघा[नक्षत्र] and a संवत्सर; that is to say, मघाभियुक्तः संवत्सरः माघः. The word माघ, in the sense of a Māgha-saṁvatsara, is formed from मघा, which is in the instrumental case, by the suffix अण्; the आ of मघा, being elided, is replaced by अ of the suffix अण्, while अ, the first vowel in मघा, undergoes वृद्धि. We have thus the expression माघसंवत्सर. This is the teaching of Pūjyapāda, Śākaṭāyana, Hemacandra and Guṇanandin.

The occurrence of a Māgha-saṁvatsara in purely literary records, apart from early inscriptions and astronomical works, is of unique interest; and its supreme importance from a chronological point of view we shall now proceed to show.

We have seen that 394 Śaka years and 7 months had elapsed at the birth of Kalkirāja. The seven months completed belong to the current Śaka year 395. The first day of the eighth month, Kārttika Śukla 1, was the day on which Kalkirāja was born, since a Śaka year commences with Caitra Śukla. The year that is actually mentioned by the Jaina writers is the expired Śaka year 394. Let us convert this into an expired Vikrama year by the addition of 135 according to the rule—

स एव पंचाग्निकुभिर्युक्तः स्याद्विक्रमस्य हि।
रेवाया उत्तरे तीरे संवन्नाम्नातिविश्रुतः ॥ २ ॥ Jyotiṣasāra

1 Cf. also यस्येति च, Pāṇini vi, 4, 148, and तिष्यपुष्ययोर्नक्षत्राणि, Vārtika on Pāṇini vi. 4. 149.

The result is[1] the Vikrama year (394 + 135 =) 529 expired. This expired Vikrama year is identical with the expired Mālava year 529, given as the second and later date in the Mandasor Inscription of Kumāragupta I and his feudatory Bandhuvarman and is expressed[2] in the following words—

वत्सरशतेषु पंचसु विशंत्य(विंशत्य)धिकेषु नवसु चाब्देषु ।
यातेष्वभिरम्य तपस्यमासशुक्लद्वितीयायां ॥

Vikrama Saṁvat 529 expired, Phālguna Śukla 2

Hence it is clear that the Mālava era is the same as the Vikrama era of B. C. 57. In order to elucidate the point further, the expired Śaka year 394 may be first converted into the corresponding Christian year by adding 78 thus—394 + 78 = 472 A. D; and then this Christian year 472 can be converted into the Mālava year 529 by adding 57—

$$472 + 57 = 529$$
$$472 = 529 - 57$$
$$\text{or } 394 + 78 = 529 - 57 = \text{A. D. } 472$$

It is thus evident that the Mālava era is the era of B. C. 57, which is known to us as the Vikrama saṁvat.

The first year in the same inscription, which is 36 years earlier, is the Vikrama year 493 expired, Pauṣa Śukla 13—

मालवानां गणस्थित्या याते शतचतुष्टये ।
त्रिनवत्यधिकेब्दानां रि(ऋ)तौ सेव्यघनस्वने ॥
सहस्यमासशुक्लस्य प्रशस्तेह्नि त्रयोदशे ।

If we subtract 135 from Vikrama year 493 expired we get Śaka 358 expired. It is therefore evident that Kumāragupta with his feudatory Bandhuvarman was reigning in Śaka 358 expired, exactly 36 years before the birth of Kalkirāja in Śaka 394 expired. The year Śaka 394 expired is a Māgha-saṁvatsara. I give below four Śaka years with corresponding cyclic years beginning with this Māgha saṁvatsara of Śaka 394 expired, according to the rule[3] of Varāhamihira—

1 पंचाग्निकु = 135 ; अग्नि = 3, कु = 1. अंकानां वामतो गतिः ।
2 Dr. Fleet's Gupta insoriptions, p. 83 ; Ind. Ant. XV. p. 198.
3 Dr. Fleet's Gupta inscriptions, Appendix III, p. 161.

Śaka	394	expired	Māgha-saṁvatsara
„	395	„	Phālguna-saṁvatsara
„	396	„	Caitra-saṁvatsara
„	397	„	Vaiśākha-saṁvatsara

The date given in the Khoh grant of Parivrājaka Mahārāja Hastin is Gupta-saṁvat 156, which is specified[1] as a Mahā-Vaiśākha saṁvatsara—

षट्पंचाशोत्तरेऽब्दशते गुप्तनृपराज्यभुक्तौ महावैशाखसंवत्सरे कार्त्तिकमासशुक्लपक्ष-तृतीयायाम् ।

The four Śaka years with corresponding cyclic and Gupta years are exhibited in the following table that the Gupta years are expired will be proved further on—

Śaka	394	expired =	Māgha-saṁvatsara =	Gupta	153	expired
„	395	„	Phālguna „	„	154	„
„	396	„	Caitra „	„	155	„
„	397	„	Vaiśākha „	„	156	„

It will be evident from the foregoing table that Gupta years can be converted into equivalent Śaka years by the addition of 241, in as much as each of the four equations stated above gives us a difference of 241. Kumāragupta I with his feudatory Bandhuvarman was thus reigning in Śaka 358, corresponding to Gupta saṁvat 117[2] and to Vikrama year 493—

Śaka 358 = Gupta saṁvat 117 = Mālava or Vikrama 493

And Kalkirāja was born 36 years later in Śaka 394, corresponding to Gupta saṁvat 153 and to Vikrama year 529—

Śaka 394 = Gupta saṁvat 153 = Mālava or Vikrama 529

It is worth noting that the birth of Kalkirāja took place only 5 years later than the latest date recorded for Skandagupta—Gupta saṁvat[3] 148, equivalent to Śaka 389,—and only one year earlier than the date[4] of his son, Kumāragupta II,— Gupta saṁvat 154, equivalent to Śaka 395.

1 Gupta inscriptions, p. 95.

2 Bharadi inscription. A. S. Progr. Rep. N. C. 1907-8 p. 39.

3 V. Smith's Early History of India, 3rd ed. p. 327.

4 Annual Progress Report of the Superintendent, Hindu and Buddhist monuments, Northern Circle, 1915, p. 6.

वर्षशते गुप्तानां सचतुःपंचाशदुत्तरे भूमिम् ।
शासति कुमारगुप्ते मासे ज्येष्ठे द्वितीयायाम् ॥

That the Gupta year mentioned in this inscription as well as the one mentioned in the Khoh grant of Mahārāja Hastin referred to above is to be taken as expired is evident from the following inscription of Budhagupta,[1] Gupta saṁvat 157 expired—

गुप्तानां समतिक्रांते सप्तपंचाशदुत्तरे ।
शते समानां पृथिवीं बुधगुप्ते प्रशासति ॥

The general conclusion is that all the Gupta years including those given in the above table must be taken as expired.

This point can be further cleared up by a comparison of the five corresponding years of the Vikrama, Śaka and Gupta eras exhibited in the following table—

Mālava or Vikrama	Śaka	Gupta
529 expired	394 expired	153
530 ,,	395 ,,	154
531 ,,	396 ,,	155
532 ,,	397 ,,	156
533 expired	398 expired	157 expired

The Gupta year 157 is specified as an expired year in the inscription of Budhagupta which has been quoted above. The difference between the expired Śaka year 398 and the expired Gupta year 157 is 241. The difference between the Śaka year 394 and the Gupta year 153 is also 241. The Śaka year 394 is known to be expired; therefore the Gupta year 153 must be taken as expired. The conclusion that forces itself upon us is that all the Gupta years mentioned in inscriptions are expired years and can be converted into corresponding expired Śaka years by the addition of 241.

We have here established five uniform equations between expired Gupta and expired Śaka years, with a difference of 241 in each case. The last equation is most important.

$$\left.\begin{array}{c}\text{Expired}\\ \text{Gupta year}\end{array}\right\} 157 = 398 \left\{\begin{array}{c}\text{Expired}\\ \text{Śaka year}\end{array}\right.$$

1 Ibid. p. 7.

This date of Budhagupta inscribed on two Buddha images is thus expressed—[1] "When the year one hundred and fifty-seven of the Guptas had expired, on the 7th day of the month Vaiśākha while Budhagupta is ruling the earth." The 7th of Vaiśākha belongs to the current Gupta year 158 corresponding to the current Śaka year 399—

Current Gupta year } 158 = 399 { Current Śaka year

Thus the difference between current Gupta and current Śaka years is also 241, the same as the difference between expired Gupta and expired Śaka years. Now the Sārnath date of Budhagupta, expired Gupta year 157, is only 8 years earlier than the date of the same Gupta king given[2] in the Eraṇ pillar inscription—

शते पंचषष्ट्यधिके वर्षाणां भूपतौ च बुधगुप्ते ।
आषाढमासशु[क्ल]द्वादश्यां सुरगुरोर्दिवसे ॥

The date is "in the year 165, on the 12th day of the bright half of Āṣāḍha, on Thursday." We are now in a position to explain this date thus—

Expired Gupta year } 165 = 406 { Expired Śaka year

"The 12th day of the bright half of Āshāḍha and Thursday" belong to the current Gupta year 166 corresponding to the current Śaka year 407—

Current Gupta year } 166 = 407 { Current Śaka year

Here we cannot take the expired Gupta year 165 as current and make it correspond with the current Śaka year 407 as, in that case, the difference between 165 and 407 would be 242 instead of 241 as required by the statements of the Jaina authorities and the Sārnath inscription of Budhagupta thus—

1 Ibid. p. 7.

2 Gupta inscriptions, p. 89.

Expired Gupta year	(*a*) 165 = (*b*) 406	Expired Śaka year
Current Gupta year	(*c*) 166 = (*d*) 407	Current Śaka year

A second reason for not making the Gupta year 165 correspond with the Śaka year 407 is that from our established equation—

Expired Gupta year	157 = 398	Expired Śaka year

it is evident that the Gupta year 165 is 8 years later than the Gupta year 157, while the Śaka year 407 is 9 years later than the corresponding Śaka year 398. A careful consideration of these facts leads to the conclusion that expired or current Gupta years can be converted into corresponding expired or current Śaka years by adding 241.

The date in the pillar inscription of Budhagupta has been the subject of calculation and controversy for more than half a century. Many scholars have attempted to interpret this date by the statements of Albērūnī, which were admitted on all hands to be conflicting. It may therefore be interesting to point out how many statements of this celebrated Mahomedan writer can now be accepted as correct. He says[1] that the era of Ballaba is subsequent to that of Śaka by 241 years. The era of the Guptas also commences the year 241 of the era of Śaka. Then he mentions the year 1088 of the era of Vikramāditya, the year 953 of the era of Śaka, the year 712 of the era of Ballaba and of that of the Guptas, as equivalent years. These statements are reliable as they are in agreement with our equation thus—

	Mālava or Vikrama		Śaka		Gupta
(*a*)	529	=	394	=	153
(*b*)	1088	=	953	=	712
	559		559		559

1 Gupta inscriptions, Introduction, p. 23 f.

The difference between Mālava 529 and Śaka 394 is 135; that between Vikrama 1088 and Śaka 953 is also 135; the difference between Śaka 394 and Gupta 153 is 241; and that between Śaka 953 and Gupta-Valabhī 712 is also 241; the difference between the Mālava year 529 and the Gupta year 153 is 376; and the difference between the Vikrama 1088 and the Gupta-Valabhī year 712 is also 376. It is also interesting to note that from the year of the birth of Kalkirāja in Śaka 394 or Gupta year 153, when the Gupta empire was still enduring, to the year A. D. 1031–32 in which Albērūnī was writing, 559 years had elapsed.[1] So that his equation (*b*) is as accurate as if it had been formed by adding 559 to each of the equivalent years of the three eras in our own equation (*a*).

An interesting peculiarity of the years of the Mālava era deserves to be noticed here. The second date in the Mandasor inscription of Kumāragupta I and Bandhuvarman is the Mālava year 529 expired, Phālguna Śukla 2. The equivalent Śaka year is 394 expired. Deduct 394 from our present Śaka year 1839 in Western India. The result is 1445. Add 1445 to 529; the result is 1974. This will be our Mālava or Vikrama year on Phālguna Śukla 2 next, in Western India. This is true according to our almanac. Let us now turn to the Mandasor inscription[2] of Yaśodharman where the expired Mālava year 589 with the season of Vasanta is thus mentioned—

पञ्चसु शतेषु शरदां यातेष्वेकान्ननवतिसहितेषु ।
मालवगणस्थितिवशात्कालज्ञानाय लिखितेषु ॥
यस्मिन्काले कलमृदुगिरां कोकिलानां प्रलापा
भिन्दतीव स्मरशरनिभाः प्रोषितानां मनांसि ।
भृङ्गालीनां ध्वनिरनुरतं भारमन्द्रश्च यस्मि-
न्नाधूतज्यं धनुरिव नदच्छ्रूयते पुष्पकेतोः ॥

प्रियतमकुपितानां रामयन्बद्धरागं
किसलयमिव मुग्धं मानसं मानिनीनां ।
उपनयति नभस्वान्मानभङ्गाय यस्मि-
न्कुसुमसमयमासे तत्र निर्मापितोयम् ॥

1 Ind. Ant, Vol. xvii, p. 213 note 1. 2 Gupta Inscr, p. 154.

Here the date is the वसन्त, i. e. चैत्र and वैशाख of the expired Mālava year 589, कुसुमसमय or पुष्पसमय being synonymous with वसन्त (Amara I, 3. 18). To-day is अक्षयतृतीया, i. e. वैशाख शुक्ल २ of the Śaka year 1839 in Western India. The expired Mālava year 589 is 60 years later than the expired Mālava year 529. Add 60 to the expired Śaka 394. The result is the expired Śaka 454 corresponding to Mālava 589. Now deduct 454 from our present Śaka year 1839 ; the remainder is 1385. Add 589 to 1385 and we get Mālava year 1974 corresponding to our present Śaka year on अक्षयतृतीया. But our Vikrama saṁvat to-day is 1973 because it is कार्त्तिकादि and will be found to be identical with the Mālava year 1974 on our next Phālguna Śukla 2, as has been shown above. This may be illustrated by the following diagram—

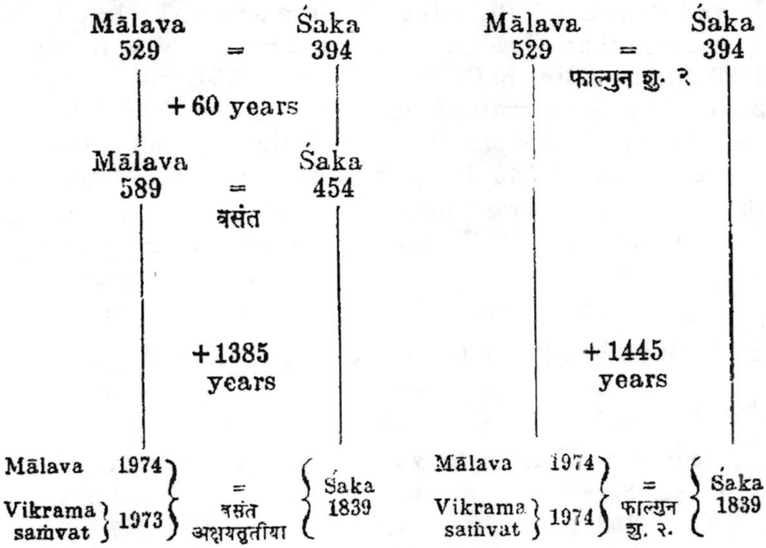

The conclusion that is forced upon us is that the years of the Mālava era in the times of the Guptas and the Hūṇas were Caitrādi Vikrama years. This will enable us to refute the opinion of Dr. Kielhorn[1] who, while admitting that the Vikrama era was called Mālava, says " The Vikrama era was Kārttikādi from the beginning, and it is

1 Ind. Ant. Vol. xx., p. 32 8ff.

probable that the change which has gradually taken place in the direction of a more general use of the Caitrādi year was owing to the increasing growth and influence of the Śaka era." This erroneous view is also shared by Dr. Fleet[1] who says—"It can hardly be doubted that the original scheme of the Vikrama years is the one commencing with the first day of the bright half of Kārttika (October–November)."

The fact that the years of the Mālava era are Caitrādi is most important. It will enable us not only to establish the absolute identity of the Gupta era with the Valabhī era, but also to ascertain the exact difference between the years of the Gupta era and of the Mālava era on the one hand, and those of the Śaka era on the other. The date of Col. Tod's Verāwal[2] inscription is Vikrama saṁvat 1320 and Valabhī saṁvat 945, Āṣāḍha vadi 13 Ravi. From Diwan Bahadur Pillai's Indian Chronology, Table x. p. 92, we learn that Āṣāḍha vadi Ravivāra falls in Śaka 1186 corresponding to Caitrādi Vikrama 1321, and is Sunday 25th May 1264 according to the Christian era. The Vikrama yea 1320 mentioned in this inscription as equivalent to Valabhī saṁvat 945 is thus southern and Kārttikādi; therefore the corresponding Caitrādi Vikrama year or Mālava year is 1321. We thus get the following equation—

	Śaka		Mālava		Valabhī
(a)	1186	=	1321	=	945

By deducting 792 from the above we get the next equation—

	Śaka		Mālava		Valabhī
(b)	394	=	529	=	153

By deducting 36 from (b) we get the following equation—

	Śaka		Mālava		Valabhī
(c)	358	=	493	=	117

We know[3] that Kumāragupta I was reigning in Gupta saṁvat 117 which is thus identical with the Valabhī year 117. The last equation also proves that the exact dif-

1 Gupta Inscriptions, Intr. p. 66 f. n. 2.

2 Gupta Inscr. Intr. p. 85.

3 A. S. Progr. Rep. N. C. 1907-08, p. 39; Ep. Ind. Vol. x, p. 70.

ference between the Gupta and Śaka years is 241; while that between the Mālava and Gupta years is 376. Here our agreement is based on Col. Tod's Verāwal inscription. This argument is easier to understand than that which is founded on the Māgha-saṁvatsara of Śaka 394 expired, and which presupposes a knowledge of the grammatical sūtras of Pūjyapāda and Śākaṭāyana. The conclusion arrived at by these two independent lines of argument is the same, namely, that the difference between Gupta and Śaka year's is 241. We have also demonstrated that the difference between current Gupta years and current Śaka years is 241. Thus—

Expired Gupta 157 = 398 Śaka expired
Current Gupta 158 = 399 Śaka current

It is of importance to note that in converting a Gupta-valabhī year into its Śaka equivalent, it is not necessary to know beforehand whether the Gupta-Valabhī year is expired or current. If the resulting Śaka is expired, the Gupta-Valabhī year must be expired. On the other hand, if the Śaka year is current, the corresponding Gupta-Valabhī year must also be current. These observations can be illustrated by the Kaira grant of Valabhī saṁvat 330 and by the Verāwal inscription of Valabhī saṁvat 927. The date in the Kaira grant is thus expressed[1]—

Saṁ. 300 30 dvi-Mārgaśira śu. 2.

Here the Valabhī year 330 can be converted into Śaka 571 by adding 241. The exact date is अधिकमार्गशीर्ष शुक्ल २. On referring to Hindu Tables we find that the intercalary Mārgaśirṣa actually falls in Śaka 571. This Śaka year is therefore current and equivalent to Valabhī 330. Our equation is thus—

Current Valabhī 330 = 571 Śaka current

The date of the Verāwal inscription of Valabhī saṁvat 927 is thus expressed[2]—

1 Gupta Inscr. Intr. p. 93.
2 Gupta Inscr. Intr. p. 91.

Śrīmad-Valabhī sa[ṁ]vat 927 Phālguna Śu. 2 Sau(Sō) mē.
By adding 241 to 927 we get the following equation—

Valabhī 927 = 1168 Śaka

By astronomical calculations the late Mr. S. B. Dikshit arrived at Śaka 1167 expired as the equivalent year. Therefore the current Śaka year is 1168, which corresponds to current Valabhī 927. Our equation therefore is—

Current Valabhī 927 = 1168 Śaka current

These two records dated in current Valabhī years are most important and interesting as they amply refute the erroneous theory of Dr. Fleet that the running difference between current Gupta-Valabhī years and current Śaka years is 242. Nor can we accept as correct his opinion that the two Vikrama years 706 and 1303 are southern and the nominal equivalents of the current Valabhī years 330 and 927 respectively. For, on a comparison with the following equations—

Śaka		Mālava		Gupta-Valabhī
394	=	529	=	153
571	=	706	=	330
1168	=	1303	=	927

it is obvious that these Vikrama years are Mālava or Caitrādi and the real equivalents of the two Valabhī years, and do not differ from southern Vikrama years, because they are coupled with the months of Mārgaśīrṣa and Phālguna in these inscriptions.

On the other hand the year 386, which is the date in the Nepal inscription of Mānadeva, is expired, because it can be converted into expired Śaka 627 by adding 241, and does not correspond to current Śaka 628, as maintained by Dr. Fleet.[1]

Alberūnī's first statement that Gupta years can be converted into Śaka years by adding 241 was perfectly accurate. But it was invalidated by a second statement which he made to the effect that the Gupta era dated from the extermination of the Guptas. This led many scholars to discredit his statements entirely.

1 Gupta Inscriptions, Intr. p. 95 ff.

Dr. Fleet's discovery of the Mandasor inscription was very interesting and important. But his attempt to prove that the Mālava era was the same as the Vikrama era of B.C. 57 was a failure and looked like the attempt of a person who has, to use Dr. R. G. Bhandarkar's words,[1] "to determine the value of one unknown quantity by means of another unknown quantity, which cannot be done." Nor was Dr. Fleet more successful in interpreting the date of the pillar inscription of Budhagupta when he said that the Gupta year 165 was a current year and that[2] "in following Alberūnī's statement and adding two hundred and forty-one what is really accomplished is the conversion of a given current Gupta-Valabhī year into an expired Śaka year, by which we obtain precisely the basis that is wanted for working out results by Hindu Tables, viz. the last Śaka year expired before the commencement of the current Śaka year corresponding to a given current Gupta-Valabhī year; and that the running difference between current Gupta-Valabhī and current Śaka years is two hundred and forty-two." That this view is erroneous will be obvious from a careful consideration of the following two equations which have been explained above—

Expired Gupta year (*a*) 165 = (*b*) 406 expired Śaka year

Current Gupta year (*c*) 166 = (*d*) 407 current Śaka year

Dr. Fleet has mistaken the expired Gupta year (*a*) 165 for a current year and made it correspond to the current Śaka year (*d*) 407 and drawn the wrong inference that the difference between current Gupta years and current Śaka years is 242 instead of 241. His final conclusion, which is also due to the above mistake, that[3] "in the absence of any distinct specification to the contrary, we must interpret the years in Gupta-Valabhī dates as current years"

1 Jour. Bom. Br. R. A. S., Vol. XVII, part II, p. 92. See Bühler's opinion, Ind. Ant. XV, p. 339, and Cunningham's letter, Ibid. p. 347.

2 Gupta inscriptions, Introd. p, 84.

3 Idem. p. 129 f.

is equally erroneous. Dr. Fleet attacks[1] Dr. R. G. Bhandarkar's view that "the addition of 241 would turn a past Gupta year into a past Śaka year; and the addition of 242, a past Gupta year into a current Śaka year." But this view, which is found to be in accordance with the statements of the Jaina authorities and the Sārnath inscription of Budhagupta, must now be accepted as final and decisive on the point at issue.

Let us turn to the date of the Morvi copper plate grant,[2] which is thus expressed—

पञ्चाशीत्या युतेतीते समानां शतपञ्चके ।
गौप्ते ददावदो नृपः सोपरागेर्कमंडले ॥

This means that the king made the grant, when 585 years of the Guptas had expired, on the occurrence of a solar eclipse. The eclipse, therefore, occurred in the current Gupta year 586. Our equation is—

Expired Gupta 157 = 398 expired Śaka.

Now the expired Gupta 585 is 428 years later than the expired Gupta 157. By the addition of 428 to both sides we get the new equation—

Expired Gupta 585 = 826 expired Śaka

The equivalent Śaka year 826 can also be obtained by adding 241 to 585. Therefore—

Current Gupta 586 = 827 current Śaka

The solar eclipse alluded to in the grant is therefore the one that occurred on the new moon of Mārgaśirṣa, Śaka 827 current, corresponding to the 10th November A. D. 904. There was a solar eclipse also in the following Śaka year 828 current, on Jyeṣṭha Bahula Amāvāsyā, corresponding to the 7th May, A. D. 905. Dr. Fleet's view that this second eclipse is the one alluded to in the grant is untenable as the Śaka year 828 is obtainable by adding 242 to the current Gupta year 586; and this is, as we have seen, against the statements of our Jaina authorities and the two Sārnath inscriptions. Nor can we accept his reading *Gopte* and his

1 Idem. p. 84, n. 1.

2 Gupta Inscr. Intr. p. 97.

explanation of it as the name of a village; for on the analogy of the expression गुप्तानां शते found in the two Sārnath inscriptions of Kumāragupta II and Budhagupta we must expect the reading गौप्ते शतपञ्चके in the Morvi grant. If the reading be गोप्ते, it should be corrected into गौप्ते. It is thus clear that Dr. Fleet's reading and interpretation of the date in the Morvi copper plate grant are positively wrong. On the other hand the decision of Dr. R. G. Bhandarkar on this interesting point is upheld by our Jaina authorities and the Sārnath inscriptions of Kumāragupta II and Budhagupta.

The connection of Kumāragupta II and Budhagupta with the main line of the Imperial Guptas may be exhibited in the following genealogical tree—

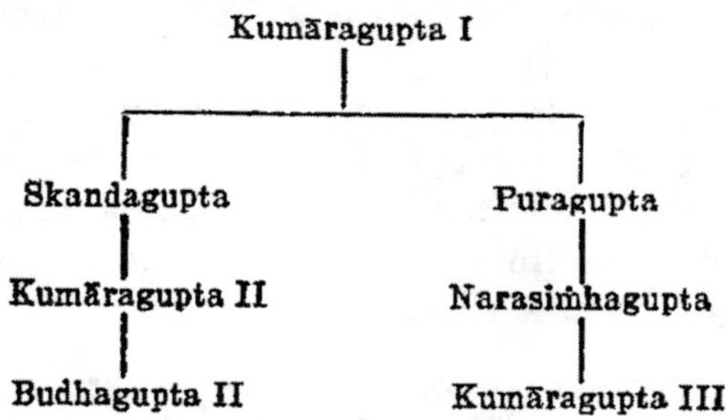

The rule that Gupta years can be converted into Śaka years by adding 241, may be illustrated thus: Skandagupta ascended the throne in Gupta saṁvat 136. In the very first year of his reign, the Gupta empire was invaded by the Hūṇas. Kālidāsa assures us that the Hūṇas, who enjoyed the reputation of being the most invincible warriors of their age, were still on the Vaṅkṣū(Vakṣū)tīra or Oxus banks, when he wrote his well-known verses. The Hūṇa empire in the Oxus Basin was founded about A. D. 450. The date of the invasion of the Gupta empire by the Hūṇas and their defeat by Skandagupta, namely the Gupta year 136, must therefore be subsequent to about A. D. 450 by a very few years. By calculating 24 years backwards from Śaka year 394, corresponding to the Gupta year 153, we arrive at Śaka 370 (=A. D. 448) corresponding to the Gupta saṃvat 129. Now the Gupta year 129 (A. D. 448) is the 36th regnal year of Kumāragupta I. In A. D. 448, in the reign of Kumāragupta I, the establishment of the Hūṇa empire in the Oxus Basin may be placed. That the year A. D. 448 is the exactly correct date of this event, while the year A. D. 450 is only approximate will be shown hereafter. The Gupta year 136 (A. D. 455) is thus only 7 years subsequent to A. D. 448. Kālidāsa's reference to the Hūṇas being the most invincible conquerors of their age, and as being still in the Oxus Basin, must have been made between A. D. 448 and A. D. 455. Kālidāsa and Skandagupta were thus contemporaries. This argument needs no elaboration here, as it has been discussed at length in the introduction to my second edition of the Meghadūta, (pp. x, xi, xii) where it is shown that the fall of the Gupta empire took place towards the close of the fifth century. Jinasena, who writes a little less than three centuries later, has preserved to the world the oldest, and therefore the most reliable, text of the Meghadūta as yet discovered, while his pupil Guṇabhadra says that the Kumārasambhava was widely read in his time and was the delight of every class of people, young as well as old.[1]

From a comparison of the Eraṇ pillar Inscription of Budhagupta and the Eraṇ Boar inscription of Toramāṇa it can be conclusively proved, as has been shown by Dr. Fleet, that[2] Toramāṇa came after Budhagupta. The latest date for Buddhagupta is Gupta saṁvat 180 corresponding to Śaka 421 or A. D. 499. Toramāṇa was the father of Mihirakula. Mihiraula was defeated by Yaśodharman who was reigning[3] in Mālava or Vikrama year 589 corresponding to Śaka 454 (A. D. 532). The first regnal year of Toramāṇa is mentioned in the Eraṇ Boar inscription, while

1 Compare, for instance, उत्तरपुराण, Chap. 59, stanza 36—

संवर्ध्य विषवृक्षं च छेत्तुं स्वयमवैति कः ।
इत्याबालप्रसिद्धं किं न वेत्सि विषभृत्पते ॥ 36 ॥

with कुमारसंभव ii. 55—

विषवृक्षोऽपि संवर्ध्य स्वयं छेत्तुमसांप्रतम् ।

2 Ind. Ant. vol XVIII, p. 227.

3 Gupta inscriptions, pp. 150, 158, 162.

the 15th regnal year of his son Mihirakula is given in his Gwālior inscription. These two regnal years must fall between Gupta saṁvat 180 and Mālava year 589, corresponding to Śaka 421 (A. D. 499) and Śaka 454 (A. D. 532) respectively, according to our Jaina authorities. It is worth noting that the inscription which records the defeat of Mihirakula by Yaśodharman is not dated. But from another inscription of Yaśodharman dated in Mālava or Vikrama year 589, the approximate date of Mihirakula is ascertained. This Mihirakula is believed by Dr. Fleet and other scholars to be identical with the famous tyrant Mihirakula, whose career has been described in such vivid colours by the Chinese traveller Hiuen Tsiang and by Kalhaṇa in the Rājataraṅgiṇī. On the other hand our Jaina authorities tell us that the Early Gupta kings were immediately succeeded by the great tyrant Caturmukha–Kalkin, Kalkin or Kalkirāja. He was a paramount sovereign(महीं कृत्स्नां स भोक्ष्यति). He was foremost among wicked men (दुर्जनादिमः), a perpetrator of sinful deeds (अक्रमकारिन्). He oppressed the world (उद्वेजितभूतलः). He asked his ministers whether there were any people on earth who did not owe allegiance to him; the reply was, none but the Nirgranthas. He thereupon issued an edict that the first lump of food offered to the Jaina community of Nirgranthas at noon every day by pious people should be levied as a tax. The Jaina Nirgranthas are allowed by the rules of their religion to take their meal at noon once a day. If any अन्तराय or difficulty occurs at that hour, they must wait for their meal till noon on the following day. The result of the tyrant Kalkirāja's edict was that the Nirgranthas were exposed to utter starvation. Unable to bear this spectacle, a demon appeared and killed the tyrant with his thunderbolt. Kalkirāja then went into the hell called Ratnaprabhā, there to live countless ages and to endure misery for a long time.[1] We may compare this account with the statement[2] of Hiuen Tsiang as regards Mihirakula—"the holy saints said, in

1 See the passage given at the end.

2 V. Smith's Early History of India, 3rd. Ed. p. 319,

pity, for having killed countless victims and overthrown the law of Buddha, he has now fallen into the lowest hell, where he shall pass endless ages of revolution."

We have seen that the tyrant Kalkirāja was a paramount sovereign. The Mihirakula of the inscriptions also was a paramount sovereign, because he bowed down before none save the god Śiva. The real meaning of the verse, in which this fact is stated, and which was misunderstood by the translators of the Gupta inscriptions, has been pointed[1] out by the present writer and by Dr. Kielhorn. Like the Mihirakula of the inscriptions the tyrant Kalkirāja came immediately after the Early Guptas; that is to say, he overthrew the Early Gupta sovereignty. The Mihirakula of the inscriptions was therefore a tyrant and must be identical with the tyrant Mihirakula of Hiuen Tsiang and of the Rājataranginī. Then again, like the tyrant Mikirakula, the tyrant Kalkirāja (A. D. 472–542)[2] was reigning in A. D. 520 when the Chinese pilgrim Song Yun visited this country, and was still on the throne when the Greek monk Cosmas came to India about A. D. 530. There is no denying the cogency of these arguments, which lead to the inevitable conclusion that Kalkirāja was only another name of the famous tyrant Mihirakula. It is to this great Hūṇa conqueror that the Jaina author Somadeva, contemporary with the Rāṣṭrakūṭa king Kṛṣṇarāja III, alludes when he says[3]—

नामुद्रहस्तोऽशोधितो वा कश्चित्स्वमण्डलविषये प्रविशेन्नि(न्नि)र्गच्छेद्वा । श्रूयते हि किल हूणाधिपतिः पण्यपुटवाहिभिः सुभटैश्चित्रकूटं जग्राह ।

The Jaina version of the story of Mihirakula has this advantage over the Buddhist and Brahmanical versions that, while the two latter afford no clue to the real date of the tyrant, the former gives the exact dates of his birth and death. Not only is the approximate date of the tyrant

1 See my paper entitled "Nṛipatuṅga and the authorship of the Kavirâjamârga." Jour. Bom. Br. R. A. S. Vol. XXII p. 82 ff; Ind. Ant. Vol. XVIII, p. 219.

2 See below, p. 217.

3 नीतिवाक्यामृत Bombay ed p. 79.

deduced from inscriptions and coins amply corroborated by the Jaina authors, but they supplement, in a material degree, the information which we owe to those two independent sources.

The famous tyrant Mihirakula, accounts of whose cruel deeds have been preserved to us in Buddhist, Jaina and Brahmanical literatures, was then born on the 1st of the bright half of the month Kārttika in Śaka 394 expired, the cyclic year being a Māgha-saṁvatsara, corresponding to A. D. 472. And he died at the age of 70 in Śaka 464 or A. D. 542. Jinasena assigns to him a reign of 42 years, while, according to Guṇabhadra and Nemiçandra, he reigned 40 years. Deducting 42 or 40 from A. D. 542 we get A. D. 500 or A. D. 502. We shall accept A. D. 502 for the initial year of Mihirakula's reign. His fifteenth regnal year must be A. D. 517. His father Toramāṇa's first year may be safely taken to be A. D. 500, coming after Gupta saṁvat 180 or A. D. 499, the latest date for Budhagupta. And the figure 52 found on Toramāṇa's silver coins corresponds to A. D. 500, the initial year of his reign. If calculated backwards, the figure 52 brings us to A. D. 448,[1] which is thus the exact date of the foundation of the Hūṇa empire in the Oxus Basin.

The tyrant Mihirakula died in A. D. 542, just a century before Hiuen Tsiang was on his travels, and exactly 241 years before Jinasena wrote his passage relating to the Guptas. Jinasena says that he owes his information to chroniclers who preceded him (कालविद्भिरुदाहृतम्). These chroniclers must be as near in time to the period of the Hūṇa sovereignty as Hiuen Tsiang himself. In the light of these facts we feel that we are in a position to discard as baseless the opinion of the Chinese pilgrim that Mihirakula lived 'some centuries previously,' as it comes into conflict with the statements of the Jaina writers, which have been shown to rest upon contemporary Gupta inscriptions. On the same ground we should reject as valueless the view of Albērūnī, admittedly a later

1 V. Smith's Early History of India, 3rd Ed. p. 316, note 3.

writer than our Jaina authorities, that the Gupta era dated from the extermination of the Guptas. This erroneous opinion of Albērūnī, coupled with his conflicting statements as to the difference between Śaka and Gupta years being 241, 242 or 243,[1] led to a fierce controversy over the epoch of the Gupta era, which has raged now for more than 78 years since 1838, when Mr. James Prinsep discussed the date of the Kahāuṁ pillar inscription of Skandagupta. A great step in advance was made when Dr. Fleet discovered his Mandasor inscriptions. But his method of proving that the Mālava era was the same as the Vikrama era of B. C. 57 left a great deal to be desired. Now that we have placed his hypothesis on a footing of certainty, unstinted praise should be given to Dr. Fleet for his interesting discovery. But that he claimed more for his discovery than was its due has been already shown. Nor should we refuse to pay a well-merited tribute to Mr. D. R. Bhandarkar for his discovery of an earlier date in the Vikrama era, namely 461, referable to the reign of Candragupta II. Mention should be made here of the synchronism between Samudragupta and the king Meghavarṇa of Ceylon discovered by M. Sylvain Lévi to whom our thanks are due. But this synchronism, valuable as it is, should be utilized not in proving the epoch of the Gupta era, as was suggested by some scholars, but in rectifying Ceylonese chronology, which is full of uncertainty, as various dates are proposed for king Meghavarṇa. Nor should we omit to express our gratitude to Mr. Hargreaves who has lately discovered the two Gupta inscriptions, one of Kumāragupta II dated Gupta saṁvat 154, and the other of Budhagupta dated Gupta saṁvat 157, which have enabled us, with the help of our Jaina authorities, to prove that the Gupta years between 153 and 157 are expired and not current years.

Thus the controversy, which has raged over the epoch of the Gupta era for more than 78 years, is finally set at rest.

1 Gupta inscriptions, Introd. p. 25; Ind. Ant. Vol. XV, p. 189.

Extract from Guṇabhadra's
Uttara-purāṇa, chap. 76

अथान्यदा महाराजः श्रेणिकः क्षायिकीं[1] दृशं ।
दधन्नत्वा गणाधीशं कुड्मलीकृतहस्तकः ॥ 387 ॥
शेषावसर्पिणीकालस्थितिं निरवशेषतः ।
आगाम्युत्सर्पिणीकालस्थितिमप्यनुयुक्तवान् ॥ 388 ॥
गणी निजद्विजाभीषुप्रसरैः प्रीणयन्सभाम् ।
गिरा गंभीरया व्यक्तमुक्तवानिति स क्रमात् ॥ 389 ॥
चतुर्थकालपर्यंते स्थिते संवत्सरत्रये ।
साष्टमासे सपक्षे स्यात्सिद्धः सिद्धार्थनंदनः[2] ॥ 390 ॥
दुःषमायाः स्थितिर्वर्षसहस्राण्येकविंशतिः ।
शतवर्षायुषस्तस्मिन्नुत्कृष्टेन मता नराः ॥ 391 ॥
समारत्निप्रमाणांगा रूक्षच्छाया विरूपकाः ।
त्रिकालाहारनिरताः सुरतासक्तमानसाः ॥ 392 ॥
परेपि दोषाः प्रायेण तेषां स्युः कालदोषतः ।
यतोस्यां पापकर्माणो जनिष्यंते सहस्रशः ॥ 393 ॥
यथोक्तभूभुजाभावाज्जाते वर्णादिसंकरे ।
दुःषमायां सहस्राब्दव्यतीतौ धर्महानितः ॥ 394 ॥
पुरे पाटलिपुत्राख्ये शिशुपालमहीपतेः ।
पापी तनूजः पृथिवीसुंदर्यां दुर्जनादिमः ॥ 395 ॥
चतुर्मुखाह्वयः कल्की राजोद्वेजितभूतलः ।
उपत्स्यते[3] मघासंवत्सरयोगसमागमे ॥ 396 ॥
समानां सप्ततिस्तस्य परमायुः प्रकीर्तितम् ।
चत्वारिंशत्समा राज्यस्थितिश्चाक्रमकारिणः ॥ 397 ॥
षण्णवत्युक्तपापंडिवर्गस्याज्ञाविधायिनः ।
निजभृत्यत्वमापाद्य महीं कृत्स्नां स भोक्ष्यति ॥ 398 ॥

1 सम्यग्दर्शन which purifies the soul permanently by entirely destroying कर्मन् or action. Cf. Tattvārtha-Rājavārtika II, 1, 2 and 10, Benares Ed. I, p. 69,

2 Mahāvīra.

3 So three Kannaḍa Mss. of the Jaina Matha, Kolhapur, and one Nāgari Ms. of the late Maṇikshet of Bombay. But I reject the reading मद्दा in some Deccan College. Mss., which gives no sense,

अथान्येद्युः स्वमिथ्यात्वपाकाविष्कृतचेतसा ।
पाषंडिषु किमस्माकं संत्यत्राज्ञापराङ्मुखाः ॥ 399 ॥
कथ्यतामिति पापेन प्रष्टव्यास्तेन मंत्रिणः ।
निर्ग्रंथाः संति देवेति ते वदिष्यंति सोपि तान् ॥ 400 ॥
आचारः कीदृशस्तेषामिति प्रक्ष्यति भूपतिः ।
निजपाणिपुटामंत्रा[1] धनहीना गतस्पृहाः ॥ 401 ॥
अहिंसाव्रतरक्षार्थं त्यक्तचेलादिसंवराः ।
साधनं तपसो मत्वा देहस्थित्यर्थमार्हतिम्[2] ॥ 402 ॥
एकाद्युपोषितप्रांते भिक्षाकालेंगदर्शनात् ।
निर्याचनां स्वशास्त्रोक्तां ग्रहीतुमभिलाषिणः ॥ 403 ॥
आत्मनो घातके त्रायके च ते समदर्शिनः ।
क्षुत्पिपासादिबाधायाः सहाः सत्यपि कारणे ॥ 404 ॥
परपाषंडिवन्नान्यैरदत्तमभिलाषुकाः ।
सर्पा[3] वा विहितावासा ज्ञानध्यानपरायणाः ॥ 405 ॥
अनृसंचारदेशेषु संवसंति मृगैः सह ।
इति वक्ष्यंति दृष्टं स्वैर्विशिष्टास्तेस्य मंत्रिणः ॥ 406 ॥
श्रुत्वा तत्सहितुं नाहं शक्नोम्यक्रमवर्तनम् ।
तेषां पाणिपुटे प्राच्यः पिंडः शुल्को विधीयताम् ॥ 407 ॥
इति राजोपदेशेन याचिष्यंते नियोगिनः ।
अग्रपिंडमभुंजानाः स्थास्यंति मुनयोपि ते ॥ 408 ॥
तदृष्ट्वा दर्पिणो नग्ना नाज्ञां राज्ञः प्रतीप्सवः ।
किं जातमिति ते गत्वा ज्ञापयिष्यंति तं नृपम् ॥ 409 ॥
सोपि पापः स्वयं क्रोधादरुणीभूतवीक्षणः ।
उद्यमी पिंडमाहर्तुं प्रस्फुरद्दशनच्छदः ॥ 410 ॥
सोढुं तदक्षमः कश्चिदसुरः शुद्धदृक् तदा ।
हनिष्यति तमन्यायं शक्तः सन्सहते न हि ॥ 411 ॥

1 अमत्र a pot; cf. पाणिपात्रो दिगंबरः ।
2 आर्हति = आहार, food.
3 वा = इव, अकृतावासाः ।

सोपि रत्नप्रभां[1] गत्वा सागरोपमजीवितः[2]।
चिरं चतुर्मुखो दुःखं लोभादनुभविष्यति ॥ 412 ॥

....

....

तनूजः कल्किराजस्य बुद्धिमानजितंजयः।
पत्न्या चालनया[3] सार्धं यातैनं शरणं सुरम्[4] ॥ 426 ॥
सम्यग्दर्शनरत्नं च महार्घं स्वीकरिष्यति।
जिनेंद्रधर्ममाहात्म्यं दृष्ट्वा सुरविनिर्मितम् ॥ 447 ॥

Extract from Trilokasāra,

Palm-leaf Ms. p. 32

इदानीं शककल्किनोरुत्पत्तिमाह—

पण छस्सय वस्सं पणमासजुदं गमिय वीरणिव्वुइदो।
सगराजो सो कल्की चदुणवतियमहिय सगमासं ॥ 840 ॥

श्रीवीरनाथनिर्वृतेः सकाशात् पंचोत्तरषट्शतवर्षाणि (६०५) पंचमासयुतानि गत्वा पश्चात् विक्रमांकशकराजो जायते तत उपरि चतुर्णवत्युत्तरत्रिशत (३९४) वर्षाणि सप्त (७) मासाधिकानि गत्वा पश्चात् कल्की जायते।

इदानीं कल्किनः कृत्यं गाथाषट्केनाह—

सो उम्मग्गाहिमुहो चउम्मुहो सदरिवास परमाऊ।
चाळीस रज्जओ जिदभूमि पुच्छइ स मंतिगणं ॥ 841 ॥

स कल्क्युन्मार्गाभिमुखश्चतुर्मुखाख्यः सप्तति वर्षपरमायुष्यश्च चत्वारिंशद्वर्ष(४०)राज्यो जितभूमिः सन् स्वमंत्रिगणं पृच्छति।

अम्हाणं के अवसा णिग्गंथा अत्थि केरिसायारा।
णिद्धणवत्था भिक्खाभोजी जहसत्थमिदिवयणे ॥ 842 ॥

1 The name of the first hell.

2 सागरोपमः=असंख्येयः Tattvārtharājavārtika III, 38, 8. (Benares Ed. II, p, 149).

3 Also called चेलना.

4 No distinction is made between सुर and असुर in these passages.

5 This means 394 according to the principle अंकानां वामतो गतिः ; see note 9. of खद्वयाष्टाद्रि (=2800) विज्ञातवादिवृंदाभिवंदितः ॥ Guṇabhadra, Uttarapurana, Chap-61.

6 This is a mistake. See my paper on the date of Mahāvīra, Ind. Ant. Vol. xii, 22.

अस्माकं के अवशा इति मंत्रिणः कथयंति निर्ग्रंथाः संति इति पुनः पृच्छति ते कीदशा इति निर्धनवस्त्रा यथाशास्त्रं भिक्षाभोजिन इति मंत्रिणः प्रतिवचनं श्रुत्वा—

तप्पाणिउडे णिवडिदपढमं पिंडं तु सुंक मिदिगेज्झं ।
इदि णियमे सचिवकदे चत्ताहारा गया मुणिणो ॥ 843 ॥

तेषां निर्ग्रंथानां पाणिपुटे निपतितं प्रथमं पिंडं शुल्कमिति ग्राह्यमिति राज्ञो नियमे सचिवेन कृते सति त्यक्ताहाराः संतो मुनयो गताः ।

तं सोढुमक्खमो तं णिहणदि वज्जाउहेण असुरवई ।
सो भुंजदि रयणपहे दुक्खग्गाहेक्क जलरासिं ॥ 844 ॥

तमपराधं सोढुमक्षमो सुरपतिश्चं(श्चा)मरेंद्रो वज्रायुधेन तं राजानं निहन्ति स मृत्वा रत्नप्रभायां दुःखग्राह्यैकजलराशिं भुंक्ते ।

तब्भयदो तस्स सुदो आजिदंजय सण्णिदो सुरारिं तं ।
सरणं गच्छइ चेलयसण्णाए सह समाहेळाए ॥ 845 ॥

तस्मादसुरपतिभयात्तस्य राज्ञः सुतो जितंजयसंज्ञितश्चेलकेसंज्ञया स्वमहिष्या सहितं सुरारिं शरणं गच्छति ।

सम्मद्दंसणरयणं हिययाभरणं च कुणदि सो सिग्घं ।
पच्चक्खं दट्ठूणिह सुरकयजिणधम्ममाहप्पं ॥ 846 ॥

सुरकृतजिनधर्ममाहात्म्यं प्रत्यक्षं दृष्ट्वा शीघ्रं सम्यग्दर्शनरत्नं हृदयाभरणं करोति ।

1 See above note 3 p. 22.

FISCAL ADMINISTRATION UNDER EARLY COḺAS

BY H. KRISHNA SHASTRI

SOME of the striking features in the study of Coḻa inscriptions, which at first arrest the attention of the student are the elaborate detail and care shown in the wording of the documents, their revenue technicalities, the corporate nature of their transactions and the incidental light which these necessarily throw on the public and private life of the Tamil people in general. The key-note of the Dravidian genius as distinguished from that of the Aryan, has evidently to be sought for in one or more of these factors of national development. I confine myself at present to putting together such information as may be available from a study of inscriptions bearing on the second of the items noted above *viz.* the revenue administration and technicalities of the Coḻa period prior to the time of Rājarāja I—not omitting of course, to make some observations where necessary on the other points as well.

Early Tamil literature does not materially add to our knowledge of this important question. All that could be said has been ably summed up by Mr. V. Kanaka Sabhai Pillai in chapter IX of his 'Tamils 1800 years ago,' where he describes the social life of the Tamil people at that remote period. Some of the salient points noted are: "The principal thoroughfares in the interior of the country were guarded by the king's soldiers and tolls were levied on these highways. The system of Government, which was far from despotic, also conduced to the public welfare. The head of the government was a hereditary monarch. His power was restricted by five councils which were known as the 'Five great assemblies.'[1] The ministers attended to the collection and expenditure of revenue and the administration of justice. Customs, tolls and land-tax formed the chief sources of revenue. Customs were levied at all

1 Apparently the assemblies here referred to are the *pañcamaṇḍalis* (corresponding to the modern *panchāyats)* mentioned in the Gupta inscriptions.

the sea-ports. Tolls were collected on the trunk-roads used by caravans and at the frontier of each kingdom. The land-tax was paid in money or in kind at the option of the farmer. One-sixth of the produce on land was the legitimate share of the king: and for water supplied by the State, a water-cess was levied from the farmers." All these statements drawn mainly from Tamil literature, receive full support, as will be shown subsequently, from the numerous inscriptions with which the Tamil country is studded. One noteworthy point, however, is that while no definite statement has been found in literature about the organisation of village assemblies which, as stated above, forms the most important feature of Dravidian civilization, the inscriptions never fail to insist upon their existence.

There is no doubt that the Tamils, who at a distant past are supposed to have migrated to the South of India from the North-east corner of the Peninsula through the Magadha territory, must have naturally imbibed much of the Magadha culture which at that period was a model for nations to imitate. The excellent work, Kauṭilya's *Arthaśāstra*, recently brought to light by the unswerving labors of Pandit R. Shama Shastri of Mysore, has in it chapters fully devoted to administration, revenue collection, taxes, etc. There were no doubt co-operative undertakings, councils of ministers, guilds of merchants and consultative bodies of village elders. But the essentially democratic spirit of village administration in matters revenue and judicial, social and religious, as appears to have distinctly existed throughout the Dravidian kingdoms, is not to be found in the *Arthaśāstra* of Kauṭilya. That corporate life and the democratic will of the people received due consideration from the Aryan law-makers cannot altogether be denied. Epigraphical evidence too is not wanting to support this supposition. The Mālavas, for instance, as early as the fourth and fifth centuries of the Christian era, had a national assembly the organisation of which was the occasion for starting a new era called the Kṛta. So was it with the Licchavis.

The earliest glimpses of Tamil civilisation available

from historical data, present a state of perfection and organisation that suouldmake us pause and think of the long ages that must have elapsed before the Tamils as a race could have attained that stage of development. In the dawn of the sixth or rather of the 7th century A. D., to which some at least of the Tamil works extant have been assigned, lived the great Coḷa king Karikāla who carried out a grand scheme of agricultural improvement by constructing flood-banks on either side of the river Cauvery with the assistance of "all his subordinate kings such as Trilocana-Pallava and others whose eyes were directed towards his lotus-like feet." It is evidently this great project, no way inferior in its conception and magnitude to similar administrative measures adopted by the highly famous statesmen of the present day, that still contributes in a great measure to "the rich fertile flats of paddy fields, groves of areca and cocoanut palms and forests of plantain trees" of the Coḷa country. In fact it must have been mainly due to Karikāla's improvement that the river Cauvery which flows through the heart of the Coḷa country, came to be described in literature as the golden river whose garland consisted of gardens and which was the prosperity of the Coḷas. Other Coḷa kings that came after Karikāla were equally great; but their contribution to the happiness of the people by way of sound administrative measures, as in the case of Karikāla, does not appear to have been much. In their time there was an upheaval of religious enthusiasm: Buddhism and Jainism which were the strong opponents of the Śaivite and Vaiṣṇavite forms of Hinduism were practically driven out of the land. The kings also took an active part in this propoganda and some of them, it may be noted, came to be considered as saints.

With Vijayālaya began a new line of Coḷa kings whose revenue administration is the subject of this contribution. Vijayālaya is assigned to the latter part of the 9th century A. D., a period about which the Pallavas of Kāñcī, who had till then been wielding suzerain power, were slowly declining and the powerful Pāṇḍyas of the farthest South were also growing weak. Vijayālaya was entitled a Parakesarivarman 'the lion to enemy kings,' and after him the successors to the Coḻa throne regularly called themselves Rājakesarivarman 'lion among kings' and Parakesarivarman alternately. The famous Rājarāja I came very nearly a century later. Between him and Vijayālaya there were many ruling sovereigns; but the most prominent of these were Āditya I, Parāntaka I, Gaṇḍarāditya, Sundara-coḻa, Parāntaka II and Madhurāntaka Uttama-coḻa. Hundreds of their records are found throughout Southern India. A perusal of their contents sufficiently indicates, in unequivocal terms, the existence of peaceful rule and an organisation of government which, as far as could be gathered, compares not unfavorably, with the conditions obtaining at present, after a distance of more than a thousand years, under the benign British rule.

Professor Krishnasvami Aiyangar (*Ancient India* pp. 163 ff.) has dealt fully with the question of Coḻa administration in the light of published records ranging in date roughly from A. D. 800 to A. D. 1200. What he has herein stated practically covers the whole field. The village assemblies, as stated already, formed a distinct feature of Coḻa administration. Full details about the organisation of these assemblies, their elective basis, qualifications for membership, disqualifications, executive committees etc. have been supplied by two very interesting inscriptions which belong to the time of Parāntaka I (A. D. 907 to about 953). It must, however, be noted that it was not for the first time in the reign of Parāntaka I that these assemblies were organised and brought into existence. The system was in vogue in much earlier times. Three classes of assemblies appear to have existed; those of Brahmans which were called *sabhās;* those of the general body of residents in a village which were called *ūrār* and those of the merchants (and professionals?) called *nagarattār.* The district assembly, *nāṭṭār* was also a body which met when, perhaps, subjects touching the interests of the whole district were discussed, or when there were no *sabhās* to represent the villages within the district. Each holder of a share in a Brahman village (called *agrahāra*) had the right to a seat in the village *sabhā;* but he was required to be well-versed in one at least of the Dharmaśāstras or Codes of law. The question of a share-holder possessing his share by purchase, present or as *strīdhana*, seems to have arisen. It was decided that even such might be represented on the village council provided that they held a full share and not a fraction of it, and had studied a whole Veda with its *pariśiṣṭas.* The co-operative and constructive principles on which an assembly had to conduct its deliberations were evidently fully recognised and no member was allowed to persistently oppose, on penalty of a fine, the proceedings of the assembly by saying 'nay, nay' to every proposal that was brought up. Refractoriness on the part of members, as distinguished from an honest difference of opinion, was much discouraged. No rules regulating the management of the other classes of assemblies, viz. *ūrār, nagarattār* and *nāṭṭār* have come to light. Evidently all general qualifications for efficient membership such as those obtained in the Brahmanical *sabhās* must have also been in force, except perhaps the knowledge of the Veda and the Mantra-Brāhmaṇa.

The thus constituted assembly of a village was known by various names such as *perumakkaḷ* 'the big children' *peruṅguri-perumakkal* 'the big children of the big assembly,' *mahāsabhā*, *parudai* (pariṣat), *mūla-paruḍai*, *piramadeyakkiḷavar* 'the old men of the Brahmadeya,' *gaṇapperumakkaḷ*, 'the big children of the gaṇa' and *āḷumgaṇattar* 'the gaṇa members ruling (the village.)'[1] The assemblies generally met in temples where often special

1 The word *gaṇa* as applied to a tribal congregation is still prevalent among many Non-Brahmanical classes of Southern India who have their own caste assemblies and *panchāyats* where several questions concerning the particular society and individual members are discussed and amicably settled. The word *yajamān* among the trade-guilds and *gaṇācārya* among others prove the existence of such corporate life.

halls were constructed for that purpose.[1] Sometimes they are said to have assembled in theatrical halls of a temple such as those that existed in the great temples at Tanjore and Tiruvidamarudūr. It was not unusual also for the village assembly to sit in council under a tamarind tree, a pepul-margossa tree or an olive tree of the village. Trees with platforms round them are a common sight in Indian villages. The regular and constitutional meetings of the village assemblies must have been partly at least responsible for the existence of these platforms. The installation also of Nāga-stones on such platforms—specially under the shade of the pepul-margossa tree—may have been found necessary in view of the belief that the Nāgas always sit in judgment over a just decision or a charitable deed. The constituents of the *sabhās* were the big men of the village, i. e. the aged elders, the *bhaṭṭas*, 'the learned people,' the *viśiṣṭas* 'the very highly pious and upright men' and temple priests. Sometimes children are also mentioned as members of a *sabhā*—evidently it might be for the purpose of picking up pot-tickets mentioned in the Uttaramallur inscriptions. Often the merchants (nagarattār), residents and professionals (urār), and district representatives (nāṭṭā) also took their seat on the Brahman assemblies—the sabhās—though in most cases these had their own independent meetings. It must be noted that the representative of the king, the local officer, and the agents of the parties interested in the business of the day, were also present at the meetings of the assembly. The tendency towards corporate life did not stop with their village councils mentioned above. It extended even to the internal management of a temple. The *padipūdamūlattār* 'those that attend on the sacred feet of God,' the *tiruvuṇṇāḻigai-uḍaiyār* or *sabhaiyār* 'those in charge of (the management of) the sacred inside (of a temple),' *danmakaṭṭaḷaiyār* 'those (in charge) of organised charities,' *tiruk-*

1 Have we to understand that the *sabhā-maṇḍapas* in almost every Hindu temple of Southern India, now supposed to be the place for Naṭarāja and the divine congregation, were primarily intended for the meetings of village assemblies?

koyiluḍaiyār, 'those (in charge) of the sacred (precincts of the) temple,' *devakanmigaḻ* 'temple servants,' *upāsakas*, *māheśvaras*, *śrī-vaiṣṇavas*, *devar-maṉrāḍigaḻ* or *devar-iḍaic-cānar*, 'the shepherds (of the temple),' etc. are frequently mentioned. In addition to these were professional guilds who settled among themselves the business that concerned their particular community.

The general assembly of the village was both a deliberative and an executive body. It met together under beat of tomtom and transacted every kind of business that concerned the local temple and the village. They sold or purchased lands on behalf of the temple and in the latter case they made the lands invariably tax-free by receiving in advance a lump amount called *irai-kāval*, the interest on which would cover the annual rent due on the land. Sometimes when the temple as purchaser was unable to pay the *irai-kāval*, they distributed the same by common consent on the whole village. They received deposits of money made on behalf of the temple or from the temple itself, or again on account of other charities, and carried out the trust from the interest accruing regularly year after year. The investments were evidently utilised for original works and improvements. They formed themselves into various committees to watch the interest of the gardens, wet and dry fields, tanks and irrigation, tolls and shop-rents, waste-lands and their reclamation, the regular management of temple services and charities etc. Once a tank having given way, the village was threatened to be flooded away. A donation was made to the tank-committee to repair the breach, and it was stipulated that the interest on that amount may be regularly handed over to the local temple. The committee was thus both a banker and a trustee. In another similar case of a breach in an irrigation canal, the banks were strengthened and perhaps also broadened by acquiring portions of lands from the adjacent landholders,—this acquisition by purchase being entrusted to the garden-supervision committee. If a canal irrigating the fields of one village had to pass through the lands of another village, the assembly of the latter interfered, stipulated the course for the canal and charged a fee of one-in-five for the privilege. A committee was once appointed by the assembly of Uttaramattūr to enquire into the purity of gold that found exchange in that village. They appointed four residents from the street called Māḍavidhi, two from the army and three from the Brahman quarter (*śaṅkarappāḍi*),—all by election. It was stipulated that the persons selected must be neither young nor old and should have the necessary experience in testing gold. This committee examined the gold for all people and were instructed not to rub the gold on the touchstone (too much). The wax on which the rubbed gold-dust was collected, was to be handed over to the tank-supervision committee without any reservation. For arrears of land-tax, the assembly was empowered even to confiscate the lands and sell them by public auction. They made no exception even if these lands happened to belong to the temple. But as Hindus interested in the temple, they provided for the various services connected with the temple by communal contributions. Before public auction, the procedure adopted was to ask, i. e. to advertise once, twice and thrice, to know if there was any to purchase the land in question. Such sales were known as 'the king's big sales'—a phrase evidently used to denote the public nature of the transaction. One record states that the sale was proclaimed twice and (the bid) called out thrice.[1] Such sales were generally adopted when the original holders of lands had given them up or had absconded owing to their inability to pay the taxes. In the latter case the assembly sold the lands by auction to recover the arrears of rent, whereas in the former, the owners themselves disposed of the lands. A wet land having become mounded up with sand owing to floods in the Cauvery, the owners neglected cultivating it for six or seven years and evidently the rent having accumulated, they asked 'are there none to purchase this land?' A person

1 For a different explanation of the phrase *irukālāvadu mukkālāvadu*, which generally occurs in sales of land, see S. I. I. Vol. III. p. 17, note. 2.

came forward, purchased it and presented the same to the temple.

The taxes on landed property consisted of collections in kind and in coin, and the king was by a right vested in him, entitled to enjoy a very large number of them. 'Whichever the king may lay his hands upon and enjoy' is the phrase that occurs in copper-plate grants and stone inscriptions in giving away to a donee the full possession of a property with all its rights and enjoyments. They consisted of a good number of items of service called *kuḍimai* (tenancy obligations) which appear to have been as strictly demanded as land-revenue (*kaḍamai*) itself. In making grants of villages to Gods and Brahmans the original holders (*kuḍis*) were first divested of their rights of tenancy, evidently it must be by compensation. In some cases the *kuḍis* were retained. From this it may be inferred that the tenants (ryots) had an a priori right over the lands they cultivated, being subject only to *kaḍamai* and *kuḍimai* or as defined in other inscriptions to *kuḍimai* 'which was tenable at the door of the tenant' and to 'the income by taxes (*varippāḍu*) which the village paid.' When a land was granted, sold or exchanged (*parivartanai*), its boundaries were clearly defined, stones and milk bush were planted for demarcation purposes and the connected documents produced. If the donation was made for the first time by the king or under his orders, the *śrīmukha* (Tamil: *tirumugam*) 'royal order' intimating the donation was received by the assembly, was honoured by 'being placed on the head,' opened and read (in the presence of all).[1] The *ājñapti* or *āṇatti* who was to execute the order of the king affixed his signature and thus made the royal order take effect. Most of the land transactions referred to in inscriptions are free donations to temples, Brahmans and charitable institutions. Sometimes the property which was thus donated was purchased with all its rights and enjoyments 'in accordance to old custom' with all land (high and low), 'where the iguana runs and the tortoise

1 The small fee that was collected in order to celebrate thus the receipt of the royal order (*tirumugam*) was called *tirumugakkāṇam*.

crawls; with (slight) excess or deficiency (if any, in measurements); with specified exemptions (*parihāra*) and declarations, and after paying the 'full amount (agreed upon) and receiving all the land defined.' The sale-amount was always calculated in gold-bullion of standard weight and fineness, or occasionally in coin. In the former case, the gold intended for currency is defined as 'marked gold,' 'red gold brilliant as fire,' 'gold passed by the king (such as *Parakesari*, *Viḍelviḍugu*, *etc.*) and weighed by the standard stone of the village or of the treasury,' 'gold 9½ carats fine which is burnt, cut, heated to the brilliancy of fire, stamped and found not to be deficient on the touchstone or the balance.' The sale deed thus effected was drawn up first on the palm-leaf (*olai*) and then engraved on stone and copper. When this was done it was declared to be final and no further document for the transfer or receipt of property was necessary to produce nor would any such, if produced, be considered valid.

Irrigation received the special attention of Coḷa administrators. Karikāla's embankments on either side of the Cauvery have been already referred to. No natural source of water seems to have been allowed to waste. Irrigation tanks and wells were scrupulously kept in proper repair. Anicuts were thrown across the rivers. A special committee on each village assembly was entrusted with tank-supervision and perhaps generally with irrigation. Numerous references are found in inscriptions to channels, sluices, embankments, canals and so forth. Every grant of land, where it happened to be under an irrigation tank or canal, was especially provided with the conditions and methods of irrigation. The distribution of water was very carefully and systematically organised. Wet lands were divided for this purpose into flats severally called *kaṇāṛṛu*, *śadiram*, *śiragu*, *śadukkam* and *pāḍagam*, and the main and sub-channels that irrigated them received names of kings, princes, chiefs or other distinguished personages. Even the foot-paths and demarcation ridges between field and field were named and recognised, so that the revenue officers from a mere description of the boundaries, and of

punishment. The exact sense of these terms has not been made out.

The king was apparenlty the highest appellate authority in his country. He had numerous officials under him to organise and manage the various departments of administration. Later Coḷa inscriptions mention very nearly twenty such departments, besides the military. Thus the Dravidians developed, from the very beginning of their dominancy in the South, a system of government which was a monarchy regulated and controlled by a democratic organisation, in which the will of the people was fully and freely represented. History repeats itself, and in the fulness of time the Dravidian genius must influence to a very large extent the present government of the land.

GAṄGAVĀḌI

BY LEWIS RICE

AMONG the Jaina States which flourished in Southern India in early times, and held their own more or less throughout the first millennium of the Christian era, Gaṅgavāḍi was one of the most interesting, and played a prominent part. It derived its name from the dynasty of the Gaṅga kings whose dominion it formed, and occupied the greater portion of the existing Mysore country. Its subjects are to this day represented by the Gaṅgaḍikāras, the largest section still of the agricultural population, their name being a contraction of Gaṅgavāḍikāra.

But, long before this part was called Gaṅgavāḍi, it had been the scene of important events in history. For it was the region through which, early in the 3rd century B. C., Bhadrabāhu the *Śrutakevali* led the Jaina migration from the north of India, in order to escape a predicted famine of twelve years. Feeling his end approaching, he sent on the body of pilgrims to Punnāṭa, a State in the south-west of Mysore, and remained at Śrāvaṇa Belgoḷa, where he died. Hither also the celebrated Maurya emperor Candra-gupta is said to have accompanied him, having abdicated for that purpose. Ministering to him in his last moments as his sole attendant, Candra-gupta, a few years later, ended his own life at the same place. It was apparently in connexion with these movements that the separation arose of the Jainas into Digambaras and Śvetāmbaras. Evidence is not wanting in support of these statements. First-hand information as to the statecraft of the period is now available in the *Arthaśāstra* of Cāṇakya, the minister of Candra-gupta, of which an only copy has lately been discovered by Shama Shastri and published in Mysore. Subsequently, not only was there a seat of the Maurya government in the north of this country in the time of Candra-gupta's grandson Aśoka, but missionaries were then sent to the southern part, under the name of Mahiṣa-maṇḍala, as well as to Vanavāsa or Banavāsi, on the north-west, in efforts to spread the religion of the Buddha.

The rise of Gaṅgavāḍi may be traced to the 2nd century A. D., and was about coincident with the fall of the Āndhras or Śātavāhanas, whose name survives in the form of Śālivāhana, which in later times came to designate the prevailing Śaka era, dating from A. D. 78. At quite a modern period Mysore is described as the Śālivāhana country, but the nature of the connexion is not clear. Still, one record of the 16th century dates itself by the Śātavāhana-śaka instead of the Śālivāhana-śaka.

Testimony to the rule of the Śātavāhanas in ancient Mysore is confined to the north-west, where they were immediately followed by the Kadambas of Banavāsi. But the remainder of this country mostly came under the Gaṅgas, and was hence known as Gaṅgavāḍi, which takes the forms Gaṅgapāḍi and Gaṅgapāṭi in Sanskrit and Tamil. After the Āndhras, the dominant overlords of the Dekkhan were the Pallavas, who also gained the maritime countries lying along the east coast. They claim to have set up the Kadambas of Banavāsi, in the 3rd century, and assumed the rôle of patrons at the coronation of certain of the early Gaṅgas.

Gaṅgavāḍi was a Ninety-six Thousand country, the remaining portions of Mysore being occupied by the Noṇambavāḍi or Noḷambavāḍi Thirty-two Thousand, in the north-east, and the Banavāsi Twelve Thousand, in the north-west. But the former of these was much later in formation than the latter,—about the 8th century. In the south-west was Punnāṭa, mentioned by Ptolemy in the 2nd century, and later known as the Punnāḍ Six Thousand. The numerical descriptions attached to the names, which are sometimes used alone, are believed to indicate the revenue value of the countries, reckoned in *niṣkas*, an obsolete currency of more than one rate, but popularly supposed to be equivalent to *varahas* or pagodas. Or else they may refer to subdivisions, or *nāḍs*, which were called Thousands. That they represent the number of villages, it is quite plain, is physically impossible, even supposing the whole areas were occupied by villages and nothing else.

The original boundaries of Gaṅgavāḍi are given as—north, Marandale; east, Toṇḍa-nāḍ; west, the ocean towards Cera; south, Koṅgu. There is no difficulty in identifying these, except the one on the north. This I have so far been unable to trace or find. But it is of importance that it should be discovered. It appears again at the time when the Gaṅga king Śivamāra-Saigoṭṭa, who had been deposed and kept in confinement by the Rāṣṭrakūṭas, was released by them and reinstated. For the record says that he was again ruling the Gaṅgavāḍi Ninety-six Thousand up to Marandale as his boundary, as if to show that the whole of his kingdom even to the original limits had been restored to him. The place was probably somewhere between the Tuṅgabhadrā and the Kṛṣṇā rivers, as one record of the time of Śrīpuruṣa indicates that his boundary then extended to the north-east of the Bellary District. Of the remaining boundaries, Toṇḍa-nāḍ is the Madras country to the east of Mysore, variously called Toṇḍa-maṇḍalam and Tuṇḍāka-viṣayā. It was a Forty-eight Thousand country. Cera, mentioned in connexion with the west, is Cochin and Travancore. It is doubtful, however, whether Gaṅgavāḍi really touched the ocean, though it was no doubt very near at certain points. Koṅgu, on the south, is Coimbatore and Salem.

The first capital of Gaṅgavāḍi was Kuvalāla, a name modified later to Kovalāla, and then to Kolāla. This is the present Kolar, in the eastern part of Mysore, and situated to the west of the Pālār river. It has passed through so many vicissitudes, and been the area of so much fighting in modern times, that few remains of antiquity are now to be found there, municipal improvements, it is feared, having swept away whatever relics there may have been. In the 3rd century the capital was removed to Talekāḍ (Talavanapura in Sanskrit), a place in the south-east of Mysore, in a bend of the river Kāverī, which encircles it on three sides. Here the capital permanently remained, until its capture in 1004 brought the Gaṅga sovereignty to an end. It is now nearly buried under sand dunes, which continue to encroach upon it. Though this was the recognized capital, the royal residence was removed in the time of Śrī-puruṣa, in the 8th century, to a more central position at Maṇṇe or Mānyapura, some 30 miles north-west of Bangalore, on the plain lying to the east of the Devarāyadurga chain of mountains, and facing Nandidroog. Such was the prosperity of the State at this period that it came to be styled the Śrī-rājya, or Fortunate kingdom.

The main river of Gaṅgavāḍi is the Kāverī (Anglicised as Cauvery[1]), the Kabœros of the Greek geographer Pliny, and designated by Hindus the Dakṣiṇa Gaṅgā, or Ganges of the south. Its name is said to be derived from the *muni* Kavera, whose daughter Kāverī was fabled to be. But the Purāṇas assign to her a divine origin. According to one account, she was a daughter of Brahmā, born as a mortal in the person of the virgin Viṣṇumāyā or Lopāmudrā, whom Brahmā allowed to be regarded as the child of Kavera-muni. In order to obtain beatitude for her adoptive father, she resolved to become a river whose waters should purify from all sin. And once a year the Ganges itself is supposed to flow underground into the Kāverī at its source, so as to cleanse the stream from the pollution of the sins of the multitudes who bathe in it. The period of this mystic confluence, in Tulā-māsa, needless to say, is signalized by a great religious festival. On the first occasion when the floods came down, as promised them by Pārvatī, and the Coorgs plunged in to bathe, so violent was the rush of the water that it twisted the knots of the women's cloths round to the back; and in this fashion, opposed to the general custom in India, the Coorg women still wear them, in commemoration (says the Purāṇa) of the event.

The river has its source in the Western Ghats in Coorg, and flows in a generally south-east direction through

1 But the proper pronunciation is that of the words *car* (with *r* silent) and *vary*.

the Mysore to the island of Śivasamudram, where it descends from the tableland to the lower level of the Madras country. Here it separates Coimbatore from Salem, and continuing through Trichinopoly, where is the island of Śrīraṅgam, reaches the sea in the delta of Tanjore. Near where it enters Mysore from Coorg is a narrow gorge, below which the stream descends some 60 to 80 feet in a succession of rapids. At Rāmanāthpur is an old ford, by which the epic hero Rāma is said to have crossed the river on his expedition to Laṅkā or Ceylon. Farther down, an extensive system of irrigation is carried on on both banks by means of miles of canals or channels, led off from dams across the river. This fertile region, under the name of the Aṣṭagrāma, was conferred on the Vaiṣṇava reformer Rāmānuja in the 11th century. In about the middle of its course through this part is the island of Śrī-Raṅga, containing the historical fortress of Seringapatam. Passing on, round the site of the ancient capital city Talekāḍ or Talakāḍ, the river arrives at the island of Śivasamudram, where it ends its career in Mysore. Here are the celebrated Falls of the Kāverī, in which the stream hurls itself down some 320 feet in two distinct falls, one on each side of the island. The one on the west is called the Gagana Chukki (sky spray), and the one on the east the Bhar Chukki (heavy spray). The former tumbles with deafening roar over vast boulders in a cloud of foam, the whole place quivering with the impact. The column of vapour rising from it may often be seen for miles. It is at this fall that the Kāverī has been harnessed for electric power. The installation was completed in 1902, the first in India, and at that time the longest line of transmission in the world. For it conveyed the power 92 miles to the Kolar gold mines, which have profited greatly by its use, and have been provided repeatedly with additional supplies. From the same source the cities of Bangalore and Mysore obtain electric lighting, and mills are operated there. The other fall is quieter, and when in flood pours over in a continuous sheet a quarter of a mile wide. It has been compared to the Horse-shoe Fall at Niagara. Beyond the Falls the reunited stream rushes on through wild gorges, so narrow as at one point to be called the Mēke-dāṭu or Goat's Leap. Farther on is the Smoking Rock, which from the middle of the stream throws up a column of perpetual spray, though the water around is free from any sign of agitation.

Among the natural features of Gaṅgavāḍi are many notable mountains. They rise up in all parts in more or less isolated peaks, known as droogs (Sanskrit *durga*). Possessing springs of water at the summit, they have in many cases been fortified and made almost impregnable, especially before the invention of artillery. The one chiefly connected with the Gaṅgas was Nandagirī, from which they had one of their titles as Nandagiri-nātha. This is the well-known Nundydroog (Nandidurga), rising to about 5000 feet, standing at the end of the mountain range in the west of Kolar. At the beginning of the 9th century a Bāṇa queen had erected the temple of Bhoga-Nandīśvara at the village of Nandi, on the northern foot, and the Kālāmukha sect of Yogins had a *maṭha* at the temple of Yoga-Nandīśvara at the summit. The fortifications of the Mahrattas on the hill were greatly extended and strengthened by Tīpu Sultān, from whom the place was captured by the British in 1791. In the 19th century it became a sanatorium and hill station.

The establishment of the Gaṅgavāḍi kingdom is attributed to the agency of a Jaina priest named Siṁhanandi, known in literature. His action was induced by the arrival of two brothers, the Jaina princes Daḍiga and Mādhava, who had been sent away by their father Padmanābha from the north to save them from a threatened invasion of his territory. With their sister Ālabbe and attendant Brahmans (presumably Jaina Brahmans) they encamped on their way at Pērūr, the one in Kaḍapa District, still distinguished as Gaṅga-Pērūr, near Siddhavaṭṭam (Sidhout of the maps). Here they met with Siṁhanandi, who being interested in their story, took them by the hand, and gave them instruction and training. In due time he procured for them a kingdom as a boon from the goddess Padmāvatī, who confirmed it with the gift of a sword. Mādhava, who was but a boy at the time, seized the sword and wielded it with such vigour that a stone pillar he struck split in two. This was recognized as a favourable omen, and Mādhava became the first king of the Gaṅga line. But the succession was continued in the descendants of Daḍiga, and they were not long in establishing their power over the Mysore country, which was apparently without a ruler then. They mostly had the second distinctive name of Koṅguṇivarmmā.

The new rulers soon came into conflict with the Mahābali or Bāṇa kings, who had probably preceded the Pallava on the east and been driven towards Gaṅgavāḍi. Their territory is described as lying to the west of the Āndhra or Telugu country, and seems to have been known as the Vaḍugavaḷi Twelve Thousand. Bṛihad Bāṇa was compelled to pay tribute by the founder of the Kadamba kingdom and the Bāṇas continued in contact with Gaṅgavāḍi for some centuries on the north-east, where the Noḷambas were opposed to them as rival.

The Gaṅgas appear to have been a hardy and manly race. Of the fourth king, his mental energy is said to have been unimpaired to the end of life, implying that he lived to a great age. Of the next king it is said that his arms were grown stout and hard with athletic exercises. The fifth and sixth were interesting characters. They were named Avinīta or Nirvvinīta and Durvvinīta. The former was the son of a Kadamba princess, and crowned while an infant on his mother's lap. He was a ruler of great activity, and on one occasion, to the consternation of his attendants, plunged into the river Kāverī and crossed it when in full flood, being known in consequence as Curcuvāyda Gaṅga. He married a Punnāḍ princess, by whom he had the son Durvvinīta whom, on the advice of his *guru*, he attempted to set aside from the succession in favour of another son, probably by a different mother. In this he was aided by the Pallava and Rāṣṭrakūṭa kings, who crowned the latter, thus striving to perpetuate their patronage of the line. But Durvvinīta was able to vindicate his rights and defeat this conspiracy. There is reason to believe that he allied himself with the Cālukyas, who were then appearing in the south, by giving his daughter in marriage to the prince of that family. If so, the issue of this union was a son named Jayasiṁha-Vallabha, whom, after capturing the Pallava king on the field of battle, Durvvinīta seated on the Pallava throne. He was engaged too in many sanguinary wars to the east.

But he was also distinguished as a scholar. For he is said to have written a commentary on the 15th Sarga of the *Kirātārjunīya*, the Sanskrit poem by Bhāravi. This Sarga is remarkable for being entirely composed in verbal puzzles and riddles. One stanza contains no consonant but *n*, with a single *t* at the end; in another, each half line read backwards is similar to the other half. He is also said to have been himself the author of a *Śabdāvatāra*, the name of a work always attributed to the Jaina grammarian Pūjyapāda, being a *nyāsa* on Pāṇini. Possibly Pūjyapāda was his preceptor. He is besides said to have made a Sanskrit version of the *Vaḍḍakathā*, that is, the *Bṛihatkathā*, which is written in the Paiśācī dialect. There is a great probability that this Durvvinīta is the one named in Nṛpatuṅga's *Kavirājamārgga* among the distinguished early Kannaḍa authors.

In the 7th and 8th centuries the Pallavas suffered heavy defeats from the Gaṅgas and the Cālukyas, and lost their power. The Gaṅga king Śrīpuruṣa took away from them the title of Permmānaḍi, which implied supremacy, and adopted it himself, handing it down to his successors. His long reign of over 50 years was the period when the Gaṅgavāḍi kingdom reached the highest point of prosperity, and was known as the Śrī-rājya or Fortunate kingdom. His dates are absolutely fixed by the Jāvali plates, which give Śaka 672 or A. D. 750 (verified by Drs. Kielhorn and Fleet) as the 25th year of his reign, corroborated by the Devarhalli plates of Śaka 698 or A. D. 776, his 50th year.[1] He removed the royal residence to Maṇṇe or Mānyapura, as before stated.

1 The Pennukoṇḍa plates, newly discovered and admitted to be genuine, dispose of objections to the early chronology.

The crest of the Gaṅgas was an elephant, and was given to them by Indra. Both Śrīpuruṣa and his successor Śivamāra were greatly interested in this animal, of which Gaṅgavāḍi or Mysore is a home, in the southern forests. The elephant *kheddahs* are a peculiarly special entertainment on the occasion of royal or viceregal visits to the State. Both the Gaṅga kings mentioned above wrote works on the management of elephants. That by Śrīpuruṣa was called *Gajaśāstra*. But Śivamāra seems to have gone far beyond. He made a deep study of the *Pālakāpyam*, a Sanskrit work by Pālakāpya or Kareṇubhū, and having obtained an insight into the subject as taught by this *yati* born from the mouth of a female elephant, embodied his own system in a poem of a high order, called *Gajāṣṭakam*, so unique in rhythm and expression that if recited before a dumb man it would enable him to recover his speech. At a later period the Yuvarāja Būtugendra is said to have been like the son of Kareṇu in his knowledge of elephants, and five times overcame in battle the Koṅgas (the Tamil people of Koṅgu or Coimbatore), who resisted his tying up elephants, and according to ancient custom he captured herds difficult to catch.

But to return to the history. The reign of Śivamāra-Saigoṭṭa, the grandson and successor of Śrīpuruṣa, was disastrous. The Rāṣṭrakūṭas, who had been invading Gaṅgavāḍi, succeeded in overcoming the Gaṅgas, never before conquered, and took the king prisoner. He was led away into captivity and the conquerors appointed their own viceroys to rule the territory. The first of these was the king Dhruva Nirupama or Dhārāvarṣa's son Kambharasa, having the title Raṇāvaloka. But in the next reign, or about 814, the Rāṣṭrakūṭas reinstated Śivamāra on his throne, the king Govinda Prabhūtavarṣa and the Pallava king Nandivarmmā officiating at his coronation. Although at first the succeeding king Nṛpatuṅga Amoghavarṣa sought again to subdue the Gaṅgas, the policy towards them changed, and matrimonial alliances brought the two families into intimate friendship. The people and their language greatly interested him, and he compiled the

Grammar called *Kavirājamārgga*, with the aid perhaps of Śrīvijaya, the oldest manuscript yet found in Kannaḍa.

The recovery of independence for Gaṅgavāḍi is attributed to Rājamalla or Rācamalla Satyavākya, who came to the throne in 817, and these names were borne as titles by many of the succeeding kings. Others took the title of his son Nītimārgga. A new era of prosperity had thus set in for the State. But contests arose on the north-east against the Bāṇas and the Noḷambas. The latter, also called Noṇambas, were a branch of the Pallavas, who, on the overthrow of the main line established themselves, under the protection of the Gaṅgas, in the north of the country. Their subjects are still represented by the Noṇabas. Intermarriages alternated with hostilities. Nītimārgga captured Bāṇarasa's Mahārājara-nāḍ, also called the Mārājavāḍi Seven Thousand, with its capital at Vallur, probably in Kadapa District. About the same time Noḷambādhirāja was, under him, ruling the Gaṅga Six Thousand, which was in Kolar District, the king's younger sister having been given to him in marriage. But the Noḷamba king Mahendra declared his independence in about 878, and proclaimed himself Mahābali-kula-vidhvaṁsana, destroyer of the Mahābali (or Bāṇa) family. He, however, in his turn was slain by the Gaṅga king Ereyappa, who took the title of Mahendrāntaka. In the end the Gaṅga king Mārasiṁha (961-974) overcame the Noḷambas and received the title of Noḷambakulāntaka. But neither of the lines was totally destroyed.

Būtuga II (938-953), the younger son of Ereyappa, had gained the throne by slaying his elder brother. He was a close friend of the Rāṣṭrakūṭa king Baddega or Amoghavarṣa II, who gave him his daughter to wife, with a dowry of four provinces in the south Bombay country. On the death of Baddega, Būtugaassisted his son Kṛṣṇa or Kannara III in securing the throne from an usurper named Lalliya. And when Kannara was at war with the Cola king Rājāditya, Būtuga rendered him a farther great service by slaying that king at Takkolam in 949, having attacked him in single combat on his elephant, For this he was rewarded with the Banavāsi Twelve Thousand province, and he may have been assisted by Kannara in gaining his own throne by getting rid of his elder brother. His daughter was married to the son of Kṛṣṇa III, and became the mother of Indra Rāja, the last of the Rāṣṭrakūṭas, who ended his life in despair at Śrāvaṇa Beḷgola in 982.

Būtuga was succeeded by his son Mārasiṁha, who continued in close alliance with the Rāṣṭrakūṭas, and while Kannara or Akālavarṣa III had engaged in extensive conquests in the south, as far as Tanjore, fought for him northwards against Gurjjara or Gujarat, and against the Western Cālukya prince Rājāditya. He also put down the Noḷambas. He retired in 973, and died in Baṅkāpura in 974. The Gaṅga dominions now embraced the whole of the Mysore country and beyond, up to the Kṛṣṇā river. In the reign of his son Rācamalla Satyavākya IV, who succeeded him, was erected by his minister and general Cāmuṇḍa Rāya, in about 983, on the highest hill at Śrāvaṇa Beḷgola, that remarkable Jaina monument and object of worship, the colossal monolith statue of Gomaṭa or Gommaṭeśvara, which in daring conception and gigantic dimensions is without a rival in India. It was no doubt intended to symbolize the triumph and stability of Jainism, but in reality was fated to be more like the memorial of an expiring faith.

For the Rāṣṭrakūṭas had gone, and the Gaṅgas were soon to follow. Fortune deserted the two principal Jain states of the south. The Coḷas, who had overwhelmed all the countries on the east up to Orissa, including the Eastern Cālukyas, and were engaged in deadly struggles with the Western Cālukyas, closed in upon Gaṅgavāḍi. The Coḷa king Rājarāja had established himself in the Kolar country by 997. His son Rājendra Coḷa, in command of his father's forces, advanced against Talekāḍ, the Gaṅga capital, and this ancient city fell in 1004, and with it the Gaṅga line came to an end as a sovereign power. The event was marked by Rājendra Coḷa assuming the title of Gaṅgaikoṇḍa Coḷa, 'the Coḷa who took Gaṅgai.'

So far as can be determined, the invasion approached by way of the valley of the Shimsha river, and a province named Cikka Gaṅgavāḍi was formed in what is now the Cannapaṭṇa country, with its capital at Ponganūr or Honganūr. The name Gaṅgavāḍi continued in use for a considerable time afterwards, but gradually dropped out in favour of the Hoysala-rājya, when the latter ousted the Coḻas in 1116. But the annals of the Gaṅgavāḍi dominion, which had endured for well nigh eight hundred years, were not inglorious, as we have seen, and it deserves to be held in remembrance by the flourishing State which now fills its place.

THE MAṆḌALA OF KHAṆḌAROHĀ

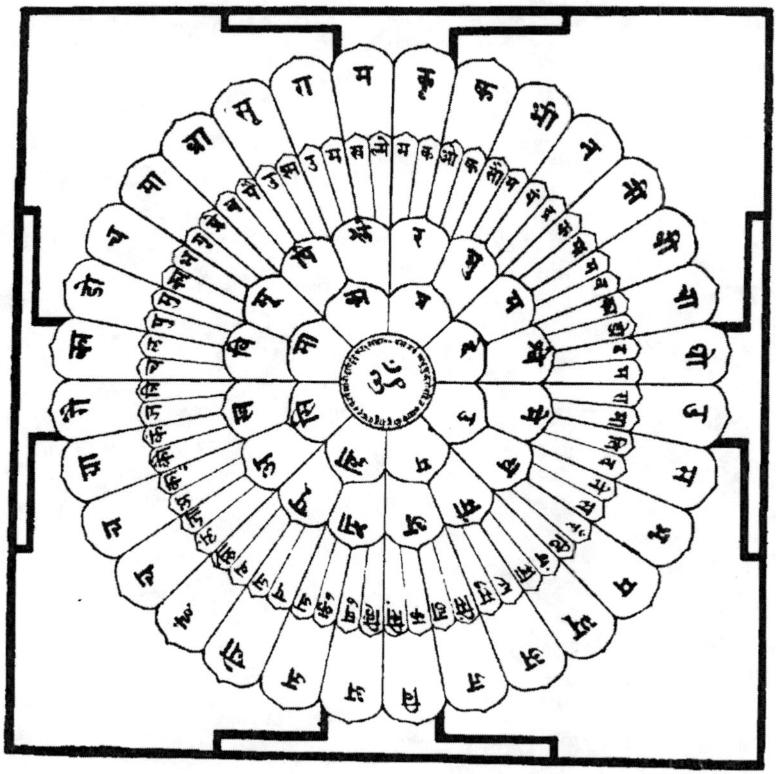

BOMBAY IN THE ELEVENTH CENTURY

BY HARAPRASAD SHASTRI

THERE is a manuscript in the Durbar Library, Nepal, written in bold and beautiful old Nevāri characters of the twelfth century of a Tāntrik work entitled the Ḍākārṇava. The manuscript is on thick Daphni paper called in Nepal Vaṁśapatra paper. The manuscript has travelled in many countries, specially Tibet, as it bears marginal notes in Tibetan smaller hand throughout. The subject matter treated of in this work is *indrajāla* or sorcery and Tāntrik worship of many spirits. The spirits worshipped are Vajravarāhī, Ḍākinī, Lāmā, Khaṇḍarohā, Rāpiṇī, Kākāsyā, Ulūkāsyā, Śvānāsyā, Śūkarāsyā, Yamadāḍī, Yamadūtī, Yamadaṁṣṭrī, Yamamathanī and others. It treats of Mantroddhāra, Kavaca, Rakṣāvidhi, Pūjāvidhi, Mudrā and so on. The language is Sanskrit of a sort, like the pigeon English of the Chinese. The authors of these Tāntrik Buddhist works hated the Brahmans for their fondness of correct Sanskrit—*suśabdavāditā.* They wrote simply for the sense—*arthasāraṇatām āśritya.* And so their language has now become as much mystic as their subject.

The fifth chapter of this book treats of the worship of Khaṇḍarohā ; but what is most interesting is her *maṇḍala* or mystic circle. This consist of five concentric circles, the whole forming an expanded lotus, with compartments marked out for petals.[1] Each petal has a letter in it. The letter is the initial letter of the name of one of the companion detities (āvaraṇa-devatā) of Kaṇḍarohā whose Mūlamantra is at the pericarp or karṇikā. The eight petals just round the pericarp form the heart of the Mantra, those following the heart form the neck. Those round the neck form the naval and those round the naval the head. The number of petals in concentric circles are altogether 8+16+64+32=120. So Khaṇḍarohā is accompanied by 120 deities. Of these 60 belong to the outer world and 60 to the inner

1 See the annexed diagram of the lotus.

world: the Macrocosom and the Microcosom. The sixty spirits representing the outer world are deities presiding over different countries, districts and cities of India and the surrounding countries, not in any definite order, as will appear from the accompanying extracts containing these names. There is an exact agreement between these names and their initial letters in the petals.

The interest of this *maṇḍala* lies in the fact that the 52nd name is *Mumbanī* and the 52nd initial letter is *Mu* in the naval, showing that there was a shrine to Devī Mumbanī in the island of Bombay. This shrine can be no other than the present shrine of Mumbā-devī on the Malabar Hills. So Ḍākārṇava in its fifth chapter speaks of the island city of Bombay and its eponymous shrine and deity.

The manuscript of Ḍākārṇava, as above mentioned, belongs to the 12th century after christ. The Tengur collection of the Tibetans contains a translation of this work, and as the collection was made in the 13th century the translation may be referred to a century earlier and the composition of the Sanskrit original to a century earlier still, i. e. to the eleventh century. It may go earlier of course. But the most cautions calculation cannot place it later than the eleventh century. So here we have the earliest mention yet known of Bombay the Gate of India and the second city of the Indian Empire. It was then a small place claiming notoriety as the seat of a goddess. In Hindu India temples and shrines used to attract population as commerce and courts do now.

Salsette and Karle in the immediate vicinity of Bombay contain cave temples which are at least as old as the 5th and 6th century of the Christian era. Those who excavated these caves must have known Bombay which is so near them and so beautifully situated and hence it is probable that they erected a temple in this island too.

Ḍākārṇava, Extracts from Adhyāya V.

अतः परं प्रवक्ष्यामि सत्त्वानां हितकाम्यया ।
खण्डरोहापदे स्थित्वा वज्रडाकः स्वयं प्रभुः ॥
चतुश्चक्रसरोजेषु नाडीशतं च विंशति ।
तेषु नामं यथान्याय्यं वक्ष्यते तत्त्वभाजनां ॥
मध्यदेशी कलिङ्गी च ओड्डु कर्णाटकीसरी ।
सौराष्ट्री मलयो वङ्गी द्रवडी च कलिङ्गकी ॥
गालवी तु महारठी वरेन्द्री कामरूपिणी ।
डोहली ढाविदेशी च भरौडी रौढ मागधी ॥
तिरभुक्ति(सत्ति) दद्दरण्डी नेपाली सरवासिनी ।
रौढी ढिक्करी वङ्गाली खाडी च हरिकेलकी ॥
सुवर्णद्वीपी सिंहली च डांमडी च कैत्तोरकी ।
सिन्धु हिमालयी बुडी कुरुत्ती जडरी पथी ॥
जर्ज्जवती वरुणा च ओरियाणलम्पाककी ।
जालन्धरी अर्बुदी च कश्मीरि कोशली कछी ॥
जयंती त्रिशक्ती चशी लहरी पूररोहिकी ।
मुम्बनी काम्बोजकी च भट्टालिकी गृहदेवती ॥
प्रेतपुरी वलभी च (वभभौच) पेलवी चोपपेलवी ।
श्मशानी उपश्मशानी महोदधितटी खसी ॥
म्लेच्छी च सर्व्वदेशकी देवी चतुःषष्टिः क्रमात् ।
नाभिचक्रेषु योगिन्यः विज्ञेया कुलनाडिकाः ॥
हृदयचक्रे तथा अष्टधूतिका सर्वगामिनी ।
प्रयागदेवकोटाश्चै उज्जयिन्यां महालक्ष्मी ॥
ज्वालामुखी सिद्धसिम्भली महिलो कौमारी पौरिकी ।
एवं सर्वहृदिस्थाने मायाकार सुक्षेत्रिणी ॥
कण्ठचक्रस्य देवीं च वर्ण्यते वरनायिकीं ।
षोडशैव महाभागा धातूनां षोडशैव तु ॥
रक्ता शुक्रा मज्ज श्वेदा मेधा चर्म मांसा अस्थी च ।
श्वायुः पूयं अन्त्रे स्त्रयंभुव विट्ट मूत्र पित्तश्लेष्मिकीं ॥
रहस्यादिपदैर्यातु ताभि सदवाहिनी ।

मस्तकेषु महादेवी चक्रे द्वात्रिंशनालिका ॥
होमक्रमेषु सर्वत्र सर्वासिद्धि महद्भुता ।
[१]कृष्ण(।) [२]करालि भी[३]भच्छी न[४]न्द्री तीता[५] विनायि[६]का ॥
[७]चाँमुण्डी घोररूपा तु उ[९]मादेवी सर[१०]स्वती ।
भद्र[११]काली महा[१२]काली स्थूल[१३]काली पर[१४]ाजिता ॥
[१५]जया विज[१६]या [१७]अजिता ज[१८]यन्ती घोर[१९]दंष्ट्री च ।
[२०]इन्द्री [२१]चण्डी चतु[२२]ष्पथी ग्राम[२३]वासिनी रौद्रि[२४]की ॥
[२५]कौम्बोजी [२६]डोम्बी च[२७]ण्डाली [२८]मातङ्गी ब्राह्म[२९]णी सूद्रि[३०]का ।
राज[३१]पुत्री [३२]महर्द्धिकी दिव्यमदपूरिका ॥
इत्येवं नाडिचक्रेषु खण्डरोहानुगामिनी ।
कथयन्तु मम स्वामी किं मया[त]त्र गामिकां ॥
धातु सर्वशरीरं तु खतुल्यकात्र भावया ।
भूभागैवर्त्त जानीयात् देशभिन्ना भूम्येक तु ॥
खण्डखण्डं गतो धातुरथवा देशहोरयः ।
ण्डकारं सूचितो तेन अण्डगर्भेषु लक्षणात् ॥
रोप्यते ह्यत्र विज्ञानं यादृशा यस्य धातुपु ।
आलयं तं विजानीयो कर्म्मखण्डरोहिका स्वयम् ॥
हार्य्यमाणं महापापं मारणो सर्वधातुकं ।
तैश्च सत्त्वान विगातीव खण्डरोहा सर्वकार्म्मिकी ॥
नायकी वरयोगिन्यां स्वसंक्रान्ता थिती पराम् ।
मीनश्चोदयकाले तु मासि(कामा) फाल्गुनके परे ॥
आवरगोदावरीद्वीपे महारागस्वभाविनि ।
नाभावकारकी देवी अद्वयपदमाश्रिता ॥
सप्तत्रिंशात्मकमध्ये उत्पद्यान्ति स्वमन्त्रजाम् ॥

ॐ वसजर्व खवुश्रुद्धरोवाहिजकाडायेकी हूंनींहूंये फट् व फटर्नस्वानी हाये हूं २ फट् २ स्वाहा ॐ ।

इदं मन्त्रप्रयोगेण मण्डनं सर्वकामिकम् ।
एकैकस्य देवीनां मध्येषु चतुश्चक्रजां ॥
उपायप्रज्ञात्मकं सर्व्वं धर्म्मोदयेषु मध्यतः ।
चतुर्द्वारसमायुक्तं तोरणं तद्विभूषितम् ॥

खाद्यमानं महामांसं भैरवनादनादितम् ।
लामाचक्रं तु गोमांसं डाकिनी दन्तिमांसकम् ॥
वाराहि सर्वमासञ्च समयसरम्वयोगतः ।
मन्त्रसद्भावतो ज्ञात्वा न मन्त्राक्षरवाचकम् ॥
सर्व्वसत्त्वेषु यद्वाद्यं तन्मन्त्र योगिनी स्मृतम् ।
यदि अक्षरिकं मन्त्रं लिपगोतीव सन्निभम् ॥
नालिकारन्ध्ररन्ध्रेषु श्वासाकारसंज्ञकम् ।
मन्त्रयानं तु चित्तं हि आपादान्त निरोधनात् ॥
देशे देशे तु संचारं मध्यदेशेषु चागतात् ।
तृप्तिः कुर्य्या स्वयन्त्रेषु घटवत् पानपावयेत् ॥
यन्त्रं श्वासने स्थित्वा तु भ्रामयेत् घ्राणचक्रवत् ।
चेतनाभ्राम्यमाणे तु मणिरन्ध्रं च पीडयेत् ॥
नवरन्ध्रेषु वीजं च भावयेद्धन्त्रादिना ।
अथवा सर्वनाडीषु मन्त्रन्यासमिहाक्षरैः ॥

म क ओ क सौ म वं द्र क मा म ख का डा ढ भ रा मा ति द ने स रँ ढि वं खा ह सु सिं डा क सिं हि वु कु ज प ज व ओ लं । जा अ का कौ कं ज त्रि च ल पु मु का भ गृ प्रे व पै उ श्म उ म ख म्ले । इति नाभिः ।

प्र दे उ म ज्वा सि मा कौ । इति हृदये ।

र सु म स्त्रे मे च मां अ स्ना पू अं स्व वि मू पि श्ले । इति कण्ठस्य च । कृ क भी न ती वि चा घो उ स भ म स्थू अ ज वि अ ज घो इ च च ग्रा रौ का डो च मा ब्रा सू रा [म] इति मस्तचक्रस्य ।

अथवा अभेयादि नामकम् ।

तेषु चाद्यक्षरं सर्व्वं देयं मस्तचक्रके ।
इदं यन्त्रं महाधीमान् प्राणवायु विधार्य्यते ॥
चक्रक्रमे सूत्रयेत् कोष्ट चतुपद्मदलाकृतिम् ।
वर्तुलाकार सर्व्वञ्च पञ्चसूत्राणि पातयेत् ॥
अष्ट षोडश चाषाष्टै द्वात्रिंश कोष्टकं मतम् ।
कर्णिकास्थानमासाद्य भ्रमणं प्राणशक्तिभिः ॥
यावातदधूती वायु तावयन्त्रमिहोच्यताम् ।

यदि वा चैव कुर्व्वीत मन्त्रं गीयति कालिकाम् ॥
घनिः प्राणसमाकीर्णा नवनाडी तु रोधयेत् ।
न रोगं न जरा न कष्टं न क्षुत्पिपासकं सदा ॥
एवमादिमनन्तं च न व्याधिं मरणादिकम् ।
पञ्चमण्डलके चाथ वाहयेत् सर्वयन्त्रकम् ॥
धातुरायतनान्यादि भक्षयेदमृतयोगवान् ।
इत्याह भगवान् स्वामी वज्रडाकस्तथागतः ॥
सर्ववीरसमायोगात् वज्रसत्वः परं सुखम् ॥

VIRŪPĀKṢA II OF VIJAYANAGAR

BY S. KRISHNASWAMI AIYANGAR

THE period intervening between the death of Devarāya II in A. D. 1449 and the accession of the first Sāḷuva, Narasiṅga or Narasiṁha, was one of darkness and there prevailed some confusion as to the succession of rulers following Devarāya. That Mallikārjuna, Immaḍi Prauḍa Devarāya, son of Devarāya II by Ponnalādevī, succeeded his father upon the throne is now placed beyond doubt by the *Gaṅgādāsapratāpavilāsam* and the copper plate in possession of Rāmacandrāpura Maṭha (Nagar 65).[1] The problem that is proposed to be taken up here is, who succeeded Mallikārjuna and what was the actual character of the succession? The further consideration of this question is rendered necessary by the discovery[2] of a copper plate grant[3] issued by Virūpākṣa on the day of his coronation in the year Śaka, *Vasu-aṣṭa-guṇa-bhū* (1388), the year Pārthiva, kārttika, kṛṣṇa-pañcamī (fifth of the dark half), about November-December of the year A. D. 1466.

The passages pertinent to this question in the book above referred to are these:—Virūpākṣa should have succeeded to the throne in Śaka 1387, according to Mr. Krishna Shastri, who seems inclined to regard him as the son of Mallikārjuna. Virūpākṣa's dates range between A. D. 1466 and 1485. What is more, Mr. Shastri rejects Professor Kielhorn's acceptance of Virūpākṣa as the son of Devarāya II by Siṁhalādevī, and would regard him rather as the son of Devarāya II's brother, Pratāpadeva, 'who acquired the kingdom from his elder brother.' The other passage is Ferishta's description of the position of Narasiṅga and the mention in the Burhan-i-Maasir

1 Epigraphia Carnāṭaka, Vol. VIII, ii, pp. 283–4. For a discussion of this point and for the whole period reference may be made to my "A little-known chapter of Vijayanagar History," Madras 1916.

2 By Mr. A. Rangaswami Sarasvati, B. A., the University Research student, working with me.

3 Printed in full at the end of this paper.

of Mālūr as a principal fort in the kingdom from which Kañcī was attacked; and the utter absence of any reference to the ruling power in all these transactions indicates a want of understanding between Narasiṅga and Virūpākṣa which would warrant the inference that Virūpākṣa perhaps came to the throne by means which did not commend themselves to the powerful viceroy.

The position then is this. Mallikārjuna died in A. D. 1465–6 or thereabouts, and his half brother succeeded, setting aside his two nephews, Rājaśekhara and Virūpākṣa. These naturally created a powerful party against him and he was not perhaps quite worthy of the exalted position.

The points actually demanding reconsideration are: (1) whether Virūpākṣa the successor of Mallikārjuna was the son of Devarāya II or of his brother Pratāpadeva; and (2) whether he actually usurped the throne setting aside the sons of Mallikārjuna, namely, Rājaśekhara and Virūpākṣa.

The Satyamaṅgalam plates[1] of Devarāya II refer to a brother (*anujanmā*) of Devarāya by name Pratāpa Deva. He was successively governor, under his elder brother, of Terukanambi in Mysore, Mulbāgalrājya, and later still of Maratakanagara prānta, the district round Vṛncīpuram (Maratakanagara). This prince pre-deceased his brother, having died in A. D. 1446.[2] He does not appear to have been associated with Ghanādrirājyam (Penukonda Government) particularly. With these facts let us proceed to examine the Śrīśailam plates with us at present. The passage pertinent to the question runs thus—

Tasya[3] Nārāyaṇīdevyām utpannaḥ śubhalakṣaṇaḥ ।
Pratāparāya ityākhyām agamat pārthivottamaḥ ॥
Guṇairanekairavanītalesmin
virājamānaḥ sukṛtāptakīrtiḥ ।
Nijāgrajāt prāpta-*Ghanādrirājyaḥ*
sādhīkṛtārthī janapārijātaḥ ॥

1 Epigraphia Indica III. p. 37 ff.

2 Rice, Śrāv. Bel. Inscrip. p. 125.

3 I. e. Vijayasya.

Tasya Siddhaladevīti bhāryā lakṣaṇasaṁyutā ।
Lakṣmīr Nārāyaṇasyeva jātā trijagadambikā ॥

Tasyāṁ Śivaḥ prādurabhūd guṇāḍhyo
nāmnā Virūpākṣa iti prasiddhaḥ ।
Rajādhirājaḥ kṣitipālamauḷir
vadānyamūrtiḥ karuṇaikasindhuḥ ॥
Nijapratāpādadhigatya rājyaṁ
samastabhāgyaiḥ parisevyamānaḥ ।
Khaḍgāgrataḥ sarvaripūn vijitya
sammodate vīravilāsabhūmiḥ ॥

There are two other inscriptions bearing upon the point. Maḷavalli 121 published in the Epigraphia Carnāṭaka III is the first; the second is the one relied upon by Rai Sahib Krishna Shastri, who in his report for the year 1914 states:—"The father of Virūpākṣa was Pratāpa or Prauḍha-Pratāpa. I have suggested (Arch. Sur. Rep. for 1907–8, p. 252, note 5) that this cannot be identical with Devarāya II as Prof. Kielhorn apparently thought (Epigraphia Indica V, Appendix II, 18 ‡ a ‡) but must be his younger brother Pratāpa Devarāya who is mentioned in the Satyamaṅgalam plates of Devarāya II as having held a high office under his royal brother. (Epig. Ind. III. p. 36). This is supported by what is stated in the present inscription, viz., that the former 'acquired the rule of the kingdom of Ghanādri (i. e. Penugonda) from his elder brother. Again, the wife of this Pratāpa and the mother of Virūpākṣa was Siddhaladevī as given in our record. Mr. Rice, however, gives the name as Siṁhaladevī in Ep. Car. Vol. III. Maḷavalli 121. It is possible that Siṁhaladevī is a mistake for Siddhaladevī. Virūpākṣa is stated in our record to have secured his succession to the Vijayanagar throne by his own prowess (*nija-pratāpāt*). Evidently there was some trouble in the succession subsequent to the death of Mallikārjuna Immaḍi-Prauḍa Dēvarāya II." This grant is dated almost exactly a year after that of the Śrīśailam plates. In respect of details these two agree; while in material particulars these two together differ from the Maḷavalli plates (of date A. D. 1474, six years later than the

Śrīśailam plates) which have in place of the first four lines—

> Tasya Nārāyaṇīdevyām *prādurāsīt yaśōdhanaḥ* ।
> *Prauḍhapratāpavibhavaḥ Pratāpākhyo mahīpatiḥ* ॥
> Guṇairanekairavanītalesmin
> virājamānaḥ sukṛtāptakīrtiḥ ।
> Nijāgrajāprāptam *anādirājyaṁ*
> sādhīkṛtārthī *vraja*-pārijātaḥ ॥

All the plates apparently make the same statement in the first two lines, namely, to Vijaya by Nārāyaṇīdevī was born a *king* called Pratāpa, because of 'the possession of mature valour.' The words *Mahīpati* and *Pārthivottamaḥ* seem unmistakably to indicate that he had been actually king. Besides the term *Prauḍha* before *Pratāpa* has been associated with the king Devarāya almost invariably to form a part of his name, while it is nothing like so closely associated with the name of his brother. The terms *anādirājyam* (immemorial kingdom) and *vrajapārijātaḥ* (the most excellent among the 'Yadus') would seem to have the same tendency. The substitution of *Ghanādri* for the word *anādi* does make a change in significance, while that of *vraja* for *jana* or vice versa does not really matter. There really is nothing so far to compell the conclusion that the person referred to is not Devarāya II. The expression *nijāgrajāt prāptam*, with the variant *nijāgrajā* for the first part, does make a material alteration which seems to have led to the Government Epigraphist taking it as referring to Devarāya II's brother Pratāpadeva. Assuming the reading *nijāgrajāt* to be the correct reading, he takes it that this part refers to Pratāpadeva son of Vijaya, who probably was the governor of Ghanādrirājyam under his brother. If, on the other hand, it is taken as referring to Devarāya II, we have no knowledge of an elder brother of his, nor of his having been governor of Ghanādri. If again it is possible to take Ghanādri with *nijāgrajā* instead of *nijāgrajāt*, the meaning would be that Devarāya II got the Penukonda viceroyalty from his elder sister, possibly Harimā referred to in a Chitaldroog record,[1] the wife of Sāḷuva Tippa who was viceroy of Mulbāgal-mahārājya (major province).

While, therefore, it is just possible that the reading may actually be the one or the other, the actual expressions used seem to refer to a monarch that ruled and not to a younger brother who did not occupy the throne at all. The decision must then rest upon the Kāñcī inscriptions[2] on which the late Prof. Kielhorn based his conclusions. The expressions actually used are Śrī-*Vīrapratāpa Devarāyamahārāyar* kumārar Mallikārjunadeva Mahārāyar (Mallikārjuna, Śaka 1387, the son of the glorious Vīrapratāpa Deva Mahārāya) in respect of Mallikārjuna; and Śrī *Devarāya Mahārāyar* kumārar śrī Virūpākṣadeva Mahārāyar (the glorious Virūpākṣadeva Mahārāya, Śaka 1392, the son of the glorious Devarāya Mahārāya).

The dropping of the term Vīrapratāpa in the second of these records cannot be held to state that Virūpākṣa was the son of Pratāpa Devarāya, as we have no warrant for assuming that this prince was ever known by the designation Devaraya, though this forms part of the name Pratāpa Deva who is also often known as Pratāparāya. The doubts and the difficulties raised by the three copper plates of Virūpākṣa notwithstanding, it would be difficult to resist the conclusion that *Mallikārjuna and Virūpākṣa were sons of Devarāya II by different wives.*

In regard to the second part of our thesis, namely, whether Virūpākṣa usurped the throne, we are at one with Rai Sahib Krishna Shastri in suspecting that there was some trouble in the succession of Virūpākṣa to the throne, whether it be after the death of Mallikārjuna or before. The expression *nijapratāpād adhigatya rājyam* justifies the suspicion, as also the attitude of the viceroys and the ascent of the Sāḷuvas to supreme power. On this point we get unexpected light from the Vaiṣṇava work Prapannāmṛtam compiled in the reign of Veṅkaṭapatirāya, who

1 Srīmān āste praśasto Vijayanṛpasuto Devarāyakṣitīndraḥ ।
Tasyāgrajāyā Harimāṅganāyāḥ prāṇeśvaraḥ Sāḷuva Tipparājaḥ ।
(Chitaldroog, 29, Ep. Car. XI).

2 Indian Antiquary XXI. p. 322.

died in the year A. D. 1614, by a disciple of the grandson of Kumāra Tātācārya, the contemporary of Rāmarāya who fell at Talikota in A. D. 1565. In writing the story of Yeṭur Siṅgarācārya, the founder of the Yeṭur section of these Tātācāryas he has the following—

Nṛsiṁhāryō mahātejāḥ sarvaśāstraviśāradaḥ ।
Eṭūrunāma nagaraṁ sa prāpa sumahāyaśāḥ ॥

....

Tasminn Eṭūrunagare kañcit kālaṁ samāsthitaḥ ।
Tasmin kāle mahātejā Virūpākṣo mahābalaḥ ॥

Śaśāsa rājyaṁ dharmeṇa vijaye nagare nṛipaḥ ।
Driṣṭvāsahiṣṇavas sarve Virūpākṣasya vaibhavam ॥

Jñātayo hiṁsituṁ yatnañ cakrire baladarpitāḥ ।
Virūpākṣo viditvātha teṣāṁ tat karma kṛtsnaśaḥ ॥

Diśāntaram avasthāya nirgatya nagarād bahiḥ ।
Gūḍho rahasi kasmiñścit kañcit kālam ināya saḥ ॥

Tataḥ sampādya mahatīṁ senāṁ sa caturaṅgiṇīm ।
Kenāpyajñātavṛttānto niśīthe sa balī mahān ॥

Vijayaṁ nagaram prāpya Virūpākṣo nṛpottamaḥ ।
Niśśeṣaṁ sarva śatrūṇāṁ vadhaṁ cakre mahābalaḥ ॥

Vijayākhye tatas tasmin nagare pūrvavat tadā ।
Rājyam praśāsayañs tasthau sarvalokamahīpatiḥ ॥

Niśīthe bāndhavas sarve tena ye nihatā nṛpāḥ ।
Piśācabhūtās te sarve putrapautrādikā janāḥ ॥

Taṁ nṛpam pīḍayāmāsur Virūpākṣaṁ divāniśam ।
Visṛjya rājabhavanaṁ Virūpākṣo mahāmatiḥ ॥

Punar anyad vidhāyāśu rājaveśma mahābalaḥ ।
Rājyam praśāsayañs tasthau tatra sarvajanais saha ॥

Pratirātram piśācānāṁ teṣāṁ kōlāhalo ravaḥ ।
Pratāpaś ca mahañs tatra śrūyate rājaveśmani ॥

Paiśācyamocanārthāya teṣām rājamahātmanā ।
Kanyāgobhūmidānāni gṛhadānānyanekaśaḥ ॥

Puṇyavratānyanekāni kṛtāny anyāni yāni ca ।
Sa tair na mōcitā dānair ghōrapaiśācyavedanā ॥

Without actually translating the passage, the substance of it may be given as follows: Nṛsiṁharāya (*vulgo*

Śiṅgarācārya) was in residence at Yeṭūr for some time having come there from Kāñcī (?). Virūpākṣa was then the ruling sovereign in Vijayanagar. His cousins and others getting jealous of his great prosperity made his position very uncomfortable. Virūpākṣa went into exile and had to bide his time. Sometime after, having collected together a large army, he attacked his enemies and destroyed all his relatives that caused him so much trouble. He then ascended the throne but the royal palace at Vijayanagar had become unfit for residence because his victims, having become *piśācas*, haunted the whole city and made life impossible. Then the story goes on to say that Śiṅgarācārya by reading the Rāmāyaṇa in the ghost-haunted part of the city, released the ghosts from the *paiśāca* life, and thus rid Virūpākṣa of this pest. Virūpākṣa's grant to this Ācārya was in gratitude for this great peace that the Ācārya gave him.

The two expressions that occur in his inscriptions, *nijapratāpād adhigatya rājyam* 'having taken possession of the kingdom by his own valour,' and *khaḍgāgratas sarvaripūn vijitya* 'having overcome all his enemies at the point of the sword,' seem but the voice from the grave of what is described in comparatively clear, though somewhat coloured, language by the hagiologist. That this expression is *saṅgrāmataḥ* 'in battle,' would alter the purport but little, though it would give the deed perhaps a dignity that it did not possess. Even in this slight change there might have been more than meets the eye. Paiśāca life is the fate of those that die 'bad deaths' (*durmaraṇa*) and death in war entitles one to *svarga* (Indra's heaven). There is one other minor change also noticeable. The coronation grant (the Śriśailam plates) has *pitryaṁ siṁhāsanam*, the throne of his father, at the worst the throne of his ancestors. This gets altered in the Maḷavalli grant into *divyaṁ siṁhāsanam* (the divine throne). Whether the alteration was made by accident or design is more than can be decided at present. The Śriśailam plates belong to Śaka 1388, the Bellary plates to the next year, and the Maḷavalli 121, to A. D. 1396.

These three grants studied comparatively in the light of the passage from the Prapannāmṛtam leave hardly any doubt that Virūpākṣa waded through slaughter to the throne; and this incident perhaps finds a distant but inaccurate echo in the story that Nuniz has to relate of the events following the death of Devarāya II. If this conclusion should turn out to be correct in the light of further research, it would remove another dark spot in Vijayanagar history and make the position of the Sāḷuvas clearer, exhibiting the Sāḷuva usurpation in the true light of a patriotic and wise act of far-seeing statesmanship.

Transcript of the
Śrīśailam Plates of Virūpākṣa

[I.2]श्रीगणाधिपतये नमः। नमस्तुंगशिरश्चुंबिचन्द्रचामरचारवे । त्रैलोक्यनगरारंभमूलस्तंभाय शंभवे ॥ मदामोदभ्रमद्भृङ्गनिवारणकरोज्वलः । अव्याद्गणपतिर्विश्वं विश्वविघ्ननिवारणः ॥ अत्युज्वलमुदाराङ्गं घृष्टिकायं बिभर्ति यः । सपायादखिलं विश्वं विष्णुरेष सनातनः ॥ अस्ति श्रीकमलालयानुजतया दीव्यन्नभोमण्डले नक्षत्राधिपतिः प्रभाभिरनिशं दिङ्मंडलोल्लासकृ(त्) । क्षीराब्धिप्रभवः कलानिधिरिति ख्यातस्सुधांशुस्स्वयं मौलौ यस्य विभूषणत्वमगमच्छंभोर्भवानीपतेः ॥ तस्यान्वयेत्र संभूतो यदुर्नाम महीपतिः । तद्वंशजेन भूरेषा वासुदेवेन पालिता ॥ अभूदस्मिन्महावंशे प्रभूतभुजविक्रमः । संजातलक्ष्मीसंपन्नः संगमो नाम भूपतिः ॥ विजित्य शत्रूनखिलान्जगत्प्रभुः सम्मोदते वीरविलाससंश्रयः । समस्तविद्यानिपुणः प्रतापी धर्मैकभूस्सर्वकलासुकोविदः ॥ अभूदस्मान्महाभूपाद्बुक्करायमहीपतिः । प्रचंडतरदोर्दंडखंडितारातिविक्रमः ॥ कर्नाटलक्ष्मीस्सविलासमास यस्मिन्महीपे महनीयकीर्तौ । भूमिस्तथैवाप वसुन्धरात्वं स्थिरेति नाम प्रथमं गुणौघैः ॥ क्षोणीपालनमेव कर्तुमनिशं जातौ त्रिलोकाधिपावेकीभूय च बुक्करायनृपतौ पीताम्बरेशावुभौ । नाम्ना चापि तयोः प्रसिद्धिमगमद्भूवल्लभः श्रीयुतः सर्वां सागरमेखलां भुवमिमां संपालयन्दीव्यति ॥ राजा हरिहराख्योसौ महादानानि षोडश । विधाय लक्ष्मीसंपन्नो भाति सर्वगुणाश्रयः ॥ तस्य मेलांबिकाजानेः प्रादुरासीद्यशोधनः । प्रतापदेव-
[II.2]रायाख्यस्तनयो विनयान्वितः॥प्रतापवह्नौ परिजृंभमाणे शुष्कास्तुरुष्का अपि यस्य राज्ञः । रिपुक्षितीन्द्राश्च निरस्तधैर्याः कान्तारवल्मीककृतात्मरक्षाः॥

तस्य देमांबिकाभर्तुः पुत्रश्शत्रुनिषूदनः । विद्याविन(य)संपन्नो वीरो त्रिजय-भूपतिः ॥ तस्य नारायणीदेव्यामुत्पन्नः शुभलक्षणः । प्रतापराय इत्याख्या-मगमत्पार्थिवोत्तमः ॥ गुणैरनेकैरवनीतलेऽस्मिन् विराजमानः सुकृताप्तकीर्तिः । निजाग्रजात् प्राप्तधनाद्रिराज्यः साधीकृतार्थी जनपारिजातः ॥ तस्य सिद्धल-देवीति भार्या लक्षणसंयुता । लक्ष्मीर्नारायणस्येव जाता त्रिजगदंबिका ॥ तस्यां शिवः प्रादुरभूद्गुणाढ्यो नाम्ना विरूपाक्ष इति प्रसिद्धः । राजाधिराजः क्षितिपालमौलिर्वदान्यमूर्ति(:) करुणैकसिन्धुः ॥ निज[प्रत]प्रतापादधिगत्य राज्यं समस्तभाग्यैः परिसेव्यमानः । खड्गाग्रतः सर्वरिपून्विजित्य संमोदते वीरविलासभूमिः ॥ खिलीकृतसुरत्राणो द्रावितान्ध्रमहीपतिः । हिंदुरायसुर-त्राणस्त्रिराजभुजयोन्नतिः ॥ वैरिराजगजेन्द्राणां पंचास्यः परभीतिकृत् । श्रित-पद्मासुधाभानु-इत्यादि बिरुदोन्नतः॥ तुंगभद्रासरित्तीरे विरूपाक्षस्य सन्निधौ। दिव्यं सिंहासनं प्राप्य पालयन्नवनीमिमां ॥ पुण्यश्लोकाग्रगण्योसौ विरूपाक्षक्षितीश्वरः। धर्मस्थानगतैस्सद्भिः संयुतो धरणीसुरैः ॥ शालिवाहननिर्णीतशकवर्षक्रमागते । वस्वष्टगुणभूयुक्ते पार्थिवाख्ये च वत्सरे ॥ कार्तिकाख्ये च मासेस्मिन्नसिते पंचमी-तिथौ । राजाधिराजसर्वज्ञो राज्ञां पर(मे)श्वरः॥ विरूपाक्षक्षितीपालो विरूपाक्षस्य संनिधौ। निजपट्टाभिषेकस्य पुण्यकाले नृपोत्तमः॥ प्रतापाह्वयविख्यातगिरे राज्ये त[II. 2]थैव च। कंनाडौशिर्माणाख्यात आतुकूरेति विश्रुतं ॥ कैला(स)स्थित एव शंभुरधुना श्रीपर्वते सर्वदा पार्वत्या सह संवसन्नातिमुदा लोकत्रयं पालयन्।यास्ति इत्यथ तस्य सेवकविधौ श्रीलिंगचक्रेश्वरः श्रीमान् पर्वतमल्लिकार्जुनमहादेवस्य पा-दार्चकः॥ कैलासोपरि ये स्थितामरगणा[द्या]वापृथिव्यां च ये मुख्यसिद्धगणम(?) न्नप्रभृतयस्तैः सार्धमद्यापि यः। वाराणस्यधिवासतामधिगतः श्रीपर्वतेयं मुद्रा श्रीसि-द्धप्रतिपन्नवैभवतया भिक्षाप्रवत्तिति(?)च॥ अंगरंगादिभोगाय पर्वमासोत्सवाय च। तपस्विभ्योन्नदानाय विरूपाक्षक्षितीश्वरः॥ ददौ स्वाभिमतावाप्त्यै श्रीगिरौ सन्नि-वासिने। प्रतापाख्यगिरे राज्ये वराहाणां चतुश्शतं ॥ अष्टरापरिविख्यात आतु-कूरेति निश्चितं । विरूपाक्षपुरं चेति प्रतिनाम्ना विधाय च ॥ सहि(पु)ण्योद-कदानधारापूर्वं यथाविधि । निधिनिक्षेपवार्यश्म आक्षिण्यागामिसंज्ञकं ॥ सिद्ध-साध्य इति ख्यातमष्टभोगैश्च संयुतं । कुल्यारामादिसंयुक्तं समस्तबालिसंयुतं ॥ ददौ पर्वतसंस्थस्य मल्लिकार्जुननामतः । दीव्यमानस्य णावस्य विरूपाक्षक्षिती-श्वरः ॥ तपस्वी स च संतुष्टः संयुतः परयामुदा । राजानमाशिषं चक्रे चिरंजीवी

भवत्विति ॥ तैस्तैस्समन्विताश्चिह्नैर्दिक्षु प्राच्यादिषु क्रमात् । सीमानो यस्याग्रहारस्य लिख्यते देशभाषया ॥ श्रीकांनाडवोलगण आतुकूर ग्रामदच्चतुस्सीमेयविवरमूडलु लोल्ललपिंनापुन्ना पुरदसीमेमेर । अनंतपुरदसीमेमेर । ब्रांहलपिंनापुरदसीमेमेर ॥ [III. 1] ब्राह्मलअनंतपुरदसीमेमेर करि वेनसीमेमेर । दुयालसीमेमेर नंदिकुट होलसीमेमेर नेतिपले होलसीमेमेर रामापुरद होलसीमेमेर रंद्रेश्वरद होलसीमे गेबुरुगमरनकुडिपोतु राजपल्लिय होलमेरेसीमे । ईशान्य दलपे जरमड्डुगेमेर । रंतिदुसिरुमलातुकू रिंगे प्रतिनामाविरूपाक्ष पुरद चतुस्सीमा ॥ भारद्वाजोयबोधीमान् चिक्कतम्मतनूभवः। बह्वृचो गंगणार्योसौ वृत्तिमेकामिहाश्नुते ॥ काश्शपो याजुषो धीमान् नारणार्यतनूभवः । रायसाधिपरंगार्यो वृत्तिद्वयमिहाश्नुते ॥ त्वष्टा श्रीमुद्दणाचार्यसूनुश्शासनलेखकः । वीरणस्सुगुणो धीमान् वृत्तिद्वयपतिः स्वयं ॥ दानपालनयोर्मध्ये दानाच्छ्रेयोनुपालनं । दानात्स्वर्गमवाप्नोति पालनादच्युतं पदं ॥ स्वदत्तां परदत्तां वा यो हरेत वसुंधरां । षष्टिर्वर्षसहस्राणि विष्टायां जायते क्रिमिः ॥ स्वदत्ताद्द्विगुणं पुण्यं परदत्तानुपालनं । परदत्तापहारेण स्वदत्तं निष्फलं ब(भ)वेत् ॥ एकैव भगिनी लोके सर्वेषामेव भूभुजां । न भोज्या न करग्राह्या विप्रदत्ता वसुन्धरा ॥ सामान्योयं धर्मसेतुर्नृपाणां काले काले पालनीयो भवद्भिः । सर्वानेतान्भाविनः पार्थिवेन्द्रान् भूयोभूयो याचते रामचन्द्रः ॥

THE JAIN TEACHERS OF AKBAR

BY VINCENT A. SMITH

THE concluding section of Āīn 30 of Book II of the *Āīn-i-Akbarī* is entitled 'The Learned Men of the Time,' who are enumerated as being 140 in number, divided into five classes. The first class, 'such as understand the mysteries of both worlds,' headed by the name of Abu-l Fazl's father, Shaikh Mubārak, ends with No. 21, Ādit (Āditya), probably a Brahmanical Hindu. The first twelve names are Muslim. Nos. 13–21 are all Hindu in form. Blochmann evidently knew nothing about the persons indicated by those nine names, as he gives no note on any one of them. No. 16, Harijī Sūr, was, as will be explained, an eminent Jain.[1]

We need not trouble ourselves now with Abu-l Fazl's second, third and fourth classes. His fifth class, 'such as understand sciences resting on testimony (*naḳl*)' comprises Nos. 100–140, all of whom, except the last two, are Musalmāns. The names of those two, Nos. 139 and 140, are given respectively as Bijai Sēn Sūr and Bhāu Chand, again without comment by Blochmann. They also were distinguished Jains.

The important fact that Akbar welcomed Jain teachers and listened to their instruction for at least twenty years has been ignored in the extremely unsatisfactory account of his life and actions given in modern history books. Indeed, this fact has been made known only by an anonymous article in an obscure publication in 1910, which will be described presently.

The erroneous notion that Buddhists took part in the debates on religion, held first in the 'Ibādat-khāna or House of Worship,[2] and subsequently in the private apartments

1 The spelling 'Jain', not 'Jaina' is used intentionally. People do not ordinarily speak Sanskrit.

2 So much erroneous nonsense has been written about the 'Ibādat-khāna that it is well to state briefly in this place the facts, which will be explained more fully in an essay to appear in an early number of the

of the palace at Fathpur-Sīkrī rests on the mistranslation of a passage in the *Akbarnāma* committed by Chalmers in his manuscript version and copied first by Elliot and Dowson and then by von Noer.

Abu-l Fazl relates that at the end of September, or early in October, 1578, the discussions in the *'Ibādat-khāna* were carried on by the representatives of many creeds. 'Sūfī, philosopher, orator, jurist, Sunnī, Shīa, Brahman, Jatī, Sīūra, Chārbāk, Nazarene, Jew, Ṣātī (Ṣatīan), Zoroastrian, and others enjoyed exquisite pleasure' (Vol. III, Chap. xlv, p. 365 of Beveridge's version). The words Jatī and Sīūra, which of course refer to Śvetāmbara Jains, were mistranslated by Chalmers, as 'Jains, Buddhists.' That error, having been adopted by Elliot and Dowson (Vol. VI, p. 59), misled von Noer, who drew the erroneous inference that 'it may be concluded with not too slight probability that there were Buddhists at Fathpur' (transl. Beveridge, I. 327,

Journal of the Royal Asiatic Society. The *'Ibādat-khāna*, or House of Worship, was built by order of Akbar early in 1575 as a debating hall for the accommodation of the doctors of rival schools of Muslim theology only. For about three years the discussions were confined to the Islamitic domain. In 1578 Akbar ceased regular attendance at the mosque, and during that year admitted Jains and representatives of sundry other sects and religions to the disputations in the 'Ibādat-khāna. In Sept. 1579 he compelled the *'ulamā* to issue the 'Infallibility Decree' which made him supreme arbiter in all disputed questions relating to Islām. Discussion on the subject in the Debating Hall thus became superfluous. In 1580, 1581, and 1582, the debates in which the Jesuits joined seem always to have been held in the private apartments of the palace.

The House of Worship was a large, commodious, handsomely decorated building, probably capable of accommodating several hundred people, erected in the gardens of the palace not far from the dwelling of Shaikh Salīm Chishtī. No trace of it has been found, and its exact site is totally forgotten. The reason for such oblivion probably is that in 1579, or soon after, the hall was demolished as being useless. Akbar had ceased to be a Musalman from about 1580; and from the beginning of 1582, when he promulgated the *Dīn Ilāhī*, his apostasy was open and avowed. He never resumed his old faith, and died as he had lived for twenty-three years, a believer in One God, represented on earth by His Imperial Majesty. All the statements in this note can be fully proved, and will be dealt with in my work on Akbar, which will be published as soon as war conditions at the Clarendon Press permit.

note). In reality, there is not a particle of evidence that any Buddhist ever attended the debates, or that Akbar acquired even the slightest knowledge of Buddhism. Abu-l Fazl himself knew little about the subject, because he could not find anybody in India competent to teach him. He says expressly:—'For a long time past scarcely any trace of them [Buddhist monks] has existed in Hindustan, but they are found in Pegu, Tenasserim, and Tibet. The third time that the writer accompanied His Majesty to the delightful valley of Kashmīr [*scil.* A. D. 1597], he met with a few old men of this persuasion, but saw none among the learned.'[1] It thus appears that Akbar never had an opportunity of meeting any learned Buddhists, and that no Buddhists took part or could have taken part in the discussions at Fathpur-Sīkrī.

But the Jain holy men undoubtedly gave Akbar prolonged instruction for years, which largely influenced his actions; and they secured his assent to their doctrines so far that he was reputed to have been converted to Jainism.

The correct name of the Jain who 'understood the mysteries of both worlds' was Hīravijaya Sūri, and the names of the two teachers mentioned by Abu-l Fazl as 'understanding sciences resting on testimony (*naḳl*),' such as religious law, traditions, and history, were Vijayasen Sūri, and Bhānucandra Upādhyāya.

We will now briefly discuss the relations of these three teachers with Akbar.

Hīravijaya

Hīravijaya, the most distinguished of Akbar's Jain instructors, who was credited with the conversion of the emperor, was born in Saṁvat 1583=A. D. 1526–7, at Pālanpur (Prahlādan Pātan), an ancient town in Gujarāt. At the age of 13 (A. D. 1539), he took up the religious life under the guidance of Vijaya Dāna Sūri, who sent him to the Deccan to study logic, in which he became proficient. In A. D. 1557 he was given the title of Vācaka at Nadulai

1 *Āīn*, vol. III, tr. Jarrett, p. 212.

or Nāradpur, and two years later was made a Sūri at Sīrohī in south-western Rājputāna. He thus became the leader of the Tapāgaṇa or Tapāgaccha section of Jain ascetics.

In the *Paṭṭāvalī* of the Tapāgaccha his biography is entered in the following terms:—

'58. Hīravijaya, who converted the emperor Akbar (*cf.* Kharatara-Paṭṭāvalī, *sub* 61), born Saṁ. 1583 Mārga° sudi 9, at Prahlādanapura; *dikshā*, 1596, Kārtika vadi 2, at Pāṭaṇa; *vāchakapada*, 1608, Māgha sudi 5, at Nāradapurī; *sūripada*, 1610, at Sīrohī; died 1652, Bhādra° sudi 11 [A. D. 1595] at Uṁnānagara.'[1]

The reference to No. 61 of the Kharatara-gaccha (ibid. p. 250) is of interest because it credits the saint Jinacandra of the Kharatara section with having 'converted the Emperor Akbar to the Jain religion.' His name is not entered in any of Abu-l Fazl's lists, and I have not found any other mention of his presence at Akbar's court.

The fame of Hīravijaya having reached Akbar's ears, the emperor sent swift messengers to summon him to court. Shihāb Khān (Shihābu-d-dīn Ahmad Khān), the Governor of Gujarāt, on receiving the imperial commands, arranged for the departure of the Sūri, who made over the charge of his community to Vijayasena. The Sūri, in strict compliance with the rules of his order, declined all the gifts and conveyances offered by the governor. He walked the whole way, much to the amazement of the emperor, who provided for his reception with great pomp. Akbar, being busy at the time, made his guest over to Abu-l Fazl, who entered on the discussion of religious subjects with him. When Akbar was at leisure, he received instruction concerning Dharma from the Sūri, who explained the nature of the five vows observed by Jain ascetics—namely, non-killing, truthfulness, refusal to accept anything not freely offered, celibacy, and abstinence from possession of wealth in the form of money, etc. The emperor pressed certain books on his guest, who accepted

1 Klatt, *Ind. Ant.*, vol. XI (1882), p. 256.

them reluctantly and then gave them to the Agra library, meaning presumably that of the Jain community at that place.

The Sūri retired to Agra for the rainy season of 1582, returning to Fathpur-Sīkrī at the beginning of the cold season. He persuaded the emperor to issue various commands in accordance with Jain doctrine, and to extend them in the following year, 1583. Fishing in the great lake called Dābar, evidently that at Fathpur-Sīkrī, was prohibited. The title of Jagadguru or World Teacher, was conferred on the Sūri, who quitted the capital in 1584, leaving Śānticandra Upādhyāya behind him at court. Hīravijaya spent the rainy season of 1585 at Allahabad, designated as Abhirāmābād,[1] and that of 1586 at Agra. During the rains of 1587 he was the guest of 'Sultān Deorah or Deodah,'[2] the chief or zemindar of Sīrohī, who was much attracted by the doctrine of the Sūri who had attained his rank as such at Sīrohī in A. D. 1553 (Saṁ. 1610). Later in the year 1587, Hīravijaya returned to Pātan (Pattan) in Gujarāt. He starved himself to death in the approved Jain fashion in A. D. 1595 at the age of sixty-nine. A *stūpa* was erected to commemorate him.

The basis of this paper is the essay by 'C' entitled 'Hīravijaya Sūri, or the Jainas at the court of Akbar,' published in a number of the *Jaina-Śāsana*, a little known periodical printed at the Angrezi Kothi, Benares City, in Vīra Saṁ. 2437=A. D. 1910, pp. 113-128. The author of that essay was the first to make public the identification of the three Jain names in Abu-l Fazl's lists. He makes extensive quotations from several metrical Sanskrit works, of

1 This name for Allahabad is quoted by 'C' from one or other of the Jain Sanskrit poems. It means 'abode of delight', and probably never was current. I have not met it elsewhere.

2 'Sultān Deorah' is a corruption of the name Surthān, a Deorā Rājpūt, who was the Rāo of Sīrohī in the reigns of Akbar and Jahāngīr, and refused to recognize the imperial supremacy. The Deorās are a branch of the Chauhāns. Akbar had sufficient control over Sīrohī to be able to pass the town when he wished to do so, as he did in 1573. See Imperial Gazetteer (1908) *s. v.* Sirohi.

which two are not mentioned by Guérinot in his *Essai de Bibliographie Jaina*, Leroux, Paris, 1906; or in the supplement to that work, entitled '*Notes de Bibliographie Jaina*' printed in the *Journal Asiatique*, Juillet – Août, 1909, pp. 47–148.

The poems cited by 'C' are:—

(1) *Jagadguru-kāvyam;*

(2) *Hīra-saubhāgyam;* by Devavimala Gaṇi, ed. by K. P. Parab (Kāvyamālā, No. 67), Bombay 1900, with the author's commentry;[1]

(3) *Kṛpārasa-kośa*: a panegyric on Akbar, composed by Sānti(Śānti)candra.

Further information about them would be welcome.

Klatt noted the following particulars concerning works connected with Hīravijaya Sūri—

'4 *Paṭṭāvalī* of the Tapā-gachchha.

The *Gurvāvalī* of Dharmasāgara-gaṇi (Saṁvat 1629) is printed in Weber, *Verz.* II, pp. 997–1015. This is the original edition of Dh. All the Poona Mss. contain the revised edition, made Saṁvat 1648 [=A. D. 1591] by the order of Hīravijaya-Sūri . . . . . Later works are— the *Paṭṭāvalī* contained in Sarga IV of Devavimala's *Hīravijaya-caritra*, see *Journ. Germ. Or. Soc.*, vol. 47, p. 315.' (Klatt and Leumann, *Ind. Ant.*, vol. XXIII (1894), p. 179).

Vijayasena Sūri and Bhānucandra Upādhyāya

We have mentioned that Hīravijaya, when starting on his long journey to court, put Vijayasena in charge of his sect or congregation, and that when Hīravijaya quitted Fathpur-Sīkrī in 1584, Sānti(Śānti)candra remained at court. He composed an eulogy of the emperor, entitled *Kṛpārasa-kośa*, 'Treasury of the Quality of Mercy' describing and praising all Akbar's merciful acts. This elaborate piece of flattery used to be read to Akbar, who was pleased with it. Late in 1587 when Śānticandra desired to return to Gujarāt, the emperor gave him *farmāns* abolishing the *jizya* tax on non-Muslims, and prohibiting

1 Guérinot, No. 433, p. 207.

slaughter of animals to a large extent. The forbidden days were extended so as to comprise half the year.

Bhānucandra continued to reside at court. His pupil Mahāmahopādhyāya Siddhicandra composed a commentary on the latter half of the *Kādambarī* of Bāṇa. He had the reputation of being able to do 108 things at a time, and so secured from Akbar the formal title of *Ḳhush-faham*, or 'Intelligent.' From the colophon to the commentary on the Kādambarī by Siddhicandra we learn, through C's quotations, that his teacher, Bhānucandra, a Mahopādhyāya, had taught Akbar 1000 names of the Sun, and had obtained from the emperor in 1593 *farmāns* abolishing the tax on pilgrims to the holy hill of Śatruñjaya at Pālitāna, and directing that all the sacred places should be made over to Hīravijaya Sūri.

Vijayasena Sūri was then invited to the court, which continued to reside ordinarily at Lahore until 1598. He vanquished 363 learned Brahmans in formal debates to Akbar's satisfaction and so earned the title of Sawāi. He made Bhānucandra an Upādhyāya or instructor, the expenses of the ceremony, amounting to 600 rupees, being defrayed by Abu-l Fazl.[1]

Probably Bhānucandra continued to reside at the court until the end of the reign in 1605. However that may be, the details given above prove conclusively that Akbar's close intercourse with Jain teachers lasted for at least twenty years, from 1578 to 1597 inclusive.

A person called Shāh Sauvarṇika Tejapāla induced Hīravijaya in 1590 to consecrate the temple of Ādīśvara or Ādinātha on the Śatruñjaya hill, the 'Shatrunja' of the *Imperial Gazetteer*, adjoining the town of Pālitāna in Kāṭhiāwāṛ. In the porch of the eastern or front entrance

1 The ordinary ascetic is called a Sādhu. 'The next step to which he can rise is that of Upādhyāya or instructor. An exceptionally clever monk may be chosen from amongst the others as teacher, when he is expected to study the scriptures and teach them to his fellow monks. Amongst the Tapāgaccha no monk can be chosen as an Upādhyāya till he has been an ascetic for at least a year' (Stevenson, *The Heart of Jainism*, p. 239). See *Āīn*, vol. III, p. 206

of that temple there is an exceptionally long Sanskrit inscription, comprising 87 verses in various metres, the composition of Hemavijaya, and dated 1650=A. D. 1593.[1]

The long record has high historical value as a trustworthy contemporary account of Akbar's dealings with his Jain teachers. It will be well first to quote Bühler's summary of the contents. He notes that the inscription enumerates sundry Jain leaders, of whom the third is Hīravijaya, and proceeds—

'(3) HIRAVIJAYA (Klatt No. 58), verses 14-24, who was called by Sāhi Akabbara [Shāh Akbar] to Mevāta, and persuaded the emperor in Saṁvat 1639 [=A. D. 1582] to issue an edict forbidding the slaughter of animals for six months, to abolish the confiscation of the property of deceased persons, the *Sujījia* tax, and a *Śulka;*[2] to set free many captives, snared birds and animals; to present Śatruñjaya to the Jainas; to establish a Jaina library (*Paustakam bhāṇḍāgāram*), and to become a saint like king Śreṇika;[3] who converted the head of the Lumpākas, Meghajī;[4] made many people adherents of the Tapāgachchha;

1 References are:—(1) short notice in Kielhorn's 'List of the Inscriptions of Northern India,' appendix to *Epigraphia Indica*, vol. V, No. 308; (2) Bühler, abstract of contents of Inscr. No. XII of 'Jaina Inscriptions from Śatruñjaya' in *Ep. Ind.*, II, p. 38, and transcript of text, ibid., pp. 50-59; (3) parts of text and transl. in 'C's' essay above cited. The translation is quoted as from '*J. B. R. S.*, August, 1844,' but really from the *Journal of the Bombay Branch of the R. As. Soc.*, for 1841. pp. 59-63.

2 'Possibly a tax on Jaina pilgrims visiting their holy places may be meant—see also Elphinstone's *History of India*, p. 339 (6th edition. The *Sujījia* tax is, of course, the *Jizya* or capitation tax on infidels) [G. B.].

3 Or Bimbisāra, the fifth Śaiśunāga king of Magadha, who is believed by the Jains to have been a zealous adherent of their religion, as well as his son Ajātaśatru (See *E. H. I.*, 3rd Ed., p. 35 *n.*, and S. V. Venkatesvara Aiyar in *Ind. Ant.*, 1916, p. 12).

4 'Regarding the Lumpākas see Bhandarkar, *Report on Sanskrit Mss.*' for 1883-4, p. 153' [G. B.]. 'C' (p. 114) states that Meghaji Ṛṣi, being convinced of his errors, became a pupil of Hīravijaya. Guérinot, abstracting Weber, writes—'7. Secte Paḍimāri (Lumpāka). Fondée par Lumpāka in Saṁvat 1508. [=A. D. 1451]. Elle a pour caractère fondamental d'être opposée au culte des images' (*Bibl. Jaina*, No. 336, p. 176),

caused many temples to be built in Gujarāt and other countries; and made many natives of that country, of Mālavā, and so forth, undertake pilgrimages to Śatruñjaya. No. CXVIII commemorates one of these pilgrimages, which was undertaken by Vimalaharsha and 200 others. The same inscription states that Hīravijaya belonged to the *Sāpha* race. He died, according to XIII by starvation, at Unnatadurga, in Saṁvat 1652, Bhādrapada Śukla 10, and his *pādukās* were erected in the same year, on Mārga. vadi 9, Monday, by Udayakarṇa of Stambhatīrtha (Cambay)[1] and consecrated by Vijayasena. (4) Vijayasena (Klatt No. 59), (verses 25–34), who was called by Akabbara [Akbar] to Lābhapura (Lahor), received from him great honours, and a *phuramāna* [*farmān*], forbidding the slaughter of cows, bulls, and buffalo-cows, to confiscate the property of deceased persons and to make captives in war; who, honoured by the king, the son of Cholī-bēgam[2] (Cholī Vegama), adorned Gujarāt. Latest date Saṁvat 1650.'

The nature of the orders issued by Akbar in conformity with the advice of his Jain monitors is sufficiently indicated by Bühler's summary of the great inscription as quoted above. The testimony of that record is fully confirmed by Badāonī, who adds that infringements of the rules concerning the killing of animals were treated as capital offences. Akbar, in adopting such rigorous measures, followed precedents set by Harṣa and various other ancient Indian kings, who preferred the life of a beast to that of a man.[3]

1 Stambhatīrtha, a Sanskritized form of Khambāyat or Khambāt.

2 Cholī or Chūlı Begam was an epithet applied to Akbar's mother, Hamıda Bāno Bēgam, on account of her painful wanderings in the desert (*chūl*), prior to her son's birth. Humāyūn conferred the title *Chūlī* on the attendants who followed him through the deserts (*Akbarnāma*), tr. (Beveridge, vol. I, p. 412).

3 The interpretation 'capital punishment' is that of Blochmann, *Āīn*, Vol. I, p. 200). Lowe renders simply 'punishment,' adding that many a family was ruined, and his property confiscated' (page 331 and Errata). Blochmann seems to have been right. For the practice of Hindu kings, see *Early Hist. of India*, 3rd ed., pp. 181, 344.

The order forbidding the confiscation of the property of deceased persons is expressed in the text of the inscription (v. 32) by the words—मोच्यमेव मृतवित्तमशेषम् 'the whole estate of the dead was to be released.' The command professed to repeal the rule of practice under which the Mogul emperors were accustomed to seize the property of any deceased subject who left an estate worth confiscating. The order of repeal, like many other benevolent enactments issued from time to time by Akbar and his successors, was not acted on. When Akbar's mother died in 1604, leaving a will directing her estate to be shared among her male descendants, the emperor disregarded her injunctions and seized the whole for himself, as Du Jarric relates.[1]

According to Badāonī (Lowe, p. 404), the legislation of A. H. 1002 (= A. D. 1593–4) provided that—

'An inspector and registrar of the effects of those who died or disappeared was to be appointed. So that if any one who died had an heir (P. 391), after it had been proved that he did not owe anything to the imperial exchequer, was not a *karorī* (tax-gatherer), or a banker receiving deposits, the heir might take possession of it; otherwise it passed into the imperial treasury; and until they got a receipt from the treasurer, they were not to bury the deceased.'

Those rules, it should be observed, were issued long after the decree obtained by the Jains which professedly abolished the confiscation of the estates of deceased persons in general terms. The modified rule of 1593 was not observed, and the protection given to the subject was illusory. There is abundant evidence that Akbar and his successors ordinarily seized all estates worth taking. There was much 'make see,' to use the Chinese phrase, about the orders repeatedly issued to abolish burdensome imposts and practices.

The *jizya* was supposed to have been abolished universally in the ninth year of the reign (1564); and when Gujarāt was annexed in 1573, the abolition should have

1 *Thesaurus*, III, 118.

taken effect in that province. But the inscription shows that it did not, and that a fresh order of abolition was required in 1593. Probably the local governor disregarded the concession made to the Jains at that date, just as he had disregarded the general orders of 1564. The Viceroys, as a matter of fact, could ordinarily do what they pleased in all questions of administration, and in many cases were personages far too powerful to be seriously checked by imperial authority, even in the days of Akbar, who was stronger than any of his successors. Unfortunately, we know little about the actual administration of Akbar's empire, but enough is on record to permit of no doubt that the noble sentiments and benevolent enactments which figure so largely in the panegyrical books were translated into practice in a manner extremely imperfect.

To sum up. Akbar never came under Buddhist influence in any degree whatsoever. No Buddhists took part in the debates on religion held at Fathpur-Sīkrī, and Abu-l Fazl never met any learned Buddhist. Consequently his knowledge of Buddhism was extremely slight. Certain persons who took part in the debates and have been supposed erroneously to have been Buddhists were really Jains from Gujarāt. Many Jains visited the imperial court or resided there at various times during at least twenty years, from 1578 to 1597, and enjoyed ample facilities for access to the emperor. The most eminent Jain teacher who gave instruction to Akbar was Hīravijaya Sūri. The two other most important instructors were Vijayasena Sūri and Bhānucandra Upādhyāya. The doings of those three persons are recorded in Sanskrit poems entitled (1) *Jagadguru-kāvyam;* (2) *Hīra-saubhāgyam;* (3) *Kṛpā-rasa-kośa;* and (4) *Hīravijaya-caritra;* as well as in the *Paṭṭāvalī* of the Tapā-gaccha section of the Jain community, and in the inscriptions at Śatruñjaya, especially the long record No. XII comprising 87 verses, composed by Hemavijaya and set up in A. D. 1593 at the Ādināth temple. The documents prove that Akbar's partial acceptance of the doctrine of *ahiṁsā*, or abstention from killing, and sundry edicts intended to give effect to that doctrine, resulted directly from the efforts of Hīravijaya and his colleagues.

The two creeds which had the most influence upon Akbar's mind from 1578 to his death in 1605 were Jainism and Zoroastrianism.

The emperor granted various favours to the Jain community. Abu-l Fazl made use of his opportunities to compile an excellent and generally accurate account of the Śvetāmbara sect, derived from personal communication with learned men of that community, especially Hīravijaya Sūri. He failed to meet any learned member of the Digambara sect, and consequently observes that his account of the Digambara peculiarities 'has been written as it were in the dark.'[1]

1 *Āīn*, tr. Jarrett, vol. III, p. 210. Mrs. Stevenson's book entitled '*The Heart of Jainism*', Oxford University Press, 1915, and *Outlines of Jainism* by Jagmanderlal Jaini, M. A., Cambridge University Press, 1916 may be recommended to students of the subject. Abu-l Fazl does not acknowledge the extent of the Jain influence on Akbar's views and practice. He confines himself to a compliment on his master's toleration, which embraced all sects, even the Jain, which the Brahmans abhorred.

SOME NOTES ON WILLIAM HAWKINS

(1607-1612)

BY H. G. RAWLINSON

THE first actual attempt to establish communication between England and the Moghal court was made by the two great pioneers of British enterprise in the East, Sir William Osborne, Lord Mayor of London, and Richard Staper, who is described on his monument at St. Helen's, Bishopsgate, as "The greatest merchant of his time and the chiefest actor in the discovery of the trades of Turkey and the East Indies." They organized a party of four Englishmen under one John Newbury, an experienced traveller who had been to the Levant and knew Arabic. Armed with a letter from Elizabeth to the Emperor Akbar, in which they were represented as being induced to undertake the journey "by the singular report of Your Imperial Majesty's humanity in these uttermost parts of the world,"[1] they sailed, on Shrove Tuesday 1583, on the *Tiger*, bound for Aleppo. This event evidently became, as it deserved to be, historic, for nearly twenty years after, Shakespeare could still make the First Witch in *Macbeth* say—

> Her husband's to Aleppo gone, master o' the *Tiger*,

and we must suppose that the remark would not have been made unless it was likely to be appreciated by the audience. Of the party which set out thus bravely, only one, Ralph Fitch, returned. He reached England on April 29th, 1591. From Aleppo they had travelled to Bagdad, Basra and Ormuz, where they were arrested by the Portuguese and sent off to Goa. At Goa one of their party settled down; the rest broke their parole, and after many

1 It is interesting to know that reports of Akbar's tolerance and culture had reached England, (doubtless through the Portuguese, though the actual source cannot be traced) at so early a date. So Mildenhall (for whom *vide infra*) writes of Akbar's "renowned kindness to Christians," as "so much blazed throughout the world that it had come into the uttermost parts of the ocean." Purchas, Ed. Maclehose, Vol. II. p. 300.

almost incredible adventures, arrived at the court of Akbar at Agra. Here another of the band was tempted to enter Akbar's service and deserted them. Newbury then arranged that he should return overland, while Fitch, the remaining member of the company, should travel to Bengal and await him there. Newbury apparently intended to fit out a ship to return and fetch Fitch, but he perished, "unknown how or where," says Purchas, some time after leaving Lahore. After Newbury's departure, Fitch set out to fulfil his part of the contract. From Agra he struck eastward, travelled down the Ganges to its mouth, took boat to Burma, (which he explored pretty thoroughly), and visited Java and the Malaccas. He returned home by the route by which he had come, touching at Ceylon on his way. His report on his travels forms a most valuable document, and is the first detailed account of the East from an English pen.[1]

In 1599, encouraged by reports of Linschoten,[2] Fitch and others, the London merchants determined to form a Company for trading with India by sea. The defeat of the Spanish Armada had seriously damaged the prestige of the Catholic powers, and the attempts to reach India by the North-west and North-east passages had proved fruitless. Hence it was resolved to try the Cape route, in defiance of the Portuguese, Papal Bulls notwithstanding.[3] At first the Merchant Adventurers were chiefly attracted by the spice trade of the Malaccas, which offered an easy way of making large profits, but in 1599 Staper renewed his attempt to establish a treaty with the Mughal Empire.

1 *The long, dangerous and memorable voyage of Mr. Ralph Fitch, merchant, of London, by the way of Tripolis in Syria to Ormuz, to Goa in East India, to Cambaia, to the river of Ganges, to Bengala, to Bacola, to Chonderi, to Pegu, to Siam, etc, begun in the year 1583 and ended in the year 1591. Apud* Hakluyt, V. 465.

2 This famous Dutchman went to Goa in the suite of the Archbishop in 1589 and befriended Fitch there. His *Itineratio* (1596) became the leading work on India. It was translated into English in 1598, and has been republished by the Hakluyt Society.

3 The Bull of Alexander VI, 1494, had given to Portugal the exclusive right to all discoveries East and South of the Azores, and to Spain all discoveries West and South of the same point. See Purchas, II, 32 ff.

John Mildenhall, who was chosen for this errand, travelled to India by the overland route through northern Persia. He took his own time over the journey, and did not reach Lahore until 1603. On reaching Agra, he was kindly received at first by Akbar, until the Jesuit mission, perceiving the dangers of Protestant rivalry to the ascendancy which they had gained over the Emperor, commenced the bitter opposition to an English alliance which they maintained so unswervingly throughout the next reign. On being asked by Akbar what they knew about the English, "they flatly answered," says Mildenhall, "that our Nation were all thieves, and that I was a spy sent thither for no other purpose to have friendship with His Majesty, but that afterwards our men might come thither and get some of his ports, and so put His Majesty to much trouble."[1] They further hindered negotiations by bribing his interpreter to abscond; but Mildenhall learnt Persian, and according to his own story, scored a brilliant diplomatic victory, "to my own great contentment, and as I hope, to the profit of my nation." Accordingly, Akbar ordered that "whatever privileges or commandments he would have, should be presently written, sealed and given, without any more delay or question." Unfortunately, the *farmān* was not forthcoming, and it is difficult to avoid the conclusion that Mildenhall was a rascal who did not scruple to invent whatever he thought might please his employers. Staper apparently thought the same, for a note in the Company's minutes for 1609 states that his application for further employment was rejected as he was "not thought fit to be engaged." He came to a bad end, for we learn from the diary of one Nicholas Withington, preserved by Purchas, that he "had been employed with three English young men, which he poisoned in Persia to make himself master of their goods, but he was likewise poisoned, yet by preservations lived for many months after, but swelled exceedingly, and so came to Agra with the value of 20,000

1 See his letter to Staper "from Casbin in Persia, Oct. 3, 1606" in Purchas, II. 299.

dollars."[1] Here he died early in 1614, having, as the Jesuits told Withington, "given all his goods to a French Protestant to marry his bastard daughter in Persia and bring up another." The Company employed Withington, Steele and others to recover property belonging to them, with partial success.

The East India Company did not, however, abandon the project. The first two "voyages" had, as we have seen, gone to the Spice Islands. When the third fleet made ready to sail, it was determined that one vessel should be sent to Surat, to establish a factory there by treaty with the Mughal Court, buy calicoes, and rejoin the rest at Bantam; by which means, writes Captain Keeling, the "General" of the expedition, they "would lay the best foundation for gain against another year that ever I heard of."[2] Surat was chosen for many reasons. As the great *entrepôt* of the Mughal Empire on the Western coast of India, it was, in the words of a contemporary traveller "a city of very great trade in all classes of merchandize, a very important sea-port, yielding a large revenue to the king and frequented by many ships from Malabar and all parts." The Portuguese had recognized this, and in 1530–1, Antonio de Silveira burnt the ships in the harbour and razed the town to the ground, killing all living things within reach. Since its conquest by Akbar in 1572, however, they had left it alone,[3] and hence it did not come under the Company's agreement not to trade with any place "in lawful and actual possession of any Christian prince at amity with England, who would not accept of such trade."

The ambassador selected for this mission was William Hawkins, a nephew of the great Sir John, the terror of the Spanish Main. He was one of eleven children, two of

1 Purchas, IV. 173. Withington came out with Captain Best in the Tenth Voyage.

2 Purchas, VI. 59.

3 By a curious oversight, the Portuguese established no factories at the Cape of Good Hope, Singapore, or Surat, all places of the utmost strategic and commercial importance.

whom, besides himself, were connected with the East India Company.[1] He had seen fighting under Fenton off Brazil and had been in the Levant, where he learnt Turkish.[2] Hawkins sailed as master of the *Hector* from Erith on March 8th 1607. Captain Keeling, on the *Dragon*, accompanied him as "General." A third ship, the *Consent*, Captain, David Middleton, sailed independently,[3] and it was well for them that they did, for they reached the Cape on July the 27th, whereas Keeling did not make it until December 17th.[4] He had been blown right out of his course to the Brazil coast, and owing to scurvy and lack of water, was forced to put into Sierra Leone to refit. Here an interesting event is recorded by Keeling. On Sept. 5th, the crew of the *Hector* acted the tragedy of *Hamlet*. On the 30th Captain Keeling asked Hawkins to dinner, "where my companions acted *King Richard II*"; and on the following day, he again "envited Captain Hawkins to a ffishe dinner, and had *Hamlet* acted abord me, wch I p'mitt to keepe my people from idleness and unlawful games, or sleepe."[5] The voyage was altogether very long and tedious. Socotra was only reached in March 1608. Here, acting on the advice of some friendly Gujarati sailors, they awaited the bursting of the S. W. Monsoon. On June 24th they parted, Keeling for Bantam and Hawkins for Surat, armed with a duplicate of the Commission under the Great Seal. He arrived on August 4th and came ashore on the 28th.

1 Giles Hawkins was a factor at Bantam; Charles was a partner in the Sixth Voyage. Markham, *The Hawkins Voyages*, xlii. note (Hakluyt Society's Publications).

2 Ibid, xliv.

3 She left Tilbury on March 12th, Purchas III. 51: *cf.* his marginal note, II. 502.

4 Keeling's Diary in Purchas, II. 508.

5 So Rundall, in *Narratives of Voyages to the North-West*, (Hakluyt Society) p. 231. This was published in 1849. Since then someone has stolen the page from Keeling's Ms. diary. For plays on board ship, *cf. The Lancaster Voyages*, p.147, where Sir Henry Middleton at Cape Verde "had a great feast and a play played," on the *Trade's Increase*, June 18th 1610.

The following interesting description of Surat as they found it, from the pen of William Finch, one of the company, is preserved by Purchas:[1]

"The city is of good quantity, with many fair Merchants' houses therein, standing twenty miles within the land upon a fair river. Some three miles from the south of the river, (where on the south side lieth a small low island overflowed in time of rain), is the bar, where ships trade and unlade, whereon at springtide is three fathom water. Over this the channel is fair to the city side, able to bear vessels of fifty tons laden. The river runs to Bramport (*Burhānpur*), others say to Musselpatan. As you come up to the river, on the right hand stands the Castle, well walled and ditched, reasonable great and fair, with a number of fair pieces, some of them of exceeding greatness. It hath one gate to the Green-ward, with a drawbridge and a small port on the river-side. The captain hath in command two hundred horse. Before this lieth the Medon (*Maidān*), which is a pleasant green, in the midst whereof is a May pole to hang lights on and for other pastimes on great Festivals.[2]

On this side the city lieth open to the Green, but on all other parts is ditched and fenced with thick hedges, having three gates, of which one leadeth to Variaw,[3] a small village where is the ford to pass over to Cambaya way. Near this village on the left hand lieth a small Aldea (village) on the river-bank, very pleasant, where stands a great Pagoda, much resorted to by the Indians. Another grate leadeth to Bramport, a third to Nonsary (*Navsāri*) a town ten cose (*kos*, two miles) off, where is made a great store of calico, having a fair river[4] coming to it. Some ten cose further lieth Gondoree[5] and a little further, Belsaca[6], the frontier town upon Daman.

1 IV. 27 ff.

2 Probably a *dīpmāl* or lampstand.

3 A hamlet on the north side of the town.

4 The Purna River.

5 Probably Gandevi.

6 Balsār.

Hard without Nonsary gate is a fair tank,[1] sixteen square, enclosed on all sides with stone steps, three-quarters of an English mile in compass, with a small house in the middest. On the further side are diverse fair tombs with a goodly paved court, pleasant to behold; behind which groweth a small grove of mango-trees, whither the citizens go forth to banquet. Some half cose behind this place is a great tree much worshipped by the Banians, where they affirm a Dew (*Deva*, god) to keep, and that it hath often times been cut down and stocked up at the Moores' command and yet hath sprung up again. Near to the Castle is the Alphandica (*alphandega*, customs house), where is a pair of stairs for lading and unlading of goods: within are rooms for keeping goods till they are cleared, the custom being two and half for goods, three for victuals, and two for money. Without the gate is a great Gondoree or Bazaar. Right before this gate stands a tree within an arbour, whereon the Fokeers (*fakīrs*), which are Indian holy men, sit in state. Betwixt this and the Castle, on the entrance of the Green, is the market for horse and cattle. A little lower, on the right over the river, is a little pleasant town, Ranele,[2] inhabited by a people called Naites,[3] speaking another language, and for the most part seamen: the houses are fair therein, with fair steps to each man's door, the streets narrow. They are very friendly to the English. Here are many pleasant Gardens, which attract many to pass there their time: and on the trees are an infinite number of great Bats which we saw at Saint Augustine's, hanging by the claws on the boughs, making a shrill noise. This fowl, the people say, engendereth in the ear: on each wing it hath an hook, and giveth the young suck."

Hawkins landed and was politely received by the local authorities, who, however, referred his case to "Mocreb

1 The Gopi Talāo.

2 Rānder, (called Ranel by Barbosa).

3 *Nāyata*, Arab merchants and sailors who settled there in 1225, Cf. Stanley's Barbosa, 67.

chan," or Mukarrab Khān, the Viceroy of Cambay and Surat, afterwards known to the English as their most relentless opponent. The messenger to Cambay was delayed by the violence of the monsoon; meanwhile, in spite of some opposition, Hawkins started to trade in such articles as might be profitably sold at Bantam; for it was decided to send the *Hector* to join Keeling as agreed on, while Hawkins himself went to Agra to present his petition. The *Hector* was soon loaded up. Master Marlow was put in command and farewells were said and Hawkins returned to his work at Surat, when "the next day,[1] going about my affairs to the great man's brother, I met with some ten or twelve of our men, of the better sort of them, very much frighted, telling me the heaviest news, as I thought, that ever came unto me, of the taking of the barks by a Portugal frigate[2] or two, and all goods and men taken, only they escaped." Finch[3] gives further details. "These frigates were Portugals, which desired one come to talk with them, and Master Bucke rashly doing it, they detained him, and after (I and Nicholas Ufflet being ashore) Master Marlowe and the rest began to flee; the cockswain would have fought, which he would not permit, but running aground through ignorance of the channel, they were taken going on the sandy island by Portugal treachery, and the fault of some of themselves,[4] nineteen with Master Bucke; but the Ginne put off the Pinnace, and notwithstanding the Portugal bullets, rowed her to Surat. Four

1 October 2nd. The passage is from Hawkins' diary, *apud* Purchas, III. 4.

2 A light galley, used for river work.

3 Finch, *apud* Purchas, IV. 20.

4 So Hawkins—But the Company thought otherwise. "We are informed by Bucke and Marlowe," they write, "that they were destitute of powder and other means to defend themselves, which was a great neglect in your part to be so secure as not to arm and animate your men thoroughly." *First Letter Book,* 316. These men were taken from Goa to the Trunk at Lisbon where they remained till 1610, in great want. *Ibid*. 306. Their crime was "trading in the East without the king of Spain's licence."

escaped by swimming and got that night to Surat, besides Nicholas Ufflet and myself, near twenty miles from the place." It subsequently transpired that the *Hector* herself had got away, only the longboat and her crew being captured; but Hawkins found himself in an awkward plight. He was surrounded by enemies. Mukarrab Khān, instigated by the Portuguese, tried to kidnap him and steal his goods. He decided that his best course was to lay his case before the Emperor at Agra; and on February 1st, 1609, he set out for the capital, leaving Finch, who was down with dysentery, to look after his goods at Surat.

After sundry attempts had been made to murder him *en route*, Hawkins presented himself to Jahāngir on April 16th at Agra. The king was pleased to see him, and Hawkins found that he could make himself understood in Turkish, which is not far removed from Turki, the ancestral tongue of the descendants of Babur. Jahāngir liked new acquaintances, especially good fellows who could hold their liquor, and Hawkins entertained him vastly with stories of his travels. No wonder the "Portugalls," who since the time of Akbar had held a distinguished position at the court, became like "madde dogges." Hawkins, Nicholas Ufflet, and the 'boy,' Stephen Gravener, became mysteriously ill, and the latter died. Thereupon Jahāngir gave his friend a wife out of the Royal Harem to cook his food, and so avoid untoward accidents in the future. This lady was a daughter of Mubarik Shāh, an Armenian Christian who had risen to distinction in Akbar's service. The marriage service was read by Ufflet, until such time as a more formal ceremony could be performed by a regular Chaplain. The king now seemed quite won over. He gave Hawkins his commission, written under his Golden Seal, to be sent to Surat, together with a stinging reproof to Mukarrab Khān for his bad behaviour to the English. Hawkins was now in high glee; he was with the king day and night (usually until the World Grasper was removed, the worse for drink, to the Harem); at the audience, he stood within the coveted Red Rails; and Jahāngir, in an outburst of friendship, went so far as to offer him, if he would stay at the court, a pension of £3,200 a year, a troop of horse, and any concessions for the Factory that he liked to ask! Finding, like Philip II of Spain, that "Achins" was a difficult name to pronounce, Jahāngir gave him the title of "Inglis Khān," (in Persia, it is the title for a Duke, Hawkins parenthetically explains). To all of which, our envoy, seeing that "it would feather my nest and do Your Worships a service," as he writes to his masters, cheerfully acquiesced.

His triumph, however, was destined to be short-lived. The nobles and the "Portugalls" were consumed with jealousy. The Viceroy of Goa sent a letter (accompanied by a handsome present) warning Jahāngir that if the English got a footing in the country, he would eventually lose his harbours and his trade altogether. This, according to Hawkins, was the cause of his downfall. "The king went from his word, esteeming a few toys which the Fathers had promised him more than his honour." "It is true," His Majesty cynically remarked, "that the commandment for the Factory was sealed and ready to be delivered; but upon letters received from Mocrebcan, and better consideration had on the affairs of his ports in Guzerat, he thought it fitting not to let him have it." Unfortunately for Hawkins there was another Englishman at Agra who kept a journal, and he supplements the story in a very different fashion, though, as there was no love lost between the two, we must, perhaps, allow something for the writer's malice. This was John Jourdain[1] of the *Ascension*, which, with the *Union*,[2] had set out in 1608 on the Company's Fourth Voyage, and had been wrecked on the shoals in the Gulf of Cambay. The survivors had found their way to Surat, where, owing to the lack of control exercised by the Master, Captain Sharpeigh, they had been

1 For details, see his Journal, edited by Foster for the Hakluyt Society, Series II, Vol. XVI.

2 The *Union* went on to Achin. After a disastrous voyage she went on the rocks off Andierne in Brittany on her return journey.

involved in various broils,[1] and had finally set out for Agra. Jourdain says that Hawkins had at first acquired popularity at Court by winning the favour of Asaf Khān, a powerful nobleman, whose sister was the famous Nūr Jahān, afterwards Jahāngir's wife, and whose daughter married Jahāngir's favourite son Prince Khurram. After a while, however, by trying to drive a hard bargain in trade, Hawkins offended the Queen Mother and Khwāja Abūl Hassan, the Chief Secretary. Abūl Hassan took his revenge in an amusing fashion. The king was a great drinker, but was ashamed of his vice, and cruelly punished those who talked of his orgies or of the part they took in them. "The king," says Jourdain, "was informed that some of his great men were bibbers of wine and that before they came to the Court daily, they filled their heads with strong drink, and commanded that upon pain of his displeasure none of his nobles that came to his court should drink any strong drink before their coming. Now Abdelhasan, knowing that Hawkins was a great drinker, feed the porter (as is supposed) to smell if he had drunk any strong drink, which is easily discerned by one that is fasting. So the chief porter finding that Hawkins had drunk, he presently carried him before the king in presence of the whole Court, where, by the mouth of Abdelhasan, being Secretary, it was told the king he had drunk strong drink. Whereat the king paused a little space, and considering that he was a stranger, he bid him go to his house, and when he came next he should not drink. So being disgraced in public, he could not be suffered to come into his accustomed place near the king, which was the cause why he went not so often to Court."[2]

1 One Tom Tucker had got drunk and killed a calf. This enraged the "Banyans," who paid a handsome sum to the authorities every year to stop cow-killing. Captain Downton found it impossible to open a beef market for the same reason (Downton in Purchas IV. 220).

2 Jourdain's Journal, p. 104 ff. Hawkins was lucky. Some unfortunate nobles, after a banquet to welcome the Persian ambassadors, boasted of the "merry night past." For this Jahāngir had them flogged almost to death. *Embassy of Sir Thos. Roe*, Ed. Foster, pp. 303–4.

Whether this was true or not, Hawkins was now out of favour. "Stay I would not, among these worthless infidels," he writes, but unfortunately Mrs. Hawkins' relatives objected to her leaving India. At first he thought of asking the Jesuits (who were ready to do anything to get rid of him) to give him a passport to settle in Goa, with full liberty of conscience, and eventually returning to England when opportunity offered. Jourdain, however, pointed out the dangers of this. News had come of the appearance of a fresh English fleet off the coast of Cambay and Jourdain proposed to go and join it. "I told him," he writes, "if he went to Goa his life would not be long, because he had much disputed against the Pope and their religion, and was apt to do the like again there, if he were urged thereunto, which would cost him his life, and the sooner because of his goods. But he answered that the Fathers had promised to get him a pass from the Viceroy, and also from the Bishop and priests, that he might use his own conscience. I told him the same cause would be his destruction, if he went. So he was persuaded to go that way and I was persuaded to go the other way, although he urged me very far, promising great wages; but his promises were of little force, for he was very fickle in his resolution, as also in his religion, for in his house he used altogether the custom of the Moors or Mahometans and seemed to be discontent if all men did not the like."[1] With this malicious hit, Jourdain parted from Hawkins on July 28th, 1611, and reached Surat in October. Here he found Sir Henry Middleton with the Sixth Voyage, his flagship being the magnificent *Trades Increase*, a great vessel of 1,100 tons, the pride of the Mercantile Navy.[2] The coast was closely blockaded by the Portuguese admiral, Don Fransisco de Soto, who refused to allow any trade with the shore, and Jourdain had some difficulty in getting on board. Hawkins followed in November, having ap-

1 Jourdain, *op. cit.* p. 161.

2 The other vessels were the *Peppercorn* (Captain, Nicholas Downton), the *Darling* and the *Samuel*.

parently taken Jourdain's advice. But he outwitted his wife's relatives in an amusing way. He persuaded the Jesuits to make him out duplicate passports, one an open one licencing him to settle down as a trader in Goa, the other a secret permit to return to England "and what agreements I made with them to be void and of none effect, but I should stay and go when I pleased." What marginal notes on "Jesuiticall Sanctitie" would a similar procedure on the part of his opponents have evoked from the worthy Purchas!

Hawkins, his wife and the other Englishman were taken on board under an armed escort, Mukarrab Khān, overawed by the Portuguese fleet, peremptorily refusing to allow a factory to be opened or any English traders to be left behind at Surat. Before starting Middleton made a most valuable discovery, acting on information supplied by Jourdain from native sources.[1] This was the location of the famous Swally Hole, a fine roadstead seven miles long and a mile broad, protected from the sea by a long sandbar. Here a fleet could ride at anchor much more safely than among the shifting shoals of the Tāpti. Swally became the port of Surat and acquired great fame.[2] Otherwise Middleton had accomplished nothing during a stay of one hundred and thirty-eight days. On his way out he had been robbed and imprisoned by the Arabs at Mocha, and he was burning for revenge. Accordingly his fleet weighed anchor and sailed along the coast to Dabul, destroying Portuguese shipping, and then crossed over to Aden and blockaded the mouth of the Red Sea. Many Mahommedan ships were held up for ransom, including the huge *Rahīmi*, a pilgrim ship belonging to the Queen Mother, which paid 15,000 reals of eight. The blockade was spoilt by the arrival of Captain John Saris with the Eighth

1 Hawkins, refusing to give his enemy any credit, says that Middleton discovered Swally "miraculously," "and never known to any of the country."

2 "The Road of Swally and the Port of Surat are fittest for you in all the Moghal's country.......The Road of Swally is as safe as a pond." Roe, *apud* Foster II. 345.

Voyage; as usual, the rival commanders could not agree, and unfortunate squabbles about precedence rendered co-operation between the two fleets impossible. On October 19th, 1612, they set sail for Tiku in Sumatra, where, in the following January, Hawkins and his wife took a passage on the *Thomas* homeward bound. They reached Saldania Road on April 2nd, and here Hawkins' diary ends. He "dyed on the Irish shore,"[1] no doubt, like so many of the adventurers of his time, of disease contracted in the East.

Hawkins' mission was, directly, a failure. He had failed to obtain from Jahāngir even the worthless *farmāns* he bestowed upon other English ambassadors. Jahāngir, convinced by the Jesuit Fathers that the English were a paltry and distant race who wanted to rob him of his trade, took no notice of him when he had exhausted his stock of novelties and good stories. The English are not even mentioned in that monarch's voluminous memoirs. Nor was any change likely to come about while the Portuguese fleet could blockade the coast at will. A decisive victory at sea was supremely necessary for English prestige. But indirectly the results were very important. Hawkins had thoroughly explored the resources of the Moghal Empire (of which he wrote a very able account) and had investigated the possibilities of Surat as the site for a factory. Hawkins may not unfairly claim to be ranked among the founders of the Indian Empire.

A few words on the adventures of the rest of the company may not be out of place. Finch died at Bagdad in trying to reach home by the overland route.[2] The ill-luck which pursued Sir Henry Middleton throughout his "tired, crost, and decayed" voyage, clung to him to the end. The "princely *Trade*," "for beauty, burthen and strength

1 Purchas, *Pilgrimage* (1626) p. 521. The mortality was very high, Downton, Middleton, Aldworth, and a host of others never saw home again. The life of a man was "two monsoons," says Ovington of Bombay, and this was true of the East in general.

2 He had been very badly treated by Hawkins, if we can believ Jourdain, *op. cit.* 157.

surpassing all merchants' ships whatsoever," ran on a coral reef, and had to be careened at Bantam. Here she was set on fire by the Javanese. The terrible climate killed most of the crew, Sir Henry being the first to go—"most of heartsore," say the old records. Jourdain found that one hundred and forty had perished, and the rest were "like ghosts or men frighted" and "scarce able to go on their legs." *Quæ regio in terris nostri non plena laboris?* is a quotation which Purchas not inaptly applies to our struggles for a footing in these Eastern seas.

Mrs. Hawkins had no difficulty in consoling herself. She had brought from Agra diamonds worth £6,000, no doubt procured by her step-father, Abraham de Duyts, Prince Khurram's court-jeweller, and the Company gave her 200 Jacobuses as "a token of their love." She married Captain Gabriel Towerson of the *Hector*, her first husband's old ship, and in 1617 returned to India with Mrs. Hudson and her maid, Francis Webb. Richard Steele and Mrs. Golding the Chaplain were her fellow passengers, Sir Thomas Roe being then at Agra as English Ambassador.

The party arrived at Agra on November 2nd, Steele having married Francis at the Cape. Mr. Golding, who was very fond of the ladies, followed them to Agra disguised as a native, for which unclerical conduct Sir Thomas Roe had him arrested. Sir Thomas disliked them all, and writes of them as follows—"I found him (Steele) high in his conceits, having somewhat forgotten me, Master Kerridge and him at wars, which I endeavoured to temper on all parts; but for his wife I dealt with him clearly, she could not stay with our safety nor his masters' content; that he had ruined his fortunes if by amends he repaired it not; that she should not travel nor live on the Company's purse; I know the charge of women, that if he were content to live himself like a merchant, as others did, frugally, and to be ordered for the Company's service and to send home his wife, he was welcome; otherwise I must take a course with both, against my nature. Having to this persuaded him, I likewise practised the discouragement of Captain Towerson about his wife (you know not the danger, the trouble, the inconvenience of granting these liberties); to effect this, I persuaded Abraham, his Father-in-law here, to hold fast; I wrote to them the gripings of this Court, the small hope of relief from his alliance, who expected great matters from him."[1] Accordingly, Gabriel Towerson let his wife return to her own people,[2] while he went to the Far East to take charge of the English Factory at Amboyna. Here he and the other factors were barbarously murdered, after nameless tortures, by the Dutch in 1623. A similar fate had already befallen John Jourdain seven years previously; the Dutch admiral treacherously shot him on his own quarter-deck, after he had surrendered to superior forces, off the town of Patani on the coast of the Malay Peninsula.

1 Embassy of Sir Thomas Roe, Ed. Foster II. 478.

2 This was in 1618. In 1619 she and her mother were "railing" at Towerson for his desertion of her, and trying to borrow Rs. 220 from Kerridge, Chief of the Surat factory. She was still worrying in 1627. *English Factories*, Ed. Foster, I, 169, 327, etc.

NOTE ON AUTHORITIES

These may be divided into (1) Miscellaneous Records and Correspondence of the East India Company; (2) Journals kept by the Voyagers themselves; (3) Selections from these Journals, with other miscellaneous matter, edited by Hakluyt and Purchas.

The Correspondence, Factory Records, Court Minutes and Letter Books of the Company are now partly available to the student, thanks to the labours of Foster, Birdwood, Danvers, Sainsbury, Forrest, and other workers in this field.

The original journals of the Voyagers have survived in a very imperfect condition, probably being neglected because Purchas and Hakluyt had published the most interesting portions of them. These precious fragments have been edited from time to time by the members of the Hakluyt Society. For our purpose the most important are the three imperfect abstracts of Keeling's voyage in Markham's *Voyage of Sir James Lancaster*, pp. 108-120, and the journals of John Jourdain and Sir Thomas Roe, edited by Mr. W. Foster.

Purchas, after the death of Hakluyt, was entrusted by Sir Thomas Smyth, the first Governor of the Company, with all its logs and journals. How he used them may be gathered from his marginal note. "This journal of Captain Keeling's and that of Captain Hawkins, written at sea-leisure, very voluminous in a hundred sheets of paper, *I have been bold so to shorten as to express only the most necessary observations for sea and land affairs.*" For this he has been somewhat severly taken to task. But the matter was very unwieldy, (in Maclehose's reprint it covers as it is twenty volumes of nearly six hundred pages each), and the standard of historical accuracy was not always what it is to-day. In the preface to Churchill's *Collection of Voyages*, John Locke wishes that "the author (Hakluyt) had been less voluminous, delivering what was really authentic and useful, and not stuffing his work with..............so many warlike exploits not at all pertinent to his undertaking, and such a multitude of articles, charters, privileges. letters, relations, and other things little to the purpose of travels and discoveries."

A CHAPTER FROM THE LIFE OF SHIVAJI

(1665-1666)

BY JADUNATH SARKAR

A little after 9 o'clock in the morning of 11th June, 1665, while Mirza Rajah Jai Sinha was holding court in his tent at the foot of Purandar fort, Raghunath Pandit, the envoy of Shivaji, came in and reported to him that the Maratha chief had arrived to offer his submission. High officers of the Mirza Rajah were sent to welcome him on the way and usher him. On entering the tent he was cordially received by Jai Sinha, while armed Rajputs stood around to guard against any treacherous movement on the part of Shivaji!

Meanwhile, the siege of Purandar was pressed on, the lower part (named Vajra-garh or Rudra-mālā) having been captured before. Some more defensive works (*Khand Kala*?=demi-lunes or horn works) were assaulted and carried by the Mughals immediately after Shiva's arrival, and the fighting could be distinctly seen from the interior of the Rajah's tent. Shiva then offered to surrender the fort and prevent useless bloodshed. Jai Sinha, therefore, ordered the fighting to cease, and sent some of his own officers with an agent of Shiva to take possession of the fort in the name of the Emperor and let the garrison depart unmolested. This was effected on the next day.

Shiva had travelled without any baggage or retinue, and therefore Jai Sinha lodged him in his office tent as his guest. Up to mid-night the two sides higgled for the terms of a permanent place. But Jai Sinha knew the strength of his position. As he wrote in his despatches to the Emperor, "I declined to abate a single fort. Gradually, after much discussion, we came to this agreement:— (*a*) That 23 of his forts, the lands of which yielded 4 lakhs of hun as annual revenue, should be annexed to the Empire; and (*b*) that 12 of his forts, including Rajgarh, with an annual revenue of 1 lakh of hun, should be left to Shiva, on condition of service and loyalty to the imperial throne."

Shivaji, however, begged to be excused from attending the Emperor's court like other nobles and Rajahs, and proposed to send his son, as his representative, with a contingent of 5,000 horse, (to be paid by means of a jagir), for regular attendance and service under the Emperor or the Mughal governor of the Deccan. This was exactly the favour shown to the Mahārāna of Udaipur. As he pleaded with Jai Sinha, "By reason of my late unwise and disloyal acts, I have not the face to wait on the Emperor. I shall depute my son to be His Majesty's servant and slave, and he will be created a Commander of Five Thousand with a suitable jagir............As for me sinner, exempt me from holding any *mansab* or serving in the Mughal army. But whenever in your wars *in the Deccan*, I am given any military duty, I shall promptly perform it."

In addition to the above terms, Shivaji made another and a conditional engagement with the Mughals: "If lands yielding 4 lakhs of hun a year in the lowlands of Konkan (Tal-Konkan) and 5 lakhs of hun a year in the uplands (Balaghat Bijapuri), are granted to me by the Emperor and I am assured by an imperial *farmān* that the possession of these lands will be confirmed in me after the expected Mughal conquest of Bijapur, then I agree to pay to the Emperor 40 lakhs of *hun* in 13 yearly instalments." He was expected to wrest these lands from the Bijapuri officers by means of his own troops.

Here we detect the shrewdness of Jai Sinha's policy in throwing a bone of perpetual contention between Shivaji and the Sultan of Bijapur. As he wrote to the Emperor, "This policy will result in a three-fold gain: *first*, we get 40 lakhs of hun or 2 krores of Rupees; *secondly*, Shivaji will be alienated from Bijapur; *thirdly*, the imperial army will be relieved from the arduous task of campaigning in these two broken and jungly regions, as Shiva will himself undertake the task of expelling the Bijapuri garrisons from them." In return for it, Shiva also agreed to assist the Mughals in the invasion of Bijapur with 2,000 cavalry of his son Shambhuji's *mansab* and 7,000 expert infantry under his own command.

These terms were reported to the Emperor for ratification, together with a letter of submission and prayer for pardon from Shiva (but really drafted by Jai Sinha's secretary Udai Raj) and a despatch from Jai Sinha recommending the acceptance of the terms and the granting of a robe of honour to Shiva. They reached Aurangzib at Delhi on 23rd June and he was pleased to accede to them all.

The treaty of Purandar being thus happily concluded, Jai Sinha on 14th June dismissed Shivaji with his son Kumar Kirat Sinha, for the transfer of his forts to Mughal hands. They reached Kondana at noon of the same day. It was evacuated by the Marathas and Kirat Sinha was left there in occupation, while Shiva moved on to Rajgarh (where he arrived on the 15th and halted for a day). On the 17th Shiva sent Shambhuji with Jai Sinha's officer Ugrasen Kachhwah from Rajgarh, and they reached Jai Sinha's camp the next day, when news arrived of the surrender of Rajgarh and four other forts.

Jai Sinha then began to make preparations for the invasion of Bijapur, in order to prevent his large army eating its bread in idleness after its recent victorious campaign against Shivaji. In September he received the Emperor's despatch accepting all his recommendations about Shiva together with a gracious *farmān* stamped with the impression of his palm) and a robe of honour for the latter. Jai Sinha invited Shiva to come and receive these marks of imperial favour with befitting solemnity. "Shivaji, then in Adil Shahi Tal-Konkan, immediately on hearing of it, travelled quickly and reached my camp on 27th September, 1665. On the 30th, I sent him, with my son Kirat Sinha and my Pay-master Jāni Khān, to advance and welcome the imperial letter on the way."

A little mummery was acted on the occasion, to satisfy the etiquette of the Mughal court: "As Shiva had worn no weapon on his person from the day when he had come like a penitent offender to wait on the Rajah to this date, Jai Sinha now gave him a jewelled sword and dagger and pressed him to put them on" (*Alamgir-namah*, 907)

The ceremony completed his restoration to the good grace of the Emperor.

Jai Sinha then dismissed Shivaji to enable him to gather his contingent of 9,000 men and make the necessary preparations for the coming campaign, promising him two lakhs of Rupees from the imperial treasury for the purpose. Shiva promised to join Jai Sinha the day before he started.

At last, on 20th November, 1665, Jai Sinha set out on the invasion of Bijapur, from the fort of Purandar. The Maraṭha contingent, 9,000 strong, under Shiva and his kinsman (*khwest*) Netuji Palkar,—"whom the Deccanis regard as a second Shivaji,"—formed the Left Centre of the Mughal army.

During the first month of the campaign, Jai Sinha's march was an uninterrupted triumph. From Purandar to Mangalbirah (Maṅgalveḍhe), a fort 32 miles north of Bijapur, the invaders advanced without meeting with any opposition; the Bijapuri forts on the way were either evacuted in terror or surrendered at call to Shiva's troops who had been sent ahead by Jai Sinha to capture them. Phaltan, about forty miles south-east of Purandar was entered on 7th December; Thathora, 14 miles north of Phaltan, on the 8th; Khāwan about a week later; and Mangalbira itself on the 18th.

The invaders marched on, and then, on 24th December, they came into touch with the enemy for the first time. Next day a Mughal detachment under Dilir Khān and Shivaji marched 10 miles from their camp and fought a Bijapuri army of 12,000 under the famous generals Sharza Khān and Khawās Khān and their Maratha auxiliaries under Jadu Rao [Ghorpure ?] of Kalian and Venkoji, the half-brother of Shivaji. The Deccanis evaded the charge of the cavaliers of Delhi, but harassed them by their "cossack tactics," dividing themselves into four bodies and fighting loosely with the Mughal divisions opposite. After a long contest, Dilir Khān's tireless energy and courage broke the enemy's force by repeated charges, and they retired in the afternoon, leaving one general (Yaqut the

Abyssinian) and 15 captains dead on the field and many flags, horses and weapons in the Mughal hands. But as soon as the victors began their return march to camp, the elusive enemy reappeared and galled them severely with rockets from the two wings and rear. The Maratha rear-guard under Netuji bore the brunt of the attack but stood its ground well. When the Deccanis hemmed Netu round and pressed him hard, he called for reinforcements from Kirat Sinha and Fath Jang Khān and with their aid repulsed the enemy. Jadu Rao of Kalian received a musket shot, of which he died in five or six days. Shivaji and his brother Venkoji fought on opposite sides !

After a two days' halt, Jai Sinha resumed his march on the 27th. The next day, after reaching the camping ground in the evening, he detached a force to attack and expel the Bijapuri army from the neighbourhood. The fight soon became general, and Jai Sinha himself had to charge the enemy's largest division. Shivaji and Kumar Kirat Sinha, seated on the same elephant, led his Van and dashed into the Deccani ranks. After a hard fight, the enemy were put to flight, leaving more than a hundred dead and many more wounded.

On 29th December, 1665, Jai Sinha arrived at Makhnapur,[1] ten miles north of Bijapur fort. Here his advanc was stopped, and after waiting for a week, he was forced to begin his retreat on 5th January, 1666, as he found his fondly hoped-for chance of taking Bijapur by a *coup de main* gone. He was not prepared for a regular siege, because, in his eagerness "to grasp the golden opportunity" of attacking Bijapur while undefended and torn by domestic factions, he had not brought any big artillery and siege materials with himself. On the other hand, Adil Shah had put the fort of Bijapur in a strong posture of defence; its walls had been repaired, large quantities of provisions and material laid in, its regular garrison augmented by 30,000 Karnatic infantry, and the country round for a radius of seven

1 In the Persian Ms. the name may be read either as *Makhanah* or as *Naythana*. The latter is a village 8 miles N. N. E. of Bijapur.

miles laid waste, drained of its water supply, and denuded of its trees. At the same time he had sent a picked force under Sharza Khān and Siddi Masaud to invade the Mughal dominions and make a diversion in Jai Sinha's rear.

On 27th January, the retreating Mughal army reached a place 16 miles from Parenda, and there halted for 24 days. Here we shall leave it, as the historian of Shivaji is not concerned with its operations any further.

On receiving the unexpected check before Bijapur, Jai Sinha looked round, to create a diversion. As he writes in a despatch to the Court, "At my request the Emperor had sent a robe of honour and jewelled dagger for Shiva, who was ready to co-operate at the siege of Bijapur, but.........I did not deem it expedient. Shiva said to me,—'If you detach me, I can go and capture for the Emperor Panhala, of which I know all the exits and entrances, while the garrison are off their guard. I shall raise so much disturbance in that district that the enemy will be compelled to divert a large force from their army to oppose me.' As his words bore promise of action, I sent him away on his promised errand."

This was about 11th January. Five days later Shiva reached the environs of Panhala, and delivered an assault on it three hours before sunrise. But the garrison were on the alert and offered a stubborn defence. A thousand of Shiva's followers fell down, killed and wounded. When the rising sun lit up the scene, Shiva at last recognised that it was madness to continue the struggle, and drew back sullenly to his own fort of Khelnā [Visālgarh], about 20 miles westwards. But his troops continued to ravage that quarter and succeeded in drawing and detaining there a force of 6,000 Bijapuris under Siddi Masaud and Randaula Khān.

The news of Shivaji's failure at Panhala reached Jai Sinha on 20th January. The evil was aggravated by the desertion of Netuji. Taking offence with Shiva for some reason or other,—probably because he deemed his valuable services and gallant feats of arms inadequately rewarded,—Netu accepted the Bijapuri bait of 4 lakhs of hun and, deserting to Adil Shah, raided the Mughal territory with great vigour and effect. Jai Sinha could not afford to lose such a man; and so he lured Netuji back (20th March) with many persuasive letters and the granting of all his high demands, viz. the *mansab* of a Commander of Five Thousand in the Mughal peerage, a Jagir in the settled and lucrative old territory of the empire (as distinct from the ill-conquered, unsettled, ever-ravaged recent annexations in the Deccan), and Rs. 38,000 in cash.[1]

Netuji's defection at the end of January, 1666, greatly alarmed Jai Sinha. If Shiva were to do the same, the entire Maratha army would swell the enemy's ranks and the Mughal invaders would be crushed between them. As he wrote to the Emperor, "Now that Adil Shah and Qutb Shah have united in mischief, it is necessary to win Shiva's heart by all means and to send him to Northern India to have audience of Your Majesty." The Emperor having consented to this proposal, Shiva was formally permitted by Jai Sinha in March to set out for the imperial court.

How Shivaji journeyed to Agra, how he asserted his dignity against the proud governor of Aurangabad, how he was received in audience by Aurangzib on 12th May, 1666, how he was forbidden the court and then placed under police guard, and how finally he escaped from Agra on 19th August and, after many romantic adventures on the way, returned to Rajgarh in December 1666, I have told in detail from all the available Persian sources, in the *Modern Review* for August 1907, pp. 153-161. A few scraps of additional information about Shiva's doings at Agra which I subsequently gleaned from the news-letters of Aurangzib's court, have been printed by Mr. G. S. Sardesai in his *Marathi Riyasat*, new edition, i. 325. It is now necessary to turn to the affairs of the Deccan, especially Jai Sinha's anxieties, plans and acts, during Shiva's absence from home.

1 Aurangzib's punishment of the traitor was stern. After Netuji had been outwardly conciliated and re-employed by the Mughals, he was suddenly arrested at Dharur, in October, 1666, sent to Delhi in chains, and forced to embrace Islam (as Muhammad Quli Khān) as the only means of saving his life, February 1667.

When, at the *darbar* of 12th May, Shivaji impatiently complained that he had not been treated by the Emperor according to his just expectations, Aurangzib wrote to Jai Sinha to state clearly and fully what promises he had made to Shivaji on behalf of the Mughal government. Jai Sinha replied enumerating and explaining the clauses of the Treaty of Purandar which I have given above. The Emperor's intentions with regard to Shiva when at Agra are thus described in a letter written by Jai Sinha's secretary, reporting the Mirza Rajah's speech: "The Emperor had excluded Shiva [from the darbar] for a few days on account of the ignorance [or disregard] of the etiquette of the imperial court which Shiva had displayed on the day of his audience. Afterwards it was his intention to.........send him back with honour and favours."

But the confidential despatches of Jai Sinha to the Emperor and the prime minister Jafar Khan show that there was much political trickery below the surface of the affair. Shiva had been sent away from the Deccan early in March, as we have seen, to guard against the possibility of his adding to Jai Sinha's troubles.

Jai Sinha's word had been pledged for the safe return of Shivaji to his home. He, therefore, was anxious to prevent the murder or even long imprisonment of Shiva at Agra. As he remarked in a letter to Bhojraj Kachhwah, evidently for communication to Kumar Ram Sinha (his representative at the imperial court), "Act in such a way [in the affair of Shiva] as to secure the safety of the imperial dominions and the sanctity of my word and your word."

After that angry scene in the Public Audience Hall of Agra fort, Shiva had been forbidden the Presence, and his intermediary at Court, Kumar Ram Sinha, had been told by the Emperor that he would have to stand bail and security for the good conduct and presence of Shiva at Agra pending further orders. Evidently Aurangzib changed his mind soon. As Jai Sinha writes to his son, "As at first the Emperor had strongly insisted that Shivaji should be taken out of your bail and security, I had hoped that, after the arrival of my former letter disavowing your responsibility for Shiva, you would be easily relieved [of your responsibility for him]. Now, I learn from the Emperor's letters that he wishes you to guard Shiva. Wait for a few days and pass the time as you have done in the past, till the decision of my prayer,—viz. either I should be retained in the command of the Deccan army with full power and adequate reinforcements or recalled to Court. Thereafter make the necessary application about Shiva [viz. your being relieved of the charge of him]."

And again, "you have written that the Emperor is thinking of leaving you at Agra in charge of Shiva, by ostensibly appointing you commandant of the fort or Faujdar [of the district]." This was exactly what Jai Sinha wanted to avoid. So, he instructed his son to beseech the Emperor to take him with him during the march, saying that he had never before been separated from the imperial company.

Aurangzib agreed to the proposal. Then the question arose, what was to be done with Shiva? Was he to be made to accompany the Emperor [as a political suspect under surveillance] or was he to be left in any fortress? On this point Jai Sinha replied,—"If the Emperor resolves to set out on a compaign, it would be expedient to leave Shiva at Agra. He ought to be conciliated and assured that he would be summoned to the court after it had arrived in the Deccan. His son should, as a matter of policy, be kept with the Emperor, in order that his followers may not be thrown into dispair, but may loyally serve us. [*H. A.* 197*a*].

A little earlier Jai Sinha had recommended a similar policy: "When I prayed that Shiva might be permitted by the Emperor to return home, affairs [in the Deccan] were in a different condition. Now that they have changed altogether [i. e. adversely for the Mughals], it is not at all politic to send him to this side. Please detain him in such a way that his officers may not despair [of his life or return home], go over to Adil Shah, raise disturbances and thus compel us to divert a force to their quarter." [*H. A.* 194*a*].

Jai Sinha was adversely spoken of in the imperial court in connection with Shiva's conduct at Agra. Here is his indignant defence of his action in relation to the Maratha hero—

"The Emperor himself had appointed me to the command of the expedition against Shiva. By the grace of God and the good luck of the Emperor, I brought it to a successful conclusion in the shortest possible time, and then, by a thousand devices I succeeded in sending him with his son to the imperial Presence. The Emperor is aware of it and yet the courtiers are saying, 'When you knew Shiva to be this sort of person, why did you send him to Court?'.........When I sent him off against Panhala, people here [i. e. my rivals in the Mughal camp] began to say that I had helped him to escape from our hands. And now that I have sent him to the Emperor's Presence, they are saying, 'Why did you send him here?' Such remarks spoil the success of the half-finished Bijapur business." [*H. A.* 194*b*–195*a*].

Jai Sinha's position was rendered infinitely worse by Shiva's escape from Agra on 19th August 1666. He had been disgraced in the eyes of the Emperor by the failure of his invasion of Bijapur. And now his son Ram Sinha was openly suspected of having connived at Shiva's flight. As he writes in bitterness, "All the plans and devices that I had employed in sending Shiva to court have been spoiled, and measureless distraction has fallen to my lot. But there is no remedy against Fate and what is written on a man's forehead. I learn from the letters of some court agents that there is a proposal to dismiss Ram Sinha from his rank (*mansab*) and jagir, because Shiva's Brahman followers, at the instigation of selfish men [my enemies at Court], have alleged that the flight of Shiva was due to the advice of Ram Sinha, and resulted from the latter's omission to watch him well. May God give death to the man who cherishes the very thought of such an act of faithlessness in his heart! Why should Shiva's men's words be believed against mine, when I had reduced him to such an extremity [in war]?" [*H. A.* 201*a*].

The anticipated return of Shivaji to the Deccan greatly added to Jai Sinha's fears. As he wrote on 5th November, 1666:—"The times are bad for me. My anxieties are ceaseless. The lying Bijapuris are wasting time [by delusive negotiations]. There is no trace or news of the fugitive Shiva. My days are passing in distraction and anxiety. I have sent trusty spies, under various disguises, to get news of Shiva." [*H. A.* 200*a*].

About this time the officers left by Shiva in the Deccan when leaving for Agra began to display ominous activity. Sayyid Masaud, the Mughal qiladar of Raigarh, wrote to Jai Sinha's Paymaster complaining of the lack of provisions etc. in the fort, and the collection of lead, gunpowder, rockets and infantry in the neighbourhood of Raigarh by some men who gave themselves out to be Shiva's followers and pretended that they intended to invade Bijapuri territory. At this alarming news Jai Sinha sent orders to provision the fort as a precaution and to hold it strongly, pending the arrival of Udai-bhān [the permanent qiladar ?]. A reinforcement of 500 infantry under Sukh-man Chauban was also ordered to be thrown into the fort if necessary. [*H. A.* 234*a* and *b*].

At last, in December, 1666, definite news was received of Shiva's arrival at Rājgarh. As Jai Sinha's secretary wrote, "Trusty spies have now brought the news that Shiva himself has arrived but is very anxious about his son who has not returned with him. He professes a determination [to submit] to the imperial government. But who knows what is in his heart? For some time past Mahadji Nimbalkar, the son of Bajāji, the Zamindar of Phaltan and son-in-law of the infernal Shiva, has been causing disturbances in the region of Poona and other places. My master [i. e. Jai Sinha] has appointed the jagirdars of that tract, such as, Tānāji Bhonsle[1] and others to Supa, Halāl Khān to Indāpur, Ghālib Khān to Chamārgunda, Hassan Khān, Abdur Rasul and other Deccanis also to that side, and Trimbakji Bhonsle and others to Raisin. Before the others could arrive at their posts, Tānāji Bhonsle went to his

1 The name may be also read as *Būbāji* or *Nānāji*.

jagir and getting an opportunity attacked Mahad, sent many of his followers to hell, captured his flag, *torah*,[1] 150 horses, arrows etc., and returning lived in peace of mind. As the Deccanis have some [unknown] need for the flag and *torah*, Mahadji trod the path of submission and humility; but Tānāji declined [to restore them]. At last four days afterwards, that wretch got help from the Bijapuris and attacked Tānāji by surprise. That loyal and martial officer fought valiantly on foot, till he fell in the Emperor's service. And Anāji (or Dātāji) Deshmukh, went to hell in the neighbourhood of Pandharpur. It is reported that Mahadji also was wounded.........Jai Sinha at first wanted to march there in person [and retrieve the disaster], but was persuaded to give up the idea, lest the Bijapuris should take advantage of his absence. So, he has decided to send Abdul Hamid with 5,000 men to that quarter. [*H. A.* 211*b*].

Then in a letter to the prime minister Jafar Khān we have an astounding proposal from Jai Sinha to entrap Shiva by a false proposal of a marriage between his daughter and Jai Sinha's son, and get him murdered during a journey to the Rajput general's camp—

"I have not failed, nor will I do so in future, to exert myself against Bijapur, Golkonda and Shiva in every possible way.........I am trying to arrange matters in such a way that the wicked wretch Shiva will come to see me once, and that in the course of his journey or return [our] clever men may get a favourable opportunity [of disposing of] that luckless fellow in his unguarded moment at that place. This slave of the Court, for furthering the Emperor's affairs, is prepared to go so far,—regardless of the praise or blame of other people,—that if the Emperor sanctions it, I shall set on foot a proposal for a match with his family and settle the marriage of my son with his daughter,—though the pedigree and caste of Shiva are notoriously low and men like me do not eat food touched by his hand (not to speak of entering into a matrimonial

1 The text reads *tarahrah* and *sarrah*.

connection with him), and in case this wretch's daughter is captured I shall not condescend to keep her in my harem. As he is of low birth, he will very likely swallow this bait and be hooked. But great care should be taken to keep this plan secret. Send me quickly a reply to act accordingly." [*H. A.* 139*a*].

This letter throws a lurid light on the political morals of the 17th century. When people argue that Afzal Khān could not have possibly intended to stab Shivaji during an interview, they should remember that the sanctimonious Jai Sinha was prepared to prove his loyalty by lowering his family honour and laying a fatal snare for Shivaji, a brother Hindu.

PALÆOGRAPHIC NOTES

BY V. S. SUKTHANKAR

IN the field of the palæography of Northern India the beginning of the sixth century of the Christian era is marked by the advent of a new epoch of alphabet which is chiefly characterised by the acute angles which show themselves at the right or lower ends of letters as well as by the wedges which are superimposed on the tops of the vertical or slanting lines, and which is therefore variously styled as the 'Acute-angled' or 'Nail-headed' alphabet.[1] The epigraphic documents of the period from the sixth to at least the beginning of the eighth century form an unbroken record of the use of this alphabet in Central and Northern India. This type was in course of time supplemented by a rival alphabet; and the characters of the inscriptions of the next century present the incipient stages of the Northern Nāgarī, the fully developed forms of which may be seen in the Kauthem (Miraj State) copper-plate grant[2] of the Cālukya king Vikramāditya V (A. D. 1009). The distinguishing features of this type are the substitution of horizontal covering strokes in place of the wedges, and right angles in place of the acute angles of the previous variety. The general course of the evolution of Nāgarī out of the acute-angled alphabet is evident enough;[3] but the determination of the actual period of transition is a problem which naturally presents certain difficulties. The earliest forms of the transition alphabet are differentiated from those of its predecessor merely by the flattening of the above mentioned wedges. These forms are supplied by the characters of the *Multāī* (Central Provinces) plates of the Rāṣṭrakūṭa Nandarāja Yuddhāsura dated in the year corresponding to A. D. 708-9, and other inscriptions of a later date. In other respects the characters of the Multāī plate link on directly to the acute-angled

1 Bühler, *Indische Palæographie*, p. 49.

2 *Indian Antiquary*, Vol. 16, pp, 15 ff.

3 Bühler, *op. cit.*, pp. 50 f,

alphabet, and Bühler was therefore perfectly right in looking upon it as the last phase of this variety.[1] The distinctive peculiarity of Nāgarī, it must be emphasised, lies in the widening of the acute angles into right angles as well as the addition of the flat top stroke which, so to say, covers the entire breadth of the letters at their upper end. Both these characteristics are unmistakably manifest in the Kaṇheri inscriptions of the Śilāhāra feudatories Pullaśakti and Kapardin II.[2] Thus upto the beginning of the eigth century (A. D. 708: the Multāī plates) the acute-angled alphabet was still current in Northern India; on the other hand, as we see from the Kaṇheri inscriptions (A. D. 851 and 877) Nāgarī had come to be used as an epigraphic alphabet by the middle of the ninth century.

We might therefore set ourselves the question, at what period does this change set in? Are there any records written in Nāgarī of a date earlier than the above mentioned Kaṇheri inscriptions[3]? Bühler was inclined to suppose that the northern Nāgarī was in use at least since the beginning of the eigth century.[4] The inscriptions which appear to lend support indirectly to this view form the following series:[5] (1) the *Sāmāngaḍ* grant[6] of the Raṣṭra-

1 Bühler, *op. cit.*, p. 50.

2 Inscriptions No. 15 and 43; see *Indian Antiquary*, Vol. 13, p. 135.

3 I wish to exclude herefrom the signature or families of signatures of Gurjara princes on the copper-plates of Kairā (of A.D. 628 and 633), of Dābhoi (A. D. 642), of Nausārī (A. D. 705) and of Kāvī (A. D. 736) appended to texts written in a southern alphabet. From these royal sign-manuals it does necessarily follow that the alphabet in question was used at that period commonly for epigraphic purposes.

4 Bühler *op. cit.*, p. 51.

5 The earliest of these is dated in A. D. 754. But Bühler argued that as an inscription from the Kanarese country, viz. the Paṭṭadkal pillar inscription of Kīrtivarman II, (*Epigraphia Indica*, Vol. 3, pp. 1 ff.) which was caused to be incised by a Brahman from Northern India, shows the mixture of the Nāgarī and acute-angled letters, we could assume the use of Nāgarī since the beginning of the eighth century. For my part, I must say, I have not been able to trace any Nāgarī letters in this inscription.

6 Edited by Fleet, *Indian Antiquary*, Vol. 11 p. 105.

kūṭa Dantidurga (Bühler, Palæographic Tables, Plate IV. Col. XXII), bearing a date corresponding to A. D. 754, from Western India; (ii) the *Dighvā-Dubaulī* Plate[1] of Mahendrapāla I; and (iii) the Bengal Asiatic Society's plate of Vināyakapāla[2] (of the imperial Pratīhāra dynasty) believed by Bühler to be dated in the years corresponding to A. D. 761 and 794-5 respectively, from Northern India. We shall presently return to a detailed consideration of the Sāmāngaḍ grant, but let us first examine the characters of the other two records a little more closely. It is true enough that we find here distinctly Nāgarī characteristics, e. g. (i) in the above-mentioned right angles of *gha* (Pl. IV, col. XXI; 10), *pa* (col. XXI; 27), *ma* (col. XXIII; 31), *ya*, (col. XXI, XXIII ; 32), and *ṣa* (col. XXIII; 37); (ii) in the flat top stroke of *pa* (col. XXIII; 27); *ma* (col. XXIII; 31), *ya* (col. XXIII ; 32), *ṣa* (col. XXIII ; 37), and *sa* (col. XXIII; 38). Of special interest is the form of *ja* (col. XXI, XXIII ; 14). In the Dighvā-Dubaulī plate it has entirely lost its original characteristic element of three parallel bars as, for instance, in the specimen[3] quoted in the immediately preceding column (XX ; 14) of the same table ; but in the other grant the transformation is still more striking. The lower portion of the letter forms a clearly developed double curve, while the (originally horizontal) middle bar is all but vertical.

Now with regard to these alleged specimens of early Nāgarī the following is to be noted. As far as the alphabet of the Dighvā-Dubaulī plate is concerned the term Nāgarī seems to me to be applied to it with doubtful propriety.[4] Bühler has classed it rightly as in instance of the Acute-angled variety.[5] The absence of the covering stroke in *gha* (col. XXI; 10), *pa* (col. XXI; 27), *ma* col. XXI ; 31, *ya*

1 See Fleet, *Indian Antiquary*, Vol. 15 p. 106.

2 *Indian Antiquary*, Vol. 15, p. 140.

3 Multāī plates ; see Fleet, *Indian Antiquary*, Vol. 18, p. 231.

4 It is called North-Indian Nāgarī by Dr. Fleet, *Indian Antiquary*, Vol. 15, p. 106.

5 Bühler, *op. cit.*, p. 50.

(col. XXI ; 32), *ṣa* (col. XXI ; 37), and *sa* (col. XXI ; 38), shows that it has not passed the transition stage, while the sporadic acute angles, for instance, in *ma* (col. XXI ; 31) and perhaps *ṣa* (col. XXI ; 37) entitle it to be considered a phase of the acute-angled alphabet. This is, however, only a matter of nomenclature. No such doubt can be entertained with regard to the copper-plate grant of the Pratīhāra-king Vināyakapāla of Mahodaya which is certainly one of the earliest instances (if indeed, not the earliest instance) of the use of Nāgarī form for epigraphic purposes as far as Northern and Central India is concerned. None the less is the conclusion of Bühler regarding the phase marked by these two plates in the evolution of Nāgarī wrong ; the reason is that both these records were considerably antedated by him. The mistake lay in the erroneous interpretation put in his time upon the syllables *saṁvatsro* forming part of the date of the record. Here the ligature *tsro* (as was first pointed out by Dr. Hoernle) must be looked upon as consisting of the *t* or *saṁvat* and *sro*, which latter apparently stands for the multiplicative factor 100, a conclusion which has now found general acceptance.[1] The numerical symbols thus correspond to the figures 955 and 988, which when referred to the Vikrama era yield the dates A. D. 898 and 931, and therefore, relegate the plate to the end of the ninth and the beginning of the tenth century respectively, that is, fully 137 years later than the date assigned to them by Bühler.

The expunging of these two records from their place at the end of Plate IV of Bühler's Tables has the effect of breaking up the series mentioned above, and with it disappears a solid block of evidence for the supposition that Nāgarī forms were commonly in use for epigraphic purposes since the beginning of the eigth century. It may be incidentally remarked that even from a consideration of the advanced forms of the plate of Vināyakapāla, this

1 An independent proof of the correctness of this view has now been supplied by the date of the newly discovered Partabgar Ins. noticed by Mr. D. R. Bhandarkar in the *Indian Antiquary*, Vol. 45 (1916), p. 122.

is a satisfactory conclusion, as the latter fits in much better in its new place near the Sūaḍoṇī[1] inscriptions from Central India, the dates of which run from A. D. 968, than in juxtaposition with the Multāī plates and the Baijanāth[2] inscription. It is, however, an extremely fortunate circumstance that in this instance the palæographic conclusion finds a substantial corroboration from an independent source of evidence.

But to return to the question of the earliest use of Nāgarī, it may be observed that the alteration in the reading of the date of the places of the Pratīhāra grants leaves in the main the thesis of Bühler untouched; for, in assigning the earliest known specimen of Nāgarī to the middle of the eigth century Bühler[3] was relying on the *Sāmāngaḍ* grant [4] of Dantidurga which purports to be dated in the year corresponding to A. D. 754; and it must be admitted that in these plates we find not the slightest trace of the wedge formation nor of the acute-angles, but on the other hand, the frequent use of top-strokes (which cover the entire breadth of the letters) and the right angles which, as remarked above, are so characteristic of Nāgarī. Moreover, as the reading of their date is beyond all doubt certain, the existence of these plates is prima facie evidence in support of Bühler's view. But on the other hand one cannot entirely ignore the fact that these plates occupy a very isolated position in the progressive development of Nāgarī. For, the next earliest records in which we again find anything like Nāgarī forms, belong to the beginning of the following century, viz. the Rādhanpur and Vaṇī copper-plate grants of the Rāṣṭrakūṭa Govinda III, issued in the year corresponding to A. D. 808; but it may be pointed out that in this grant of Govinda III, the Nāgarī characters are used not exclusively as in the alleged grant of Dantidurga,

1 Bühler, *op. cit.*, plate V, col. VII.

2 Bühler *op. cit.*, plate V, col. I.

3 Bühler *op. cit.*, p. 51.

4 *Indian Antiquary*, Vol. 11, pages 106 ff., and facsimllie 5; *Indian Antiquary*, Vol. 6, p. 59; Vol. 11, p. 158.

but side by side with others which are distinctly acute-angled. This distinction is worth noting : and I shall shortly have occasion to refer to it again.

As remarked above, there can be no possibility of doubt concerning the reading of the date of the Sāmāngaḍ grant: it is given both in words and numerical figures which tally with each other admirably. But this circumstance does not exclude the possibility that the plates may not actually belong to the year to which they refer themselves; and, in my opinion, the date is too early by at least a hundred years, if not more. It is true that the space of a century often does not make an appreciable difference in palæographic matters. Moreover, while tracing the minute changes in the shape of individual letters even of co-eval documents, we are by the nature of the circumstance forced to utilise for purposes of comparison alphabets from whatever locality they happen to be preserved, which is not the most satisfactory basis of comparison. We must further reckon with the personal indiosyncrasies of the engraver which are mostly an indeterminate factor. It is therefore right to add here that the following remarks regarding the age of the Sāmāngaḍ grant are made with the diffidence which the circumstances call for.

We shall now turn to the alphabet of this alledged grant of Dantidurga and examine it more minutely with a view to determine the standard of development reached by it. From what I have just said it follows that the best course would have been to select for comparison such documents as belong to the same epoch and are executed in the same part of the country. I should have preferred therefore to cite for comparison two copper-plate charters of the Rāṣṭrakūṭa king Kṛṣṇarāja I which have recently been brought to light : the one found at Taḻegāon (Poona district) has been briefly reviewed in the *Progress Report of the Archæological Survey, Western Circle*, for the year ending March 1910; but the other found at Bhāndak (Chandā District, Central Provinces) has as yet received no further publicity beyond the bare mention of its discovery,

It is regrettable therefore that it is not possible to reproduce them here and make them available for the examination of the reader, as no description can adequately take the place of a facsimilie. Out of the plates which have already been edited, and which lend themselves for use in this connection, the Daulatābād plates[1] of the Rāṣṭrakūṭa Śaṅkaragaṇa (dated in the Śaka year 715 corresponding to A. D. 793) are as suitable as any other. When these two sets of plates are placed side by side it will be noticed at once that there is a wide gap separating their alphabet. The characters of the Sāmāngaḍ grant are far in advance of those of the Daulatābād plates which are executed nearly forty years later than the alleged date of the former grant. The difference between them is now the more difficult to explain as the advanced types of the Dighvā-Dubaulī and Vināyakapāla plates are no longer available for bridging over the intervening gap.

A comparison between the alphabets of the two plates reveals the following points of difference between them. In place of the covering stroke of the letters *gha*, *pa*, *ma*, *ya* and *ṣa* of the Sāmāngaḍ grant we have ornamental protuberences in the other plate. As regards *gha* it is worth noting that an example of the tripartite open form (in line 4, twice) of the Daulatābād plates can be seen in as late a record as the Pehvā Praśasti[2] which is assigned by Bühler himself to cir. A. D. 900. Characteristic of a later epoch is the form of *ja* in the Sāmāngaḍ grant which originally and even in the Multāī plates (A. D. 708–9) consisted of three nearly parallel bars connected at one end. Subsequent development of the letter is as follows. The lowest bar develops a notch at its free end, and the middle inclines downwards. Incidentally it may be observed that this is the form of *ja* in the Bhāndak plate of Kṛṣṇarāja I (A. D. 772). In the Vināyakapāla plate the notch develops into a curve, so that the lower portion of the letter forms a

1 Ed. D. R. Bhandarkar, *Epigraphia Indica* Vol. 9, pp. 193 ff., and facsimilie.

2 Bühler, *op. cit.*, Plate V, col. III.

double curve, while the (originally horizontal) middle bar is all but vertical. The change is perfectly gradual, and is, I think, a good index of the age of the document. The *ja* of the Daulatābād plates marks an intermediate stage between the two limits: the lowest bar is slightly bent backwards, while the middle bar, though inclined downwards, is near its point of attachment almost horizontal. In the Sāmāngaḍ plates, however, the typical *ja* shows further progress in so far as the lowest bar is bent double, while the middle bar is well on its way to become vertical. Most noticeable and important are the characteristic acute angles in the Daulatābād plates, as, for instance, in *ma*, *ya*, *la* and *sa*. In the Sāmāngaḍ grant, on the other hand, the acute angles have widened into right angles. Thus with respect to the Sāmāngaḍ grant the Daulatābād plate of Śaṅkaragaṇa will have to be looked upon as a retrograde type. But the latter are no exception in this respect. In fact, an examination of the hitherto published records of the century intervening between the Sāmāngaḍ grant (alleged date A. D. 754) and the Kaṇheri inscriptions (cir. A. D. 850) will prove that it is not possible to produce a single instance of an inscription which is on the same stage of graphic development as the plates of Dantidurga. The alphabet of every other inscription of this period will appear archaic or retrograde in comparison with the Sāmāngaḍ grant.[1]

It may be at once admitted that there could be no exception taken to the circumstance that an inscription contains some forms which are slightly more advanced than those of other records of the same or even slightly later period. In the above-mentioned grants of Govinda III, for instance, we find side by side types with wedges and those

1 See for instance, Kielhorn, *List of Inscriptions of Southern India*, Nos. 794, 808, 809, 835, 867. In these examples it will be found that the top stroke is attached to the left vertical of the letter and does not cover the entire breadth of it unless the vowel sign is appended to the letter, in which case the sign was drawn in continuation of the top stroke. Another feature is the sporadic presence of acute angles in the letters *gha*, *pa*, *ma*, *ya*, etc.

with long covering strokes, that is to say, a mixture of acute-angled and another more advanced alphabet. While on the other hand the Gwalior inscription[1] of Bhoja, which is roughly fifty years later in date, shows forms which are on the whole acute-angled. This is quite natural. In the case of the Sāmāngaḍ grant, however, the outstanding consideration for suspecting its authenticity is the circumstance that it contains not merely advanced forms, but that these are used to the entire exclusion of others which must have been current at the epoch. The use of the advanced forms is not arbitrary: the regularity with which they recur shows that they had become fixed types at the time the document was concocted. The consideration that further search will bring to light other records which will supply the missing links seems to me to be a futile consolation. At any rate I should say that an essential preliminary condition for re-establishing the impugned authenticity of this grant will be the actual discovery of a sufficient number of dated records which will supply forms which can bridge over the gulf between the epoch marked by, let us say, the Multānī plates and the Sāmāngaḍ grant. Unless and until evidence of this nature is forthcoming, one might, in my opinion, legitimately doubt if the plates belong to the epoch to which they refer themselves.

Another fact which corroborates the suspicion is the following. It is a matter of common experience that forged plates are generally very inaccurate as regards their orthography. The reason for this may be that the text which was being copied was not familiar to the executors of the forgery. Be that as it may, if this be any criterion, it will have to be admitted that the Sāmāngaḍ grant stands the test very badly, as the text of that record is in a lamentably corrupt condition. Dr. Fleet's transcript does not show all the mistakes of the original; for instance, the very first syllable of the first verse (line 1) Dr. Fleet reads as *sa*; it is as a matter of fact a clear *śa*. In l. 8 the third syllable is *va;* Dr. Fleet transcribes it with *vi*. But

1 Bühler *op. cit.*, Plate V, col. II.

there are worse blunders than these in the text. The half verse beginning with *nītāvadhe* etc. (l. 17) has been mutilated beyond recognition[1] as a comparison with the Bhāndak grant of Kṛṣṇarāja will prove. But the most significant blunder is the one in the verse beginning with *Śrīmadyuva* (l. 16). The first quarter of this verse must in the original have read something like *Śrīmad-Bhuvagaṇā nāma.* The forger having misread the ligature *dbhu* as *dyu*, must have added conjecturally *ti* after *va* so as to comply the word *yuvati* and then, in order to adjust the number of syllabic instants of the quarter, proceeded to convert the final *ma* into an *anusvāra.* In doing so, however, he obliterated completely the word Bhavagaṇā, the name of the queen, a word which the writer probably did not know at all. Significant is also the fact that the Sāmāngaḍ grant is the only early Rāṣṭrakūṭa grant so far discovered in which verses *Sabhrūvibhaṅga* etc., and *Kāñcīśa* etc. (ll. 23 ff.) occur in this order; elsewhere the latter preceeds the former. It is unnecessary however to labour the point any further.

Lastly, I should like to call attention to the use of decimal figures in expressing the date of the Sāmāngaḍ grant. Is this an anachronism? That is no doubt a difficult question to answer. The Sāmāngaḍ grant is certainly no longer the earliest known specimen in which the decimal notation comes into use, as remarked by Dr. Fleet thirty-four years ago. But it would be, if genuine, still one of the few inscriptions of a date earlier than the ninth

1 *Indian Antiquary,* Vol. 11, p. 112 ff.—

Sāmāngaḍ (Dr. Fleet's transcript)—

Nītāvadhe(? *the*)*mivāśeṣajagataḥ pālitāyati*[*ḥ**] 1. Dr. Fleet does not translate the dubious *nītāvadhemiva*; the rest he renders with: 'who protected the expanse of the whole world.'

Bhāndak plates (verse 12)—

Nītāvarthamivāśeṣajanatāprārthitāyati[ḥ*] 1. Translation: '(From her he obtained a son) like unto material well-being: (*artha*) from (i. e. as a result of) righteous conduct (*nīti*), (a son who was at it were) the future (prosperity) prayed for by the whole of mankind.'

century in which decimal notation is used.[1] As far as the grants of the successors of Dantidurga are concerned, it may be noted that in both the (unpublished) records of Kṛṣṇa I, the Alās plates[2] (A.D. 770) of Yuvarāja Govinda II, and all the plates of Govinda III upto the Śaka year 735 (i. e. A. D. 813) and the majority of his other records,[3] the date is given merely in words. A noteworthy exception is a record of the Rāṣṭrakūṭa Kakkarāja of Gujarāt of the year A. D. 757 where the date is expressed both in words and numerical figures. But in this instance the symbols which are employed, be it remembered, are not decimal as in the Sāmāngaḍ grant, but letter-numerals. But with reference to the use of the decimal notation I may add that in view of the mode of dating of the Gurjara inscription[4] of the Kalacuri year 346 (A. D. 594), of the Valabhī inscription[5] of the Gupta year 365 (?) (i. e. A. D. 685?) and some others, one might surmise that the Gurjaras and perhaps their neighbours in Gujarāt had adopted the more advanced system of decimal notation much earlier than their contemporaries further south. We know however so little definite about the early use of this notation in India that it would be unwise to enunciate a solution which happens to suit a particular case. I leave it therefore here as an open question whether we can legimately assume the prevalence of the use of decimal notation in the heart of the Southern Maratha country as early as the eighth century, especially in epigraphic records which admittedly affected a certain amount of archaism. Worth noting however is the fact that even to Bühler the forms of the numerals in the Sāmāngaḍ grant appeared to be 'strongly modified cursive forms.'[6] But here again we are on shaky ground for want of sufficient material on which to base a definite conclusion.

1 Bühler, *op. cit.*

2 Ed. D. R. Bhandarkar, *Epigraphia Indica*, Vol. 6, p. 209 and plates.

3 See Kielhorn, *List of the Inscriptions of Southern India.*

4 Ed. Dhruva, *Epigraphia Indica*, Vol. 2, pp. 19 ff., and plate.

5 *Journal of the Bengal As. Soc.*, Vol. 7, p. 968.

6 Bühler, *op. cit.*

In this connection, one is irresistibly reminded of the Dhiniki plate[1] of Jāikadeva of Saurāṣṭra bearing the date V. [79]4 corresponding to A. D. [73]7. In this instance also, the numerals expressing the date are decimal and the alphabet is a well developed form of Nāgarī. The details of the date, however, leave (in the concurring judgment of Kielhorn and Dr. Fleet) no doubt as to its being a forgery.[2] It is unfortunate, therefore, that the details of the date of the Sāmāngaḍ grant are not capable of verification.

Taking all things into consideration, the balance of evidence points, in my opinion, strongly to the conclusion expressed above, viz. that the Sāmāngaḍ grant is spurious. This conclusion, if granted, would have the immediate result of taking the epoch of the use of Nāgarī in epigraphic documents backward by at least a hundred years. For, as remarked above, if we leave out of consideration the Sāmāngaḍ grant, the next earliest inscriptions which are written throughout in Nāgarī are the Kaṇheri inscriptions of the Śilāhāra princes Pullaśakti and Kapardin II. These nearly co-eval inscriptions exhibit the regular use of top-strokes covering the entire breadth of the letters as well as rectangles (as opposed to the wedges and acute angles) in *gha* (Bühler's Palæographic tables, plate V, col. V; 13), *pa* (col. V; 30), *ya* (col. V; 35), *ṣa* (col. V; 40) and *sa* (col. V; 41). The *Rādhanpur* and *Vaṇī* plates of Govinda III. which contain a mixture of both the acute-angled and transition types appear now in a different light. They do not represent a retrograde movement but a progressive one. Preceding as they do by about fifty years the earliest known inscriptions in which Nāgarī forms are exclusively employed, they represent a true transition stage.

As the outcome of the analysis here undertaken, we arrive at the following conclusion. The very earliest dated inscriptions hitherto known, which are written throughout in Nāgarī characters are the inscriptions (cir. A. D. 850) of

1 *Indian Antiquary*, Vol. 12, p. 155 and plate.

2 See references under Kielhorn, *List of the Inscriptions of Northern India*, No. 8.

the Śilāhāra princes, from the Kaṇheri Caves in Western India. These show (i) the top-stroke covering the entire breadth of the letter, and (ii) rectangular corners. Transition stages leading upto these forms have been already discussed. In these the top stroke never covers the entire breadth of the letters, while some characters retain their former acute angles; the form of *ja* is also a significant index. The subsequent course of the development of Nāgarī in Western India can be traced with the help of the below-noted inscriptions of the Rāṣṭrakūtas of Mālkheḍ and Lāṭa belonging to the period cir. A. D. 850–950. A minute examination of these records will also provide further support to the inference that the Kaṇheri inscriptions should be placed at the middle point of the evolution of the Nāgarī out of the acute-angled alphabet. Following are the inscriptions above referred to:

1. Kielhorn's Southern List No. 77, Śaka 789 (A. D. 867). The Bāgumrā plates of the Mahāsāmantādhipati Dhruvarāja II—Dhārāvarṣa-Nirupama of Gujarāt—regarding the alphabet of which Bühler remarks (*Ind. Ant.* Vol. 12, p. 181) that the letters resemble those of the Sāmāngaḍ plates.

2. Ibid No. 81, Śaka 810 (A. D. 888). The Bāgumrā plate of the feudatory Rāṣṭrakūṭa Kṛṣṇarāja Akālavarṣa of Gujarāt. In this instance the top-stroke covers the entire breadth of the letter, and rectangular corners are prominent.

3. Ibid Nos. 86–87, Śaka 836 (A. D. 914). The Bāgumrā plates of the Rāṣṭrakūṭa Mahārājādhirāja Indra III. Here the development of Nāgarī along the two main lines indicated above is completed.

4. Ibid No. 91, Śaka 852 (A. D. 930). The Cambay plates of the Rāṣṭrakūṭa Mahārajādhirāja Govinda IV. This superbly engraved record may be looked upon as a standard to which the Nāgarī of the tenth century was tending.

5. Ibid No. 92, Śaka 855 (A. D. 933). The Sāṅglī plates of the Rāṣṭrakūṭa Mahārājādhirāja Govinda IV the cha-

racters of which are of the same type as the Bāgumrā inscriptions of Indra III.

6. Ibid No. 94, Śaka 867 (A. D. 945). The Sālotgi (Bijāpur District) pillar inscription of the reign of the Rāṣṭrakūṭa Kṛṣṇa III, Akālavarṣa. The forms are perhaps somewhat more archaic than those of the plates mentioned above.

Additional reference will be found in Bühler's *Indische Palaeographie*, p. 51.

So much for the earliest use of Nāgarī in Western India. Regarding its use in Northern India, I should like to add the following observation which arises directly out of a fact noted above. Bühler's mislection of the date of the Vināyakapāla plate, as we have seen, led him into an error regarding the period at which this alphabet became an epigraphic alphabet in Northern India. Having thus erroneously dated this instance of the use of Nāgarī in A. D. 794–5 he found that the succeeding, that is the ninth, century was practically bare of Nāgarī inscriptions, and had to admit that it was not till the middle of the tenth century that this alphabet comes again into general use in that part of India. Bühler was, I think, substantially right in saying that in Northern and Central India the Nāgarī appears first in the copper-plate grant of Vināyakapāla, but that event has to be dated in A. D. 931. It remains to determine the transitional stages during the latter part of the ninth and beginning of the tenth century; but it would appear as if there are no Nāgarī inscriptions belonging to the eighth or even the early part of the ninth century from Northern India.

Grammar and Philology

BHAGVADGĪTĀ FROM GRAMMATICAL AND LITERARY POINTS OF VIEW

BY V. K. RAJWADE

A claim is sometimes made for the Bhagvadgītā that, besides being a philosophical or rather ethical work, it is one of the best poems of the world. I intend to subject this claim to criticism in this paper and find out how far it can be sustained.

Mammaṭa who is the highest authority on Sanskrit poetics defines poetry as a conglomerate of words and sense free from faults, possessed of distinctive qualities and containing figures of speech. Jagannātha who is the next best authority on the same subject improves on this definition as he subordinates sense to expression. Poetry according to him is word or expression conveying charming sense. European writers also attach the same importance to style. One of them (Puttenham) calls it the image of man, for 'man is but his mind, and as his mind is tempered and qualified, so are his speeches and language at large.' Dryden says: 'In poetry the expression is that which charms the reader and beautifies the design.' Coleridge's definition of good prose is—proper words in their proper places—and of good verse—the most proper words in their proper places. 'The words in prose ought to express the intended meaning and no more; if they attract attention to themselves, it is, in general, a fault. But in verse the words, the media, must be beautiful and ought to attract notice.' Wordsworth says: 'It is unphilosophic to call language or diction the dress of thoughts; I would call it the incarnation of thoughts.' De Quincey, commenting on this, remarks: 'If language were merely a dress, then you could separate the two. But you can no more deal thus with poetic diction than you can with soul and body. The union is too subtle, the intertexture too ineffable—each co-existing not merely *with* the other, but each *in* and *through* the other.'

Mr. Hudson Maxim, who has criticised current definitions of poetry, says : 'Poetry obeys the law of conservation of energy. By poetry a thought is presented with the utmost economy of word-symbols.' He approvingly quotes Herbert Spencer's statement: 'As language is the vehicle of thought, there seems reason to think that in all cases the friction and inertia of the vehicle deduct from its efficiency, and that in composition the chief, if not the sole thing to be done is to reduce this friction and inertia to the smallest possible amount. Economy of the recipient's attention is the secret of effect, alike in the right choice and collocation of words, in the best arrangement of clauses in a sentence, in the proper order of its principal and subordinate propositions, in the judicious use of simile, metaphor, and other figures of speech, and even in the rhythmical sequence of syllables.' 'But,' says Mr. Maxim, 'language is not merely a vehicle of thought ; it is also an instrument for the conversion of energy into pleasurable emotions. Considered as a vehicle of thought, that language is best which utilises, with the greatest economy, the maximum of energy of both hearer and speaker in the production of pleasurable emotions as concomitants of the thought conveyed.' Anything that increases the friction and inertia of the vehicle—every fault of grammar and diction for instance—causes a waste of the recipient's energy and thus lessens the pleasurable emotion. Mammaṭa mentions all such faults in the seventh section of the Kāvyaprakāśa and gives illustrative examples.

All writers—poets included—should scrupulously avoid faults of grammar. In Sanskrit युध्, यत्, रम्, पू (1st and 4th conj.), च्यु, स्था with अव, वृत् with नि, and लभ् are Ātmanepada, and कांक्ष्, व्रज्, विश् and इष् are Parasmaipada ; but in the Gītā they are almost always used in the *wrong pada*. विज् with उद् is once (v. 20) used in the Parasmaipapa. निवासिष्यसि (xii. 8) ought to be निवत्स्यसि. मा शुचः (xvi. 5) means 'do not be pure.' As the sense is 'do not be sad,' it ought to be मा शोचः or मा शाचीः. प्रसविष्यध्वं (iii. 10) is quite unaccountable. प्रासविष्यध्वं is conditional. There is no warrant for using this mood with

मा and dropping the अ, for मा is used before the aorist (माङि लुङ्) and the imperfect (स्मोत्तरे लङ् च) only. Besides there is not even the मा here. In यमः संयमतां (x. 29) the correct form is संयच्छतां. It is difficult to say whether हे सखेति (xi. 41) is an instance of *wrong sandhi* or wrong vocative, whether the author thought सख to be the vocative singular of सखि like राम or whether he dropped the इ of इति after सखे for the sake of the metre. The latter conjecture is probably the right one, for we have प्रियः प्रियायार्हसि (xi. 44) where there is a double sandhi viz. प्रियायाः+अर्हसि = प्रियाया अर्हसि = प्रियायार्हसि. We have also शक्यः + अहं = शक्य अहं in xi. 48 and 54. Sandhi is neglected in मय्येव अत ऊर्ध्वं (xii. 8). सेनानीनां (x. 24) ought to be सेनान्यां. It is doubtful whether ब्राह्मणाः in ब्राह्मणास्तेन वेदाश्च (xvii. 23) refers to the caste or to the Brāhmaṇa portions of the Vedas. In the latter case it ought to be ब्राह्मणानि. If it be the caste, there is no reason why it should precede the Vedas and sacrifices. That objection would not arise against the second interpretation, as the Brāhmaṇas are part and parcel of the Vedas.

सर्वेभ्यः पापकृत्तमः (iv. 36) and न तस्मात्प्रियकृत्तमः (xviii. 69) are *wrong cases* as also तेषां के योगवित्तमाः (xii.1). सर्वेषां-°षु पापकृत्तमः, न तस्मात्प्रियकृत्तरः and तेषां के योगवित्तराः are the right expressions. In the last only two kinds of persons are compared. There is no authority for the dative in सत्यं ते प्रतिजाने (xviii. 65), for it does not fall under प्रत्याङ्भ्यां श्रुवः. योगस्य जिज्ञासुः (vi. 44) and धर्मस्य अश्रद्दधानाः (ix. 3) ought to be योगं जिज्ञासुः and धर्मे or धर्मे अश्रद्दधानाः and मद्भक्तेषु अभिधास्यति (xviii. 68) should be मद्भक्तान् or मद्भक्तेभ्यः अभिधास्यति. The verb नम् governs the accusative while the particle नमस् governs the dative. गरीयसे ब्रह्मणोऽप्यादिकर्त्रे नमेरन् (xi. 37) is wrong. In वक्तुमर्हस्यशेषेण दिव्या ह्यात्मविभूतयः (x. 16) and हन्त ते कथयिष्यामि दिव्या ह्यात्मविभूतयः (x. 19) विभूतयः should be विभूतीः. मे श्रुणु (x. 1 etc.) and मे निबोध (xviii. 13) seem to be influenced by Prākrit expressions. एतत् संशयं (vi. 39) and इदं महिमानं (xi. 41) may be misreadings. In प्रकृतेः क्रियमाणानि etc. (iii. 27) कर्माणि seems to be the object of कर्ता which however is a noun; कर्माणि must be कर्मणां. कर्म in iv. 24, कर्माणि in v. 10, पुरुषं in viii. 8, and मां in ix. 14 and 22 and in xii. 6 have to be construed twice. This fault recurs in a few other places also.

In न हि प्रपश्यामि ममापनुद्यात् (ii. 8), अपनुद्यात् should be अपनुदेत्, because no benedictive is wanted here. In v. 21 and xv. 3 and 4 there is nothing to connect the two halves of the stanzas. The Ātmanepada in i. 1 (अकुर्वत), iii. 12 (दास्यन्ते), iii. 21 and iv. 37 (कुरुते), and ix. 27 (कुरुष्व), and the Parasmaipada in xvi. 15 (दास्यामि) are meaningless, as also the future forms in ii. 52 (गन्तासि) and in xviii. 69 (भविता).

There are many instances of *clumsy or intricate constructions.* Some typical ones are the following—

अस्माकं तु विशिष्टा ये तान्निबोध द्विजोत्तम ।
नायका मम सैन्यस्य संज्ञार्थं तान्ब्रवीमि ते ॥ १.७

How are we to construe नायका मम सैन्यस्य ? It cannot be अस्माकं सैन्यस्य ये विशिष्टा नायकाः, because मम shall have to be neglected and also because it would be a far-fetched construction. A way out of the difficulty would be to understand ये before नायकाः in the second line. Similarly कैर्मया सह योद्धव्यमस्मिन्रणसमुद्यमे (i. 22) stands disconnected. There is nothing to connect it with the preceding half or the succeeding stanza. The queerest stanza is ii. 67—

इन्द्रियाणां हि चरतां यन्मनोऽनुविधीयते ।
तदस्य हरति प्रज्ञां वायुर्नावमिवाम्भसि ॥

For an intelligible construction we have to alter the forms of words as well as to supply certain links.[1] यो बुद्धेः परतस्तु सः (iii. 42) = यस्तु बुद्धेः परतः सः is incomplete ; यः really is unnecessary, for the construction can be बुद्धेः परतस्तु सः (आत्मा). कर्मणो ह्यपि बोद्धव्यं (iv. 1) really means कर्म हि बोद्धव्यं. In v. 21—

बाह्यस्पर्शेष्वसक्तात्मा विन्दत्यात्मनि यत्सुखं ।
स ब्रह्मयोगयुक्तात्मा सुखमक्षय्यमश्नुते ॥

यत्सुखं requires for its correlative तत्सुखं. The construction should be बाह्यस्पर्शेष्वसक्तात्मा आत्मनि यत्सुखं विन्दति तत्सुखमक्षय्यं तच्च ब्रह्मयोगयुक्तात्मा अश्नुते ; सः has no place in this sentence.[2] In xi. 27 and 28 विशन्ति has two objects, viz. त्वां and वक्त्राणि. In ii. 35—

भयाद्रणादुपरतं मंस्यंते त्वां महारथाः ।
येषां च त्वं बहुमतो भूत्वा यास्यसि लाघवम् ॥

1 यदा (यत्) मनः चरन्ति इंद्रियाणि (चरतां इंद्रियाणां) अनुविधत्ते (अनुविधीयते) तदा (understood) तत् अस्य प्रज्ञां हरति.

2 Equally clumsy or intricate are viii. 2, 9 and 10, x. 39 second half, and xviii. 60.

we have a tough construction, for येषां is a stumbling block. If येषां be altered to तेषां the difficulty may be got over. In ये चैव सात्त्विका भावा राजसास्तामसाश्च ये । मत्त एवेति तान्विद्धि etc. (vii. 12) तान् should be ते, which should be placed somewhere before इति. In (vii. 21)—

यो यो यां यां तनुं भक्तः श्रद्धयार्चितुमिच्छति ।
तस्य तस्याचलां श्रद्धां तामेव विदधाम्यहम् ॥

there is nothing corresponding to यां यां तनुं. We expect तस्यां तस्यां तन्वां; तामेव must be omitted. The Stanza दिव्यमाल्यांबरधरं (xi. 11) is intended to be construed with xi. 9 and 10 but cannot be so constructed, for all the adjectives qualify देवं which has no syntactical connection with दर्शयामास or ऐश्वरं रूपं. Three constructions seem to be mixed up in xviii. 21 पृथक्त्वेन तु यज्ज्ञानं etc. यत्तुज्ञानं पृथक्त्वेन (वर्तते) तज्ज्ञानं राजसं विद्धि; or यज्ज्ञानं सर्वेषु भूतेषु नानाभावान्वेत्ति तत् etc.; or यज्ज्ञानं नानाभावान् पृथग्विधान् वेत्ति तत् etc. The worst example is perhaps xviii. 50—सिद्धिं प्राप्तो यथा ब्रह्म तथाप्नोति निबोधं मे where आप्नोति is misplaced. It should have beed सिद्धिं प्राप्तो यथा ब्रह्माप्नोति तथा मे निबोध. It violates the rule that the words of one sentence ought not to be mixed up with those of another.

The components of certain *compounds* have been misplaced as those of अनलार्कौ (=अर्कानलौ xi. 17), जन्मकर्मफलप्रदां (=कर्मफलजन्मप्रदां ii. 43, where कर्मफल or जन्म may be omitted), चैलाजिनकुशोत्तरं (=कुशाजिनचैलोत्तरं vi. 11), धनमानमद (=मानधनमद xvi. 17), and दिव्यानेकोद्यतायुधं (=अनेकदिव्योद्यतायुधं xi. 30, to suit the other adjectives). Compounds like मदर्पणं(ix. 27), दिव्यगन्धानुलेपनं (xi.11), ब्रह्मसंस्पर्शं (सुखं vi. 28) are bad and cannot be regularly dissolved. It is hard to say whether कामहैतुकं (xvi. 8) and अहैतुकं (xviii.22) are compounds or Taddhits; in either case there is no rule to explain them. The suffix वत् can be used only in three cases, viz. तेन तुल्यं क्रिया चेद्वतिः, तत्र तस्येव and तदर्हं. None of these sūtras is applicable in कृत्स्नवत् (xviii. 22) and in अयथावत् (xviii. 31). The third case may explain अयथावत् if यथा is used for याथार्थ्यं, i. e. as a noun. यतात्मवान् (xii. 11) and अनादिमत् (xiii. 12) are considered wrong, for the rule is that वत् etc. should not be added where a Bahuvrīhi compound can give the intended meaning (न कर्मधारयान्मत्वर्थीयो बहुव्रीहिश्चेत्तदर्थप्रतिपत्तिकरः); यतात्मा and अनादि are quite significant: at least यतात्मा is, while अनादिमत् might be the negative of आदिमत्.

दीर्घसूत्री (xviii. 28) is in the same category. Amara gives दीर्घसूत्र which is correct by the above rule.

Mammaṭa insists on the use of proper *correlatives*, but the Gītā uses तस्य for अस्य and vice versa, यस्य for तस्य, एभ्यः for तेभ्यः, एतत् for तत्, and ततः for तदा. Sometimes wrong words are used, as for instance विसृज्य for उत्सृज्य, and संविग्न for उद्विग्न (i. 47), योगैः for योगिभिः (v. 5), द्वैध for द्वैत (v. 25), स्पर्शन for स्पर्श or स्पर्शेंद्रिय and रसन for रसना (xv. 9), अभ्यसन for अभ्यास (xvii. 15), मनीषिणां for मनुष्याणां (xviii. 5), अन्यथा for अन्यत् (xiii. 11), प्रमुखतः for संमुखे (i. 25). अमृतं शृण्वतः (x. 18), एतै र्द्वारैर्विमुक्तः (xvi. 22) and सुखसंगेन बध्नाति (xiv. 6) are instances of careless Sanskrit, while अपात्रेभ्यो दीयते (xvii. 22) is unidiomatic.

The Gītā offends against economy of words most egregiously by interspersing *expletives* like च, एव, अपि, तु, हि, उत, ह and other meaningless single words plentifully, and by using expressions that in no way add to or emphasize the meaning. For instance एव is used about eighty times when no restriction or certainty is intended. In लोकसंग्रहमेवापि संपश्यन् कर्तुमर्हसि (iii. 20) we have both एव and अपि, which, if not used as expletives, would contradict each other. By एव Arjuna would be compelled to look to the preservation of society alone but by अपि he would have an additional motive for his activity. Like Janaka he would secure salvation and like Kṛṣṇa he would preserve society by action. One of these two must be omitted. Again तु when not expletive signifies distinction. It is doubtful if it has any meaning in उभयोरपि दृष्टोऽतस्त्वनयोस्तत्त्वदर्शिभिः (ii.16) and in अविनाशि तु तद्विद्धि (ii.17). In the first case तु leads one to expect a distinction between the two lines as though the author wanted to differentiate the philosophical view from the popular view, but as current or traditional explanations go no such differentiation can be discovered. In the second case तु again raises the same expectation but does not satisfy it. Similarly अपि in the first case seems to say—whereas according to popular view only *one* thing has an end (अंत), according to philosophers both have an end. But the whole point of अपि and तु is lost when अंत is made to mean निश्चय or real nature.

Sometimes एव and च are repeated to fill up gaps. दिव्य, आत्मन् and अव्यय in their various forms सर्वशः, अशेषतः and पृथक् are also made to serve the same purpose. We have in one and the same sentence सर्वं and अखिल (iv. 33), सततं and नित्यशः (viii. 14), नमस्कृत्वा and प्रणम्य (xi. 35), पुनः and भूयः (xi. 39), अचल and ध्रुव (xii. 3), and उक्त्वा twice (ii. 9). In सुहृन्मित्रार्युदासीनमध्यस्थद्वेष्य (vi. 9) we have three pairs, the components of each having the same meaning. The परं भावमजानंतो ममाव्ययमनुत्तमं of vii. 24 is altered to परं भावमजानंतो मम भूतमहेश्वरं (ix. 11), but one fails to see the necessity of the alteration; moreover भूतमहेश्वरं is hard to construe and interpret. It is simply a stop-gap or a filler. Sometimes these fillers spoil the sense as in प्राणांस्त्यक्त्वा धनानि च as though riches were dearer to the warriors than life, or in आवृतं ज्ञानमेतेन···कामरूपेणानलेन च (iii 39) as though fire would envelop but not burn knowledge, or in तत्रैवं सति कर्तारमात्मानं केवलं तु यः (xviii.16) where केवलं qualifying आत्मानं would make the आत्मन् an agent in company with certain other factors, whereas the Gitā says emphatically नान्यं गुणेभ्यः कर्तारं (xiv. 19) and यः पश्यति तथात्मानमकर्तारं (xiii. 29). Again one of the constituents of दैवी संपत् 'divine or blessed character' is said to be नातिमानिता (xvi. 3). Did the writer approve of *some* portion of pride but not of over much? It is clearly opposed to अमानित्व in xiii. 7.

Another source for filling out is a host of vocatives such as हृषीकेश, गुडाकेश, कमलपत्राक्ष, अनघ, परंतप, महाबाहो, भारत, भरतर्षभ, पार्थ, कौंतेय, अर्जुन, धनंजय, अरिसूदन, पुरुषर्षभ, कुरुसत्तम, कुरुप्रवीर, सव्यसाचिन्, देहभृतां वर, and of epithets like वीर्यवान्, नरपुंगव, समितिंजय, परमेष्वास; at times a stanza has two or even three vocatives as for instance भूतभावन भूतेश देवदेव जगत्पते x. 15 which is simply a string of such expletives. In xvi. 19 the plural संसारेषु and in iv. 26 संयमाग्निषु serve apparently the same purpose of filling out.

Prepositions are still another source: प्र and सं seem to be prominently the favourites of the author who uses each of them some fifty times[1] without adding to or altering the sense of the verbal forms, though that is the object

1 No references are here given everywhere as the forms could easily be located from the valuable word-index to the Gitā supplied at the end of the Anandashram edition (No. 34).

generally served by prepositions. Thus प्र prefixed to ध्मतुः, पश्यामि, दुष्यंति, वदंति, सिध्येत्, व्यथित, जानाति, निधाय, द्विषंतः, ईप्सु, and उच्यते; —सं to जनयन्, जायते, अभिगच्छति, आचरन्, आरंभ, तरिष्यति, अतीतानि, उत्थ, दृश्यंते, उद्धर्ता, प्रवृत्तानि, अतीत्य, स्मृत्वा and उद्भव;—परि to शुष्यति, दह्यते, अवतिष्ठते, उपासते, समाप्यते, चिंतयन्, त्याग, and ज्ञाता;—अनु to पश्यामि, सज्जते, चिंतयन्, स्मर, दर्शन, संततानि, and प्रपन्न;—अभि to अहन्यत, असूयंतः, उत्थान, जानाति, प्रवृत्त, युक्तानां, अधिक, अर्च्, and रत;—वि to कंपितं, निवर्तंते, मुह्यति, भ्रम, मोक्ष्यसे, वर्जित, अपेत, दाहिनः, and लग्न;—and नि to हत्वा, वध्यते, गच्छति, and बोध—do not bring out any special sense. जायते is similarly used with the prefixes अभि, उप and सं. Sometimes two prepositions are prefixed superfluously, as for instance वि and अति to तरिष्यति (ii. 52) and वि and अप to आश्रित्य (ix. 32). प्रकीर्त्या is the same as कीर्त्या, प्रपश्य as पश्य, समाहर्तुं as संहर्तुं, and समायुक्त is संयुक्त. Sometimes wrong prepositions are used, as परि for आ in परिचक्षते (xvii. 13), उप for अव in उपधारय (vii. 16), प्र for आ in प्रसक्त (xvi. 16) and सं for वि in समाप्नोषि (vi. 40). प्रत्यनीक (xi. 32) is the opposite of and not the same as अनीक. दुर्निरीक्ष्यं (xi. 17) should be दुरीक्ष्यं. Similarly गृह्यते is without नि in vi. 35, युज्यते without प्र in xvii. 26 and श्रिताः without आ in ix. 12. A complete list would be four times as large.

Though so lavish of expletives, the Gītā does not seem to mind lacunæ. प्रमुखतः is wanted after महीक्षितां (i. 25), अपि after आततायिनः (i. 36), तत् to correspond to यत् in ii. 8, इव after स्वर्गद्वारं (ii. 32), तदा in ii. 58, अपि after अन्यत्र (iii. 9), and also after either विगुण or स्वनुष्ठितात् (iii. 35), अति before जाग्रतः (vi. 16), इव after प्रियायाः and अपराधं before सोढुं (xi. 44), यः before त्यजेत् (xviii. 8), and तस्मै after अभ्यसूयति (xviii. 67). In xi. 28 some such words as क्षुब्धं is required to qualify समुद्रं, which would thus come into line with वक्त्राणि which is qualified by अभिविज्वलंति.

We should expect the Gītā to be honey-combed with purple passages, if it were a poem and a poem worthy of being placed in the highest class of poetry. A philosophical poem is a misnomer if the philosophy is not allegorized. The Gītā has not the slightest pretention to allegory. Its aim is to convince by argument and not to visualize. except in one place. The appeal almost everywhere is to reason and when it occasionally does appeal to emotion, it does so, because emotion on those occasions cannot be divorced from reason. The immortality of the soul is a theme where reason alone would be impotent but for its ally, viz. emotion. Here it must be acknowledged that emotion is the highest kind of reason. Other such passages are ii. 55–59 about the स्थितप्रज्ञ, iii. 17–18 about the आत्मतृप्त, v. 14–20 about the ज्ञानी. Lower in scale are i. 28–46 where Arjuna is overwhelmed with grief, ii. 45–53 about कर्माधिकार, vi. 18–23 about अकर्म, vi. 39–40 about ज्ञान, v. 8–13 about action being due to *indriyas*, vi. 29–32 where the Yogin sees Brahma everywhere, ix. 22–34 about the true devotee, xii. 12–19 and xiv. 23–26 about the ज्ञानी, and xvi. 4–26 where the two kinds of mental endowment, divine and diabolical, are spoken of. Still lower in scale are ii. 39–44 about the unified and diversified wills, iii. 20–24 where the enlightened perform acts for the preservation of society, and vi. 14–19 where the true Yogin is defined. None of these passages is pure gold, most of them being tarnished more or less by defects. All the poetic passages taken together number two and fifty lines at the most, the rest baing mere versified prose.

If there is one subject that is more amenable to poetic treatment than any other, it is the greatness of the soul. It is capable of putting the mind into the highest divine afflatus and demands vast knowledge and operation of all the faculties. The passages we have referred to above are too meagre and the artist would feel happy if he were given larger elbow-room such as he would find in chapters x. and xi. Everything that is great in the universe being an incarnation or manifestation of the deity ; and the divine vision or revelation : these are subjects that would delight, inspire and exercise any poetic genius. The way in which an artist deals with these topics would show his mettle. Even Kālidāsa, Bhavabhūti, Bāna, Shakespere, Milton, Shelley would have been on their trial and yet there is not the slighest doubt that they would have acquitted themselves worthily, endoweded as they were with an inexhaustible store of images and a faculty that knew how to work on those images. They would have given a lifelike description and produced an immortal picture, the main characteštic of which would have been unity in the midst of vastness. The question before us is whether the author of the Gītā has brought together the best possible images, whether he has marshalled them in due order and whether he leaves on our mind an effect of unity and vastness.

Towards the end of chapter x, the Bhagavān says that he has mentioned only illustrative examples of his greatness, that in fact everything that is grand, or splendid or powerful is a portion of his light. Yet there are things in this chapter that possess none of these qualities. Some no doubt are grand, as the Himālayas, the ocean and the Ganges; some splendid as the sun and the moon; and some powerful, as the wind, the fire, the lion, the eagle and the crocodile. A few of these again may have two characteristics or even all the three, as for instance kings and such mythical beings as Indra, Kubera, Prahlāda, Airāvata and Uccaiśravas. But by which of these qualities shall we characterize the Sāma-veda, the Bṛhatsāma, Bṛhaspati, Bhṛgu, and Nārada? These are simply the best of their class. The letter अ, the Dvandva compound, and the month Mārgaśīrṣa happen to be the first though not necessarily the best of their series. Again कीर्ति, श्री, etc. are considered best among women because they happen to be feminine in speech. But the heroines and noble ladies of our epics—a mere utterance of whose names soon after waking in early morning is deemed auspicious—Sītā, Tārā, Anasūyā, Maṇḍodarī, Sāvitrī, Damayantī and Tārāmatī of blessed memory, Urvaśī, Rambhā and Śakuntalā unsurpassed in beauty, Sarasvatī the goddess of speech: these have been forgotten; so also are Rāma the ideal hero, son and husband, Hanumān celebrated for devoted self-sacrificing service, Rāvaṇa notorious for undying hatred of Rāma, Lakṣmaṇa the type of devoted brotherhood, Hariścandra true to his word, Dharma, conscience incarnate, and Nala. The Architect and the Physicions of the gods are conspicuous by their absence. If the Aśvattha is the best of trees, Soma is the best of creepers. But the latter has been passed over. Instead of these we have

वाद and द्यूत which are mere acts, दंड and नीति which are means, चेतना a common characteristic of creatures, etc. What sort of greatness do these possess and what sort of pride or pleasure can Kṛṣṇa or for that matter any one feel in calling himself 'gambling' which is simply a civilized form of filching? It is rather strange that Kṛṣṇa, Arjuna and Vyāsa who are so intimately connected with the story of the Mahābhārata and Gītā should be mentioned as the best of their clan, family or class. Can they be so detached from self, so impartial as to look upon themselves in that light?

A few things have been dragged in for mere alliteration as पवनः पवतां, कालः कलयतां and वादः प्रवदतां. It is this love of alliteration that has betrayed the author into a solecism like यमः संयमतां where संयमतां should be संयच्छतां. This correct form would read as well, but then the meritricious ornament would be missed. The writer cannot forget his own trade; like a pedant he must bring in the alphabet and grammar, which last is of a seamy character as we have seen above. No one can trace the source of his statement that the Dvandva is the first of compounds. In a description of divine greatness one expects order and progressiveness, the absence of which is felt everywhere. The Vedas, the gods, the senses and animate creatures are spoken of in stanza 22, trees and divine sages in 26, weapons, cows, lust and snakes in 28, demons and calculators in 30, purifiers, warriors, aquatic creatures and rivers in 31, letters, compounds, eternity and the creator in 33, death and such pretty damsels as fame, wealth, speech in 34 : Many would be amazed at finding themselves in such queer company. Cows, how soever tolerant, would not put up with the society of snakes. Order there is none. Any quarter, any half, any couplet may be placed anywhere, the writer's chief anxiety being how to complete the couplet. Great things and small have been simply huddled up.

To illustrate greatness the author starts with the all pervasive soul and the statement 'I am the beginning, the end and the middle of creatures' (x. 20, which is repeated in

32 with the substitution of creations for creatures'). This must lead to an anti-climax if there be any order. To leave an abiding, clear impression small things should have been stated first, and these should have led up gradually to great and greater things till the whole enumeration culminated in the description of the universal soul. The author should have followed some logical method. As it is, it is nothing but a miserable welter. It is a small objection to say that half the things mentioned are fabulous.

The description of divine greatness in chapter x fills Arjuna with an ardent desire to visualize that greatness. Yet very few things mentioned in that chapter are seen in the universal vision. No particular gods are referred to except Brahmā who is seated in the lotus and the Aśvins. Poor Ṛṣis jostle in company with serpents. The splendour of the vision would be equalled if a thousand suns shone simultaneously in the sky. In this transcendental blaze Arjuna sees innumerable arms, legs, bellies, mouths, jaws, and eyes, and into the cavernous mouths warriors on either side rushing and encountering death like moths rushing into burning fire. The vision occupies all interspace between earth and sky and all the directions and yet curiously wears a crown and carries in hand the mace and the disc like the ordinary Kṛṣṇa, and like him too is clad in resplendent garments, decked with garlands and annointed with scented pigments. This gay image is absolutely incongrous with the monstrous many-armed, many-legged, many-mouthed, many-jawed, and many-bellied apparition which terrifies Arjuna and the three worlds. With strange forgetfulness Arjuna desires to see Kṛṣṇa with the traditional crown and the other fixtures in stanza 46. Are we to suppose that it was a moving picture as in a cinematograph wherein Kṛṣṇa appeared now gay and now frightful ? It is a pity that with his endowment of a divine sight Arjuna saw only arms, legs etc. and gods demigods, sages and demons all agog with terror. Even a modern writer like the author of the Vyaṅkaṭeśa-stotra could imagine countless worlds penetrating space. Even Milton could think of worlds on worlds revolving. In spite of stellar systems by far greater than the one with which we are familiar, planets other than the earth, Saturn with its rings, comets with tails and the golden galaxy, the universe of Arjuna was narrowed down to three worlds. What are countless arms and other physical appendages in comparison with these marvels or even with such earthly phenomena as mountains, volcanoes and oceans? Could the mutability and perishableness of the universe have been less impressive, had these grander images been pressed into service? Arjuna could have seen worlds resolving into nebula and new worlds forming out of it. His attention is however confined to the traditional three worlds and their contents, to the sun and the moon, to the mythical gods, demigods and giants, to sages and serpents. He is struck dumb at this insignificant vision and bows in front, behind (?), and on all sides (?), and repeats his bows a thousand times and again and again. Throughout he talks like a driveller, and in very bad Sanskrit. The interlocutors and Vyāsa are Hindus to their very tips. The whole vision is steeped in Hindu mythology and Hindu belief, whereas a vision of the universe ought to transcend all such limitations. It ought to surpass all the discoveries, past and future, of astronomy and other cognate sciences. It ought to be truth itself. Like the preceding chapter this too deals in fabulous matter. It moreover abounds in slovenly unclassical Sanskrit and in mistakes of grammar some of which have been pointed out above. It is a failure both in respect of style and vision and, along with the preceding chapter and a few others, appears immaterial. The first stanza of the new chapter seems to connect it with chapter ix or even with chapter vi.

The test of good poetry lies in renewal and increase of pleasure at every fresh perusal. But one is pained to state that the Gītā does not satisfy this test. The imperfections by far out number the beauties.

It may be said that when a work is enshrined in faith and becomes an object of veneration to millions, it has a claim to be considered invulnerable and that faults of grammar, style and reason are impertinent. Such a view is intelligible and deserves respect. Men of faith would and should ignore this criticism completely as I should be sorry to hurt their feelings. But when men take their stand on reason and not on faith and assert that the Gītā has spoken the last word on ethics and that it is the best poem in the world, they lay themselves open to attack. These people ought to demonstrate that the defects shown in this paper are no defects, that the style is the most poetical style according to the most authoritative definitions of poetry, or that these definitions are wrong. Exigencies of verse is no excuse, for Sanskrit literature abounds in verse that is scrupulously correct and chaste. There is no reason why Vyāsa should trip where, not to speak of Kālidāsa and his compeers, even lesser artists have succeeded.

I must explain my own position. Our old writers did not scruple to write in the name of Kṛṣṇa or Śiva as the old Hebrew prophets spoke and wrote in the name of Jehova. They felt that God spoke to mankind through them, that they were mere transmitters of God's will. Inspired though they thought themselves to be, they could not transcend the limitations of their knowledge. Their ignorance and knowledge, their superstition and faith, the tradition and faith in which they had been nurtured came into play and left their impress on their work.

INFLUENCE OF ANALOGY IN SASNKRIT

BY V. S. GHATE

EVERY language, as it passes through the different periods of its growth, is seen to undergo a multiplicity of changes. Such changes consist not only in the addition of new words from different sources, or of new ideas due to a general progress in thought, but in altering the very form of the words already existing and their signification. Thus if we look to a language like English or Marathi, we shall see that the language as it is at present is quite different in form from what it was a few centuries ago, so that one knowing the Marathi of to-day, may not necessarily be able to read with equal ease, the Marathi of the 13th or the 14th century.

Such linguistic changes are found to be not merely accidental or whimsical, but governed by certain phonetic laws which can be established after a careful study of the different stages of a language, and a comparison of more than one language passing through a similar course. How and why such phonetic laws came to govern a particular language, it is difficult to say. As language is a mechanical product, the result of the particular vocal organism, a difference, of course qualitative, in the structure of the organism may lead to a difference in pronunciation, which, in the course of time, may substantially alter the form of the product. It is thus that different dialects come into existence. Race and climate may have their share in this work of change, but very generally, it is the desire for ease of utterance, the natural tendency to economize vocal effort, which accounts for it a good deal.

Such phonetic laws which belong to the so-called science of Philology, are not, however, laws in the sense in which, the laws of Mathematics and natural sciences are laws. In the case of the latter, you can predict with certainty the result that would follow, when you know the law holding in the particular case. The laws can never fail, as long as all the conditions and the qualifications required are there intact. With language, however, the case is different. Every phonetic law has a large number of apparent exceptions. In the first place, any phonetic law is true only with a particular language, under particular environments of time and place. But, even in this limited sphere, the law fails us several times. Why is it so ? It is due to the very nature of language which these laws have to govern. In linguistic change there are not only physical elements, but psychological elements also. The mechanism which finally produces language is at first set into work by the human will. Thus there are always two factors, mutually opposed to some extent, that are at work in the development of a language. Phonetic laws, mainly relating to the physical element, tend to produce variety; but at the same time the psychological factor is at work, which tends to produce simplicity out of variety, of course as far as it is consistent with intelligibility. The less bound we are by tradition, the more free is the psychological factor, and the greater the scope for analogy. Thus the apparent exceptions to any particular phonetic law do not at all affect the truth of the law, but only tend to confirm it; since they can be explained as due to the other element, very generally by means of analogy. Analogy proceeds to work in some such way;—if there is a likeness of signification, why should there not be a likeness of form ? If there is a likeness of function, why should there not be a likeness of form ? Thus, if we have a word like *brother*, why should we not have words like *father* and *mother*, because all are equally words of relationship? It must be noted here that the form '*brother*' is phonetically regular, while '*fader*' and '*mader*' would be the phonetically regular forms. But we have instead *father* and *mother* due to form-association with *brother*. If we have a form like *pituḥ*, why not also have *patyuḥ* and *sakhyuḥ*, since all the three words express relationship; though *pituḥ* can be phonetically explained, while *patyaḥ* and *sakhyaḥ* should be the phonetically regular forms ? It is thus that analogy works to produce simplicity out of variety; it tends to the unification of the grammatical system, and the simplification of the mechanism of speech. Thus to account for linguistic change, merely the doctrine of the strict order in phonetic development is not sufficient; it must be complemented by the doctrine of analogy. It is the object of this paper to illustrate the working of this factor of analogy from Sanskrit, to show how the apparent exceptions to certain phonetic rules are only due to analogy.

It may be said here that there cannot possibly be any scope for analogy as far as Sanskrit is concerned, because, since the time of Pāṇini's grammar, supplemented by the works of Kātyāyana and Patañjali, every writer and speaker of Sanskrit has tried to conform as exactly as possible to the rules laid down; and that Sanskrit has ceased to be a spoken language in the full sense of the word, i. e. amongst the masses. So, there being no linguistic change possible, there is no scope for analogy.

So far the statement is true. But there is another point of view of looking at Sanskrit. If we look at the past history of the Sanskrit language, at the various stages as represented by the Vedas, the Brāhmaṇas, the Upaniṣads, and the epics, we cannot but observe a gradual linguistic change going on. As a descriptive grammar of the Sanskrit language (i. e. a grammar which brings together and classifies all the grammatical facts of a language at a particular stage), Pāṇini's work cannot be surpassed. But there are other kinds of grammar which are more interesting and valuable. A historical grammar of Sanskrit, for instance, regarding classical Sanskrit in relation to the Sanskrit of the Vedas and the epics on the one hand, and to the Prākrit dialects on the other hand, would testify to an immense linguistic change, and to the working of analogy. We can go still further and consider Sanskrit in relation to Avesta, Greek and Latin, which have been now conclusively proved to be sister-languages, at first so many dialects springing from the common parent, the Indo-German language (which has so far of course only a hypothetical existence). Thus in addition to a descriptive and a historical grammar, there can be a philological or comparative grammar of Sanskrit; and here there would be even a greater scope for linguistic change and the working of analogy. For convenience's sake, I mean to restrict myself to this last sphere only; that is to say, I shall try to illustrate the working of analogy, in so far as Sanskrit is considered as one of the members of the Indo-germanic family.

It is now conclusively proved that the vowel *a* in Sanskrit sometimes represents an original *a*, e. g. Sanskrit *ájati* is Greek ἄγει, sometimes an original *e*, e. g. Sanskrit *ásti* is Greek ἔστι, and lastly an original *o*, e. g. Sanskrit *páti* is Greek πόσις. Immediately connected with this phenomenon is another, viz. that the original velar and labio-velar sounds are represented in Sanskrit sometimes by the velar (or guttural) and sometimes by the palatal sounds. Thus, Sanskrit *karkaṭa* = Greek καρκίνος and Sanskrit *yuga* = Greek ζυγόν. But Sanskrit *ca* = Greek τε = Latin *que*; and Sanskrit *jyā* = Greek βιός = Lithuanian *gìjà*. This difference in the representation in Sanskrit of the original *k*, *g*, *gh* sounds, i. e. sometimes as *k*, *g*, *gh*, but sometimes as *c*, *j*, *h*, is accounted for by the law of Palatalisation. According to this law, an original guttural is palatalised in Indo-Iranian, if it is followed by the vowels, *i*, *ī*, *e*, or an *a* or *ā* which represents an original *e*, or the consonant *y*. Otherwise it remains unchanged, i. e. if followed by *u* *ū* *o*, or an *a* or *ā* which represents an original *o* or *a* or any other consonant. It is this law which is at the root of the phenomenon of a mutual exchange of the gutturals and the palatals so often seen in the forms of one and the same root or stem. Thus, for instance, in the form *cakāra*, the perfect 1st person singular of the root *kṛ* or *kar*, we see that the *k* is changed to the corresponding palatal *c* in the reduplicative syllable; so also in *jaghāna*, we have *gh* in the original root-syllable, while we have *j* the corresponding un-aspirated palatal in the reduplicative syllable. And this difference of representation can be easily explained if we know that the vowel *a* in the reduplicative syllable represents an original *e* which is also the vowel of reduplication in Greek, and that the *ā* in the root-syllable represents an original *o* which is the strong vowel corres-

The form *tulayati* is regular, as is shown by the corresponding form τελαμών ; but it has also led to another form *tolayati*, on the analogy of the root *budh* leading to *bodhayati*. The real character of the *u* (which is not original, but which has come in secondarily in the same way as *turayati* from *tṛ*) was lost sight of, and it was confounded with an original *u*. So also the form *Sphoṭayati* from *Sphuṭ* can be explained only as due to analogy, because the cerebral *ṭ* in *Sphuṭ* clearly shows that the *u* is not original but has come in the place of the *ṛ* necessary for the cerebralisation.

The treatment of the Sanskrit *j* and *h* is very interesting. We find that these two sounds are found to behave in two different ways, especially at the end of roots, under similar circumstances. Thus, to take the two roots *yuj* and *yaj*, we have from the former such forms as *yóga*, *yuktá*, *yúgvan*, *yokṣyati* ; but from the latter, such forms as *yajña*, *yájvan*, *yaṣṭave*, *ayāṭ*. In the same way the root *duh* gives such forms as *dugdhá*, *su-dugha*, *adhok* ; while the root *lih* gives *līḍhá*, *leha*, *aleṭ*. Thus it is found that there are really two series : one, the original palatals (e. g. in *yaj* and *lih*) and the other, the secondary palatals derived from the original velars, which reassert themselves before certain sounds, like the *ta* of the past passive participle.

This distinction which is found in Sanskrit is also confirmed by the different representation of the two series in Avesta where *z* represents the original palatals *j* and *h*, while *g* or *j* represents the secondary palatals. Thus corresponding to Sanskrit *yajati* and *vahati*, Avesta has *yazaiti* and *vazaiti* ; while corresponding to *hanti*, it has *jainti*. Now, many times in Sanskrit, the two series get interchanged under the influence of analogy ; that is to say, the *h* of the old palatal series behaves as if it were of the secondary palatal series, and vice versa. Thus the root *muh*, the *h* of which is a secondary palatal, has not only the phonetically regular form *mugdha* showing the original guttural, but, by its side, it has also *mūḍha* on the analogy of *līḍha*. On the other hand, the root *dih* the *h* of which is an original palatal, as is shown by the forms in Avesta (e. g.

daēz, dišta), has the form *digdha*, instead of the phonetically regular *dīḍha*.

Before the hard consonants of the palatal, lingual and dental class, there is inserted, after a final *n*, a sibilant of each of these classes respectively, before which the *n* becomes *anusvāra*. Thus *tān* + *taṇḍulān* gives *tāṅstaṇḍulān*. Now this insertion of a sibilant, which is regularly observed in classical Sanskrit, but not very often in the Veda, is not at all arbitrary, but it really involves a historical survival. In a large majority of cases, the final *n* is an original *ns*. Thus, for instance, the accusative plural termination of the *a*, *i*, and *u* stems was originally *ns* but afterwards, the *s* was dropped, conferring a compensatory lengthening on the preceding vowel. The same fact is confirmed by Greek, where we have φίλονς, accus. plu. of φίλος, afterwards becoming φίλους with the ν dropped and the preceding vowel extended. The original *ns* is also proved by a peculiar Sandhi in the Veda, where a final *ān*, *īn*, *ūn* or *ṛn* followed by a vowel is treated as if it were a nasalised vowel followed by a visarga. Thus, *mahān* + *asi* gives *mahāṅ-asi* ; *raśmīn-iva* gives *raśmīṅriva*. In classical Sanskrit, however, this insertion of a sibilant after a final *n* is almost generalised ; that is to say, extended to those cases even where there is no historical justification for the presence of the *s*. Thus because we have *gacchan* + *tatra* = *gacchaṅstatra* (the original form being *gacchans*), we have also by analogy, *a-bharan* + *tatra* = *abharaṅstatra*, or *kasmin* + *cit* = *kasmiṅścit*, without any real reason for the *s*. This transference by analogy is facilitated by the fact that the original presence of the *s* was altogether forgotten, and the insertion of the sibilant was looked upon as only arbitrary, without any etymological reasons. Thus if we have it in one case, why not have it in other cases also, apparently similar ?

A phenomenon of an external Sandhi is often transferred to an internal Sandhi, under the influence of analogy. Thus a final mute, when followed by a nasal, often becomes a corresponding nasal, instead of a corresponding soft unaspirate. Thus we have *tat* + *mama* = *tanmama*.

The same is afterwards extended to forms like *anna*, *chinna* etc., where the *d* of the root becomes *n* before the following nasal; so also we have forms like *mṛṇmaya;* though otherwise, in similar cases of internal Sandhi, we have forms like *udnaḥ* from *udan*, *vidma* from *vid*, *garutmant* and so on.

Another illustration of a similar transference of external Sandhi to internal, is supposed to be provided by such forms as *havirbhiḥ*, *manobhiḥ*, etc. The final *s* of *havis* and *manas* is treated as if it were a regular visarga at the end of a word ; though, really speaking, the *s* ought to be softened before the following soft consonant; and the forms should be *havidbhiḥ* coming from an original *havizbhiḥ* and *manadbhiḥ* coming from *manazbhiḥ*. So also we should have *havikṣu* and *manatsu*, as expected phonetically, but we have *haviḥṣu* and *manaḥsu* instead. These may be regarded as instances of transference by analogy, but perhaps these forms may imply some historical survival too. It is held that most of the so called suffixes (of declension as well as of conjugation) were once independent words and were afterwards, by their constant association with other words, gradually knocked down into abbreviated suffixes. Thus the visarga in the forms above may be a survival of this fact. It is to be noted also that in the Padapāṭha of the Vedic texts, such forms as *havirbhiḥ* are written with the mark ऽ (avagraha) inserted between *haviḥ* and *bhiḥ*, implying that they are two members of a compound word. The designation *pada* (base) in such cases, may also have something to do with this.

Coming more particularly to declension, we have very interesting instances of the influcence of analogy. The declension of pronouns has very much influenced that of nouns, and amongst nouns, the *a* and *n* stems have very much influencd the rest. The original instrumental singular termination was *ā* not only with consonant stems, but even with vowel stems. Thus we have in the Veda forms like *yajñā*, *mahitvā*. But even in the Veda, and regularly in classical Sanskrit, the *a* stems have as a rule the termination *na* with the change of the final *a* of the stem to *e*. Now, this is nothing but a case of transference from the pronoun, where the *na* is original, as we see from forms in the related language. Thus corresponding to *tena*, (or *tyena* in Veda), we have old Persian *tya-nā*, Gothic *þan*. (This suffix *na* is very probably the same as appears, for instance, in Sanskrit *cana*, *vinā*, *kuruta-na* (in Veda), or in Latin *pōne*).

The forms of the Nominative plural of *a* stems like *devāsaḥ* by the side of *devāḥ* which alone is found in classical Sanskrit, are also due to the influence of what is called the proportionate analogy. In the case of consonant stems, the nominative plural has an *as* in addition to the form of the nominative singular (the suffix *s* being dropped). So it might have been argued that just as the nom. sing. *marut* gives the nom. plu. *marutaḥ*, so the nom. sing. *devaḥ* should give *devāsaḥ*—[*marut* : *marutaḥ* :: *devas* : *devāsaḥ*]. Or perhaps this may be a case of adding double endings ; as for instance, we have *mahatvatā* in Veda, *children* in English, *ἕμε-ν-α* in Greek, or *dāsya-tva*, often used in modern Marathi.

The accusative plural form of *a* stems may also be similarly explained, as being due to analogy. Thus *devaḥ* : *devam* :: *devāḥ* : *devān* ; or it may be a case of compensatory lengthening as said above.

The Vedic instrumental plural of *a* stems is also influenced by other stems. Thus the original form should be, for instance, *devaiḥ*, as is clearly shown by the Greek *φίλοις* ; but by its side we have *devebhiḥ*, which is due to the analogy of *agnibhiḥ*, *Śatrubhiḥ*, etc.

The original genitive plural termination is *ām* not only with consonant stems, but also with vowel stems, as is shown by the Greek *ἵππων* and the Latin *deum*. But Sanskrit has instead *ānām* for *a* stems, from which it is then transferred to *i* and *u* stems. In the Ṛgveda, we have only a very small number of examples of simple *ām* instead of *ānām*, like *caratām* for instance. Now this *ānām* was transferred to *a* stems from the feminine *ā* stems, which acquired it in the first instance from the *n* stems. Thus to take two words *ātman* and *bālā*, *ātman* has forms like *ātmabhiḥ*, *ātmasu* and *ātmanām;* the word *bālā* has also *bālābhiḥ*, *bālāsu*; then why should it not also have *bālānām ?* Thus, *ātmabhiḥ*: *ātmasu* : *ātmanām* :: *bālābhiḥ* : *bālāsu* : *bālānām*. And this transference by analogy must have been facilitated by the nominative singular forms *ātmā* and *bālā*, which are exactly alike. Another reason must have been that the suffix *ām* would give the form *bālām* which can not be distinguished from the accu. sing. form. Afterwards it was transferred to *a* stems, probably owing to the similarity of form in the nom. plural. Thus, *bālāḥ*: *bālānām* :: *devāḥ*: *devānām*. In old Persian also, we have *bagānām* from *baga* (= a god).

The neuter nom. plural of *a* stems is also influenced by the *n* stems. The original suffix is *ā*, as shown by Vedic forms like *yugā* and Gothic *juka* and Latin *iuga*. But the *n* stems in the Veda had both kinds of forms like *dhāmā* and *dhāmāni*, which must have given rise to such forms as *yugāni* by the side of *yugā*; and afterwards, as the *n* stems had only the regular forms like *nāmāni*, the *a* stems also preserved only forms like *yugāni*, the forms like *yugā* being completely lost. Afterwards the same was transferred to neuter stems in *i*, *u* and *ṛ*.

The instr. sing. of the feminine stems in *ā* is also influenced by the pronominal declension. The original form is found in Vedic Sanskrit, e. g. *aśvā* instr. sing. of *aśvā* (fem), corresponding to which we have also forms like κρύφᾱ, λάθρᾱ in Greek. But later we have *aśvayā* on the model of *tayā*, which is probably the original form with pronouns, as appears from the corresponding old Lithuanian *taja* and old Bulgarian *toją*.

The loc. singular *aśvāyām* was probably formed to distinguish the regular *aśvāi* from the dat. sing. which would also be *aśvāi*; and afterwards the forms *aśvāyai* and *aśvāyāḥ* of the dat. and abl. sing. were modelled after *devyām*, *devyai* and *devyāḥ*.

The instr. sing. forms of *i* and *u* stems are also modelled after *n* stems. Thus instead of directly adding *ā* to the stem, we have forms like *agninā* and *śatruṇā*, on the analogy of *balinā* and *āyunā* from *balin* and *āyun* respectively. Thus, *balibhiḥ*: *baliṣu* : *balinā* :: *agnibhiḥ*: *agniṣu*: *agninā*. This analogy was perhaps facilitated by some words which were both *i* and *in* stems.

The neuter stems in *i* and *u* are very much influenced by the *n* stems, before vowel-terminations. Thus we have forms like *vāriṇā*, *vāriṇe* and so on, exactly like *baline*, *balinaḥ*. This transference was best facilitated by the identity of the forms for the nom. plu.; for we had already forms like *vārīṇi*, instead of the Vedic *vārī*, which came to exist on the analogy of forms like *yugāni*.

Nouns ending in *ṛ*, like *pitṛ*, *mātṛ*, present a very interesting illustration of the influence of analogy. They were originally stems ending in *ar*, as is shown by the related languages. Thus Sk. *pitár* = Gk. *πατέρ* = Lat. *pater*; and several case-forms also agree in all these languages. But coming to the accusative and the genitive plural, we have in Sanskrit forms like *pitṛṣu* and *pitṛṇām*; whereas we should expect, as phonetically regular, *pitraḥ* and *pitrām*, corresponding to the allied forms *πατέρας* and *πατρών*. It was the similarity of the forms *pitṛbhiḥ* and *pitṛṣu* to *agnibhiḥ* and *agniṣu*, which must have brought this change. Thus, *agnibhiḥ* : *agniṣu* : *agnīn*: *agnīnām* :: *pitṛbhiḥ* : *pitṛṣu* : *pitṝn* : *pitṝṇām*. So also *mātṝḥ* (f.) was due the analogy of *matīḥ*; and *dātṝṇi* (neuter) was in the same way influenced by *vārīṇi*; until at last the original character of the stems as ending in *ar* was forgotten, and they were regarded as regular vowel-stems ending in *ṛ*.

So also the nasal in the neuter nom. plural of *as* stems like *manas* is not original, but is due to the analogy of the stems in *mant* and of words like *pratyañc*, where the nasal is original. Thus *dhīmat*: *dhīmanti* :: *manas*: *manāṁsi* (instead of *manāsi*); and then the nasal was further extended to nouns like *haviṣ* and *cakṣuṣ* which give *havīṁṣi* and *cakṣūṁṣi*.

Coming to conjugation we find that in Sanskrit *mi* is the termination of the 1st pers. sing. present, throughout all the conjugations, whether they have a thematic vowel or not. But originally there was a distinction. The thematic verbs had *o*, while it was only the non-thematic verbs that had *mi*. Thus we have in Greek φέρω, Latin *fero*, Gothic *baira*, which should be in Sanskrit *bharā* instead of the actually existing *bharāmi*; (It is to be noted that this form in *o* is probably preserved in the Vedic subjunctive forms like *bravā* and the old Avestic *spasyā* corresponding to Latin *specio*); while we have εἰμί corresponding to Sk. *asmi* and Avesta *ahmi*. In Sanskrit, however, this distinction was lost, and *mi* was applied throughout, under the influence of some such analogy as—*dviṣmaḥ* : *dveṣmi* :: *bharāmaḥ* : *bharāmi*; or *dviṣe*: *dveṣmi*:: *bhare*: *bharāmi*.

So also the suffix of the 1st pers. sing. of the imperfect is *m* which should appear as a nasal consonant after a vowel but as a vowel *a* after a consonant. Thus in Greek, we have ἔ-φερο-ν corresponding to *á-bhara-m* ; but ἦα (=ἦσα = *ēs-m̥*) which should be *āsa* in Sanskrit; but instead, we have *āsam*, only on the analogy of *á-bharam*.

In the potential, *yā* and *ī* are the suffixes added to non-thematic verbs before the strong and weak personal terminations respectively ; thus we have in Greek εἴην (= original εσ-ιη-ν) and old Latin *siem* corresponding to Sanskrit *syām*, in the 1st pers. sing. But in the 1st pers. plural, we have εἶμεν (=orig. ἐσ-ι-μεν) and Latin *s-ī-mus* which should correspond phonetically with *sīma* in Sanskrit: but instead we have *syāma*. So also τιθε-ίη-ς corresponds to *dadhyāḥ*, but τιθε-ῑ-μεν should correspond to *dadhīma*, but instead we have *dadhyāma*. Thus the *yā* originally peculiar to the strong terminations is, in Sanskrit, extended to weak terminations also, on the analogy of the conjugation of thematic verbs, and because the personal terminations were found to be sufficient to distinguish one form from the other, without there being the necessity of any difference in the stem.

A similar tendency is seen, for instance, in the imperfect of the root *as* 'to be'. In the present, the original difference of vowel-gradation in the stem before strong and weak terminations is preserved. Thus we have, *ás-mi*, but *s-máḥ* *ás-ti* but *s-ánti*, just as we have with the root *i* 'to go', *é-mi* but *i-màḥ*. In the same way, in the imperfect, we should have *ās-am* (=*a*+*as–am*) but *a-s-ma* (=*a*+*s–ma*), but we have instead *āsma*; that is to say, the singular has extended its form of the stem, throughout, on the analogy of the thematic verbs.

The Sanskrit root meaning 'to hear' is originally *śru*, which is preserved is *śrutá*, *śrótum*, and the *u* also appears in Gree κλυτός and Latin *in-clutus*. But the *ru* is changed to *ṛ* in the conjugation. Thus we have *śṛṇó-mi*, *śṛṇu-máḥ* etc. One possible explanation suggested is that in the form *śṛṇu*, the original *ru* followed by an *u* in the immediately next syllable, (*śruṇu*) must have been at first changed to *ṛ* by dissimilation, in order to avoid two syllables with *u*; and then this *ṛ* must have been perhaps extended by analogy, to even the strong forms, which had *ṇo* instead of *ṇu*.

Another result of the influence of analogy is the phenomenon of the transference of roots from one conjugation to another. Thus the verbs *tiṣṭhāmi*, *pibāmi*, *jighrāmi* must have originally belonged to the reduplicating class or the third conjugation, the roots being *sthā*, *pā* and *ghrā*. But as we have for instance *bhavāmi*, *bhavāmaḥ*, *bhavasi*, so why not also have *tiṣṭhāmaḥ*, *tiṣṭhasi*? And the change of the reduplicating syllable both in regard to the consonant and the vowel must have weakened their tie to the reduplicating class; and finally they came to be looked upon as belonging to the first class. In the same way, verbs like *kṛntati*, *muñcati*, which originally must have belonged to the seventh conjugation, afterwards came to be looked upon as belonging to the thematic class. The same is the case with verbs like *cakās* and *jakṣ* which originally belonged to the reduplicating class (the roots being *kās* and *ghas*) but which afterwards were transferred to the second conjugation.

In Greek and other European languages, the vowel of the reduplication syllable in the Perfect is *e*. Thus we have in Greek δέ-δορκα, κέκλιται, in old Latin, *memordi*, *cecidi*. This *e* was phonetically represented by *a* in Sanskrit. Thus, *dadarśa*, *jaghāna*. Afterwards the original character of this *a* being forgotten, the reduplication-vowel became *a*, *i*, *u*, according as the vowel of the root was *a*, *i*, *u*. Thus if *han* gives *jaghan*, why should *nī* not give *ninī* or *su*, *suṣu*? Thus the reduplication-vowel was regularly assimilated to the root-vowel. The original condition of the reduplication-vowel is preserved in the form *babhūva* (orig. *bebhūva*) instead of *bubhūva*, and in the Vedic *sasūva* instead of the classical *suṣūva*. A similar assimilation is found in Latin also, e. g. *momordi* for *memordi*, *pupugi* for *pepugi*. The reduplication-vowel in the third conjugation was originally *i*, as is shown by τίθημι, ἵστημι in Greek, and also by the Sanskrit forms *tiṣṭhāmi*, *jighrāmi* etc. But this was also subjected to the influence of the perfect reduplication and thus the reduplication vowel came to be assimilated to the root-vowel.

The perfect forms like *pecima*, *tenima* are apparently anomalous; but can be explained as due to analogy. The change of the root-vowel *a* to *e* was phonetically just in the case of, for instance, *sedima* which was originally *sazdima*, (= *sa-s(a)d-i-ma*) the *a* suffering a compensatory lengthening, and the *z* being dropped. Compare, for instance, *edhi*, the imperative 2nd pers. sing. of *as*, which corresponds to *azdhi* in Avesta). So also in the case of *yemima*, the *e* is phonetically regular; for the form was originally *ya-im-ima*, *im* being the weak grade or samprasāraṇa of *yam*. The original character of the *e* in such cases was, in the course of time, forgotten; and then it was extended to forms like *tenima*, where it had no phonetic explanation. The Vedic form *paptima* instead of the classical *petima* testifies to the fact that this extension of *e* was a later result of the influence of analogy.

As regards the non-conjugational tenses, Sanskrit grammarians have a three-fold division of roots, *seṭ*, *aniṭ* and *weṭ*, according as an *i* is inserted or not or is inserted optionally between the stem and the personal terminations. There are hard and fast rules regarding this insertion of *i*. But the original Indo-germanic language does not seem to know this distinction, as appears from Greek, Latin and even the Avesta. It is a question how this distinction came to exist and to occupy such a prominent place in Sanskrit. One explanation suggested is that the distinction must have at first started from the so-called dis-syllabic roots, which existed from the beginning, as distinguished from the mono-syllabic roots. Thus *śruta* and *śro-tum* arise from the root *śreu̯*; but *bhūta* and *bhavi-tum*, from *bheui* or *bhavi*. Thus the *i* naturally found its place in the case of these dis-syllabic roots. So from the root *jenə* or *jani* we have a perfect form *jajñ-i-ma*, from the root *rudə* or *rudi*, we have *rurud-i-ma*. This second vowel of the root is represented in Greek sometimes, as for instance, in τετρόφαμεν, λελοίπαμεν, (instead of λέλοιπμεν). Afterwards, by analogy, the *i* was extended in Sanskrit to other roots which were not at all originally dis-syllabic. Thus we have,

jajāna : *jajñima* } :: *dadarśa* : *dadṛśima*
or, *ruroda* : *rurudima* } :: and *vavarta* : *vavṛtima*,

although the roots *dṛś* and *vṛt* are mono-syllabic. The same is the case with the aorist and the future. Thus with the root *jṛ* or *jari*, which is dis-syllabic, we have *a-jāriṣam* (cf. Greek ἐγήρα-σα); and then the *i* was extended to other monosyllabic roots by analogy. In *vartiṣyāmi*, the *i* is due to analogy only and is not phonetically just, the root being mono-syllabic. In the same way, the *i* in the case of past passive participles and infinitives is to be explained.

The *ṣ* Aorist (6th variety) is a curious illustration of analogy. A root like *bhās* gave a form like *a-bhāsi-ṣam* in the usual way; but later *bhā* and *bhās* were confounded and the form *a-bhāsiṣam* was taken to have come from *bhā*. Then by analogy, the formation was extended to other roots ending in *ā*, and we have such forms as *a-yāsiṣam* etc.

A similar working of analogy is seen in the case of causals in *p*, like *sthāpayāmi*, *dāpayāmi* etc. A root like *dīp* gave in the regular way *dīpayati*, which was afterwards confounded as being the causal of another root *dī*. Then the *p*-formation was extended to other cases like *yāpayāmi*. The root *i* 'to go' gives not only *āyayati* but *āpayati*, due to some such analogy as *sthita* : *sthāpayāmi* : : *itu* : *āpayāmi*. Or perhaps the *p* causal formation may be due to a confusion of the denominative with the causal. Thus, for instance, from the noun *dīpa* 'a lamp' is formed the denominative *dīpayati*, which was afterwards taken to be a causal from *dī*, exactly in the same way as, from the nouns *pāla* and *ghāta* are formed the denominatives *pālayati* and *ghātayati*, which were afterwards taken to be direct causals of the roots *pā* and *han*.

So far, I have adduced some of the instances from Sanskrit grammar which illustrate the influence of analogy, and these too I could not deal with exhaustively within the limits of an article. Many more instances can be added; but I think that what has been said so far, may be quite sufficient to give an idea as to what a powerful factor analogy is in the formation of a language, side by side with the working of phonetic rules. Its influence is too great to be neglected; and those who are daunted by the numerous exceptions to a phonetic rule and allow their faith in the science of language to waver will do well to remember this fact.

There is a good deal of literature on the subject of analogy; but in most of such works Greek and Latin play an important part, while Sanskrit has a subordinate place. In the comparative grammars of Indo-European languages the space for any particular language is necessarily limited; and as far as I know, analogy by itself with special reference to Sanskrit is nowhere treated. I hope, therefore, that this enumeration of some examples of analogy from Sanskrit, though brief and rough, will have its usefulness.

A PROPOS DE LA RACINE LUBH

PAR A. MEILLET

LE dialecte de l'Inde sur lequel repose la langue du Ṛgveda est celui du Nord-Ouest, donc celui qui est le plus voisin de la région iranienne. Il veut la peine d'examiner si ce dialecte n'offre pas avec l'iranien certains points de contact.

Parmi les points de contact, le plus frappant sans doute est le traitement de l'ancienne liquide indo-européenne *l*. Comme l'iranien, la langue du Ṛgveda ignore la liquide *l*, qui y est confondue avec *r*; par example, en regard du *linquō* 'je laisse,' le védique=*ṛṇakti*, et en face du gotique *filu*: 'beaucoup,' il a *purú*.

Le parler d'autres régions de l'Inde avait conservé la distinction de *r* et de *l*; et le sanskrit classique, qui représente un type védique employé par des hommes de régions diverses, a souvent introduit des formes avec *l*; par example, en lieu du latin *lingō*, le Ṛgveda a une racine *rih* (soit *réḻhi*), tout comme l'avestique a une racine *riz*; mais le sanskrit classique a *lih* (soit *leḍhi*) avec *l*, comme le latin, le grec, le germanique, le slave, l'arménien. C'est l'une des innovations, qui montrent le mieux le caractère composite du sanskrit classique.

Si, dans une racine comme *rih*, qui avait *r* dans le Ṛgveda, le sanskrit classique a introduit *l*, à plus forte raison on conçoit que *l* figure dans une racine inconnue du Ṛgveda. C'est ce qui arrive pour la racine *lubh*; cette racine ne se trouve pas dans la partie ancienne du Ṛgveda, on signale seulement une forme *lobháyanti* de causatif dans le maṇḍala x du Ṛgveda. C'est pour cela que cette racine qui commençait par *l* en indo-européen—qu'on compare gotique *ljap* 'cher,' latin *lubet* 'il plaît',—existe en sanskrit seulement avec *l* initiale. C'était une racine inconnue au dialecte du Nord-Ouest.

Il n'y a pas là un simple hasard : inconnue au Nord-Ouest de l'Inde, cette racine indo-européenne l'était aussi à l'iranien, où l'on n'en signale aucune trace. A la concordance entre les traitements phonétiques de *l* dans l'Iran et dans le Nord-Ouest de l'Inde, s'ajoute ici une concordance du vocabulaire, qui merite l'attention.

On trouverait sans doute quelques autres cas analogues à celui-ci. Par example, le groupe de mots *lakṣam*, *lakṣma* etc. n'a aucun correspondent connu en iranien ; il est à peine représenté dans le Ṛgveda, surtout dans les parties anciennes ; et le fait qu'il présente *l* montre que, dans le Ṛgveda, il appartint au petit nombre des éléments empruntées à des parlers autres que ceux du Nord-Ouest.

Bien que l'iranien, d'une part, et les langues de l'Inde de l'autre, forment deux ensembles qui s'opposent nettement, il semble donc que, en une certaine mesure, les parlers du Nord-Ouest, dont le Ṛgveda offre la forme la plus ancienne, fournissent une transition entre l'indien et l'iranien.

A PROPOS DE L'ACCENT D'INTENSITE EN INDO-ARYEN

PAR JULES BLOCH

DANS un ouvrage sur *la formation de la langue marathe*, dont la guerre a retardé la publication,[1] je me suis cru autorisé à écarter de l'explication historique toute théorie phonétique fondée sur l'hypothèse d'un accent d'intensité.

Lorsqu'on examine l'évolution phonétique de l'indo-aryen, dans son ensemble, il est impossible de ne pas être frappé de l'analogie des altérations subies par les voyelles dans cette famille et dans la famille romane; dans les deux groupes, les voyelles finales des polysyllabes sont tombées, tandis que les pénultièmes ont subsisté; le timbre des voyelles intérieures s'est altéré. Or, en ce qui concerne le roman, on sait par quelques témoignages anciens, et surtout par la concordance universelle des divers dialectes modernes, que ces altérations ont été déterminées par un accent d'intensité pénultième, combiné avec un contre-accent initial; cet accent a succédé en latin à un ton o accent de hauteur, dont la place dans le mot dépendait de la quantité des syllabes finales. Rien de plus naturel, semble-t-il, que de supposer qu'en moyen-indien aussi, il s'est développé un accent d'intensité remplaçant le ton védique disparu. Ainsi M. Bhandarkar (Wilson lectures, p. 152) écrit: "la syllable pénultième est renforcée dans tous nos dialectes par un accent qui tend à faire allonger cette syllabe et à faire tomber la voyelle finale." C'est à peu près la formule romane.

Mais d'abord l'exemple du roman peut être trompeur. Les mêmes effets peuvent provenir de causes différentes: ainsi en scandinave la chute d'une voyelle finale peut suffire à déterminer l'allongement de la voyelle précédente,

1 Toutefois la partie dogmatique, qui a servi de thèse du doctorat, a été communiquée à plusieurs amis; M. Turner en a même dès à présent discuté le chapitre concernant l'accent dans J.R.A.S., 1916, p. 203 et suiv.

et l'on sait que la chute des voyelles finales est un phénomène général, indépendant de l'accentuation. De même, en latin le ton seul est à l'origine de l'abrègement des voyelles longues atones dans *Apollĭnis*, *ancŏra*, *būtĭrum*, qui sont des emprunts aux formes grecques Ἀπόλλωνος, ἄγχῡρα, βούτῡρον.

De plus, outre que le détail des faits n'est pas entièrement comparable dans les deux groupes de langues, l'analogie est forcée dans le principe même. La place du ton en latin est déterminée par la quantité de la syllabe pénultième; le ton, et à sa suite l'accent roman, portent sur cette pénultième si elle est longue, sur l'antépénultième, si la pénultième est brève. En védique, au contraire, l'accentuation est indépendante de la quantité des syllabes et de la forme du mot; elle a une valeur non phonétique, mais grammaticale et sémantique. De ce fait, ou l'accent pénultième supposé du moyen-indien doit être considéré comme une innovation, et le rapprochement avec la famille romane s'évanouit; ou l'on est amené à compliquer la première hypothèse d'hypothèses subordinaires pour expliquer comment le ton védique à place libre a pu aboutir en moyen-indien à un accent à place fixe.

Dans ce second cas on voit se manifester entre les deux histoires qu'on prétend rapprocher une différence nouvelle et grave, lorsqu'il s'agit de l'accent: différence de clarté. Les règles de l'accent roman se découvrent aisément à la simple inspection des dialectes modernes; elles sont précises et simples, les effets en sont plus ou moins violents suivant les régions, mais il sont constants. C'est ce qui se produit dans les langues comportant un accent d'intensité. Ainsi le simple examen du grec moderne révèle un accent prenant la place du ton ancien. De même, il est aisé de reconnaître qu'en germanique le ton ancien a cédé la place à un accent initial. Dans l'Inde, rien de pareil; les théories se contredisent et s'établissent mal; pas plus que pour la période ancienne, les faits ne sont établis, de façon sûre, pour la période moderne.

Il paraît donc prudent de s'abstenir d'alléguer des observations insuffisantes et contradictoires pour étayer une hypothèse historique qui n'est pas indispensable pour l'explication qu'elle prétend fournir.

Par contre, l'examen des faits contemporains mériterait d'être repris, abstraction faite de tout préjugé historique, de toute construction théorique, et de façon indépendante dans les divers dialectes.

C'est aux indigènes qu'il faut, de préférence, remettre le soin de cette enquête. Dans toute étude de linguistique descriptive, il arrive assez vite un moment où l'oreille d'un étranger hésite, quand elle ne va pas jusqu'à l'induire en erreur, et dans l'étude de l'accent en particulier, les habitudes linguistiques d'observateur risquent de fausser gravement les résultats de son enquête. Si l'on a admis que le sanscrit classique comportait un accent d'intensité, au moins dans les récitations modernes, ce n'est pas un hasard: ce sont deux Allemands, Haug et Bühler, qui ont fait les premières expériences, et ils ont confondu les alternances de longues et de brèves qui fournissent le rythme traditionnel du sanscrit, avec des variations d'intensité;[1] or les enregistrements phonographiques de récitations sanscrites n'ont donné aucune trace d'intensité: ceci ne fait que confirmer l'avis d'indigènes consultés. De même, Sir George Grierson, dans une lettre qu'il m'a fait l'honneur de m'addresser jadis, supposait que les Anglais qui n'entendent pas d'accent dans les langues de l'Inde, sont trompés par le fait que l'accent ne s'y trouve pas comme en anglais, rapproché le plus possible de l'initiale.

On sait, d'autre part, que les appareils enregistreurs ne fournissent pas le moyen de noter l'accent, comme ils donnent, par exemple, la hauteur ou la quantité. L'intensité mécanique d'un phonème dépend de l'amplitude et de la fréquence des vibrations; mais ce sont là des phénomènes qui varient suivant la hauteur et l'articulation même du phonème: ainsi pour un même débit d'air une voyelle fermée est moins intense qu'une voyelle ouverte; pour un même débit d'air aussi un son est d'autant plus intense

1 J'en avais fait l'observation avant la guèrre "la formation de la langue marathe" p. 51.

qu'il est plus élevé. Du reste l'intensité mécanique, et même la perceptibilité auditive ne se confondent pas avec l'intensité telle que la sent le sujet parlant; elles y contribuent, mais il faut compter en outre avec les rapports prévus comme normaux entre l'intensité des divers éléments du langage pour un débit sans accentuation, et avec les altérations de ces rapports reconnus comme dépendants de l'accentuation. Ces appréciations délicates échappant à l'appareil mécanique, il est indispensable de s'addresser à l'auditeur averti.

Une première enquête s'impose : déterminer dans quelle mesure le phénomène, s'il se réalise, est conscient aux sujets parlants. Il ne faut pas s'attendre à trouver souvent chez eux une notion claire de l'accent; la plupart des grammaires indigènes omettent même entièrement la question, mais le cas peut se présenter. Au témoignage de Sir George Grierson, le pandit Choṭu Rām Trivedī connaissait l'accent, et lui donnait, "en *Bhāṣā*" le nom d'*udātta*; par contre un Panjabi cultivé, mais qui n'avait jamais réfléchi à la question, disait au même savant que l'accent chez lui s'appelait *dabāū* "pression": il est vrai qu'un autre Panjabi consulté par moi ignore le mot dans cette acception. Enfin, en bengali, c'est (au témoignage de Mr. J. D. Anderson) *jor* "force", qui désigne l'accent, par opposition à *surer uṭhaū o nāmān* "l'élévation et l'abaissement de la voix."

Du reste, à défaut de l'existence d'un terme plus ou moins technique pour le désigner, à défaut même de la conscience de sa réalité, l'accent peut être sensible de façon indirecte : en français où il est à peine perceptible, il subsiste pourtant en ce sens que dans le débit normal, il apparaît comme fautif, s'il est mal placé : *épouvantable* paraît expressif, parce qu'exceptionnel : *épouvantáble* avec un accent violent, apparaîtra comme emphatique, mais normal; *épouvántable* est nettement barbare. Autre fait: à Paris, dans le débit populaire, la pénultième s'allonge et devient plus intense: *quat(re) sous lā liv(re)*; dans le Français provincial de l'Est, cet accent pénultième est bien marqué et courant; à un Français normal cet accent paraît ridicule. Des faits de ce genre permettent de déterminer l'existence psychique et la place de l'accent. Il faut, de plus, s'attendre à trouver des perturbations d'accent dues à la place du mot dans la phrase ou à la valeur psychologique même de la phrase. Ainsi on sait qu'en bengali le début d'un groupe de mot reçoit à la fois un ton plus haut, une intensité plus forte et une quantité plus longue, indépendemment de toute intention rhétorique: *ār kaṣṭa bārai nā*: "n'ajoutez pas à mes ennuis." *Bāra bhāla kathā*: "c'est une *trés* bonne histoire" se prononcer *Báura bhāla kathā*, inversement *kathāṭā bara bhālo*: "l'histoire est très bonne."

C'est là l'origine du *Chi-chi English*, le défaut caractéristique de tout étudiant bengali, à ses débuts dans l'apprentissage de l'anglais.—Dans d'autres langues, l'accent, s'il existe de façon sensible, pourra être déplacé pour des raisons d'emphase: en français, le mot de valeur d'une phrase reçoit un accent initial, surtout s'il débute par une consonne occlusive ou spirante, (Rondet. El. de phonétique, p. 251) *párdon*, *beaúcoup*, *énórmément*. On trouvera peut-être dans l'Inde de faits analogues; il s'agira d'en déterminer la généralité.

Enfin, si l'on sait observer sans se laisser guider—ou tromper—par une hypothèse historique préconçue, on s'apercevra peut-être que l'accent n'aura pas la même intensité et ne sera pas soumis aux mêmes lois dans tous les dialectes. M. Turner apporte (J. R. A. S., 1916, p. 212) une observation intéresante: les Guzratis disent que les Marathes chantent en parlant, tandis que pour un Marathe, le Guzrati a un débit saccadé. D'autre part Navalkar qui nie l'accent en marathe signale dans cette langue un ton initial qui pourrait bien s'accompagner aussi d'une faible intensité: *tethẽ rāhāvẽ*: "il faut rester là"; il semble que le panjābi possède même un *staccato* à l'italienne: on prononce *càlan* comme s'il y avait un *tašdīd*, c'est à dire presque *càllan* (communication de Sir George Grierson).

Il est en effet naturel de prévoir des divergences dans les différentes langues et même à l'intérieur de chaque langue. L'accent n'est pas un phénomène stable : ainsi le ton indo-européen avait disparu dès la période la plus ancienne du latin; plus tard l'intensité initiale du latin archaïque a cédé le pas à un ton nouveau déterminé par la quantité des finales; ce ton du latin classique est devenu un accent, qui en français devient insensible ou instable; enfin, en français contemporain on assiste à la naissance d'une nouvelle accentuation encore mal définissable. Combien de variations ne peut-on pas s'attendre à trouver dans un pays où l'indo-aryen ne s'est pas répandu partout à la même date, ni avec la même rapidité, et où les langues qu'il a remplacées ont pu, en s'éteignant, laisser, comme il arrive constamment, des empreintes profondes sur le système phonétique de la langue nouvelle! Il n'est pas interdit de prévoir que l'étude de l'accent, menée de façon désintéressée et indépendante dans chaque région, peut servir non seulement à préciser ou rectifier nos notions sur l'indo-aryen médiéval, mais à éclairer de lumières indirectes l'histoire de la colonisation linguistique de l'Inde.

Kāvya and Alaṅkāra

DATE OF ŚŪDRAKA'S MṚCCHAKAṬIKA

BY K. C. MEHENDALE

THE attempts hitherto made by distinguished Orientalists and Sanskrit scholars to settle the date of the Mṛcchakaṭika—of that kingly playwright Śūdraka—have resulted in more or less plausible conjectures. This is quite natural in consideration of the unsettled state of Indian chronology and the meagre and elusive data available from evidence both internal and external.[1] Pischel is said to have been once inclined to ascribe the play to Bhāsa; but later on he gave up this view in favour of a bold theory that Daṇḍin, the author of Kāvyādarśa, wrote the play. The reasons adduced by him in support are palpably wrong. He has not correctly understood the passage[2] from the commentary of Pratīhārendurāja on Udbhaṭa's Kāvyālaṅkārasaṅgraha, and he has quite missed the point of the learned and rather long drawn discussion introduced by Daṇḍin in connection with the well-known verse लिम्पतीव तमोऽङ्गानि वर्षतीवाऽञ्जनं नभः at Kāvyādarśa iii. 226–234. Evidently Daṇḍin is here quoting the verse which many previous writers on Alaṅkāra were misled by the presence of the particle *iva* in regarding as containing the figure Upamā. Daṇḍin strongly controverts this view and conclu sively proves that the figure in question is Utprekṣā. Peterson[3] asserted that the Mṛcchakaṭika belonged to a period when "people had begun to forget how to write good Sanskrit" and consequently Daṇḍin who quotes it cannot be a very old writer (*cir.* 6th century A. D.)!

Prof. K. B. Pathak holds that the Prākrit as found in the Mṛcchakaṭika is older than that occurring in the three dramas of Kālidāsa, and that threfore Śūdraka must be

1 Ind. Antiquary for March 1911, pp. 87-89.

2 Pischel's ed. of Rudraṭa's Śṛṇgāratilaka page 18, and Udbhaṭa's Kāvyālaṅkārasaṅgraha p. 26 (Nir. Sag. ed.)—अतः एव दण्डिना लिम्पतीव........ निष्फलतां गता इत्यादिर्गर्भीकृतातिशयोत्प्रेक्षाभेदत्वमेव महता प्रपञ्चेनाभ्यधायि.

3 Preface to Daśakumāracarita part III, p. 7 (Bom. Sk. Series).

considerably anterior to Kālidāsa. This view appears to be probable in the light of the accidental coincidence of the fourth distich of the Mṛcchakaṭika, ix. 33, with the fourth distich of the Kālidāsa's Kumārasambhava, ii. 32, (धूमकेतुरिवोत्थितः). Of course it is hazardous to establish any case of borrowing on the strength of this isolated agreement. The custom of self-immolation as prescribed for the *sarva-svāra* sacrifice, the mention of the promulgators of the science of thieving, the description of the paraphernalia of burglary, the reference to the successful rescue of Udayana by his trusted and devoted minister Yaugandharāyaṇa, the Indramakha festival, the Ratna-ṣaṣṭhī fast and vow observed by Dhūtā, the four modes of ordeals, the law-giver Manu quoted, the representation, on the stage, of sleeping and strangling in direct violation of the rules of Bharata, the use of the technical terms of gambling together with the employment of the words पायशापिण्डलक, गड्ढी, शत्ती, कण्णाटकलह, वैशिकी and वरंडलंबुअ the exact signification of which has been lost and which have gone out of vogue, the flourishing state of Buddhism and the attitude of tolerance towards it, a Brahman allowed to take a Śūdrā as a lawful wife unto himself—a practice strictly prohibited in the Kali age: all these facts in their cumulative effect easily lend themselves to establish the antiquity of the play. Messrs. Raddi Shastri and Paranjpye, in the Introduction to their edition of the play, have assigned it to the first century before Christ.

Lovers of Sanskrit cannot but be greatful to Mr. T. Ganapati Shastri, Curator of Sanskrit Manuscripts in the Palace Collection, Travancore State, to whom belongs the credit of bringing to light the plays of Bhāsa till then regarded as irrecoverably lost in the abyss of time. It is an undoubted fact that the *Chārudatta* formed a unit in the नाटकचक्र of Bhāsa. It is referred to by Abhinavagupta (*cir.* 1000 A. D.) in his Nāṭyavedavivṛti. Abhinavagupta, while commenting on the 13th stanza of the 19th chapter of Bharata's Nāṭyaśāstra alias Nāṭyaveda, says[1]—

1 This commentary, the Nāṭyavedavivṛti, is still unpublished; and I owe this quotation to the kindness of Mr. T. Ganapati Shastri.

सर्वस्येव हि कार्यस्य प्रारब्धस्य फलार्थिनः
एता अनुक्रमेणैव पञ्चावस्था भवन्ति हि ॥

ननु मानुषव्यापारे नायकस्य तत्सचिवादेर्वा भवन्त्वेता अवस्थाः प्रतिनायकेऽप्येवम् तत्र परमसदुपायापेक्षया यत्र तु दैवायतं फलं वर्ण्यते तत्र कथम्। न च वर्ज्यतां पुरुषकारमात्राभिमानिनां दैवमवजानानां चार्वाकादिमतमेयुषां सः। दैवबहुमानव्युत्पत्तये हि पुरुषकारोऽप्यफलस्तदभावोऽपि सफलः प्रदर्शनीयः। अत एव दरिद्रचारुदत्तादिरूपकाणि तद्विषयाणि। तस्माद्दैवायत्तत्वे कथमेतदवस्थापञ्चकं तत्परिहर्तुमाह सर्वस्यैव हीति। दैवादागच्छतोऽपीत्यर्थः। तत्राऽपि हि यद्यप्यभिनायको न वर्तते तथापि यत्र फलं भवति तत्रावश्यमवस्थाभिर्भाव्यम्। स एव च परं फलेन तदानीमर्थी भवति यमर्थमधिकृत्य प्रवर्तत इति हि प्रयोजनलक्षणं वदन्ति।

The *Cārudatta* printed in the Trivendrum Sanskrit Series is evidently a fragment, though the remark अवसितम् appears in the colophon of one Ms. A reference to the Sarasvatīkaṇṭhābharaṇa[1] (*cir.* 1050 A. D.), Pariccheda v, stanzas 599–600 shows that Bhoja is quoting from a work and that too a drama in which Viṭa is addressing Śakāra. The passage of similar import from the Mṛcchakaṭika deserves being placed side by side for the purpose of useful comparison. Moreover the following passages from the *Cārudatta* unmistakably shadow forth matter for further acts of the play which Bhāsa must have woven into it—

(*a*) पापं कर्म च यत् परैरपि कृतं तत्तस्य सम्भाव्यते (चा° i. 6);

(*b*) संवाहकः—(स्वगतम्) णिउणं खु पच्चाचक्खिदो ह्मि। को हि णाम अप्पणा किदं पच्चुअआरेण विणासेदि। (ibid. ii p. 44);

(*c*) सज्जलकः—नरः प्रत्युपकारार्थी विपत्तौ लभते फलम्।
द्विषतामेव कालोऽस्तु योऽस्या भवतु तस्य वा ॥
(ibid. iv. 7);

(*d*) गणिका—भणेहि अत्तं जदा अय्यचारुदत्तो अभिसारइदव्वो तदा मण्डेमि त्ति।
(ibid. iv. p. 71);

(*e*) गणिका— एहि इमं अलंकारं गण्हिअ अय्यचारुदत्तं अभिसरिस्सामो।
चेटी— अज्जुए तह। एदं पुण अभिसारिआसहाअभूदं दुद्दिणं उण्णमिदं।
(ibid. iv, p. 86).

1 Page 740, ed. Jibananda—

मान्यः कलत्रवान् भुक्तविभवो गुणवान् विटः।

स यथा—

शकार किं प्रार्थनया प्रावारेण मिषेण वा।
अकार्यवर्जं मे ब्रूहि किमभिष्टं करोमि ते ॥

Cf. Mṛcchakaṭika (Bom. Sk. Series), p. 340—विटः। नाहं करोमि वर्जयित्वा स्वकार्यम्.

It also deserves to be noted that the *Cārudatta* is not wound up with the usual concluding benediction. Thus we can infer that Bhāsa must most probobly have completed the *Cārudatta*. Or perhaps the copy of the Mṛcchakaṭika which Bhoja used might have contained the passage referred to above in place of the correspondidg reading in the editions of the Mṛcchakaṭika. But the latter alternative seems to be unlikely in as much as even the two Mss. E and K, which hailed from Saugor and Jeypore,—Central India,—and on which the late Mr. N. B. Godabole relied for his edition of the Mṛcchakaṭika, contain no trace of that reading. In this connection it also deserves to be mentioned that the Sarasvatīkaṇṭhābharaṇa reads the 22nd verse of the Mṛcchakaṭika Act viii. as—

पलिच्चले लम्बदशाकलाअं पाआलअ शुत्तशदेहिं छत्तं ।
मंशञ्च खादु तुह तुट्ठि कादुं चकुश्चुकुश्चकुचुकुश्चुकुत्ति ॥

and that this reading is not found in the editions.

From the considerations set forth above it would not be unsafe, in the present state of our knowledge, to conclude that the *Cārudatta* of Bhāsa was the original which Śūdraka worked up into his Mṛcchakaṭika. It is, however, an unfortunate circumstance that the *Cārudatta* has been recovered only in part and that we are thus left in the dark in respect of the full and adequate material which otherwise would have been available to us from the remaining portion of the *Cārudatta* for settling the *terminus a quo* of the Mṛcchakaṭika and incidentally furnishing additional data for determining the much discussed date of Bhāsa himself.

The *terminus ad quem* for the Mṛcchakaṭika is settled by the following passages from the Avaloka[1] of Dhanika—

(*a*) विप्रादीनां शांततैव न ला़लित्यम् । यथा मालतीमाधवमृच्छकटिकादौ माधवचारुदत्तादिः ।

(*b*) यथा वा—मखशतपरिपूतं गोत्रमुद्भासितं यत् etc.

(*c*) कितवद्यूतकारादिधूर्तसंकुलं तु मृच्छकटिकादिवत्संकीर्णप्रकरणम् ।

(मृच्छ० X. 12).

1 Daśarupa, Nir. Sāg. ed. pages 45, 90.

This Dhanika was one of the literary circle at the court of Parmār Muñja of Malva (A. D. 974-995).[1] Dhanika thus belongs to the end of the tenth century, which is thus the later limit of the Mṛcchakaṭika. The earlier limit is however not so easy to settle. Vāmana[2] (*cir.* 775 A. D.) in his Kāvyālaṅkārasūtravṛtti supplies two quotations which have an important bearing upon this line of inquiry—

(*a*) यासां बलिर्भवति मद्गृहदेहलीनां
हंसैश्च सारसगणैश्च विलुप्तपूर्वः ।
तास्वेव पूर्वबलिरूढयवाङ्कुरासु
बीजाञ्जलिः पतति कीटमुखावलीढः ॥

(*b*) द्यूतं हि नाम पुरुषस्याऽसिंहासनं राज्यम् ।

The first quotation appears in a modified form in the Mṛcchakaṭika Act i.; but it rathers agrees more with Bhāsa's Cārudatta, Act i. 2. The second occurs in the Mṛcchakaṭika Act ii. but, strangely enough, it is not found in the Cārudatta. These facts, taken in conjunction with Vāmana's remark[3] that the works of Śūdraka and others supply copious illustrations of the artistic characteristic of composition called Śleṣa, clearly lead to the conclusion that Śūdraka was, in the latter half of the eighth century already known as an author with a recognised place in the realm of letters. From the way in which Vāmana is giving the above quotations it appears quite probable that Śūdraka must have written the Mṛcchakaṭika. Except the latter drama and a solitary verse[4] no other work of Śūdraka is as yet known to the Sanskrit world of letters.

Having established so much let us see if we can possibly derive any further light to help us in this investigation from Bāṇa's Kādambarī and Harṣacarita. It is significant that Bāṇa in the introductory verses prefixed to the

1 Ind. Antiquary xxxvi, pp. 168-170 and J. R. A. S. xv, 175.

2 Nir. Sag. ed. pp. 60 and 56.

3 Ibid. p. 33—शूद्रकादिरचितेषु प्रबन्धेष्वस्य भूयान्प्रपञ्चो दृश्यते.

4 No. 1271, Vallabhadeva's Subhāṣitāvali—त्यागो हि सर्वव्यसनानि हन्तीत्यलीकमेतद्भुवि संप्रतीतम्।' जातानि सर्वव्यसनानि तस्यास्त्यागेन मे मुग्धविलोचनायाः ॥ शूद्रकस्य.

Harṣacarita eulogizes Bhāsa the dramatist, and omits Śūdraka. It is well known to Sanskrit scholars that the basis of Bāṇa's Kādambarī is the Bṛhatkathā of Guṇāḍhya, of which there exist two faithful and independent renderings in Sanskrit: the Bṛhatkathāmañjarī and the Kathāsaritsāgara. Bāṇa, in writing his masterpiece of romance, has changed the name of the hero of the original Kathā from king Sumānasa (or Sumanas) of Kāñcanapurī to king Śūdraka of Vidiśā. Now is this substitution haphazard or deliberate? Bāṇa in his Harṣacarita[1] mentions a Śūdraka one of whose emissaries deprived Candraketu the lord of the Cakoras and his minister of life. This information does not help us; so is the case with the hero of the Kādambarī where he is described as the fountainhead of all polite arts and as a sovereign possessing all the advantages of power and position,—no reference or indication is however given as to his authorship or as to his being blessed with a son. This description evidently savours of being technical and stereotyped. The dynastic lists given in the Purāṇas and collected by Mr. F. G. Pargiter make no mention of any Śūdraka. Kṣīrasvāmin[2] (cir. 1075 A. D.) while commenting on Amara ii. 8. 2 gives a list of Cakravartins among whom the following names occur—

विक्रमादित्यः साहसाङ्कः शकान्तकः ।
शूद्रकस्त्वग्निमित्रो वा हालः स्याच्छालिवाहनः (*v. l.* सातवा°) ॥

In the commentary on the Vākyapadīya of Bhartṛhari a king Śūdraka is mentioned—लोकेऽपि राजपुरुष इत्युक्ते कस्य राज्ञः शूद्रकस्येति प्रश्नोत्तरयो राजपदार्थप्रविभागः etc. The author of the commentary Hṛdayaṅgamā, while commenting[3] on Daṇḍin's Kāvyādarśa i. 15 makes mention of a Śūdraka: सदाश्रयम्—हर्षशूद्रकोदयनादिसत्पुरुषसमाश्रयम्. A Śūdraka (*v. l.* Śūdṛka), whose life was written conjointly by Rāmila and Somila, is mentioned by Rājaśekhara.[4] All these references go to

1 Harṣacarita, p. 270 (Bom. Sk. Series).

2 Mr. G. K. Oak's ed. of Amarakośa with the commentary of Kṣīrasvāmin, p. 122.

3 Kāvyādarśa, ed. by Prof. M. Rangacharya, p. 14.

4 R.G. Bhandarkar's Report on the Search for Sk. Mss., 1887-91, p.x.

prove that a great king named Śūdraka was known to old Indian tradition, which information is already vouched for by the writer of the Prelude to the Mṛcchakaṭika. There Śūdraka is said to have lived for one hundred years and ten days. The Āin-i-Akbarī of Abdul Fazal mentions, among kings of Bengal, a king of the Khatri caste named *Sadhrak* whose reign lasted for 91 years.[1] Abdul Fazal assigns 2418 years to the reigns of 24 Khatri princes of Bengal 'who kept aflame the torch of sovereignty from father to son in succession.' All this is on its very face unhistorical. The other items of information about Śūdraka given in the Prelude are that he was a Kṣatriya par excellence, that he performed the horse-sacrifice which involved him in many hostilities, and that he possessed boundless and resourceful energy (अगाधसत्त्व). The writer of the Prelude has used the Perfect (परोक्षे लिट्) in describing Śūdraka. The latter must therefore have lived a considerable time before him. In the present state of our knowledge it is very difficult to exercise reservation in the matter of accepting such information. It may be that Śūdraka may have, for ought may turn up to the contrary, come upon the swelling tide of the vigorous Brahmanic revival so gloriously inaugurated by the Gupta emperors. The Rājataraṅgiṇī mentions a Śūdraka who was distinguished by eminent courage and energy.[2] Kalhana appears to regard him as coming after Vikramāditya. It is very difficult to say exactly who this Vikramāditya is. The contemporaneity of Mātṛgupta, Pravarasena II, Meṇṭha (or Bhartṛmeṇṭha) and Vikramāditya, indicated by Kalhaṇa, and reminiscences of which are preserved in Sanskrit literary tradition, makes it highly probable that this Śūdraka may have lived about 550–600 after Christ, the second well-known blank in Indian history. This literary tradition is preserved in the anthologies of Jalhaṇa (cir.

1 The Āin-i-Akbari of Abdul Fazl translated by Col. H. S. Jarrett, Vol. II, pp. 144-146.

2 Rājataraṅgiṇī (Bom. Sk. Series), iii. stanza 343—संत्यज्य विक्रमादित्यं सत्त्वोद्रिक्तं च शूद्रकम्। त्वां च भूपाल पर्याप्तं धैर्यमन्यत्र दुर्लभम॥

13th century), Śārṅgadhara and Vallabhadeva. The verse—

लिम्पतीव तमोङ्गानि वर्षतीवाञ्जनं नभः ।

is ascribed to Vikramāditya by Jalhaṇa and Vallabhadeva, while in the Sārṅgadharapaddhati it is ascribed to Vikramāditya and Menṭha jointly. The verse occurs in the Bālacarita and the Cārudatta of Bhāsa, and consequently the amusing mess of the anthologists and the conjuctures of Pischel may be safely passed over.

It may thus be seen that the Mṛcchakaṭika of Śūdraka had not attained that degree of celebrity in the time of Bāṇa which would merit a necessary and complimentary reference to it in the beginning of the Harṣacarita. It may also appear that before the Pañcatantra in its two recensions was compiled, the Mṛcchakaṭika had already been a popular work. In Pañcatantra I, the 14th and the 15th stanzas of the Mṛcchakaṭika Act iv are reproduced. Also the 90th stanza in Tantra II is a reproduction of Mṛcchakaṭika iii. 25. The Pañcatantra in its present form cannot be earlier than Dāmodara Gupta's Sambhalīmata (*cir.* 775 A. D.) and Rudraṭa's Sṛṅgāratilaka (*cir.* 850) in as much as the stanzas पर्यङ्कः स्वास्तरणः (799) and सार्धं मनोरथशतैस्तव धूर्त कान्ता (i. 41) occur in Tantra I. 174 and Tantra IV. 8 respectively. So long as the remaining portion of the Cārudatta of Bhāsa, viz. from the fifth act to the conclusion, remains unrecovered, it may not be of much avail to interpret and discuss for the purpose of this paper the evidence supplied by the judicial astrology, the court-trial and the state of Buddhism in the Mṛcchakaṭika. Provisionally we may assign Śūdraka to the middle of the sixth century after Christ.

" The world is worldly usage.

" Tradition of words, lexicology of meanings, metre, doctrines of the arts, and of love, politics and so on are the sciences.

" From tradition of words comes word-suggestion.

" From lexicology of meanings comes certitude of the import of words :

" Since what is not allowed is not allowable.

" From metre comes decision of metrical doubt.

" From doctrine of arts, realization of the essence of the arts.

" From doctrine of love, (realization) of the procedure of love.

" From politics, (realization) of policy and impolicy.

" Also therefrom comes ingenuity of incident.

" Miscellaneous are perception of aim, application, attendance upon seniors, trial, fancy and attention.

" Perception of aim is acquaintance with other poets.

" Application is exertion in composing poetry.

" Attendance upon seniors is listening to those who are authorities in teaching poetry.

" Trial is adoption and rejection of words,

[Com. To this effect there is the verse—

" So long is there adoption and rejection, while the mind wavers :

" Once settled the word's retention, straight Sarasvatī's work is perfect.

" When the words are beyond suffering replacement,

" The expert in wording call that word-ripeness.]

" Fancy is the seed of poesy.

" Attention is concentration of mind.

" This is by means of place and time.

" The place is solitude,

" The time the fourth watch of the night ".

Vāmana's commentary does not appreciably amplify this scheme, which, especially in the particularization of time and place, is sufficiently definite, without, however, going counter to the dictates of nature. No doubt there are night poets and morning poets : whether the former or the latter are meant, perhaps Vāgbhaṭa (see below 'early hours') may help to decide.

It is, however, the Jaina writers who let us participate most particularly in the secrets of the poetic studio. I commence with the two Vāgbhaṭa's and end with Hemchandra, who gives the fullest directions.

The author of the *Vāgbhaṭālaṅkāra*, son of Soma, (first half of the 12th century) expounds as follows (I. 3 sqq.):—

" Cause thereof (*i. e.* of poetry) is fancy, and culture its adornment.

" Application effects its abundant outflow—so the saying of the old poets.

" Furnishing suggestions of tranquil words and adaptation of new matter,

" The flashing thought of a good poet is fancy, towards every point alert.

" Unusual intelligence, based upon instruction in the doctrines

" Of words, morals, action, love and so forth is termed culture.

" Incessant devotion to poetic composition under a senior

" Is known as practice : thereof we expound some little of the procedure.

" By a string of words having charm of composition, but void of meaning

" One should master in view of poesy the metres one and all.

" Afterwards comes weight through combination, non-omission of *visarga*,

" And avoidance of failure of *sandhi*, these being causes of charm of composition. (*Illustration follows.*)

"If, owing to inexperience, adaptation of new matter fails to present itself,

"One should practise even in conversation the art of giving form to meaning. (*Illustration follows.*)

"Composing another's matter would also be practice in poetic usage :

"It is not advisable, since thereby the poet becomes a thief.

"However, in *samasyā* (verse-filling) a taking of another's poetry may be a merit in a poet :

"For he makes new matter joining on thereto.

"Tranquillity of mind, fancy, early hours, application,

"Insight into various Śāstras—these are the cause of sense-inspiration.

"With a view to detail of the subject to be described let him acquire readiness in combining it

"With attributes or with sentences, such as similes etc. in the second half."

The author suggests practice in the arts of expansion and compression, and notes certain conventions relating to the Sanskrit language and the usage of the poets (*kavi-saṅgati*).

The other Vāgbhaṭa, the son of Nemikumāra who belongs to the 14th (?) century, in his *Kāvyānuśāsana* gives to the poetic conventions ('absence of flower and fruit in the Aśoka tree', 'opening of the blue lotus etc. in the daytime,' 'darkness that can be handled', 'whiteness of fame and laughter,' etc.—things affirmed or ignored without regard to fact) the prior place, and then proceeds to the actual training. His matter being identical with that of Hemachandra, an earlier authority to whom we hasten, we give only his brief text without the explanations and examples in his commentary (I., page 12 of the edition in the Kāvyamālā 43).

" Training is 'shadow-dependence' upon the poems " of great poets, sometimes by way of 'imaging,' " sometimes by way of 'copy-sketch,' sometimes by " 'corporeal resemblance,' sometimes by 'foreign- " city-entrance' likeness—these in progressive sequ- " ence; dependence in one line, two, three; depend- " ence in sayings; verse-filling and word-replacing; " practice with meaningless words and so on.

" Among these 'imaging' is where the sense is the " same, but the form, by different expressions, is " other.

" 'Copy-sketch' is where with only a certain " amount of difference there is an appearance of dis- " tinction of the one from the other.

" Where even with difference of subject there is, " owing to extreme similarity, an impression of " identity, that is 'corporeal resemblance.'

" Where the poem's actual capital is one, but the " garnishing is widely different, that is 'foreign-city- " entrance' likeness."

Hemachandra, the celebrated Jaina polygraph (12th century A. D.), whose Kāvyānuśāsana with his own commentary has been published, like the works of the two Vāgbhaṭas, in the Kāvyamālā series (No. 71, Bombay, 1901), commences with 'fancy' (*pratibhā*), 'culture' (*vyutpatti*), and 'practice' (*abhyāsa*), and then goes on to deal with 'training' (*śikṣā*), pp. 8 sqq.—

" Non-mention of even the actual, mention of even " the not-actual, restriction, dependence in the form " of 'shadow and so on,' etc., are the trainings.

" *Of even the actual* : *i. e.*, of genus, substance, " quality, action, and so on, *non-mention*. *Of even the* " *not actual* : *i. e.*, of genus and so on, as before *men-* " *tion*. *Restriction* : *i. e.*, confining to one application " a more widely applicable genus and so on. '*Shadow-*

" *dependence*' by way of a sort of 'imaging,' 'painted " copy-sketch,' 'corporeal equivalence,' 'foreign- " city-entrance' likeness. In virtue of the *and so on* " dependence in word, line etc., as may seem proper, " upon another poem. In virtue of the *etc.*, filling- " up verses and so on. These are the trainings."

from Commentary (omitting illustrative verses):—

" *Shadow* : *i. e.*, of the sense. *Dependence* thereupon is " in some cases *by way of imaging* . . . as is said—

" Where the sense is the same entirely, but the setting is in other expressions,

" That poem, not fundamentally different, would be a sort of 'imaging.'

" In some cases by way of 'copy-sketch' . . . as is said—

" Through a moderate elaboration of particulars a subject appears as if different;

" Such a poem is by experts in the matter termed a 'copy-sketch.'

" In some cases by way of 'corporeal equivalence' . . . . . . as is said—

" Where despite difference of matter identity is apprehended through extreme resemblance,

" That poem, similar by 'corporeal equivalence,' even clever men compose.

" In some cases by way of 'foreign-city-entrance' likeness . . . . . . as is said—

" Where there should be substantial identity, but the garnishing is widely divergent,

" That poem, similar by 'foreign-city-entrance', may be enjoyed by good poets,

" And of these four the superiority is in ascending order.

The commentary then proceeds to illustrate the borrowing of a word, a line, two lines, three lines, but would not allow four lines (a whole verse), which it describes as complete theft. It then deals with the borrowing of part of a word, and of a phrase or saying (*ukti*), and continues:

> "Should it be apprehended that this (borrowing of a phrase or saying) should not be advised, since they say—
>
> "'By lapse of time a man's other thefts may pass;
> "'Word-theft passes not away even to sons and grandsons.'
>
> "This is met by the 'as may seem good' of the text. "'This man is unknown, I am known,' 'This man is "without position, I have position,' 'The putting "forward of this is inappropriate in him, appropriate "in me,' 'This man's words are like tonic (*guḍūcī*), "mine are like wine' (*i. e.*, our style and aim are "different), 'This man disregards the specialities "of dialect, I regard them,' 'This is obsolete,' 'This "had a foreign author,' 'This has a worn-out subject "(or 'occasion'),' 'This was composed by a mere "barbarian'—for these and such reasons you may "acquiesce in word-plunder and matter-plunder, so "says Avantisundarī. And they say—
>
> "'No poet-person but is a thief, no trader-person but is a thief:
> "'Without reproach he thrives who knows how to conceal.
>
> "'One poet is a creator, an adapter another,
> "'A coverer-up another, a developer.
> "'Whoso here in word, sense, saying, should discern somewhat novel,
> "'And copy something old, be he looked upon as a great poet.'"

We then proceed to deal with *samasyā* (filling-up verses), and the conventional ideas of poetry in detail.

The last part of this extract brings us close to the subject of plagiarism, that penumbra of literary craft. Literature, being a traditional, social, and developing art in which the new has to incorporte somehow and to imply the old, must always include this debatable borderland. It might be interesting to classify the cases, psychologically, ranging from unconscious suggestion, positive and negative to habitual harpyism and careers which are 'one long appropriation clause,' or according to the object appropriated, word, idea, quotation, use of a metre, subject and so forth. Our Indian theorist does not go far into the matter. It must be confessed that, though he stops short of 'I take what is good for me where I find it,' he allows his appropriator a fair latitude. But upon reflexion the reader will admit that in most of the excuses which he accepts there is a good deal of human nature, and that they have often prevailed in practice outside of India.

The thief proper was, however, clearly an apprehended danger, and his character is distinguished in a verse of Bāṇa's *Harṣacarita* (Introductory Verses, 6).

> "By modifying phrases and hiding the signs of authorship
>
> "The poet, unacknowledged among good men, is divined a thief."

But he figures in prefaces seldom in comparison with the poet's more usual enemies, the *khala*, or hostile critic, and the *piśuna*, the envious man.

What was the object that our poet set before himself, and what was the judgment to which he appealed? The oldest writers (except Bhāmaha), seem to have mentioned only fame (*kīrti*) and delight (*prīti*, *pramoda*, *ānanda*) as the purpose of poetry; and herewith Daṇḍin (I. 105), Vāmana (I. 5), Bhoja (I. 2), and Rudraṭa (I. 21-2), seem to be content. But before long it became customary (see Bhāmaha, ll. 2599, *Kāvyaprakāśa* I. 2, Vāgbhaṭa II., I. 2, *Sāhityadarpaṇa*, I. 2, *Ekāvali* I. 9, *Alaṅkāraśekhara* I. 1) to add 'wealth' (*dhana*), 'social accomplishment,' 'escape from ills,' 'instruction,' and generally the *trivarga* (profit, pleasure, virtue); later even the *caturvarga* (anticipated by Bhāmaha) which adds *mokṣa*, the liberation of the soul.

The *trivarga* or *caturvarga* is a consequence of the correct use of words, 'since a single word properly used and understood is a source of all good in this world and the next,' while 'instruction' is defined as like the teaching of a mistress *(kāntātulyatayopadeśa)*, 'Be like Rāma, not like Rāvaṇa,' in contrast with that of the scriptures and the sciences, which command as a lord or advise as a friend. This reminds us of Matthew Arnold's 'Charm is the poet's alone.' Some writers, like Vāgbhaṭa I., (I. 2) and Hemacandra (p. 4) demur to items of the traditional enumeration, commonly illustrated by examples, on the ground that such objects are not characteristic of poetry, but realizable by other means.

The Sanskrit poet was fully conscious of the truth contained in Horace's verse that there were 'kings before Agamemnon,' but that their names have perished for lack of a sacred poet. Daṇḍin writes (I. 5) that—

> "The image of the glory of ancient kings, through finding in speech a mirror,
> "Though they be no longer here, itself, behold, does not wane."

to the same effect Rudraṭa (I. v. 5)—

> "For when the fruit of their deeds, heaven, etc., is exhausted by time,
> "Not even the names of kings would exist, were there not good poets."

and an anthology verse runs (*Subhāṣitāvalī* v. 150, cf. also 160, 167, 186)—

> "The hundred-weights of gold, the throngs of rutting elephants
> "Bestowed by Great Harṣa upon Bāṇa's merits, where are they now?
> "But his glories, limned by Bāṇa in his flowing verse,
> "These pass not, I trow, even at the aeon's waning, to decay."

Indeed, it is plain that our poets looked in general to the favour of courts. Even their 'instruction as by a mistress' is designed for the "tender" minds of princes and great men, which might not tolerate the undiluted lessons of science and history. Lively pictures of such literary diversion at courts are familiar to us in the amusing *Bhojaprabandha* and in Hemacandra's *Prabandha-cintāmaṇi* (as also in Persian literature).

But the less exalted lover of literature is not overlooked. This is the *rasika* or *sahṛdaya*. Hemacandra defines him (p. 3)—

> "The *sahṛdaya* is one whose mind-mirror being made
> "spotless by practice in studying poetry, he has with
> "a sympathy of heart a fitness for identifying him-
> "self with the matter described;"

and he adds that 'the poet himself, who, according to Bhoja's commentator likewise (*Sarasvatīkaṇṭhābharaṇa*, I. 2), is also a spectator (*sāmājika*) of his own work, has taste of the sentiment (*rasa*) only in his enjoying phase, since being poet is apart from being enjoyer.' The anthologies express vividly the victorious effect of good poetry, as in (*Subhāṣitāvali* 163, cf. 158 and 165)—

> "What poetry is that that should not stir the heart, as if it had drunk much wine,
>
> "Should not by force of its sentiment thrill the hair even of those with minds befogged by envy,
>
> "Make the head tremble, the cheeks redden, the eyes fill with tears,
>
> "Mainstay the voice intent on chanting out the imagined theme?"

The poets and critics from whom these extracts have been taken were not employing a language that could be called dead, not even a language holding the position of Latin in Europe during the middle ages. In a sense they were artificial. They were carefully schooled; they practised assiduously, like Stevenson. They appealed to an instructed audience; and they were competitive. Hence we must not judge from a modern standpoint their adherence to old themes, their conventionality in ideas and expressions, of which a small selection is to be found in Dr. Otto Walter's *Ubereinstimmungen in Gedanken, Vergleichen und Wendungen beiden indischen Kunstdichtern von Vālmīki bis auf Māgha*, Leipzig, 190—(A dictionary of such things was long ago proposed by the writer of this paper). Undoubtedly they made ample use of their note-books and collectanea; and how many of the constant *śleṣas*, for instance, can boast a life of a thousand years! The envious man is always double-tongued like the snake and has poison in his mouth; the king's toe-nails are always polished by the jewels in the crowns of prostrate rivals; affection (*rāga*) is always redness (*rāga*), and fame is always whitening the heavens. This is the poetical convention (*saṅgati*), which naturally was the whole stock-in-trade of the poor poet (*kukavi*), who belonged only to the genus; when the great (*mahākavi*) or creative (*utpādaka*) poet makes use of such things, we must think of his audience, which knew them very well and concentrated its attention upon the new turn given to them, or the rival whom, as in the case of Māgha with Bhāravi, he was bent upon outdoing. He is engaged upon a work of art. Though his range is narrow, his fancy (*pratibhā*) is real and fertile, as any anthology will most abundantly show. His sentiment is not artificial or 'complicated', but natural. His work is, as he says, 'a special creation free from the laws of destiny' (*Kāvyaprakāśa*, I. 1); and so it is not 'life'; but in quality, form and content it is literature, which is more truly perhaps an antidote to life.

PRE-DHVANI SCHOOLS OF ALAṄKĀRA

BY V. V. SOVANI

IN the opening portion of Alaṅkārasarvasva Rājānaka Ruyyaka (Maṅkhaka, according to Pandit T. Ganapati Shastri of Trivandrum), before giving the view of the Dhvanikāra, briefly reviews the opinions of Bhāmaha, Rudraṭa, Vāmana, Udbhaṭa, Vakroktijīvitakāra, and Bhaṭṭanāyaka relating to the Dhvani doctrine to show the stage at which criticism had arrived before the advent of the Dhvani School. In the present paper an attempt has been made to show that there were three schools of criticism before the Dhvani school appeared on the horizon, viz. (1) the Rasa school, (2) the Vakrokti school or the school of Alaṅkāras, and (3) the Rīti school or the school of Guṇas.

Samudrabandha in his commentary[1] on the Alaṅkārasarvasva thus classifies the schools of criticism—

इह विशिष्टौ शब्दार्थौ काव्यम् । तयोश्च वैशिष्टचं धर्ममुखेन व्यापारमुखेन व्यङ्गचमुखेन वेति त्रयः पक्षाः । आद्येऽप्यलङ्कारतो गुणतो वेति द्वैविध्यम् । द्वितीयेऽपि भणितिवैचित्र्येण भोगकृत्त्वेन वेति द्वैधम् । इति पञ्चसु पक्षेष्वाद्य उद्भटादिभिरङ्गीकृतो द्वितीयो वामनेन तृतीयो वक्रोक्तिजीवितकारेण चतुर्थो भट्टनायकेन पञ्चम आनन्दवर्धनेन । व्यक्तिविवेककाराभिमतस्त्वनुमानपक्षः सिद्धान्तप्रदर्शनसमनन्तरं विचारासहत्वेन दूषितत्वाद् मङ्खुकस्य पूर्वपक्षत्वेनाप्यनाभिमत इत्याहुः । एषु प्रस्थानेषु स्वाभिमतं प्रस्थानं तस्य सर्वैरङ्गीकरणीयतां च दर्शयितुमेषामुपन्यासः ।

I will try to show that Vakroktijīvitakāra may be included in the Alaṅkāra school, as he merely elaborates Bhāmaha's Vakrokti.[2] Bhaṭṭanāyaka, on the other hand, is the exponent of Bharata's Rasa school, as will be shown presently. So the former views belong to the three different schools of criticism, obtaining before the rise of Dhvani.

The Rasa school: The oldest writer extant of this school is the sage Bharata, whose views we learn from chapters vi, vii and xvi of his Nāṭyaśāstra. Bharata's conception of poetry is dramatic,[3] and it is upheld by Vāmana in

1 Trivandrum Sanskrit Series edition, page 4. 2 Bhāmaha ii. 85.

3 Nāṭyaśāstra xvi. 118, always quoted from the Kāvyamālā edition.

i. 3. 30–32 and by Abhinavagupta in his commentary on the sixth chapter of the Nāṭyśāstra, where he says—काव्यं तावन्मुख्यतो दशरूपकात्मकमेव ।···सर्गन्बधादौ हि नायिकाया अपि संस्कृतैवोक्तिरित्यादि बहुतरमनुचितम्.

Bharata deals with Rasas and Bhāvas in chapters vi and vii and treats of 36 lakṣaṇas, 4 poetical tropes, and 10 poetical excellences in chapter xvii. Of these the 36 lakṣaṇas or dramatic embellishments were later included under alaṅkāras[1] or under guṇas and alaṅkāras.[2] Guṇas, doṣas and alaṅkāras were all subordinated to Rasas by Bharata.[3] That Rasa is predominant in poetry is seen from Bharata's statement[4]—न हि रसादृते कश्चिदर्थः प्रवर्तते. At the beginning of chapter vii Bharata says—वागङ्गसत्त्वोपेतान् काव्यार्थान् भावयन्तीति भावाः and Abhinavagupta in his commentary on the same explains it thus—काव्यस्यार्थो रसाः। अर्थ्यन्ते प्राधान्येनेत्यर्थः। न त्वर्थशब्दोऽभिधेयवाची। स्वशब्दानभिधेयत्वं हि रसानां ध्वनिकारादिभिर्दर्शितम्.

The genesis of Rasa is thus illustrated by Bharata[5]—अत्राह—यदाऽन्योन्यार्थसंभूतैर्विभावानुभावव्यञ्जितैरेकोनपञ्चाशता भावैः सामान्यगुणयोगेनाभिनिष्पद्यन्ते रसास्तत्कथं स्थायिन एव भावा रसत्वमाप्नुवन्ति। उच्यते ···। बह्वाश्रयत्वात्स्वामिभूताः स्थायिनो भावाः। ······। यथा नरेन्द्रो बहुजनपरिवारोऽपि स एव नाम लभते नान्यः सुमहानपि पुरुषस्तथा विभावानुभावव्यभिचारिपरिष्कृतः स्थायिभावो रसतां लभते. Here we may note that the underlined expressions anticipate the *vyañjanā* function of the Dhvani theory as also the *bhāvakatva* function advocated by Bhaṭṭanāyaka.

The Rasābhāsas do not seem to be formally recognised by Bharata, though he appears to have hinted at them,[6] as we learn from Abhinavagupta's commentary Abhinavabhāratī on the Nāṭyaśāstra, ch. vi, which is partially reproduced in the Dhvanyālokalocana.[7] We next meet with them in the Kavyālaṅkārasaṅgraha of Udbhaṭa (iv. 6) where they receive the designation *ūrjasvin*, and we encounter them

1 Kāvyādarśa ii. 367, and Daśarūpaka iv. 84 with Avaloka.

2 Sāhityadarpaṇa, ch. vi. p. 332, Durgaprasad's edition.

3 Nāṭyaśātra, xvi. 104.

4 Ch. vi. p. 62; cf. also Bharata vii. 7.

5 Ch. vii. p. 70.

6 Vide ch. vi. 40—शृङ्गारानुकृतिर्या तु स हासः।

7 Page 23 and 66, Nir. Sag. edition.

again in the Dhvanikārikā ii. 3, the first half of which is attributed to Śṛṅgāratilaka with a diffrent line for the latter half by the author of Pratāparudrayaśobhūṣaṇa.[1]

Before passing further we may note that according to Bharata, as interpreted by his commentator Abhinavagupta, Rasa was the very essence of Nāṭya. Abhinavagupta in explaining Nāṭya-rasa in the concluding portion of the prose, just before verse 33 of chapter vi, says—नाट्यात्समुदायरूपाद् रसाः । यदि वा नाट्यमेव रसाः रससमुदायः । नाट्य एव च रसाः । काव्येऽपि नाट्यायमान एव रसः काव्यार्थः ।

We also find the same in the Dhvanyāloka,[2] where Ānandvardhana says—एतच्च रसादितात्पर्येण काव्यनिबन्धनं भारतादावपि सुप्रसिद्धमेवेति प्रतिपादयितुमाह—scil. ध्वनिकारिका, ch. iii. 33, to support which statement Abhinavagupta in his Locana, p. 182, cites from Bharata—वृत्तयः काव्यमातृकाः (Nāṭyaśāstra, xx. 62, where we read वृत्तयो नाट्यमातरः). To depict Rasa, it is necessary to observe the rules of propriety (aucitya) and hence Bharata has laid down that the hero of a Nāṭaka must be well known and exalted.[3]

Bharata's lakṣaṇas are all illustrated in the Sāhityadarpaṇa under lakṣaṇas and nāṭyālaṅkāras by Viśvanātha.[4] The four poetical figures are illustrated with their subdivisions by Bharata himself.[5] Bharata's ten poetical defects may also be learnt from the third chapter of Daṇḍin's Kāvyādarśa. It is not so very easy, however, to understand very clearly what Bharata's guṇas actually mean. For example, Professor Hermann Jacobi[6] asserted that Bharata's prasāda guṇa was identical with Daṇḍin's samādhi guṇa, proposing to read 'mukhya' instead of 'mukha' in Bharata xvi. 95. It seems, however, that Bharata meant by prasāda 'a sly hint' or 'suggestion,' as illustrated by Prasannarāghavā, prologue, stanza 7, and is thus similar to the figure Mudrā of Candrāloka

1 Page 90, K. P. Trivedi's edition. 2 Ch. iii. p. 181.

3 Dhvanyāloka, ch. iii. p. 149 ; Nāṭyaśāstra xviii. 10.

4 Pages 316-332, Durgaprasad's edition.

5 Nāṭyaśāstra xvi. 41-82.

6 Z. D. M. G. lxiv. p. 138, continued footnote.

and Kuvalayānanda.[1] My view is based on the restatement of Bharata's view and its illustration in Hemacandra's Alaṅkāracūḍāmaṇi on his own Kāvyānuśāsana.[2] Bharata's ten poetical excellences are defined and illustrated, as contrasted with Vāmana's and Daṇḍin's, in the Alaṅkāracūḍā maṇi of Hemacandra, pages 195—200. As Hemacandra has largely borrowed from older works—such as the Kāvyamīmāṅsā of Rājaśekhara, chapters ix, xiv–xviii, Rudraṭa's Kāvyālaṅkāra (in Alaṅkāracūḍāmaṇi, chapters v and vii), Mahimabhaṭṭa's[3] Vyaktiviveka, Abhinavagupta's statement of the views of Bhaṭṭalollaṭa, Daṇḍin, Śrīśaṅkuka, Bhaṭṭanāyaka, Bhaṭṭatota and himself (as found in his commentary on the sixth chapter of the Nāṭyaśāstra in the course of the explanation of Rasalakṣaṇa)—therefore, I venture to think that this comparative view of Bharata's, Daṇḍin's, and Vāmana's guṇas also is based on some older and authoritative work, possibly the sixteenth chapter of Abhinavagupta's commentary on the Nāṭyaśāstra, which, among others, is wanting in the manuscript of the Trivandrum Palace Library.

Bharata's doctrine that Rasa is the essential factor in poetry is accepted by Rudrabhaṭṭa in his Śṛṅgāratilaka i. 5-6 and in the stanzas attributed to him in the Pratāparudrayaśobhūṣaṇa.[4] It is also accepted in the Agnipurāṇa,[5] in Rudraṭa's Kāvyālaṅkāra,[6] in Rājaśekhara's Kāvyamīmāṅsā Kavirahasya,[7] as well as in Bhojadeva's Sarasvatīkaṇṭhābharaṇa.[8] So all these may be said to belong to the Rasa school. Bhaṭṭanāyaka the author of Hṛdayadarpaṇa (a commentary on Bharata's Nāṭyaśāstra, as appears from the opening portion of the Abhinavabhāratī) holds practically the same view, as may be inferred from Abhinavagupta's observations in Locana.[9] Professor H. Jacobi says in the Introduction (pages 5 and 17) to his translation

1 Vide pages 146–147, Nirnayasagar edition.
2 Page 196, Kāvyamālā edition.
3 Pages 43-55, Trivandrum Sans. Series edition.
4 Pages 90 and 334–335 in K. P. Trivedi's edition.
5 Chapter 336 verse 33, chapter 338 verses 9-11.
6 Chap. xii. 2, as explained by Namisādhu.
7 Chap. iii. p. 6.
8 Chap. v. 8.
9 Pp. 11, 12, 15 68.

of Dhvanyāloka that Udbhaṭa also held that Rasa was predominant in poetry, as can be seen from Kāvyālaṅkāra-saṅgraha vi. 17. Now on the 77th page of the Nirnayasagar edition of the same, we see that the above-mentioned verse is not from Udbhaṭa, but is a citation from some other writer in Pratīhārendurāja's vṛtti, as it is introduced by तदाहुः. Further the verse can have no logical place in Udbhaṭa's Compendium as Samudrabandha in his commentary on the Alaṅkārasarvasva (page 4) says distinctly that Udbhaṭa gives prominence to alaṅkāras. Lastly Udbhaṭa has included Rasavat, Preyaḥ, and Ūrjasvin among alaṅkāras. Hence Udbhaṭa belongs to the Alaṅkāra school. Udbhaṭa was the Sabhāpati of king Jayāpīḍa of Kāśmīra (779-813 A. D.), as accepted by Professor H. Jacobi in his paper, *On the Vakrokti and the Antiquity of Dandin.*[1]

I have spoken of the *Rasa school of Bharata*, because Bharata has made guṇas, doṣas, and alaṅkāras subordinate to Rasa on the ground that they constitute the *vācika abhinaya* or *anubhāva*, which necessarily calls forth Rasa, as can be seen from the Rasalakṣaṇasūtra[2] and also the definitions of anubhāva (vii. 5), and abhinaya (viii. 6) and its subdivisions (viii. 9). Vācika abhinaya is treated by Bharata in chapters xiv-xx; and chapter xvi, which deals with lakṣaṇas, alaṅkāras, doṣas and guṇas, comes naturally under vācika abhinaya. The Dhvani school as well as Bhaṭṭanāyaka's Hṛdayadarpaṇa are in agreement with Bharata on this point, and may be said to have only developed the teaching of Bharata, as can be seen from the passage from Nāṭyaśāstra, chapter vii, cited above. Even Mahimabhaṭṭa says in Vyaktiviveka[3]—काव्यस्यात्मनि सञ्ज्ञिनि रसादिरूपे न कस्यचिद्विमतिः. The only difference between the Dhvanikāra, Bhaṭṭanāyaka, and Mahimabhaṭṭa was as regards the *function par excellence* which is operative in poetry.

Bharata's Nāṭyaśāstra stands at the beginning of the Christian era and may be much older, as shown by

1 Z. D. M. G. Vol. xliv, page 138.

2 Chapter vi, page 62.

3 Page 22, Trivandrum Sanskrit Series edition.

Professor E. J. Rapson in his article 'Drama (Indian)' in the Encyclopædia of Religion and Ethics.[1] Rudrabhaṭṭa seems to be considered as the predecessor of Rudraṭa,[2] and Rudraṭa is assigned to the middle of the ninth century A. D. by Professor R. Pischel in the Introduction to his edition of the Śṛiṅgāratilaka (pp. 12 and 26), a date accepted by Professor H. Jacobi and confirmed by Rājaśekhara's mention[3] of Rudraṭa's Kākuvakrokti figure (Rudraṭa ii. 16). The treatment of poetics in Agnipurāṇa, chapters 336-347, knows not the Dhvani theory at all and therefore its treatment of poetics is of the Pre-dhvani stage, like that of Rudrabhaṭṭa's Śṛṅgāratilaka and Rudraṭa's Kāvyālaṅkāra. Further Ānandavardhana cites two verses on page 222 of the Dhvanyāloka which are found in Agnipurāṇa, chapter 338, stanzas 10-11; and chapter 344, stanzas 14-15. Dhvani or Ākṣepa is given as a Śabdārthālaṅkāra, while the Kavirājamārga of Nṛpatuṅga or Amoghavarṣa, written shortly after 814 A. D.,[4] mentions Dhvani as a figure of speech, as shown by Professor K. B. Pathak in his edition of the work in the Bibliotheca Carnatica: Bhaṭṭanāyaka's Hṛdayadarpaṇa, Rājaśekhara's Kāvyamīmāṅsā, and Bhojadeva's Sarasvatīkaṇṭhābharaṇa are, on the other hand, all later than the Dhvanikāra, as they all notice the views of Ānandavardhana, the author of Dhvanyāloka. Mahimabhaṭṭa's Vyaktiviveka is professedly a criticism of Dhvanyāloka.

The Alaṅkāra school: The oldest extant writer of this School is Bhāmaha whose work, the Kāvyālaṅkāra, has been published as an Appendix in Mr. Trivedi's edition of the Pratāparudrayaśobhuṣaṇa. Bhāmaha is to be placed before Daṇḍin, as shown by Professor H. Jacobi in his article on Vakrokti above cited. Mr. Trivedi also

1 Volume 4, page 886, §§ 3 and 4.

2 Translation of Dhvanyāloka, pages 56-57, footnoote 3.

3 In his Kāvyamīmāṅsā Kavirahasya, page 31, Gaekwad Oriental Series edition.

4 Vide Journal B. B. R. A. S. Vol. xx, p. 304.

has collected presumptive evidence for the same in his Introduction to Pratāparudriya and Bhāmaha, (pp. xxxii-xxxv). The mention of the Nyāsakāra by Bhāmaha in vi. 36-37 need not disturb the above conclusion, because in the Harṣacarita of Bāṇa we find on page 86(Nir. Sag. ed.)—कृतगुरुपदन्यासा: which is explained in Śaṅkara's Saṅketa as—कृतोऽभ्यस्तो गुरुपदे दुर्बोधशब्दे न्यासो वृत्तिर्विवरणं (sic. वृत्तिविवरणं) यैः. Hence it follows that Bāṇa clearly refers to the Nyāsa on Pāṇinisūtravṛtti, from which we can see that it was already studied in the earlier part of the seventh century A. D. by students of Pāṇini. Bhāmaha seems to refer in iii. 55 to Raghu xiv. 7–8, and in i. 42f. to Meghadūta and hence is probably later than Kālidāsa (who, according to Professor K. B. Pāthak[1], flourished in the latter half of the fifth century A. D.). Bhāmaha therefore is probably of the same age as Bāṇa, because Bhaṭṭi seems in xxii. 34 to allude to Bhāmaha ii. 20. Further Bhaṭṭi seems in canto x to illustrate Bhāmaha's figures of word and sense, in canto xi his mādhuryaguṇa, in canto xii his Bhāvika alaṅkāra as the pre-eminent excellence of composition, in canto xiii his Sanskrit and Prākrit Kāvya and in cantos x-xiii his Prasādaguṇa as shown by Jayamaṅgalā thereon, which confirms the same thing. Now Bhaṭṭi lived at the end of the sixth and towards the beginning of the seventh century A. D., as stated by Professor H. Jacobi in his paper above referred to.

The main point of difference between Bharata's system and Bhāmaha's school is that while according to Bharata the all-absorbing element of poetry is Rasa (Nāṭyaśāstra vii. 7), it is Vakrokti according to Bhāmaha (Bhāmahālaṅkāra ii. 85), Vakrokti being the basal principle of all Alaṅkāras, among which Rasas also are included. Bhāmaha's idea of Vakrokti can be clearly understood from Bhāmahālaṅkara i. 23, 34, 36 ; ii. 85–86 ; v. 66 ; vi. 23, in addition to ii. 81–84. In vi. 23 Bhāmaha characterises poetic speech as *vakra*, and in i. 5. a poet is said to be 'one who possesses Imagination.' From ii. 81 we can see

1 Vide his Introduction to his second edition of Mehghadūta, p xi.

that *vakra* connotes 'addressing itself to superhuman images, which exist only in the poet's world,' as becomes quite clear from Pratīhārendurāja's exposition.[1] In i. 30 Bhāmaha says that all the subdivisions of poetry mentioned by him in i. 16–30 are admissible to the designation of Kāvya in so far as they possess *vakrasvabhāvokti* or imaginative speech. In ii. 86 Bhāmaha says that Hetu, Sūkṣma, and Leśa are not poetic figures, since they are not enlivened by Vakrokti. The following from Rasagaṅgādhara[2] throws light on Bhāmaha's position—

अत्र वदन्ति । काव्यलिङ्गं नालङ्कारः । वैचित्र्यात्मनो विच्छित्तिविशेषस्याभावात् । सं हि जन्यतासंसर्गेण कविप्रतिभाविशेषस्तन्निर्मितत्वप्रयुक्तश्चमत्कृतिविशेषो वेति उक्तम् । न चानयोरन्यतरस्याप्यत्र संभवः । हेतुहेतुमद्भावस्य वस्तुसिद्धत्वेन कविप्रतिभानिर्वर्तितत्वायोगात् ।

Udbhaṭa accepts Kāvyaliṅga as a figure (vi. 7).

The charming feature of a composition is called by Bhāmaha (iii. 52) the figure Bhāvika, which visualises objects both past and future. The sources of this life-like representation are the prespicuity of language, excellent acting and striking, exalted and novel ideas (Bhāmaha iii. 53). Now the prespicuity of language is the *prasāda guṇa* of Bhāmaha ii. 3. The other factors of Bhāvika originate in *atiśayokti* or *vakrokti* ; for, according to Bhāmaha (ii. 85) objects are discovered to our vision by Vakrokti (सैषा सर्वत्र वक्रोक्तिरनयाऽर्थो विभाव्यते), or are rendered suitable factors of Rasa. Both these senses seem to be justified, because in Nāṭyaśāstra chapter vii Bharata says—विभावितं विज्ञातमित्यनर्थान्तरम् while Abhinavagupta says in his Dhvanyālokalocana (page 208)—प्रमदोद्यानादिर्विभावतां नीयते विशेषेण च भाव्यते रसमयीक्रियत इति—while explaining Bhāmahas's सैषा सर्वत्र वक्रोक्तिरनयाऽर्थो विभाव्यते. Bhāmaha has used *vibhāvyate* in this double sense in order that the Alaṅkāras and the Rasas may both originate in Vakrokti. Vākrokti first renders objects vivid to the imagination, and subsequently the Rasas are rendered *apparent* (रसवद्दर्शितस्पष्टश्रृङ्गारादि रसम्—

1 Kāvyālaṅkārasaṅgraha, pp. 40–42, Nir. Sagar edition.

2 Page 470, Kāvyamālā edition.

Bhāmaha iii. 6). This is further elucidated by Abhinavagupta's observation[1] in Locana, paga 69,—काव्येऽपि च लोकनाट्यधर्मिस्थानीये स्वभावोक्तिवक्रोक्तिप्रकारद्वयेनालौकिकप्रसन्नमधुरौजस्विशब्दसमर्प्यमाणविभावादियोगादियमेव रसवार्ता, and by Alankārasarvasvakāra's observation—स्फुटप्रतीत्युत्तरकालं तु साधारण्यप्रतीतौ स्फुटप्रतीतिनिमित्तक औत्तरकालिको रसवदलङ्कारः स्यात्. However, Bhāmaha did not consider that Rasa was invariably present in a poem. What must be present in a poem as such is Vākrokti or imaginative speech only (Bhāmaha i. 30). The following observations of Jagannātha[2] shed further light on Bhāmaha's view—

काव्यजीवितं चमत्कारित्वं चावशिष्टमेव । ... । यत्तु रसवदेव काव्यमिति साहित्यदर्पणे निर्णीतम् तन्न । वस्त्वलङ्कारप्रधानानां काव्यानामकाव्यत्वापत्तेः । न चेष्टापत्तिः । महाकविसम्प्रदायस्याकुलीभावप्रसङ्गात् ।

Hence Jagannātha[3] defined Kāvya as रमणीयार्थप्रतिपादकः शब्दः while Bhāmaha's definition[4] is शब्दार्थौ सहितौ काव्यं युक्तं वक्रस्वभावोक्त्या.

Bhāmaha does not distinguish between Guṇas and Alaṅkāras, because he calls the Bhāvika figure a Guṇa as well.[5] This is made explicit[6] by his commentator thus—समवायवृत्त्या शौर्यादयः संयोगवृत्त्या तु हारादय इत्यस्तु गुणालङ्काराणां भेदः । ओजःप्रभृतीनामनुप्रासोपमादीनां चोभयेषामपि समवायवृत्त्या स्थितिरिति गड्डलिकाप्रवाहेणैवेषां भेद इति. However, Udbhaṭa (iv. 2, 6, 8) differs from Bhāmaha (iii. 5, 7, 10) regarding प्रेयः, ऊर्जस्विन्, and समाहित. Udbhaṭa further considers that Bhāvas are indicated by their own names, by their factors, by their ensuants, and by the accessories singly or collectively, while Rasas are indicated by their names, factors, ensuants, accessories, and permanent feelings singly or collectively.[7]

Vakroktijīvitakāra[8] has further developed the Vakroti

1 Page 180, Kāvyamālā ed. 2 Rasagaṅgādhara, Kāvyamālā ed., p. 7

3 Ibid. page 4. 4 Bhāmaha, i. 16 and i. 30. 5 Ibid. iii. 32.

6 Mammaṭa, Kāvyaprakāśa chapter viii, pages 566–570, Zalkikar's 2nd ed. Vide also Alaṅkāracūḍāmaṇi by Hemacandra, Kāvyamālā, p. 17.

7 Kāvyālaṅkārasaṅgraha, pages 48-49.

8 See Alaṅkārasarvasva p. 8 (Kāvyamālā ed.) with Jayaratha thereon, pp. 8-9 with Samudrabandha thereon; also Vyaktiviveka, pages 28 37, 58 and 64; and Vyaktivivekavicāra pages 16, 36, 37 and 43–44. Vakroktijīvitakāra is also alluded to by Kāmadhenu, page 6, on Vāmana I.i. 1.

of Bhāmaha, so as to make it cover the entire domain of Dhvani. From Alaṅkāravimarśinī of Jayaratha,[1] we learn that Vakroktijīvitakāra *Kuntaka* (Vyaktivivekavicāra, pp. 16 and 32) rejected such figures as Yathāsaṅkhya on the same grounds as those of Bhāmaha (ii. 86).

Dhvanyālokalocana thus criticises[2] the doctrine of Vakrokti—यदि तावदतिशयोक्तेः सर्वालङ्कारेषु सामान्यरूपता सा तर्हि तादात्म्यपर्यवसायिनीति तदव्यतिरिक्तो नैवालङ्कारो दृश्यत इति कविप्रतिभानं न तत्रापेक्षणीयं स्यात्। अलङ्कारमात्रं च न किंचिद् दृश्यते। अथ सा काव्यजीवितत्वेन तु विवक्षिता। तथाप्यनौचित्येपि निबध्यमाना तथा स्यात्। औचित्यवती जीवितमिति चेद् औचित्यनिबन्धनं रसभावादि मुक्त्वा नान्यत्किञ्चिदस्तीति तदेवान्तर्भासि मुख्यं जीवितमित्यभ्युपगन्तव्यं न तु सा।

Vakroktijīvitakāra is later in age than Dhvanikāra, as stated by Jayaratha.[3]

The Rīti school: The chief writers of this school were Daṇḍin and Vāmana. Daṇḍin is already shown to be posterior to Kālidāsa and belongs to the latter half of seventh century, after Christ.[4] Vāmana is said to be identical with the minister of king Jayāpīḍa of Kāśmīra (779–813 A.D.) by Professor H. Jacobi in his paper above referred to.

The doctrine of Rīti was older than Bhāmaha, who refers to the Vaidarbha and Gauḍīya styles of poetry (Bhāmaha i. 31–36) as recognised by writers on poetics who prefered the former in spite of many excellent ideas in the latter. Bhāmaha (i. 34) says that a Vaidarbha kāvya is merely melodious to the ear like singing, is naive, tender, transparent but wanting in imaginative expressions and charming ideas. That this description of Vaidarbhī by Bhāmaha was not off the point is seen[5] from the dictum—

1 Alaṅkārasarvasva, page 8. 2 Page 208, Kāvyamālā ed.

3 Alaṅkāravimarśinī, Kāvyamālā, p. 12.

4 Professor K. B. Pathak in his Introduction to the second edition of Meghadūta, page xiii, citing Indian Antiquary for 1912, page 237.

5 Compare also the vṛtti on Alaṅkārasūtra i. 2. 21 and Bihlaṇa in Vikramāṅkadevacarita i. 9.

विपञ्चीस्वरसौभाग्या वैदर्भी रीतिरिष्यते—in Vāmanavṛtti on Alaṅkāra-sūtra i. 2. 11.

Daṇḍin was the first, as far as we know, to distinguish between the Vaidarbhī and the Gauḍiyā and to show that the former was for very good reasons adjudged the better of the two (Kāvyādarśa i. 41–100). Other writers like Rudraṭa (ii. 5–6) considered that the Vaidarbhī was devoid of any Samāsas or compounds, while Gauḍīyā had the longest compounds. This does not seem to be the case, because in the Kāvyādarśa i. 84, which gives an illustration of Vaidarbhī style, there is a long compound extending over the first half of the stanza, although the compond is easily understood and elegant.[1] Daṇḍin thus contrasts the two styles of poetry—Vaidarbhī is well-knit, intelligible, even, chiming, mild, compact, and heightened ; while the Gauḍiyā is highly alliterative, stiff, non-harmonious, harsh, impetuous, bombastic, and exaggerated. Kānti or heightened speech which, Daṇḍin says, is a Guṇa of the Vaidarbhī style,is thus contrasted with Atyukti or exaggeration of the Gauḍīyā style.[2] This Kānti of Daṇḍin is the Atiśayokti or Vakrokti of Bhāmaha, chastened by propriety, as we can see from Dhvanyāloka and Dhvanyālokalocana, pages 207–208. So we see that what was considered essential in poetry was an Alaṅkāra for Bhāmaha, while the same, chastened by propriety, was considered a Guṇa by Daṇḍin. Further, Daṇḍin considered that Samādhi or metaphor, which he thought of as a Guṇa[3] was the all-in-all in poetry[4] and was observed by all the poets.

The ten poetic excellences were considered as the very life or breath of the Vaidarbhī style, while poetic tropes were considered as the attributes of poetry which contributed to its grace. Poetry was defined by Daṇḍin as a set of words, regulated by agreeable sense or idea.[5] The definition of poetry by Daṇḍin is very close to Jagannātha's definition in Rasagaṅgādhara.[6]

Daṇḍin's conception of Rasa was objective and was

1 Kāvyādarśa i. 83.
2 i. Ibid, 85-92.
3 Ibid, i. 93.
4 Ibid, i. 100.
5 Ibid, i. 10.
6 Page 4, Kāv. ed.

the same as Bhaṭṭalollaṭa's, as explained by Abhinavagupta in the Abhinavabhāratī on chapter vi of Bharata's Nāṭyaśāstra, where he says—एवं क्रमहेतुमभिधाय रसविषयलक्षणसूत्रमाह— विभावानुभावव्यभिचारिसंयोगाद् रसनिष्पत्तिः । अत्र भट्टलोल्लटप्रभृतयस्तावदेवं व्याचख्युः । विभावादिभिः संयोगः अर्थात्स्थायिनस्ततो रसानिष्पत्तिः । अत्र विभावश्चित्तवृत्तेः स्थाय्या(त्मिका)या उत्पत्तौ कारणमनुभावाश्च न रसजन्या अत्र विवक्षिताः । तेषां रसकारणत्वेन गणनानर्हत्वात् । अपि तु भावानामेव येऽनुभावा व्यभिचारिणः (ते) चित्तवृत्त्यात्मकत्वाद्यद्यपि न सहभाविनः स्थायिना तथापि वासनात्मतेह विवक्षिता । दृष्टान्तेऽपि व्यञ्जनादिमध्ये कस्यचिद्वासनात्मता स्थायिवदन्यस्योद्भूतता व्यभिचारिवत् । तेन स्थाय्येव विभावानुभावादिभिरुपचितो रसः स्थायी भवत्वनु(प)चितः । स चोभये (मुख्यया वृत्त्या रामादाव)नुकार्येनुऽकर्तर्यविचारानुसन्धानबलादिति'। चिन्तरानानाश्चा(sic. चिरन्तनानाञ्चा)यमेव पक्षः । तथाहि दण्डिनाऽस्यालङ्कारलक्षणेऽभ्यधायि—रतिः शृङ्गारताङ्गता । (प)रूपबाहुल्ययोगेनेति (Kāvyādarśa, ii. 281), अधिरुह्य परां कोटिं कोपो रौद्रात्मतां गतः (Ibid, ii. 283) इत्यादि.[1] This objective view of Rasa, namely that it was produced in the original hero primarily and in the actor secondarily, and was developed by factors, ensuants, and accessory feelings, otherwise remaining as instinct—was responsible for the subordinate position given to Rasa in the Alaṅkāra school as well as the Rīti school.

It was Vāmana, who perfected the system of Daṇḍin, and who is considered the authority in the Rīti school. In his Vṛtti on Alaṅkārasūtra I. i. 1, Vāmana says—काव्यशब्दोऽयं गुणालङ्कारसंस्कृतयोः शब्दार्थयोर्वर्तते । भक्त्या तु शब्दार्थमात्रवचनोऽत्रगृह्यते. Now of the two embellishers Guṇas and Alaṅkāras, Guṇas are the essential factors of poetic charm, which is only heightened by poetic tropes (Alaṅkārasūtra III. i. 1-3). According to Vāmana I. 2. 6 (रीतिरात्मा काव्यस्य) 'style is the soul of poetry.' Kāmadhenu[2] thus explains the aphorism—व्याचष्टे—रीतिर्नामेति । रिणन्ति गच्छन्ति अस्यां गुणा इति रीयते क्षरत्यस्यां वाङ्मधुधारेति वा रीतिः । अधिकरणार्थे क्तिन् प्रत्ययः । करङ्कगात्रकल्पकर्कशतर्कवाक्यवैलक्षण्यप्रकटनप्रगल्भस्फुरत्ताहेतुः कश्चन स्वभावोऽत्रात्मेति उच्यते. Rīti is thus that distinct character of poetry which sharply separates it from philosophical writings, which are harsh and wanting in life as a dead body. Rīti is further defined and analysed in i. 2. 7-8 as—विशिष्टा पदरचना रीतिः । विशेषो गुणात्मा.

1. Vide page 57 of the Alaṅkāracūḍāmaṇi of Hemacandra on his own Kāvyānuśāsana, where this is reproduced almost verbatim.

2 Kāvyālaṅkārasūtravṛtti with Kāmadhenu, pp. 15-16, Vāṇīvilāsa ed.

Vāmana said perhaps that it was no doubt true that we did not find distinct Rasa in every poetical piece, and hence if our investigation included into its domain all varieties of poetry, we must make our definition wide enough to cover the sphere of those varieties of poetry also, which developed no Rasa. He, however, emphasized the necessity of distinguishing between those characteristics of poetry which are quite essential, and those which are of secondary importance. These essential characteristics he further divided into verbal or formal, and material. The verbal attributes prepare a suitable vehicle for poetic images, so that even a slightly charming idea is greatly appreciated when conveyed by the elegant style Vaidarbhī.[1]

Vāmana made a great advance over the Alaṅkāra school by including Rasas among the necessary characteristics of poetry. Daṇḍin had allowed Rasas to be included among Alaṅkāras.[2] He had meant by Mādhurya absence of vulgarity[3] and did not contemplate the inclusion of Rasas under Mādhurya as he himself explicily says in ii. 292. Now Vāmana, who had great partiality for dramatic poetry[4] saw that Rasas were among the essential properties of poetry and included them under Kānti.[5] Absence of vulgarity was considered as essential but was included under Udāṛatā.[6]

Another improvement he made, which is also important to note. Daṇḍin had included Bhāvika, the property of the entire composition, among the Alaṅkāras, just as Bhāmaha did in Kāvyālaṅkāra iii. 52–53. The Bhāvika of Daṇḍin (ii. 364–366) was analysed into the Arthagunas, Śleṣa (iii. 2. 4) the fifth variety of Ojas (iii. 2. 2, vṛtti), Samatā (iii. 2. 5), Samādhi (iii. 2. 6-9) Mādhurya (iii. 2. 10), and lastly Arthavyakti (iii. 2. 13).

The Rīti school is given the credit of having dimly

1 Alaṅkārasūtra i. 2. 21.

2 Kāvyādarśa ii. 275; ii. 280–292.

3 Ibid. i. 51, i. 62, and ii. 292.

4 Alaṅkārasūtra i. 3. 30-33.

5 Ibid. iii. 2. 14.

6 Ibid. iii. 2. 12.

perceived the true nature of poetry by the Dhvanikāra.[1] The criticism which Mammaṭa has made on Vāmana's view[2] is not very convincing ; and Mammaṭa's own system is open to a similar criticism, as is clearly shown by Kāmadhenu.[3] The difference between the Dhvani school and the Rīti school is thus summarised by Kāmadhenu[4]—रीतिध्वनिवादमतयोरियांस्तु भेदः—तत्र प्रथमे रीतिरात्मा काव्यस्य तद्व्यवहारप्रयोजका गुणाः । चरमे तु ध्वनिरात्मा स एव तद्व्यवहारप्रयोजक इति । उभयत्राप्यात्मनिष्ठा गुणाः । शब्दार्थयुगलं शरीरम् । तन्निष्ठा अलङ्कारा इति च सर्वमविशिष्टम् ।

Both the Alaṅkāra school and the Guṇa school have left their impression on the Kāvyaprakāśa of Mammaṭa, as can be seen from Mammaṭa's definition of Kāvya (i. 4). The Kāvyaprakāśa is considered the standard work on the Dhvani system of poetics, and therefore the commentators try to justify its views everywhere. However, here the commentators have not quite succeeded in showing the consistency of the definition.[5] The definition becomes quite intelligible when we remember that Mammaṭa was influenced by Vāmana (III. i. 1–3), although no doubt Mammaṭa considered Guṇas as primarily attributes of Rasas and only secondarily of letters.[6] To a less extent he was influenced by the Alaṅkāra school, as he allows a Kāvya to be devoid of Alaṅkāras in a few cases.[7] However Bhāmaha's Vakrokti does appear in Kāvyaprakāśa, under the name of Prauḍhokti[8]—प्रौढोक्तिमात्रनिष्पन्नशरीरोऽर्थशक्त्युद्भवो ध्वनिः ।

1 Dhvanyāloka, Kāvyamālā edition, iii. 52, page 231.

2 Kāvyaprakāśa, chapter viii, pages 571–572 (Bom. Sk. Series) 2nd ed.

3 On Vāmana's Alaṅkārasūtra iii. 1. 4 on pages 72-73 of the Kāvyālaṅkārasūtravṛtti, Vāṇīvilāsa edition.

4 Ibid. page 72. 5 Vide Zalkikar's second edition, pages 19–21.

6 Vide Kāvyaprakāśavṛtti on viii. 1. 7 Kāvyaprakāśa i. 4.

8 Chapter iv. pages 160-161, as also Dhvanyāloka, pages 105–106.

SOME NOTES ON BHĀMAHA

BY K. P. TRIVEDĪ

THE oldest writer[1] on poetics whose work is at present available is Bhāmaha. He is quoted with great reverence by learned authors like Ānandavardhana, Abhinavagupta, Mammaṭa, Hemacandra, Jayamaṅgalākāra, Pratihārendurāja, and others; and is given the first place among old Ālaṅkārikas by Alaṅkārasarvasvakāra,[2] Vidyādhara,[3] and Vidyānātha.[4] The object of this paper is to make a somewhat critical survey of Bhāmaha's work[5] with a view to examine the grounds on which he is held in such great reverence by subsequent authors of profound learning.

The broad line of distinction between ancient and later Ālaṅkārikas is that the former attach much importance to the *guṇas* and the *alaṅkāras*. The suggested sense in their opinion goes simply to contribute to the beauty of the expressed sense, which is predominant. Owing to this undue importance attached by them to the *alaṅkāras*, the very works of Bhāmaha and Udbhaṭa go by the names of "Kāvyālaṅkāra" and and "Kāvyālaṅkārasārasaṅgraha" respectively.

Bhāmaha has divided his work into six *paricchedas* or sections. At the end of his work he enumerates the subjects that he has dwelt upon in these sections. Five topics have been treated in six sections as under—

1 That he is older than Daṇḍin is clearly shown by me in the Introduction to my edition of the *Pratāparudrayaśobhūṣaṇa* in the Bombay Sanskrit Series and also in my article on the "Priority of Bhāmaha to Daṇḍin" in the Indian Antiquary, Vol. XLII, October 1913, pp. 258-264.

2 इह हि तावद्भामहोद्भटप्रभृतयश्चिरंतनालंकारकाराः प्रतीयमानमर्थं वाच्योपस्कारकतयालंकारपक्षनिक्षिप्तं मन्यन्ते । अलं० सर्व०, p. 3.

3 यत् पुनरलंकारकोटिनिविष्टत्वं वस्तुध्वनेरुद्भावयन् भामहादयस्तदपि विचारविधुरम् । एका० p. 30 (Bom. Sans. Series).

4 पूर्वेभ्यो भामहादिभ्यः सादरं विहिताञ्जलिः । प्रताप०, p. 4 (Bom. Sans. Series).

5 The *Kāvyālaṅkāra*, printed as an Appendix to my edition of the Pratāparudra.

1 *Kāvyaśarīra* or the body of poetry, in 60 verses;
2 *Alaṅkāras* or figures of speech, in 160 verses;
3 *Doṣas* or demerits in composition, in 50 verses;
4 *Nyāyanirṇaya* or settling the logic of poetry, in 70 verses; and
5 *Śabdaśuddhi* or grammatical purity, in 60 verses.

The importance of the cultivation of good poetry is very well shown by Bhāmaha in the following verse—

धर्मार्थकाममोक्षेषु वैचक्षण्यं कलासु च।
प्रीतिं करोति कीर्तिं च साधुकाव्यनिबन्धनम्॥

Mammaṭa's well known verse काव्यं यशसेऽर्थकृते° exactly corresponds to this. The only additional idea in it is that poetry instructs a man gently and lovingly, like a beloved. In his *Ekāvalī* Vidyādhara shows that the Vedas are प्रभुसंमित—like a lord—owing to the authoritative manner in which they direct the reader to follow certain rules, and are शद्बप्रधान—having words as predominant—since even a slight change of words in them would be productive of sins;[1] that mythological works are मित्रसंमित—like a friend—since they advise us in a friendly way, and are अर्थप्रधान—having sense as predominant; and that lastly poetry is कान्तासंमित—like a beloved—since it advises us in a delicate manner, and is ध्वनिप्रधान—having the suggested sense as predominant, words and their primary sense being both made subordinate to the powers of suggestion.[2]

Abhinavagupta's remarks on the verse धर्मार्थकाममोक्षेषु° are worth reading.[3] He observes that though the cultivation of poetry gives proficiency (vyutpatti) in arts, the most prominent fruit of its cultivation is pleasure. What is meant to assert is that vyutpatti or proficiency comes from the study or the cultivation of other works of literature also, but poetry gives pleasure in addition to it. The

1 ईषत्पाठान्यथापाठे प्रत्यवायस्य दर्शनात्--*Ekāvalī*, Bom. Sans. Series, p. 13.

2 शद्बार्थौ गुणतां नीत्वा व्यञ्जनप्रवणं यतः—Ibid., p. 15.

3 श्रोतॄणां व्युत्पत्तिर्यद्यप्यस्ति यथोक्तम्—धर्मार्थकाम° इति तथापि प्रीतिरेव प्रधानम्। अन्यथा प्रभुसंमितेभ्यो वेदादिभ्यो मित्रसंमितेभ्यश्चेतिहासादिभ्यो कोऽस्य काव्यरूपस्य व्युत्पत्तिहेतोर्जायासंमितत्वलक्षणो विशेष इति प्राधान्येनानन्द एव उक्तः। चतुर्वर्गव्युत्पत्तेरपि चानन्द एव पार्यन्तिकं मुख्यं फलम्। ध्वन्या० p. 12.

English poet Cowper has very well expressed this pleasure on the part of poets even when their work of the selection of appropriate words is beset with great trouble. His excellent lines are worth quoting—

> There is a pleasure in poetic pains
> Which only poets know. The shifts and turns,
> The expedients and inventions multiform
> To which the mind resorts, in chase of terms,
> Though apt, yet coy and difficult to win,
>
> . . . .
>
> Are occupations of the poet's mind
> So pleasing and that steal away the thought
> With such address from themes of sad import,
> That, lost in his own-musings, happy man !
> He feels the anxieties of life, denied
> Their wonted entertainment,—all retire.

Bhāmaha winds up his first section by similar ideas, comparing the work of poets to that of a garland-maker, in as much as both have to take up what is good and reject what is bad and to select proper places for proper objects. His concluding verse is—

> एतद्ग्राह्यं सुरभिकुसुमं ग्राम्यमेतान्निधेयं
> धत्ते शोभां विरचितमिदं स्थानमस्यैतदस्य ।
> मालाकारो रचयति यथा साधु विज्ञाय मालां
> योज्यं काव्येष्ववहितधिया तद्वदेवाभिधानम् ॥

Lord Macaulay in his Essay on Milton expresses the same idea when he speaks of the magical influence of poetry. He says—"We often hear of the magical influence of poetry. The expression in general means nothing; but applied to the writings of Milton, it is most appropriate. His poetry acts like an incantation.........Change the structure of the sentence, substitute one synonym for another and the whole effect is destroyed." This felicity of expression—the unchangeableness of words—is what Sanskrit writers on poetics call *maitrī*, *śayyā*, or *pāka*. Vidyānātha's definition of *śayyā* is—

> या पदानां परान्योन्यमैत्री शय्येति कथ्यते । प्रता° p. 67.

It is the repose of words in their mutual favourableness like the repose of the body in a bed. The mutual friendship of words so close that they cannot be replaced by their synonyms constitutes what is called *śayyā*. Mallinātha[1] explains it as under—

पदानां परिवृत्तिवैमुख्यं विनिमयासहिष्णुत्वम् । एतदेव मैत्री शय्येति चाख्यायते यथास्मदीयश्लोके चंद्रोदये—

निशाकरकरस्पर्शान्निशया निर्वृतात्मना ।
अमी स्तम्भादयो भावा व्यज्यन्ते रज्यमानया ॥

Here we cannot replace निशया by क्षपया—अत्र निशादिपदस्थाने क्षपादिपदान्तरप्रक्षेपे पदानां परस्परमैत्रीभङ्गः ।

This is one sort of *pāka*, viz. *śabda-pāka* or maturity of expression that comes from a long study of good poetic works. But this felicity of expression, *vāg-vidagdhatā* as Bhāmaha calls it, is useless without a high poetic power, which comes very rarely to some one only from poetic genius of a very high order. By itself it is like possessing wealth without modesty and night without the moon—

विनयेन विना का श्रीः का निशा शशिना विना ।
रहिता सत्कवित्वेन कीदृशी वाग्विदग्धता ॥
गुरूपदेशादध्येतुं शास्त्रं जडधियोऽप्यलम् ।
काव्यं तु जायते जातु कस्यचित् प्रतिभावतः ॥ भामहालंकार १. ४–५

Thus what is wanted in poetry is not *śabda-pāka* alone but *artha-pāka* also. अर्थपाक is अर्थगम्भीरिमा—depth of sense. It is of various sorts, of which द्राक्षापाक and नारिकेलपाक are mentioned by Vidyānātha (प्रता॰ p. 67)—

अर्थगम्भीरिमा पाकः स द्विधा हृदयंगमः ।
द्राक्षापाको नारिकेलपाकश्च प्रस्फुटान्तरौ ॥

These varieties are brought about by different tastes of different poetic sentiments, like varieties of food. Without *pratibhā* or poetic genius such a charm in expression and sense (शब्दचमत्कार and अर्थचमत्कार) cannot be brought about, and Bhāmaha therefore very rightly says—

काव्यं तु जायते जातु कस्यचित् प्रतिभावतः ।

That is, *pratibhā* is absolutely necessary for the composition of poetry ; it is found in some one only, and in

1 *Tarala* on the *Ekāvali* pp. 22—23. The following verse of Mallinātha describing the rise of the moon seems to be from his रघुवीरचरित,

him also not at all times (जातु–कदाचिदेव). It is only in a few happy hours, when a man is fired by poetic genius of a superior kind, that he is able to compose what deserves to be called poetry.

Mammaṭa also places *pratibhā* which he calls *śakti* as the first and the most important of all the requisites for the composition of poetry.[1] Now *pratibhā* is defined as intelligence that buds forth in new and newer sprouts. The verse which defines it, defines also *kavi* and *kāvya* as under—

प्रज्ञा नवनवोन्मेषशालिनी प्रतिभा मता ।
तदनुप्राणनाजीवद्वर्णनानिपुणो कविः ॥
तस्य कर्म स्मृतं काव्यम्——हेमचन्द्र's काव्यानु°, p. 3

In the opinion of the above writer a poet is one who is skilled in the description animated by poetic genius; and his composition is known as poetry. Though Bhāmaha, like the above author, attaches much importance to *pratibhā*, he does not ignore other essential requisites of a secondary nature for the composition of poetry. He mentions them in the following verses—

शब्दश्छन्दोऽभिधानार्था[2] इतिहासाश्रयाः कथाः ।
लोको युक्तिः कलाश्चेति मन्तव्याः काव्यगैर्ह्यमी (?) ॥
शब्दाभिधेये विज्ञाय कृत्वा तद्विदुपासनाम् ।
विलोक्यान्यनिबन्धांश्च कार्यः काव्यक्रियादरः ॥ १. ९–१०

Thus one who desires to be a poet must know words, prosody, powers and senses of words, mythological stories, the world, arguments, and arts; he must also wait upon poets and study the works of others.

1 Compare—शक्तिर्निपुणता लोकशास्त्रकाव्याद्यवेक्षणात् ।
काव्यज्ञशिक्षयाभ्यास इति हेतुस्तदुद्भवे ॥ काव्यप्र° १. ३

The singular form हेतुः shows that शक्ति, निपुणता and अभ्यास are the combined causes for the composition of poetry.

2 Bhaṭṭodbhaṭṭa, who has composed a commentary called *Bhāmaha-vivaraṇa*, explains the word अभिधान as शब्दानामभिधानमभिधाव्यापारो मुख्यो गुणवृत्तिश्च । ध्वन्यालोक p. 10. Should it not be explained as अभिधानमभिधाव्यापारः । उपलक्षणमिदम् । तेन लक्षणव्यञ्जनयोरपि ग्रहणमित्यर्थः? For as I shall show further on Bhāmaha is not ध्वन्यभाववादी—one who does not believe in the existence of the suggested sense—as Mallinātha puts him down in his *Tarala* on the *Ekavalī*.

In his sixth ullāsa in which Mammaṭa examines the characteristics of *śabda-citra* and *artha-citra* poetry—as to whether there is any charm of sense in a *śabda-citra* poem or any charm of words in an *artha-citra* poem—he asserts that there are both the charms in both kinds of poetry, but that in a *śabda-citra* poem the charm of sense is subordinate to that of words, while in an *artha-citra* poem the charm of words is subordinate to that of sense. In support of his statement he quotes the following verses of Bhāmaha—

रूपकादिरलंकारस्तस्यान्यैर्बहुधोदितः ।
न कान्तमपि निर्भूषं विभाति वनितामुखम् ॥
रूपकादिमलंकारं बाह्यमाचक्षते परे ।
सुपां तिङां च व्युत्पत्तिं वाचां वाञ्छन्त्यलंकृतिम् ॥
तदेतदाहुः सौशब्द्यं नार्थव्युत्पत्तिरीदृशी ।
शब्दाभिधेयालंकारभेदादिष्टं द्वयं तु नः ॥१. १३–१५

These verses are quoted by Mammaṭa without the name of the author. Sarasvatītīrtha rightly attributes them to Bhāmaha; while Vivaraṇakāra is wrong in ascribing them to Dhvanikāra. In these Bhāmaha sets forth the views of some old Ālaṅkārikas. Some writers on poetics, says Bhāmaha, have mentioned *Rūpaka* and many such figures as ornaments of poetry; because even the handsome face of a lady does not look splendid if it be devoid of ornaments. Others, however, consider *Rūpaka* and other figures to be external. They desire the charmingness of nouns and verbs to constitute an ornament of poetry. This they call *sauśabdya*—felicitous expression. In their view charmingness of sense is not so pleasant. But in our view both are to be accepted; because there are two sorts of figures: those that adorn words and those that adorn sense. Bhāmaha is of opinion that words and sense both constitute the body of poetry—शब्दार्थौ सहितौ काव्यम् (ix. 16)—and not words alone. Daṇḍin and Jagannātha attach undue importance to words. The former defines poetry as—इष्टार्थव्यवच्छिन्ना पदावली, while the latter as—रमणीयार्थप्रतिपादकः शब्दः काव्यम्. Mammata follows Bhāmaha and considers word and sense both as constituting poetry—तददोषौ शब्दार्थौ.

The following verse from Bhāmaha is quoted by many writers such as Ānandavardhana, Mammaṭa, and Hemacandra—

सैषा सर्वत्र वक्रोक्तिरनयार्थो विभाव्यते ।
यत्नोऽस्यां कविना कार्यः कोऽलंकारोऽनया विना ॥ २. ८५

Here *vakrokti* means a charming and suggestive expression. It is synonymous with लोकातिक्रान्तगोचरं वचः which Bhāmaha uses in defining the figure *Atiśayokti*—

निमित्ततो वचो यत्तु लोकातिक्रान्तगोचरम् ।
मन्यन्तेऽतिशयोक्तिं तामलंकारतया यथा ॥ २. ८१

which says that when words are used in an ordinary manner in which people in general without a poetic turn of mind use them, there is no *vaicitrya*, no charm, and consequently no figure of speech. It is only when they are used in a charming sense, in an extraordinary manner which remotely suggests something very charming, that we have what we call a figure of speech. *Vaicitrya* of word and sense which Bhāmaha means by *vakrokti* is essential to constitute an Alaṅkāra. He says—

वक्राभिधेयशब्दोक्तिरिष्टा वाचामलंकृतिः । २. ३६

and also further on—

वाचां वक्रार्थशब्दोक्तिरलंकाराय कल्पते । ६. ६६

Abhinavagupta explains this (ध्वन्या॰ p. 208) as under—

शब्दस्य हि वक्रता अभिधेयस्य च वक्रता लोकोत्तीर्णेन रूपेणावस्थानमित्ययमेवासावलंकारस्यालंकारान्तरभावः ।

According to later writers on poetics the figure *Atiśayokti* is found under one of these five conditions: (1) when things different are described as not different (भेदेऽप्यभेदः); (2) when the object under description is conceived to be another than what it is, in other words, when things not different are described as different (अभेदेऽपि भेदः); (3) when connection is described between objects where there is no connection (असंबन्धेऽपि संबन्धः); (4) when non-connection is put forth between objects where there is connection (संबन्धेऽप्यसंबन्धः); and (5) when the sequence of cause and effect is reversed. Bhāmaha does not like to enter into minute divisions and distinctions. Of the two instances of this figure given by him, the first, viz.—

स्वपुष्पच्छविहारिण्या चन्द्रभासा तिरोहिताः ।
अन्वमीयन्त भृङ्गालिवाचा सप्तच्छदद्रुमाः ॥ २. ८२

corresponds to the figure *Sāmānya* of Mammaṭa; and the second, viz.—

अपां यदि त्वक् शिथिला च्युता स्यात् फणिनामिव ।
तदा शुक्लांशुकानि स्युरङ्गेष्वम्भसि योषिताम् ॥ २. ८३

corresponds to यद्यर्थातिशयोक्ति of Mammaṭa or असंबन्धेऽपिसंबन्धातिशयोक्ति of Alaṅkārasarvasvakāra. The latter is a broader division and comprehends the former as observed by Mallinātha in his Tarala.[1] Hemacandra remarks that since in almost all figures, we have *Atiśayokti*, it is unnecessary to take *Mīlita*, *Ekāvalī*, *Nidarśanā*, etc. as quite separate figures—तां विना प्रायेणालंकारत्वायोगादिति न सामान्यमीलितैकावलीनिदर्शना विशेषाद्यलंकारोपन्यासः श्रेयान् । हेमचन्द्र, काव्यानु॰, p. 267. But this view is not proper; for if it be accepted, it would do away with the necessity of many other divisions of figures, such as *Samāsokti*, *Ākṣepa*, and *Paryāyokti*. Nay, such an *Atiśayokti* is found even in *Upamā* and *Utprekṣā*, as Bhāmaha himself explains—

इष्टं चातिशयार्थत्वमुपमोत्प्रेक्षयोर्यथा ।
पुञ्जीभूतमिव ध्वान्तमेष भाति मतङ्गजः ॥
सरः शरत्प्रसन्नाम्भो नभःखण्डमिवोज्झितम् ॥ २. ५०-५१

What is meant by Bhāmaha is that *vaicitrya* or charmingness of expression is necessary to constitute a figure. When this charmingness is extraordinary it makes up the figure called *Atiśayokti*. Thus in *Atiśayokti*, there is always a *vyañgya*—remotely suggested sense—which is charming. Though this kind of charming suggestiveness of sense is found in many figures, still their varieties are based upon an additional charm peculiar to each figure.

1. काव्यप्रकाशकारस्तु भेदेऽभेदः, अभेदे भेदः, यद्यर्थशब्दप्रयोगादसंभावितार्थान्तरकल्पनं, कार्यकारणपौर्वापर्यमङ्गश्चेत्येवं चातुर्विध्यं सिद्धान्तयांचकार । तदपि चिन्त्यम् । ....तत्राद्ये (पुष्पप्रवालोपहितं यदि स्यात्' इत्यादौ) असंभावितोऽर्थः पुष्पप्रवालयोर्मुक्ताफलविद्रुमयोश्च संबन्ध एव यादिशब्देन संभाव्यते इत्यसंबन्धे संबन्धभेद एवायम् । द्वितीये (राकायामकलंकं चेत्' इत्यादौ) तु अकलंकं चोदिति कलंकासंबन्ध इन्दोश्चेच्छब्देन संभाव्यत इति संबन्धेऽप्यसंबन्धभेद एवायम् । एवं स्थिते सामान्ये विशेषस्यान्तर्भाव उचितः विशेषे वा सामान्यस्य तदत्रभवन्त एव विदांकुर्वन्तु । तस्मादस्मदुक्तः पञ्चधा विभाग एव न्याय्य इत्यलम्—p. 237 (Bom. Sans. Series).

Premacandratarkavāgīśa[1] also after quoting Bhāmaha's सैषा सर्वत्र वक्रोक्तिः and another verse to the same effect by another authority, viz—

कस्याप्यतिशयस्योक्तिरित्यन्वर्थविचारणात् ।
प्रायेणामी अलंकारा भिन्ना नातिशयोक्तितः ॥

very rightly observes—

एवं सर्वत्रातिशयोक्तिसद्भावेऽपि वैचित्र्यान्तरेणालंकारान्तरव्यपदेशः । वैचित्र्यान्तराभावे त्वतिशयोक्तिव्यपदेश इति बोध्यम् ।

From the following remarks[2] of Ānandavardhana it is clear that Bhāmaha is not ध्वन्यभाववादी or one who denies the existence of ध्वनि, as Mallinātha considers him to be—

भामहेनाप्यतिशयोक्तिलक्षणे यदुक्तम्—सैषा सर्वत्र वक्रोक्ति°—तत्रातिशयोक्तिर्यमलंकारमधितिष्ठति कविप्रतिभावशात् तस्य चारुत्वातिशययोगोऽन्यस्य त्वलंकारमात्रतैवेति सर्वालंकारशरीरस्वीकरणयोग्यत्वेनाभेदोपचारात् सैव सर्वालंकाररूपेत्ययमेवार्थोऽवगन्तव्यः । तस्याश्चालंकारान्तरसंकीर्णत्वं कदाचिद्वाच्यत्वेन कदाचिद्व्यङ्ग्यत्वेन ।

Furtheron, p. 211, it is rightly observed—

सर्वथा नास्त्येव सहृदयहृदयहारिणः काव्यस्य स प्रकारो यत्र न प्रतीयमानार्थसंस्पर्शेन सौभाग्यम् ।

It is because there is no *vakrokti* in them that Bhāmaha rejects *Hetu*, *Sūkṣma*, and *Leśa* as figures, though they are accepted by others—

हेतुश्च सूक्ष्मो लेशोऽथ नालंकारतया मतः ।
समुदायाभिधानस्य वक्रोक्त्यनभिधानतः ॥ २. ८६

The word वक्रोक्त्यनभिधानतः in this verse clearly shows that according to Bhāmaha's opinion words first express the primary sense and then the remotely suggested sense (वक्रोक्तेरप्यभिधानं भवति). In other words, the remotely suggested sense does exist; but it is subordinate to the primary sense. Bhāmaha thus comes under the class described by Ānandavardhana as भाक्तमाहुस्तमन्ये (ध्वन्या०, p. 2). The *Vṛtti* on this (p. 10) is clear—यद्यपि च ध्वनिशब्दसंकीर्तनेन काव्यलक्षणविधायिभिर्गुणवृत्तिरन्यो वा न कश्चित् प्रकारः प्रकाशितस्तथापि गुणवृत्त्या काव्येषु व्यवहारं दर्शयता ध्वनिमार्गो मनाक् स्पृष्टो लक्ष्यत इति परिकल्प्यैवमुक्तम्—भाक्तमाहुस्तमन्य इति ।

The following are a few of the excellent verses, which are Bhāmaha's own composition given by him as illustrations—

1 Kāvyādarśa, Premacanda's edition p. 223.
2 Dhvanyāloka, pp. 207-208.

अहं त्वा यदि नेक्षेय क्षणमप्युत्सुका ततः ।
इयदेवास्त्वतोऽन्येन किमुक्तेनाप्रियेण तु ॥ २. ६९
वहन्ति गिरयो मेघानभ्युपेतान् गुरूनपि ।
गरीयानेव हि गुरून् बिभर्ति प्रणयागतान् ॥ २. ७४
स्कन्धवानृजुरव्यालः स्थिरोऽनेकमहाफलः ।
जातस्तरुरयं चोच्चैः पातितश्च नभस्वता ॥ २. ८०
छायावन्तो गतव्यालाः स्वारोहाः फलदायिनः ।
मार्गद्रुमा महान्तश्च परेषामेव भूतये ॥ ३. १७
उन्नता लोकदयिता महान्तः प्राज्यवर्षिणः ।
शमयन्ति क्षितेस्तापं सुराजानो घना इव ॥ ३. १८
अयं मन्दद्युतिर्भास्वानस्तं प्रति यियासति ।
उदयः पतनायेति श्रीमतो बोधयन् नरान् ॥ ३. ३३
अनलंकृतकान्तं ते वदनं वनजद्युति ।
निशाकृतं प्रकृत्यैव चारोः का वास्त्यलंकृतिः ॥ ३. ५०

Unlike the later writers—Daṇḍin, Vāmana, and Bhoja, who accept ten *guṇas* or poetic merits, Bhāmaha betrays higher taste and critical faculty by accepting only three: *mādhurya*, *ojas*, and *prasāda*. Mammaṭa follows him and accepts these three only, stating that the rest are included in them. Of these *mādhurya* is defined by Bhāmaha[1] as—

श्रव्यं नातिसमस्तार्थं काव्यं मधुरमिष्यते । २. ३

Mammaṭa and Hemacandra take objection to this definition. They state that a poem with *prasāda* is also *śravya* ; so the definition is open to the fault of *ativyāti*—

श्रव्यत्वं पुनरोजः प्रसादयोरपि । काव्यप्र०, 8. 68

द्रुतिहेतुत्वं माधुर्यस्य लक्षणं न तु श्रव्यत्वम् । ओजः प्रसादयोरपि श्रव्यत्वात् । तेन श्रव्यं नातिसमस्तार्थशब्दं मधुरमिष्यते इति माधुर्यलक्षणत्वेन श्रव्यत्वं यद्भामहेनोक्तं तन्न युक्तमित्यर्थः—काव्यानु०, p. 201. I think that there is not much force in this objection. *Śravya* means pleasant to hear; the adjective नातिसमस्तार्थम् prevents the *ativyāpti* of the definition to *ojas* which has *samāsabhūyastva*. *Prasāda* is the simplicity or rather lucidity of a poem, so great that it may be grasped even by women and children. Mammaṭa has made the degree of pleasantness clear by stating that this poetic merit is the cause of the

1 Pradīpakāra in his commentary attributes this definition to one Bhāskara—भास्करस्तु श्रव्यत्वं माधुर्यस्य लक्षणमाह स्म तदयुक्तम्—काव्यप्रदीप, p. 329.

melting of the mind (द्रुतिकारणम्). It is said that there are only three conditions of the mind generated by nine poetic sentiments. They are: 1 *druti*—melting or dissolution of the mind as on hearing a poem suggestive of the sentiments of love, grief, and tranquillity; 2 *vistāra*—expansion or firing up of the mind as on hearing a poem suggesting the sentiments of valour, wrath, and repulsion; and 3 *vikāsa*—the budding forth of the mind as on hearing a poem suggestive of the sentiments of humour, wonder, and terror.

The definition of *prasāda* as given by Bhāmaha is far superior to that of any other writer, Mammaṭa included. I give the definitions of Bhāmaha and Mammaṭa below, so that the reader will at once see the superiority of the former to that of the latter—

आविद्वदङ्गनाबालप्रतीतार्थं प्रसादवत् ॥ काव्यालंकार, २. ३
श्रुतिमात्रेण शद्बात्तु येनार्थप्रत्ययो भवेत् ।
साधारणः समग्राणां स प्रसादो गुणो मतः ॥ काव्यप्र० ८

Bhāmaha's verse shows that a poem with *prasāda* must be such as can be comprehended by all, from the learned right up to women and children. Simplicity and lucidity are acknowledged by all nations to be the first essentials of excellent poetry. Out-of-the-way words and involved constructions must be shunned. That Bhāmaha is very strong on this point is evident from the following additional verse—

काव्यान्यपि यदीमानि व्याख्यागम्यानि शास्त्रवत् ।
उत्सवः सुधियामेव हन्त दुर्मेधसो हताः ॥ २.२०

by which verse he expresses his displeasure for artificial poetry like *prahelikā*. Śrīvatsāṅka-miśra (10th century) in his Introduction to *yamakaratnākara* attributes this verse to Bhāmaha. There is a verse in the Rāvaṇavadha of Bhaṭṭi where almost the same words occur, though the idea is quite the reverse. It is as under—

व्याख्यागम्यमिदं काव्यमुत्सवः सुधियामलम् ।
हता दुर्मेधसश्चास्मिन् विद्वत्प्रियतया मया ॥ भट्टि० २२.३४

Unlike Bhaṭṭi, Bhāmaha is of opinion that poetry should

be so lucid that it might be understood by all, not by the learned alone.

The instances given to illustrate figures of speech are mostly Bhāmaha's own composition[1] and the cases where he has borrowed them from other authors are clearly acknowledged. That Bhāmaha was a man of independent views and did not like to slavishly endorse the views of others is evident from the concluding verse of the third Pariccheda—

गिरामलंकारविधिः सविस्तरः स्वयं विनिश्चित्य धिया मयोदितः ।
अनेन वागर्थविदामलंकृता विभाति नारीव विदग्धमण्डला ॥ ३. ५७

That Bhāmaha at the same time knew and consulted a good many writers on poetics is evident from the names of the ancient writers quoted by him,[2] writers so old that their names, except that of Medhāvin, are not found in any works available to us. Many other writers are alluded to under the words *anya*, *apara* and *kiñcit*.[3] Notwithstanding his vast erudition, sound scholarship and independent judgment, Bhāmaha had no pride, as is clear from the following—

न दूषणायायमुदाहृतो विधिर्न चाभिमानेन किमु प्रतीयते ।
कृतात्मनां तत्त्वदृशां च मादृशो जनोऽभिसंधिं क इवावभोत्स्यते ॥ ४. ५१

And it is these virtues that have been chiefly instrumental in his being held in high esteem by subsequent writers of great learning and sound judgment.

1 Compare स्वयंकृतैरेव निदर्शनैरियं मया प्रक्लृप्ता खलु वागलंकृतिः ।
अतः परं चारुरनेकधापरो गिरामलंकारविधिर्विधास्यते ॥ २. ९६

2 Thus प्रहेलिका सा ह्युदिता रामशर्माच्युतोत्तरे 2. 19; राजमित्रे यथोदितम् 2. 45; रत्नवर्धनस्य after 2. 47; रामशर्मणः after 2. 58; मेधाविनोत्प्रेक्षाभिहिता क्वचित् 2. 88; समाहितं राजमित्रे यथा क्षत्रिययोषिताम् 3. 10 etc.

3 Compare— यदुक्तं त्रिप्रकारत्वं तस्याः कैश्चिन्महात्मभिः । २. ३७
स्वभावोक्तिरलंकार इति केचित् प्रचक्षते । २. ९३
उत्प्रेक्षावयवं चान्ये संसृष्टमपि चापरे ।
भाविकत्वं च निजगुरलंकारं सुमेधसः ॥ ३. ४
धीरन्त्यशब्दविषयावृत्तवर्णाहितस्मृतिः ।
वाक्यमित्याहुरपरे......................४. ६
पुनरुक्तमिदं प्राहुरन्ये शब्दार्थभेदतः ॥ ४. १२

Technical Sciences

AN ANCIENT MEDICAL MANUSCRIPT FROM EASTERN TURKESTAN

BY A. F. RUDOLF HOERNLE

THIS paper deals with two extracts from a medical manuscript discovered, with other manuscript treaures, by Sir Aurel Stein in the "Cvess of the Thousand-Buddhas" near Tun-huang, during his second tour of exploration in Eastern Turkestan. A full account of his discoveries in that locality may be read in the second volume of his *Ruins of Desert Cathay*, pp. 159 ff.

The manuscript is written on thick coarse paper, and consists of 71 folios. It is arranged in the fashion of an Indian pothī, except that the circlet surrounding the string-hole through which the binding cord is passed in the case of the pothī, is here a mere conventional survival, there being no string-hole. The folios measure $11\frac{3}{4} \times 3\frac{3}{8}$ inches, with five lines of writing in black cursive Khotanese script. The writing is guided by faint straight lines, and bounded by similar straight lines on the right and left, which mark it off from narrow lateral margins, about half an inch wide. The folios are numbered, in the usual way, in the middle of the left margin on the obverse sides; but they have also a second numbering on the same side within the blank circlets, above mentioned. The marginal numbers run from 44 to 116, and the interior numbers from 1 to 71. This shows that the existing manuscript is merely the continuation of another which is missing. What the subject of this missing portion, on fols. 1 to 43, may have been, is not known. though of course the probability is that it was also medical. In any case, the salutation formula with which the existing portion begins on fol. 44, as well as the interior numbering which begins with 1, shows that the preceding missing portion, whatever its subject may have been, must have contained the text of a separate treatise. Clearly what exists is a portion of a collective pothī. How much more that pothī may have contained is also unknown; for the last existing folio does not give the conclusion of the treatise to which it belongs.

In three respects our manuscript possesses a special interest. In the first place it is of a secular character, containing a series of medical formulae for the cure of various diseases, while most of the other manuscripts, or fragments of manuscripts, discovered in E. Turkestan, have a religious character, containing portions of the Buddhist Canon. Secondly, it is written in a hitherto unknown species of Iranian language, which up to the middle of the 8th century A. D. was spoken in the territory of Khotan, but since that date has fallen into utter oblivion. Thirdly, it is written in a peculiar cursive script which, for the purpose of secular use, developed in the Khotan territory from a type of the Gupta script introduced from India along with Buddhist religious literature. What this cursive Khotanese script looks like may be seen from the accompanying Plate, which shows the obverse and reverse sides of the 1st and 21st folios of the manuscript. For further information on the subject of language and script the Introduction may be consulted to the First Volume of my *Manuscript Remains of Buddhist Literature in Eastern Turkestan*; also chapter III of the Introduction to my edition of the *Bower Manuscript*, reprinted in the *Indian Antiquary*, vol. XLII, where all needful references to other books will be found.

A further point of interest in our manuscript is that, in addition to the Khotanese medical formulary, it contains the original Sanskrit text of the work from which it is translated, almost verbally, into the Khotanese language. This circumstance furnishes us with a very useful key to the understanding of such Khotanese words of secular import, as naturally fall outside the range of Khotanese translations from Buddhist religious literature.

The original Sanskrit text is written in an exceedingly barbarous type of that language, which presents problems of its own. Neither the name of the treatise, nor that of its author is disclosed in the surviving portion of the work. That portion contains many formulae which cannot be traced in any of the Sanskrit medical treatises of India, known to me; certainly not in the three standard works of Caraka, Suśruta, and Vāgbhaṭa. The first formula, quoted in this paper, is an example of this class. But it contains also a few formulae which can be identified in Indian standard works; and of these the second formula, quoted in this paper, is an example. This formula is the so-called *Tryūṣaṇa-ghṛta*, which occurs in the chapter on Cough (*kāsa*) in the *Caraka-saṁhitā*, as printed by Jīvānanda in his first edition of 1877, on p. 732. It occurs also on fol. 320*b* of the famous Nepalese Ms. of N. E. 303, or A. D. 1183, the oldest known manuscript of the Saṁhitā, and on fol. 551*b* of the Tübingen Ms. 458 of the 16th century A. D. The chapter on Cough is one of those which were added to the original treatise of Caraka by the Kashmirian Dṛḍhabala, whose date falls somewhere in the 8th or 9th century A. D. (see my *Studies in Indian Medicine, Part I*, p. 16). For his additions, as he himself admits, Dṛḍhabala utilized a number of then existing treatises (see *ibid*, p. 2). It does not seem impossible that he knew and utilized the Sanskrit medical formulary which in our manuscript is translated into the Khotanese language. If he did so, he did naturally (at his time of day) "edit" the formulae which he extracted in that fairly correct Sanskrit in which they now appear in Caraka's Saṁhitā. This hypothesis is more probable than the other that the author of the Khotanese work turned the fairly correct Sanskrit of his original into the barbarous Sanskrit of his own composition. The use of barbarous Sanskrit points to a rather early date. Early Buddhist writers, as existing Mahāyāna treatises show, were not capable of writing good Sanskrit. A medical writer, moreover, without much Brahmanic culture, would naturally write a more or less barbarous Sanskrit.[1] In fact, such writers would employ what may be called a northern vernacular Sanskrit on a linguistist level similar to the vernacular, now known as Pāli. Thus, like the

1. Another good example of such barbarous Sanskrit may be seen in a fragment of an astrological treatise, edited by Dr. Thomas, in Vol. I of my *Manuscript Remains of Buddhist Literature in E. Turkestan* p. 121.

latter, the northern vernacular drops final consonants, as in *dadyā* (*dadyāt*), Pāli *dajjā* (fol. 44*b*^iii^); inserts superfluous anusvāras, as in *viṁṣa* (fol. 44*a*^iii^) for *viṣa*; and admits a great variety of changes in vowels, such as *vāraṇā* (fol. 44*a*^v^) for *vāriṇā*, *saidha* (fol. 44*a*^i^) for *siddha*, *kūkūmasyaṁ* (fol. 44*b*^i^) for *kuṁkumasya*, *tvacisya*, (fol. 44*b*^i^) for *tvacasya*, *baudhasya* (fol. 45*a*^i-ii^) for *buddhasya*, etc; the change of *a* for *i*, and *ū* for *u* being particulary frequent. (On the usages of Pāli, in all these respects, see Kuhn's Pāli Grammar, pp. 21 ff., E. Müller, pp. 3 ff, 21 ff.) Such considerations tend to suggest that our Sanskrit formulary is a very early composition of a North-Indian medical man, who, to judge from the salutation (*namo Buddhasya*) in the mantra on fol. 45*a*^i-ii^ must have been a Buddhist, though the salutation formula at the head of his treatise (fol. 44 *a*^i^) is of a more neutral character, as would befit a layman. But, no doubt, the barbarism of the original treatise has been much aggravated by the carelessness, or illiteracy of the scribe who copied the existing manuscript, and who introduced numerous senseless blunders, such as *kecaindad* (fol. 44 *a*^ii^) for *kecaid* (*kecid*), *kūṣṭasya* (fol. 44 *b*^ii^) for *kūṣṭaṁ* (*kuṣṭhaṁ*) *ca*; *bilvā* (fol. 64 *a*^v^) for *piṣṭvā*, etc. They are all, noted in the foot-notes to the two extracts; but some of them, for the present, defy correction, and thus impede the reading and understanding of the text. What adds to the difficulty in such cases is that the scribe is peccable even in copying the corresponding clauses of the translation into his own native Khotanese language, so that the student is forsaken in respect of help from either side, Sanskrit and Khotanese. This happens, *e. g.*, in the opening passage of fol. 44*a*^i-ii^. In fol. 44*a*^iv^ the scribe has missed out a syllable in *rbīśāṁ* for *harbīśāṁ*, in fol. 64 *a*^iv^ he writes *śṭī* for *śaṭī*, etc., Other difficulties are created for the student by the scribe's occasional confounding of two akṣaras of similar shape, such as *pha* and *ha*, in *viṁṣâpaphā* (fol. 44*a*^iii^) for *viṁṣâpahā*, or *ya* and *gha*, in *prrayātta* (fol. 46*a*^i^) for *prraghātta* (*praghāta*), etc.; and by his inordinate proclivity to insert the anusvāra in and out of season, as in *upaṁryaṁpari* (fol. 44 a^{iii}) for *uparyupari*, *naṁladaṁsyaṁ* (fol. 44 a^{v}) for *naladasya*, etc. Occasionally, also, he inserts a superfluous *r*, as in *kūṁrkūṁna* (fol. 44 b^{i}) for *kuṁkuma* *pūrttanā* (fol. 45b^{iv}) for *pūtanā*; *ghrrattārthi* (fol. 64 a^{v}) for *ghrrattātti* (*ghṛtāt*). In addition, there are for the student certain pitfalls inherent in the Khotanese cursive script, especially the difficulty of distinguishing between *n*, *nn*, and *t*, *tt*; *e.g.*,*ttasya* (fol. 45 a^{i}) for *tasya*, and *nnasya* (fol. 47 a^{iii}) for *nasya* are written exactly alike; likewise between long *ā* (distinguished in this paper typographically by accented *á*) and *u*; *e. g.*, *nīlámttpala* (fol. 44 b^{iii}) for *nīluttpala* (*nīlôtpala*).[1] Other difficulties of this kind are peculiar to the cursive script of our manuscript; such as the practical identity of the symbol for virāma with the symbol for *i*, *ī*, *e*. Thus the apparent *saddhamī* in fol. 44a^{i}, *bhavatte* in fol. 44 a^{v}, *ghrrattātti* in fol. 64 a^{v},) really represent *saddham*, *bhavet*, *ghrattat*, etc.

A striking peculiarily of our manuscript is the total absence of the well-known double dot which indicates a sound intermediate between *a* and *i* (or *ĕ*). It is one of the distinguishing marks of the ordinary Khotanese script and language; yet, in our manuscript, it is totally absent. To what cause this neglect of the double dot is due, whether to a mere personal whim of the scribe, or to a peculiarity of some local dialect, or linguistic period, is not apparent at present. It has not been observed by me in any other Khotanese manuscript.

The arrangement of the following two extracts is as follows: (1) a romanized transcript of the text its Sanskrit clauses being printed in italic type; (2) a restoration of the Sanskrit portion into ordinary popular (not classic) Sanskrit; (3) an English translation of the Khotanese portion.

1 See my article in Journal, RAS., 1915, p. 487.

FIRST EXTRACT

[Fol. 44 *a*][i] *Saddhamī*[1] *namau brrahmaṇe-*[2] aurga ttā brrahmāṁ hālai=*namau saidhavaidyādharāṁṇāṁ-* aurga ttā saidhavaidhyādarāṁ rasaṇā hālai=*bhagavāṁ brraṣmī*[ii] *ttarvma*[3] [=] jasta beysi ttatta hve si ttū ttā mahajsā = *brrūṇū*[4] *ttā*[5] *vakṣyāṁme Jīvakaṁ*[5] *sarvaṁthā* = pūja vā hvāṁñū ttā harbaiśa padya=*ye kecainda*[iii] *d*[6] *agadā siṁte*[7] =cabure heca[8] agade : *jaṁbudvīpe viṁṣâpaphā-* jaṁbvīyi bipā[9] hiṁśākye—*upaṁryaṁpari sarvi ṣā*[10] uskātta u[iv]skātta rbīśāṁ[11] agadāṁ myāṁña=*ahaṁ vakṣyāṁmi ttabh*[12] *brruṇu* =ayse ttā hvāṁñū tvā pū=*parapilavasyaṁ catvāre:*[2] parapilava tcau mā[v] cāṁgyi = *catvārau naṁladaṁsyaṁ ca* = tcahau mācāṁgyi gaṁdhanalaṁdha = *caṁdanasyaṁ*[13] *catvāri*=caṃdaṁ tcau mācāṁga=*catvārau agarā*[14] *bhavatte:*[1] tcahau

1 Read *saddham*, and l. 5, *bhavet*.

2 Interpunction is made here and elsewhere by a single or double comma (prone), or by a single or double dot (like visarga), corresponding to the modern single or double bar ; a double bar, in addition to the double comma, however, occurs on fol. 45 *a*[i]. Where the Ms. omits interpunction, it is added within square brackets.

3 Reading of *ttarvma* very uncertain. 4 Corruption of *varṇaṁ*.

5 Omit both *ttā* and *Jīvakaṁ* ; the former is a Khot. intrusion ; the latter does not occur in the Khot. version ; both are in excess of the metre. 6 Read *kecaid*, om. *nda*.

7 The original in the Ms. seems to have been *sāṁte*, afterwards altered to *siṁte*.

8 Apparently a total blunder for *hame* ; *ca* and *ma* are not unlike in cursive script ; hence in rev. l. 5 probably *marajsai* to be read for *carajsai*. 9 Perhaps read *biṣa*.

10 Read *sarviṣā* (*sarveṣāṁ*) ; the interpunction is misplaced, and *ṣā* turned into the Khot. pronoun *ṣā*.

11 Read *harbīśāṁ*. 12 Read *tad*.

13 Insert *ca* to satisfy the metre. It is inadvertently missed out by reason of the following *ca* of *catvāri*. Similarly in rev. l. 1 read *pātca*, its *tcā* being missed out by reason of the following *tca* of *tcahau*.

14 Orig. reading was *agare* ; afterwards altered to *agarā*.

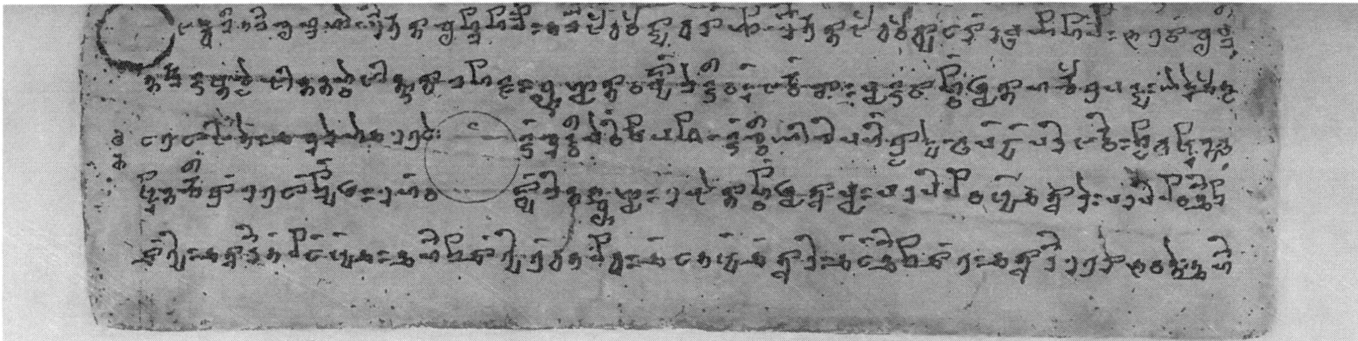

Obverse

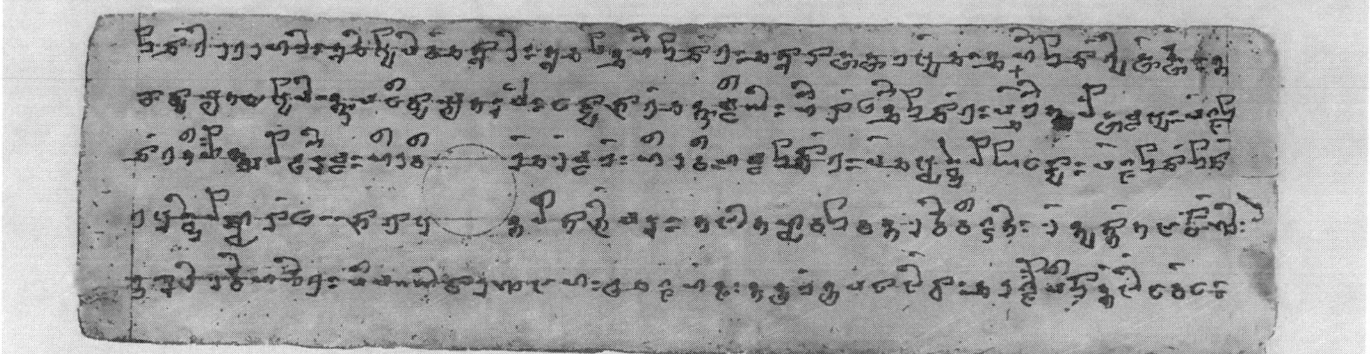

Reverse

[Fol. 44*b*][i] mācāṁgi agara hami = *tvacisyâpi vaṁ*[1] *catvāri* = tvaca pā tcahau mācāṁga = *catvārá kūkūmasyaṁ ca* tcahau mācāṁgyi kūṁrkūṁma *tta*[ii]*thā vyāghrranakhasyâpi* = ttū padī vyāghrranaka ṣai = *dadyā bhāgaṁ cattūṣṭīyi* = haurāṁña tcau mācāṁga = *paṁ*+[2] *ca mautpalaṁ kūṣṭasya*[3] = paṁjsa mā[iii]cāṁga nīláṁttpala u kauṣṭa = *hīravīraṁ ca aṁṣṭamaṁ*: hīravī haṣṭa mācāṁga = *paṁca sūkṣmelayā dadyā* = paṁjsa mācāṁ[4] mācāṁ[iv]ga sukṣmila hūrāṁña -- *bhāgā suttalītā*[5] *bhiṁṣaka*[6] = nasina hūvamāvatta arvi vījani = *aṁnny*[7] *attāṁna sarvāṁṇi* :[v] ttaburi arvi harbiśa = *pīpayayi*[8] *vāraṇa saha* = ucajsa haṁtsa = *ttattra maṁttrapadā siṁdhā*: carajsai pīrmāttaṁ siṁdavaṁda =

[Fol. 45*a*][i] *brrūṇū vakṣyāṁma Jīvakaṁ* = pū cveva hvāṁñūṃ tta vātcaṁ tatta arvi ṣāña u ṣā agada = ‖ *tadyathā kiśi kiśi kiśa laṁbi hilī hilīṁ namau*[ii] *baudhasya siṁdhyaṁttū maṁttrapaṁdāṁni*[9] *svāhā* = aga ttāyi ttauvi = ṣā vīja caāṁ tvā agada śū hye = *īmi maṁttram ūdāhari*: tta āṁnayāṁda[iii] ṣa maṁdrra hvañai = *śūca samāhyina būtvā* = surai vī hūysīnau tta hamāṁña [=] vasvi samāhye = śi tvāva nasāṁñi [=] *pūṣyayaugena*[iv] *budamāṁ* = pviśa nakṣattra vīra bvāṁma ya vījina = ṣa kiri = *ttasya karmagūṇā krraitsnā* = ttye agadi hīyi kira bviṁjsi aha[v]rīnaka – *brrūṇū vakṣyāṁma Jīvaki* = pū aysi ttā hvāṁñūṁ Jīvā = *sarvaraugaprraśamanī*-harbīśāṁ āchāṁ naṣi ṁmāka = *samā*.

[Fol. 45*b*][i] *sā gagattáttama*[10] = haṁbicajsasaṁ ṣā ag[a]da pīrmāttama hvava pūviṁsthartai ttā hvāṁñāṁ = *yiṣū*

1 Read *ca*.

2 *Ca*, having been inadvertently omitted, is inserted below the line, and the place of insertion marked above by a cross; similar cases are in fol. 45*b*[v] and fol. 46*a*[v].

4 Omit one *mācāṁ*.

3 Read *kūṣṭaṁ ca*, as required by grammar and by Khot. version.

5 Read *satulita*, as shown by Khot. *hūvamāvatta*.

6 Read *bhiṁsak* (*bhiṣak*) to satisfy metre.

7 Read *dravyāṁny* (*dravyāṇi*) as required by metre and Khot. *arvi*.

8 The akṣara *ya* is imperfectly formed; perhaps the reading *pīpayi* is intended, i. e. *pīpayet* for *pāyayet*. Its Khot. equivalent is omitted.

9 In order to satisfy the metre (if the clause is part of a verse) two syallbles have to be omitted, reading either *mantrāṇi* or *padāni*.

10 Blundered for *jagattáttama*, i.e. vernacular Skr *jagata* and *uttama*.

rgauṣū bhiṁṣajya [=] kāṁmyāṁ āchāṁ[ii] vī ṣa arva 1: *diva-gaṁdhayikṣiṣū*[1] = jasta gaṁdharvi yakṣa = *prrītta dārūṁ-ṇā rakṣasā* = prrīyi bīysāṁnā rakṣaysi = [iii]*sarvabhūttava-kāriṣū* = harbīśāṁ būvajāṁ āchāṁ vīra—*lalāṭim*[2] *ūpaye* = sā agada haṁdrrauja pīsilyāṁ[iv]ña = *śāṁmyatti sarvavittāṇ-ḍā*: naṣamāraṁjsa harbiṁśa vittāla = *pūrttanā krraittavi-dhaka* = būvau[3] kūra hīra = *khākhau*[v]*da śviva śāṁmyatt* = cāṇūṁjsa[4] pātca biṁśa naṣamāri = *grrahā yau ca sudūraṇa*[5] [=] kāṁma ra jsāṁna tta grra*hā* cū vīhī $\underset{\text{bi}}{+}$ ysāṁnā = *sarvi*[6]

[Fol. 46*a*][i] *suprrayāttârthaṁ*[7] = harbīśāṁ pahijāṁmī udaśāyi = *agadā samūdāhyattī* = [8]sā agada hvava ṣṭi = *hala halaiṣū saṁyūhttaṁ* [=][ii]cu halāhala binaskva īde = *vaṣāpi-ttaṣū dārāṇā*[5] = cū vā eha ttrraikṣa bīāī = *pītta śīttaṁna ttauyina*: khāśāṁña[iii] pvāyi ucana = *sattyā cavitti*[9] *narava-ṣaṁ* = ttanī thyau vīnabe hamāre—*banavidaṣū gāttriṣū* = ca vā aṁga ttana[iv] rvaha tcasta u hvasta = *āyū vaṣi*[10]*dūṣatti* [=] prraha raṇḍyaujsa bivūḍau = *vrraṇâlaipannimāttreṇa* = vīraṇāṁ bai[v]da sakhalyāṁña masvāṁñajsa = *vrraṇadīṣū*[11] *prramūcatta* = vīraṁ hīye gaṁjsajsa gūśta = *jantavá ye ca drraiṣṭā*[12] *sya* = kāṁma $\underset{\text{ra}}{+}$ jsāṁna â-

1 Read *gaṁdharva*, and satisfy the metre.

2 The pāda is short by two syllables; read *lalāṭa-taṭam*.

3 Probably read *būvanna* (Skr. *pūtanā*), the akṣaras *u* and *nna* being not very dissimilar.

4 The akṣara *ṇū* is imperfect in the original; it might be meant for *yū*, but *cāṇū* is reminiscent of Skr. *caṇḍa*.

5 Read *dāruṇā*.

7 Read *suprraghāttârthaṁ*.

6 Read *sarviṣām* (*sarveṣām*); *i* for *e* is not unfrequent in this Ms. see *yikṣisū* and *vakāriṣa* in ll. 2 and 3; possibly the two vowels were not clearly written in the original Ms. from which our scribe copied. After *sarvi* there is a washed out akṣara, but it looks rather like *na*.

8 Read *samūdāhṛttī*; akṣaras *hya* and *hṛ* much alike; moreover the original spelling was *°hyatte*, but *e* is washed out and replaced by *ī*.

9 Read *bhavati* or *bhāvet*, as shown by the Khot. *hamāre*; also read *sadyo*, for Khot. *thyau*; and *narvaṣaṁ* (*nirviṣaṁ*). But the metre of the pāda is out of order; it either runs *sadyo bhavati narvaṣaṁ*, or *sadyo bhavet naravaṣaṁ*.

10 Read *doṣā*.

11 Read *vaṣiṇa* (*viṣeṇa*) to satisfy the metre.

12 Read *klaiṣṭā* (*kliṣṭa*); akṣaras *drr* and *ke* much alike; read *syā* (*syāt*).

[Fol. 46*b*][i] phīḍā prraṁṇāṁ hamāṁde = *yaurā*[1] *parame dūrūṇā* = bīysāṁṇā bīhī ttraikṣa = *daheyū vaṣṭamāttrāṁṇi*[2] = cu hvāṁṇḍa pada[ii] jsīda dūṣṭa masu = *tteṣāṁm apavaṣākhyā*[3] = ttyāṁ hīyai pābe pahaiśaeṁ = *yasyi hastagattā naittyaṁ*[4] = ca ttye baida ṣa agada[iii] hamāve = *pāpa ttasya na jāyatti* = ttye herī vīśūṁna hīra na hamāre = *sarva ca sūdayi cârthaṁ* = harbīśai hāva saijī[iv]di : *pūtayiśta*[5] *na jāyitte* = pātca pātcī upadrrava na ysyāre = *ye va gaura vabai diṣṭhai*[3] = cū bīysāṁnai bena dūṣṭi = *vaṣa*[v] *ṣvastāsu śāṁṇittā*[3] = bena umya āphīḍe hūṁñajsi : *tteṣāṁ kākapadaṁ mūrdhaṁ* = ttyāṁjsa vasalaka tcerā ttera baidi = *krraitvā dadyā*

[Fol. 47*a*][i] *gadauntā*[6] = tcera ttera vīra haurāṁñai ṣa agada = *mūkhatas tū ttrayau dadyā baidavau*[7] = ehiṁ drrai kane ṣa agada haurāṁña—*nasta ttraye*[7] = ha[ii]ysgvā drrai kane : *agaḍena va*[8] *līpeti* = ttye agada sakhalyāṁñāṁmejsa = *ttatta saṁjīvattaṁ supttaṁ* = ṣa bina mauḍa hve paskyāṣṭa būjvaiye = *ttra*[iii] *būkīdinnaṁ daṣṭi*[9] = gūṇāysyāṁ sajājva dūrṣṭaṁ = *lūttāṁ mūṣakaṁ veśte*[9] [=] cū vīśūṁnnyāṁ dūṣṭa u mūlāṁ drrvāṁṇḍyaujsa = *nnasyapāṁnaṁ*[iv] *janâlaipā*[10] [=] haysgvā khaśa arja[11] saṁkhalyūñaṁ[=]*vadhaṁnnā narvaṣe bhavi* : dyenaṁjsa vī naube hame = *strīṇāṁ va*[8] *mūḍhagarbhāṁṇāṁ* – kāṁma tta strīye cū haṁ[v] jyāramaichām āvāmaichīde. *yauvalepaṁ prradūpaye* – ttyām pūrāṁña saṁkhalyāṁña u[12] haurāṁña : *vasucakayāṁ ghaurāyāṁ* = ca vā pejsa vasuja ī : [vi] *dadyā ṣṇana vāraṇā* : grrāmmye ucajsa hūrāṁña : *rakṣa karṣu*[13] *ca bālāṁnāṁ* [=] āysdīrja tcairai ṣīkalakām = *suprrajāṁnāṁ prrajāyitte* = śaraśaram

1 Read *ghaurā* (*ghorā*). 2 Apparently read *uṣṭa*, burnt.
3 Text irremediably corrupt. 4 Omitted in the Khot. version.
5 Corrupt; perhaps read *pūtayaś ca*.
6 Pāda short by one syllable; perh. read *gadauṇtakā* (*gandântakaṁ*).
7 The text of this śloka is quite out of order, and wants two syllables.
8 Read *ca*. 10 Read *pāṁnâṁjanâ*.
9 Both pādas are short by one syllable, and otherwise corrupt; possibly *ttrabūkīdittaṁ*.
11 Perhaps read *aṁja*, or *aṁjana*.
12 The akṣara *u* is here out of place; its right place is below in the 6th line, where it is required to complete the blundered reading *ṣṇana* and to satisfy the metre; the correct reading is *uṣṇana* (*uṣṇena*).
13 *Karṣa* makes no sense; probably read *kuryā* (*kuryāt*).

[Fol. 47*b*][i] jsa pūra ysyāṁre cvai baida bīḍi : *yūvaṁd arthavarṣa*[1] *pava* = caṁdai kṣamī hama yi bi khāśe [=] *tarva*[2] *ṣau*[3] *kūrvattaṁ kṣaprri* = ta ṣa bevai padīme thyau [=][ii] haṣṭa[4] vī dīra na īdi = *vrraikṣa aidrrârthinar*[2] *yathā* = khu Śakrrana paśā āśūna bahya-bījevetta ṣā·agada bījevāki = *bhagava*[iii] *ttau bhāṣitta Svastakaṁ nnāṁma mahâgada samâptta* = jasta beysina hvava Svastaka nāṁma agada dāśyā ॥

RESTORATION OF THE SANSKRIT TEXT[5]

Siddham । namo Brahmaṇe namo Siddha-vidyādharāṇām॥

[Fol. 44*a*]

Bhagavāṁ abravī[d] yoga-varṇaṁ vakṣyāmi sarvathā ।[6]
ye kecid agadā santi Jambudvīpe viṣâpahā[ḥ] ॥ 1 ॥
Upary-upari sarveṣāṁ ahaṁ vakṣyāmi tad-varṇaṁ ।
paripelavasya[7] catvāri catvāro naladasya ca ॥ 2 ॥
Caṁdanasya[ca] catvāri catvāro agarā bhavet ।
tvacasyâpi ca catvāri catvāro kuṁkumasya ca ॥ 3 ॥

[Fol. 44*b*]

Tathā vyāghranakhasyâpi dadyā[d] bhāgaṁ catuṣṭayaṁ
paṁcam[8]ôtpala-kuṣṭhaṁ ca hiriveraṁ ca aṣṭamaṁ[8] ॥4॥
Paṁca sūkṣmelayā dadyā[d] bhāgā sutulitā bhiṣak ।
dravyāny etāni sarvāṇi pāyaye[d] vāriṇā saha ॥5 ॥

1 Read *tarṣa*, thirst.

2 Read *tāva* (*tāvat*), and similarly in l. 2, *ârthinā*.

3 Read *sau* (*so*) ; the cerebralization probably due to the analogy of Khot. *ṣa*.

4 Probably read *hāṣṭa*, 'here'.

5 This is merely a rendering into the more common vernacular not classic Sanskrit, to facilitate the understanding of the very barbarous text of the Ms.

6 The orig. text is irremediably corrupt. The emendation is suggested by the Khot. *hve*, he said. The spelling *brrūṇū* for *varṇaṁ* is very curious, but its genuineness is confirmed by its occuring four times in the same clause, fol. 44*a*[ii] *a*[iv], 45*a*[i] *a*[v], and by its equivalence to Khot. *pūja* or *pū*.

7 So in both, Skr. and Khot. texts, but it is in excess of the metre by one syllable ; the shorter form *paripela* which would suit, however, also exists ; see M. Williams' Skr. Dict.

8 *Paṁcama* and *aṣṭama* are treated as aggregatives, like *paṁcaka* and *aṣṭaka*.

Tatra mantrapadā siddhā varṇaṁ vakṣyāmi Jīvaka [ḥ] ı

[Fol. 45*a*]

Tadyathā ı kiśi kiśi kiśa laṁbi hilī hilīṁ ı namo Buddhasya ı
Siddhyaṁtu mantrāṇi svāhā ı imaṁ mantram udāhare[t]ıı6
Śucasamādhinā bhūtvā Puṣyayogena buddhimāṁ ı
tasya karmaguṇā kṛtsnā varṇaṁ vakṣyāmi Jīvaka[ḥ] ıı7ıı
Sarvarogapraśamanaṁ samāsā[d] gaganôttamaṁ ı

[Fol. 45*b*]

yeṣu rogeṣu bhaiṣajyaṁ - - - - - - - - - ıı8ıı[1]
Devagaṁdharvayakṣeṣu pretadāruṇarakṣasāṁ ı
Sarvabhūtavikāreṣu lalāṭa-[taṭa]m upaye[t] ıı9ıı
Śāmyati sarvavitāṇḍā pūtanākṛtyavedhaka ı
Khārkhoda śvita śāmyati grahā ye ca sudāruṇā ıı10ıı
Sarveṣāṁ supraghātârthaṁ agada[ḥ] samudāhṛtaḥ ı

[Fol. 46*a*]

halāhaleṣu saṁyuktaṁ viṣapīteṣu dāruṇam ıı11ıı
Pītaṁ śītena toyena sadyo bhavati nirviṣaṁ ı
bāṇaviddheṣu gātreṣu āyur viṣeṇa dūṣyate ıı12ıı
Vraṇâlepanamātreṇa vraṇadoṣaḥ pramucyate ı
jantūnāṁ ye ca kleśāṁ[ḥ][2]syā[d] ghorāḥ paramadāruṇā[ḥ]
ıı13ıı [Fol. 46*b*]

1 The omission of the 4th pāda in śl. 8, and of the 3rd pāda in śl. 20, might seem to compensate each other. But if that be so, the metre of all the ślokas after the 8th is out of order. Now at the place of the missing 3d pāda in sl. 20, the Khot. text has the remark *haṭṣa vī dīra na īdit* i.e., in this there is no failure, which does not occur in the Skr. text and which we rendered by the pāda *asmin akuśalaṁ nâsti*. As to the missing 4th pāda of śl. 8, one expects a demonstative clause to complement the preceding relative clause, and the clause *ttā hvāṁñāṁ*, i.e. "that I shall say" in the Khot. text does seem to suggest that a complement such as *bhavet, tūny ahaṁ vakṣyāmi* has droped out of the Skr. text.

2 The Ms. has *jantavá ye ca drraiṣṭa* (*klaiṣṭā*) which does not agree with the following clause. The emendation is suggested by the Khot. version which does agree with it.

Daheyu[r] uṣṭamātreṇa teṣām apavaṣākhyā[1] ı
yasya hastagataṁ nityaṁ pāpaṁ tasya na jāyate ıı14ıı
Sarvaṁ ca sādhaye[d] arthaṁ pūtayaś ca[2] na jāyante ı
ye ca ghorā [vabaidiṣṭhai vaṣaṣvastāsu[3]] śoṇite ıı15ıı
Teṣāṁ kākapadaṁ mūrdhni kṛtvā dadyā[d] gadântakaṁ ı
[Fol. 47*a*]
mukhataś tu trayo dadyā[d] bindavo vā nastas tttrayo ıı16ıı
Agadena ca limpeta tataḥ saṁjīvati suptaḥ ı
mūtrabhū-kīṭena daṣṭo lūtāmūṣakeṇa veṣṭa[ḥ] ıı 17 ıı[4]
Nasyapānâṁjanâlepā[d] vidhinā nirviṣo bhave[t] ı
strīṇāṁ ca mūḍhagarbhāṇāṁ yonilepaṁ pradāpaye[t] ıı18ıı
Visūcikāyāṁ ghorāyāṁ dadyā[d] uṣṇena vāriṇā ı
rakṣāṁ kuryā[c][5] ca bālānāṁ suprajānāṁ prajāyitā ıı19ıı
Yāvad arthatarṣa[ḥ] pive[t] tāva[t] sa kurvati kṣipraṁ ı
-------- ı vṛkṣaṁ Indrârthinā yathā ıı 20 ıı
Bhagavato bhāṣita Svastaka nāma mahâgada[ḥ] samāpta[ḥ]
ıı :: ıı

1 The Ms. is here quite corrupt, and its metre is short by one syllable; but for the present I am unable to suggest an emendation, as the meaning of the Khot. version is unknown.

2 The Ms. text has *pūtayiśta* (or *pūnayiśta*) which is not intelligible. The emendation is suggested by the Khot. version *pātca pātcī upadrrava* which seems to mean "after-troubles."

3 The Ms. readings *vabaidiṣṭhai* and *vaṣaṣvastāsu* are quite corrupt; they correspond respectively to Khot. *bena dūṣṭi* and *bena umya*, which however themselves are doubtful; *umya* seems to mean 'latent', Skr. *supta*; and Skr. *vabai* and *vaṣa*, both representing Khot. *bena*, might be corruptions of *viṣa*, poison. The reference seems to be to the so-called *dūṣī-viṣa*, or slow poison settled in the blood, in the treatment of the last or most severe stage (*vega*) of which the *kākapada* incision is recommended in *Caraka-saṁhitā*, Cik. Sth., xxv, verses 29, 61, 64 (Jīv. 2nd ed. pp. 725, 727) and in *Suśruta-saṁhitā*, K. Sth., II, v. 48, and V, vv. 21, 22, 42, 43 (Jīv. 5th ed. pp. 567, 580, 582).

4 Both text and metre of śl. 17*b* are badly corrupted in the Ms. The doubtfully suggested emendation is based on the Khot. version.

5 The Ms. reading *karṣa* makes no sense. The emendation is suggested by the Khot. *tcairai*.

TRANSLATION[1]

[Fol. 44*a*][i] Reverence towards Brahman! Reverence towards the Siddhas, Vidyādharas, (Ṛṣis).[2]

The divine blessed one (Jīvaka)[3] thus spake: [ii] Of this formula I will speak the praises in every way.[4] [iii] Whatever antidotes there are in Jambudvīpa, [iv] of the topmost among all of them, of that I will now say the praises. Of Paripelava (*Cyperus rotundus*) four parts,[v] and four parts of Gandha-nalada (fragrant *Nardostachys Jatamansi*, Indian spikenard); of Candana (*Santalum album*, sandel wood) four parts; [fol. 44*b*][i] four parts of Agaru (*Acquilaria Agallocha*, aloe wood) there should be; of Tvaca (*Cinnamomum zeylanicum*, bark of cinnamon) also four parts; four parts of Kuṁkuma (*Crocus sativus*, saffron); [ii] moreover of Vyāghranakha (*Unguis Odoratus*, lit. fragrant tiger-claw) let be given four parts; five [iii] parts of Nīlôtpala (*Nymphaea stellata*, blue lotus), and of Kuṣṭha (*Saussurea auriculata*, Indian costus), of Hrīvera (*Pavonia odorata*, a fragrant root) eight parts; five parts of [iv] Sūkṣmelā (*Elletaria Cardamomum*, Malabar or small cardamom) should be added, well-weighed by the physician (lit. expert in drugs). [v] All these drugs should (be drunk)[5] with water. At that moment an effective sacred formula (comes in); [fol. 45*a*]; its

1 As close to the Khot. text as possible, irrespective of style.

2 Khot. *raṣaṇā*, which is not in the Skr. text, and is doubtful; perhaps *ṛṣīṇāṁ*.

3 Jīvaka is only in the Skr. text, not in the Khot. version; but he occurs in both texts below (fol. 45*a*[v]). He is represented as the author of the formula. For other examples of formulae of Jīvaka, see my edition of the Bower Ms., pp. 178, 180. Of course, the term *bhagavāṁ*, Khot. *jasta beysa* might refer to Buddha, in which case *Jīvaka* would have to be taken in the vocative case, as addressed by Buddha; but the term *bhagavat* is in the treatises of Caraka, Suśruta, and others regularly applied to great medical authorities, such as Dhanvantari, Ātreya, Nimi; and, anyhow, it implicitly marks the formula as one of Jīvaka's.

4 Translated as suggested by the Khot. *hve*, he said, Skr. *abravīt* The Skr. text is here irremediably corrupt.

5 Inadvertendly omitted in the Khot. version; the Skr. has *pīpayayi* (*pāyayet*); the Khot. would be *khāśāṁña*.

praises (i. e. terms), as follows, I (Jīvaka) shall say, along with each of the drugs and the antidote[1]: "Kiśi kiśi etc. reverence be to [ii] Buddha, may successful be the charm-words, Svāhā!" The physician, when he prepares the antidote should reverently[iii] say this mantra, in purity, well disposed. [iv] The wise physician should be in pure samādhi, in one state (of mind)[2] concentrated, at the time of the Puṣya asterism. As to its works; of the[v] complete virtues of the works belonging to this antidote, I Jivaka will now say the praises. Of all diseases it is a healer; [fol. 45*b*][i] among the whole number of antidotes this is said to be the most excellent in the universe. I will now say in what diseases[ii] it is a remedy. In all diseases due to Devas, Gandharvas, Yakṣas, Pretas, frightful Rakṣasas,[iii] Bhūtas this antidote is to be applied to the forehead.[iv] It gives relief from all Vetālas, Pūtanās, attacks by witchcraft;[v] it gives relief from Khārkhoda magic, leprosy. Whatever Grahas there are, most terrible, [fol. 46*a*][i] for the purpose of defeating them all this antidote is declared.[ii] In contact with Halāhala, which indeed is the most terrible (of poisons taken) by the mouth,[3] it is to be drunk[ii]) with cold water; upon that it (i. e. Halāhaḷa) becomes innocuous. If any limb[iv] by a (poisoned) arrow is struck and wounded, and life by its poison is endangered, (then) by merely smearing it on the wound, the mischief attaching to the wound is expelled. Whatever [fol. 46*b*][i] disease

1 Conjectural translation. Apparently the Mantra is to be repeated along with the addition of each drug, and again at the completion of the whole prescription. This is suggested by the clause which follows the Mantra, though the meaning of the phrase *agattāyittauvi* is not intelligible.

2 The "one" state of mind is "I am brahman"; see *Śabdakalpadruma*, vol. v, p. 271, col. 3, *ahaṁ brahmêty avasthānaṁ samādhir iti gīyate.*

3 The Khotanese interpretation has *eha ttraikṣa*, lit. mouth terrible. If *eha* is the same as *ehiṁ* in fol. 47*a*[i] where it renders Skr. *mukha*, mouth, it would seem that a word meaning "drunk" is omitted, corresponding to Skr. *viṣapīta*, poisonous drink.

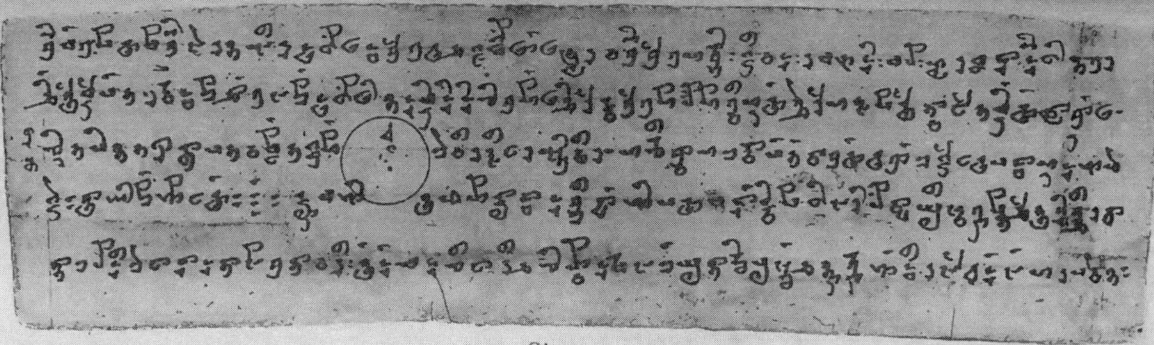

Obverse

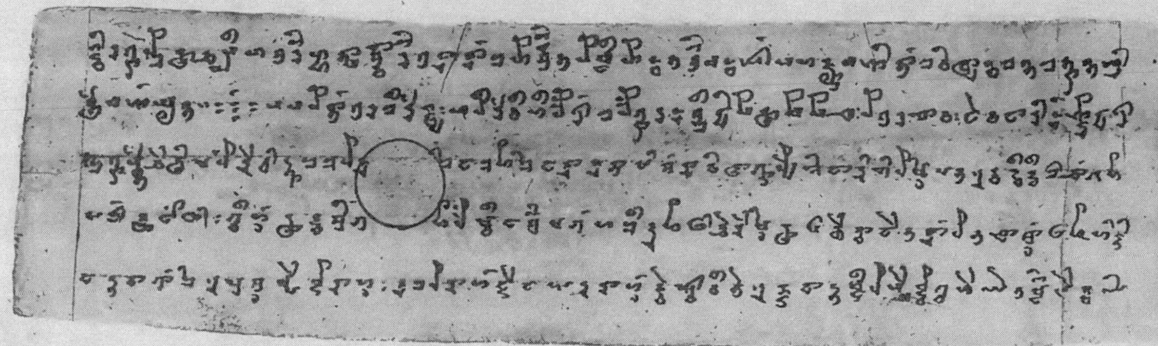

Reverse

of living beings there may be, frightful, very terrible, which[ii] burn men like fire, their mischief it counteracts.[1] In whosesoever hands this antidote is, with respect to him there are no threats of danger;[2] all his objects prosper;[iv] nor do any rotten things spring up. If by dreadful corrupt poison[v] latent diseases are in the blood,[3] for them a kākapada (Crow's foot) incision is to be made on the head; [fol. 47*a*][i] having been made, this antidote is to be given. By the mouth three drops of this antidote should be given, by the nose three drops. Upon being anointed with this antidote, a patient (lit. a man), without consciousness, again revives.[iii] If any one is stung by ordure-born insects, or attacked by spiders or rats,[4] by (this antidote in the form of an) errhine, potion,[iv] eyesalve, ointment, properly administered, he becomes quit of poison. Whenever women are[v] suffering from difficult labour, to their genitals it should be applied. When there is a case of severe cholera,[iv] it should be given with warm water. It affords protection to children, and [fol. 47*b*][i] when successfully sons are to be born, it gives support. Whatever desiring, any one drinks, of that it procures accomplishment quickly;[ii] in this there is no failure; just as the tree (did) for Indra (Śakra) desirous of deliverance.[6] This antidote or destro yer (of diseases) does (truly) destroy.[iii] Here the (great) antidote, named Svastaka, spoken by the Divine Blessed One, ends.

SECOND EXTRACT

[Fol. 64*a*][iv] Drrūṣaṇi ttraphalā drrākṣā kaśmīryāṁni parūṣakāṁ dvi pāṭhi sarilaṁ vyāghrrī svagūpttā caittraki

1 Conjectural translation; the Skr. text is corrupt, and the Khot. version unknown.

2 Here the Khot. *viśāṁna hīra* renders the Skr. *pāpa*, evil angury.

3 The Skr. text is corrupt, and the Khot doubtful; see foot-note 3. on p. 426.

4 The exact meaning of the text is doubtful, *exc.* spiders and rats.

5 This seems clearly to be the meaning of the text, though I do not know to what mythological story it refers.

śṭi[1] radhā[v] ttāmalakī medā kākanāsā śattāvari : ttraṁkaṁṭaka bīdārī ca bilvā[2] karṣasamam ghrrattārthi[3] prrasthaṁ cattūrgūṇaṁ ksīra saidha kaṁsaṁhara pavetta =

[Fol. 64*b*][i] jvira gūlma rūca plīha śarau hṛt pārśvā raugaká[4] kāṁmalârśau nalaṣṭīlā kṣata śauṣa kṣayâṁpaha Drrūṣaṇi nāṁma vikhyātam attam anuttami[ii] ttraiṣaṇaṁ ghrratta ‖ *Papala nnūṁgara mīraijya: halīrai vīhīlai āṁmalai gūra kaśmīryi pārūṣā pāṭha: lagarabāva: devadāri kāṁṇḍārya ā[iii]tmagūpttai caittri ṣalaṁ raidhi ttāmalaka mida mahāmida*[2] *kākanāsi śaṁrāvi ttrāgūlye bidāri bila ṣi pana arva dvi dvi mācāṁga hā*[iv] *samūṁ kūṭāṁñi: gvīhaṁ rū dva śiṁga hālai ṣvīda śau ṣagaṁ hamīḍa hāñi tcerai ṣi rū pāchai nvādaina kāṁlana khāśūṁña phahiji*[v]*da*[5] *ttavā gáṁmi apuśa*[6] *ṣpaijā rāha: kāmala rāhaṁ*[7] *jaida ysara*

1 Read *śaṭī*.

2 Read *piṣṭvā*. The reading *bilvā*, involves a curious problem. All Indian authorities (see footnote 4, p. 431) read *piṣṭvā* and count only 19 ingredients, while our Ms. text, with its *bilvā*, counts 20; and its count seems supported by the fact that it renders Skr. *bilvā* by Khot. *bila*. But, on the other hand, it renders Skr. *piṣṭvā* by Khot. *kūṭāṁñi*. Now, the insertion of both, *bilvā* and *piṣṭvā* in the Skr. text is incompatible with its metre, while the omission of *piṣṭvā* in favour of *bilvā* is not compatible with its sense. On the whole the probability seems to be that the Indian reading is correct, and that our Ms. is wrong; and that its wrong reading is due not so much to the author of the Khot. version, as to the scribe of our Ms., who, moreover (as the footnotes show), is guilty of numerous other blunders. He would seem to have misread *bilvā*, and inserted the supernumerary ingredient *bila* to suit his misreading. The supernumerary *mahāmida* is probably also due to him. It is not in the Skr. text.

3 Read *ghrrattātti*; for *ghrrattātt* with virāma indicated by *i*.

4 Read *rauganu* (*roganut*), and below, in *l.* 5, *guṁmi* (*gulma*); in both cases with *á* for *u*.

5 Read *pahijida*; cf. fol. 46*a*[i]. 6 Read *arūśa*, as in fol. 52*b*[ii].

7 Read *rūhaṁ*, as elsewhere.

rūhaṁ tvesvā[1] *vīne*[2] *arja vāttaṣṭīla paijvāgvahaiye naṣṭāusai kṣaye*

[Fol. 65*a*][i] *pīreḍa: ttrūṣala*[3] *nāṁma rūṁ bausta ṣṭe viṁsthārī* ॥ ॥

RESTORATION OF THE SANSKRIT TEXT[4]

Tryūṣanaṁ triphalāṁ drākṣāṁ kāṣmaryāni parūṣakam ।
dve pāṭhe saralaṁ vyāghrīṁ svaguptāṁ citrakaṁ śaṭim ॥1
Ṛddhiṁ tāmalakīṁ medāṁ kākanāsāṁ śatāvarīm ।
trikaṇṭakāṁ vidāriṁ ca piṣṭva karṣasamaṁ ghṛtāt ॥ 2 ॥
Prasthaṁ caturguṇaṁ kṣīraṁ siddhaṁ kāsaharaṁ pivet ।
jvara-gulm-âruci-plīha-śiro-hṛt-pārśva-roga-nut ॥ 3 ॥
Kāmal-ârśo-'nilāṣṭhīlā-kṣata-śoṣa-kṣay-âpaham ।
tryūṣanaṁ nāma vikhyātam etad ghṛtam anuttamam ॥4॥

TRANSLATION OF THE KHOTANESE TEXT

(The three acrids, viz.) long pepper, dry ginger, black pepper, (the three myrobalans, viz.) chebulic, beleric emblic, grapes, (fruits of) Kāśmarya (*Gmelina arborea*), Parūṣaka (*Grewia Asiatica*), Pāṭhā (*Stephania hernandifolia*), Lagara-

1 Read *pesvā*, as in fol. 52*b*[ii].

2 Owing to confusion, by the Khot. scribe, of Khot. *kamala*, head with Skr. *kāmalā*, jaundice, the latter is omitted after *vine*.

3 Probably read *ttrūṣaṇa*.

4 See *Caraka-saṁhitā*, chap. on *kāsa*, p. 732 of Jīvānanda's 1st ed. of 1877, which is supported by the oldest known Mss. In his 2nd ed. of 1896, *devadāru* is printed for *sarala*. The latter is supported, so far as I know only by such late Indian authorities, as Ind. Off. Ms. 359 (fol. 99 *b*) Deccan Coll. Ms. 925 (fol. 292*a*) and Sena ed.,p. 762 ; but it is now shown to have the respectable support of our old Khot. Ms. Anciently the two trees seem to have been taken as identical, though now they are treated as different, *Pinus longifolia* (*sarala*) and *Cedrus Deodara* (*devadāru*). The 2nd ed. prints also *brāhmī* for *vyāghrī* for which I know no authority. An altogether different *tryūṣaṇa* formula occurs in the chap. on *gulma* of *Caraka-saṁhitā* (Jīv. 1st ed., p. 513, 2nd ed. p. 488), adopted in *Aṣṭâṅga Hṛdaya*, II, 252, *Vaṅgasena*, p. 473, *Siddhayoga*, p. 271, *Cakradatta* (Sena ed.), p 348.

bāva[1] (root of Rāsnā, *Vanda Roxburghii*), Devadāru (*Cedrus Deodara*), Kaṁṇḍārya (Vyāghrī, *Solanum xanthocarpum*), Ātmaguptā (*Mucuna pruriens*), Citraka (*Plumbago Zeylanica*), Śaṭī (*Curcuma Zedoaria*), Ṛddhi (unknown), Tāmalakī (*Phillanthus Niruri*), Medā and Mahāmedā (both unknown), Kākanāsā (*Asclepias curassavica*), Śaṁrāvi (Śatāvari, *Asparagus racemosus*), Trāgūlye (Trikaṇṭaka, *Hygrophila spinosa*), and Bidāri (*Batatas paniculata*):[2] these several drugs, each equal to two mācāṁga,[3] should be ground, and together with two śiṁga[3] of cow's ghee and one ṣaga[3] of cow's milk made into paste. This ghee, having been boiled over a slow fire, at the right time should be drunk. It cures fever, abdominal tumours, distate for food, disease of the spleen. It overcomes headache. It removes diseases of the chest, pains in the sides,[4] piles, tumours due to deranged air-humour, wasting sores, consumption, general waste. This is the excellent, widely-famed ghee, named Tryūṣaṇa.

1. The "two Pāṭhā" of the Skr. text are in the Khot. version taken to mean *pāṭhā* and *rāsnā*. In India they are now identified with *pāṭhā* and *pāṭala* (*Vaidyaka-śabda-sindhu*, p. 594), or with *pāṭhā* and *śvāsāri*, (*Rājanighaṇṭu*, Ānandāśrama ed., p. 20).

2 Here is illegitimately added *Bila* (Skr. *vilva*, *Aegle Marmelos*).

3 Mācāṅga is equal to a tolaka or half a karṣa; śiṁga, to one prastha; and ṣaga to one āḍhaka or four prastha.

4 Here the Skr. text inserts *kāmalā*, a kind of jaundice, which is inadvertently missed out in the Khot. version, apparently due to the similarity of its name to the Khot. name *kamala-rāha* for headache. The Khot. name for *kāmalā* is *hākau-rauga* (fol. 53aii).

KIRĪṬA-MUKUṬA

BY RAMBHADRA OJHA

THE words *kirīṭa* and *mukuṭa* are not foreign to the Hindu ear. From the learned scholar down to the menial the expressions sound familiar and seem to convey some definite ideas; and yet when one is asked to give a descriptive definition of either of them one is simply embarrassed and finds that the terms are too technical to be explained even with the help of so many dictionaries or *kośas*. An attempt is made in the following pages to discuss briefly the three possible views that can be held in this connection: namely, (1) that *kirīṭa* and *mukuṭa* are mere synonyms; (2) that they are two quite distinct things; and (3) that *kirīṭa* is a kind of *mukuṭa*.

As to the first position that *kirīṭa* and *mukuṭa* are identical, it would seem that that is the current view in the matter. The Amara-kośa (ii. 6. 102)—

अलङ्कारस्त्वाभरणं परिष्कारो विभूषणम् ।
मण्डनं चाथ मुकुटं किरीटं पुन्नपुंसकम् ॥

gives the words as synonyms and the commentators on Kāvyas and Purāṇas have followed suit and disposed of the words by explaining *kirīṭa* as *mukuṭa* and *mukuṭa* as *kirīta*; but none of these commentators have anywhere entered into an elaborate description of these two terms, the reason probably being that in Purāṇas such as the Bhāgavata, which are most popular in the country, the words *kirīṭa* and *mukuṭa* are found used each by itself; as for example the in Bhāgavata x. 3. 10—

महार्हवैदूर्यकिरीटकुण्डलत्विषा परिष्वक्तसहस्रकुन्तलम् ।
उद्दामकाञ्चयङ्गदकङ्कणादिभिर्विरोचमानं वसुदेव ऐक्षत ॥
स्पृष्ट्वा चतुर्मुकुटकोटिभिरङ्घ्रियुग्मं नत्वा मुदश्रुसुजलैरकृताभिषेकम् ।

and very rarely if at all are they used together in the same context. This last circumstance might have induced the commentators to make a distinction between the two.

Examples of the use of these terms together and in the same context are not however wanting. In the Skanda-

Purāṇa we meet with the following description of Balabhadra, the elder brother of Kṛṣṇa—

हलचक्राब्जमुसलधारिणं वनमालिनम् ।
हारकुण्डलकेयूरकिरीटमुकुटोज्ज्वलम् ॥

In the *Pṛthugadya* Rāmānujācārya says—किरीटमुकुटचूडावतंसमकरकुण्डल इति; and in the Krama-dīpikā likewise we find the following stanza—

इन्दीवरनिभं सौम्यं पद्मपत्रायतेक्षणम् ।
स्निग्धकुण्डलसम्भिन्नकिरीटमुकुटोज्ज्वलम् ॥

These and similar passages shake our confidence in the theory of the identity of the *kirīṭa* and the *mukuṭa*.

The *kirīṭa* appparently was a resplendent head-gear worn on occasions like cornations of kings. Thus Arjuna was called a *kirīṭin,* but never a *mukuṭin*, and in the Mahābhārata Arjuna explains the genesis of the name thus—

पुरा शक्रेण मे बद्धं युध्यतो दानवर्षभैः ।
किरीटं मूर्ध्नि सूर्याभं तेनाहुर्मां किरीटिनम् ॥

and at the time of the coronation of Śrī Rāmacandra we are told in the Rāmāyaṇa that—

किरीटेन ततः पश्चाद्वसिष्ठेन महात्मना ।
ऋत्विग्भिर्भूषणैश्चैव समयोक्ष्यत राघवः ॥

E. B. Havell in his "Indian Sculpture and Painting" reproduces the illustration of Avalokiteśvara's *kirīṭa* as old as 1000 years, while A. K. Kumara Swami in his journal "Viśvakarmā" illustrates the *mukuṭa* of Natarāja of similar antiquity. The illustrations differ, thereby implying that *kirīṭa* and *mukuṭa* were different.

In the temples and Rāsamaṇḍalis of North India including मथुरा, वृन्दावन etc. two different head-gears known as *kirīṭa* and *mukuṭa* are worn one above the other by images as well as actors to the present day, and this custom prevalent there affords additional ground for the same view.

Lastly, it must be mentioned that Jīva Gosvāmi, a well known commentator on the Bhāgvata, says explictly—किरीटं त्रिकोणपत्रावलिरूपं मुकुटं तु समस्तकचावरकमिति भेदः and this remark of his establishes directly that the two head-gears are different.

All these arguments, interesting as they are, are not very convincing to one who would rely on nothing but a strictly technical work on the subject. But the task of tracing out a technical work dealing with head-gears in general is hard, and that of explaining the same is harder still. Our biggest libraries are poor in Mss. of Śilpa Śāstra, and most the Mss. that do exist are quite silent on the topic of the *mukuṭa*. The Purāṇas and Upa-Purāṇas have a lot to say about *Chhatra*, *Cāmara* and *Siṁhāsana* but disappoint us keenly in respect of the *mukuṭa*, so familiar and yet so difficult to define.

In the Baroda Central Library there is a Ms. of a work called the Aparājita-pṛcchā and in the Tanjore Palace Library that of another work called Śilpa-śāstra which is ascribed to so venerable a name as that of Viśvakarman himself. The Mss. give a detailed treatment of head-gears in general and of the *mukuṭa* in particular, but they are so hopelessly corrupt that it is practically impossible to make much sense out of them.

However, there is another work called Mānavasāra or Mānasāra, Mss. of which are preserved in the Libraries of Bombay, Poona, Tanjore, Madras, Trivandrum, and Calcutta. The India Office Library in London also contains a copy of it, and it is reported to be still in the possession of a number of sculptors in South India, who cousult it to the present day in making images of gods, etc.

The text of the Mānasāra dealing with the subject under discussion is not entirely free from error, and I have to acknowledge here the help I have derived from Mr. T. Gopinath Rao M. A. of the Travancore State who unfolded to me many of the technicalities of this work.

The text of the Mānasāra is at the very outset clear enough to enable one to finally discard the two theories discussed above and to establish a third, viz. that *kirīṭa is neither identical with nor different from mukuṭa but is only a kind of it* ; in other words, that there are many kinds of *mukuṭas* of which *kirīṭa* is one. As the text of our Ms. explains—

देवानां भूपतीनांश्च मौलिलक्षणमुच्यते ।
जटामौलिः किरीटश्च करण्डश्च शिरस्त्रकम् ॥
कुन्तलं केशबन्धश्च धम्मिल्लालकचूडकम् ।
मुकुटं तदिति ख्यातं तत्तदाधारमानतः ॥

This theory having thus been established on the basis of an original and technical work on the subject, it is no longer necessary to make much of the statements of commentators and lexicographers quoted above, who evidently did not think it essential for their immediate purpose of bringing the meaning of their texts home to their readers or of stringing together a list of approximate synonyms for the guidance of students, to discuss the technical side of the question; they were perhaps themselves in the dark about the real things connoted by these words.

The expression *kirīta-mukuṭa* as it occurs in some of the passages above cited can now be explained as—किरीटाख्यं मुकुटम्—the मुकुट known as किरीट. It avoids confusion by specifying the kind of *mukuṭa* meant.

Similarly if the same illustration is spoken of now as *kirīṭa* and now as *mukuṭa* or if different illustrations are given answering to the *kirīṭa* and the *mukuṭa* we must imagine that it is a case of calling the thing now by its special name and now by its general name.

The origin of the custom that has sprung up in North India of using two different things which go by different names *kirīṭa* and *mukuṭa* is still in the dark. It may be that names of ornaments and other gears are, like dialects, local, and it is not improbable that the *mukuṭa* of the North differed from that of the South. But this does not seem to be likely; for the terms in question had their import fixed by the Śāstras and special technical treatises which have had currency throughout the length and breadth of India, as the disribution of the Mss. themselves shows.

The full text of the Mānasāra dealing with the subject of *kirīṭa* and *mukuṭa* is given below—

KIRĪṬA-MUKUṬA

भूपानाञ्च शिरोनाहतुल्यं तन्मुकुटोदयम् ॥
भूपानां मुकुटोत्सेधः षड्विंशतिविभाजितः ।
फालपट्टोदयः पञ्चभागश्चूडं तदर्धकम् ॥ १ ॥
पूरिमोत्सेधपञ्चांशो मूलता तु षडंशिका ।
तदूर्ध्वं चाग्रपट्टं स्यात् त्रिपादांशत्रिवेदिकम् ॥ २ ॥
पट्टाधश्चोर्ध्वदेशे तु पादांशोनत्रिवेत्रकम् ।
तदूर्ध्वं पद्ममेकेन त्र्यंशेन मुकुलोदयः ॥ ३ ॥
मुकुटान्तात् पट्टिकान्तमेवमूर्ध्वं शिरोमणिः ।
वेत्रादिकुड्मलान्तः स्यात् शिखामण्युदयः स्मृतः ॥ ४ ॥
अधोवेत्रादधोदेशे रत्नदामावृतांशकम् ।
वृत्ताकारं तु सर्वाङ्गं युक्त्या तत्रैव योजयेत् ॥ ५ ॥
अन्यत्र सर्व देशे तु तरङ्गाकृति कारयेत् ।
तरङ्गाकारमध्ये तु पुष्परत्नैश्च शोभितम् ॥ ६ ॥
पूरिमस्य द्विपार्श्वे च मकरैश्च विभूषितम् ।
तन्मध्ये रत्नबंधः स्याद्वाह्ये वल्लिभिरावृतः ॥ ७ ॥
मकरस्यास्य देशे तु मकरान्मकरान्तरम् ।
मौलिबन्धनवल्ल्यैव मुक्तादामैरलङ्कृतम् ॥ ८ ॥
ललाटपट्टतुङ्गं तच्च चतुर्भागं विभज्यते ।
एकांशः पट्टभागः स्यात् सर्वरत्नैश्च बंधयेत् ॥ ९ ॥
तस्याधो रत्नदामैश्च ललाटोर्ध्वेऽर्धचन्द्रवत् ।
कर्णपत्रसमायुक्तः श्रोत्रोर्ध्वे कर्णपुष्पयुक् ॥ १० ॥
तस्मात्तु लम्बनं दाम सर्वरत्नैरलङ्कृतम् ।
पूरिमस्य त्वधोदेशे चूडरत्नादि विन्यसेत् ॥ ११ ॥
चतुःपूरिमसंयुक्तं कर्णोर्ध्वे पार्श्वपूरिमम् ।
शिरःपृष्ठोर्ध्वदेशे तु पृष्ठपूरिमसंयुतम् ॥ १२ ॥
शिरोनाहत्रिभागैकं शिरश्चक्रं प्रकीर्तितम् ।
चक्राकारं तु संयुक्तं सर्वरत्नादि विन्यसेत् ॥ १३ ॥
एतत्किरीटमुकुटं सर्वालङ्कारसंयुतम् ॥

I shall not attempt to translate the passage; it has been explained by Mr. T. A. Gopinatha Rao in his "Elements of Hindu Iconography" pages 26 ff, and I have perpared an illustration of the *kirīṭa* which will give the reader a correct notion on the subject. The *kirīṭa* here shown is the very likeness of thousands of *kirīṭa-mukuṭas* old and new in the temples of Southern India.

The only thing that now remains to be considered is the following text of the बृहत्संहिता, which however is not the description of a *mukuṭa.*

पट्टः शुभदो राज्ञां मध्येऽष्टावङ्गुलानि विस्तीर्णः ।
सप्त नरेन्द्रमहिष्याः षड् युवराजस्य निर्दिष्टः ॥
चतुरङ्गुलविस्तारः पट्टः सेनापतेर्भवति मध्ये ।
द्वे च प्रसादपट्टः पञ्चैते कीर्तिताः पट्टाः ॥
सर्वे द्विगुणा यामा मध्यादर्धेन पार्श्वविस्तीर्णाः ।
सर्वे च शुद्धकाञ्चनविनिर्मिताः श्रेयसो वृद्ध्यै ॥
पञ्चशिखो भूमिपतेस्त्रिशिखो युवराजपार्थिवमहिष्योः ।
एकशिखः सैन्यपतेः प्रसादपट्टो विना शिखया ॥

The author explicitly describes here the *paṭṭa* and not the *mukuṭa* but भट्टोत्पल the commentator takes *paṭṭa* here as equal to *mukuṭa* and thus gives rise to a doubt as to the real nature of the head-gear; but the following quotation from the Bhāgavata Purāṇa—

भारं परं पट्टकिरीटजुष्टमप्युत्तमाङ्गं न नमेन्मुकुन्दम्

where the words पट्ट and किरीट occur together, clearly indicates that both of them are important head-gears and may be worn simultaneously. *Paṭṭa*, though it has several meanings, cannot mean here an ordinary silk or thread band for a turban, as this cannot be mentioned in the same breath with *kirīṭa* and a thing to be proud of. *Paṭṭa* must be something almost as good as *kirīṭa* and a thing to be worn in some cases with and in others without *kirīṭa*. This is also evident from the following passages from the Agni-Purāṇa—पट्टबंधं च कारयेत् । राज्ञो मुकुटबन्धं च, and from the Baudhāyana Gṛhyasūtra—पट्टं वा मुकुटं वा करोति. The passage from Bhaṭṭotpala therefore has no bearing on the problem before us.

A quite explicit statement in the matter is also made by Bharata in his Nāṭyaśāstra (p. 235, Kāvyamālā ed.), where he says—

त्रिविधा मुकुटा ज्ञेया दिव्यपार्थिवसंश्रयाः ।
- - - - - - - - - - - - - - - - -
उत्तमा ये च दिव्यानां तेषां कार्याः किरीटिनः ॥

and though his classification might seem to differ he nevertheless holds that *kirīṭa* is a sub-variety of the *mukuṭa*, and this is the final conclusion that seems most acceptable.[1]

1 This article was the result of a Commission appointed by His Highness the Maharaja of Alwar to investigate from all points of view the question of the relation of the *kirīṭa* to the *mukuṭa*. A further light on the matter is earnestly solicited.

A STANZA FROM PĀṆINI'S ŚIKṢĀ

BY G. S. KHARE

THE Pāṇinīya Śikṣā contains the following stanza—

उदात्ते निषादगान्धारावनुदात्त ऋषभधैवतौ ।
स्वरितप्रभवा ह्येते षड्जमध्यमपञ्चमाः ॥ १२ ॥

which is also given in the Nāradī Śikṣā in an identical form. The Yājñavalkya Śikṣā has the following in stead—

उच्चौ निषादगान्धारौ नीचावृषभधैवतौ ।
शेषास्तु स्वरिता ज्ञेयाः षड्जमध्यमपञ्चमाः ॥ ७ ॥

which in substance means the same thing. But precisely to understand what is meant by saying that the udātta requires the notes niṣāda and gāndhāra, the anudātta, the ṛṣabha and dhaivata, and the svarita, the remaining three: ṣaḍja, madhyama and pañcama, it would be necessary to get some Vedic distich chanted to the accompaniment of a musical instrument. I selected for the purpose the very first line इषे त्वोर्जे त्वा of the Taittirīya Saṁhitā and I give below a plate expressing the result of the same in the the staff notation which has been adopted by Mr. E. Clements in his "Introduction to the study of Indian music."

इ षे त्वो र्जे त्वा वा य वः स्थो पा य वः स्थ दे वो वः स वि ता

प्रा र्प॑ य तु श्रे ष्ठ त मा य क र्म॑ णे

At the outset I may explain that a syllable without any mark is to be chanted on a higher note by a semitone than that on which a syllable with a horizontal line below is chanted; and that a syllable with a vertical line above is to be chanted on a note higher by a major tone than the first. Thus the whole of the Taittirīya Saṁhitā requires only three notes for the purpose of chanting. The mode of chanting the Ṛk Saṁhitā is slightly different, but all the same it requires three notes. The chanters commence with different bases but they chant on three notes only. Writers on Sanskrit grammar call these modes of accents (*svaras*) udātta, anudātta and svarita respectively. Experts in this branch of chanting are at one with modern students of the Vedic lore in the matter of the exact sense of these three technical terms. This agreement is bound to result in correctly finding out the sense of the stanzas from the Śikṣās quoted above. Naturally enough, the ancient and authoritative writers of Indian music have employed these three terms in their treatises and have assigned definite meanings to them: the udātta is to be chanted on niṣāda or gāndhāra notes, the anudātta on ṛṣabha or dhaivata notes, and the svarita on ṣaḍja, madhyama, or pañcama notes. The stanzas from the Śikṣās say the same thing in effect, in that they assign two notes to each of the three terms. Thus they have constituted two alternative sets of notes: ṛṣabha, gāndhāra, and madhyama or dhaivata, niṣāda and ṣaḍja for anudatta, udātta and svarita respectively. In addition to these six notes the authors of the Śikṣās have assigned pañcama for the svarita; but they do not give the corresponding notes for the anudātta and the udātta. As the svarita is represented by pañcama, the anudātta and the udātta would naturally be represented by antara (a vikṛta svara) and madhyama respectively.

It is necessary to bear in mind that the above notes are of the older musical scale followed by Bharata and Śārṅgadeva, and that they will not coincide with the same notes of the present musical scale. The values of these older notes have already been determined by the late Sharadaprasad Ghosh[1] of Bengal, by Mr. Nagojirao of Coimbatore, and by Messrs. Krishnajee Ballal Deval,[2] E. Clements,[3] and Fox Strangways. Rao Bahadur Prabhakar Ramkrishna

1 Modern Review, Vol. x, page 384.

2 *A Lecture on the musical scale of Ratnākara.*

3 *Introduction to the study of Indian Music,* page 77.

Bhandarkar of the Indore Medical Service has also given the same values in the Epigraphia Indica, Vol. XII, pages 223 to 228—

षड्ज	ऋषभ	गांधार	मध्यम	पंचम	धैवत	निषाद	षड्ज	octave
1	$\frac{10}{9}$	$\frac{32}{27}$	$\frac{4}{3}$	$\frac{3}{2}$	$\frac{5}{3}$	$\frac{16}{9}$	2	

Ellis's cents—

0	182	294	498	702	884	996	1200

According to the present scale the anudātta will be represented by major sixth $\frac{15}{16}$ (B) or major third $\frac{5}{4}$ (E), the udātta would be represented by fundamental note (C) or Fourth $\frac{4}{3}$ (F), and the svarita would be represented by major second $\frac{9}{8}$ (D) or fifth $\frac{3}{2}$ (G). The result of our investigation about the subject will be grasped at a glance from the following table—

Vedic Syllables		वा	य	वः
Terms employed by writers of grammar		Anudātta	Udātta	Svarita
Terms employed by old writers on Music	First set	ऋषभ $\frac{10}{9}$	गांधार $\frac{32}{27}$	मध्यम $\frac{4}{3}$
	Second set	धैवत $\frac{5}{3}$	निषाद $\frac{16}{9}$	षड्ज 2
Terms employed by present musicians	First set	Major third $\frac{5}{4}$	Fourth $\frac{4}{3}$	Fifth $\frac{3}{2}$
	Second set	Major sixth $\frac{15}{8}$	Octave 2	Major second $\frac{9}{8}$

From the above it conclusively follows that the present mode of chanting the Taittirīya Saṁhitā is substantially in agreement with the dicta given in the Śikṣās and that this marked agreement indirectly proves the correctness of the interpretation of the stanzas from the Śikṣās quoted above. The old authorities on Sanskrit grammar by their use of these technical terms also support the present mode of chanting the Vedas. As the text of the Vedas has come down to us almost in its pristine purity, so also has the mode of chanting them, there being an undisturbed and unbroken continuity of tradition in the matter.

GUPTA STYLE OF ARCHITECTURE AND THE ORIGIN OF ŚIKHARA

BY E. B. HAVELL

ORIENTAL Scholars have always treated the Gupta period from a sectarian point of view as the period which marks the revival of Brahmanism and the decline of Buddhism—a period of conflict between the Brahman Pandit 'orthodox Hindu' and the Buddhist bhikku. It is not easy to determine exactly what 'orthodox Hinduism' meant at different periods of Indian history, but to ignore the fact that Brahmans always took a leading part in the organisation of the Saṅgha and in formulating the doctrines of Buddhist religious schools seems to me a great historical error.

In Aśoka's time a Brahman member of the Buddhist Saṅgha was, from an Indian point of view, an 'orthodox Hindu,' and in making sectarian rivalries and disputes the keynote to the interpretation of Indian history one is liable to fall into the common error of seeing Indian things through European spectacles. The Indian war-lords of the Gupta dynasty were not putting themselves forward, like Aśoka, as religious teachers: they were full-blooded Aryans of the historic Licchavi clan who rallied the Kṣatriya clans to the defence of the Āryāvarta against the Turks and Huns of those days who were threatening the existence of Aryan Empire in India. The fact that their adversaries were Buddhists was not the point at issue at all, for the majority of the Aryan warriors were probably also Buddhists. The dominant historical event of the Gupta period was an Indo-Aryan or national revival, not a sectarian or religious one. That this connoted a revival of Sanskrit learning was a natural consequence, for Sanskrit probably had never ceased to be the court language of the Aryans when a Brahman or Kṣatriya was the ruler, though Buddhist kings followed the commandment of the Blessed One in conducting all the affairs of the Saṅgha through the medium of the vernaculars.

We may, therefore, take it that the culture of the Gupta period which found expression in the building of royal temples and palaces was also distinctively Indo-Aryan. Fergusson in his History of Indian Architecture[1] brings all Hindu temples crowned with the curvilinear spire or śikhara under the category of Indo-Aryan; but at the same time he asserts positively that 'no one can accuse the pure Aryans of introducing this form into India, or of building temples at all, or of worshipping images of Śiva or Viṣṇu, with which these temples are filled.'

He maintains that the śikhara-temple is a sure indication 'of the existence, past or present, of a people of Dasyu extraction.' This I take to be a huge mistake vitiating his whole theory of the history of Indian architecture. The śikhara is Indo-Aryan not only because it is found mostly in Northern India, or the ancient Āryāvarta, but because it was introduced into India by the early Aryans and was peculiarly their own contribution to Indian building traditions. Fergusson's statement contains, I believe, this much of truth that with the early Aryans the building crowned by a śikhara was not a temple but an Aryan chieftain's fortress-palace, where he as the spiritual leader of his people conducted the tribal sacrifices.

I have discussed this question in my recent book on the Ancient and Mediæval Architecture of India and the further study of the subject only strengthens my conviction that this is the true statement of the case. It is known that the Aryans ruled in Babylonia for six hundred years from about B. C. 1746, and their gods were the Vedic Gods, Sūrya, Varuṇa, Indra, and the Aśvins.[2] We have two important sculptural records of Mesopotamian architecture showing the ancient form of a royal fortress-palace. One is the famous stele of Nurām-Sin, now in the Louvre, and the other, one of the sculptures figured in

1 Introduction, p. 14.

2 Hall's Early History of the Near East, p. 201.

Layard's Nineveh (Pl. 16, 2nd series) and decribed as the palace of Sennacherib. Both of these show the characteristic spire of the śikhara temple. In the former it is crowned with a sun emblem. The Indian śikhara is also crowned by a sun emblem, the so-called āmalaka or fruit of the blue water-lily, Viṣṇu's sacred symbol.[1] We know that the chief god of the Aryans in Mesopotamia was Sūrya and the earliest Indian images show us that the concept of Viṣṇu was a development of the early Aryan ideas of Sūrya. Viṣṇu and Sūrya are always represented in Indian sculpture as Aryan warrior-kings and the Vaiṣṇava cult is essentially a Kṣatriya one centred in the idea of *bhakti*, the loyalty of the Aryan to his spiritual king, Viṣṇu-Sūrya. It was natural, therefore, that the primitive ritual of the cult was centred round the fortress-palace of the tribal chieftain, the *maṇḍapa* of which was both the council house of the Aryan sabhā and the place where tribal religious ceremonies were performed. The king's throne was under the śikhara—where the image of the deity is now placed—and the śikhara itself was originally a watch-tower generally pierced by sun-shaped loop-holes where the archers of the royal body-guard were stationed. The European term 'horse-shoe' applied to these loop-holes by Fergusson is as misleading as most European terms are when applied to Indian things.

The curvilinear form of the śikhara was derived from the fact that a similar watch-tower or platform for the royal body-guard was often constructed of wooden poles or bambus and built over the great fighting car of the chieftains, which was the rallying point of the Kṣatriyas in battle. Hence we often see that the Indian śikhara-temple is carved with stone wheels representing the wheels of the royal fighting car, or the 'tank' of ancient Aryan warfare.

If these hypotheses are correct the corollary will be that the Gupta period which marked the revival of Aryan

1 It is significant that the same symbolism appears in Aśoka's imperial standards, the *dhvaja-stambhas* upon which his edicts were inscribed.

political domination in northern India would be distinguished by the building of many śikhara-temples dedicated mostly to Viṣṇu-Sūrya or his avatars, Kṛṣṇa the hero of the Kṣatriya epic, the Mahābhārata, or Rāma the hero of the Rāmāyaṇa, rather than to Śiva, the Great God of the Brahmans, though the latter were no doubt staunch supporters of the Aryan revival. It will also follow that the innumerable śikhara-temples which are so characteristic of Northern Indian architecture, so far from defining the limits of a Dasyu on non-Aryan province, afford the most conspicuous proof of the political and spiritual supremacy of the Aryans in the Āryāvarta.

NOTES ON ANCIENT HINDU SHIPPING

BY RADHAKUMUD MUKERJI

IN the present paper I mean to contribute some notes on ancient Hindu shipping which would form a supplement to my larger work on the *History of Indian Shipping* and at the same time break some new ground. By way of introduction I should like to cite the following remarks I made elsewhere[1]—

The History of Indian Shipping and Maritime Activity dispels to a great extent the prevailing misconception that the Hindus have never been a practical people, that while they have succeeded so well in the sphere of speculation, they have fared very badly in the sphere of action. The misconception is due to the fact that our study of ancient Hindu culture-history has mostly confined itself to its subjective aspects: to the records it presents of mental, moral and spiritual development, and has not adequately attended to its objective or positive aspects: the records of material progress and secular achievements. And yet we have abundant testimony of these in the results achieved by the ancient Hindus in such scientific and practical subjects as Medicine, Surgery, Applied Chemistry, Pharmacy, or in the many arts of civilised life like Architecture, Sculpture, Painting, Metallurgy, Dyeing, or in the numerous handicrafts which established the dominance of India in the ancient commercial world.

That dominance was mainly secured by her shipping and maritime activity which supplies one of the best proofs of the practical capacities of the Hindu genius in days of yore. Navigation, whether inland or oceanic, is one of the most difficult of arts, and the pursuit of that art in ages long before the application of steam to locomotion must have multiplied its difficulties, which could only have been

1 Lantern Lecture on Ancient and Indian Shipping at Government House, Darjeeling, delivered on the 15th of June, 1916, in the presence of Lord and Lady Carmichael.

met by a corresponding amount of daring, enterprise, skill and resourcefulness. To show how far the pursuit of that art was successful I will quote only two testimonies :

A French writer, F. B. Solvyns, writes in his *Les Hindous* (1811): 'In ancient times the Indians excelled in the art of constructing vessels and the present Hindus can in this respect still offer models to Europe—so much so that the English, attentive to everything which relates to naval architecture, have borrowed from the Hindus many improvements which they have adapted with success to their own shipping. The Indian vessels unite elegance and utility and are models of patience and fine workmanship.'

Similarly that distinguished Englishman, Sir John Malcolm, writing in the J. R. A. S., Vol. I, says: 'Indian vessels are so admirably adapted to the purposes for which they are required that, notwithstanding their superior science, Europeans have been unable, during an intercourse with India for two centuries, to suggest or at least to bring into successful practice, *one* improvement.'

These witnesses may perhaps be exaggerating in their enthusiasm but that their statements contain a kernel of truth will be clear from a consideration of the evidence on the subject as set forth in my above-mentioned work.

The evidence in one respect however is defective in quantity, though not perhaps in quality, for it is quite conclusive so far as it goes. The defect is in regard to the *direct* Indian evidence which is meagre in volume as compared with the *indirect* Indian evidence, i. e. references and allusions to ships or voyages which are so abundant in Indian literatures, such as Sanskrit and Pāli.

The fact is that though ancient India can boast of considerable naval enterprise, the only important piece of direct evidence on the subject that is available in our present state of knowledge is that embodied in the Ms. called *Yuktikalpataru* which, in one of its chapters, deals directly with boats and ships and gives details about their construction, varieties, measurements, sizes, decoration and accommodation. As the only repository of this direct evidence the Ms. deserves a critical notice for its unique importance.

Three copies of the Ms. I have been able to trace up-to now. One is in the Calcutta Sanskrit College Library, the second in the library of the late Maharaja Sir J. M. Tagore, as mentioned by Dr. Rajendralal Mitra in his *Notices of Sanskrit Mss.*, Vol. I, no. CCLXXI, and a third copy is in the possession of Mahāmahopādhyāya Adityaram Bhattacharyya M. A., Pro-Vice-Chancellor, Benares Hindu University.[1] All the copies are in agreement (so far at least as the shipping portion goes) except in respect of mistakes in copying. I have used the Pāṇini Office copy for purposes of this notice.

The work was compiled by Bhoja Nṛpati from older works. The author states that he has carefully extracted the substance of the writings of various sages and expanded it into the present work.[2] The Ms. mentions a namesake of the author from whom it frequently quotes, mostly in agreement but sometimes in difference too, as shown by the expression *Bhojas tu* occuring in several places in the Ms.[3] This proves that Bhoja, the author of the Ms., is distinct from, and lived later than, the Bhoja whom the Ms. cites as an authority. Moreover the Ms. is based upon many other authorities besides Bhoja, who are all cited on the subjects in which they are the traditional masters. Thus—

I. (1) Bṛhaspati [fol. 2] and
(2) Uśanaḥ [fol. 2]

are cited on *Nīti* or Polity, but there is no reference to the various schools and leaders of political thought mentioned by Kauṭilya, such as Bharadvāja, Viśālākṣa, Parāśara, Piśuna, Kauṇapadanta, Vātavyādhi, Bahudantīputra, etc.

1 A copy of this was made by the Pāṇini Office, Allahabad, and kindly lent to me by the courtesy of Major B. D. Basu, I. M. S. (Retired), the proprietor.

2 *Nānā-muni-nibandhānāṁ sāram ākṛṣya yatnataḥ* । *Tanute Bhoja-nṛpatir Yukti-kalpatarum mude* ॥

3 E. g., fol. 22, fol. 28, etc.

II. (3) Parāśara [foll. 11, 26, 98 etc.] and
(4) Bhaviṣya Purāṇa

are the authorities cited on *Vāstu* or the art of building houses and cities;

III. (5) Garuḍa Purāṇa [fol. 39]

is cited on *Ratna* or jewels and precious stones;

IV. (6) Lauhapradīpa [fol. 75]
(7) Śārṅgadhara [fol. 75]
(8) Nāgārjuna [fol. 76]
(9) Vātsya [foll. 71, 97, 102] and
(10) Lauhārṇava [fol. 77]

are the various authorities cited on *Āyudha* or arms and weapons;

V. (11) Śālihotra [fol. 98]

is cited on *Aśva* or horses; and

VI. (12) Pālakāpya [fol. 100, 102] and
(13) Garga [fol. 102]

are cited as authorities on *Gaja* or elephants.

With regard to Nāgārjuna who is cited as an authority on arms and weapons it is important to note that Alberuni also speaks of a Nāgārjuna who was a famous chemist of Somanāth and composed a book which 'contains the substance of the whole literature on the subject.' He lived nearly a hundred years before Alberuni, i.e. before A. D. 873. See *Alberuni*, I. 189.

The Ms. treats of the following topics: polity, forts, cities, houses, seats, umbrellas, clothes, ornaments, jewels, arms, horses, elephants, domesticated animals, and conveyances.

As already stated, the author of the Ms. calls himself Bhoja Nṛpati and the inference may be made that he is identical with the famous Bhojarāja of Dhārā [1018–1060 A. D.] in which case the Bhoja whom the Ms. cites will be a mere writer. A second inference has been made by Dr. Rājendralāl Mitra that the Bhoja quoted by the Ms. is identical with the Bhoja Rājā of Dhārā renowned for his literary work and patronage, in which case Bhoja Nṛpati, the author of the Ms., will be a later and a lesser king. There is no conclusive evidence in the Ms. in favour of either theory.

The most interesting part of the Ms. is that which treats of the classification[1] of vessels into (A) *Special* or those which venture out into the open main and (B) *Ordinary* or those confined to the inland waters, as well as of the varieties under each class according to their differences in sizes or the measurements of their dimensions. These measurements turn on the meaning of the term *rājahasta* used in the text, on which I made the following remarks in my *Indian Shipping*: "Opinions of Sanskrit scholars whom I have consulted differ as to the exact meaning of the passages above quoted from the Ms. According to some the word *rāja* means *candra* = 1, and *hasta* = 2, so that *rājahasta* stands for the number 21. But according to others with whom I agree *rāja* = 16, for in the works on Astronomy *mahībhṛt* or *rāja* is often used to indicate that number. I have made the calculations given above on the basis of the second interpretation." The conjecture about the possible meanings of the term is however rendered unnecessary by the discovery in the Ms. itself of a passage which explains it. The passage runs thus: *Rājñaḥ svahastair daśabhī rājahasta udāhṛtaḥ* [folio 10] which defines *rājahasta* as equivalent to ten cubits. On this basis the measurements given in the Ms. for the various types of vessels, ocean-going or otherwise, work themselves out as follows[2]—

A. Class I: *Ordinary*

	Names of sub-classes	Length in cubits	Breadth in cubits	Height in cubits
I.	Kṣudrā	10	2·5	2·5
II.	Madhyamā	15	7·5	7·5
III.	Bhīmā	25	12·5	12·5

1 सामान्यश्च विशेषश्च नौकाया लक्षणद्वयम् ।

2 राजहस्तमितायामा तत्पादपरिणाहिनी ।
तावदेवोन्नता नौका क्षुद्रेति गदिता बुधैः ॥

	Names of sub-classes	Length in cubits	Breadth in cubits	Height in cubits
IV.	Capalā	30	15	15
V.	Paṭalā	40	20	20
VI.	Bhayā	45	22·5	22·5
VII.	Dīrghā	55	27·5	27·5
VIII.	Patrapuṭā	60	30	30
IX.	Garbharā	70	35	35
X.	Mantharā	75	37·5	37·5

B. Class II: *Special Sea-going*

(a) *Dīrghā*

	Names of sub-classes	Length in cubits	Breadth in cubits	Height in cubits
I.	Dīrghikā	20	2·5	2
II.	Taraṇī	30	3·75	3
III.	Lolā	40	5	4
IV.	Gatvarā	50	6·25	5
V.	Gāminī	60	7·5	6
VI.	Tarī	70	8·75	7
VII.	Jaṅghālā	80	10	8
VIII.	Plāvinī	90	11·95	9
IX.	Dhāriṇī	100	12·5	10
X.	Veginī	110	13·75	11

अतः सार्द्धमितायामा तदर्द्धपरिणाहिनी ।
त्रिभागेणोत्थिता नौका मध्यमेति प्रचक्षते ॥
क्षुद्राथ मध्यमा भीमा चपला पटला भया ।
दीर्घा पत्रपुटा चैव गर्भरा मन्थरा तथा ॥
नौकादशकमित्युक्तं राजहस्तैरनुक्रमम् ।
एकैकवृद्धैः सार्द्धैश्च विजानीयाद् द्वयं द्वयम् ॥
उन्नतिश्च प्रवीणा च हस्तादर्धांशलक्षिता ।
अत्र भीमा भया चैव गर्भरा चाशुभप्रदा ॥
मन्थरापरतोयास्तु तासामेवाम्बुधौ गतिः ।
दीर्घा चैवोन्नता चेति विशेषे द्विविधा भिदा ॥
राजहस्तद्वयायामा अष्टांशपरिणाहिनी ।
नौकेयं दीर्घिका नाम दशाङ्गेनोन्नतापि च ॥
दीर्घिका तरणिर्लोला गत्वरा गामिनी तरिः ।
जंघाला प्लाविनी चैव धारिणी वेगिनी तथा ॥
राजहस्तैकैकवृद्धा नौकानामानि वै दश ।
उन्नतिः परिणाहश्च दशाष्टांशमितौ क्रमात् ॥
ऊर्ध्वानूर्ध्वास्वर्णमुखी गार्भिणी मन्थरा तथा ।
राजहस्तेकैकवृद्ध्या नाम पञ्चत्रयं भवेत् ॥

(β) *Unnatā*

	Names of sub-classes	Length in cubits	Breadth in cubits	Height in cubits
I.	Ūrddhvā	20	10	10
II.	Anūrddhvā	30	15	15
III.	Suvarṇamukhī	110	20	20
IV.	Garbhiṇī	50	25	25
V.	Mantharā	60	30	30

Some of the Pāli texts are repository of important direct evidence regarding Indian shipping. They do not usually give actual measurements of the different dimensions of vessels, but they enable us to infer the sizes of vessels from the number of passengers they give, which is a rare characteristic in the corresponding Sanskrit texts. The *Rājāvalī* mentions that Prince Vijaya with his retinue was banished by his father from Bengal in a fleet of ships carrying more than 700 passengers. The *Si-yu-ki* [ii. 241] mentions a ship carrying 501 persons, nearly all merchants. The ship in which the bride of Vijaya and her party came to Ceylon carried nearly 800 persons.[1] The ship of the *Janaka-Jātaka* carried 700 persons besides the Buddha; that of the *Valāhassa-Jātaka* carried 500 merchants; that of the *Samaudda Vānija-Jātaka* accommodated a whole village of absconding carpenters numbering 1000; that of the Punna brothers provided room for 300 merchants and their large cargo of timber,[2] that of the two Burmese merchant-brothers conveyed full 500 cart-loads of their own goods besides others' cargo,[3] while that of the *Mahājanaka-Jātaka* had on board 7 caravans with their beasts. The only measurements given of a ship are those of the ship of the *Saṅkha-Jātaka* which was 800 cubits in length, 600 in breadth, 20 fathoms in depth and had three masts. The *Dāṭhādhātuvaṁsa* describes a ship bound for Ceylon as firmly constructed with planks served together with ropes with a well-rigged, lofty mast, a

1 Turnour's *Mahāwanso*, 51.

2 Hardy *Manual of Buddhism*, 57, 260.

3 Bigandet's *Life of Godama*, 101.

spacious sail and a skilful captain. The *Divyāvadāna* mentions several merchant vessels laden with goods, one of which carried 500 merchants.

The next line of direct evidence is that furnished by the nautical terms mentioned in Sanskrit literature. Macdonell and Keith's *Vedic Index* gives us a clue to such terms in Vedic literature. Thus, *aritra* is the word in Vedic literature for 'oar' by which boats were propelled. Ṛgveda i. 116. 5 and *Vājasaneyī Saṁhitā* xxi, 7 make mention of a vessel with 100 oars and a boat (*nau*) is said to be propelled by oars (*aritra-paraṇīm* in Ṛgveda x. 101, 2; cf. *Śatapatha Brāhmaṇa* iv. 2, 5, 10). The rower of a boat is called *aritṛ* in Ṛv. ii. 42. 1 and ix. 95. 2; *dyumna* is used in the sense of raft in Ṛv. viii. 19. 14. In the compound *nau-maṇḍa* the *maṇḍa* denotes the two nidders of a ship (*Śatapatha Brāhmaṇa* ii. 3. 3, 15). In later literature (cf. *Amarakośa*) the words for boat-pole or oar are *naudaṇḍa*, *kṣepaṇī*, *aritra* and *kenipātaka*. The words *kṛpaka*, *guṇavṛkṣaka* and *naubandhana* stand for ship-anchorage (*Amarakośa*), *Naukarṇa* is the hem of a ship and *nau-karṇa-dhāra* is the helmsman.[1] A sailor is called *naukarmajīvih* in Manu x. 34, and *naujīvika* in Varāhamihira's *Bṛhat-saṁhitā*, Ch. VII. A bridge of boats is called *naukarma* in *Divyāvadāna* as well as *nausaṅkrama*. The Pāli *Abhidhānappadīpikā* (verse 664) mentions *lakāra*, *vatakāra* and *piya* as parts of a ship.

The *Arthaśāstra* of *Kauṭilya*, from the abundance of its nautical terms, deserves special mention. In the first place, water-routes in general are divided into the three following classes—(1) the ordinary river routes as well as artificial water-ways or canals, called *kulyā*; (2) the routes for coastal traffic carrying on inter-portal communications, called *kulapatha*; (3) the ocean-routes called *saṁyānapatha* (Book VII).—Secondly, the following classes of ships and boats are mentioned suiting the purposes of both inland and oceanic navigation—

1 Varāhamihira, *Bṛhat-saṁhitā*, Ch. 5.

(1) *Saṁyātyaḥ nāvaḥ*, i. e. ocean-going vessels. It is mentioned that these ships had to pay tolls (*śulka*) at the harbours (*kṣetra*) at which they touched (Book II). *Amarakośa* defines a *sāṁyātrika* as a merchantman, *potavaṇik*.

(2) *Pravahaṇa*, which is another name for sea-going vessels or more properly merchantmen (Book I). It is thus defined in the commentary on *Uttarādhyāya-sūtra*, p. 246: *Sāmudrikāḥ vyāpāriṇaḥ mahāsamudram pravahaṇais taranti*, i. e. sea-going merchants cross the main by means of *pravahaṇa*.

(3) *Śaṅkha-muktā-grāhiṇyaḥ nāvaḥ*, which were boats used for pearl-fishing (Book II).

(4) *Mahānāvaḥ*, which were the larger vessels for use in the large rivers that were navigable throughout the year (ibid).

(5) *Kṣudrakāḥ nāvaḥ*, which were smaller boats for use in small and shallow rivers that overflowed in the rains (ibid).

(6) *Hiṅsakāḥ*, i. e. pirate ships and boats which, according to harbour regulations, should be pursued and destroyed.

Lastly, there are also names for different officers of the ship. The captain is called *śāsaka*, the steersman *niyāmaka*,[1] the man who is to vale out water is called *utsecaka*, and the sailors handling the nidder and rope are called *dātra-raśmi-grāhaka* (ibid). The officer in charge of the king's Admiralty is called *nāvādhyakṣa*, lit. the superintendent of ships, while there is mentioned another officer who is the superintendent of ocean mines.

1 Cf. Amarakośa, *Niyāmakāḥ potavāhāḥ*.

fection and ethical nobility of manhood to which they daily aspire. Krishna may be praised by the millions, notwithstanding his immoralities; and Rama may be extolled and even loved for his limited virtue; Yudhistra may be called "Dharman," notwithstanding his unrighteous passion for the dice. But Christ only, in the eyes of modern educated India, stands the perfect test of character. All over the land, Hindus of culture, of serious thought, and of ambition to reach after high ethical standards see in Jesus Christ the only inspiration and immaculate example of life that all history, myth, and legend present. And there is not a town in India to-day where there are not found these men of power and influence who are studying eagerly the life of Jesus, are pondering over the Gospel narratives; and are reading such books of Christian devotion as Thomas à Kempis's "Imitation of Christ." This last-named book is now being translated by a Brahman gentleman, a friend of the writer, and published by a Hindu firm for its Hindu readers! I have known such men for many years, and am assured that their tribe is increasing; they are men who for the first time have found the deepest yearnings of their soul answered in the example of Jesus.

Ask any of them for their reason, and they will tell

you that Christ is of the East, like themselves, and that His example appeals to them with unique power.

In India, the ideal of life has been one of restraint. Starting with the conviction that human life is an unmixed evil, the restraint of passion and the elimination of every human emotion (the best as well as the worst) has been to the Hindu the goal and consummation of life. Nothing can be more inadequate than this; and the Hindu is beginning to feel it. Jesus represents Culture *and* Restraint. With him the restraint of the lower passions is with a view to the culture of the higher. The man of sin must die, that the man of God may live and prosper. This is the Christ ideal, as opposed to the Brahmanic. And the leaven of this ideal of life is spreading all over India and is transforming the aspirations of millions. There is nothing more inspiring or comforting than the assurance which we have that the Christ life is becoming the dominant ideal among the classes of India, as it is to a less degree among the masses.

A Brahman gentleman had the presumption to say to me, recently, that he and his fellow-Brahmans and other Hindus were able to understand the Christ much better than we of the West. He also claimed that they could understand the deep significance and the